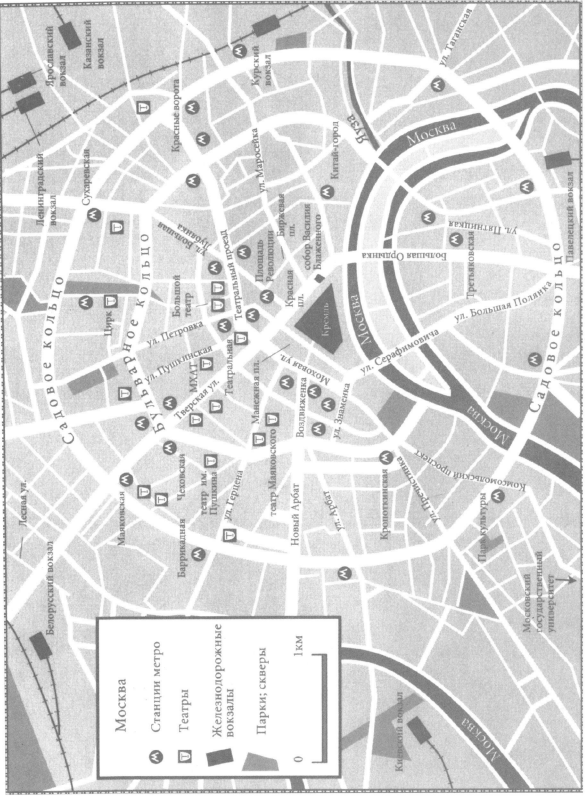

Москва

Ⓜ Станции метро

🎭 Театры

▬ Железнодорожные
     вокзалы

▬ Парки; скверы

0 _____ 1КМ

Ярославский вокзал
Казанский вокзал
Ленинградский вокзал
Сухаревская
Красные ворота
Курский вокзал
ул. Таганская
Москва
ул. Маросейка
Китай-город
Павелецкий вокзал
Садовое кольцо
ул. Пятницкая
большая Ордынка
ул. Третьяковская
ул. Большая Полянка
Биржевая пл.
собор Василия Блаженного
Площадь Революции
Красная пл.
Кремль
Москва
ул. Серафимовича
Бульварное кольцо
Театральный проезд
Большой театр
ул. Петровка
Театральная
Театральная пл.
Мохован ул.
ул. Знаменка
Воздвиженка
Манежная пл.
МХАТ
ул. Пушкинская
Тверская ул.
театр им. Пушкина
ул. Герцена
театр Маяковского
Новый Арбат
ул. Арбат
Кропоткинская
ул. Пречистенка
Комсомольский проспект
Маяковская
Чеховская
Баррикадная
Белорусский вокзал
Лесная ул.
Садовое кольцо
Парк культуры
Московский государственный университет
Киевский вокзал
МОСКВА

BOOK ONE

НАЧАЛО

Second Edition

Sophia Lubensky
State University of New York—Albany

Gerard L. Ervin
Ohio State University, Emeritus

Larry McLellan
University of California, Santa Barbara

Donald K. Jarvis
Brigham Young University

Boston   Burr Ridge, IL   Dubuque, IA   Madison, WI   New York   San Francisco   St. Louis
Bangkok   Bogotá   Caracas   Kuala Lumpur   Lisbon   London   Madrid   Mexico City
Milan   Montreal   New Delhi   Santiago   Seoul   Singapore   Sydney   Taipei   Toronto

McGraw-Hill Higher Education ⚛

*A Division of The **McGraw-Hill** Companies*

This is an ⊏⫾⫾ book

NACHALO, Book 1

Published by McGraw-Hill, an imprint of The McGraw-Hill Companies, Inc., 1221 Avenue of the Americas, New York, NY 10020. Copyright © 2001, 1996, by The McGraw-Hill Companies, Inc. All rights reserved. No part of this publication may be reproduced or distributed in any form or by any means, or stored in a database or retrieval system, without the prior written consent of The McGraw-Hill Companies, Inc., including, but not limited to, in any network or other electronic storage or transmission, or broadcast for distance learning.

This book is printed on acid-free paper.

1 2 3 4 5 6 7 8 9 0 DOW DOW   0 9 8 7 6 5 4 3 2 1 0

ISBN 0-07-365515-5 (Student Edition)

ISBN 0-07-230966-0 (Instructor's Edition)

Vice president/Editor-in-chief: *Thalia Dorwick*
Senior sponsoring editor: *Leslie Hines*
Marketing manager: *Nick Agnew*
Associate project manager: *David Sutton*
Senior production supervisor: *Richard DeVitto*
Director of design: *Stuart Paterson*
Cover design: *Andrew Ogus*
Photo research coordinator: *Nora Agbayani*
Photo researcher: *Susan Friedman*
Compositor: *Interactive Composition Corporation*
Senior supplement coordinator: *Louis Swaim*
Typeface: *10/12 Minion*
Printer: *RR Donnelley & Sons Company*

Because this page cannot legibly accommodate all the copyright notices, page 408 constitutes an extension of the copyright page.

Library of Congress Cataloging-in-Publication Data
[Nachalo] / Sophia Lubensky . . . [et al.].—2nd ed.
    p. cm.
  1st ed. by Sophia Lubensky, Gerard L. Ervin, and Donald K. Jarvis.
  Includes index.
  ISBN 0-07-365515-5
    1. Russian language—Textbooks for foreign speakers—English. I. Lubensky, Sophia.

PG2129.E5 L8 2000
491.782'421—dc21   00-061676

http://www.mhhe.com

CONTENTS

УРОК 1 ДОБРО ПОЖАЛОВАТЬ В РОССИЮ! 1

О РОССИИ

СЛОВА, СЛОВА, СЛОВА. . .

УЧИСЬ УЧИТЬСЯ

APPENDICES   339

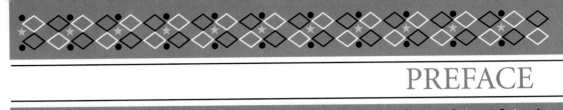

Welcome to the Second Edition of **НАЧАЛО.**

This is Book 1 in a complete package of instructional materials for students who are beginning Russian. Response to the first edition of **НАЧАЛО** was overwhelmingly positive. **НАЧАЛО** was the first Russian program to integrate video into the teaching of language and culture. The program struck a chord with instructors and students around the world who were drawn in to the engaging storyline of an American student, Jim, and his Russian friends. **НАЧАЛО** has been used by thousands of beginning Russian students since it was first published in 1996.

НАЧАЛО provides a balanced approach, integrating current and useful vocabulary with functionally based grammar explanations derived directly from the storyline. In addition, grammar is "spiraled" in its presentation. That is, a grammar point is treated in a limited way when it first occurs, then is expanded upon when it appears in more advanced forms in later readings. Throughout the text, small-group and partner/pair activities encourage students to use Russian in meaningful, communicative situations because in our experience, students' proficiency in Russian develops better and faster when there is a true balance between structure and communication.

❖ CHANGES IN THE SECOND EDITION

In responding to feedback about the first edition of **НАЧАЛО,** we have endeavored to incorporate suggested changes that will enhance the text's approach while retaining the key features that were praised by reviewers. The visual *Guided Tour through* **НАЧАЛО** (pages xxi–xxiv) explains all major features, some of which are new. Changes in the Second Edition include the following:

- The new design and four-color photographs enhance students' learning experience.
- The text has been streamlined by reducing the number of lessons in Book 1 and Book 2. Now each book consists of seven lessons, and Book 2 ends with a video epilogue that students can view on their own.
- The Second Edition offers extensively revised grammar explanations and exercises based on user feedback, including a more consolidated and comprehensive presentation of case forms. Much of the grammar has been resequenced to provide a more holistic initial presentation of forms than was offered in the first edition.

Exercises have been modified to move from form-focused, mechanical activities to open-ended, communicative activities following each grammar point.

- Each Lesson now ends with tinted pages containing an active vocabulary list, a grammar checklist, a grammar consolidation, and one or more optional supplemental reading texts.

- Each of the four Parts in a Lesson is now marked with a colored tab for ease of reference.

- New thematic, visual openers (**С ЧЕГО НАЧАТЬ?**) begin each Part with a short visual display related to a theme of that Part. This feature, which reinforces vocabulary acquisition through lexical association, should be of particular help to more visual learners.

- **КУЛЬТУРА РЕЧИ** (along with **ЧТЕНИЕ** and **ГРАММАТИКА И ПРАКТИКА**) is now a major section in each Part of the lesson. It includes several new repeating rubrics that focus on development of speaking skills.

- Book 2 contains a new *reVERBerations* rubric in the grammar sections to help students focus on the increasing complexities of the Russian verbal system.

- Notes (**О РОССИИ**) about contemporary Russian culture and society have been revised to reflect recent developments and current issues in Russia.

- Exciting new ancillaries include a colorful and engaging CD-ROM and a text-specific Website. See *Program Components* for a description of all the ancillaries.

❖ ORGANIZATION OF THE STUDENT TEXT

The fourteen lessons in **НАЧАЛО** are divided into Book 1 (Lessons 1–7) and Book 2 (Lessons 8–14 and Epilogue). Lesson 1 of Book 1 is an introduction to the Russian language. It uses simple greetings, basic vocabulary, visual displays, and classroom phrases to present the basic sound and writing systems of the language. The remaining lessons of Book 1 and all lessons in Book 2 follow a consistent format:

- **Lesson Opener.** This page introduces the lesson with photographs and a summary of the story line in each Part as well as a general description of what students will be learning to say and do.

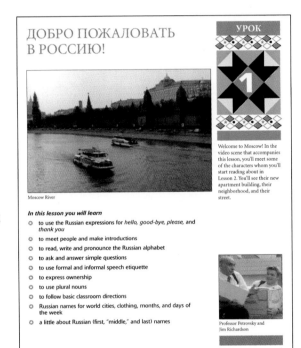

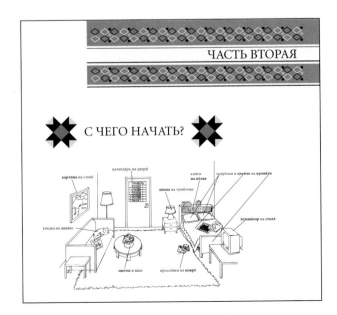

- **ЧАСТИ** *(Parts)*. There are four parts to each lesson, each essentially containing the following:

- **С ЧЕГО НАЧАТЬ?** *(Visual Opener)*. A new thematic visual opener introduces each Part with a short display related to a theme of that Part.

ЧТЕНИЕ

bad

here / I'll be right there!

beautiful

cat

tomcat

it seems

SCENE A: ИЗВИНЍТЕ, ЭТО ВЃША СОБЃКА!

(The staircase, second floor. The Silins are leaving.)

НАТЃЛЬЯ ИВ. Какóй ýжас! Квартѝра мáленькая и **плохáя.°** И сосéд музыкáнт.

СЕРГÉЙ ПЕТР. Квартѝра хорóшая и сосéди хорóшие, Натáша. *(Shouts.)* Лéна, ты где?

ЛÉНА. *(From inside the apartment.)* Я **тут,°** пáпа! **Сейчáс!°** Бéлка!

(Sasha comes down the stairs carrying a cat. Lena appears with Belka, who starts barking.)

СÃША. Извинѝте, это вáша собáка? Какáя **красѝвая°**!

ЛÉНА. Моя. Её зовýт Бéлка. А это вáша **кóшка?°** Какáя большáя!

СÃША. Это **кот.°** Его зовýт Матвéй. Или Мóтя. А я Алексáндр. Сáша.

ЛÉНА. Елéна. Лéна.

СÃША. Óчень прѝятно. Мы, **кáжется,°** сосéди.

SCENE B: НÓВЫЕ АДРЕСÃ

All

entrance

third / Downstairs

(Grandma Kruglov is sitting on a bench talking to a neighbor.)

— **Всё°** домá нóвые. Нóвые квартѝры, нóвые сосéди, нóвые адресá . . . Вот это наш дом. Сосéди хорóшие. Вон наш сосéд, профéссор Петрóвский, и Джим, его аспирáнт. Джим америкáнец. А это наш **подъéзд°**. Квартѝра нóмер дéсять, **трéтий°** этáж. **Внизý°** живýт Сѝлины. Их дочь студéнтка. **Журналѝстка.¹** Мой внук Сáша — тóже студéнт. Пианѝст. *(They hear the piano being played.)* Это Сáша! Он óчень хорóший пианѝст!

УПРАЖНÉНИЕ 3   Под микроскóпом: *Adjective endings*

Without looking back at the text, see if you can supply the missing adjective endings. Then check your answers against the original text in Scene A above.

1. Ка_____ ýжас! Квартѝра мáленьк_____ и плох_____!
2. Квартѝра хорóш_____ и сосéди хорóш_____, Натáша!
3. Извинѝте, это вáша собáка? Как_____ красѝв_____!
4. А это вáша кóшка? Как_____ больш_____!

- **ЧТЕНИЕ** (*Reading*). The reading material is presented in the form of a play, an ongoing story that helps tie together each of the four Parts within the Lesson. In many lessons, one of the readings is in prose form.

- **Под микроскóпом** (*Under the Microscope*). New exercises follow each reading and focus on a grammatical or lexical feature from an earlier lesson or as an introduction for the current lesson.

- **ГРАММАТИКА И ПРАКТИКА** (*Grammar and Practice*). Grammar topics are generally introduced with examples from the readings. Additional examples often accompany the explanations, which are deliberately short and uncomplicated. Each is followed by at least one exercise suitable for in-class use, including form-focused mechanical exercises, interactive "information gap" activities, and open-ended, communicative activities.

Icons identify audio and video recordings, pair/group activities, and info-gap activities.

ГРАММАТИКА И ПРАКТИКА

2.1. AN INTRODUCTION TO VERB CONJUGATION: ЖИВЁТ, ЖИВÝТ

Здесь **живýт** Сѝлины.   *The Silins live here.*
Их собáка Бéлка тóже **живёт** здесь.   *Their dog Belka lives here too.*

In English we say *I live* but *he/she lives*, adding an *-s* to the verb form when the subject is *he* or *she*. Changing the verb form so that it agrees with its subject is called *conjugation*. (Note from the examples that in Russian the subject of a sentence may sometimes follow its verb. See next section on word order.) The only new conjugated forms in this reading are **живёт** (for **он** or **онá** subjects), and **живýт** (for **онѝ** subjects).[4] Note that **кто** always takes a singular verb form (like **живёт**), even if a plural answer is expected, such as **Сѝлины.**

УПРАЖНÉНИЕ (EXERCISE) 4   Verb endings

Supply the correct verb ending to the following:

1. Вóва жив_____ там.
2. Бáбушка и дéдушка жив_____ здесь.
3. Кто там жив_____?
4. Там жив_____ Круглóвы.
5. Где он жив_____?
6. Её семья жив_____ там.

2.2. WORD ORDER IN QUESTIONS AND ANSWERS

— **Кто** там живёт?   *"Who lives there?"*
— Там живёт **Вóва.**   *"Vova lives there."*

English usually requires a strict word order of subject first, verb second, and any remaining sentence elements last: <u>Who</u> hit the ball? <u>John</u> did. Does <u>Stacy</u> live here? No, <u>Laurel</u> does. In Russian, important and/or new information is usually placed toward the end of the sentence.

— Здесь живёт **Сáша?**   *"Does Sasha live here?"*
— Нет, здесь живёт **Вóва.**   *"No, Vova lives here."*

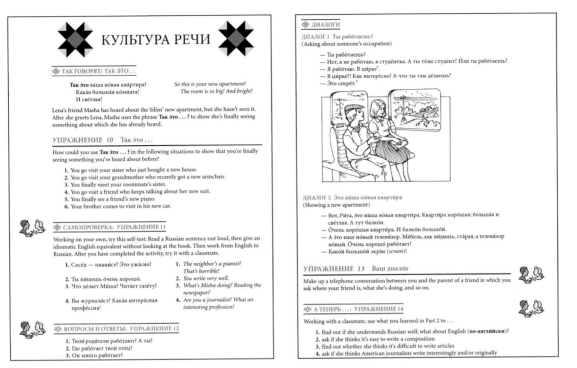

- **КУЛЬТУРА РЕЧИ.** Useful, high-frequency conversational elements focus on the development of speaking skills. Each **КУЛЬТУРА РЕЧИ** section includes **ТАК ГОВОРЯТ, САМОПРОВЕРКА, ВОПРОСЫ И ОТВЕТЫ, ДИАЛОГИ, Ваш диалóг,** and **А ТЕПЕРЬ . . .**

- **ИТАК . . .** Each lesson ends with tinted pages containing:

  - **НОВЫЕ СЛОВА.** A list of all active vocabulary presented in the chapter.

  - **ЧТО Я ЗНАЮ, ЧТО Я УМЕЮ.** A grammar checklist for students to use to review the major grammar topics of the lesson.

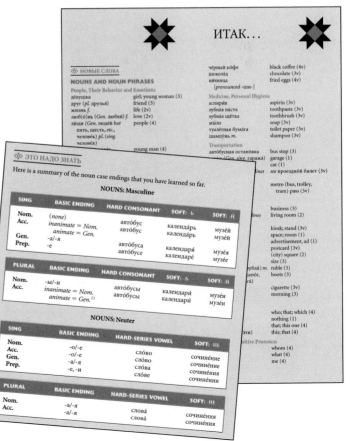

- **ЭТО НАДО ЗНАТЬ.** Periodic grammar consolidations of nouns, adjectives, verbs, and other forms presented to date.

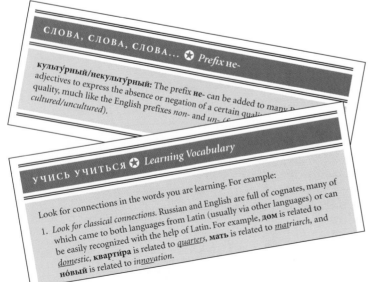

⟡ ДОПОЛНИТЕЛЬНЫЕ ТЕКСТЫ

A. EVENTS CALENDAR

МУЗЫКА

Четверг, 23 октября
Камерный Бетховен
Фортепианный квартет "Клавиоль" в составе: Игорь Гусельников (фортепиано), Дина Ахънова (скрипка), Марина Судзиловская (альт) и Сергей Судзиловский (виолончель) — играет камерные произведения Бетховена.
Музей Скрябина, 18.30. 241 19 01. Бол. Николопесковский пер., 11, Ⓜ «Смоленская»

Четверг, 23 октября
Владимир Спиваков
Художественный руководитель камерного оркестра «Виртуозы Москвы» играет сольную скрипичную программу. У рояля — корейский пианист Кун Ву Пек.
Концертный зал им. Чайковского, 19.00. 299 36 81, 299 39 57. Триумфальная пл., 4/31, Ⓜ «Маяковская»

Пятница, 24 октября
Дед и внук
Скрипачи Виктор и Игорь Пикайзен, альтист Игорь Найдин из квартета им. Бородина и камерный оркестр "Cantus firmus" под управлением Александра Хургина.
В программе — произведения Моцарта.
Малый зал Московской консерватории, 19.00. 229 77 95. Бол. Никитская, 13, Ⓜ «Библиотека им. Ленина», «Охотный ряд», «Арбатская»

ОПЕРА

Среда, 22 октября
«Любовь к трём апельсинам» С. Прокофьева
Режиссёр Пйтер Устинов. Спектакль сделан в европейской манере. Доминируют стильные модёрновые декорации Олега Шейнциса.
Большой театр, 19.00. 292 00 50, 292 99 86. Театральная пл., 1, Ⓜ «Театральная», «Охотный ряд»

Воскресенье, 26 октября
«Сказка о царе Салтане» Н. Римского-Корсакова
В спектакле Александра Тителя много режиссёрской фантазии и театральных трюков.
Музыкальный театр им. К. С. Станиславского и В. И. Немировича-Данченко, 12.00. 229 06 49, 229 83 88. Б. Дмитровка, 17, Ⓜ «Чеховская»

Вторник, 28 октября
Дивертисмент Россини
Фрагменты комических опер Россини «Севильский цирюльник» и «Итальянка в Алжире». Кроме того, впервые на московской сцене звучат фрагменты менее известных у нас опер композитора, в том числе уникальный хор спасшихся евреев из оперы «Моисей в Египте».
Новая опера, 19.00. Репетиционная сцена. 911 14 40. Таганская, 40/42, Ⓜ «Марксистская»

Музыка
1. Which composer's work will be performed at the **Музей Скрябина**?
2. Which musicians will be performing in this quartet? Give the Russian words.
3. Where will **Владимир Спиваков** be performing?
4. What is the name of his chamber orchestra?
5. What instrument will he be playing?
6. What is the name of the country his accompanist is from?
7. What is the relationship between **Виктор** и **Игорь Пикайзен**?
8. What instrument(s) do they play?
9. Which composer's music will they perform?

Опера
1. Who is the composer of **«Любовь к трём апельсинам»** [*The Love for Three Oranges*]?
2. What is the name of the venue where this opera is being performed?
3. Which venue is presenting music by an Italian composer?
4. What is the Italian composer's name?
5. Who is the composer of **«Сказка о царе Салтане»** [*The Tale of Tsar Sultan*]?
6. Which opera would you go to if you want to see a matinee?
7. What are the phone numbers of the **Большой театр**?

- **ДОПОЛНИТЕЛЬНЫЕ ТЕКСТЫ.** Optional supplemental texts including schedules for performing arts or sporting events, maps, diagrams, tongue twisters, short magazine articles and reviews, poems, songs, and advertisements.

In addition, the following special features appear at various places in the lessons:

- **О РОССИИ** (*About Russia*). Concise cultural observations about contemporary Russian societal and behavioral norms and formal elements of Russian culture that expand on the cultural information in the readings.

❖❖❖ О РОССИИ ❖❖❖❖❖❖❖❖❖❖❖❖❖❖❖❖❖❖❖❖

ШАХМАТЫ

Сергей Петрович и Вова играют в шахматы.

Chess (**шахматы**; always plural) in Russia is a national passion. The names of such grand masters as Karpov and Kasparov are known all over the world by anyone who has even a passing acquaintance with the game. Any major international tournament will have Russians prominent among its top contestants, and most of the world champions of the past 50 years have been from Russia and the Soviet Union. In Russia itself, top chess players are treated with the same respect afforded practitioners of the more physical sports; in fact, chess is among the 60-some officially recognized sports— right up there with soccer (**футбол**), swimming (**плавание**), and figure skating (**фигурное катание**). Here are the names of the chess pieces (**фигуры**): *pawn* = **пешка**, *rook/castle* = **ладья**, *knight* = **конь** (*m.*), *bishop* = **слон**, *queen* = **ферзь** (*m.*), *king* = **король** (*m.*). Oh, and **шах/мат** (*check/mate*), "the king is dead" (from Persian).

Гарри Каспаров

❖❖❖❖❖❖❖❖❖❖❖❖❖❖❖❖❖❖❖❖❖❖❖❖❖❖❖❖

СЛОВА, СЛОВА, СЛОВА... ✪ *Prefix* не-

культурный/некультурный: The prefix **не-** can be added to many adjectives to express the absence or negation of a certain quality, much like the English prefixes *non-* and *un-* (*cultured/uncultured*).

УЧИСЬ УЧИТЬСЯ ✪ *Learning Vocabulary*

Look for connections in the words you are learning. For example:

1. *Look for classical connections.* Russian and English are full of cognates, many of which came to both languages from Latin (usually via other languages) or can be easily recognized with the help of Latin. For example, **дом** is related to *domestic*, **квартира** is related to *quarters*, **мать** is related to *matriarch*, and **новый** is related to *innovation*.

- **СЛОВА, СЛОВА, СЛОВА . . .** (*Words, words, words . . .*). Offers a special focus section on word families and vocabulary items needing commentary or clarification.

- **УЧИСЬ УЧИТЬСЯ** (*Learn to Study*). These study tips provide students with hints about effective language-learning practice.

PROGRAM COMPONENTS

Available to adopters and to students:

- The *Student Edition* of both Books 1 and 2 is packaged with the *Listening Comprehension Program,* a free audiocassette or audio CD that contains the readings of each lesson.

- The *Video Guide* provides pre- and postviewing exercises to keep students actively involved as they watch the video dramatization.

- The combined *Workbook/Laboratory Manual,* by Ruth Warner, University of Northern Colorado, has been extensively revised. It now offers an increased emphasis on contextualized and open-ended activities. Intended for use as homework, the Workbook portion presents written exercises for each grammar point in the text. The Laboratory Manual portion contains listening and speaking exercises.

- The *Student Audio Program,* available on either audio CD or audiocassette, correlates with the Laboratory Manual portions of the *Workbook/Laboratory Manual.*

- A multimedia *CD-ROM* offers a variety of innovative exercises focusing on the storyline as well as functional activities with the linguistic and cultural information contained in each lesson.

- A text-specific *Website* provides links to other culturally authentic sites and expands upon the themes of each lesson.

- A *Practical Guide to Language Learning,* by H. Douglas Brown, San Francisco State University, provides beginning foreign-language students with a general introduction to the language-learning process.

- The *Rand-McNally New Millennium World Atlas on CD-ROM,* available for student purchase, contains detailed maps along with visuals and textual information (in English) about key events in history, famous figures, important cities, and so on. The detail and information provided significantly enhance the foreign-language experience from a cultural, historical, and geographical perspective.

Available to adopters only:

- The *Annotated Instructor's Edition* for each book includes teaching hints; *Reading Introduction*—three or four factual questions in Russian about each reading that students can be expected to answer; expansions on grammar topics and usage; and helpful ideas for classroom activities that enrich the exercises. In addition, answer keys are provided for the form-focused activities that are intended for classroom use.

- The *Video Program,* professionally filmed on location in Moscow, presents selected scenes from the storyline comprising the readings in the Lessons, offering students an engaging way to see and hear the story they are following in the text.

- The *Instructor's Manual/Tapescript/Testing Program* offers extensive teaching suggestions, transparency masters of selected illustrations from the *Student Edition,* a *Testing program* (consisting of two alternate tests with answer keys for each lesson), audioscripts for the listening comprehension and speaking exercises, and an *Answer key* to the written exercises in the *Workbook/Laboratory Manual.*

- A *training/orientation manual* for use with teaching assistants, by James F. Lee, University of Indiana at Bloomington, offers practical advice for beginning language instructors and language coordinators.

CAST OF CHARACTERS

Characters in the framework of the storyline include the following:

Professor Petrovsky and his American graduate student, **Jim.** Jim already speaks Russian fairly well because this is not his first trip to Russia. But, as you'll see, he still has a lot to learn . . . and is having a good time doing so!

The **Silin Family,** consisting of **Mr. and Mrs. Silin,** their daughter, **Lena,** who studies journalism, her little brother, **Vova,** and their dog, **Belka.**

Grandma and **Grandpa Kruglov** and their grandson, **Sasha,** a piano student at a Moscow conservatory, whose tastes run from classical to jazz.

Tatyana Dmitrievna, who rents out a room in her apartment to two young women, **Tanya** and **Sveta.**

Viktor, a hustling young entrepreneur of the post-Soviet era, who always seems to know how to provide hard-to-find goods and services.

ACKNOWLEDGMENTS

Many organizations and individuals made significant contributions to the production of **НАЧАЛО** and its ancillary materials. Early funding was received from the Geraldine Dodge Foundation, the National Endowment for the Humanities, the U.S. Department of Education, and the Defense Language Institute. These funds were administered through the Office of the Vice President for Research, University at Albany, State University of New York; we are grateful to Dr. Jeanne Gullahorn for her unwavering support. The College of Humanities at Brigham Young University and the Department of Slavic and East European Languages and Literatures at the Ohio State University were very generous with research assistance and logistical and communications support. Substantial funding specifically for the video, whose enhancement to this set of materials will immediately be clear to all, was received from the Film Committee of Brigham Young University.

The authors would like to thank many of our colleagues for their numerous contributions to the development of textbook and ancillary materials. Special thanks to Audra Starcheus, for her many hours of careful editing and cross-checking; and to Jennifer Marks Bown, Erin Diehm, Stacey Gordon, Lisa and Michael Kelly, William G. Koseluk, Betty Lou Leaver, Katia McClain, Slava Paperno, David Patton, Christopher Putney, Anelya Rugaleva, Adonica Sendelbach, Igor Sharanov, and Ruth Warner.

In addition, the publishers wish to acknowledge the suggestions received from the following instructors and professional friends who reviewed parts of the manuscript of the first edition, second edition, or both:

Valentina Abdelrahim-Soboleva
  Lincoln University
Tatiana Akishina
  University of Southern California
Deborah L. Barshay
  Bridgewater State College
Daniel Bayer
  University of Southern California
Yelena Belyaeva-Stander
  St. Louis University
Kathleen E. Dillon
  California Polytechnic School,
  Pasadena

Svetlana Elnitsky
  St. Michael's College
W. G. Fiedorov
  Knox College
Melissa Frazier
  Sarah Lawrence College
Carol A. Hart
  Ohio State University
Alexander G. Kostina
  Rhodes College
Lisa Little
  University of California,
  Berkeley

Elena Litvinenko
  Defense Language Institute, Monterey,
  California
Lawrence K. Mansour
  United States Military Academy
Rebecca E. Matveyev
  Lawrence University
Mark D. McLean
  North Harris College
Frank J. Miller
  Columbia University
Gerorge Mitrevski
  Auburn University
Frederick Patton
  West Chester University

Eric D. Roston
  Columbia University
Louise Rozwell
  Monroe Community College
Caroline Scielzo
  Montclair State University
Margaret Simontor
  Albertson College
Daniel Stearns
  University of Chicago
Harry Walsh
  University of Houston
Irina I. Wood
  Skagit Valley College

The appearance of their names in this list does not necessarily constitute their endorsement of the text or of its methodology.

  It would be impossible for us to overstate the contribution to the project that was provided at McGraw-Hill by Thalia Dorwick, whose patience, encouragement, guidance, and sound advice sustained us throughout our work. Special thanks are also due to the editorial, design, and production staff at McGraw-Hill, especially Leslie Hines, Gregory Trauth, Diane Renda, Francis Owens, David Sutton, Rich DeVitto, Nora Agbayani, and Louis Swaim for all of their patience and dedication to a complex project.

  Finally, to family and friends who listened to us, supported us, and tolerated us during the years of planning, writing, and revising, we offer the deepest gratitude of all.

ДОБРО ПОЖАЛОВАТЬ В РОССИЮ!

Moscow River

Welcome to Moscow! In the video scene that accompanies this lesson, you'll meet some of the characters whom you'll start reading about in Lesson 2. You'll see their new apartment building, their neighborhood, and their street.

In this lesson you will learn

✪ to use the Russian expressions for *hello, good-bye, please,* and *thank you*

✪ to meet people and make introductions

✪ to read, write and pronounce the Russian alphabet

✪ to ask and answer simple questions

✪ to use formal and informal speech etiquette

✪ to express ownership

✪ to use plural nouns

✪ to follow basic classroom directions

✪ Russian names for world cities, clothing, months, and days of the week

✪ a little about Russian (first, "middle," and last) names

Professor Petrovsky and Jim Richardson

ЧАСТЬ ПЕРВАЯ

❖ 1.1. GETTING ACQUAINTED (CASUAL)

Look at the illustrations below and read the English translations. Then listen to your instructor read the Russian phrases. The symbol 🎧 indicates material recorded on your textbook CD or audiocassette. Listen frequently to each recording to develop your listening and speaking skills.

*TAMARA: Hi! My name is Tamara. And yours?
PAVEL: Hi! My name is Pavel. Pasha.

*PAVEL: Who's that?
TAMARA: I don't know.

*TAMARA: What's her name?
PAVEL: Galina.

*TAMARA: What's his name?
GIRLFRIEND: Yan.

EXERCISE 1   Introductions

Using the first picture on page 2 as a model, learn the names of the students in your class. (The symbol 🗣 indicates a conversational exercise.)

2

❖ 1.2. NEW LETTERS AND SOUNDS: GROUP A

There are 33 letters in the Russian (Cyrillic) alphabet. Most represent sounds similar to those of English. Although there are often close similarities, exact sound equivalences between languages are rare. Listen to your teacher and tapes carefully and imitate them. Writing practice is provided in the workbook. Each Russian word has only one stressed syllable. Since the printed form of the word gives no hint about which syllable is stressed, this book will mark all stresses. The preceding dialogues contain 21 of the 33 Russian letters.

М, К, Т, А, О are similar to English letters in print and sound.

М, м	Тама́ра	Similar to English [m]
К, к	кто	Similar to English [k], but without the puff of air following; closer to the [k] in *skin* than in *kin*
Т, т	приве́т	Similar to English [t], but with the tongue touching the back of the upper teeth, and without the puff of air following; closer to the [t] in *stop* than in *top*
А, а	как	Similar to the [a] in *father* in these locations: (1) in the stressed syllable (as in Тама́ра); (2) in the syllable immediately preceding the stress (as in Гали́на); and (3) as the first letter of a word; elsewhere "uh," similar to the [a] in *about* (as in the last syllable of Тама́ра)
О, о	кто	In the stressed syllable, similar to the [o] in *shore*; similar to the [a] in *father* in these locations: (1) in the syllable immediately preceding the stress (as in зову́т); (2) as the first letter of a word; elsewhere "uh," similar to the [a] in *about* (as in э́то)

В, Н, Р, У, Е look like English letters, but represent different sounds.

В, в	зову́т	Similar to English [v]
Н, н	Гали́на	Similar to English [n], but with the tongue touching the back of the upper teeth
Р, р	Тама́ра	A flapped [r], similar to the casual American pronunciation of [d] in *widow*
У, у	зову́т	Similar to English [u] in *Luke* or *jukebox*
Е, е	приве́т	In a stressed syllable, similar to the [ye] in *yet* in these locations: (1) at the beginning of a word; (2) after a vowel; elsewhere in a stressed syllable, similar to the [e] in *yet*;
		In an unstressed syllable, similar to the [yi] in *Yiddish* in these locations: (1) at the beginning of a word (as in его́); (2) after a vowel; elsewhere in an unstressed syllable, similar to the [i] in *bit* (as in меня́)

З, Б, П, Г, Л, Ш, Э, И, Ё, Ю, Я do not look like English letters.

З, з	зову́т	Similar to English [z]
Б, б	тебя́	Similar to English [b] as in *cab*
П, п[1]	приве́т	Similar to English [p], but without the puff of air following; closer to the [p] in *spin* than in *pin*
Г, г	Гали́на	In most instances, similar to English [g] in *get, big*; however, in the words **его́** and certain others, it is pronounced like English [v]
Л, л	Па́вел	Similar to English [1] in *dull*
Ш, ш	Па́ша	Similar to English [sh] in *shore*
Э, э	э́то	Similar to English [e] in *bet*
И, и	Гали́на	Similar to English [i] in *magazine*
Ё, ё	её	Similar to [yo] in *York*
Ю, ю	зна́ю	Similar to [yu] in *yule*
Я, я	Ян	In a stressed syllable, similar to the [ya] in *yacht* in these locations: (1) at the beginning of a word; (2) after a vowel; elsewhere in a stressed syllable, similar to the [a] in *yacht* (as in меня́);
		In an unstressed syllable, similar to the [yi] in *Yiddish* at the beginning of a word; at the end of a word, similar to the [yu] in *yuppie* (after a vowel) or the final [a] in *pizza* (after a consonant); elsewhere in an unstressed syllable, similar to the [i] in *bit*

EXERCISE 2   Word recognition

The following words are made from the 21 letters you have already encountered. As your instructor reads words at random, fill in the blank with the order in which you hear them. Try to guess their meaning.

1. ——— Аме́рика
2. ——— Норве́гия
3. _3_ тра́ктор
4. ——— Украи́на
5. _6_ ка́мера
6. ——— зе́бра
7. _1_ Петербу́рг
8. ——— актёр
9. _9_ ро́за
10. ——— Япо́ния
11. ——— ю́мор

12. _7_ Юпи́тер
13. ——— коло́ния
14. ——— контра́кт
15. _8_ Герма́ния
16. _5_ Коре́я
17. _2_ эква́тор
18. _10_ ветера́н
19. ——— кенгуру́
20. ——— партнёр
21. ——— Во́лга
22. _4_ Вашингто́н

---

[1]You may recognize this letter, and some of the others, as derived from the Greek alphabet.

STUDY TIP ⭐ *Space Out Your Practice*

Athletes and musicians know the value of regular, daily workouts and practice sessions. The same applies to language students. For example, listen to your tapes repeatedly; they become much easier the second or third time around. Use flash cards several times a day: ten minutes here, ten minutes there. Do your written homework each day: Regular daily contact with Russian makes for far better learning than once- or twice-a-week marathon cram sessions.

EXERCISE 3   Cyrillic scramble

Below are some of the words from Exercise 2, with their letters mixed up. Unscramble them and write them out in cursive. Use capital letters as necessary.

1. зора (a flower)   *роза*
2. приюте (a planet)   *Юпитер*
3. антевер (an old soldier)   *Ветеран*
4. бреза (an animal)   *Зебра*
5. магрения (a country)   *Германия*
6. транкокт (a written agreement)   *Контракт*
7. груберепт (a city)   *Петербург*

EXERCISE 4   Countries and regions

Place the countries into the correct regions.

	Asia	Latin America	Africa	Europe
Аргенти́на	[ ]	[x]	[ ]	[ ]
Ира́н	[x]	[ ]	[x]	[ ]
Ку́ба	[ ]	[x]	[ ]	[ ]
Маро́кко	[ ]	[ ]	[x]	[ ]
Ве́нгрия	[ ]	[ ]	[ ]	[ ]
Пана́ма	[ ]	[x]	[ ]	[ ]
Перу́	[ ]	[x]	[ ]	[ ]
Япо́ния	[ ]	[ ]	[ ]	[ ]

❖❖ 1.3. CASUAL GREETINGS AND INTRODUCTIONS

Привёт! is a casual greeting like *Hi!* Students and friends commonly greet one another this way, but it is inappropriate for students to use this greeting with teachers. (Formal greetings are presented in the next section.)

Как тебя зовут? (*literally, How do they call you?*) is the informal way of asking *What is your name?* To answer with your own name, say **Меня зовут** . . . (*literally, Me they call* . . .), and fill in your name. In this context, **зовут** (*they call*) never changes in form, regardless of whose name is given.

А тебя? (*And you?*) is conversational; its full form is **А как тебя зовут?**

Это, an unchanging pronoun, is used in Russian to ask about something or point something out. It corresponds to *This is, That is, These are, Those are* . . .

What's his/her name?　There are several ways to ask someone the name of another person.

Кто это?	*Who is that/this?* (Russian does not normally express *am, are, is.*)
Как **его** зовут?	*What's his name?*
Как **её** зовут?	*What's her name?*

The answer to this question can vary, depending on the situation.

Это . . .	*That's/This is* . . .
Его зовут . . .	*His name is* (*they call him*) . . .
Её зовут . . .	*Her name is* (*they call her*) . . .
Не знаю.	*I don't know.*

EXERCISE 5　Greetings, getting acquainted

What can you say when

1. you greet someone your own age casually?
2. you want to ask the name of a student to whom you have just begun talking?
3. you see a man you don't know and ask a friend what his name is?
4. you see a woman you don't know and ask a friend what her name is?
5. you've been asked who someone is and want to say what his or her name is?
6. you've been asked who someone is and don't know his or her name?

EXERCISE 6　Introducing yourself (casually)

Following the examples in the illustrations at the beginning of this Part, introduce yourself to several other people in the class. Then ask them if they know the name of someone you have not met. Try to use as many of the various question-and-answer combinations as you can.

ЧАСТЬ ВТОРАЯ

❖ 1.4. ГЕОГРАФИЯ†

Го́род: Санкт-Петербу́рг, Нью-Йо́рк, Монреа́ль . . .

Страна́: Росси́я, США (Соединённые Шта́ты Аме́рики), Кана́да . . .

Контине́нт: Австра́лия, А́зия, А́фрика, Евро́па, Се́верная (*North*) Аме́рика, Ю́жная
(*South*) Аме́рика . . .

Река́: Амазо́нка, Миссиси́пи, Нил . . .

EXERCISE 1   Геогра́фия

A number of world cities are indicated on the map. As your instructor reads them
aloud, check off the ones you recognize in the small boxes next to each name on
the map. 🖐

✧ 1.5. NEW LETTERS AND SOUNDS: GROUP B

Some of the eight new letters introduced in this group do not look like English letters, but most of them represent sounds that have English counterparts. Listen carefully and imitate your teacher and the tape.

Ф, С, Д, Ч, Ж, Й, Х, Ь

Ф, ф	Фра́нк**ф**урт	Similar to English [f]
С, с	Бо́**с**тон	Similar to English [s]; compare English words spelled with [c] such as *ice*
Д, д	Ло́н**д**он	Similar to English [d], but with the tongue touching the back of the upper teeth
Ч, ч	**Ч**ика́го	Similar to English [ch] in *cheap*
Ж, ж	Ри́о-де-**Ж**ане́йро	Similar to the [zh] sound at the end of *mirage* or the middle of *vision*
Й, й	На**й**ро́би	A "glide," like English [y] when following vowels: **ой** (*boy*), **ей** (*hey*), **ай** (*guy*), **уй** (*buoy*). This letter represents a consonant, not a vowel.
Х, х	**Х**ано́й	Similar to German [ch] in *Bach*
Ь, ь	Монреа́**ль**	**мя́гкий знак** *soft sign* has no sound of its own; softens the preceding consonant[2]

Э́то бу́ква (*letter*).

Э́то звук (*sound*).

Э́то сло́во (*word*).

✧ 1.6. NAMES AND NICKNAMES

Full first names for Russian men typically end in a consonant; full names for women typically end in **-а** or **-я**. For both genders, nicknames typically end in **-а** or **-я**. **Са́ша, Ва́ля, Же́ня,** and a few other nicknames can be either men's or women's names, like *Pat* or *Chris* in English.

EXERCISE 2   Hearing and recognizing names

You are in Russia, and a Russian friend has invited you to a party. She is telling you the names of some people you will meet there. Circle the names you hear as your instructor reads them.

---

[2]This "softening," also called "palatalization," will be discussed in Part 4 of this lesson. Pronunciation of soft consonants is best learned by listening to your instructor and the tapes.

MEN'S NAMES		WOMEN'S NAMES	
~ Сáша	Ми́ша	Сáша	Мáша
Бóря	Ди́ма	Вáля	Зи́на
Тóля	Гéна	Áля	Лéна
— Алёша	Кóля	˘ Вéра	Йра
~ Волóдя	Пéтя	Зóя	Кáтя
Слáва	Юра	⌣ Жéня	~ Люба
Ви́тя	Олéг	Гáля	Тáня
Яша	Илю́ша	Тамáра	˘ Свéта

◆ 1.7. PATRONYMICS AND LAST NAMES

он			**онá**		
Николáй	Михáйлович	Лáзарев	Надéжда	Михáйловна	Лáзарева
и́мя	óтчество	фами́лия	и́мя	óтчество	фами́лия

A full Russian name consists of three parts. The first name (**и́мя**) is given by the parents. The second element, the *patronymic* (**óтчество**), is the name of the person's father with a suffix, usually **-ович** or **-евич** for males and **-овна** or **-евна** for females. If the father's name is **Ивáн**, for example, the patronymic for his son(s) is **Ивáнович,** for his daughter(s) is **Ивáновна.** The patronymic is usually used with the complete form of the first name when speaking to adults, especially in formal situations. School and university students in Russia always address their teachers by first name and patronymic (**и́мя и óтчество**).

— Меня́ зову́т Николáй Ивáнович Лéбедев. Извини́те (*Excuse me*), а как вáше (*your*) и́мя и óтчество?
— Мариáнна Петрóвна.

The last element is the family name (**фами́лия**). Most family names have different forms for males and females. For example,

MALES	FEMALES
Соколóв	Соколóва
Мали́нин	Мали́нина
Покрóвский	Покрóвская

EXERCISE 3   Famous patronymics

What is the first name of the father of each of these famous Russians?

1. Лев Николáевич Толстóй (author)
2. Áнна Андрéевна Ахмáтова (author)
3. Модéст Петрóвич Му́соргский (composer)
4. Алексáндр Сергéевич Пу́шкин (author)
5. Илья́ Ефи́мович Рéпин (artist)
6. Пётр Ильи́ч Чайкóвский (composer)
7. Валенти́на Влади́мировна Терешкóва (first woman cosmonaut)
8. Дми́трий Ивáнович Менделéев (scientist)
9. Васи́лий Васи́льевич Канди́нский (artist)

EXERCISE 4   Male or female?

Indicate whether the following names refer to men (M), women (W), or both (B).

1. _____ Га́ля
2. _____ Ви́тя
3. _____ Серге́й Петро́вич
4. _____ Викто́рия Ви́кторовна
5. _____ Ната́лья Я́ковлевна
6. _____ Са́ша
7. _____ Ива́н Никола́евич

EXERCISE 5   Gender markers

One must get used to distinguishing last names from patronymics, and masculine from feminine forms. Below are some feminine last names and patronymics; write in their masculine forms, then answer the questions:

EXAMPLE: Ива́новна   *Ива́нович*

1. Пано́ва   _____
2. Кругло́ва   _____
3. Миха́йловна   _____
4. Петро́вна   _____
5. Никола́ева   _____
6. Влади́мировна   _____

a. Which three pairs are last names?
b. Which three pairs are patronymics?

❖❖ 1.8. FORMAL GREETINGS AND INTRODUCTIONS

Look at the illustrations below and read the English translations. Then listen to your instructor read the Russian phrases.

*MAN: Hello! My name is Michael Smith.

*WOMAN: Hello! Nadezhda Mikhailo[...]sed to meet you.
 MAN: Nice to meet you

Здра́вствуйте!   Like most languages, Russian makes more of a distinction between formal and informal speech than English does. When a young person meets an older person or someone of higher status, such as a teacher, the familiar **Приве́т!** is inappropriate (as is **тебя́** in **Как тебя́ зову́т?**). **Здра́вствуйте** is used instead. Russians say **Здра́вствуйте!** only once a day to a given person. If they see that person again on the same day, Russians usually just nod, if no verbal exchange is otherwise needed. If you forget and greet someone with **Здра́вствуйте** a second time in the same day, it may surprise him or her.

Наде́жда Миха́йловна   Unless they know each other very well, adult Russians address one another by first name (here **Наде́жда**) and patronymic (here **Миха́йловна**). There are no Russian equivalents of Mr., Mrs., Miss, or Ms. in everyday use. (You'll learn more about names in Lesson 2.)

EXERCISE 6   Introducing yourself (formally)

Working with a classmate, follow the example above to act out a situation where you meet a new instructor, **Серге́й Миха́йлович** or **Мари́на Па́вловна.** Take turns playing each role.

❖ 1.9. REQUESTING, GIVING, AND RECEIVING

The word **Пожа́луйста** can mean *Please, Here you are,* and *You're welcome!* Use it when making a request and when giving something to someone. Use **Спаси́бо** (*Thank you*) when receiving an item or favor.

*WOMAN: Coffee, please.
WAITER: Here you are.
WOMAN: Thanks.
WAITER: You're welcome.

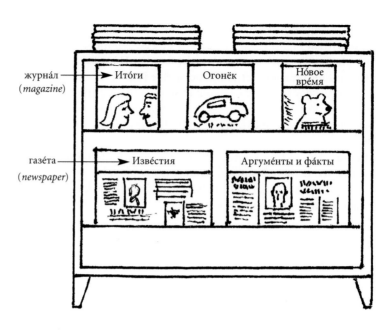

журна́л
(*magazine*)

газе́та
(*newspaper*)

EXERCISE 7   Пе́пси и пирожо́к, пожа́луйста

Working with a classmate, take the parts of salesperson and customer. Practice purchasing items from the menu and from the newsstand.

МЕНЮ́

ко́фе	конья́к	пирожо́к (*pirozhok—small filled pastry*)
чай (*tea*)	вино́ (*wine*)	бутербро́д (*sandwich*)
сок (*juice*)	шампа́нское	наполео́н (*layered custard pastry*)
пе́пси	пи́во (*beer*)	моро́женое (*ice cream*)

❖ 1.10. INFORMAL GREETINGS: "HI, HOW ARE THINGS?"

О́ЛЯ.	Приве́т, Са́ша!	"*Hi, Sasha!*"
СА́ША.	О́ля! Приве́т!	"*Olya! Hi!*"
О́ЛЯ.	Как дела́?	"*How are things?*"
СА́ША.	Хорошо́, спаси́бо.	"*Fine, thanks.*
	А у тебя́?	*And with you?*"
О́ЛЯ.	Ничего́.	"*Not bad.*"

Use the informal question **Как делá?** (*How are things?*) with your friends, family, and fellow students. Note that an instructor might ask this of a student, but the reverse is inappropriate. Typical responses are **Хорошó** (*Fine*) and **Ничегó** or **Неплóхо** (*Okay, not bad*). Note that the -г- in **Ничегó** is pronounced [**v**]. Other possible responses include:

Как делá?

| Óчень хорошó | Неплóхо (Ничегó) | Плóхо | Óчень плóхо |

If you say either **Плóхо** or **Óчень плóхо,** a Russian would probably react with concern and ask what's the matter. Unless you are prepared to explain a misfortune, it's best to stick with (**Óчень**) **хорошó** or **Ничегó.** The familiar form of the natural follow-up question is **А у тебя?** Since the question **Как делá?** implies **у тебя** "*with you*," the follow-up question also contains this phrase: **А у тебя?** "*And with you?*"

EXERCISE 8   Informal greetings

Working with classmates, substitute your own names in the dialogue on page 12 and greet one another.

◈◈ 1.11. PRONUNCIATION: STRESSED VS. UNSTRESSED «О» AND «А»

Stress is very important in Russian. With a solid understanding of phenomena associated with stress, many "irregularities" in Russian pronunciation and spelling turn out to be part of a pattern. A good way to begin learning about stress is to note that certain vowel letters under stress receive a very "full" pronunciation, while their pronunciation in unstressed syllables is "reduced." Here are some examples of stressed and unstressed **o** and **a**:

YOU SEE:	YOU SAY:	
	STRESSED ("full" pronunciation)	**UNSTRESSED** ("reduced" pronunciation)
a	• "ah" (second syllable of Тамáра)	• "ah" immediately before the stressed syllable (first syllable of Тамáра) **or** as the first letter in a word (first letter of **а**спирáнт) • "uh" elsewhere (last syllable of Тамáр**а**)
o	• "oh" (last syllable of хорош**ó**)	• "ah" immediately before the stressed syllable (second syllable of хор**о**шó) **or** as the first letter in a word (first letter of **о**кеáн) • "uh" elsewhere (first syllable of х**о**рошó)

Don't try to memorize these pronunciation descriptions as "rules." The point in presenting them is to help you make sense out of what you will hear native speakers of Russian say. Most Russians are, of course, totally unaware of any such "rules"—to them it's just normal speaking. But if you listen closely, you will hear them make these distinctions almost without exception. Through careful listening and mimicry of what you hear, these pronunciation habits of Russian will become second nature to you as well.

◈ 1.12. FORMAL GREETINGS: "HELLO. HOW ARE YOU?" (FORMAL AND INFORMAL YOU—ВЫ, ВАС **AND** ТЫ, ТЕБЯ́)

Здра́вствуйте!

А́ННА ПЕТРО́ВНА.	Здра́вствуйте, Са́ша!	*"Hello, Sasha!"*
СА́ША.	Здра́вствуйте, А́нна Петро́вна!	*"Hello, Anna Petrovna!"*
А́ННА ПЕТРО́ВНА.	Как у вас дела́?	*"How are you?"*
СА́ША.	Хорошо́, спаси́бо.	*"Fine, thank you."*

Like many European languages, Russian has a formal and informal distinction in its words for *you* and for related words like *your*. The formal variant of *you* as in **Как у вас дела́?** (as well as the subject form **вы**, which will be introduced in Part 3) is used between adults, by children addressing adults, or when any younger person (such as a student) addresses an older person (such as a teacher). It also expresses the plural *you*, the way to address a group of people. The informal variant of *you*, as in **Как тебя́ зову́т?** (as well as the subject form **ты**, which will be introduced in Part 3) is used in families, among close friends and young people, and when addressing God, a child, or a pet. Here's a good rule of thumb: If you are at all in doubt about how to address someone, it's best to use the formal register.

   Как у вас дела́? (*How are things with you?*)   The instructor, **А́нна Петро́вна,** has used the complete, formal version of **Как дела́?** Note her use of **у вас** rather than the familiar **у тебя́.** Note also that Sasha does not ask her **Как у вас дела́?** He is following the general Russian rule that in formal situations the higher-status individual is usually the one who asks any personal questions.

Asking someone's name.   Use **Как тебя́ зову́т?** when addressing a child or an animal. Young people up through university age also typically use this informal register with one another. In other situations, one should use a more formal phrasing such as **Извини́те, как вас зову́т?** or **Извини́те, как ва́ше и́мя и о́тчество?** (The phrase **и́мя и о́тчество** is often pronounced without «**и**» and is often spelled with a hyphen to reflect colloquial pronunciation: **и́мя-о́тчество.**)

Извини́те, как вас зову́т?

EXERCISE 9   Formal or informal

You are a student on your first visit to Russia. Decide whether the language register *you* use in these situations should be formal or informal.

		FORMAL	INFORMAL
EXAMPLE:	You're at a welcoming party thrown for your group by the Russian students and you are getting acquainted with them.	☐	☒
1.	You meet the English instructor at the Russian students' school and greet her in Russian.	☐	☐
2.	You meet the younger brother or sister of the student with whom you will be staying.	☐	☐
3.	You meet the parents of the student with whom you will be staying.	☐	☐
4.	You go into a store and ask the clerk to point you to the bread section.	☐	☐
5.	A young man comes up to you on the subway and, sensing that you are a foreigner, begins speaking with you.	☐	☐
6.	You are on the street and bump into an elderly woman by accident.	☐	☐
7.	A small child looks lost in the city park. You offer to help.	☐	☐

EXERCISE 10   Formal greetings

Working with classmates, choose one of you to be the instructor, and practice formal greetings. Then choose one of you to be a little boy named **Во́ва** or a little girl named **Ма́ша** and practice informal greetings.

❖❖ 1.13. SAYING GOOD-BYE

*See you later!

*Good-bye.

The formal-informal distinction in greetings is reflected also in good-byes. **До свида́ния** is the more formal expression, while **Пока́** is informal and usually implies that you expect to see the person again soon.

EXERCISE 11   Saying good-bye

How would you say good-bye to

    1. your teacher at the end of class?
    2. your classmates at the end of class?
    3. your roommate when leaving for class?
    4. your family when going off to attend college in another state?
    5. the maid as you leave your hotel?
    6. your taxi driver as you leave the cab?

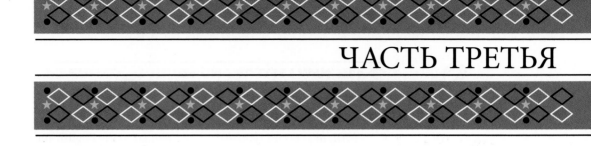

❖❖ 1.14. WHAT TO WEAR?

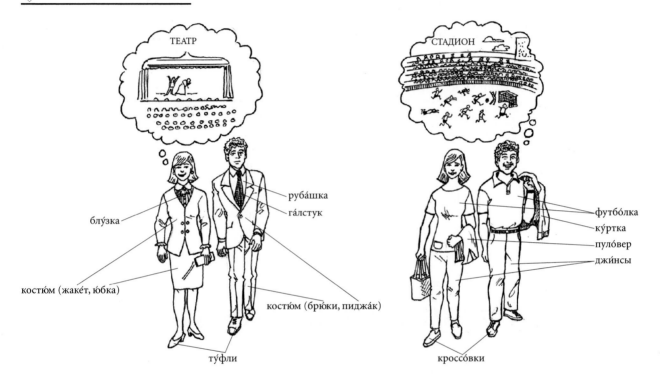

ТЕАТР

СТАДИОН

блу́зка

руба́шка
га́лстук

костю́м (жаке́т, ю́бка)

костю́м (брю́ки, пиджа́к)

ту́фли

футбо́лка
ку́ртка
пуло́вер
джи́нсы

кроссо́вки

EXERCISE 1   Packing list

The pictures above and the list below include some items you have brought to Russia. As you unpack, your "roommate" (a classmate) names some things. Circle what you hear your "roommate" say.

ша́пка	*hat*
сапоги́	*boots*
носки́	*socks*
плащ	*raincoat*
пальто́	*overcoat*
пла́тье	*dress*
перча́тки	*gloves*
ма́йка	*tank top*
фуфа́йка	*sweat shirt*
сви́тер	*high-neck sweater*

❖❖ 1.15. NEW LETTERS AND SOUNDS: GROUP C

Here are the four remaining letters of the Russian alphabet.

Щ, Ц, Ы, Ъ

Щ, щ	борщ (*borsch*)	Similar to the English combination [sh-sh] in *fresh sheets*
Ц, ц	пи́цца (*pizza*)	Similar to the English [ts] sound in *bats, pizza*
Ы, ы	вы (*you*)	Similar to English [ih] in *bit, tip, witch,* but with the tongue pulled further back
Ъ, ъ	подъе́зд (*entrance*)	**тве́рдый знак** *hard sign* indicates that a [y] sound (as in *you* or *yes*) precedes the following vowel

EXERCISE 2   Countries and currencies

Match the name of the currency with the country. (Some currencies are associated with more than one country.)

1. _____ до́ллар		а. Аме́рика
2. _____ ие́на		б. А́нглия
3. _____ ли́ра		в. Герма́ния
4. _____ ма́рка		г. Испа́ния
5. _____ пе́со		д. Ита́лия
6. _____ рубль		е. Кана́да
7. _____ франк		ж. Ме́ксика
8. _____ фунт (*pound*)		з. Росси́я
9. _____ песе́та		и. Фра́нция
		к. Япо́ния

❖❖ 1.16. ASKING AND ANSWERING QUESTIONS

a) — Кто э́то? Э́то Алексе́й Урма́нов?[3]
— Да, э́то Урма́нов.
— Нет, э́то не Урма́нов, э́то
  Илья́ Кули́к.

b) — Вы врач?   *"Are you a doctor?"*
— Нет, я музыка́нт.   *"No, I'm a musician."*

c) — Он студе́нт?   *"Is he an undergrad?"*
— Нет, он не студе́нт. Он аспира́нт.   *"No, he's not. He's a grad student."*

Нет means *no.* Use **не** *not* to negate a specific element in the sentence.

Articles: There are no definite (*the*) or indefinite (*a, an*) articles in Russian.

---

[3]Russian uses a dash (—) to indicate the beginning of a remark in a dialogue. No special mark is used at the end of the remark.

To be: The verb equivalents of present-tense forms *am, is, are* are generally not expressed.

Pronouns: Pronouns substitute for nouns. Here are the Russian pronouns used when referring to people:

я *I*		**мы** *we*	
ты *you* (informal)		**вы** *you* (formal or plural)	
он *he* / **она́** *she*		**они́** *they*	

Verbs are usually accompanied by pronouns in Russian, although **я** is frequently omitted in the phrase **Не зна́ю** *I don't know.* Note that Russians do not capitalize **я** (*I*) unless it is the first word of a sentence.

    Студе́нт means a male undergraduate student at a college or university; a female undergraduate student is **студе́нтка.**

    Аспира́нт and **аспира́нтка** are used to refer to graduate students. When speaking about students in general or about mixed groups, the masculine forms are used.

EXERCISE 3   Asking and answering questions

Working with two classmates, follow the models of the preceding dialogues to discuss the identity of other students in the classroom, or of other people whose pictures you might have with you in a newspaper, magazine, book, and so on.

❖ 1.17. INTONATION IN WH-QUESTIONS

In Russian, as in English, many questions begin with a question word (such as **где, кто, что, как**). These can be collectively referred to as WH-questions, because many of the corresponding question words in English begin with wh- (cf. *who, what, when, where, why*). The intonation of WH-questions in Russian differs markedly, however, from that in English. Diagrammatically the Russian intonation might be presented this way:

LEVEL	WH-QUESTIONS
High *Mid* *Low*	КТО э́то?

The focal word is pronounced higher than mid-level and the pitch falls sharply on the stressed syllable. As the preceding example shows, the focal point of a WH-question may be the question word itself, but usually it is the stressed syllable in the final word of the question, as in following examples:

LEVEL	WH-QUESTIONS	
High *Mid* *Low*	Как де- ЛА́?	Как вас зо- ВУ́Т?

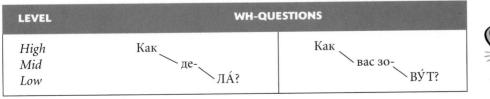

Now that you know what to listen for, pay close attention to your teacher and the tapes and you'll quickly learn to use this intonation quite naturally.

1.18. INTONATION IN YES/NO QUESTIONS AND STATEMENTS: ЭТО НИ́НА? VS. ЭТО НИ́НА.

Only intonation enables one to distinguish between the question **Э́то Ни́на?** and the statement **Э́то Ни́на.** Yes/no questions and statements both start at mid-range; then they differ: to ask yes/no questions (those not containing a question word), sharply raise the pitch of the stressed syllable of the word you are asking about. To answer a question or make a statement, start at mid-range and drop to the low range on the last stressed syllable of the sentence.

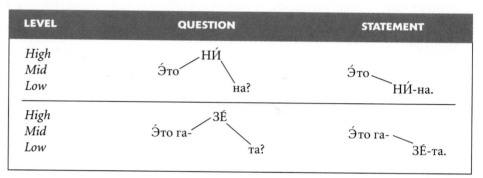

LEVEL	QUESTION	STATEMENT
High	НИ́	
Mid	Э́то	Э́то
Low	на?	НИ́-на.
High	ЗЕ́	
Mid	Э́то га-	Э́то га-
Low	та?	ЗЕ́-та.

EXERCISE 4   Question or statement?

Do you hear a question or a statement? Circle what you hear.

1. Э́то Ни́на?   Э́то Ни́на.
2. Она́ студе́нтка?   Она́ студе́нтка.
3. А́нна здесь (*here*)? А́нна здесь.
4. Марк до́ма (*at home*)? Марк до́ма.
5. Бори́с студе́нт?   Бори́с студе́нт.
6. Он аспира́нт?   Он аспира́нт.
7. Э́то Ко́ля?   Э́то Ко́ля.

EXERCISE 5   Ка́рта ми́ра (*World map*)

Working with a classmate, point out continents, countries, and cities on the maps at the beginning of Part 2 and inside the back cover of the book. Practice asking and answering questions such as the following:

1. Э́то Евро́па (А́зия, А́фрика . . .). Евро́па (А́зия, А́фрика . . .) — э́то континéнт?
2. — Э́то Украи́на?
   — Да, э́то Украи́на.
   — А э́то?
   — Э́то Росси́я (А́нглия, Аме́рика, Кана́да, Аргенти́на, Фра́нция, Брази́лия. . .)

❖ 1.19. DISCUSSING LOCATION: WHERE, HERE, AT HOME

ВИТА́ЛИЙ.	Здра́вствуйте! Э́то Мари́на Петро́вна?
МАРИ́НА ПЕТРО́ВНА.	Да. Здра́вствуйте. Кто э́то? Э́то Андре́й?
ВИТА́ЛИЙ.	Нет, э́то не Андре́й. Э́то Вита́лий. Мари́на Петро́вна, Ната́ша до́ма?
М. П.	До́ма. (*Shouting.*) Ната́ша! (*No response.*) Ната́ша, где ты?
НАТА́ША.	Я здесь, ма́ма. (*Whispering.*) Кто э́то?
М. П.	Э́то Вита́лий. (*Into the phone.*) До свида́ния, Вита́лий.
ВИТА́ЛИЙ.	До свида́ния, Мари́на Петро́вна.
НАТА́ША.	(*Picks up the phone.*) Вита́лий, приве́т!

Some possible responses to the question **где?** (*where?*) include **здесь** (*here*) and **до́ма** (*at home*). One can be **до́ма** without being physically inside the house (**дом**), as when washing the car or relaxing in the yard.

EXERCISE 6   On the phone

Working with two classmates, create a phone dialogue based on this model: one person calls a friend whose parent answers the phone; the caller asks if the friend is at home and then the friend comes to the phone. Include the location words **где, здесь, до́ма** in your dialogue. Remember to use a first name and patronymic that reflect whether the friend's mother or father is speaking.

◆ 1.20. ASKING THE NAME OF SOMETHING

—Что это? (*What's that?*)
—Это? Это ру́чка.
—А э́то?
—Это газе́та и письмо́.
—А что э́то?
—Это кни́га и журна́л.
—А э́то?
—Это каранда́ш.

EXERCISE 7   Что э́то?

Working with a classmate, practice asking and answering the questions **Что э́то?**, **Это _____?, А э́то?** Point to items in the room that you know, or select items from the illustration above. Ask a "wrong" question occasionally (for example, point to a newspaper and ask, **Это кни́га?**).

EXERCISE 8   Это Аме́рика?

Working with a classmate and a map, take turns asking and answering questions about various places. Ask a "wrong" question occasionally, as in the following example:

EXAMPLE: — (*Pointing to Africa.*) Это Аме́рика?
— Нет, э́то не Аме́рика. Это А́фрика.
— А э́то? (*Pointing to Australia.*) Это Анта́рктика?
— Нет! Это Австра́лия!

❖❖ 1.21. GRAMMATICAL GENDER

As you have already learned, **он, она** refer to *he, she,* expressing biological gender. But these words also express grammatical gender. That is, for inanimate nouns, English has one pronoun, *it,* while Russian, like many other European languages, has three: **он, она,** and **оно**. To choose the right pronoun to replace an inanimate noun, you must know the noun's *grammatical gender* (masculine, feminine, or neuter), which has nothing to do with biology! For instance, **журнал** (*magazine*) is masculine and can be replaced by the masculine pronoun **он; газета** (*newspaper*) is feminine and corresponds to the feminine **она;** and the neuter **письмо** (*letter*) requires the neuter **оно**. Gender is not reflected, however, in the plural: **они** (*they*) is used for all genders.

The pronoun endings hint at ways to tell grammatical gender in the dictionary form (the Nominative case) of nouns.

ОН (*he, it*)	Nouns ending in a consonant, including **-й,** are masculine:		
	Иван	*Ivan*	журнал	*magazine*
	город	*city*	континент	*continent*
	музей	*museum*		

ОНА́ (*she, it*)	Nouns ending in **-а** or **-я** are generally feminine:		
	Наташа	*Natasha*	Москва	*Moscow*
	студентка	*female student*	блузка	*blouse*
	фамилия	*last name*		

ОНО́ (*it*)	Nouns ending in **-о** or **-е** are neuter:		
	письмо	*letter*	слово	*word*
	отчество	*patronymic*	упражнение	*exercise*

ОНИ́ (*they*)	**-ы** and **-и** are two common endings for plural:		
	журналы	*magazines*	газеты	*newspaper*
	студенты	*students*	книги	*books*

Remember, however, that regardless of the ending on the noun, biology takes precedence over grammar: Most men's nicknames (**Дима**) and some words for male relatives (**папа** *dad*) end in **-а** or **-я,** but are still masculine. (Note also that most nouns ending in **-ь** are feminine. In this textbook, gender of nouns ending in **-ь** is always marked.)

Finally, a special word about the dictionary form (Nominative case) of a noun: You will encounter it in two contexts:

1. As the subject of a sentence.
— Где газета?
— Газета там.

2. As a predicate Nominative:
Иван — студент.
Лариса Михайловна — врач.

EXERCISE 9   Nouns by gender and number

Write **он** before the masculine nouns, **она́** before the feminine nouns, **оно́** before the neuter nouns, and **они́** before the plural nouns.

1.	_____ ру́чка	*pen*
2.	_____ журна́л	*magazine*
3.	_____ окно́	*window*
4.	_____ кни́га	*book*
5.	_____ кни́ги	*books*
6.	_____ газе́та	*newspaper*
7.	_____ молоко́	*milk*
8.	_____ кварти́ра	*apartment*
9.	_____ студе́нт	*(male) student*
10.	_____ студе́нтка	*(female) student*
11.	_____ мо́ре	*sea*
12.	_____ роди́тели	*parents*
13.	_____ стул	*chair*
14.	_____ доска́	*chalkboard*
15.	_____ часы́	*clock; watch*
16.	_____ каранда́ш	*pencil*
17.	_____ рюкза́к	*backpack*
18.	_____ очки́	*glasses*
19.	_____ джи́нсы	*jeans*
20.	_____ блу́зка	*blouse*
21.	_____ сви́тер	*high-neck sweater*
22.	_____ футбо́лка	*T-shirt*
23.	_____ пуло́вер	*V-neck sweater*

EXERCISE 10   Он (она́, оно́, они́) здесь (до́ма)

Using the list of clothing and accessories in Exercise 1, write down five items on a piece of paper. Your list represents a "suitcase" which you have "packed" and brought with you, and the items you listed are «**здесь**». Anything you did not list is «**до́ма**». Then see if you can find three other students in the class who packed at least three of the same items in their suitcase that you did.

EXAMPLE:	You:	Где джи́нсы? (*item on your list*)
	Classmate:	Они́ здесь. (*pointing to his list*)
		or
		Они́ до́ма.

❖ 1.22. PLURALS OF MASCULINE AND FEMININE NOUNS

— Кто э́то?
— Э́то студе́нты и .... аспира́нты.

журна́л журна́лы

кни́га кни́ги

— Что э́то?
— Э́то кни́ги и журна́лы.

The basic plural ending for masculine and feminine nouns is **-ы.**[4] It is added after the final consonant of masculine nouns and replaces the final **-a** on feminine nouns. The plural ending is spelled **-и** when the final consonant of the word (after dropping any vowel ending) is one of the following: **г, к, х** (referred to as *velars*); or **ж, ч, ш, щ** (known as *hushers*). Sometimes there are also stress shifts, which are largely unpredictable. Here is a summary of the basic pluralization pattern for masculine and feminine nouns[5]:

---

[4]Pluralization of neuter nouns will be presented when you know more neuter nouns. You already know one neuter plural: **дела́** (in **Как дела́?** *How are things?*), which is the plural form of **де́ло.**
[5]This spelling rule, which can be referred to as the «**кни́ги**» rule, will be presented in more detail in Lesson 2.

	SINGULAR (dictionary form)	PLURAL ENDING	EXAMPLES
Masculine and feminine nouns	студе́нт журна́л газе́т–а бу́кв–а	Delete final vowel; add **–ы/–и**	студе́нт–ы журна́л–ы газе́т–ы бу́кв–ы
	звук каранда́ш студе́нтк–а кни́г–а		зву́к–и карандаш–и́ студе́нтк–и кни́г–и

EXERCISE 1   Making plurals

Write the plural forms of these nouns.

EXAMPLE:
блу́зка   _блу́зки_

1. студе́нт _____
2. футбо́лка _____
3. журна́л _____
4. студе́нтка _____
5. кни́га _____
6. газе́та _____
7. ру́чка _____

8. телефо́н _____
9. компью́тер _____
10. зе́бра _____
11. тигр _____
12. офице́р _____
13. до́ллар _____

❖❖ 1.23. EXPRESSING OWNERSHIP

Э́то моя́ кни́га!*

Нет! Не твоя́, а моя́!

*он: It's my book!
она́: No! It's not yours. It's mine!

Мой, твой, наш, ваш *my, your (informal), our, your (formal or plural)*   These words change form to match the gender and number of the thing owned. For example:

мой журна́л	*my magazine*	на́ш журна́л	*our magazine*
мо**я** кни́га	*my book*	на́**ша** кни́га	*our book*
мо**ё** письмо́	*my letter*	на́**ше** письмо́	*our letter*
мо**и́** кни́ги	*my books*	на́**ши** кни́ги	*our books*
(**твой** follows the **мой** pattern)		(**ваш** follows the **наш** pattern)	

Be sure to pronounce the plural forms **мои́** and **твои́** with two distinct syllables [mah-EE, tvah-EE], placing the stress on the second syllable to distinguish these words from the one-syllable forms **мой, твой**. In Russian, every vowel makes a syllable, even when two vowels appear together.

Note that the possessive pronoun endings are similar to noun endings: The masculine forms (**мой, наш**) end in a consonant (remember, **-й** is a consonant); the feminine forms (**моя́, на́ша**) end in **-а/-я**; the neuter forms (**моё, на́ше**) end in **-е/-ё** (**ё** can be considered a variant of **-о**); and the plural forms end in **-и**.

Его́, её, их   Like their English counterparts, Russian third-person possessive pronouns **его́** (*his*), **её** (*her*), and **их** (*their*) never change to agree with the noun they modify[6]: For example, **его́ каранда́ш, его́ кни́га, его́ письмо́, его́ кни́ги** mean *his pencil, his book, his letter, his books*; **её каранда́ш, её кни́га, её письмо́, её кни́ги** mean *her pencil, her book, her letter, her books*. How would you say *their pencil, their book, their letter, their books*?

Here is a summary of the possessive adjectives, with a typical noun for each gender:

MEANING	MASCULINE	FEMININE	NEUTER	PLURAL
my	мой журна́л	моя́ кни́га	моё письмо́	мои́ журна́лы
your (*informal*)	твой журна́л	твоя́ кни́га	твоё письмо́	твои́ журна́лы
his (*does not change*)	его́ журна́л	его́ кни́га	его́ письмо́	его́ журна́лы
her (*does not change*)	её журна́л	её кни́га	её письмо́	её журна́лы
our	наш журна́л	на́ша кни́га	на́ше письмо́	на́ши журна́лы
your (*formal or pl.*)	ваш журна́л	ва́ша кни́га	ва́ше письмо́	ва́ши журна́лы
their (*does not change*)	их журна́л	их кни́га	их письмо́	их журна́лы

EXERCISE 2   Э́то твой . . . ?

In a group of four or five students, swap several items for which you know the names. One student picks up something from another student's desk and asks **Э́то твоя́ кни́га?** (**Э́то твой каранда́ш?**) The person addressed responds **Да, э́то моя́ кни́га,** or if it belongs to someone else, **Нет, э́то его́/её кни́га,** pointing out the correct owner. The person who began the exchange then hands this item back to its owner, asking again **Э́то твоя́ кни́га?** and getting a response from its owner **Да, моя́.**

---

[6]The possessives **его́, её, их** are identical in form to the personal pronouns you learned in the phrases **Как его́ (её) зову́т?**

❖ 1.24. В АЭРОПОРТУ́ (*At the airport*)

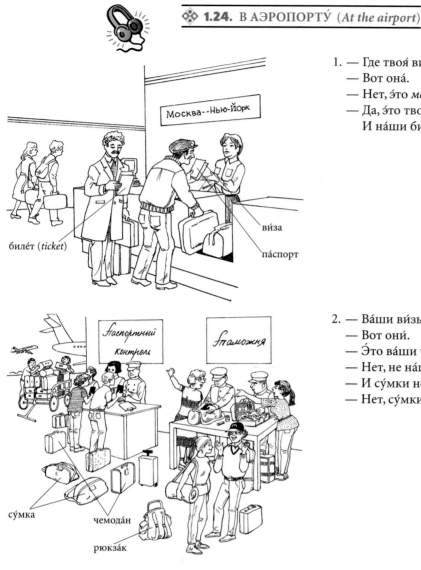

билéт (*ticket*)
ви́за
пáспорт

1. — Где твоя́ ви́за?
   — Вот онá.
   — Нет, э́то *моя́* ви́за.
   — Да, э́то твоя́ ви́за. А вот моя́ ви́за. И мой пáспорт. И нáши биле́ты.

2. — Вáши ви́зы, пожáлуйста.
   — Вот они́.
   — Э́то вáши чемодáны?
   — Нет, не нáши. Нáши чемодáны (*pointing*)—там.
   — И су́мки не вáши?
   — Нет, су́мки нáши! И рюкзаки́ нáши.

су́мка
чемодáн

рюкзáк

EXERCISE 3   Где . . . ?

Working with a classmate, create an airport dialogue based on one of the preceding models. Include some of the following items: **билéт, ви́за, пáспорт, рюкзáк, су́мка, чемодáн.** Try making some of the words plural.

What is the name of this airline company?

❖ 1.25. PRONUNCIATION AND SPELLING: PALATALIZATION (SOFTENING) OF CONSONANTS

The symbol **ь** (called **мягкий знак,** or *soft sign*), though soundless itself, represents a sound modification that you can usually hear and should always try to imitate. Without it, you will have a pronounced foreign accent in Russian and will even be misunderstood in some cases. Moreover, this phenomenon—called *palatalization* or *softening*—explains much about the way Russian words are spelled.

Most Russian consonant sounds have not one, but two spoken forms: a hard (unpalatalized) form and a soft (palatalized) form. Many words are distinguished simply by whether a consonant sound in them is palatalized or not. The presence of the **-ь** after the final consonant in the following words indicates that each word ends in a palatalized (soft) consonant.

HARD CONSONANTS	SOFT CONSONANTS
ма**т** (*swearing*)	ма**ть** (*mother*)
говори**т** (*he/she speaks*)	говори**ть**(*to speak*)
е**л** (*he ate*)	е**ль**(*fir tree*)
бы**л** (*he was*)	бы**ль**(*true story*)

The **ь** symbol is not the only way palatalized consonant sounds are indicated in writing. Another way—when a palatalized consonant sound is followed by a vowel sound—is with a *soft-series vowel letter*. Here again, accurate pronunciation is important because pronunciation makes a difference in meaning.

VOWEL LETTERS	VOWEL LETTERS
FOLLOWING HARD CONSONANTS	FOLLOWING SOFT CONSONANTS
(*HARD-SERIES VOWELS:* а, э, о, у, ы):	(*SOFT-SERIES VOWELS:* я, е, ё, ю, и):
мать (*mother*)	**мя**ть (*to wrinkle*)
мэ́ры (*mayors*)	**ме́**ры (*measures*)
жи**во́**т (*stomach*)	жи**вё**т (*he/she lives*)
лук (*onion*)	**лю**к (*trap door*)
был (*he/it was*)	**би**л (*he beat*)

Listen carefully as your instructor pronounces the pairs of words in the lists above and try to imitate the distinctions between them as closely as you can.

EXERCISE 4   Listening for hard and soft consonants

Listen as your instructor reads each pair of words. Then, as your instructor pronounces one of each pair, indicate whether you heard the hard or the soft consonant.

HARD	SOFT
1. стал	сталь
2. брат	брать
3. ел	ель
4. мат	мать
5. говори́т	говори́ть
6. был	бил
7. в зал	взял
8. мать	мять
9. живо́т	живёт

❖❖ 1.26. PRONUNCIATION AND SPELLING: MORE ON SOFT-SERIES VOWELS

The soft-series vowels actually serve two different functions. As discussed above, when they follow a consonant, they indicate that the consonant is soft. Elsewhere, such as after a vowel or at the beginning of a word, they indicate the presence of a distinct **й**-onset similar to that in **yacht, yet, York, yule**, when four of these letters **я, е, ё, ю** (*but not* **и**) are pronounced. Some examples you have seen already include:

> after a vowel: мо**я** (*my*), твоё (*your*), зна́**ю** (*I know*)
> at the beginning of a word: **я** (*I*), **ю**бка (*skirt*)

❖❖ 1.27. PRONUNCIATION: STRESSED VS. UNSTRESSED «Е» AND «Я»

Like the vowels **о** and **а**, the vowels **е** and **я** also vary according to whether they are stressed (pronounced with a "full" pronunciation) or unstressed (pronounced with a "reduced" pronunciation). As you saw in the preceding Parts, the soft-series vowels **я, е, ё, ю** can indicate the softness of a preceding consonant, or the presence of a distinct **й**-onset at the beginning of a word or after a vowel. Here are some examples of stressed and unstressed **е** and **я**. Remember, you should try mimicking what you hear rather than memorizing these descriptions as rules:

YOU SEE:	YOU SAY:	
	STRESSED ("full" pronunciation)	**UNSTRESSED** ("reduced" pronunciation)
е	• *at the beginning of a word or after a vowel:* [yeh] *as in* **е́**хать *to go, ride* • *after a soft consonant:* [eh]: прив**е́**т	• *at the beginning of a word or after a vowel:* [yih] *as in* **е**го́ • *after a soft consonant:* [ih] *as in* мен**я́**
я	• *at the beginning of a word or after a vowel:* [yah] *as in* **Я**н, **я́**блоко *apple,* при**я́**тно • *after a soft consonant:* [ah] *as in* мен**я́**	• *at the beginning of a word:* [yih] *as in* **я**нва́рь *January* • *after a vowel at the end of a word:* [yuh] *as in* Росси́**я** • *after a soft consonant at the end of a word:* [uh] *as in* и́м**я** • *after a soft consonant elsewhere:* [ih] *as in* де́с**я**ть *ten*

WORD STUDY ✪ *Days and Months*

дни неде́ли	ме́сяцы	
понеде́льник	янва́рь	ию́ль
вто́рник	февра́ль	а́вгуст
среда́	март	сентя́брь
четве́рг	апре́ль	октя́брь
пя́тница	май	ноя́брь
суббо́та	ию́нь	дека́брь
воскресе́нье		

EXERCISE 5   Days (and months) of our lives

Days of the week and months of the year include many examples of palatalization. Repeat these words after your teacher or the tape. Note that Monday is considered the first day of the week on a Russian calendar.

	ЯНВАРЬ	ФЕВРАЛЬ	МАРТ
Пн	6 13 20 27	3 10 17 24	3 10 17 24 31
Вт	7 14 21 28	4 11 18 25	4 11 18 25
Ср	1 8 15 22 29	5 12 19 26	5 12 19 26
Чт	2 9 16 23 30	6 13 20 27	6 13 20 27
Пт	3 10 17 24 31	7 14 21 28	7 14 21 28
Сб	4 11 18 25	1 8 15 22	1 8 15 22 29
Вс	5 12 19 26	2 9 16 23	2 9 16 23 30

	АПРЕЛЬ	МАЙ	ИЮНЬ
Пн	7 1 21 28	5 12 19 26	2 9 16 23 30
Вт	1 8 1 22 29	6 13 20 27	3 10 17 24
Ср	2 9 1 23 30	7 14 21 28	4 11 18 25
Чт	3 10 1 24	1 8 15 22 29	5 12 19 26
Пт	4 11 1 25	2 9 16 23 30	6 13 20 27
Сб	5 12 1 26	3 10 17 24 31	7 14 21 28
Вс	6 13 20 27	4 11 18 25	1 8 15 22 29

месяц

	ИЮЛЬ	АВГУСТ	СЕНТЯБРЬ
Пн	**7 14 21 28**	4 11 18 25	1 8 15 22 29
Вт	**1 8 15 22 29**	5 12 19 26	2 9 16 23 30
Ср	**2 9 16 23 30**	6 13 20 27	3 10 17 24
Чт	**3 10 17 24**	7 14 21 28	4 11 18 25
Пт	**4 11 18 25**	1 8 15 22 29	5 12 19 26
Сб	**5 12 19 26**	2 9 16 23 30	6 13 20 27
Вс	**6 13 20 27**	3 10 17 24 31	7 14 21 28

неделя

	ОКТЯБРЬ	НОЯБРЬ	ДЕКАБРЬ
Пн	**6** 13 20 27	3 10 17 24	**1 8 15 22 29**
Вт	**7** 14 21 28	4 11 18 25	2 9 16 23 30
Ср	1 **8** 15 22 29	5 12 19 26	3 10 17 24 31
Чт	2 **9** 16 23 30	6 13 20 27	4 11 18 25
Пт	3 **10** 17 24 31	7 14 21 28	5 12 19 26
Сб	4 **11** 18 25	1 8 15 22 29	6 13 20 27
Вс	5 **12** 19 26	2 9 16 23 30	7 14 21 28

год

STUDY TIP ⭐ *Words in a Series*

While it is not usually advisable to memorize new words in a particular order, items that typically occur in a series, such as days of the week and months of the year, are an exception. Most of us know these words in series and cannot recite them backwards, for example, without thinking carefully. Paradoxically, you may find that memorizing a series from the final element forward (the principle of *backward buildup*) is effective if the list is not too long: **воскресе́нье; суббо́та, воскресе́нье; пя́тница, суббо́та, воскресе́нье; четве́рг, пя́тница, суббо́та, воскресе́нье;** and so on.

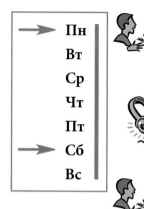

| Пн → |
| Вт |
| Ср |
| Чт |
| Пт |
| Сб → |
| Вс |

EXERCISE 6   Как по–рýсски . . . ?

Referring to the list of months and days of the week, practice asking a
classmate how to say the name of a certain month or day in Russian. Use the
phrase «**Как по–рýсски . . . ?**» as in the following example:

— Как по-рýсски «Monday»?
— Понедéльник.
— А как по-рýсски «Saturday»?
— Суббóта.

EXERCISE 7   Какóй (*what*) сегóдня день?

Working with a classmate and the calendar at the beginning of this section, point to a
day and ask which day it is, using the following dialogues as models. Be sure to ask a
"wrong" question occasionally!

1. — Кáтя, какóй сегóдня день? Средá?
   — Нет, сегóдня втóрник.
2. — Сегóдня четвéрг?
   — Да, четвéрг. Сегóдня четвéрг, а **зáвтра** (*tomorrow*) пя́тница.
3. — Сегóдня воскресéнье?
   — Нет, сегóдня не воскресéнье, а суббóта.

WORD STUDY ★ *Joining and Contrasting: И vs. А*

И Joining	**А** Joining and contrasting	**А** Contrasting
Он студéнт, и я студéнт.	Он студéнт, а я аспирáнт.	Он студéнт, а не аспирáнт.
*He's a student **and** I'm a student.*	*He's an undergrad **and** I'm a grad student.*	*He's an undergrad, not a grad student.*

While English *and* is usually used to join things (as in *My friend **and** I went to a movie yesterday, **and** then we went out to eat*), it is sometimes used to join and contrast at the same time (as in *I want to paint the kitchen yellow **and** my roommate wants to paint it green*). These two uses of English *and* are expressed with different words in Russian. To simply join things, one uses **и**: Вот мой пáспорт **и** моя́ ви́за. To join things while contrasting them, one uses **а**: Сегóдня четвéрг, **а** зáвтра пя́тница.

Russian uses **а** to juxtapose things or correct/modify a statement; note that English usually does not use *and* for this type of contrast: Сегóдня не четвéрг, **а** средá. *Today's not Thursday, it's Wednesday.*

As you've already seen, **а** is also used to introduce follow-up statements or questions:

— Как делá?   "How're things (with you)?"
— Неплóхо. **А** у тебя́ (у вас)?   "Not bad. And with you?"

WORD STUDY ⊗ *Cognates*

Russian and English share thousands of words; such words shared between two languages are called *cognates*. These may have been borrowed from the other language (**компью́тер, баскетбо́л;** *vodka, troika*) or may have entered both languages from a third source (**сестра́, три, февра́ль, биоло́гия**). Both Russian and English have borrowed heavily from the classical languages and from French.

EXERCISE 8   Reading cognates

See if you can tell what the following cognates mean. Then match them with the proper category. Try to read them aloud with Russian pronunciation. (Because Russian cognates often sound quite different from their English equivalents, printed cognates are often easier to recognize then spoken ones.)

1. _____ коме́та, метеори́т, Марс, раке́та
2. _____ бана́н, жира́ф, витами́н, зе́бра
3. _____ А́зия, Аме́рика, А́рктика, тро́пики
4. _____ геоло́гия, матема́тика, психоло́гия, фи́зика
5. _____ компью́тер, при́нтер, дисплей́, мото́р, тра́ктор

а. биоло́гия
б. астроно́мия
в. геогра́фия
г. те́хника
д. о́бласти нау́ки (*academic fields*)

EXERCISE 9   Review of greetings, introductions, and farewells

What do you say in the following instances?

1. You're on the way to class and say good-bye to your roommate.
2. You arrive at class and greet your teacher.
3. The student who sits next to you comes in and sits down.
4. Class is over. Say good-bye to your classmate.
5. Say good-bye to your teacher.
6. At lunch your roommate is talking to someone you don't know. Ask what his or her name is. Your roommate says, "This is Bill (or Jane, Sara, etc.)."
7. Bill asks what your name is.
8. You and Bill each say, "Nice to meet you."

WORD STUDY ✪ *Following Classroom Directions*

Here are some directions that your instructor will use repeatedly in class.

Иди́те сюда́.	*Come here.*
Иди́те к доске́.	*Go to the board.*
Откро́йте кни́гу на страни́це . . .	*Open your book to page . . .*
Повтори́те!	*Repeat.*
Чита́йте!	*Read.*
Слу́шайте!	*Listen.*
Пиши́те!	*Write.*
Продолжа́йте!	*Continue.*
Смотри́те!	*Look!*

STUDY TIP ✪ *Learning Vocabulary*

Part of learning any new language is learning new words. Here are some suggestions that may help you.

1. *Make flash cards.* Write the English on one side, Russian on the other. Practice going both ways, from English to Russian and from Russian to English. When you've gone through the deck, shuffle the order and do it again. As you learn words well, remove them from the deck so you will encounter the harder words more often. Make cards not only for English/Russian vocabulary practice, but also for grammar practice, such as for singular/plural.

2. *Learn phrases.* Rather than learning only isolated words, practice phrases. For example, try learning **я не зна́ю, кто она́** (*I don't know who she is*) as one phrase rather than as five separate words. Include these phrases in your flash card deck.

3. *Practice out loud.* Although it is not always convenient to be saying words and phrases aloud, do so when you can.

4. *Practice in writing.* When you think you know most of your words and phrases orally, try writing them out from your flash cards.

5. *Use images.* For instance, as you are learning **до́ма** you might picture yourself sitting at home in your favorite room. As you are learning **меня́ зову́т,** you might imagine introducing yourself to a new classmate or your teacher.

ИТАК…

At the end of each lesson is a list of words that you should learn to use actively.[7] Abbreviations on these lists include the following: *f.* = feminine; *indecl.* = indeclinable; *m.* = masculine; *neut.* = neuter; *lit.* = literally; *pl.* = plural; *sing.* = singular.[8]

NOUNS

Name and Profession

врач	physician; doctor (3)
и́мя *neut.*	(first) name (2)
музыка́нт	musician (3)
о́тчество	patronymic (2)
фами́лия	last name (2)

Clothes

блу́зка	blouse (3)
брю́ки	pants; trousers (3)
га́лстук	tie (3)
джи́нсы	jeans (3)
жаке́т	(woman's) jacket (3)
костю́м	suit (3)
кроссо́вки	sneakers (3)
ку́ртка	(casual) jacket (3)
пиджа́к	(man's) suit jacket (3)
пуло́вер	V-neck sweater (3)
руба́шка	shirt (3)
сви́тер	(high-neck) sweater (3)
ту́фли	shoes (3)
футбо́лка	T-shirt; sport shirt (3)
ю́бка	skirt (3)

Food

бутербро́д	sandwich (2)
буфе́т	snack bar (2)
ко́фе *m. indecl.*	coffee (2)
меню́ *neut. indecl.*	menu (2)
моро́женое *noun, decl. like adj.*	ice cream (2)
пирожо́к	pirozhok (*small filled pastry*) (2)
сок	juice (2)
чай	tea (2)

Studies

аспира́нт/аспира́нтка	(male/female) graduate student (3)

бу́ква	letter (*of the alphabet*) (2)
газе́та	newspaper (2)
журна́л	magazine; journal (2)
звук	sound (2)
каранда́ш	pencil (3)
кни́га	book (3)
письмо́	letter (3)
ру́чка	pen (3)
сло́во	word (2)
студе́нт/студе́нтка	student (3)
упражне́ние	exercise (3)

Travel

биле́т	ticket (4)
ви́за	visa (4)
па́спорт	passport (4)
рюкза́к	backpack; knapsack (4)
су́мка	bag (4)
чемода́н	suitcase (4)

Time

год	year (4)
день *m.*	day (4)
календа́рь *m.*	calendar (4)
ме́сяц	month (4)
неде́ля	week (4)

Months

янва́рь *m.*	January (4)
февра́ль *m.*	February (4)
март	March (4)
апре́ль *m.*	April (4)
май	May (4)
ию́нь *m.*	June (4)
ию́ль *m.*	July (4)
а́вгуст	August (4)
сентя́брь *m.*	September (4)
октя́брь *m.*	October (4)
ноя́брь *m.*	November (4)
дека́брь *m.*	December (4)

---

[7] The **Но́вые слова́** lists at the end of each lesson include only active vocabulary. Russian-English and English-Russian vocabulary lists at the end of Book 1 and Book 2 include both active and passive vocabulary.

[8] The number in parentheses following each English gloss indicates the Part, or **Часть,** where the word is first actively introduced in the lesson.

Days of the Week

понеде́льник	Monday (4)
вто́рник	Tuesday (4)
среда́	Wednesday (4)
четве́рг	Thursday (4)
пя́тница	Friday (4)
суббо́та	Saturday (4)
воскресе́нье	Sunday (4)

Space

геогра́фия	geography (2)
го́род	city; town (2)
контине́нт	continent (2)
океа́н	ocean (2)
река́	river (2)
страна́	country (2)

Geographical Names

Австра́лия	Australia (2)
А́зия	Asia (2)
Аме́рика	America (2)
А́фрика	Africa (2)
Вашингто́н	Washington (2)
Евро́па	Europe (2)
Кана́да	Canada (2)
Лос-А́нджелес	Los Angeles (2)
Москва́	Moscow (2)
Нью-Йо́рк	New York (2)
Росси́я	Russia (2)
Санкт-Петербу́рг	St. Petersburg (2)
Се́верная Аме́рика	North America (2)
Сиэ́тл	Seattle (2)
США (Соединённые Шта́ты Аме́рики)	USA (United States of America) (2)
Чика́го	Chicago (2)
Ю́жная Аме́рика	South America (2)

Other Nouns

стадио́н	stadium (3)
теа́тр	theater (3)

PRONOUNS

кто	who (1)
что	what (3)
Э́то …	That's (This is) …; Those (these) are … (1)

Personal Pronouns

я	I (3)
ты *informal*	you (3)
он	he; it (3)
она́	she; it (3)
оно́	it (3)
мы	we (3)
вы *formal or pl.*	you (3)
они́	they (3)

POSSESSIVES

мой (моя́, моё, мой)	my; mine (4)
твой (твоя́, твоё, твой)	your; yours (4)
его́	his; its (4)
её	her; hers; its (4)
наш (на́ша, на́ше, на́ши)	our; ours (4)
ваш (ва́ша, ва́ше, ва́ши)	your; yours (4)
их	their; theirs (4)

VERBS

зна́ю (*dictionary form:*[9] знать)	I know (1)

ADVERBS

вот	here (is/are) (4)
где	where (3)
до́ма	at home (3)
за́втра	tomorrow (4)
здесь	here (3)
как	how (1)
непло́хо	quite well (2)
о́чень	very (2)
пло́хо	badly (2)
сего́дня	today (4)
там	there (4)
хорошо́	well (2)

OTHER

а	and (1)
да	yes (3)
и	and (3)
не	not (1)
нет (*used at the beginning of a negative response*)	no (3)

IDIOMS AND EXPRESSIONS

До свида́ния!	Good-bye! (2)
Здра́вствуйте!	Hello! (2)
Извини́те	Excuse me. (2)
Как ва́ше и́мя и о́тчество?	What's your name and patronymic? (2)
Как дела́?	How're things? How are you doing? (2)

---

[9]For nouns, pronouns, and adjectives the dictionary form is the Nominative case; for verbs, it is the infinitive (equivalent to English forms with "to" such as *to know*).

Как по-ру́сски . . . ?

What's the Russian for . . . ? (4)

Как тебя́ (его́, её, вас) зову́т?

What is your (his, her, your *formal*) name? (1)

Как у тебя́ (у вас) дела́?

How are things (with you)? How are you doing? (2)

Како́й сего́дня день?

What day is today? (4)

Кто э́то?

Who's that (this)? (1)

Меня́ (его́, её) зову́т . . .

My (his, her) name is . . . (1)

Ничего́. (*in response to* Как дела́?)

Okay; all right; not (too) bad (2)

О́чень прия́тно! (*when meeting someone*)

Pleased to meet you; Nice to meet you. (2)

пожа́луйста

1. please; 2. You're welcome! 3. Here you are. (2)

Пока́! *informal*

Bye! See you later. (2)

Приве́т! *informal*

Hi! Hello there! (1)

Спаси́бо.

Thank you; Thanks. (2)

Хорошо́, спаси́бо. (*in response to* Как дела́?)

Fine, thanks. (2)

Что э́то?

What's that (this)? (3)

❖ GRAMMAR CHECKLIST

Use this checklist to mark off what you've learned in this lesson:

- ☐ The Russian alphabet (Parts 1, 2, and 3)
- ☐ How to meet and greet people in Russian (Parts 1 and 2)
- ☐ Addressing people formally vs. informally (Part 2)
- ☐ How to say good-bye (Part 2)
- ☐ The structure of Russian names (Part 2)
- ☐ Asking the name of and identifying someone/something (Part 3)
- ☐ How to request, give, and receive something (Part 2)
- ☐ How to ask and tell location: **где, здесь, там, до́ма** (Part 3)
- ☐ How to express ownership: **мой, твой, его́, её, наш, ваш, их** (Part 4)
- ☐ How to ask and answer questions with and without question words (Part 3)
- ☐ Intonation in WH-questions (Part 3)
- ☐ Statement intonation vs. yes/no question intonation (Part 3)
- ☐ Differentiating between hard and soft consonants in pronunciation and spelling (Part 4)
- ☐ Pronunciation of stressed and unstressed vowels (Parts 2 and 4)
- ☐ The concept of grammatical gender (Part 3)
- ☐ How to make things plural (Part 4)
- ☐ Using **и** and **а** for joining and contrasting (Part 4)

❖ SUPPLEMENTAL TEXTS

A. ГОРОДА́ И РЕ́КИ

Locate the following cities on the map on the inside back cover of your textbook and find out which rivers flow through each city.

EXAMPLE: го́род: Санкт-Петербу́рг   река́: Нева́

1. Арха́нгельск
2. Ирку́тск
3. Красноя́рск
4. Москва́
5. Новосиби́рск
6. Омск
7. Росто́в
8. Сара́тов
9. Хаба́ровск
10. Яку́тск

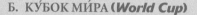

СКОРОГОВО́РКА (*tongue twister*)

Наша река́ широка́, как Ока́.   *Our river is as wide as the Oka River.*

Б. КУ́БОК МИ́РА (***World Cup***)

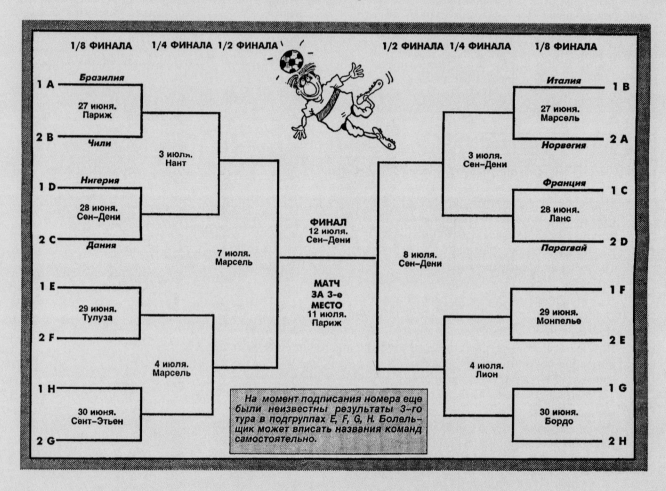

This chart shows which nations' soccer teams are competing to play in the quarter finals of the **Ку́бок ми́ра.** Look at the chart and find answers to the following questions:

1. Which countries will be playing in the following games:
   a. June 27 in Marseilles
   б. June 27 in Paris
   в. June 28 in Saint-Denis
   г. June 28 in L'Anse
2. In which cities will the quarterfinals be held? On which dates?
3. In which cities will the semifinals take place? On which dates?
4. When and where will the third place match occur?
5. When and where will the final match take place?

НАШ НОВЫЙ ДОМ

In this lesson you'll read about the main characters as they move into their new apartment building and become acquainted with one another. In Parts 2 and 3, you'll see the Silin family on video as they look over their new apartment, and you'll meet their upstairs neighbors, the Kruglovs, and their grandson, Sasha, who is a musician. It'll be clear that at least as far as Mrs. Silin is concerned, *all is not well. . . .*

Это папа и дети.

In this lesson you will learn

- ✪ to say where someone lives
- ✪ to count to twelve
- ✪ to use plurals
- ✪ to describe people and objects
- ✪ to express delight and dismay
- ✪ some important features of Russian pronunciation
- ✪ to use Russian names and nicknames
- ✪ some background on the Russian alphabet

Лёна и Вова

ЧАСТЬ ПЕРВАЯ

С ЧЕГО НАЧАТЬ?

УПРАЖНЕНИЕ (EXERCISE) 1 Which relatives can you identify?

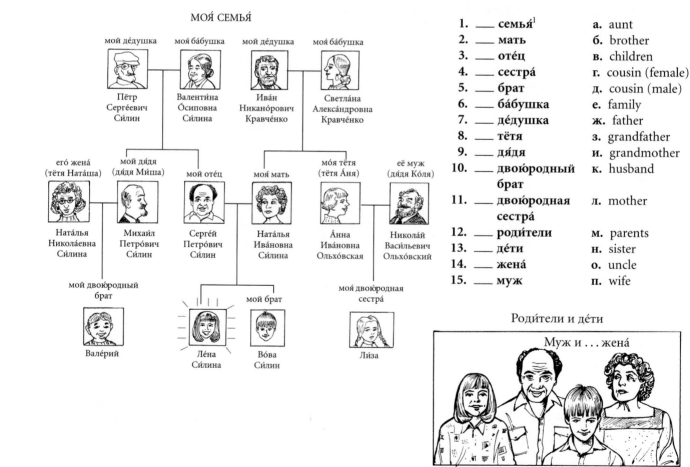

МОЯ́ СЕМЬЯ́

мой де́душка — Пётр Серге́евич Си́лин
моя́ ба́бушка — Валенти́на О́сиповна Си́лина
мой де́душка — Ива́н Никано́рович Кравче́нко
моя́ ба́бушка — Светла́на Алекса́ндровна Кравче́нко

его́ жена́ (тётя Ната́ша) — Ната́лья Никола́евна Си́лина
мой дя́дя (дя́дя Ми́ша) — Михаи́л Петро́вич Си́лин
мой оте́ц — Серге́й Петро́вич Си́лин
моя́ мать — Ната́лья Ива́новна Си́лина
мо́я тётя (тётя А́ня) — А́нна Ива́новна Ольхо́вская
её муж (дя́дя Ко́ля) — Никола́й Васи́льевич Ольхо́вский

мой двою́родный брат — Вале́рий
Ле́на Си́лина
мой брат — Во́ва Си́лин
моя́ двою́родная сестра́ — Ли́за

1. ___ семья́[1]   a. aunt
2. ___ мать   б. brother
3. ___ оте́ц   в. children
4. ___ сестра́   г. cousin (female)
5. ___ брат   д. cousin (male)
6. ___ ба́бушка   e. family
7. ___ де́душка   ж. father
8. ___ тётя   з. grandfather
9. ___ дя́дя   и. grandmother
10. ___ двою́родный   к. husband
    брат
11. ___ двою́родная   л. mother
    сестра́
12. ___ роди́тели   м. parents
13. ___ де́ти   н. sister
14. ___ жена́   o. uncle
15. ___ муж   п. wife

Роди́тели и де́ти

Муж и . . . жена́

Сестра́ и брат

---

[1]In all visual displays, new words that you should learn actively are boldfaced.

In all reading passages, new words that you should learn are boldfaced. These words appear in the end-of-lesson vocabulary list. Words whose meaning you should be able to guess are followed by a †. Words and phrases marked with a ° are translated in the margin.

◈ ЗДЕСЬ ЖИВУ́Т°

 live

Это наш **дом**°² наш **но́вый**° дом.

Наш но́вый **а́дрес**†: Москва́, **у́лица** Лесна́я,° дом **три**,° **кварти́ра**° . . .

Вот кварти́ра **шесть**.° Здесь живу́т Си́лины: Ната́лья Ива́новна, Серге́й Петро́вич, их **дочь**° Ле́на и **сын**° Во́ва. Их **соба́ка**° Бе́лка **то́же**° **живёт**° здесь. Ле́на — студе́нтка, Во́ва — **шко́льник.**°³ Их **но́мер телефо́на**° . . .

building / new
у́лица. . . Lesnaya Street /
   three / apartment
six
daughter / son / dog / also /
   lives
schoolboy / но́мер. . . phone
   number

А вот кварти́ра **де́сять.**° Здесь живу́т муж и жена́ **Кругло́вы**° и их **внук**° Са́ша. Са́ша студе́нт, **пиани́ст.**†

ten
муж. . . Mr. and Mrs. Kruglov
grandson

Это **профе́ссор**† Петро́вский, Илья́ Ильи́ч Петро́вский. Его́ кварти́ра там, **но́мер**† **пять.**° Его́ но́мер телефо́на. . . А это Джим, его́ аспира́нт. Джим — **америка́нец.**† Его́ фами́лия Ри́чардсон.

five

---

²The word **дом** refers to large apartment buildings as well as single-family dwellings.
³**Ле́на — студе́нтка, Во́ва — шко́льник.** A dash is often used to separate two nouns that would be connected by present tense forms of "to be" (*am, are, is*), which are not generally expressed in Russian.

УПРАЖНЕНИЕ (EXERCISE) 2 Под микроско́пом (*Under the microscope*) A: Pronouns

The following nouns occur in this reading. Give an English equivalent for each noun and then indicate which pronoun would be used to replace that noun.

	SINGULAR			PLURAL
	M (он)	N (оно́)	F (она́)	(они́)
1. а́дрес _____	☐	☐	☐	☐
2. аспира́нт _____	☐	☐	☐	☐
3. дочь _____	☐	☐	☐	☐
4. внук _____	☐	☐	☐	☐
5. дом _____	☐	☐	☐	☐
6. Кругло́вы _____	☐	☐	☐	☐
7. муж _____	☐	☐	☐	☐
8. жена́ _____	☐	☐	☐	☐
9. соба́ка _____	☐	☐	☐	☐
10. студе́нтка _____	☐	☐	☐	☐
11. сын _____	☐	☐	☐	☐
12. у́лица _____	☐	☐	☐	☐
13. фами́лия _____	☐	☐	☐	☐
14. шко́льник _____	☐	☐	☐	☐
15. Си́лины _____	☐	☐	☐	☐
16. кварти́ра _____	☐	☐	☐	☐

УПРАЖНЕНИЕ (EXERCISE) 3 Под микроско́пом (*Under the microscope*) Б: Family relationships

What are the relationships between the following people?

1. _____ Во́ва Си́лин и Ле́на Си́лина   **а.** мать и сын

2. _____ Степа́н Евге́ньевич Кругло́в и Са́ша Кругло́в   **б.** оте́ц и дочь

3. _____ Серге́й Петро́вич Си́лин и Ната́лья Ива́новна Си́лина   **в.** брат и сестра́

4. _____ Ната́лья Ива́новна Си́лина и Во́ва Си́лин   **г.** ба́бушка и внук

5. _____ Алекса́ндра Никола́евна Кругло́ва и Са́ша Кругло́в   **д.** де́душка и внук

6. _____ Серге́й Петро́вич Си́лин и Ле́на Си́лина   **е.** муж и жена́

ГРАММАТИКА И ПРАКТИКА

2.1. AN INTRODUCTION TO VERB CONJUGATION: ЖИВЁТ, ЖИВУ́Т

Здесь **живу́т** Си́лины.	*The Silins live here.*
Их соба́ка Бе́лка то́же **живёт** здесь.	*Their dog Belka lives here too.*

In English we say *I live* but *he/she lives,* adding an *-s* to the verb form when the subject is *he* or *she.* Changing the verb form so that it agrees with its subject is called *conjugation.* (Note from the examples that in Russian the subject of a sentence may sometimes follow its verb. See next section on word order.) The only new conjugated forms in this reading are **живёт** (for **он** or **она́** subjects), and **живу́т** (for **они́** subjects).[4] Note that **кто** always takes a singular verb form (like **живёт**), even if a plural answer is expected, such as **Си́лины.**

УПРАЖНЕ́НИЕ (EXERCISE) 4   Verb endings

Supply the correct verb ending to the following:

1. Во́ва жив_____ там.
2. Ба́бушка и де́душка жив_____ здесь.
3. Кто там жив_____?
4. Там жив_____ Кругло́вы.
5. Где он жив_____ ?
6. Её семья́ жив_____ там.

2.2. WORD ORDER IN QUESTIONS AND ANSWERS

— **Кто** там живёт?	*"Who lives there?"*
— Там живёт **Во́ва.**	*"Vova lives there."*

English usually requires a strict word order of subject first, verb second, and any remaining sentence elements last: <u>Who</u> hit the ball? <u>John</u> did. Does <u>Stacy</u> live here? No, <u>Laurel</u> does. In Russian, important and/or new information is usually placed toward the end of the sentence.

— Здесь живёт **Са́ша?**	*"Does Sasha live here?"*
— Нет, здесь живёт **Во́ва.**	*"No, Vova lives here."*

In the above example, **Во́ва,** being the answer to the question, comes last in the sentence even though it is the subject. However:

— Са́ша живёт **здесь?**	*"Does Sasha live here?"*
— Нет, Са́ша живёт **там.**	*"No, Sasha lives there."*

Here the answer to the question is **там,** so it comes last.

---

[4]You've already seen the **-ут** ending of **живу́т** in the phrase **Как тебя́ зову́т?**, which literally means *How do <u>they</u> call you?*, even though the word *they* is not expressed in this particular question.

УПРАЖНЕНИЕ (EXERCISE) 5 Word order

As the neighbors are moving into the new apartment they're asking questions about one another. Make up answers that they might hear.

ОБРАЗЕЦ (EXAMPLE):
— Кто там живёт?   — *Там живу́т Си́лины.*

1. — Си́лины живу́т здесь?   — _____

2. — Как его́ зову́т?   — _____

3. — Здесь живёт Ле́на?   — _____

4. — Её зову́т Ни́на?   — _____

УПРАЖНЕНИЕ (EXERCISE) 6 Кто там живёт?

Working with a classmate, take turns pointing to an apartment in the diagram and asking questions about who lives where. Refer back to the reading if necessary. Remember to focus on putting new or important information at the end of the sentence.

ОБРАЗЕЦ (EXAMPLE):   (Pointing to an apartment in the diagram)
Кто там живёт? → Там живёт/живу́т (*name*).

№ 7	№ 8	№ 9	№ 10
№ 3	№ 4	№ 5	№ 6
№ 1		№ 2	

СЛОВА, СЛОВА, СЛОВА... ✪ *Numerals 0–12*

Here are the numerals zero through twelve with some hints on related words.

0 ноль (*null*)[5]
1 оди́н
2 два (*dual*)
3 три (*triangle*)
4 четы́ре (*tetrahedron*)
5 пять (*pentagon*)
6 шесть (*sextet*)

7 семь (*seven*)
8 во́семь
9 де́вять
10 де́сять (*decimal*)
11 оди́ннадцать (*оди́н + на + де́сять*)
12 двена́дцать (*две + на + де́сять*)

---

[5]**Нуль** is also correct. Both **ноль** and **нуль** are masculine.

УПРАЖНЕНИЕ (EXERCISE) 7 Telephone numbers

A seven-digit Russian telephone number (**но́мер телефо́на**) is written ###–##–##.
Write your telephone number in the Russian style and exchange it with a classmate.
Use the following phrases:

— Како́й твой но́мер телефо́на? *"What's your telephone number?"*
— Мой но́мер телефо́на . . . А твой? *"My telephone number is . . .*
And yours?"

After writing down someone's telephone number, show it to him or her to be sure you
got it right. You might ask **Пра́вильно?** (*Is this correct?*)

 КУЛЬТУРА РЕЧИ

❖ ТАК ГОВОРЯТ: ВА́Ш А́ДРЕС?

If you're studying in Moscow or St. Petersburg, you'll probably have to give out
your address now and then. Here's how such a dialogue might sound in a formal
situation:

— Ваш а́дрес?
— Санкт-Петербу́рг, у́лица Пу́шкина, дом шесть, кварти́ра три.
— Спаси́бо.
— Пожа́луйста.

УПРАЖНЕНИЕ (EXERCISE) 8 Ва́ша фами́лия?

This is the first of many activities for which you and a classmate will fill in information
gaps for each other. One of you has information on this page and the other will find
complementary information in the chart for this exercise in Appendix K at the back of
the book.

One of you is visiting an important Russian official. The other student plays the
guard on duty, who will not let visitors in until they provide relevant information
about themselves. As the "guard" asks the following questions, the "visitor"
responds with his or her own name and the address and phone number given in
Appendix K. After the guard writes down the responses, the visitor should check to
see that the address and phone number are written correctly. Then switch roles and
continue.

1. Ва́ша фами́лия?
2. Ва́ше и́мя?
3. Ваш а́дрес?
4. Ваш но́мер телефо́на?

	ГО́РОД	У́ЛИЦА	ДОМ	КВАРТИ́РА	НО́МЕР ТЕЛЕФО́НА
1.	_____	_____	__	__	_____
2.	Ту́ла	Садо́вая	12	9	31–59–42
3.	_____	_____	__	__	_____
4.	Санкт-Петербу́рг	Куби́нская	5	6	527–49–38
5.	_____	_____	__	__	_____
6.	Новосиби́рск	Байка́льская	4	1	67–44–85

❖ САМОПРОВЕ́РКА: УПРАЖНЕ́НИЕ (EXERCISE) 9

You've been assigned to work as a Russian-English interpreter. Working with a classmate, try this self-test: read a Russian sentence out loud, then give an idiomatic English equivalent without looking at the book. Then work from English to Russian.

1. — <u>Здесь</u> живу́т Кругло́вы?
2. — Нет, Кругло́вы живу́т там, кварти́ра де́сять.
3. — А кто живёт здесь?
4. — Здесь живу́т Си́лины.
5. — А как вас зову́т?
6. — Ле́на Си́лина.
7. — А како́й ваш но́мер телефо́на?

1. *"Is this where the Kruglovs live?"*
2. *"No, the Kruglovs live there, apartment ten."*
3. *"So who lives here?"*
4. *"The Silins live here."*
5. *"And what's your name?"*
6. *"Lena Silina."*
7. *"And what's your phone number?"*

❖ ВОПРО́СЫ И ОТВЕ́ТЫ: УПРАЖНЕ́НИЕ (EXERCISE) 10

Working with a classmate, take turns asking and answering the following questions:

1. Как тебя́ зову́т?
2. Ты студе́нт и́ли аспира́нт? (студе́нтка и́ли аспира́нтка)?
3. Како́й твой но́мер телефо́на?
4. Твой оте́ц музыка́нт? (*if so . . .*) Пиани́ст? (*if not . . .*) А кто он? Врач? Диплома́т[†]? Президе́нт[†]? Бизнесме́н[†]?
5. А твоя́ мать то́же музыка́нт? (*if so . . .*) Пиани́стка? (*if not . . .*) А кто она́? Врач? Ветерина́р[†]? Сена́тор[†]? Инжене́р[†]?

❖ ДИАЛОГИ

Here and each time you encounter a section labeled **Диалóги** in this textbook, note the communicative purpose of each dialogue. As you practice each dialogue, think of changes you might want to make to personalize it.

ДИАЛОГ 1 Здесь живёт . . . ?
(Asking where someone lives)

— Э́то кварти́ра шесть?
— Да.
— Здесь живёт Во́ва Си́лин?
— Здесь.
— А кто ещё живёт здесь?
— Его́ роди́тели, сестра́ Ле́на и их соба́ка Бе́лка.

ДИАЛОГ 2 Как её зову́т?
(Finding out someone's identity)

— Как её зову́т?
— А́нна Смит.
— Она́ америка́нка?
— Нет, но её муж — америка́нец.

УПРАЖНЕНИЕ (EXERCISE) 11   Ваш диало́г

Working with a classmate, make up a dialogue in which you knock at a door, ask for someone, and are told that this is not his or her apartment.

❖ А ТЕПЕРЬ . . . : УПРАЖНЕНИЕ (EXERCISE) 12

Working with a classmate, use what you learned in Part 1 to . . .

1. find out what his name is
2. find out what his phone number is
3. (pointing to an apartment in the diagram on p. 44) find out who lives there
4. (pointing to people in Lena's family tree on p. 40) find out the identity of those people and their relationship to Lena

ЧАСТЬ ВТОРАЯ

С ЧЕГО НАЧАТЬ?

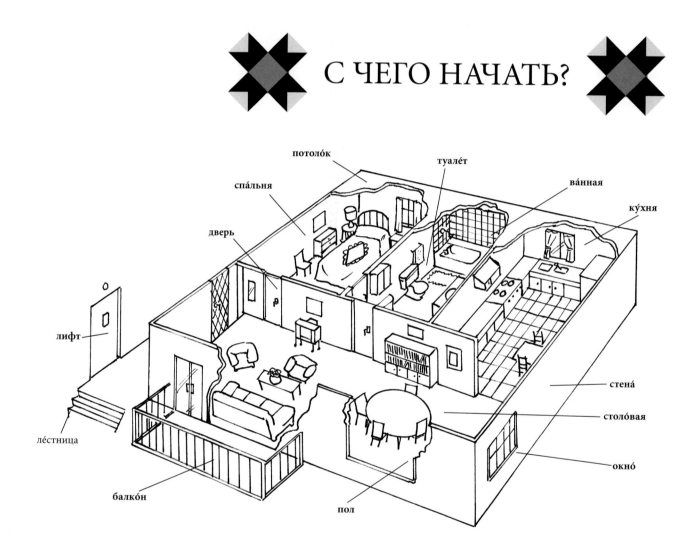

потолок
туалет
ванная
спальня
кухня
дверь
лифт
стена
столовая
лестница
окно
балкон
пол

УПРАЖНЕНИЕ 1 Дом, кварти́ра, ко́мната . . .

Use a separate piece of paper to sort the vocabulary in this picture into three groups: 1) parts of a building (**дом**); 2) areas in an apartment (**кварти́ра**); 3) things in a room (**ко́мната**).

ЧТЕНИЕ

❖ SCENE A: КАК ТЕБЯ́ ЗОВУ́Т?

(Vova and a few children of different ages (7–9 years old) are outside looking up at the apartment building.)

ДЕ́ВОЧКА.°	*(Counts the stories.)* Два, три, четы́ре . . . **Вон**° наш **эта́ж**° и на́ши о́кна.° **Спра́ва**° — столо́вая. А **сле́ва**° — моя́ **ко́мната.**° *(Pointing)* Вон моё окно́. *(To a little boy.)* А где твои́ о́кна?
МА́ЛЬЧИК.°	А мой дом не здесь.
ДЕ́ВОЧКА.	А где?
МА́ЛЬЧИК.	**Далеко́.**° У́лица Орды́нка.
ВО́ВА.	Орды́нка — э́то **центр**!° **Э́то здо́рово!**°
ДЕ́ВОЧКА.	*(To the little boy.)* А где твоя́ **ма́ма**†?
МА́ЛЬЧИК.	Ма́ма до́ма. И **па́па.**† А де́душка и ба́бушка здесь. *(Pointing to a man and a woman who are talking to Sasha and the Kruglovs.)* Вот они́.
ВО́ВА.	*(Gesturing toward Sasha.)* А кто э́то?
ДЕ́ВОЧКА.	Я зна́ю! Э́то Са́ша Кругло́в и его́ де́душка и ба́бушка. Они́ на́ши **сосе́ди.**°
МА́ЛЬЧИК.	Са́ша музыка́нт. *(Mimicking the adults.)* О́чень **хоро́ший**° пиани́ст. *(The Kruglovs and the rest of the group walk up.)*
КРУГЛО́ВА.	**Ну**° вот, э́то наш но́вый дом.
КРУГЛО́В.	*(Adjusting his hearing aid.)* А? **Чей**° дом?
КРУГЛО́ВА.	Наш, наш!

Little girl / Over there / floor windows / On the right / on the left / room

Boy

Far away

downtown / Э́то. . . That's great!

neighbors

good

Well

Whose

❖ SCENE B: НА́ША НО́ВАЯ КВАРТИ́РА

(The Silins are looking around their new apartment.)

НАТА́ЛЬЯ ИВ.	*(Unhappily)* И э́то на́ша но́вая кварти́ра?
СЕРГЕ́Й ПЕТР.	Да, Ната́ша, о́чень хоро́шая кварти́ра.
НАТА́ЛЬЯ ИВ.	Нет, ко́мнаты о́чень **ма́ленькие.**°
СЕРГЕ́Й ПЕТР.	Ко́мнаты ма́ленькие? Нет, они́ **больши́е.**°

small

big

What a	НАТА́ЛЬЯ ИВ.	**Кака́я**° ма́ленькая ку́хня!
		(*Lena and Vova are looking at one of the rooms.*)
	ВО́ВА.	Моя́ ко́мната!
	ЛЁНА.	Нет, э́то моя́ ко́мната.
		(*The Silins again.*)
	НАТА́ЛЬЯ ИВ.	И туале́т ма́ленький.
	СЕРГЕ́Й ПЕТР.	Нет, туале́т большо́й.
		(*They hear a piano being played.*)
Како́й. . . *How awful!*	НАТА́ЛЬЯ ИВ.	Что? Сосе́д — музыка́нт? **Како́й у́жас!**°

УПРАЖНЕ́НИЕ 2   Под микроско́пом : Scanning for information

Write (in Russian) the name of the person who fits each description.

1. _____ does not like the new apartment.
2. _____ is a music student.
3. _____ doesn't hear very well.
4. _____ is not pleased at having a musician for a neighbor.
5. _____ thinks the rooms in the new apartment are big.
6. _____ are deciding who'll get a certain room.
7. _____ lives with his grandmother and grandfather.

ГРАММА́ТИКА И ПРА́КТИКА

СЛОВА́, СЛОВА́, СЛОВА́… ✪ *Adjectives as Nouns*

ва́нная	*bathroom*
столо́вая	*dining room*

Some words that Russian treats as nouns were originally <adjective + noun> phrases from which the noun has been dropped over time. (When English-speaking students refer to a final exam as a *final* they are doing exactly the same thing.) In the above cases, the word **ко́мната** is not used, but it explains why these nouns all have the form of feminine adjectives. Another adjective commonly used as a noun is this one:

ру́сский, -ая, -ое, -ие	*Russian (adj.)*
ру́сский	*a Russian man*
ру́сская	*a Russian woman*
ру́сские	*Russians*

◈◈ 2.3. PLURALS OF NEUTER NOUNS

Как **дела?**   *How are things?*

окно́

Вот на́ши **о́кна.**   *Here are our windows.*

о́кна

As you know, singular neuter nouns end in **-o** (a hard-series vowel) and **-e** (a soft-series vowel). The basic ending for pluralizing neuter nouns also has two variants, one spelled with a hard-series vowel (**-a**) and one spelled with a soft-series vowel (**-я**). Choosing the proper variant is completely predictable: if the singular noun ends in a hard-series vowel, drop it and add the hard-series plural ending **-a;** if the singular ends in a soft-series vowel, drop it and add the soft-series plural ending **-я.** Here are some examples of nouns you know. Note that stress shifts are common when two-syllable nouns ending in **-o** are pluralized.

	SINGULAR FORM	PLURAL ENDING	PLURAL FORM
Neuter nouns	окн-о́		о́кн-**а**
	письм-о́	-а	пи́сьм-**а**
	сло́в-о		слов-**а́**
	пла́ть-е *dress*	-я	пла́ть-**я**
	упражне́ни-е		упражне́ни-**я**

УПРАЖНЕНИЕ 3   Plurals of neuter nouns

Here are some nouns you already know or will be learning in the coming lessons. Don't try to memorize them now, but use them to practice making plurals. Add stress marks: nouns that shift their stress (this is unpredictable) are marked [!].

ОБРАЗЕЦ: сло́во [!]   *word*   __слова́__   *words*

1. вино́ [!] *wine*   _____ *wines*
2. зда́ние *building*   _____ *buildings*
3. кре́сло *armchair*   _____ *armchairs*
4. ме́сто [!] *place*   _____ *places*
5. общежи́тие *dormitory*   _____ *dormitories*
6. окно́ [!] *window*   _____ *windows*
7. свида́ние *date*   _____ *dates*
8. письмо́ [!] *letter*   _____ *letters*
9. суеве́рие *superstition* _____ *superstitions*
10. упражне́ние *exercise*   _____ *exercises*

❖❖ 2.4. WHOSE: ЧЕЙ, ЧЬЯ, ЧЬЁ, ЧЬИ

— А? **Чей** дом?	*"Huh? Whose house?"*
— Наш, наш!	*"Ours, ours!"*
— **Чей** э́то стол?	*"Whose table is that?"*
— Э́то мой стол.	*"It's my table."*

The forms of **чей** (*whose*), like the forms of **мой,** agree with the nouns they modify: **чей** (masc.), **чья** (fem.), **чьё** (neut.), **чьи** (pl.). A typical response to a **чей** question begins with Э́то . . . : **Э́то мой журна́л.** Note that the pronoun Э́то in both the question and the answer does not change form.

Masc.	— **Чей** э́то балко́н? Твой?	Fem.	— **Чья** э́то кни́га? Твоя́?
	— Да, мой.		— Да, моя́.
Neut.	— **Чьё** э́то письмо́? Твоё?	Pl.	— **Чьи** э́то ту́фли? Твои́?
	— Да, моё.		— Да, мои́.

УПРАЖНЕНИЕ 4   Sorting clothing

You've just rented an apartment with two friends. In the move-in process some of your belongings got mixed up. Complete the sentences below, inserting the correct form of *whose* (**чей, чья, чьё, чьи**). (If you don't remember some of these words, look back at Lesson 1, Part 3, Exercise 1 on page 17.)

ОБРАЗЕ́Ц: *Чьи* э́то джи́нсы?

1. _____ э́то брю́ки?
2. _____ э́то га́лстук?
3. _____ э́то ку́ртка?
4. _____ э́то блу́зка?
5. _____ э́то пла́тье (*dress*)?

6. _____ э́то костю́м (*suit*)?
7. _____ э́то руба́шка?
8. _____ э́то кроссо́вки?
9. _____ э́то ту́фли?
10. _____ э́то ю́бка?

УПРАЖНЕНИЕ 5   Whose . . . ?

Using the following list of words, make up **чей** (**чья, чьё, чьи**) questions and answer them with possessives. Practice with some plurals.

окно́	студе́нт	роди́тели
ба́бушка	сло́во	де́душка
письмо́	газе́та	журна́л
соба́ка	кни́га	упражне́ние

ОБРАЗЕ́Ц: кварти́ра → — Чья э́то кварти́ра? (Чьи э́то кварти́ры?)
                            — Э́то моя́ кварти́ра. (Э́то мои́ кварти́ры.)

❖ 2.5. ADJECTIVES: GENDER AND NUMBER

Э́то наш **но́вый** дом.	*This is our new building.*
Э́то на́ша **но́вая** кварти́ра.	*This is our new apartment.*

Like the possessives **мой, твой, наш, ваш,** and the question word **чей,** adjectives show the same gender and number as the noun they are used with:

GENDER/NUMBER	POSSESSIVES	ADJECTIVES
masculine	мо-й костю́м (*suit*)	но́в-**ый** костю́м
feminine	мо-я ку́ртка	но́в-**ая** ку́ртка
neuter	мо-ё пла́тье (*dress*)	но́в-**ое** пла́тье
plural	мо-й джи́нсы	но́в-**ые** джи́нсы

Russian words can best be understood in terms of stems and endings: an adjective like **но́вый,** for example, is composed of the stem **нов-** and the masculine ending **-ый.** Think of **-ый, -ая, -ое,** and **-ые** as the basic adjective endings that have some slight variations. For example, when the masculine ending is stressed, it is spelled **-о́й,** as in **Большо́й теа́тр.**

Adjectives are shown in dictionaries and vocabulary lists in the masculine form: **но́вый, ма́ленький,** and **большо́й** are all masculine forms. They all end in -й, which is a consonant. So the general noun principle—if it ends in a consonant, it is masculine—holds for adjectives, too. If you know the dictionary form (masculine) of an adjective, you can automatically derive the feminine, neuter, and plural forms by replacing the masculine ending (**-ый/-ий/-ой**) with the appropriate feminine (**-ая**), neuter (**-ое**), or plural (**-ые**) endings:

masculine	но́в-ый	ма́леньк-ий	больш-о́й
feminine	но́в-ая	ма́леньк-ая	больш-а́я
neuter	но́в-ое	ма́леньк-ое	больш-о́е
plural	но́в-ые	ма́леньк-ие	больш-и́е

❖ 2.6. SPELLING RULES

Russian spelling rules are strictly applied to the endings of nouns, verbs, and adjectives. Three spelling rules are particularly useful at this point. Note that they primarily concern spelling, not pronunciation.

1. **«Кни́ги» rule:** Always write **и** (never **ы**) after **г, к, х; ж, ч, ш, щ.** Notice that two groups of consonants are involved in this rule: the letters **г, к, х** (representing *velar* sounds) and **ж, ч, ш, щ** (representing sounds called *hushers.*) Examples:
   • In plural noun endings: **кни́г-а** and **кни́г-и, ма́льчик** and **ма́льчик-и, эта́ж** and **эта́ж-и.**
   • In masculine and plural adjective endings: **ма́леньк-ий, хоро́ш-ий** and **ма́леньк-ие, хоро́ш-ие.**

2. **«Хоро́шее» rule:** *Unstressed* **о** becomes **е** after **ж, ч, ш, щ** and **ц.** This rule involves the hushers plus **ц.** Examples:
   - In neuter adjective endings: **хоро́ш-ее,** because the ending is unstressed.
   - Spellings like **большо́й** and **большо́е** are correct because the **-о** in the ending is stressed.

3. **«Роя́ли» rule:** Always write **и** (never **ы**) to replace **-ь, -й, -я** in forming noun plurals.

The **«роя́ли»** rule is not really a spelling rule that you need to memorize; instead it is a reminder that the same ending is often spelled with two variants. In Part 1 of this lesson, you learned two variants of the ending for plural neuter nouns, one with a hard-series vowel (**-а**) and one with a soft-series vowel (**-я**). Masculine and feminine plurals also have two variants: the basic ending is the hard-series vowel **-ы** (**журна́л** and **журна́л-ы, газе́т-а** and **газе́т-ы**), but the soft-series counterpart of this sound (**-и**) is also used in certain cases:

- For words that end in a soft sign: (*masc.*) **роя́л-ь** *piano* and **роя́л-и;** (*fem.*) **двер-ь** and **две́р-и.** Using the soft variant of the ending indicates that the final **-л-** is soft, and the **-ь** is no longer needed.
- For words that end in the soft consonant **-й: музе́-й** *museum* and **музе́-и.** The consonant **-й-** is usually not written between two vowels.
- For words that end in the soft-series vowel **-я: ку́хн-я** and **ку́хн-и.** In the singular, the soft-series ending **-я** indicates that the consonant **-н-** is soft; in the plural, using the soft-series ending **-и** indicates the same thing.

УПРАЖНЕНИЕ 6   Spelling rules

Fill in the missing Russian letters and be sure to apply the spelling rules when necessary. See if you can guess the unfamiliar words.

THE «КНИ́ГИ» RULE (Insert Ы or И)	**THE «ХОРО́ШЕЕ» RULE** (Insert О or Е)	**THE «РОЯ́ЛИ» RULE** (Insert Ы or И)
1. моско́вск___й (relates to Moscow)	7. больш___ окно́	11. Plural of ку́хня = _____
2. универса́льн___й (It's about everything.)	8. Больш___й теа́тр (famous theater in Moscow)	12. Plural of кварти́ра = _____
3. ш___мпанзе́ (You might see one in a zoo.)	9. Но́в__ ру́сск___ сло́во (a Russian-language newspaper published in the United States)	13. Plural of музе́й (*museum*) = _____
4. ж___ра́ф (another zoo-dweller)	10. хоро́ш___ ра́дио[†]	14. Plural of а́рмия[†] = _____
5. дж___нсы (popular kind of pants)		15. Plural of дверь = _____
6. г___та́ра (common musical instrument)		

УПРАЖНЕНИЕ 7   Disagreeing, contradicting

Your younger sister is at the age that whatever you say, she will disagree with you. Using the words below, provide the contradictions she might offer.

нóв-ый (-ая, -ое, -ые)   vs.   стáр-ый (-ая, -ое, -ые) *old*
хорóш-ий (-ая, -ее, -ие)   vs.   плох-óй (-áя, -óе, -úе) *bad*
больш-óй (-áя, -óе, -úе)   vs.   мáленьк-ий (-ая, -ое, -ие)

ОБРАЗЕЦ: — Это хорóшая квартúра. — *Нет, это плохáя квартúра!*

1. — Это большóе окнó.   — _____
2. — Это мáленький туалéт.   — _____
3. — Это стáрые джúнсы.   — _____
4. — Это хорóший роя́ль (*piano*). — _____
5. — Это её стáрый áдрес.   — _____
6. — Это плохáя рýчка.   — _____
7. — Это нóвое слóво.   — _____
8. — Это хорóшая газéта.   — _____
9. — Это нóвый дом.   — _____

СЛОВА, СЛОВА, СЛОВА... ✪ *Adjectives and Nouns*

Similar to English, adjectives in Russian may precede nouns or follow them. When adjectives precede nouns, they form noun phrases such as **мáленькие кóмнаты** *small rooms*. When adjectives follow nouns, they form complete sentences with the help of the verb "to be" (not expressed in the present tense in Russian): **Кóмнаты мáленькие** *The rooms are small*.

УПРАЖНЕНИЕ 8   \<Adjective + noun\> combinations

In the left column are adjectives; in the right column are nouns. Work with a classmate to make up at least ten \<adjective + noun\> combinations. (The gender/number endings of the adjectives reflect the spelling variations you just learned.) Check your answers by seeing if another pair of students can come up with the same combinations you have when you supply the English phrase.

ОБРАЗЦЫ: большóй дом   *big house*
            мáленькая квартúра   *small apartment*

ADJECTIVES		NOUNS	
нóв-ый (-ая, -ое, -ые)	*new*	газéта	*newspaper*
дорог-óй (-áя, -óе, -úе)	*expensive*	дом	*house; building*
больш-óй (-áя, -óе, -úе)	*big; large*	квартúры	*apartments*
мáленьк-ий (-ая, -ое, -ие)	*small*	внук	*grandson*
хорóш-ий (-ая, -ее, -ие)	*good; nice*	студéнт	*student*
		журналúстка	*(female) journalist*
		кýхня	*kitchen*
		окнó	*window*

Ты́ но́вая студе́нтка?

УПРАЖНЕ́НИЕ 9   Describing people

Using the adjectives you know and those in the following list, describe your friends, family members, or famous people to a classmate:

ОБРАЗЕ́Ц: Мой брат Джон серьёзный и энерги́чный.

You may also use the intensifier **о́чень** with the adjectives if you wish: **Моя́ сестра́ о́чень тала́нтливая.**

культу́рный	такти́чный
некульту́рный	нетакти́чный
романти́чный	тала́нтливый
серьёзный	цини́чный
несерьёзный	энерги́чный
	эксцентри́чный

СЛОВА́, СЛОВА́, СЛОВА́... ✪ *Prefix* не-

культу́рный/некульту́рный: The prefix **не-** can be added to many Russian adjectives to express the absence or negation of a certain quality, or the opposite quality, much like the English prefixes *non-* and *un-* (for example, *cultured/uncultured*).

КУЛЬТУРА РЕЧИ

❖ ТАК ГОВОРЯТ: Э́ТО

As the Kruglovs are moving into the new apartment, one of the neighbor's children uses **Э́то . . .** to identify them: **Э́то Са́ша Кругло́в и его́ де́душка и ба́бушка.**

УПРАЖНЕНИЕ 10   Э́то . . .

If you were the person listed first in the following exercise, how would you identify the person listed second?

ОБРАЗЕ́Ц: Во́ва Си́лин/Ле́на Си́лина   — *Э́то моя́ сестра́.*

1. Ната́лья Ива́новна Си́лина/Ле́на Си́лина   — _____
2. Ле́на Си́лина/Серге́й Петро́вич Си́лин   — _____
3. Серге́й Петро́вич Си́лин/Во́ва Си́лин   — _____
4. Во́ва Си́лин/Ната́лья Ива́новна Си́лина   — _____
5. Ле́на Си́лина/Во́ва Си́лин   — _____
6. Са́ша Кругло́в/Алекса́ндра Никола́евна Кругло́ва   — _____
7. Алекса́ндра Никола́евна Кругло́ва/Степа́н Евге́ньевич Кругло́в   — _____
8. Степа́н Евге́ньевич Кругло́в/Алекса́ндра Никола́евна Кругло́ва   — _____
9. Степа́н Евге́ньевич Кругло́в/Са́ша Кругло́в   — _____
10. Са́ша Кругло́в/Степа́н Евге́ньевич Кругло́в   — _____

❖ САМОПРОВЕРКА: УПРАЖНЕНИЕ 11

Working on your own, try this self-test: Read a Russian sentence out loud, then give an idiomatic English equivalent without looking at the book. Then work from English to Russian. After you have completed the activity, try it with a classmate.

1. Спра́ва моя́ ко́мната.
2. Где мои́ пи́сьма?
3. Чьё э́то окно́?
4. Э́то наш но́вый дом.
5. На́ша кварти́ра о́чень хоро́шая.

1. *My room is on the right.*
2. *Where are my letters?*
3. *Whose window is that?*
4. *This is our new apartment building.*
5. *Our apartment is very nice.*

❖ ВОПРОСЫ И ОТВЕТЫ: УПРАЖНЕНИЕ 12

Working with a classmate, take turns asking and answering the following questions:

1. Твоя́ кварти́ра хоро́шая?
2. А ку́хня больша́я?
3. А сосе́ди хоро́шие?
4. Они́ музыка́нты?
5. Сосе́д-музыка́нт — э́то хорошо́ и́ли пло́хо?

❖ ДИАЛОГИ

ДИАЛОГ 1 На́ша но́вая кварти́ра
(Making strong contrasts)

— Ва́ша но́вая кварти́ра больша́я?
— Больша́я, но (*but*) плоха́я (*bad*). А ва́ша?
— На́ша ма́ленькая, но хоро́шая.

ДИАЛОГ 2 Ты наш но́вый сосе́д?
(Meeting a new neighbor)
A child greets an older person on a staircase.

— Здра́вствуйте!
— Здра́вствуй! Ты наш но́вый сосе́д?
— Да. (*Pointing to an apartment door.*) Вот на́ша кварти́ра.
— А как тебя́ зову́т?
— Пе́тя. А вас?
— Никола́й Ива́нович.

УПРАЖНЕНИЕ 13 Ваш диало́г

Create a dialogue in which you and a friend discuss the positive and negative features of an apartment you're thinking of renting.

❖ А ТЕПЕРЬ . . . : УПРАЖНЕНИЕ 14

Working with a classmate, use what you learned in Part 2 to . . .

1. find out how things are going
2. ask if her room or apartment is nice
3. ask if her building is new
4. find out whose letters are on her desk
5. (pointing to something in the picture of the apartment building at the beginning of this Part) ask if this is the kitchen (bathroom, elevator, staircase, window, wall, and so on)

С ЧЕГО НАЧАТЬ?

магнитофо́н · часы́ · кни́жные по́лки · роя́ль · дива́н · поду́шка · кофе́йный сто́лик

УПРАЖНЕНИЕ 1   Да и́ли нет?

Which items from the Kruglovs' apartment do you have where you live?

	ДА	НЕТ
1. кофе́йный сто́лик	☐	☐
2. роя́ль	☐	☐
3. магнитофо́н (*tape recorder*)	☐	☐
4. дива́н	☐	☐
5. поду́шка	☐	☐
6. часы́	☐	☐
7. кни́жные по́лки	☐	☐

ЧТЕНИЕ

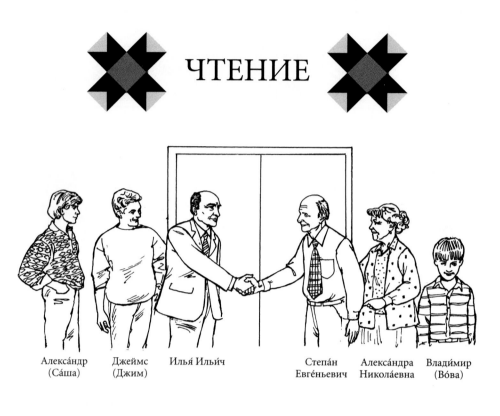

Алекса́ндр (Са́ша) Джеймс (Джим) Илья́ Ильи́ч   Степа́н Евге́ньевич Алекса́ндра Никола́евна Влади́мир (Во́ва)

Да́вайте. . . *Let's introduce ourselves.*

❖ SCENE A: ДАВА́ЙТЕ ПОЗНАКО́МИМСЯ°

(The new neighbors get acquainted.)

Dear	БА́БУШКА.	**Дороги́е**° сосе́ди, дава́йте познако́мимся! Мы Кругло́вы, Алекса́ндра Никола́евна и мой муж, Степа́н Евге́ньевич. А э́то наш внук Са́ша.
	СА́ША.	Алекса́ндр.
or	ДЖИМ.	Вас зову́т Са́ша **и́ли**° Алекса́ндр?
	ДЕ́ДУШКА.	Алекса́ндр его́ зову́т. И Са́ша то́же.
	ПРОФЕ́ССОР.	*(Accidentally bumping into Grandpa.)* Извини́те, пожа́луйста.
That's okay.	ДЕ́ДУШКА.	**Ничего́.**°
Познако́мьтесь. . . *I'd like you to meet. . .*	ПРОФЕ́ССОР.	**Познако́мьтесь, э́то**° Джим, мой аспира́нт. Он америка́нец. А меня́ зову́т Илья́ Ильи́ч Петро́вский.
	ДЖИМ.	А я Джеймс. Джеймс Ри́чардсон. *(To Sasha.)* Вы — Са́ша и Алекса́ндр, а я — Джим и Джеймс.
	ВО́ВА.	Ха́у ду ю ду, Джим! Я Во́ва, Влади́мир.
	ДЖИМ.	О́чень прия́тно. *(Lena enters.)* А кто э́то?
	ВО́ВА.	Э́то Ле́на, моя́ сестра́.
	БА́БУШКА.	*(To Grandpa and Sasha.)* Каки́е хоро́шие сосе́ди!

❖ SCENE B: ЗДЕСЬ ЖИВЁТ МУЗЫКА́НТ?

(Sergei Petrovich and Natalya Ivanovna have gone upstairs to the Kruglovs'.)

СЕРГЕ́Й ПЕТР. И НАТА́ЛЬЯ ИВ.	Здра́вствуйте!
БА́БУШКА И ДЕ́УШКА.	Здра́вствуйте!
СЕРГЕ́Й ПЕТР.	Здесь живёт музыка́нт?
ДЕ́ДУШКА.	Да, э́то мой внук. (*Inviting them to come in.*) А кто вы?
СЕРГЕ́Й ПЕТР.	А мы ва́ши сосе́ди, Си́лины. Э́то моя́ жена́.
НАТА́ЛЬЯ ИВ.	О́чень прия́тно.
ДЕ́ДУШКА.	(*Not hearing.*) Кто-кто?
СЕРГЕ́Й ПЕТР.	(*Loudly.*) Моя́ жена́, Ната́лья Ива́новна.
ДЕ́ДУШКА.	А, **о́чень рад**.° Кругло́в. Алекса́ндра Никола́евна Кругло́ва, моя́ жена́.
НАТА́ЛЬЯ ИВ.	(*To Sasha, distressed.*) **Так**° вы музыка́нт . . .
СА́ША.	Да, я студе́нт, пиани́ст.
НАТА́ЛЬЯ ИВ.	Нет, **э́то ужа́сно!**°
БА́БУШКА.	(*Offended.*) **Почему́**° ужа́сно? Са́ша — хоро́ший пиани́ст.
НАТА́ЛЬЯ ИВ.	Да?

о́чень. . . *pleased to meet you*

So

э́то. . . *that's horrible!*

Why

(Later at the Silins. Natalya Ivanovna and Lena hear a piano being played.)

ЛЕ́НА	Кака́я хоро́шая му́зыка†!
НАТА́ЛЬЯ ИВ.	**Как гро́мко он игра́ет!**°

Как. . . *He plays so loud!*

УПРАЖНЕ́НИЕ 2   Под микроско́пом: Adjectives and Possessives

The two scenes in this reading contain several examples of <adjectives (or possessives) + nouns>. Write down as many as you can find and indicate their gender or number.

	SINGULAR			PLURAL
	M (он)	F (она́)	N (оно́)	(они́)
ОБРАЗЕ́Ц: мой муж	[X]	[ ]	[ ]	[ ]
1. _____	[ ]	[ ]	[ ]	[ ]
2. _____	[ ]	[ ]	[ ]	[ ]
3. _____	[ ]	[ ]	[ ]	[ ]
4. _____	[ ]	[ ]	[ ]	[ ]
5. _____	[ ]	[ ]	[ ]	[ ]
6. _____	[ ]	[ ]	[ ]	[ ]
7. _____	[ ]	[ ]	[ ]	[ ]
8. _____	[ ]	[ ]	[ ]	[ ]
9. _____	[ ]	[ ]	[ ]	[ ]
10. _____	[ ]	[ ]	[ ]	[ ]

ГРАММАТИКА И ПРАКТИКА

❖❖ 2.7. WORD ORDER WITH ТО́ЖЕ

Здесь живу́т Си́лины. Их соба́ка Бе́лка **то́же** живёт здесь.	*The Silins live here. Their dog Belka lives here too.*
— Джим аспира́нт.	*"Jim is a graduate student."*
— Во́ва **то́же** аспира́нт?	*"Is Vova a graduate student too?"*

То́же links new information to preceding information of a similar type in a similar context; **то́же** usually follows the new information.

УПРАЖНЕНИЕ 3 Я то́же . . .

You haven't met your roommate yet. All you know about him is what someone else is telling you—and it turns out you're a lot alike. Respond to each statement using **то́же**.

> ОБРАЗЕ́Ц: Его́ зову́т Са́ша.
>
> *Меня́ то́же зову́т Са́ша.*

1. Его́ оте́ц — врач.
2. Его́ мать — музыка́нт.
3. Она́ пиани́стка.
4. Са́ша — студе́нт.
5. Его́ сестра́ аспира́нтка.
6. Их дя́дя — тала́нтливый архите́ктор[†].

УПРАЖНЕНИЕ 4 Он (она́) то́же . . . ?

Working in small groups, describe yourself, a classmate, or a famous person with a single adjective from the list in Part 2, Exercise 9, on page 56. Then, using **то́же**, name someone in the class who can also be described with the same adjective. Remember to make the adjectives agree in gender with the people you describe.

> ОБРАЗЕ́Ц: Джон о́чень тала́нтливый. Мэ́ри то́же тала́нтливая.

❖❖ 2.8. SOME UNUSUAL PLURALS

Note these unusual plural forms, many of which refer to family members. The last three items in the list represent a small but commonly used group of masculine nouns that form their plurals by adding a stressed **-a** (or **-я** if the noun ends in a soft sign).

брат—бра́тья	сын—сыновья́	сосе́д—сосе́ди
сестра́—сёстры	дочь—до́чери	профе́ссор—профессора́
жена́—жёны	мать—ма́тери	дом—дома́
муж—мужья́	оте́ц—отцы́	а́дрес—адреса́

УПРАЖНЕНИЕ 5   Plural nouns and adjectives

Add plural endings to the nouns and adjectives in the following story about a new home.

1. Это наш дом. Дом хоро́ший и сосе́д____ хоро́ш____, но здесь о́чень ма́леньк____ кварти́р____.

2. Мо____ сёстр____ живу́т не здесь.

3. Их но́в____ кварти́р____ о́чень хоро́ш____.

4. Там бо́льш____ ко́мнат____ и хоро́ш____, бо́льш____ ку́хн____.

5. Они́ рабо́тают (*work*), и их муж____ то́же рабо́тают.

6. Мо____ бра́т____ живу́т недалеко́ (*not far*).

7. Их кварти́р____ то́же хоро́ш____, но там ма́леньк____ко́мнат____.

8. Они́ рабо́тают, и их жён____ то́же рабо́тают.

9. А я не рабо́таю. Мои́ сын____ — шко́льники, а мои́ до́ч____ ещё (*still*) ма́леньк____.

УПРАЖНЕНИЕ 6   Ва́ша семья́

Bring in a photo of your family or make a drawing of them using stick figures, and label each person with a Russian term such as **моя́ мать, мой оте́ц, мой брат, моя́ сестра́.** Show your photo or drawing to your classmate. Your classmate will ask about each person: **Кто э́то?** or **Э́то твой оте́ц?** Answer, give his or her name, and tell that person's relationship to you. (**Э́то мой брат. Его́ зову́т Том.**)

◈ 2.9. "FLEETING VOWEL" (-ЕЦ) NOUNS AND NATIONALITY WORDS

Nouns like **америка́нец** and **оте́ц** drop the **-e-** from the last syllable in their plural forms: **америка́нец → америка́нцы, оте́ц → отцы́,** thus retaining the same number of syllables as in the singular. There is a large number of such nouns—often called "fleeting vowel" nouns—including many masculine nouns of nationality. The feminine, plural, and adjectival forms related to these nouns form a large subgroup. Here are just a few of the many nationalities that follow this pattern:

MALE (ending -ец)	FEMALE (ending -ка)	PLURAL (males or mixed group; ending -цы)	ADJECTIVAL FORM (ending = suffix -ск- + adjective ending for gender)
америка́н-ец	америка́н-ка	америка́н-цы	америка́нск-ий (-ая, -ое, -ие)
кана́д-ец	кана́д-ка	кана́д-цы	кана́дск-ий (-ая, -ое, -ие)
мексика́н-ец	мексика́н-ка	мексика́н-цы	мексика́нск-ий (-ая, -ое, -ие)

In the glossary, fleeting vowel nouns are indicated thus: **америка́н(е)ц.** Note that the **-ец** form when pluralized (**-цы**) denotes both a group of males and a mixed group of males and females. (A group of females only would have the expected plural form: **америка́нки, кана́дки, мексика́нки.**) Finally, note that nouns and adjectives of nationality are not capitalized, except as the first word of a sentence (though place names are capitalized: **Аме́рика, Кана́да, Ме́ксика**).

УПРАЖНЕНИЕ 7   Nations and nationalities

Following the example, complete this table of nouns of nationality as related to the countries of origin.

	COUNTRY	MALE	FEMALE	PLURAL (MIXED)
ОБРАЗЕЦ:	Япо́ния	япо́нец	_япо́нка_	_япо́нцы_
1.	Испа́ния	_____	_____	испа́нцы
2.	Ита́лия	_____	италья́нка	_____
3.	Перу́	перуа́нец	_____	_____
4.	Герма́ния	_____	_____	не́мцы
5.	Украи́на	_____	украи́нка	_____
6.	Ирла́ндия	ирла́ндец	_____	_____

УПРАЖНЕНИЕ 8   Ва́ши интере́сы

For each topic below, circle a number between 1 (low) and 5 (high) to indicate how much you know (or would like to learn) about it. Then compare your ratings with those of your classmates to see if anyone else shares any of your top three interests.

1. америка́нские маши́ны (*cars*)	1 2 3 4 5
2. европе́йская архитекту́ра†	1 2 3 4 5
3. италья́нская о́пера†	1 2 3 4 5
4. мексика́нская ку́хня (*cuisine*)	1 2 3 4 5
5. неме́цкая (*German*) филосо́фия†	1 2 3 4 5
6. ру́сская литерату́ра†	1 2 3 4 5
7. францу́зское шампа́нское (*champagne*)	1 2 3 4 5
8. япо́нский язы́к (*language*)	1 2 3 4 5

СЛОВА, СЛОВА, СЛОВА... ✪ *Multiple Meanings*

A single word often has multiple meanings, each of which might be expressed by a different word in a foreign language. For example, *cooking* in English can refer to an activity (*Does he enjoy cooking?*) or a style of cuisine (*Do you like Mexican food?*). By contrast, the Russian word **ку́хня** can refer to a kitchen (**Кака́я ма́ленькая ку́хня!**) or to a particular kind of cuisine or cooking (**мексика́нская ку́хня**) but not to the activity of preparing food.

КУЛЬТУРА РЕЧИ

❖ ТАК ГОВОРЯТ: ПОЗНАКО́МЬТЕСЬ!

In this lesson the professor introduces Jim to the neighbors: **Познако́мьтесь, э́то Джим, мой аспира́нт.** You already know the phrase **О́чень прия́тно,** which is used when introductions are made. Another phrase that can be used in this situation is **О́чень рад** (for male speakers) or **О́чень ра́да** (for female speakers).

УПРАЖНЕ́НИЕ 9   Познако́мьтесь!

Working in groups of three, practice using these phrases to make introductions in the following situations:

1. Introduce your sister to your professor.
2. Introduce your neighbor to your grandfather.
3. Introduce a parent to your new neighbor.

❖ САМОПРОВЕ́РКА: УПРАЖНЕ́НИЕ 10

Working on your own, try this self-test: Read a Russian sentence out loud, then give an idiomatic English equivalent without looking at the book. Then work from English to Russian. After you have completed the activity, try it with a classmate.

1. Дава́йте познако́мимся!
2. Извини́те, пожа́луйста.
3. Каки́е хоро́шие сосе́ди!
4. Ваш брат музыка́нт? Мой брат то́же музыка́нт.
5. Са́ша хоро́ший пиани́ст.

1. *Let's introduce ourselves!*
2. *Excuse me, please.*
3. *What nice neighbors!*
4. *Your brother's a musician? My brother's a musician, too.*
5. *Sasha is a good pianist.*

❖ ВОПРО́СЫ И ОТВЕ́ТЫ: УПРАЖНЕ́НИЕ 11

Working with a classmate, take turns asking and answering the following questions:

1. Твои́ сосе́ди — врачи́? Музыка́нты? Ветерина́ры[†]? . . .
2. Они́ америка́нцы? (Ру́сские? Кана́дцы? Мексика́нцы?)
3. Как их зову́т?
4. Они́ хоро́шие сосе́ди?
5. Их кварти́ра больша́я и́ли ма́ленькая?
   (*и́ли:* Их дом большо́й и́ли ма́ленький?)

❖❖ ДИАЛОГИ

ДИАЛОГ 1 Óчень приятно!
(Making introductions; *two young people and an older gentleman*)

ВОЛÓДЯ.	Максим Петрóвич, познакóмьтесь, это мой друг (*friend*) Сергéй.
МАКСИ́М ПЕТРÓВИЧ.	Здрáвствуйте, Сергéй, óчень приятно.
ВОЛÓДЯ.	Сергéй, Максим Петрóвич — наш сосéд.
СЕРГÉЙ.	Óчень приятно, Максим Петрóвич.

ДИАЛОГ 2 Вы брат и сестрá?
(Getting acquainted; *a teenager talks to two adults.*)

ОЛÉГ.	Вы нáши сосéди?
МАРИ́А МИХÁЙЛОВНА.	Да.
ОЛÉГ.	А как вас зовýт?
МАРИ́А МИХÁЙЛОВНА.	Мари́я Михáйловна и Пётр Михáйлович.
ОЛÉГ.	Вы брат и сестрá?
ПЁТР МИХÁЙЛОВИЧ.	Нет, (*laughing*) мы муж и женá.

УПРАЖНÉНИЕ 12 Ваш диалóг

Working with two other students, create a conversation in which you and a friend, walking across campus, meet one of your professors. You introduce your friend to the professor and mention to the professor something interesting about your friend.

❖❖ А ТЕПÉРЬ . . . : УПРАЖНÉНИЕ 13

Working with a classmate, use what you learned in Part 3 to . . .

1. introduce him to your sister
2. find out if his apartment is large
3. find out if his neighbors are nice
4. find out if they're also students
5. find out if his parents are American

С ЧЕГО НАЧАТЬ?

УПРАЖНЕНИЕ 1 Домашние животные

1. **Живо́тные** means *animals* and **дома́шние** comes from the word **дом,** so what do you think is being advertised here?
2. What kind of animals are mentioned in the ad?
3. Which breeds?
4. You know the word **врач.** What is the short form of the phrase **ветерина́рный** (*veterinary*) **врач?**
5. Which **но́мер телефо́на** could you pass on to a friend who has been looking for a puppy (**щено́к**)?

ДОМАШНИЕ ЖИВОТНЫЕ

- **ВЕТПОМОЩЬ**. Круглосуточно. 310-16-20
- Стрижка. 466-74-68
- Ротвейлеры. 429-04-26
- Йоркшир-терьеры. 753-68-32
- **Профессиональная дрессировка** собак. Исправление поведения. Выезд на дом. 399-43-48
- Щенки **шарпея**. 407-75-26
- **Ветврач.** 134-70-15
- Аргентинские мастифы. 144-19-56
- **ВЕТПОМОЩЬ**. 310-16-60

Плю́сы и ми́нусы†

Ста́рая (*old*) кварти́ра	Новая кварти́ра
ста́рый дом	но́вый дом
кварти́ра плоха́я	кварти́ра хоро́шая
плохи́е **магази́ны** (*stores*)	хоро́шие магази́ны
но (*but*):	но:
метро́ бли́зко (*nearby*)	метро́ далеко́

УПРАЖНЕНИЕ 2 Плю́сы и ми́нусы

You are trying to decide whether to stay in your old apartment or move to another one. A friend suggests the two of you write down all the pluses and minuses of each option. On a separate piece of paper, make two columns: **Ста́рая кварти́ра** and **Но́вая кварти́ра.** Working with a classmate, list the **Плю́сы** (such as **Университе́т бли́зко**) and **ми́нусы** (such as **Магази́ны плохи́е**) for each apartment. Describe the street, house, apartment, rooms, neighbors, transportation (**тра́нспорт**), proximity to the university, and so on.

ЧТЕНИЕ

❖ SCENE A: ИЗВИНИ́ТЕ, Э́ТО ВА́ША СОБА́КА!

(The staircase, second floor. The Silins are leaving.)

bad	НАТА́ЛЬЯ ИВ.	Како́й у́жас! Кварти́ра ма́ленькая и **плоха́я.**° И сосе́д музыка́нт.
	СЕРГЕ́Й ПЕТР.	Кварти́ра хоро́шая и сосе́ди хоро́шие, Ната́ша. *(Shouts.)* Ле́на, ты где?
here / I'll be right there!	ЛЕ́НА.	*(From inside the apartment.)* Я **тут,**° па́па! **Сейча́с!**° Бе́лка!

(Sasha comes down the stairs carrying a cat. Lena appears with Belka, who starts barking.)

beautiful	СА́ША.	Извини́те, э́то ва́ша соба́ка? Кака́я **краси́вая**°!
cat	ЛЕ́НА.	Моя́. Её зову́т Бе́лка. А э́то ва́ша **ко́шка?**° Кака́я больша́я!
tomcat	СА́ША.	Э́то **кот.**° Его́ зову́т Матве́й. И́ли Мо́тя. А я Алекса́ндр. Са́ша.
	ЛЕ́НА.	Еле́на. Ле́на.
it seems	СА́ША.	О́чень прия́тно. Мы, **ка́жется,**° сосе́ди.

❖ SCENE B: НО́ВЫЕ АДРЕСА́

(Grandma Kruglov is sitting on a bench talking to a neighbor.)

All — Все° дома́ но́вые. Но́вые кварти́ры, но́вые сосе́ди, но́вые адреса́ . . . Вот э́то наш дом. Сосе́ди хоро́шие. Вон наш сосе́д, профе́ссор Петро́вский, и Джим, его́ аспира́нт. Джим америка́нец. А э́то наш **подъе́зд**°. Кварти́ра но́мер де́сять, **тре́тий**° эта́ж. **Внизу́**° живу́т Си́лины. Их дочь студе́нтка. **Журнали́стка.**† Мой внук Са́ша — то́же студе́нт. Пиани́ст. *(They hear the piano being played.)* Э́то Са́ша! Он о́чень хоро́ший пиани́ст!

entrance
third / Downstairs

УПРАЖНЕ́НИЕ 3   Под микроско́пом: Adjective endings

Without looking back at the text, see if you can supply the missing adjective endings. Then check your answers against the original text in Scene A above.

1. Ка___ у́жас! Кварти́ра ма́леньк___ и плох___!

2. Кварти́ра хоро́ш___ и сосе́ди хоро́ш___, Ната́ша.

3. Извини́те, э́то ва́ша соба́ка? Как___ краси́в___!

4. А э́то ва́ша ко́шка? Как___ больш___!

ГРАММАТИКА И ПРАКТИКА

О РОССИИ

USE OF NICKNAMES

Алекса́ндр его́ зову́т. И Са́ша то́же.

Although the first name and the patronymic are used to address adults in formal situations, among friends and family Russians use nicknames, which is like our practice of calling James "Jim" or "Jimmy" and Rebecca "Becky." Note that in Part 3, Scene A, **Алекса́ндра Никола́евна** called her grandson **Са́ша,** but he chose to use the full form of his name, **Алекса́ндр,** to introduce himself to Jim. (A list of nicknames is presented in Lesson 1, Part 2, Exercise 2 on page 9, as well as in the following exercise.)

УПРАЖНЕНИЕ 4   First names and nicknames

Match the names with their nicknames by making good guesses. Indicate which you think are men's names and which are women's names.

1. _____ Алексе́й	**а.** И́ра		
2. _____ Бори́с	**б.** Алёша		
3. _____ Валенти́на	**в.** Бо́ря		
4. _____ Ви́ктор	**г.** Лю́ба		
5. _____ Генна́дий	**д.** Пе́тя		
6. _____ Дми́трий	**е.** Ви́тя		
7. _____ Екатери́на	**ж.** Ди́ма		
8. _____ Еле́на	**з.** Ми́ша		
9. _____ Зинаи́да	**и.** Ле́на		
10. _____ Ири́на	**к.** Ка́тя		
11. _____ Любо́вь	**л.** Ге́на		
12. _____ Михаи́л	**м.** Зи́на		
13. _____ Пётр	**н.** Ва́ля		

СЛОВА, СЛОВА, СЛОВА… ✪ *Ordinal Numerals: First–Fourth*

Квартúра нóмер дéсять, трéтий этáж.

CARDINAL NUMERALS	ORDINAL NUMERALS	
одúн	пéрв–ый (–ая, –ое)	first
два	втор–óй (–áя, –óе)	second
три	трéт–ий (–ья, –ье)	third
четы́ре	четвёрт–ый (–ая, –ое)	fourth

Ordinal numerals (those that show rank or order rather than quantity) are adjectives. You've already seen (and possibly heard) those numerals in use: **Пéрвый урóк, Вторóй урóк, Часть пéрвая, Часть вторáя,** and so on. The winners of contests and competitions are often referred to as having won **пéрвое мéсто** (*place*), **вторóе мéсто,** and so on.

Познакóмьтесь, э́то моя́ собáка!

❖❖ 2.10. EXCLAMATIONS

Какáя красúвая собáка!　　　　　*What a beautiful dog!*

If a friend of yours has just bought a car, is wearing a new shirt or blouse, or has moved into a new apartment, you might want to say something like, *What a nice car* (*shirt, apartment*)! Russians do the same thing, using a particular intonation that you can hear and mimic from your instructor and your tapes. To make an exclamation of this type, the adjective **какóй** (**какáя, какóе, какúе**) is used with adjectives and/or nouns as in the following examples:

CONSTRUCTION	EXAMPLES	
⎧**Какóй**⎫ ⎧+ adjective + noun⎫ ⎨**Какáя**⎬ ⎨+ adjective⎬ ⎪**Какóе**⎪ ⎪+ noun⎪ ⎩**Какúе**⎭ ⎩ ⎭	Какáя красúвая собáка!	*What a beautiful dog!*
	Э́то вáша собáка?	*Is that your dog?*
	Какáя красúвая!	*She's so beautiful!*
	Какáя собáка!	*What a dog!*

❖ 2.11. INTONATION IN EXCLAMATIONS

LEVEL	EXCLAMATION
High	краСИВая со-
Mid	Какая
Low	бака!

УПРАЖНЕНИЕ 5   Endings and intonation

How would you say the following:

1. What a nice house!
2. What a big kitchen!
3. What small rooms!
4. What a nice dog!
5. What a small apartment!
6. What a beautiful house!

УПРАЖНЕНИЕ 6   Intonation: Кака́я хоро́шая!

Using words from the following table (or others that you may know), what would you say in the following instances?

ОБРАЗЕЦ: (Your friend has just moved into a new apartment.)
Кака́я больша́я!

		де́вочка
	большо́й (-а́я, -о́е, -и́е)	дом
	ма́ленький (-ая, -ое, -ие)	кварти́ра
какой	краси́вый (-ая, -ое, -ые)	роди́тели
кака́я	хоро́ший (-ая, -ее, -ие)	ко́мната
како́е	некраси́вый (-ая, -ое, -ые)	маши́на
каки́е	тала́нтливый (-ая, -ое, -ые)	кот
	энерги́чный (-ая, -ое, -ые)	соба́ка
	???[6]	у́лица
		???

1. Your sister just brought home a cat (or a dog).
2. Your parents have bought you a new car (**маши́на**).
3. They finally finished paving the street in front of your house.
4. They just finished building the biggest house in the neighborhood.
5. Your brother just finished building a tiny model car.
6. ???

---

[6]Here and elsewhere the ??? symbol invites you to create your own examples.

УПРАЖНЕНИЕ 7   Intonation

Work with a classmate, using the following sentences and the corresponding sentences in Appendix K. Take turns reading them aloud. When a sentence is read to you, indicate whether you have heard a statement, a question, or an exclamation.

	STATEMENT	QUESTION	EXCLAMATION
1. Это моя́ ба́бушка.	☐	☐	☐
2. Это твой дом?	☐	☐	☐
3. Са́ша до́ма?	☐	☐	☐
4. Кака́я больша́я маши́на (*car*)!	☐	☐	☐

◈◇◈ О РОССИИ ◈◇◈◈◇◈◈◇◈◈◇◈◈◇◈◈◇◈◈◇◈

WHERE DID THE RUSSIANS GET THEIR ALPHABET?

In A.D. 863, two brothers named Cyril and Methodius were sent by the Byzantine emperor as missionaries to spread the Christian faith to Slavic tribes in what is now the Czech Republic. In connection with this mission, they developed an alphabet and translated parts of the Gospels and the liturgy (worship service) into the local Slavic dialect. Their translation was a bold step, for at that time Greek and Latin were the primary languages used for ecclesiastical purposes.

After Cyril and Methodius died, some of their disciples worked their way southeast, spreading and strengthening Christianity among southern Slavs in what is now Serbia and Bulgaria. A little over a century later, in A.D. 988, Grand Prince Vladimir of Kiev accepted the Byzantine version of Christianity for himself and his Eastern Slavic people.

The alphabet that lies at the source of several modern Slavic alphabets, including Russian, is called Cyrillic in honor of these pioneer linguists. Cyrillic reflects the strong influence of written Greek, which dominated cultural life in the eastern half of the medieval Christian Church.

◈◇◈ 2.12. VOICED AND VOICELESS CONSONANTS

Many languages have consonants that can be grouped into pairs whose members differ only by whether one's voice is used to pronounce them. English has *z–s, v–f, d–t,* and so on. Many Russian consonants occur in similar voiced-voiceless pairs: **з–с, в–ф, д–т,** and so on. Here is a chart of voiced-voiceless paired consonant sounds as they are written in Russian:

VOICED		VOICELESS		VOICED		VOICELESS
б	—	п		в	—	ф
д	—	т		з	—	с
г	—	к		ж	—	ш

❖❖ 2.13. FINAL DEVOICING: THE "STROGANOFF EFFECT"

Speakers of Russian do not pronounce voiced consonants at the end of a word. Instead, where a voiced consonant is written they pronounce its voiceless counterpart. This has been called the "Stroganoff Effect," because the final sound of the name **Стро́ганов** is the voiceless [f], not the voiced [v] that is written. You should learn to automatically devoice final consonants as well; failure to do so will give you a marked accent in Russian.

УПРАЖНЕНИЕ 8   The Стро́ганов effect

Listen as your instructor pronounces the following words. Then write the Cyrillic letter that represents the *sound* you hear at the end of each word.

ОБРАЗЕЦ: де**д** → [т]

1. му**ж**   → [   ]
2. Кругло́**в**   → [   ]
3. сосе́**д**   → [   ]
4. Рахма́нино**в**   → [   ]
5. ра**д**   → [   ]
6. хле**б**   → [   ]
7. Белгра́**д**   → [   ]
8. эта́**ж**   → [   ]
9. метеоро́ло**г**   → [   ]
10. Ки́е**в**   → [   ]
11. Пари́**ж**   → [   ]

❖❖ 2.14. ASSIMILATION: THE "VODKA EFFECT"

Just as Russian speakers unconsciously devoice word-final consonants, English speakers unconsciously pronounce a final written -s as a [z] sound following a voiced consonant (compare *kits* and *kids*, *backs* and *bags*, *mops* and *mobs*). This process is called *assimilation*, in which the normally voiceless [s] takes on the voicing of the preceding consonant. Speakers of Russian also unconsciously assimilate neighboring consonants, but in Russian the second consonant dominates or influences the first. This has been called the "Vodka Effect," because the word **во́дка** is pronounced as if it were written **во́[т]ка:** The letter **д** is pronounced as a voiceless [**т**] because it is followed by the naturally voiceless [**к**].

УПРАЖНЕНИЕ 9   The во́дка effect

Listen as your instructor pronounces the words below, in which two consonants occur together. Then write the Cyrillic letters that represent the *sounds* you hear as the underlined consonants are pronounced.

ОБРАЗЕЦ: а**вт**о́бус → [фт]
            баске**тб**о́л → [дб]

1. за́**вт**ра   [   ]   **5.** рю**кз**а́к   [   ]
2. остано́**вк**а   [   ]   **6.** фу**тб**о́л   [   ]
3. Петро́**вс**кий [   ]   **7.** а́**вт**ор   [   ]
4. по**вт**ори́те   [   ]   **8.** бей**сб**о́л   [   ]

УПРАЖНЕНИЕ 10   Categories

Can you guess what these words mean? Sort them into the following categories. Each category (except one!) has four associated cognates: The Arts, The Earth, Economics, Military, Politics, Science, Sports, Technology, and Weather.

авиа́ция	бюдже́т	кандида́т	моде́м	температу́ра
актри́са	ви́рус	капита́н	офице́р	те́ннис
артилле́рия	волейбо́л	кли́мат	президе́нт	термина́л
балери́на	генера́л	компа́ния	премье́р-мини́стр	термо́метр
бале́т	генера́тор	конститу́ция	при́нтер	хокке́й
банк	гене́тика	лаборато́рия	солда́т	эква́тор
биоло́гия	геогра́фия	майо́р	субси́дия	эколо́гия
бокс	дра́ма	метеоро́лог	танк	эпице́нтр

КУЛЬТУРА РЕЧИ

❖❖ ТАК ГОВОРЯТ: ИЗВИНИ́ТЕ

Извини́те, э́то ва́ша соба́ка?   *Excuse me, is that your dog?*

Извини́те can be used to apologize for bumping into someone, or to get someone's attention when you'd like to ask a question, as in **Извини́те, как вас зову́т?**

УПРАЖНЕНИЕ 11   Извини́те

Working with a classmate, use **Извини́те** in short exchanges based on the following situations:

1. you want to find out if this is the third floor
2. you accidentally bump into someone on the street
3. you want to find out where Professor Petrovsky lives
4. you want to find out the name of the person sitting beside you
5. someone tells you that you dialed the wrong phone number
6. you've entered an office building and are looking for the elevator
7. you're in a restaurant and need to find out where the bathroom is

❖❖ САМОПРОВЕ́РКА: УПРАЖНЕНИЕ 12

Working on your own, try this self-test: Read a Russian sentence out loud, then give an idiomatic English equivalent without looking at the book. Then work from English to Russian. After you have completed the activity, try it with a classmate.

1. Э́то твоя́ (ва́ша) ко́шка? Кака́я краси́вая!
2. А чья э́то соба́ка? То́же твоя́ (ва́ша)?
3. Кака́я ма́ленькая кварти́ра! Како́й у́жас!

1. *Is that your cat? It's so beautiful!*
2. *And whose dog is that? Is it also yours?*
3. *What a small apartment! How horrible!*

4. Твоя́ (ва́ша) кварти́ра то́же ма́ленькая? Э́то ужа́сно!

5. Вас зову́т Ната́ша? О́чень прия́тно. А меня́ зову́т Алексе́й.

4. Is your apartment also small? That's awful!

5. Your name's Natasha? Nice to meet you. My name's Alexei.

❖ ВОПРОСЫ И ОТВЕТЫ: УПРАЖНЕНИЕ 13

You are considering renting a new apartment, but you need to ask the rental agent some questions about it first. Remember to speak formally.

1. Э́то но́вый дом?

2. Ко́мнаты хоро́шие?

3. О́кна больши́е?

4. И ку́хня больша́я?

5. Метро́ бли́зко?

6. А магази́ны?

❖ ДИАЛОГИ

ДИАЛОГ 1   Хоро́шая профе́ссия[†]!
(Getting acquainted)

— Извини́те, как вас зову́т?

— Кристи́на.

— Како́е краси́вое и́мя[7]! А я Татья́на, Та́ня. Я архите́ктор.[†]

— Хоро́шая профе́ссия,[†] Та́ня! А я исто́рик.[†]

— Кака́я интере́сная профе́ссия!

ДИАЛОГ 2   Кто здесь живёт?
(Establishing who lives where)

— Кто здесь живёт?

— Здесь живу́т Кругло́вы. Их внук Са́ша то́же живёт здесь.

— А Джим то́же живёт здесь?

— Нет, он живёт не здесь.

УПРАЖНЕНИЕ 14   Ваш диало́г

Working with two classmates, make up your own dialogue in which a friend visits your home for the first time. She meets your father or mother and comments on your cat or dog.

---

[7]**И́мя** (*name*) is one of a small group of neuter nouns that end in **-мя**. If you're ever unsure about the gender of a word in context, check to see if any adjectives are used with it; in this instance, the neuter adjective ending **-ое** (**краси́вое и́мя**) shows that the noun is neuter.

❖❖ А ТЕПЕРЬ . . . : УПРАЖНЕНИЕ 15

Working with a classmate, use what you learned in Part 4 to . . .

1. make a positive exclamation about her new apartment
2. make a negative exclamation about her neighbor
3. get her attention and (pointing at a dog) ask if that's her dog
4. ask if the metro is nearby
5. apologize for bumping into her

УЧИСЬ УЧИТЬСЯ ✪ *Learning Vocabulary*

Look for connections in the words you are learning. For example:

1. *Look for classical connections.* Russian and English are full of cognates, many of which came to both languages from Latin (usually via other languages) or can be easily recognized with the help of Latin. For example, **дом** is related to _domestic_, **кварти́ра** is related to _quarters_, **мать** is related to _matriarch_, and **но́вый** is related to _in<u>nov</u>ation_.

2. *Look for foreign connections.* If you have studied another modern foreign language (particularly French), you'll find many borrowed words, such as **эта́ж** and **журна́л**.

3. *Learn to spot Russian connections.* Once you know **оди́н** and **де́сять,** you can see _one-on-ten_ in **оди́н-на-дцать. Двена́дцать** is formed from **две** + **на** + **де́сять.** (What do you think _thirteen_ would be? How about _fifteen, sixteen,_ and _seventeen_?)

4. *Look for logical connections.* Often it helps to learn pairs of words (**брат/сестра́, большо́й/ма́ленький**), semantic groupings of words (**дом, кварти́ра, эта́ж, ко́мната, ку́хня . . .**), and series of words (numbers, days of the week, and so on) rather than learning each word in isolation.

5. *Invent your own connections.* If it helps you to imagine an impossible younger brother when learning **брат,** don't fight the link. If you hear a dog's "bark" in the word **соба́ка,** fine. (Such memory aids, or _mnemonics,_ are useful no matter what you are studying.)

ИТАК…

❖ НОВЫЕ СЛОВА

These are the words from this lesson you should learn actively. A "**v**" indicates that the word was introduced in the visual opener (**С чего начать?**).

NOUNS

Family, Family Members, Children

ба́бушка	grandmother (1v)
брат (*pl.* бра́тья)	brother (1v)
внук/вну́чка	grandson/ granddaughter (1)
двою́родная сестра́	cousin (female) (1v)
двою́родный брат	cousin (male) (1v)
де́вочка	(little) girl (2)
де́душка	grandfather (1v)
де́ти *pl.*	children (1v)
дочь (*pl.* до́чери) *f.*	daughter (1)
дя́дя *m.*	uncle (1v)
жена́ (*pl.* жёны)	wife (1v)
ма́льчик	boy (2)
ма́ма	mom; mother (2)
мать (*pl.* ма́тери) *f.*	mother (1v)
муж (*pl.* мужья́)	husband (1v)
от(е́)ц[8] (*pl.* отцы́)	father (1v)
па́па	dad (2)
роди́тели *pl.*	parents (1v)
семья́ (*pl.* се́мьи)	family (1v)
сестра́	sister (1v)
сын (*pl.* сыновья́)	son (1)
тётя	aunt (1v)

Neighborhood, Location, and Transportation

а́дрес (*pl.* адреса́)	address (1)
магази́н	store; shop (4v)
метро́ *neut. indecl.*	subway; metro (4v)
но́мер (*pl.* номера́)	number (1)
у́лица	street (1)
центр	downtown (2)

House and Apartment

балко́н	balcony (2v)
ва́нная *noun, declines like adj.*	bathroom (2v)
дверь *f.*	door (2v)
дом (*pl.* дома́)	1. house; 2. building (1)
кварти́ра	apartment (1)

ко́мната	room (2)
ку́хня	kitchen (2v)
лифт	elevator (2v)
окно́ (*pl.* о́кна)	window (2v)
подъе́зд	entrance (*to a building*) (4)
пол (*pl.* полы́)	floor (2v)
потол(о́)к (*pl.* потолки́)	ceiling (2v)
сосе́д (*pl.* сосе́ди)/сосе́дка	neighbor (2)
спа́льня	bedroom (2v)
стена́ (*pl.* сте́ны)	wall (2v)
столо́вая *noun, declines like adj.*	dining room (2v)
туале́т	bathroom; restroom (2v)
эта́ж (*pl.* этажи́)	floor; story (2)

Furniture

дива́н	couch (3v)
кни́жная по́лка	bookshelf (3v)
поду́шка	pillow; cushion (3v)
роя́ль *m.*	piano (3v)

Pets

кот (*pl.* коты́)	tomcat (4)
ко́шка	cat (4)
соба́ка	dog (1)

Studies and Professions

журнали́ст/журнали́стка	journalist (4)
пиани́ст/пиани́стка	pianist (1)
профе́ссор (*pl.* профессора́)	professor (1)
шко́льник/шко́льница	schoolboy/schoolgirl (1)

Other Nouns

америка́н(е)ц/америка́нка	an American (1)
магнитофо́н	tape recorder, tape player (3v)
ру́сский/ру́сская (*pl.* ру́сские) *noun, declines like adj.*	a Russian (2)
часы́ *pl.*	clock; watch (3v)

[8]Certain nouns such as **отец** drop the final vowel when endings are added. This will be indicated in the glossaries by putting the vowel in parentheses.

PRONOUNS

чей (чья, чьё, чьи)	whose (2)

ADJECTIVES

большо́й	big; large (2)
дорого́й	dear (3)
како́й . . .	what a . . . (2)
краси́вый	beautiful; good-looking (4)
ма́ленький	small; little (2)
но́вый	new (1)
плохо́й	bad (4)
ру́сский	Russian (2)
ста́рый	old (4v)
хоро́ший	good; nice (2)

ADVERBS

бли́зко *used as predicate*	(it's /that's) near; (it's/that's) close (4v)
внизу́	downstairs (4)
далеко́	far; far away (2)
почему́	why (3)
сле́ва	on the left (2)
спра́ва	on the right (2)
то́же	also; too (1)
тут	here (4)

NUMERALS

ноль (*or* нуль) *m.*	zero (1)
оди́н	one (1)
два	two (1)
три	three (1)
четы́ре	four (1)
пять	five (1)
шесть	six (1)
семь	seven (1)
во́семь	eight (1)
де́вять	nine (1)
де́сять	ten (1)
оди́ннадцать	eleven (1)

двена́дцать	twelve (1)
пе́рвый	first (4)
второ́й	second (4)
тре́тий	third (4)
четвёртый	fourth (4)

VERBS

живёт, живу́т (*dictionary form* жить)	he/she/it lives, they live (1)
игра́ет (*dictionary form* игра́ть)	he/she plays (3)

OTHER

вон	(over) there (2)
и́ли	or (3)
ну	well (2)
так *particle*	so; then (3)

IDIOMS AND EXPRESSIONS

Дава́йте познако́мимся.	Let's introduce ourselves; Let's get acquainted. (3)
ка́жется *parenthetical*	it seems (4)
Как гро́мко он игра́ет!	He plays so loud! (3)
Како́й у́жас!	That's horrible!; How awful! (2)
муж и жена́ Кругло́вы	Mr. and Mrs. Kruglov; the Kruglovs, husband and wife (1)
Ничего́ (*in response to an apology*).	That's OK; That's all right. (3)
но́мер телефо́на	(tele)phone number (1)
О́чень рад.	Pleased/Nice to meet you. (3)
Познако́мьтесь, э́то . . . (*when introducing someone*)	I'd like you to meet . . . ; Meet . . . ; Let me introduce . . . (3)
Сейча́с! (*when being called by someone*)	I'll be right there! (4)
Это здо́рово!	It's/That's great! (2)
Это ужа́сно!	It's/That's horrible!; How awful! (3)

❖❖ ЧТО Я ЗНАЮ, ЧТО Я УМЕЮ

Use this checklist to mark off what you've learned in this lesson:

☐   What is meant by *verb conjugation* (Part 1)
☐   How to ask and answer some types of questions (Part 1)
☐   How to ask and answer *whose* (ownership) questions (Part 2)
☐   About making exclamations (Part 4)
☐   About words that have multiple meanings (Part 3)
☐   Using some kinds of adjectives as nouns (Part 2)
☐   Adjective endings that show gender and number (Part 2)

☐ How to pluralize neuter nouns (Part 2)
☐ Some nouns with unusual plurals (Part 3)
☐ Plurals of -ец nouns (Part 3)
☐ Word order with adjectives and nouns (Part 2)
☐ Word order with тóже (Part 3)
☐ Some uses of the prefix не- (Part 2)
☐ Some spelling rules (Part 2)
☐ Pronunciation in Russian: assimilation and devoicing (Part 4)

❖ ЭТО НАДО ЗНАТЬ

А. ADJECTIVE SUMMARY TABLE

	MASCULINE	FEMININE	NEUTER	PLURAL
Adjectives	как-óй	как-áя	как-óе	как-úе
	нóв-ый	нóв-ая	нóв-ое	нóв-ые
	мáленьк-ий	мáленьк-ая	мáленьк-ое	мáленьк-ие
	больш-óй	больш-áя	больш-óе	больш-úе
	хорóш-ий	хорóш-ая	хорóш-ее	хорóш-ие
Possessives	че-й	чь-я	чь-ё	чь-и
	мо-й	мо-я́	мо-ё	мо-и́
	тво-й	тво-я́	тво-ё	тво-и́
	наш	нáш-а	нáш-е	нáш-и
	ваш	вáш-а	вáш-е	вáш-и

Б. NOUN PLURALS

1. Masculine

a. Most common: after a hard consonant, add -ы:

журнáл— журнáлы   студéнт—студéнты

b. Fleeting vowel (many nationalities): drop -e-, add -ы:

канáдец—канáдцы   отéц—отцы́

c. «Кни́ги» spelling rule often comes into play:

внук—вну́ки   эта́ж—этажи́

d. Word-final -ь or -й: drop -ь or -й, add -и («роя́ли» rule):

роя́ль—роя́ли   музéй—музéи

e. Stressed -á subset (not predictable):

áдрес—адресá   дом—домá

2. Feminine

a. Most common: drop final -а/-я, add -ы/-и:

кварти́ра—кварти́ры   фами́лия—фами́лии

b. «Кни́ги» spelling rule often comes into play:

кни́га—кни́ги   студéнтка—студéнтки

c. Word-final -ь: drop -ь, add -и («роя́ли» rule):

дверь—двéри

3. Neuter

a. Most common: drop final -о/-е, add -а/-я:

слóво—словá   упражнéние—упражнéния

b. Stress shifts (especially on two-syllable words) are common and unpredictable:

окнó—óкна   письмó—пи́сьма

❖ ДОПОЛНИ́ТЕЛЬНЫЕ ТЕ́КСТЫ

ПЕ́РВЫЙ РЕЙС (*VOYAGE*) СОВРЕМЕ́ННОГО (*MODERN*) «ТИТА́НИКА»

I. Before you begin . . .

1. To what famous ocean liner is this modern ship being likened? Find and circle the name of that ship.
2. What types of accommodations might you find on a cruise ship?
3. What other services might be provided?
4. Have you ever traveled on a cruise ship?

II. Look at the diagram and answer the following questions focusing on the boldfaced headings.

1. What is the name of this ship?
2. How does it compare in size to an *Airbus* airplane?
3. Find the Russian equivalents of *cruise liner, passenger cabins, luxury cabin.*
4. How many cabins are on the ship?
5. How many kinds of cabins are available? How do you think they're different?
6. Find the places where one can eat on board the ship.
7. What athletic facilities are available? (Hint: **бассе́йн** = *pool*)
8. Find the Russian phrase for *night club.*
9. What other entertainment facilities are available?

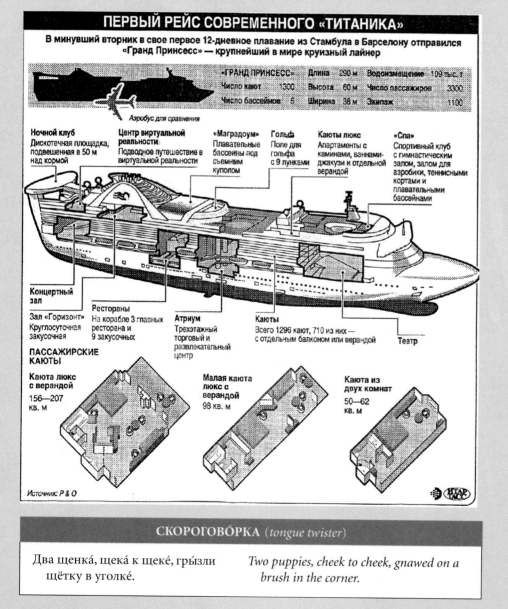

ПЕРВЫЙ РЕЙС СОВРЕМЕННОГО «ТИТАНИКА»

В минувший вторник в свое первое 12-дневное плавание из Стамбула в Барселону отправился «Гранд Принсесс» — крупнейший в мире круизный лайнер

«ГРАНД ПРИНСЕСС»	Длина	290 м	Водоизмещение	109 тыс. т
Число кают	1300	Высота	60 м	Число пассажиров	3300
Число бассейнов	5	Ширина	38 м	Экипаж	1100

Аэробус для сравнения

Ночной клуб
Дискотечная площадка, подвешенная в 50 м над кормой

Центр виртуальной реальности
Подводное путешествие в виртуальной реальности

«Маградоум»
Плавательные бассейны под съемным куполом

Гольф
Поле для гольфа с 9 лунками

Каюты люкс
Апартаменты с каминами, ваннами-джакузи и отдельной верандой

«Спа»
Спортивный клуб с гимнастическим залом, залом для аэробики, теннисными кортами и плавательными бассейнами

Концертный зал
Зал «Горизонт» Круглосуточная закусочная

Рестораны
На корабле 3 главных ресторана и 9 закусочных

Атриум
Трехэтажный торговый и развлекательный центр

Каюты
Всего 1296 кают, 710 из них — с отдельным балконом или верандой

Театр

ПАССАЖИРСКИЕ КАЮТЫ

Каюта люкс с верандой
156—207 кв. м

Малая каюта люкс с верандой
98 кв. м

Каюта из двух комнат
50—62 кв. м

Источник: P & O

ИТАР ТАСС

МЫ И НАШИ СОСЕДИ

Это на́ши сосе́ди.

In Part 1, Lena and her mother talk about Lena's choice of a career in journalism. Then in Part 2, Lena's friend, Masha, drops by the new apartment and they discuss the young pianist upstairs. In Part 3, Lena and Vova have a little spat over their differing tastes in music; and in Part 4, which you'll see on video, Professor Petrovsky and Stepan Evgenyevich Kruglov get acquainted and take a tour of the new neighborhood.

In this lesson you will learn

- ⊛ to express actions in the present tense
- ⊛ to tell where you live and work
- ⊛ to express opinions
- ⊛ to talk about objects of action
- ⊛ to express going somewhere
- ⊛ to talk about playing sports
- ⊛ to make polite inquiries
- ⊛ to talk about home furnishings, music, and places around town
- ⊛ about music in Russia
- ⊛ how Russian is related to other languages

Вот мы здесь. . .

ЧАСТЬ ПЕРВАЯ

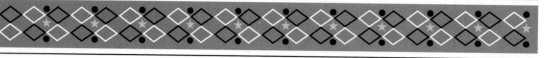

 С ЧЕГО НАЧАТЬ?

Серге́й Петро́вич **на рабо́те.**
Он **мно́го рабо́тает.**

Ната́лья Ива́новна **отдыха́ет.**
Она́ **чита́ет** три́ллер.

Во́ва **пи́шет сочине́ние.**

Ле́на и Бе́лка **гуля́ют.**

УПРАЖНЕНИЕ 1   Кто что де́лает? (*Who is doing what?*)

Match the character with the action.

1. _____ Во́ва
2. _____ Ле́на и Бе́лка
3. _____ Ната́лья Ива́новна
4. _____ Серге́й Петро́вич

а. отдыха́ет и чита́ет три́ллер
б. рабо́тает
в. гуля́ют
г. пи́шет сочине́ние

УПРАЖНЕНИЕ 2   Verbs

Match the actions.

1. _____ отдыха́ет
2. _____ пи́шет сочине́ние
3. _____ рабо́тает
4. _____ гуля́ют
5. _____ чита́ет три́ллер

а. are taking a walk
б. is resting
в. is writing a composition
г. is reading a thriller
д. is working

ЧТЕНИЕ

❖ ИНТЕРЕ́СНАЯ[†] ПРОФЕ́ССИЯ[†]

(At the Silins'.)

НАТА́ЛЬЯ ИВ.	Ле́ночка,° что ты **де́лаешь**°?
ЛЕ́НА.	Пишу́ **статью́.**°
НАТА́ЛЬЯ ИВ.	**Опя́ть**° статью́?
ЛЕ́НА.	Да . . .Э́то моя́ **курсова́я рабо́та.**°
НАТА́ЛЬЯ ИВ.	А-а, курсова́я . . . А **кака́я**° **те́ма**°?
ЛЕ́НА.	Те́ма **тру́дная**°: «**В**° ци́рке».°
НАТА́ЛЬЯ ИВ.	«В ци́рке»? **Ра́зве**° э́то тру́дная те́ма? Ведь[1] все **зна́ют,**° что тако́е цирк.°
ЛЕ́НА.	И́менно **поэ́тому,**° ма́ма! **Кро́ме того́,**° **на́до** писа́ть **интере́сно,**° **оригина́льно,**° а э́то **нелегко́.**°
НАТА́ЛЬЯ ИВ.	**Понима́ю . . .**° **Что ж,**° те́ма **интере́сная**[†]. **И вообще́** у тебя́ интере́сная профе́ссия.°

(Telephone rings.)

НАТА́ЛЬЯ ИВ.	**Рабо́тай,**° до́ченька.° *(She goes to the other room to pick up the phone.)* Алло́.° Да, я. Здра́вствуйте, Ми́ша. Что? Нет, он **уже́**° до́ма. Что мы де́лаем? Ле́на пи́шет статью́, я чита́ю, а Серёжа и Во́ва **игра́ют в ша́хматы.**° **Что-что**?° Кто выи́грывает°?

(Vova's triumphant voice from the other room) Шах°!

НАТА́ЛЬЯ ИВ.	*(Smiling.)* **По-мо́ему,**° Во́ва. Да, **сейча́с.**° *(Shouts).* Серёжа, **телефо́н**[†]!

(Vova's voice from the other room) И мат°!!!

Ле́на *(affectionate)* / что. . .
  what are you doing / article
Again
курсова́я. . . *term paper*
what / topic
difficult / At / circus
Really. . .? / все. . . *everybody
  knows /* что. . . *what a
  circus is*
И́менно. . . *That's precisely
  why /* Кро́ме. . . *Besides
  (that) / you have to /
  interestingly /
  creatively / not easy*
I understand / Well / И. . .
  *And you have an interesting
  profession anyway.*
*Keep working / daughter
  (affectionate)*
Hello / already / игра́ют. . .
  *are playing chess / Beg your
  pardon? / is winning*
Check!
I think / right away[2]
checkmate

---

[1]**Ведь** is a particle used for emphasis. Its meaning is roughly equivalent to *after all,* but very often it is not translated.
[2]Used colloquially, with the verb omitted, in the meaning "(I'll get him) right away."

УПРАЖНЕНИЕ 3　　Под микроско́пом: Feminine adjective/
　　　　　　　　　　　　　noun phrases

The preceding reading contains several feminine nouns used with adjectives. You know that an adjective can precede a noun (**но́вая кварти́ра** *new apartment*), or it can follow a noun, with an implied present tense of the verb "to be" (**кварти́ра но́вая** *the apartment is new*). Look back at the text and make a list of as many examples as you can find of each type.

❖ 3.1. VERBS: PRESENT TENSE

Ле́на, что ты **де́лаешь?**　　　　　　　*Lena, what are you doing?*
Чита́ешь?　　　　　　　　　　　　　　*Reading?*

Whereas English has several verb forms that describe an action going on at the present time (*she reads, she is reading, she has been reading*), Russian has only one form for the present tense: **она́ чита́ет**.

❖ 3.2. -ЕШЬ VERBS: BASIC (ЧИТА́ТЬ) TYPE

The largest group of Russian verbs are conjugated like **чита́ть** (*to read*). Most of these verbs have a stem ending in a vowel (such as **чита́-** or **гуля́-**), and unstressed endings, most of which begin with **-е-**. This type of verb can be called a **-ешь** verb, after the ending of its **ты** form. (Some books call this the "first conjugation.") Study this pattern carefully in the table below. For clarity, each form is separated into stem and ending. Other verbs of this type include **де́лать, отдыха́ть, гуля́ть, знать, понима́ть,** and **рабо́тать.** Note that most infinitives (dictionary forms) end in **-ть.**

PRESENT TENSE OF ЧИТА́ТЬ (*to read*)	
я	чита́-**ю**
ты	чита́-**ешь**
он, она́	чита́-**ет**
мы	чита́-**ем**
вы	чита́-**ете**
они́	чита́-**ют**

УПРАЖНЕНИЕ 4   Using basic -ешь verbs

Write the correct ending for the following verbs:

1. Мой брат — шко́льник. Он ещё не (*not yet*) рабо́та_____. Моя́ сестра́ — студе́нтка. Она́ то́же не рабо́та_____. Мои́ роди́тели рабо́та_____. Ба́бушка — пенсионе́рка (*retiree*). Она́ уже́ не (*no longer*) рабо́та_____.

2. И́ра пи́шет: «Мой па́па рабо́та_____. Он журнали́ст. Ма́ма не рабо́та_____, она́ студе́нтка».

3. Ты рабо́та_____? А я не рабо́та_____. Что ты де́ла_____? Ты пи́шешь статью́? Мы понима́_____, что писа́ть статью́ нелегко́. Ты понима́_____, почему́ э́то нелегко́? Я э́то понима́_____. И вы э́то то́же понима́_____.

Он рабо́тает и́ли отдыха́ет?

❖❖❖ 3.3. -ЕШЬ VERBS: ЖИТЬ VARIATION

Здесь **живёт** музыка́нт?   *Does a musician live here?*

A much smaller but still significant group of **-ешь** verbs has a stem ending in a conso-nant (such as **жив-**) and stressed endings, most of which begin with **-ё-**.[3] An example of this type is **жить** (*to live*). Some students and teachers find it helpful to refer to verbs with this end-stressed pattern as "**-ёшь** verbs." Note that **ё** occurs only in stressed syllables.

PRESENT TENSE OF ЖИТЬ (*to live*)	
я	жив-у́
ты	жив-ёшь
он, она́	жив-ёт
мы	жив-ём
вы	жив-ёте
они́	жив-у́т

---

[3]Russians seldom write the two dots over the letter **e** (**ё**), but you should do so where appropriate to remember the pronunciation.

УПРАЖНЕНИЕ 5 Я живу́ здесь

Fill in the blanks with the correct verb ending. Mark the stress or add the dots over the **ë**.

ПЁТР ПЕТРО́ВИЧ.	Ты жив_____[1] здесь?
ПЕ́ТЯ.	Да, я жив_____[2] здесь.
ПЁТР ПЕТРО́ВИЧ.	А твоя́ сестра́? Где она́ жив_____[3]? То́же здесь?
ПЕ́ТЯ.	Да, она́ то́же жив_____[4] здесь. А где вы жив_____[5]?
ПЁТР ПЕТРО́ВИЧ.	Я жив_____[6] не здесь.

WORD ORDER ✪ *in WH-Questions*

Где она́ живёт?	*Where does she live?*
Где живёт Ка́тя?	*Where does Katya live?*

In WH-questions a pronoun subject usually precedes the verb; a noun subject will usually follow the verb the first time it is mentioned.

❖❖ 3.4. TELLING WHERE SOMEONE LIVES: THE PREPOSITIONAL CASE

— Где ты живёшь? **В Санкт-Петербу́рге?**	*"Where do you live? In St. Petersburg?"*
— Нет, я живу́ **в Москве́.**	*"No, I live in Moscow."*
Серге́й Петро́вич **на рабо́те.**	*Sergei Petrovich is at work.*

To tell where someone lives (works, and so on) or where someone (or something) is located, Russian generally uses the prepositions **в** and **на,** with **в** being used mostly with physical locations (in a city, at a university) and **на** used mostly with events (at a football game, at work). There are some exceptions to this principle, however, such as **на по́чте** (at the post office), that you will learn quickly. In addition, **на** is used to show location *on* (on the table). The ending of the location word changes to show its function. This particular change is called *declension* and this declined form is called the *Prepositional case* (as distinct from the *Nominative case,* which is the dictionary form. Altogether there are six cases in Russian.) The Prepositional case is so called because it always follows a preposition.

The basic Prepositional case ending for singular nouns is **-e.** Just a few types of nouns take **-и.** Here is a summary of Prepositional case forms for singular nouns:

	NOMINATIVE CASE (dictionary form)	PREPOSITIONAL CASE ENDING	EXAMPLES
Neuter «-ие» type **Feminine «-ия» type** **Feminine «-ь» type**	упражнéни-е Росси́-я двер-ь	Delete final vowel or -ь; add -и	в упражнéни-**и** в Росси́-**и** на двер-**и́**
All other types	Но́вгород концéрт музé-й *museum* роя́л-ь письм-ó Москв-á рабóт-а семь-я́	Delete final vowel, -й, or -ь; add -e	в Но́вгород-**е** на концéрт-**е** в музé-**е** на роя́л-**е** в письм-**é** в Москв-**é** на рабóт-**е** в семь-**é**

City names that are indeclinable, obviously foreign, or not very well known are often presented in the construction <**в гóроде** + the Nominative case> of the city name: **в гóроде Таллахáсси, в гóроде Вýдсток.** State names are commonly put into a similar construction, with **в штáте . . .: в штáте Нью-Йóрк, в штáте Флори́да.** Canadians would, of course, say, **в прови́нции . . .: в прови́нции Онтáрио.**[4]

УПРАЖНÉНИЕ 6   Где ты живёшь?

By using the phrases **Где ты живёшь?** or **Ты живёшь в** [*city name*]**?,** find out in what cities and states your classmates live. Then find out where members of their families live.

PRONUNCIATION ✪ *Assimilation of Prepositions*

Prepositions carry meaning on their own, but they are usually pronounced as if they were simply part of the following word. This is particularly evident with single-letter prepositions like **в.** To avoid a marked foreign accent, learn to pronounce the preposition **в** as part of the next word; the number of syllables is the same, with or without the preposition. Remember, too, what you learned about voicing assimilation in Lesson 2, Part 4: before voiceless consonants, **в** is pronounced as [ф]. Not all consonants have voiced and voiceless counterparts; the consonants **х, ц, ч, щ** are voiceless, so **в** is pronounced as [ф] when the following word begins with one of these four letters. The consonants **л, м, н, р** are voiced, and all vowels are voiced, so **в** is pronounced as a voiced [в] when it precedes one of these sounds.

YOU SEE . . .
в Амéрике
в Гермáнии
в письмé
в Канáде

YOU SAY . . .
ва-МЕ-ри-ке
вгер-МА-ни-и
фпись-МЕ
фка-НА-де

---

[4]When giving more than one geographic location, start with the larger context and then give the more specific: **Я живý в штáте Миссýри, в гóроде Сент-Лýис.**

УПРАЖНЕНИЕ 7   Я живу́ в . . .

Listen as your instructor reads the following sentences and indicate whether the preposition is pronounced as [**в**] or [**ф**].

ОБРАЗЕЦ: в Ки́еве   →   [ф]Ки́еве

1. Я живу́ в Пятиго́рске.   → [   ]
2. Я живу́ в Ви́тебске.   → [   ]
3. Я живу́ в Ха́рькове.   → [   ]
4. Я живу́ в Ми́нске.   → [   ]
5. Я живу́ в Ташке́нте.   → [   ]

6. Я живу́ в Донéцке.   → [   ]
7. Я живу́ в Ирку́тске.   → [   ]
8. Я живу́ в Ку́рске.   → [   ]
9. Я живу́ в Но́вгороде.   → [   ]

PRONUNCIATION ✪ *Buffer Vowels*

Single-letter prepositions like **в** are written with an inserted vowel **о** (called a *buffer vowel*) before words that begin with certain consonant clusters, especially those that begin with **в** or **ф**. Here are some examples:

во Фра́нции
во Владивосто́ке

УПРАЖНЕНИЕ 8   Кто где живёт?

Complete the following sentences, using the country names in the list provided. Add the preposition **в** (or **во**) as required. Then be prepared to read the sentences out loud.

Амéрика
Афганиста́н
Ира́н
Кана́да

Непа́л
Румы́ния
Фра́нция
Япо́ния

ОБРАЗЕЦ: Мéксика → <u>Мексика́нцы живу́т *в Мéксике.*</u>

1. Кана́дцы живу́т_____.
2. Америка́нцы живу́т_____.
3. Францу́зы живу́т_____.
4. Афга́нцы живу́т_____.
5. Ира́нцы живу́т_____.
6. Япо́нцы живу́т_____.
7. Непа́льцы живу́т_____.
8. Румы́ны живу́т_____.

◈ 3.5. -ЕШЬ **VERBS:** ПИСА́ТЬ **VARIATION**

Я **пишу́** статью́.   *I'm writing an article.*

A third type of **-ешь** verb has a stem ending in a consonant (such as **пиш-**) and *shifting* stress. When a verb has shifting stress, the pattern is always the same: the stress occurs on the ending of the **я** form (**я пишу́**) and then shifts one syllable back onto the stem for the other forms. An example of this type is **писа́ть** (*to write*).

PRESENT TENSE OF ПИСА́ТЬ (*to write*)	
я	пиш-у́
ты	пи́ш-ешь
он, она́	пи́ш-ет
мы	пи́ш-ем
вы	пи́ш-ете
они́	пи́ш-ут

УПРАЖНЕНИЕ 9   Мы пи́шем курсовы́е

Fill in the blanks and note stresses:

МА́МА. Что ты пи́ш _____ [1]?
ЛЁНА. Я пиш _____ [2] статью́.
МА́МА. А что де́ла _____ [3] Во́ва?
ЛЁНА. Он пи́ш _____ [4] письмо́.
МА́МА. А Ма́ша и Са́ша? Что они́ пи́ш _____ [5]?
ЛЁНА. Они́ пи́ш _____ [6] курсовы́е.

❖❖ 3.6. VERB STRESS PATTERNS (SUMMARY)

The verbs **чита́ть, жить,** and **писа́ть** demonstrate the three main stress patterns of Russian verbs.

Stem stress means that the stress is always on the stem (**чита́-ю, чита́-ешь,** . . . **чита́-ют**).

Ending stress means that the stress is always on the ending (**жив-у́, жив-ёшь,** . . . **жив-у́т**).

Shifting stress means that the stress is always on the ending of the **я** form and then shifts back to the stem for the other forms (**пиш-у́, пи́ш-ешь,** . . . **пи́ш-ут**).

❖❖ О РОССИИ ❖❖❖❖❖❖❖❖❖❖❖❖❖❖❖

ША́ХМАТЫ

Серге́й Петро́вич и Во́ва игра́ют в ша́хматы.

Га́рри Каспа́ров

Chess (**ша́хматы;** always plural) in Russia is a national passion. The names of such grand masters as Karpov and Kasparov are known all over the world by anyone who has even a passing acquaintance with the game. Any major international tournament will have Russians prominent among its top contestants, and most of the world champions of the past 50 years have been from Russia and the Soviet Union. In Russia itself, top chess players are treated with the same respect afforded practitioners of the more physical sports; in fact, chess is among the 60-some officially recognized sports—right up there with soccer (**футбо́л**), swimming (**пла́вание**), and figure skating (**фигу́рное ката́ние**). Here are the names of the chess pieces (**фигу́ры**): *pawn* = **пе́шка,** *rook/castle* = **ладья́,** *knight* = **конь** (*m.*), *bishop* = **слон,** *queen* = **ферзь** (*m.*), *king* = **коро́ль** (*m.*). Oh, and **шах/мат** (*check/mate*), "the king is dead" (from Persian).

КУЛЬТУРА РЕЧИ

❖ **ТАК ГОВОРЯТ: РА́ЗВЕ…?**

— Те́ма тру́дная: «В ци́рке».
— «В ци́рке»? Ра́зве э́то тру́дная те́ма? Ведь все зна́ют, что тако́е цирк.

"The topic is difficult. 'At the circus.'"
"'At the circus'? Is that really a difficult topic? After all, everybody knows what a circus is."

The word **ра́зве** is used in follow-up questions. It may express doubt, skeptical attitude, or surprise about something previously stated or discussed. It may be used when something just stated differs from or contradicts what the speaker thinks. In the preceding example, it expresses Natalya Ivanovna's doubt or skeptical attitude that **«В ци́рке»** is indeed a difficult topic.

УПРАЖНЕНИЕ 10   Ра́зве…?

How would you translate the following exchanges with **ра́зве**?

1. (*Two neighbors talking in their courtyard see an important-looking man come out of the entranceway and get into a limo.*)
   — Кто э́то?
   — Э́то наш депута́т Ду́мы (*legislative deputy*).
   — Ра́зве он живёт в на́шем до́ме?
2. (*Two neighbors talking*)
   — Кака́я краси́вая ко́шка!
   — Э́то на́ша Мыши́льда.
   — Ра́зве у вас (*you have*) ко́шка, а не соба́ка?
3. (*A student shows her roommate a photo of a young woman pushing a baby carriage along a bridge.*)
   — Кто э́то?
   — Э́то моя́ сестра́.
   — А кака́я э́то река́?
   — Се́на (*the Seine*).
   — Се́на? Ра́зве твоя́ сестра́ живёт в Пари́же?

❖ **САМОПРОВЕРКА: УПРАЖНЕНИЕ 11**

Working on your own, try this self-test: Read a Russian sentence out loud, then give an idiomatic English equivalent without looking at the book. Then work from English to Russian. After you have completed the activity, try it with a classmate.

1. — Серге́й Петро́вич, что вы де́лаете? Чита́ете?
   — Нет, я пишу́ письмо́.

2. — Где живу́т твои́ роди́тели?
   — Они́ живу́т в Росси́и, во Влади́мире.

1. *"Sergei Petrovich, what are you doing? Reading?"*
   "No, I'm writing a letter."

2. *"Where do your parents live?"*
   "They live in Russia, in Vladimir."

3. Ты понима́ешь второ́й вопро́с?
Понима́ешь? А я не понима́ю.

3. *Do you understand the second question? You understand* (it)? *I don't.*

4. — Бо́ря, что ты де́лаешь?
Чита́ешь?
— Да, чита́ю статью́ «Футбо́л
в Аме́рике».

4. *"Borya, what are you doing? Reading?"*
"Yes, I'm reading an article: 'Soccer in America.'"

❖ ВОПРОСЫ И ОТВЕТЫ: УПРАЖНЕНИЕ 12

Working with a classmate, take turns asking and answering the following questions:

1. Ты рабо́таешь? Где?

2. Где рабо́тает твоя́ мать? А твой оте́ц?

3. Где живу́т твои́ роди́тели?

4. Где живёт твоя́ сестра́ (твоя́ ба́бушка . . .)?

5. Где живёт твой брат (твой де́душка . . .)?

6. Где рабо́тает твой брат? А твоя́ сестра́?

НОВАЯ ГАЗЕТА
№ 6 (478)
16 — 22 февраля 1998 г.

3

Профессия: мама

Э́то интере́сная профе́ссия? Тру́дная профе́ссия?

❖ ДИАЛОГИ

ДИАЛОГ 1 Что ты де́лаешь?
(Asking what someone is doing)

— Что ты де́лаешь?
— Пишу́ сочине́ние.
— А Са́ша что де́лает?
— Чита́ет газе́ту.

ДИАЛОГ 2 Где вы живёте?
(Asking where someone lives)

— Вы живёте в Москве́?
— Нет, в Санкт-Петербу́рге. А вы?
— Я живу́ в Но́вгороде.
— В Но́вгороде? Мои́ роди́тели то́же живу́т в Но́вгороде.

УПРАЖНЕНИЕ 13   Ваш диало́г

Working with a partner and using familiar expressions, write a dialogue in which you are on the phone with a friend. Each of you should find out what the other is doing.

❖ А ТЕПЕРЬ . . . : УПРАЖНЕНИЕ 14

Working with a classmate, use what you learned in Part 1 to . . .

1. find out where he lives
2. find out if he works (and if so, whether he works a lot)
3. ask where his family lives
4. find out whether his parents work (and if so, where)

С ЧЕГО НАЧАТЬ?

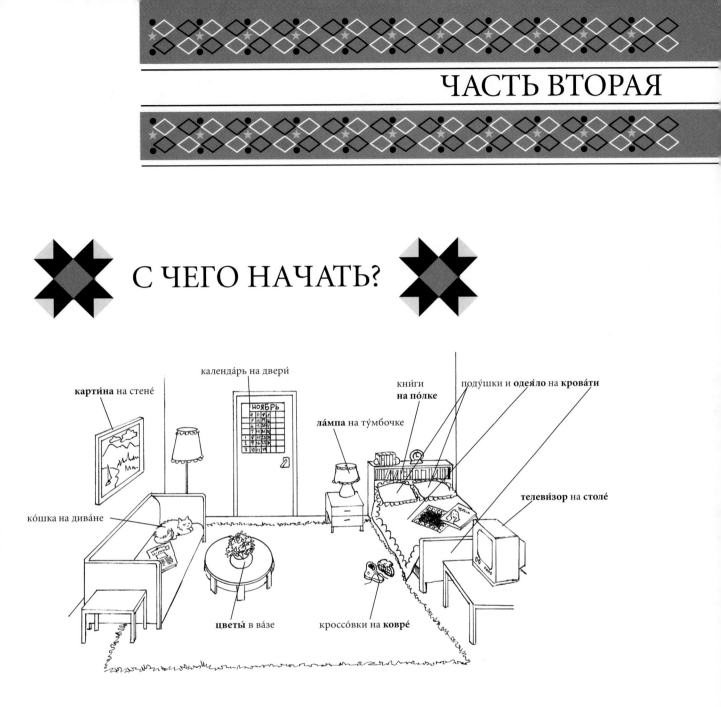

карти́на на стене́

календа́рь на двери́

ла́мпа на ту́мбочке

кни́ги на по́лке

поду́шки и одея́ло на крова́ти

телеви́зор на столе́

ко́шка на дива́не

цветы́ в ва́зе

кроссо́вки на ковре́

УПРАЖНЕНИЕ 1   А где карти́на?

Working with a classmate, take turns asking and answering questions about where things are in the room shown above. Include the labeled items, then make up some other questions based on words you already know.

ОБРАЗЕ́Ц: — Где кни́ги?
                — На по́лке. А где карти́на? (...)

✦ ЧТЕНИЕ ✦

nice   ❖❖ СОСЕ́Д **СИМПАТИ́ЧНЫЙ**°?

(Lena's friend Masha comes to visit. Natalya Ivanovna answers the door and invites her in.)

	МА́ША.	Здра́вствуйте, Ната́лья Ива́новна!
Добрый. . . *Good afternoon /*	НАТ. ИВ.	**До́брый день,°** Ма́ша. **Заходи́°**!
Come in!	МА́ША.	А Ле́на до́ма?
Mystery	НАТ. ИВ.	Да, она́ на балко́не. Детекти́в° чита́ет. *(Shouts.)* Ле́на!
		(Lena walks in.)
	ЛЕ́НА.	Ма́ша, приве́т!
Так. . . *So this is*	МА́ША.	Приве́т, Ле́нка! **Так э́то°** ва́ша но́вая кварти́ра? *(See looks around.)*
bright		Кака́я больша́я ко́мната! И **све́тлая°**!
	ЛЕ́НА.	А э́то на́ша но́вая ме́бель.
Excellent / furniture /	МА́ША.	**Отли́чная° ме́бель**! **И́мпортная,°** **коне́чно°**?
Imported / of course	ЛЕ́НА.	Стол, **сту́лья°** и **кре́сло°** и́мпортные, ла́мпы то́же. А дива́н, **как**
chairs / armchair		**ви́дишь,°** ста́рый.
как. . . *as you can see*		
		(Piano music is heard.)
	МА́ША.	Э́то что — телеви́зор?
	ЛЕ́НА.	Нет, э́то сосе́д.
	МА́ША.	Как хорошо́ игра́ет! Где он рабо́тает?
	ЛЕ́НА.	Он не рабо́тает, он студе́нт, пиани́ст.
	МА́ША.	Симпати́чный?
Кака́я. . . *What difference does*	НАТ. ИВ.	*(Overhears Masha's question.)* **Кака́я ра́зница,°** симпати́чный он и́ли
it make?		нет! Сосе́д-музыка́нт — э́то ужа́сно! *(Still annoyed.)* **Да́же° е́сли°** он
Even / if		симпати́чный!

УПРАЖНЕНИЕ 2   Под микроско́пом: Spot the verbs

Write down as many verb forms as you can find in the reading.

	Subject	*Verb*
ОБРАЗЕ́Ц:	она́	де́лает

_____   _____

_____   _____

_____   _____

_____   _____

_____   _____

ГРАММАТИКА
И ПРАКТИКА

❖ 3.7. ACCUSATIVE CASE OF NOUNS

Я чита́ю **статью́.**   *I am reading an article.*

Suppose you are reading a book. If someone asks what you are doing, you would answer, "I am reading a book." In this instance, *I* is the subject, *am reading* is the verb, and *book* is the direct object. A direct object receives the action of the verb. In the following sentences, the words *song, house,* and *car* are direct objects because they receive the action of the verb: *He's singing a song; They built a house; The Joneses want a new car.*

The same word order—*subject-verb-object*—is common in Russian. However, in Russian, word order is not the primary indicator of subjects and objects, as it is in English (compare *The cat bit the dog* with *The dog bit the cat*); rather, different cases distinguish Russian subjects from objects.[5] The *subject* of a verb is in the *Nominative* case, which is the form found in a dictionary. The *direct object* of a verb is in the *Accusative* case. Most Accusative case forms (both singular and plural) are identical to their Nominative case forms, though there are some important exceptions to this principle. Here is a summary of Accusative case forms. (Remember what you have learned about the hard/soft series vowels.)

---

[5]English once had the kind of case system that Russian and many other languages still have. About the only place we see cases in English now, however, is in our pronouns: *I* and *me, he* and *him, she* and *her,* and so on.

	NOMINATIVE CASE (dictionary form)	ACCUSATIVE CASE ENDING	EXAMPLES
«-а/-я» **feminine and masculine types in the singular**	кни́г-а стать-я́ Росси́-я дéдушк-а дя́д-я	Delete final vowel -а/-я; add -у/-ю	кни́г-**у** стать-**ю́** Росси́-**ю** дéдушк-**у** дя́д-**ю**
All other types, singular and plural (except masculine singular animates and all plural animates, which will be covered in later lessons)	<u>Singulars</u> журна́л роя́ль мать мéбель письм-о́ упражнéни-е <u>Plurals</u> журна́л-ы роя́л-и дом-а́ газéт-ы кни́г-и профéсси-и пи́сьм-а упражнéни-я	No change No change	журна́л роя́ль мать мéбель письм-о́ упражнéни-е журна́л-ы роя́л-и дом-а́ газéт-ы кни́г-и профéсси-и пи́сьм-а упражнéни-я

УПРАЖНЕНИЕ 3   Recognizing cases

Underline each noun and indicate whether it is the subject (S) or the direct object (DO) in the sentence or clause. Pay attention to the word order in each sentence.

1. — Что дéлает Кóля[1]?
   — Он читáет журнáл.[2]
   — А что ты читáешь?
   — Я читáю кни́гу.[3]
   — А где моя́ статья́[4]?
   — Бáбушка[5] читáет твою́ [*your*, Acc.] статью́.[6]
2. — Натáша[7] пи́шет письмó[8]?
   — Нет, письмó[9] пи́шет мáма.[10] А Натáша[11] пи́шет статью́.[12]
   — А что ты пи́шешь — письмó[13] и́ли статью́[14]?
   — Я пишу́ сочинéние.[15]
   — Пéтя[16] тóже пи́шет сочинéние[17]?
   — Нет, он слу́шает му́зыку[18] (*listening to music*).

УПРАЖНЕНИЕ 4   Это логи́чно? (*Is it logical?*)

Complete each of the following sentences with the words in parentheses, changing endings if necessary. *One of the words in each sentence does not make sense. Find and delete that item.*

1. Ма́ша чита́ет (журна́л, фильм, газе́та, кни́га).
2. Я пишу́ (каранда́ш, кни́га, статья́, му́зыка).
3. Это и́мпортный (дива́н, стол, профе́ссор, то́стер†).
4. Мы слу́шаем (*listen to*) (джаз†, му́зыка, ра́дио†, ша́хматы).
5. А где ва́ша америка́нская† (ме́бель, газе́та, ла́мпа, ко́мната)?

УПРАЖНЕНИЕ 5   Sentence-builder contest

Working in groups of two or three, see how many sentences (including questions) you can make up in five minutes, using subjects, verbs, and objects from the table below. (Hint: Not all combinations will work, but there are over a hundred correct possibilities.)

SUBJECTS	VERBS	OBJECTS
ста́рый пиани́ст	игра́ть	газе́та
Ви́ка и её сын	писа́ть	джаз†
вы	понима́ть	журна́л
Ма́ша и я	слу́шать (*listen to*)	кла́ссика†
ма́ленькие музыка́нты	чита́ть	кни́га
мои́ бра́тья и я	знать	конце́рт†
наш сосе́д		му́зыка†
моя́ сосе́дка профе́ссор Ми́ллер		письмо́
они́		ра́дио†
по́льский гитари́ст†		рок†
ру́сский саксофони́ст†		статья́
Степа́н и Лари́са		
ты		
я		

❖ 3.8. ADVERBS RELATED TO ADJECTIVES

Как **хорошо́** игра́ет!   *He plays so well!*

In English, many adjectives have corresponding adverbs in *-ly*. For example, we use *beautiful* (adjective) to describe a song and *beautifully* (adverb) to describe how the song was sung. Russian has the same kind of regularity: Russian adjectives (in **-ый, -ая,** and so on) often have corresponding adverbs in **-o**. Thus, with almost no effort you can now describe not only things (using adjectives), but also actions (using adverbs). Stress occasionally moves from one syllable to another when the adverb is formed:

ADJECTIVE NOMINATIVE CASE (dictionary form)	ADVERB ENDING	EXAMPLES
оригина́льн-ый хоро́ш-ий плох-о́й	Delete adjective ending; add -o	оригина́льн-**о** хорош-**о́** пло́х-**о**

УПРАЖНЕНИЕ 6   Она́ хорошо́ пи́шет по-ру́сски?

Make sentences by combining a subject with the correct form of the verb modified by an adverb (formed from the adjective in the middle column).

ОБРАЗЕЦ: Мари́на   /хоро́ший/   /писа́ть/
→ Мари́на хорошо́ пи́шет.

1. Джим   /хоро́ший/   /понима́ть по-ру́сски/
2. Мой брат   /неплохо́й/   /чита́ть и писа́ть/
3. Са́ша   /хоро́ший/   /игра́ть джаз/
4. Во́ва   /неплохо́й/   /игра́ть в ша́хматы/
5. Наш телеви́зор   /хоро́ший/   /рабо́тать/
6. Мы   /хоро́ший/   /знать наш го́род/

❖ 3.9. EXPRESSING OPINIONS: *IT'S EASY!*

Predicate forms that look identical to adverbs can be used in combination with **э́то** or **как** to express your opinion about something:

Э́то ужа́сно! *It's/That's terrible!*   Э́то легко́! *It's/That's easy!*
Как ужа́сно! *How awful!*   Э́то хорошо́! *It's/That's good!*
Как тру́дно! *How hard!*

УПРАЖНЕНИЕ 7   Expressive reactions

Using expressions from the list below, react to or comment on the situations that follow.

Серьёзно? (*Really? Seriously?*)   О́чень интере́сно!
Э́то хорошо́!   Э́то ужа́сно!
Э́то легко́!   Как тру́дно!

ОБРАЗЕЦ: Just before your big trip, the airlines go on strike → Э́то ужа́сно!

1. Your sister's fiancé lost the engagement ring he'd just bought for her.
2. Your teacher says she thought she saw Elvis at a gas station this morning.
3. A friend asks about a math assignment that you've been working on.
4. Someone tells you about an earthquake in a friend's hometown.

5. A friend asks if the magazine article you've been reading is interesting.
6. Your friend asks whether it's difficult to do a simple routine on the computer.
7. You found out that your grandmother sent you $100 just when you need money for textbooks.

УПРАЖНЕНИЕ 8   Это ужа́сно!

Working in small groups, develop three situations such as those in the previous exercise, then ask how students in other groups might react in Russian.

УПРАЖНЕНИЕ 9   Импортная ме́бель

— Где де́лают э́ту (*this*) ме́бель?
— В Росси́и, . . .

Working with a classmate, use <**в** + Prepositional> to tell in which countries the furniture in the preceding ad is made.

КУЛЬТУРА РЕЧИ

❖❖ ТАК ГОВОРЯТ: ТАК Э́ТО…

Так э́то ва́ша но́вая кварти́ра?　　　*So this is your new apartment?*
Кака́я больша́я ко́мната!　　　　　　*The room is so big! And bright!*
И све́тлая!

Lena's friend Masha has heard about the Silins' new apartment, but she hasn't seen it. After she greets Lena, Masha uses the phrase **Так э́то…?** to show she's finally seeing something about which she has already heard.

УПРАЖНЕ́НИЕ 10　Так э́то…

How could you use **Так э́то…?** in the following situations to show that you're finally seeing something you've heard about before?

1. You go visit your sister who just bought a new house.
2. You go visit your grandmother who recently got a new armchair.
3. You finally meet your roommate's sister.
4. You go visit a friend who keeps talking about her new suit.
5. You finally see a friend's new piano.
6. Your brother comes to visit in his new car.

❖❖ САМОПРОВЕ́РКА: УПРАЖНЕ́НИЕ 11

Working on your own, try this self-test: Read a Russian sentence out loud, then give an idiomatic English equivalent without looking at the book. Then work from English to Russian. After you have completed the activity, try it with a classmate.

1. Сосе́д — пиани́ст? Э́то ужа́сно!

2. Ты пи́шешь о́чень хорошо́.
3. Что де́лает Ми́ша? Чита́ет газе́ту?

4. Вы журнали́ст? Кака́я интере́сная профе́ссия!

1. *The neighbor's a pianist? That's horrible!*
2. *You write very well.*
3. *What's Misha doing? Reading the newspaper?*
4. *Are you a journalist? What an interesting profession!*

❖❖ ВОПРО́СЫ И ОТВЕ́ТЫ: УПРАЖНЕ́НИЕ 12

1. Твои́ роди́тели рабо́тают? А ты?
2. Где рабо́тает твой оте́ц?
3. Он мно́го рабо́тает?
4. А где рабо́тает твоя́ мать? А ты?
5. Ты мно́го чита́ешь?
6. Что ты чита́ешь — газе́ты, журна́лы, детекти́вы[†]…?

❖ ДИАЛОГИ

ДИАЛОГ 1 Ты рабо́таешь?
(Asking about someone's occupation)

— Ты рабо́таешь?
— Нет, я не рабо́таю, я студе́нтка. А ты то́же студе́нт? Или ты рабо́таешь?
— Я рабо́таю. В ци́рке.[†]
— В ци́рке?! Как интере́сно! А что ты там де́лаешь?
— Э́то секре́т.[†]

ДИАЛОГ 2 Э́то на́ша но́вая кварти́ра
(Showing a new apartment)

— Вот, Ри́та, э́то на́ша но́вая кварти́ра. Кварти́ра хоро́шая: больша́я и све́тлая. А тут балко́н.
— О́чень хоро́шая кварти́ра. И балко́н большо́й.
— А э́то наш но́вый телеви́зор. Ме́бель, как ви́дишь, ста́рая, а телеви́зор но́вый. О́чень хорошо́ рабо́тает!
— Како́й большо́й экра́н (*screen*)!

УПРАЖНЕНИЕ 13   Ваш диало́г

Make up a telephone conversation between you and the parent of a friend in which you ask where your friend is, what she's doing, and so on.

❖ А ТЕПЕ́РЬ . . . : УПРАЖНЕНИЕ 14

Working with a classmate, use what you learned in Part 2 to . . .

1. find out if she understands Russian well; what about English (**по-англи́йски**)?
2. ask if she thinks it's easy to write a composition
3. find out whether she thinks it's difficult to write articles
4. ask if she thinks American journalists write interestingly and/or originally
5. find out if she knows where another student in the class lives
6. find out where she lives and where her parents live
7. find out if she knows who lives in Washington

С ЧЕГО НАЧАТЬ?

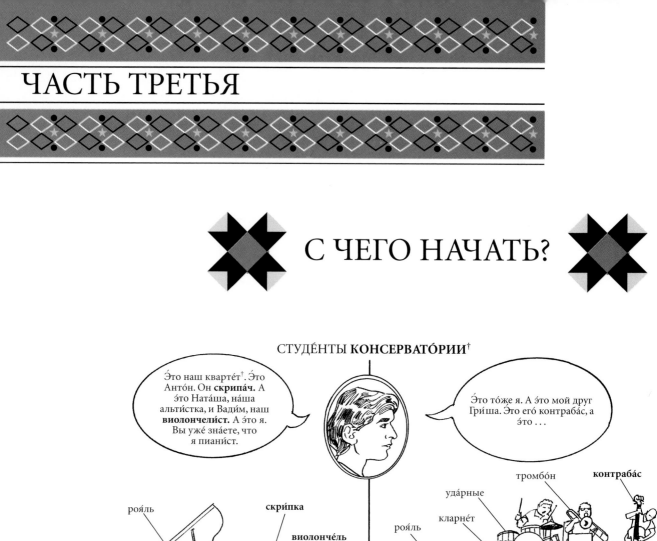

СТУДЕ́НТЫ **КОНСЕРВАТО́РИИ**†

Э́то наш кварте́т†. Э́то Анто́н. Он **скрипа́ч**. А э́то Ната́ша, на́ша альти́стка, и Вади́м, наш **виолончели́ст.** А э́то я. Вы уже́ зна́ете, что я пиани́ст.

Э́то то́же я. А э́то мой друг Гри́ша. Э́то его́ контраба́с, а э́то . . .

роя́ль

скри́пка

виолонче́ль

альт

У́ТРОМ. . .
[In the morning . . .]

тромбо́н

контраба́с

уда́рные

кларне́т

роя́ль

саксофо́н

труба́

фле́йта

. . .И ВЕ́ЧЕРОМ
[. . .and in the evening]

УПРАЖНЕ́НИЕ 1   Музыка́нты и музыка́льные инструме́нты

Match the terms for musical instruments and musicians.

1. _____ роя́ль
2. _____ скри́пка
3. _____ саксофо́н
4. _____ фле́йта
5. _____ уда́рные
6. _____ альт
7. _____ виолонче́ль
8. _____ **гита́ра**†

а. флейти́ст/флейти́стка
б. виолончели́ст/виолончели́стка
в. пиани́ст/пиани́стка
г. гитари́ст/гитари́стка
д. альти́ст/альти́стка
е. скрипа́ч/скрипа́чка
ж. уда́рник
з. саксофони́ст

ЧТЕНИЕ

Дома́шнее. . .
*homework
assignment*

❖ ДОМА́ШНЕЕ ЗАДА́НИЕ°

(*Vova, with earphones on, is reading something in the living room. Lena appears in the doorway.*)

ЛЁНА.   Во́ва, я иду́° в° апте́ку.° (*Vova does not hear her.*) Во́ва! Во́ва!!!

am going / to / drugstore

(*Vova takes off his earphones.*)

ВО́ВА.   А? Что?

ЛЁНА.   Я иду́ в апте́ку.

ВО́ВА.   Оке́й.[†]

ЛЁНА.   (*She looks at the earphones, then at the magazine he is reading.*) Во́ва, ты чита́ешь и́ли слу́шаешь°?

listening (to something)

ВО́ВА.   Не «и́ли», а «и»: я чита́ю *и* слу́шаю. И пишу́.

ЛЁНА.   Что ты чита́ешь?

ВО́ВА.   Статью́. О́чень интере́сная статья́: «**Америка́нский**[†] **рок-конце́рт**[†] в Москве́».

ЛЁНА.   А что ты слу́шаешь?

ВО́ВА.   Америка́нский рок-конце́рт в Москве́.

ЛЁНА.   Не понима́ю.

ВО́ВА.   Ну почему́ ты не понима́ешь? Я чита́ю статью́ «Америка́нский рок-конце́рт в Москве́» и слу́шаю **му́зыку**[†] — америка́нский рок-конце́рт в Москве́.

ЛЁНА.   **Тепе́рь**° понима́ю. А что ты пи́шешь?

Now

ВО́ВА.   Сочине́ние. Это моё дома́шнее зада́ние. Те́ма — «Мой **люби́мый**° **компози́тор**».°

*favorite
composer*

ЛЁНА.   И кто твой люби́мый компози́тор?

ВО́ВА.   Би́лли Джо́эл.

ЛЁНА.   А кто э́то?

ВО́ВА.   (*Scornfully.*) Ле́на, как ты **ма́ло**° зна́ешь! (*Importantly.*) Это **замеча́тельный**° америка́нский компози́тор! И пиани́ст! (*Music by Mussorgsky is heard from above. Lena listens.*) Что ты де́лаешь?

*little
wonderful*

ЛЁНА.   Я то́же слу́шаю му́зыку. Но э́то не рок, э́то **класси́ческая**[†] му́зыка. **Му́соргский**.° Слу́шай.°

Mussorgsky (a nineteenth-century Russian composer) / Listen

ВО́ВА.   Му́соргский? Како́й Му́соргский? Это Са́ша Кругло́в, наш сосе́д.

ЛЁНА.   (*Sarcastically.*) Во́ва, как ты мно́го зна́ешь!

УПРАЖНЕНИЕ 2   Под микроскóпом: Dictionary forms of verbs

Below are several sentences taken directly from this reading. To the right of each sentence fill in the dictionary form (infinitive) of the verb.

ОБРАЗЕЦ: Как ты мáло знáешь!   *знать*

1. Почемý ты не понимáешь?   _____
2. Что ты дéлаешь?   _____
3. Что ты пи́шешь?   _____
4. Что ты слýшаешь?   _____
5. Что ты читáешь?   _____
6. Я слýшаю мýзыку.   _____
7. Я читáю статью́.   _____

ГРАММАТИКА И ПРАКТИКА

❖ 3.10. GOING PLACES: VERBS OF MOTION AND DESTINATIONS

Я идý в аптéку.   *I'm going to the drugstore.*

To express the idea of going somewhere in Russian, you must learn two things:

a) The verbs to express *going*.
b) How to express the *destination*.

It's easiest to learn these two items together, so you can practice things you'll actually want and need to say.

Going verbs. Russian draws a distinction between going somewhere on foot and going somewhere by vehicle (or where the use of a vehicle is implied by the length of the trip, such as going from St. Petersburg to Moscow or traveling abroad). Here are the two verbs:

ИДТИ́

Они́ **идýт** в аптéку.

ÉХАТЬ

Они́ **éдут** в Москвý.

GOING BY FOOT (INCLUDING TRIPS IN TOWN WHERE NO VEHICLE IS IMPLIED OR STATED):		GOING BY VEHICLE (INCLUDING TRIPS OF DISTANCE THAT IMPLY THE USE OF A VEHICLE):	
	идти́		éхать
я	ид-у́	я	éд-у
ты	ид-ёшь	ты	éд-ешь
он, она́	ид-ёт	он, она́	éд-ет
мы	ид-ём	мы	éд-ем
вы	ид-ёте	вы	éд-ете
они́	ид-у́т	они́	éд-ут
(**Идти́** is a -**ёшь** verb, just like **жить**.)		(**Éхать** is a consonant-stem -**ешь** verb, very much like **писа́ть**.)	

Destinations. English often expresses the difference between location and destination by using a different preposition: *He lives <u>in</u> Moscow* (<u>in</u> shows location) vs. *He is going <u>to</u> Moscow* (<u>to</u> shows destination). Russian generally expresses this distinction by using the same preposition and putting a different case ending on the noun: **Он живёт в <u>Москве́</u>** (Prepositional case shows location) vs. **Он éдет в <u>Москву́</u>** (Accusative case shows destination).

To express *going to a certain place,* you'll generally use the prepositions **в** and **на** followed by the destination in the Accusative case. The preposition **в** is used mostly for physical destinations (*to a city, to a restaurant*) and **на** is used mostly for events (*to a football game, to work*) and to open spaces (*to a stadium, to a bus stop*). Again, there are some exceptions to this principle, such as **на по́чту** (*to the post office*). To ask *where someone is going,* use the "where to?" question word **куда́**. Note that there is a special word for going *home,* **домо́й**. Here are some examples:

— КУДА́ ТЫ ИДЁШЬ? — Я ИДУ́...	— А КУДА́ ТЫ ИДЁШЬ? — Я ИДУ́...
...в теа́тр.	...на стадио́н.
...в университе́т.[†]	...на рабо́ту.
...в шко́лу (*to school*).	...на по́чту. (!)
...в магази́н.	...на конце́рт.
...в парк.[†]	...на бале́т.[†]
...в консервато́рию.	...на заня́тия (*to class*).

УПРАЖНЕНИЕ 3   Куда́ вы...?

Complete this dialogue with forms of the verb **идти́** and be prepared to translate the exercise into English.

— Здра́вствуйте! Куда́ вы _____[1]?

— До́брый день! Мы _____[2] в парк, а пото́м (*then*) на стадио́н. А вы?

— Мы _____[3] в библиоте́ку (*library*), а Пе́тя — в университе́т.

— Ма́ша, ты то́же _____[4] в университе́т?

— Нет, я _____[5] на заня́тия (*to class*). А вот _____[6] на́ша ба́бушка. Ба́бушка, куда́ ты_____[7]?

— Я _____[8] домо́й (*home*).

УПРАЖНЕНИЕ 4   Куда́...?

Complete this dialogue with forms of the verb **éхать** and be prepared to translate the exercise into English.

> (*At the railroad station*)
>
> — Куда́ вы _____,[1] Алексе́й Влади́мирович?
> — В Но́вгород. Наш сын живёт в Но́вгороде. А вы?
> — А я _____[2] в Москву́, там живу́т мои́ вну́ки.
> — Ва́ша жена́ _____[3] с ва́ми (*with you*)?
> — Нет, жена́ не _____,[4] она́ до́ма.

Куда́ они́ иду́т?

УПРАЖНЕНИЕ 5   Куда́ ты идёшь?

On your way across campus, you run into several of your friends. Use the verb **идти́** with the prepositions **в** and **на** (+ Accusative of destination) to find out who is going where. Possible destinations are given below in the Nominative case:

> ОБРАЗЕ́Ц: — Куда́ ты идёшь?
> — В апте́ку. А ты?
> — На рабо́ту.

В... (апте́ка, университе́т, консервато́рия, теа́тр, центр (*downtown*), магази́н)

На... (рабо́та, конце́рт, по́чта (*post office*), стадио́н, бале́т[†])

❖ 3.11. DON'T OVER-"DO" IT

English often uses the auxiliary *do* to ask questions and to express negatives:[6]

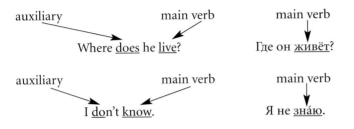

Russian has no "do" auxiliary; it uses just the main verb in these instances: —**Где он живёт?** —**Я не зна́ю.** Reserve the Russian verb **де́лать** for use as a main verb: **Что он де́лает?** (*What's he doing?*)

УПРАЖНЕНИЕ 6   Де́лать and *do*

How would you render the following short sentences in English? (There may be more than one possibility.) Take note of the main verb in each sentence and compare it with the Russian. Which English versions would require a form of the auxiliary *do*?

1. Где рабо́тает твой сосе́д?

2. Я не понима́ю, что́ э́то.

3. Где они́ живу́т?

4. Она́ мно́го чита́ет?

5. Когда́ (*when*) ты слу́шаешь ра́дио[†]?

6. Мы не зна́ем, где они́ живу́т.

УПРАЖНЕНИЕ 7   -ешь endings: я, ты, он (она́), они́

Supply the correct verb endings.

1. Ми́ша мно́го чита́____. Когда́ (*when*) он не рабо́та____, он чита́____.

2. Я понима́____, что на́до мно́го чита́ть. А ты э́то понима́____?

3. Что ты пи́ш____? Статью́?

4. Нет, я пиш____ курсову́ю.

5. По-мо́ему, ты мно́го рабо́та____. А Ми́ша то́же мно́го рабо́та____?

6. Ми́ша и его́ друг (*friend*) Же́ня о́чень мно́го рабо́та____.

7. А мы рабо́та____ ма́ло. Но мы мно́го отдыха́____.

8. Поэ́тому Ми́ша и Же́ня зна́____ о́чень мно́го, а вы зна́____ о́чень ма́ло.

❖ 3.12. GIVING AND SOLICITING OPINIONS

— Кто выи́грывает?   "*Who's winning?*"

— **По-мо́ему**, Во́ва.   "*Vova, I think.*"

To emphasize that you are expressing your opinion, use the parenthetical phrase **по-мо́ему**. If you want to ask someone his or her opinion about something, you can begin your question with **Как по-ва́шему (по-тво́ему)**. See the following example where an infinitive phrase (**писа́ть кни́ги**) is used with a predicate form (**тру́дно**) to

---

[6]Older forms of English—preserved for us in plays and poetry from the 1800s and earlier—did not use these *do* constructions. You will recognize such phrases as *What think you?* and *I know not* as correct for that time, though they may sound dated and bookish now.

ask whether one thinks doing something is difficult (easy, interesting, and so on):

Как по-твóему, писáть книги
трýдно?

*What do you think, is writing
books difficult?*

УПРАЖНЕНИЕ 8   Трýдно? Легкó? Интерéсно?

Combine an infinitive phrase with one of the predicate forms **трýдно, легкó** (*easy*), or **интерéсно** to ask your classmates what they think about the following activities. Introduce your question with **Как по-твóему,** . . . and use **по-мóему** in your answer. Try to find out which activities the class as a whole would consider to be difficult, easy, or interesting.

ОБРАЗЕЦ: писáть статьи́

— Как по-твóему, писáть статьи́ трýдно?
— Нет, по-мóему, э́то легкó.

1. писáть сочинéние
2. читáть журнáлы
3. игрáть в шáхматы
4. рабóтать в Лас-Вéгасе
5. жить в Санкт-Петербýрге
6. читáть детекти́вы†

КУЛЬТУРА РЕЧИ

❖ ТАК ГОВОРЯ́Т: ПО-МÓЕМУ

In this Part, you learned that **по-мóему** can be used to show that you are expressing your own opinion.

УПРАЖНЕНИЕ 9   По-мóему

You've been asked to conduct a public opinion survey. One student will conduct the survey and another will respond to the questions, using **по-мóему**. Switch roles after the first four questions. When you finish the following suggestions, make up some additional questions.

ОБРАЗЕЦ: — Как по-вáшему, рýсский язы́к (*language*) трýдный?
          — По-мóему, рýсский язы́к не óчень трýдный.

1. Как по-вáшему, врач — э́то хорóшая профéссия? А ветеринáрный† врач?
2. Как по-вáшему, все мáленькие дéти симпати́чные?
3. Как по-вáшему, математи́ка† трýдный предмéт (*subject*)? А литератýра†?
4. Как по-вáшему, Гáрри Каспáров хорошó игрáет в шáхматы?
5. Как по-вáшему, трýдно/интерéсно игрáть джаз?
6. Как по-вáшему, трýдно игрáть в баскетбóл так, как (*like*) игрáет Мáйкл Джóрдан?
7. Как по-вáшему, читáть дитекти́вы интерéсно?
8. Как по-вáшему, где хорошó жить?

❖❖ САМОПРОВЕРКА: УПРАЖНЕНИЕ 10

Working on your own, try this self-test: Read a Russian sentence out loud, then give an idiomatic English equivalent without looking at the book. Then work from English to Russian. After you have completed the activity, try it with a classsmate.

1. — Что де́лает Ви́ка?

— Пи́шет письмо́.

— А Ю́ра?

— Чита́ет кни́гу.

2. — Ле́на чита́ет газе́ту?

— Нет, газе́ту чита́ет Во́ва.

— А что де́лает Ле́на?

— Пи́шет статью́.

3. — Ты идёшь на рабо́ту?

— Нет, в апте́ку. А вы куда́ идёте?

— Сейча́с мы идём на по́чту, а пото́м на стадио́н.

— Пока́!

4. — Куда́ вы е́дете? В Но́вгород?

— Нет, мы е́дем в Петербу́рг. Там живёт наш сын.

1. *"What's Vika doing?"*

"Writing a letter."

"What about Yura?"

"Reading a book."

2. *"Is Lena reading the paper?"*

"No, Vova's reading the paper."

"So what's Lena doing?"

"Writing an article."

3. *"Are you going to work?"*

"No, to the drugstore. Where are you going?"

"Right now we're going to the post office and then to the stadium."

"See you later!"

4. *"Where are you going? To Novgorod?"*

"No, we're going to Petersburg. Our son lives there."

❖❖ ВОПРОСЫ И ОТВЕТЫ: УПРАЖНЕНИЕ 11

1. Кто твой люби́мый компози́тор?

2. Джаз — э́то хоро́шая му́зыка? А рок?

3. Ты хорошо́ зна́ешь америка́нский рок? А ру́сский?

4. Кто твой люби́мый музыка́нт?

5. Кака́я твоя́ люби́мая рок-гру́ппа?

Рок-конце́рт в Москве́.

❖ ДИАЛОГИ

ДИАЛОГ 1 Дома́шнее зада́ние
(Discussing a homework assignment)

— Приве́т, Андре́й! Что ты де́лаешь?
— Дома́шнее зада́ние.
— Како́е?
— Фи́зику†.
— Зада́ние большо́е?
— Большо́е и тру́дное.

ДИАЛОГ 2 Куда́ вы е́дете?
(Asking where someone is traveling to)

Three friends meet in a train station.

— Приве́т, А́ня! Приве́т, Ко́ля! Куда́ вы е́дете?
— Са́ша, приве́т! Мы е́дем в Во́логду. Наш дя́дя там рабо́тает.
— Во́логда! Э́то краси́вый го́род.
— О́чень краси́вый. А ты куда́ е́дешь?
— Я? Я е́ду в Кострому́. Там живёт моя́ ба́бушка.
— Кострома́! Как интере́сно! И на́ша ба́бушка там живёт!

УПРАЖНЕНИЕ 12   Ваш диало́г

You and a friend run into each other unexpectedly on the street. Ask where your friend is going. Your friend responds, then asks where you are going. You respond, then you both say good-bye and continue on your way.

❖ А ТЕПЕРЬ…: УПРАЖНЕНИЕ 13

Working with a classmate, use what you learned in Part 3 to . . .

1. find out what he's reading (writing, listening to)
2. ask which newspapers he reads
3. find out which magazines he reads
4. say where you're going today and ask him if he's going there too
5. ask where he's going today
6. say you're going to New York (Los Angeles, Chicago, . . .) tomorrow and ask him if he's going there too

С ЧЕГО НАЧАТЬ?

КТОКУДА́ ИДЁТ (*WHO IS GOING WHERE*)

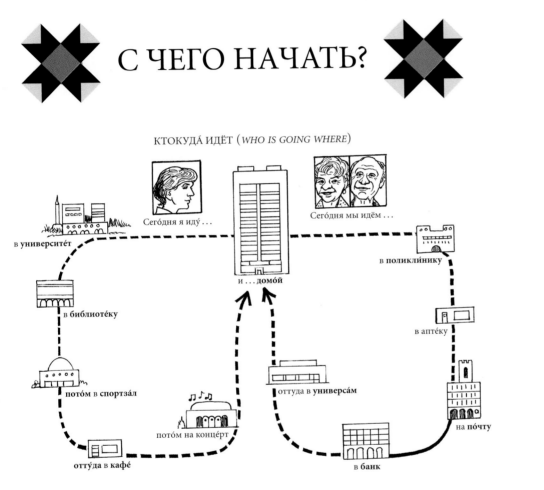

Сего́дня я иду́ . . .

Сего́дня мы идём . . .

в университе́т

в поликли́нику

в библиоте́ку

и . . . ДОМО́Й

в апте́ку

пото́м в спортза́л

оттуда в **универса́м**

пото́м на концёрт

на по́чту

отту́да в кафé

в банк

УПРАЖНЕНИЕ 1   Куда́ вы идёте?

Work in groups of three or four students and refer to destinations in the picture. One student asks the group collectively where they are going today. The second student tells where he is going; a third student repeats where the previous student is going and then adds where she is going. The next student continues, repeating first the destinations of the previous students. Continue until someone forgets a destination. Then repeat the exercise, with a different person asking where everyone is going tomorrow.

СА́РА.	Куда́ вы идёте сего́дня?
МАЙКЛ.	Я иду́ в спортза́л.
БРА́НДОН.	Майкл идёт в спортза́л, а я иду́ в библиоте́ку.

✖ ЧТЕНИЕ ✖

Здравствуйте; Илья Ильич!

neighborhood

❖❖ НАШ **МИКРОРАЙÓН**°

(The professor walks out of their building with Jim.)

куда́... Where are you going now?
ПРОФ. Джим, куда́ вы **сейча́с**°? В университе́т?

are arriving (by plane) / tennis players
ДЖИМ. Нет, Илья́ Ильи́ч, я е́ду в **аэропóрт.**† В Шереме́тьево.[7] Сегóдня прилета́ют° на́ши тенниси́сты.° Вы игра́ете в **те́ннис,**† Илья́ Ильи́ч?

but / prefer / watch
ПРОФ. Игра́ю, **но**° плóхо. Предпочита́ю° смотре́ть°, как игра́ют хорóшие тенниси́сты. Джим, а вы зна́ете, как е́хать в аэропóрт?

ДЖИМ. Конéчно, Илья́ Ильи́ч!

(They say good-bye. Jim leaves. The professor approaches Grandpa Kruglov, who is sitting on a bench outside.)

ПРОФ. Здра́вствуйте!

(Kruglov does not hear him.)

ПРОФ. *(Louder.)* Здра́вствуйте!

КРУГЛÓВ. Здра́вствуйте, Илья́ Ильи́ч!

ПРОФ. Извини́те, а как вас зовýт?

КРУГЛÓВ. Степа́н Евге́ньевич.

section of town
останóвка... bus stop
ПРОФ. Извини́те, Степа́н Евге́ньевич. Вы уже́ зна́ете наш **райóн**°? Где тут магази́н, где пóчта, где апте́ка, где **останóвка автóбуса**°?

map
Look
groceries / milk / sausage / bread / A... Are you headed there?
КРУГЛÓВ. А вот **ка́рта.**° *(He opens a map, points.)* Это наш микрорайóн. **Смотри́те,**° Илья́ Ильи́ч. Вот мы здесь, вот наш дом, а вот магази́н. Это **продýкты**° — молокó,° колбаса́,° хлеб.°[8] А вы туда́°? Я тóже.

---

[7]**Шереме́тьево** is Moscow's major international airport.
[8]Russian stores are often labeled simply with the kind of goods they carry: **Продýкты, Молокó, Óбувь, Сувени́ры,** and so on.

	(*They start walking . . .*) Вот проду́кты, а там — остано́вка авто́буса.	
ПРОФ.	Степа́н Евге́ньевич, **вы не зна́ете**°, тут есть° апте́ка?	вы. . . *Do you happen to know. . . ? / тут. . .? Is there. . . here?*
КРУГЛО́В.	Да, **ря́дом**.° (*They keep walking.*) Вот тут.	*right nearby*
ПРОФ.	А по́чта где?	
КРУГЛО́В.	По́чта **напра́во**°. На́ша по́чта **небольша́я**°. Больша́я далеко́, а ма́ленькая ря́дом.	*to the right / not too big*
ПРОФ.	Понима́ю. **Зна́чит**,° по́чта здесь, апте́ка напра́во, а наш дом — **нале́во**.°	*So to the left*
КРУГЛО́В.	Нет, Илья́ Ильи́ч, апте́ка — нале́во, а наш дом — напра́во.	

УПРАЖНЕ́НИЕ 2   Под микроско́пом: Кто куда́ идёт?

Look back to the visual opener (**С чего́ нача́ть?**) and the reading and find the Russian equivalents for the following destinations. Answer the question **Кто куда́ идёт?** using different subjects, conjugating the verb **идти́** accordingly; use «**в/на** plus the Accusative case» to show destination:

ОБРАЗЕ́Ц: Я иду́ в университе́т.

university	library
store	gym
post office	concert
drugstore	outpatient clinic
bank	

ГРАММАТИКА И ПРАКТИКА

О РОССИИ

ПО́ЧТА

По́чта напра́во. На́ша по́чта небольша́я.

Although **по́чта** in Russia and a post office in the United States are functionally similar, there are differences in the services they provide. A **по́чта** in Russia is not just a place to buy stamps (**ма́рки**) and send letters (**пи́сьма**) and packages (**посы́лки; бандеро́ль** [*f.*] for a package containing books), but also it provides a number of other important communications services: one can send telegrams (**телегра́ммы**) and make intercity or international phone calls. Because the use of credit cards and the writing and sending of checks is still relatively limited in Russia, the money order (**де́нежный перево́д**) is another frequently used postal service. Hence the location of the **по́чта** is quite important to nearby residents.

INTONATION ✪ *Или Questions*

Во́ва, ты чита́ешь и́ли слу́шаешь?

И́ли-type questions present a choice between two alternative answers. The intonation of these questions typically starts at mid-level, then jumps up so that the stressed syllable of the first alternative is the high point. The sentence then drops back to the mid-level, and on the stressed syllable of the second alternative it drops to the lowest level. Thus it is the stressed syllables of the two alternatives that have the greatest contrast.

LEVEL	QUESTION
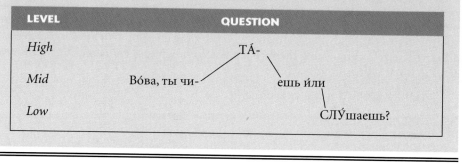

УПРАЖНЕНИЕ 3   И́ли-intonation practice

Each of the following questions presents a choice between two alternative answers. Underline the stressed syllable in the first of the two alternatives, then practice reading the questions aloud.

ОБРАЗЕ́Ц: Си́лины живу́т в кварти́ре но́мер <u>пять</u> и́ли в кварти́ре номер шесть?

1. А здесь кто живёт: профе́ссор Петро́вский и́ли Кругло́вы?
2. Ле́на студе́нтка и́ли аспира́нтка?
3. Са́ша Кругло́в пиани́ст и́ли компози́тор?
4. Му́соргский — э́то класси́ческая му́зыка и́ли рок?
5. В како́й аэропо́рт е́дет Джим: в Шереме́тьево и́ли во Вну́ково?
6. Илья́ Ильи́ч хорошо́ игра́ет в те́ннис и́ли не о́чень?
7. Кто хорошо́ зна́ет микрорайо́н: Степа́н Евге́ньевич и́ли Илья́ Ильи́ч?
8. По́чта далеко́ и́ли не о́чень далеко́?

❖ 3.13. PLAYING A SPORT

Вы **игра́ете в те́ннис?**	*Do you play tennis?*
Серёжа и Во́ва **игра́ют в ша́хматы.**	*Seryozha and Vova are playing chess.*

Игра́ть (*to play*) is a regular -**ешь** verb. *To play a particular sport* is **игра́ть в** followed by the name of the sport in the Accusative case. A number of sports are recognizable from English:

футбо́л	хокке́й	те́ннис
бейсбо́л	баскетбо́л	пинг-по́нг
волейбо́л	гандбо́л	гольф

When a Russian says **футбо́л,** however, she is referring to soccer (what Europeans call "football"). The game known as "football" in America is called **америка́нский футбо́л** in Russian. Russians also often include **ша́хматы** (*chess*) when they list popular sports.

УПРАЖНЕ́НИЕ 4   Ты игра́ешь в волейбо́л?

By asking **да/нет** or **и́ли** questions, find five classmates who play five different sports.

ОБРАЗЕ́Ц: — Ты игра́ешь в волейбо́л?
— Нет, но я игра́ю в те́ннис.

СЛОВА́, СЛОВА́, СЛОВА́ . . . ✪ *И–А–НО*

Я чита́ю, **и** Ле́на (то́же) чита́ет.	*I'm reading and Lena's reading (too).*
Я чита́ю, **а** Ле́на пи́шет статью.	*I'm reading and Lena's writing an article.*
Я игра́ю в те́ннис, **но** не о́чень хорошо́.	*I play tennis, but not very well.*

Recall what you learned about **и** and **а** in Lesson 1: **и** simply joins things while **а** joins them and may imply a contrast. A third conjunction, **но,** links two elements by emphasizing a contrast (or even a contradiction) between them. Compare the following:

Мой брат живёт и рабо́тает в Москве́.	*My brother lives and works in Moscow.*
Мой брат живёт в Москве́, а рабо́тает в Подо́льске.	*My brother lives in Moscow and/but works in Podol'sk.*
Ко́мната ма́ленькая, но све́тлая.	*The room's small, but bright.*

◈◈ 3.14. SUBORDINATE CLAUSES WITH ГДЕ, КТО, ЧТО, ПОЧЕМУ́, КАК

Я зна́ю, **где она́** живёт.	*I know where she lives.*
Я не зна́ю, **кто здесь** живёт.	*I don't know who lives here.*
Я не понима́ю, **что они́ де́лают.**	*I don't understand what they're doing.*
Я зна́ю, **что он** живёт здесь.	*I know that he lives here.*
Я понима́ю, **почему́ он э́то** де́лает.	*I understand why he does that.*
Вы зна́ете, **как е́хать в аэропо́рт?**	*Do you know how to get to the airport?*

The sentence *I know where you live* consists of two clauses: the main clause, *I know,* and the subordinate clause, *where you live.* Subordinate clauses are formed similarly in Russian, except that they are almost always preceded by a comma. Note that **что** beginning a subordinate clause is translated as either *what* or *that.* When **что** means *what,* it is pronounced with a stressed [**o**]; when it means *that,* the vowel is not stressed. Note also that **кто** is always singular.

УПРАЖНЕНИЕ 5   Meaning of subordinate clauses

Underline the subordinating conjunction in each of the sentences below, then translate each sentence into English. In which sentence(s) does **что** mean *that*, and in which does it mean *what*?

1. Вы зна́ете, кто живёт в кварти́ре но́мер шесть? А в кварти́ре но́мер пять?
2. Вы зна́ете, что Си́лин и Петро́вский — сосе́ди?
3. Вы зна́ете, где рабо́тает профе́ссор Петро́вский?
4. Ле́на сейча́с не балко́не. Вы зна́ете, что она́ де́лает?
5. Кто зна́ет, где живёт Са́ша?
6. Кто говори́т (*says*), что Са́ша хорошо́ игра́ет?
7. Вы зна́ете, кто говори́т (*says*), что Са́ша хорошо игра́ет?

УПРАЖНЕНИЕ 6   Subordinate clauses

Complete the sentences below with **что, как, где.**

1. Я зна́ю, _____ тебя́ зову́т. Тебя́ зову́т Мари́на. А ты зна́ешь, _____ меня́ зову́т?
2. Я зна́ю, _____ твой брат — пиани́ст. А ты зна́ешь, _____ моя́ сестра́ — то́же пиани́стка?
3. Я зна́ю, _____ ты живёшь. Я зна́ю, _____ ты живёшь тут. А ты зна́ешь, _____ я живу́?
4. Мы зна́ем, _____ ба́бушка до́ма.
5. Мы не зна́ем, _____ сейча́с на́ши роди́тели.
6. А ты зна́ешь, _____ сейча́с твои́ роди́тели и _____ они́ де́лают?

УПРАЖНЕНИЕ 7   Перево́д

Translate the following sentences into Russian.

1. You know where I live.
2. Do you know where I live?
3. This is your neighbor. Do you know her name?
4. I know where she works. I know that she is a doctor.
5. And does she know who you are?
6. Do you know that her brother is a pianist?
7. I don't know how he plays.
8. What is this? Your term paper? I understand that the topic is very difficult.

Как по-вашему, это муж и жена? Куда они едут? А потом куда?

милый   *dear*
мебельный=мебельный магазин

КУЛЬТУРА РЕЧИ

❖ ТАК ГОВОРЯТ: ВЫ НЕ ЗНАЕТЕ, …?

Вы не знаете, тут есть аптека?

Do you (happen to) know if there's a drugstore here?

The word **не** before **знаете** in questions softens the inquiry. This variant is used when the person asking is not sure what response she is going to get. The following activity includes questions with both **Вы знаете, …?** and **Вы не знаете, …?**

УПРАЖНЕНИЕ 8   Вы (не) зна́ете, . . .

You are an insurance investigator and must do a little snooping. Ask a classmate these questions.

1. Вы зна́ете, кто ва́ши сосе́ди?

2. Вы зна́ете, как их зову́т?

3. Вы не зна́ете, где они́ сейча́с?

4. Вы не зна́ете, они́ рабо́тают и́ли нет?

5. Вы зна́ете, где они́ рабо́тают?

6. Вы не зна́ете, каки́е газе́ты они́ чита́ют?

◆ САМОПРОВЕРКА: УПРАЖНЕНИЕ 9

Working on your own, try this self-test: Read a Russian sentence out loud, then give an idiomatic English equivalent without looking at the book. Then work from English to Russian. After you have completed the activity, try it with a classmate.

1. — Ты не зна́ешь, где живёт
Ле́на Си́лина?
— В кварти́ре №[9] 9.
— Нет, там живу́т Ивано́вы. А вот
идёт Ма́ша. Она́ зна́ет.

2. — Вы хорошо́ игра́ете в ша́хматы?
— Непло́хо. А вы?
— О́чень пло́хо. А моя́ сестра́
о́чень хорошо́ игра́ет.

3. Ваш дом большо́й, а наш —
ма́ленький.

4. Я зна́ю, где она́, но не зна́ю,
что она́ де́лает.

1. *"Do you happen to know where
Lena Silina lives?"*
"In Apartment #9."
*"No, the Ivanovs live there. But
here comes Masha. She'll know."*

2. *"Do you play chess well?"*
"Not badly. And you?"
*"Very poorly. But my sister
plays very well."*

3. *Your building's large and ours is
small.*

4. *I know where she is, but I don't
know what she's doing.*

---

[9]This abbreviation, based on a Latin alphabet *N* followed by a raised and underlined <u>o</u>, is pronounced **но́мер** and is used with building numbers, hotel room numbers, bus route numbers, and the like.

❖ ВОПРОСЫ И ОТВЕТЫ: УПРАЖНЕНИЕ 10

1. Наш университе́т/ко́лледж большо́й?

2. В университе́те есть спортза́л? А стадио́н здесь есть?

3. Спортза́л хоро́ший? Большо́й?

4. На́ши студе́нты игра́ют в футбо́л в спортза́ле и́ли на стадио́не?

5. А где они́ игра́ют в баскетбо́л?

6. А ты игра́ешь в баскетбо́л? А в футбо́л? А в бейсбо́л? А в ша́хматы?

❖ ДИАЛОГИ

ДИАЛОГ 1 Вы не зна́ете, где . . . ?
(Asking for directions)

— Вы не зна́ете, где по́чта?

— Вот она́, нале́во.

— А магази́н?

— Магази́н напра́во.

— Спаси́бо.

— Пожа́луйста.

ДИАЛОГ 2 А где по́чта?
(Asking about locations)

— Ты уже́ зна́ешь наш микрорайо́н?

— Да.

— Остано́вка авто́буса далеко́?

— Нет, она́ ря́дом.

— А где по́чта?

— По́чта далеко́.

— А магази́ны? Они́ то́же далеко́?

— Нет, магази́ны ря́дом.

УПРАЖНЕНИЕ 11   Ваш диало́г

Create a dialogue between two college students. One student, who has just moved into a new apartment, is asking the other what's in the neighborhood.

❖ А ТЕПЕРЬ . . . : УПРАЖНЕНИЕ 12

Working with a classmate, use what you learned in Part 4 to . . .

1. ask whether she is going to the gym (the post office) today

2. ask whether she is going to the university tomorrow

3. find out when she is going to the library—today or tomorrow?

4. say you're going to a concert and find out if she is also going

5. find out if she already knows the neighborhood

6. ask if she happens to know where the bus stop is

7. ask why she is going (use **éхать**) to the airport

8. say what sport you play and find out if she does too

9. find out whether she plays basketball; if so, ask if she plays well

10. ask if she knows where you're going today (she should take a guess; correct her if she's wrong)

УЧИСЬ УЧИТЬСЯ ✪ *Studying with a Friend*

Many students find it helpful to study with a classmate. Here are some ideas to help make that study time effective.

1. *Take parts in the readings and dialogues,* first reading out loud with the tapes (to help you develop an ear for intonation and rate of speech), then practicing out loud with each other. Switch parts.

2. *Quiz each other on vocabulary and phrases,* using the vocabulary list at the end of the chapters or your flash cards. Be sure to quiz each other on phrases as well as words.

3. *Do "back translations":* Select a sentence from a reading or dialogue, say it to your classmate in English, and let her translate it back into Russian. Then have your classmate do the same for you.

4. *Beat the clock:* Choose a category (for example, your room, your family, meeting a new student in your class, and so on) and see how many words, questions, and expressions relating to the category the two of you can come up with in three minutes.

5. *Review older exercises:* Without looking at an answer key or corrected homework pages, see if you can redo a textbook or workbook exercise you completed a few days or weeks ago.

 # ИТАК…

❖❖ НОВЫЕ СЛОВА

NOUNS

Neighborhood

автóбус	bus (4)
аптéка	drugstore; pharmacy (3)
аэропóрт	airport (4)
банк	bank (4v)
кафé *neut. indecl.*	café (4v)
микрорайóн	neighborhood (4)
останóвка автóбуса	bus stop (4)
поликлúника	outpatient clinic (4v)
пóчта	post office (4v)

райóн	district; section (of town) (4)
универсáм	supermarket (4v)

Furniture, Apartment

картúна	picture; painting (2v)
ков(ё)р (*pl.* коврьí)	carpet; rug (2v)
крéсло	armchair; easy chair (2)
кровáть *f.*	bed (2v)
лáмпа	lamp (2v)
мéбель *f.*	furniture (2)
одея́ло	blanket (2v)
пóлка	shelf (2v)
стол	table (2v)
стул (*pl.* стýлья)	chair (2)

телеви́зор	television (set) (2v)
телефо́н	telephone (1)
цвет(о́)к (*pl.* цветы́)	flower (2v)

Food

колбаса́	sausage (4)
молоко́	milk (4)
проду́кты *pl.*	groceries (4)
хлеб	bread (4)

Studies, Books, Work

библиоте́ка	library (4v)
дома́шнее зада́ние	homework (assignment) (3)
ка́рта	map (4)
курсова́я (курсова́я рабо́та) *noun, declines like adj.*	term paper (1)
профе́ссия	profession (1)
рабо́та	work (1v)
сочине́ние	composition (*a written assignment*) (1v)
статья́	article (1)
те́ма	topic; subject; theme (1)
университе́т	university (4v)

Music, Entertainment

виолончели́ст/ виолончели́стка	cellist (3v)
виолонче́ль *f.*	cello (3v)
гита́ра	guitar (3v)
гитари́ст/гитари́стка	guitarist (3v)
компози́тор	composer (3)
консервато́рия	conservatory (3v)
контраба́с	double bass; bass; bass viol (3v)
конце́рт	concert (3)
му́зыка	music (3)
рок	rock (music) (3)
саксофо́н	saxophone (3v)
саксофони́ст	saxophonist (3v)
скрипа́ч/скрипа́чка	violinist (3v)
скри́пка	violin (3v)
труба́	trumpet (3v)

Sport, Hobbies

спортза́л	gym; gymnasium (4v)
те́ннис [*pronounced* тэ-]	tennis (4)
ша́хматы	chess (1)

ADJECTIVES

америка́нский	American (3)
замеча́тельный	wonderful; marvelous (3)
и́мпортный	imported (2)
интере́сный	interesting (1)
како́й	which; what (kind of) (1)
класси́ческий	classical (3)
люби́мый	favorite (3)
небольшо́й	not large (4)
отли́чный	excellent (2)
све́тлый	bright; light (2)
симпати́чный	nice; likable (2)
тру́дный	difficult; hard (1)

VERBS[10]

гуля́ть (гуля́-ю, гуля́-ешь, . . . гуля́-ют)	to walk; to go for a walk; to take a walk (1v)
де́лать (де́ла-ю, де́ла-ешь, . . . де́ла-ют)	to do (1)
е́хать (е́д-у, е́д-ешь, . . . е́д-ут)	to go (*by vehicle*); to ride; to drive (3)
жить (жив-у́, жив-ёшь, . . . жив-у́т)	to live (1)
знать (зна́-ю, зна́-ешь, . . . зна́-ют)	to know (1)
игра́ть (игра́-ю, игра́-ешь, . . . игра́-ют)	to play (1)
идти́ (ид-у́, ид-ёшь, . . . ид-у́т)	1. to go; 2. to walk (3)
отдыха́ть (отдыха́-ю, отдыха́-ешь, . . . отдыха́-ют)	to rest (1v)
писа́ть (пиш-у́, пи́ш-ешь, . . . пи́ш-ут)	to write (1v)
понима́ть (понима́-ю, понима́-ешь, . . . понима́-ют)	to understand (1)
рабо́тать (рабо́та-ю, рабо́та-ешь, . . . рабо́та-ют)	to work (1v)
слу́шать (слу́ша-ю, слу́ша-ешь, . . . слу́ша-ют)	to listen (to) (3)
смотре́ть[11]	to look (at); to watch (4)
чита́ть (чита́-ю, чита́-ешь, . . . чита́-ют)	to read (1v)

---

[10]Endings for **я, ты, они** forms (the so-called "key forms") are given in parentheses. Hyphens divide stems and endings, not syllables.

[11]For the time being use **смотре́ть** in the infinitive only.

ADVERBS

вéчером	in the evening (3v)
домóй (*indicates direction*)	home (4v)
интерéсно	interestingly; engagingly (1)
кудá (*indicates direction*)	where (to) (3)
мáло	little; few (3)
мнóго	much (1v)
нáдо	(one) has to; (one) must (1)
налéво	to the left; on the left (4)
напрáво	to the right; on the right (4)
нелегкó	(it's/that's) not easy (1)
опя́ть	again (1)
оригинáльно	creatively (1)
оттýда	from there (4v)
потóм	1. then; after that; 2. later (on) (4v)
поэ́тому	that's why; therefore; so (1)
ря́дом	(right) nearby; next door (4)
сейчáс	1. now; right now; (4) 2. right away; at once (1)
тепéрь	now (3)
тудá (*indicates direction*)	there (4)
ужé	already (1)
ýтром	in the morning (3v)

PREPOSITIONS

в 1. (+ *Acc.—to denote a destination*)	to; into (3)
2. (+ *Prep.—to denote location*)	in; at (1)
на 1. (+ *Acc.—to denote a destination*)	to (3)
2. (+ *Prep.—to denote location*)	on (2v)
3. (+ *Prep.—at an event, an open place, and so on*)	at; in (1v)

CONJUNCTIONS

éсли	if (2)
но	but (4)
что	that (4)

OTHER

дáже *particle*	even (2)
рáзве	really? (1)

IDIOMS AND EXPRESSIONS

Вы не знáете …? *used when a person asking for information does not know what response will be given*	Do you (happen to) know …? (4)
Дóбрый день!	Good day!; Good afternoon! (2)
Заходи́!	Come in! (2)
знáчит *parenthetical*	so; then (4)
И вообщé … *used to introduce a statement which is more general than what precedes it*	and … anyway (1)
игрáть в шáхматы	to play chess (1)
как ви́дишь (как ви́дите)	as you can see (2)
какáя рáзница?	what's the difference?; what difference does it make? (2)
конéчно *parenthetical*	of course (2)
крóме тогó *parenthetical*	besides (that); moreover (1)
по-мóему *parenthetical*	in my opinion (1)
Смотри́те!	Look! (4)
Так э́то …	So this is (these are)… (2)
что ж	well (1)
Что-что?	Beg your pardon? (1)

❖❖ ЧТО Я ЗНАЮ, ЧТО Я УМЕЮ

Use this checklist to mark off what you've learned in this lesson:

- ☐ How to conjugate **-ешь/-ёшь** verbs with stem, ending, and shifting stress (Part 1)
- ☐ Noun endings in the Prepositional case (Part 1)
- ☐ How to describe location with **в/на** and Prepositional case (Part 1)

☐ Pronunciation of **в** before a consonant (Part 1)
☐ Use of **во** before certain consonant clusters (Part 1)
☐ Noun endings in the Accusative case (Part 2)
☐ Use of the Accusative case for direct objects (Part 2)
☐ Use of the motion verbs **идти** and **éхать** (Part 3)
☐ How to describe destination with **в/на** and Accusative case (Part 3)
☐ About word order in WH-questions (Part 3)
☐ Expressing English "do" in Russian (Part 3)
☐ How to form adverbs from adjectives (Part 2)
☐ How to express opinions with **Как ...** and **Это ...** (Part 2)
☐ Giving and soliciting opinions (Part 3)
☐ Expressing doubt about something you're told: **Рáзве** (Part 1)
☐ How to talk about playing a sport (Part 4)
☐ About subordinate clauses (Part 4)
☐ Intonation in **и́ли** questions (Part 4)
☐ More about joining and contrasting with **и, а,** and **но** (Part 4)
☐ Making polite inquiries: **Вы не знáете** (Part 4)
☐ What to say when you finally see something you've been hearing about: **Так э́то** (Part 2)

❖ ЭТО НАДО ЗНАТЬ

A. VERB PATTERNS: THE -ЕШЬ/-ЁШЬ CONJUGATION

The so-called **-ешь/-ёшь** conjugation (also known as first conjugation) is one of the two major verb patterns in Russian. Learning just a few basic things about it opens up thousands of verbs for your use. The fundamental thing to remember is that verb conjugations differ in two ways:

1) stem type
   a) vowel stem
   b) consonant stem

2) stress pattern
   a) stem stress
   b) ending stress
   c) shifting stress

With these distinctions in your mind, the patterns of Russian verb conjugations stand out very clearly. Here is a table summarizing the endings of the **-ешь/-ёшь** conjugation; the **-ё-** variants occur when the ending is stressed:

SUMMARY OF ENDINGS FOR THE -ЕШЬ/-ЁШЬ CONJUGATION

	VOWEL STEM (читá-)	CONSONANT STEM (жив-)
я	-Ю	-У
ты	-ЕШЬ/-ЁШЬ	
он, онá, онó	-ЕТ/-ЁТ	
мы	-ЕМ/-ЁМ	
вы	-ЕТЕ/-ЁТЕ	
они́	-ЮТ	-УТ

Since you often cannot tell from looking at an infinitive what its conjugation pattern is (although you'll soon be able to make good guesses), you need to learn the **я, ты,** and **они** forms (the so-called "key forms") along with the infinitives—especially for consonant stem verbs. Here are examples of **-ешь/-ёшь** verbs you have seen so far. Compare them with the table above:

EXAMPLES OF VERBS OF THE -ЕШЬ/-ЁШЬ CONJUGATION

	VOWEL STEM	**CONSONANT STEM**		
		Stem stress	**Ending stress**	**Shifting stress**
Infinitive	чита́ть	éхать	жить	писа́ть
я	чита́-ю	éд-у	жив-у́	пиш-у́
ты	чита́-ешь	éд-ешь	жив-ёшь	пи́ш-ешь
они́	чита́-ют	éд-ут	жив-у́т	пи́ш-ут
Other infinitives that follow this pattern (you should add to this list as you learn more verbs):	гуля́ть де́лать знать игра́ть отдыха́ть понима́ть рабо́тать слу́шать		идти́ ид-у́, ид-ёшь, ид-у́т	

Б. NOMINATIVE AND ACCUSATIVE

Singulars. Except for animate masculine nouns (about which you will learn more in Lesson 5), masculine and neuter nouns are identical in their Nominative (dictionary) and Accusative forms. Masculine and feminine nouns that end in **-a** or **-я** change their ending to **-y** or **-ю,** respectively. Examples:

NOMINATIVE SINGULAR
1. Где журна́л? Он там?
2. Где кни́га? Она́ там?

ACCUSATIVE SINGULAR
1. Я чита́ю журна́л.
2. Я чита́ю кни́гу.

Plurals. Except for animate nouns of all genders, Accusative plural forms are identical to their Nominative plural forms (see Lesson 2 **Ита́к. . .** for a summary of Nominative plural forms). Examples:

NOMINATIVE PLURALS
1. Где мои́ журна́лы и кни́ги?

ACCUSATIVE PLURALS
1. Моя́ сестра́ всегда́ (*always*) чита́ет мои́ журна́лы и кни́ги.

В. DESTINATION vs. LOCATION

As a general principle, verbs of motion and destinations are associated with the *Accusative* case, while locations are associated with the *Prepositional* case.

Examples:

DESTINATION
(Accusative case)

1. Мы е́дем в Москву́.
2. А́нна идёт в цирк.

LOCATION
(Prepositional case)

1. Мы живём в Москве́.
2. А́нна уже́ в ци́рке.

❖ ДОПОЛНИТЕЛЬНЫЕ ТЕКСТЫ

EVENTS CALENDAR

МАЙКЛ НАЙМАН ЕДЕТ В МОСКВУ

Английский композитор Майкл Найман со своим оркестром выступит с концертами в Москве. Майкл Найман родился 23 марта 1944 года в Лондоне. По окончании Королевской Музыкальной Академии долгое время занимался музыкальной критикой: именно Майкл Найман впервые ввел термин «минимализм» для описания музыки. Успех пришел к нему после создания музыки к фильму Питера Гринуэя «Контракт рисовальщика» (1982). Сотрудничество с режиссером продолжилось при работе над фильмами «Отсчет утопленников» (1988), «Повар, вор, его жена и ее любовник» (1989), «Книги Просперо» (1990). Майкл Найман также написал музыку к фильму Джейн Кемпион «Пианино» (1992).
3 июня концерт состоится в Большом зале консерватории с программой: музыка из фильмов «Контракт рисовальщика», «Повар, вор, его жена и ее любовник», «Пианино», «Книги Просперо», «Отсчет утопленников», музыка к компьютерной игре «Энеми зироу».

Начало в 19.00.
Справки и заказ билетов по т.: 928-06-42, 928-80-33

1. What kinds of information would you expect to find in a short article taken from an events calendar?
2. Look at the headline, the photo, and the first line of the text to get as much basic information as possible: who? what? where?
3. Glance at the body of the article. What kinds of information do you think are included here?
4. What kind of music would you guess this person is best known for?
5. Do you recognize any of the directors or films for which he composed music?
6. What time does the concert begin?
7. а. Как вы ду́маете (*think*), кто э́то на фотогра́фии†?
  б. Кто он?
  в. Куда́ он е́дет?
  г. Его́ орке́стр† то́же е́дет в Москву́?
  д. Майкл На́йман — англи́йский компози́тор и́ли америка́нский?

СКОРОГОВО́РКА *(tongue twister)*

На горе́ Арара́т растёт кру́пный виногра́д.	*Large grapes grow on Mount Ararat.*

УРОК 4

ВЫ ГОВОРИТЕ ПО-РУССКИ?

Концéртный зал и́мени Чайкóвского

In Part 1, which is on video, the neighbors complain to Sergei Petrovich, the building manager, about some construction problems in their new apartments. In Part 2, Sasha thinks he might be disturbing the neighbors by playing the piano too loudly. In Part 3, everyone meets Jim, who saves the day for Vova and Belka. In Part 4, Lena and Jim discuss the problems of going to school and simultaneously holding down a job.

Сосéди

In this lesson you will learn

- ✪ to express possession
- ✪ to say that something or someone is missing, lacking or absent
- ✪ to say what musical instruments people play
- ✪ to express actions in the past
- ✪ to say what languages you speak
- ✪ to express permission and prohibition
- ✪ to say where you go to school
- ✪ to talk about what you know how to do
- ✪ about classical music, higher learning, and housing construction in Russia
- ✪ how Russian is related to other languages
- ✪ to react appropriately to compliments

С ЧЕГО НАЧАТЬ?

НА́ШИ НО́ВЫЕ КВАРТИ́РЫ

холоди́льник

телеви́зор

пылесо́с

то́стер

микроволно́вая печь

ми́ксер

стира́льная маши́на

буди́льник

— **У вас есть** телеви́зор?
— Да. **У нас** большо́й но́вый телеви́зор.

| У вас есть. . . . ? | *Do you have . . . ?* |
| У меня́ / у нас. . . | *I have / we have* |

ЧТЕНИЕ

horrible

❖ У НАС **УЖА́СНЫЕ**° **ПРОБЛЕ́МЫ**†

(The professor, Aleksandra Nikolaevna Kruglova, and another neighbor named Tatyana Dmitrievna enter Silin's office.)

	ПРОФЕ́ССОР.	До́брый день! Кто здесь **дире́ктор**†?
	СЕРГЕ́Й ПЕТР.	А, сосе́ди! До́брый день! Я дире́ктор.
	ТАТЬЯ́НА ДМ.	Здра́вствуйте!
horror	ПРОФЕ́ССОР.	На́ши но́вые кварти́ры — э́то **у́жас**°!
nightmare	ТАТЬЯ́НА ДМ.	Э́то **кошма́р**°!
	АЛЕКСА́НДРА НИК.	Да . . .
That's wonderful!	СЕРГЕ́Й ПЕТР.	У вас но́вые кварти́ры! У меня́ то́же. **Прекра́сно**°!
то. . . that is	ПРОФЕ́ССОР.	Я не зна́ю, кака́я у вас кварти́ра. Но у меня́ — у нас, **то есть**°,
У. . . they have		и **у них**°(*pointing to the neighbors*) — ужа́сные пробле́мы.
	СЕРГЕ́Й ПЕТР.	У вас пробле́мы?
	ПРОФЕ́ССОР.	*(Exasperated.)* Да!
	СЕРГЕ́Й ПЕТР.	Каки́е у вас пробле́мы?
It's impossible / to open	ПРОФЕ́ССОР.	**Невозмо́жно**° откры́ть° о́кна.
to close	АЛЕКСА́НДРА НИК.	А две́ри невозмо́жно закры́ть.°
У. . . I have a bathtub / there's no /	ТАТЬЯ́НА ДМ.	У меня́ есть **ва́нна,**° но **нет**° воды́.°
water / У. . . I don't have	АЛЕКСА́НДРА НИК.	А у меня́ нет° ва́нны!
У. . . She doesn't have . . . /	ПРОФЕ́ССОР.	**У неё**°1 нет ва́нны, а у меня́ нет **ду́ша.**°
shower / what (do you	СЕРГЕ́Й ПЕТР.	*(Making an attempt at humor.)* А **заче́м**° ва́нна, заче́м душ,
need . . .) for		е́сли нет воды́?
	ПРОФЕ́ССОР.	Ужа́сный пол, ужа́сные сте́ны, ужа́сные о́кна.
	ТАТЬЯ́НА ДМ.	Нет ду́ша, нет воды́.
	АЛЕКСА́НДРА НИК.	Ужа́сные две́ри!
	СЕРГЕ́Й ПЕТР.	Дороги́е сосе́ди! У нас но́вый дом! И но́вые пробле́мы.

СЕРГЕ́Й ПЕТР. *(While talking, nudges the visitors toward the door.)*
Пробле́мы небольши́е: у вас нет ва́нны, у вас нет ду́ша, у вас о́чень плохо́й пол . . . Э́то, коне́чно, пло́хо. Но у нас но́вый дом! И э́то прекра́сно!

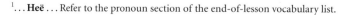

---

1. . . **Неё** . . . Refer to the pronoun section of the end-of-lesson vocabulary list.

УПРАЖНЕНИЕ 1 Под микроскопом: Это хорошая квартира?

Check the boxes in the chart below to indicate the features that would make an apartment good or bad. Then see if you can add one or two ideas of your own.

	Это очень хорошо!	Это неплохо.	Это ужасно!
1. Магазины близко.	☐	☐	☐
2. Остановка автобуса тоже близко.	☐	☐	☐
3. Сосед — музыкант.	☐	☐	☐
4. Там не работает лифт.	☐	☐	☐
5. Комнаты большие, светлые.	☐	☐	☐
6. Двери и окна невозможно закрыть.	☐	☐	☐
7. Балкон большой.	☐	☐	☐
8. Ванна есть, но нет воды.	☐	☐	☐
9. В квартире нет телефона.	☐	☐	☐
10. Рядом живут симпатичные студенты.	☐	☐	☐
11. В доме есть химчистка (*dry cleaners*).	☐	☐	☐
12. ???	☐	☐	☐

ГРАММАТИКА И ПРАКТИКА

◇◇◇ О РОССИИ ◇◇◇◇◇◇◇◇◇◇◇◇◇◇◇◇◇◇◇◇◇◇◇◇◇◇◇◇◇◇◇◇◇◇◇

ПРОБЛЕМЫ И БЮРОКРАТЫ†

У нас новый дом! И новые проблемы!

Housing construction has long been one of the key issues in Russia, especially in the major cities. New structures—ranging from modest apartment buildings like the one shown in the video to deluxe models for those who can afford such accommodations—are springing up everywhere. The quality of construction is improving, which is a welcome development: under the Communist system (1917 to 1991) a much higher priority was given to quantity and meeting the goals set by bureaucrats than to quality and consumer satisfaction. Consequently, most adult Russians have had experiences with cheaply made goods and shoddy construction, and many Russians find a certain gallows humor in telling or hearing stories about it.

Новый дом; новые квартиры

❖❖ 4.1. POSSESSION (*TO HAVE*): У ТЕБЯ ЕСТЬ ТЕЛЕВИЗОР?

— У тебя́ есть телеви́зор?	*"Do you have a TV?"*
— Да, есть.	*"Yes, I do."*

To ask about or express possession, Russians most often use the following construction:

<Preposition **у** + possessor + **есть** + item>
(in Genitive case)   (in Nominative case)

This construction takes the place of an actual verb such as *to have*. It uses a new case about which you will learn more, the *Genitive* case. In the example above, **тебя́** is the Genitive form of **ты**. The thing possessed (**телеви́зор**) is left in the Nominative case because it is the grammatical subject of the sentence. Finally, the element **есть** is an unchanging form that can be equated to *there is, there are*.

You already know most of the Genitive case pronoun forms: they are identical to the Accusative case forms used in questions and answers about names, such as **Как вас (тебя́) зову́т? Меня́ (его́, её) зову́т . . . .** The only difference is that when the third-person pronouns (**его́, её, их**) are governed by the preposition **у**, they are prefixed with the letter **н**: **его́** becomes **него́**, **её** becomes **неё**, **их** becomes **них**.

Here is a table of examples using this construction:

NOMINATIVE (for reference)	"POSSESSOR" PHRASE («у» + Genitive)		+ ЕСТЬ +	THING POSSESSED (in Nominative)
я	у меня́	*I have*		пылесо́с
ты	у тебя́	*you have*		соба́ка
он	у него́	*he has*		гита́ра
она́	у неё	*she has*		брат
мы	у нас	*we have*	есть	компью́тер†
вы	у вас	*you have*		часы́
они́	у них	*they have*		буди́льник
кто	у кого́	*who has*		???

УПРАЖНЕНИЕ 2   Who has what?

Below is a dialogue between two children. Fill in the blanks with the Russian equivalent.

— __У нас есть__ телеви́зор. А у вас?
　　　We have

— _____[1] телеви́зор! А компью́тер _____[2]?
　　We also have　　　　　　　　　　　　　　　　　do you have

— Коне́чно! И компью́тер, и при́нтер.† Мой па́па — программи́ст.†
_____[3] большо́й компью́тер и есть но́утбук.† А твой па́па
　　He has
то́же программи́ст?

— Нет, он музыка́нт. А ма́ма — программи́ст, и _____[4]
　　　　　　　　　　　　　　　　　　　　　　　　　　she also has
большо́й компью́тер и но́утбук.

❖❖ 4.2. INTONATION IN ЕСТЬ QUESTIONS AND ANSWERS

Correct intonation is crucial when asking "Do you have . . . ?" and similar questions. When asking about the existence of something, for example, the word **есть** must be the high point of the question.

LEVEL	THE QUESTION	THE ANSWER
High	ЕСТЬ	
Mid	У тебя́ со-	Да. *or* Есть. *or* Да,
Low	ба́ка?	есть.

УПРАЖНЕНИЕ 3   У тебя́ есть микроволно́вая печь?

Think of an item that you possess and for which you know the word in Russian. Then see how many of your classmates also possess that item.

ОБРАЗЕЦ: СТУДЕ́НТ А.   У тебя́ есть . . . (*your item*)?

СТУДЕ́НТ Б.   Да, есть [*or* Нет.] А у тебя́ есть . . . ?

УПРАЖНЕНИЕ 4   У тебя́ есть холоди́льник, а у меня́ есть гита́ра

Working in groups of three or four, take turns stating things you and others in your group have. Mention your own possessions if you can.

ОБРАЗЕЦ: СТУДЕ́НТ А.   У меня́ есть холоди́льник.

СТУДЕ́НТ Б.   (*to* А) У тебя́ есть холоди́льник, а у меня́ есть гита́ра.

СТУДЕ́НТ В.   (*to* А) У тебя́ есть холоди́льник, (*to* Б) у тебя́ есть гита́ра, а у меня́ есть роя́ль.

Now select one spokesperson for your group to tell the rest of the class what the members of your group have (**У неё есть холоди́льник, у него́ есть гита́ра, а у меня́ есть роя́ль**).

❖❖ 4.3. GENITIVE OF NOUNS: *MISSING, LACKING* = <НЕТ + GENITIVE>

У неё **нет ва́нны**, а у меня́ **нет ду́ша**.   *She doesn't have a bathtub, and I don't have a shower.*

У меня́ есть ва́нна, но **нет воды́**.   *I have a bathtub, but no water.*

To say that something is missing or that you don't have something, use <**нет** + Genitive> of the thing(s) lacking. Note that a sentence could have two Genitive forms for two different reasons, and no Nominative at all (as in **У них нет ва́нны**). This is also the construction to use in expressing that someone is not present, e.g.:

— Где Вади́м?   *"Where's Vadim?"*

— Вади́ма нет. (Его́ нет.)   *"Vadim's not here. (He's not here.)"*

In the table below, note that feminine and neuter Genitive noun forms often look like their corresponding Nominative plural forms, but lack the stress shifts that are common for many Nominative plural forms (for example, Genitive singular **окна́,** but Nominative plural **о́кна**). Note also that what you have learned about hard/soft endings (pp. 29–30) and spelling rules (pp. 53–54) explains what at first may seem like a lot of variation in the endings.

	NOMINATIVE CASE (dictionary form)	GENITIVE CASE ENDING	EXAMPLES (Здесь нет...)
Masculine and neuter	телеви́зор Вади́м душ Серге́-й роя́л-ь окн-о́ упражне́ни-е	Delete final vowel [in neuter] or -ь [in masculine]; Add -а/-я	телеви́зор-**а** Вади́м-**а** ду́ш-**а** Серге́-**я** роя́л-**я** окн-а́ упражне́ни-**я**
Feminine (and "masquerading masculines")	вод-а́ Мари́н-а ру́чк-а ку́хн-я двер-ь Во́в-а дя́д-я	Delete final vowel or -ь; add -ы/-и	вод-**ы́** Мари́н-**ы** ру́чк-**и** ку́хн-**и** двёр-**и** Во́в-**ы** дя́д-**и**

УПРАЖНЕ́НИЕ 5   Чего́ нет? (*What's missing?*)

For each remark in the **А** column, respond with a complaint in the **Б** column, choosing the one logical word that completes the complaint and putting it in the right case.

ОБРАЗЕ́Ц: СТУДЕ́НТ А. Како́й замеча́тельный микрорайо́н!
СТУДЕ́НТ Б. Да, но здесь нет_____*по́чты*_____! (ми́ксер, по́чта, сочине́ние)

СТУДЕ́НТ А
1. Како́й краси́вый дом!

2. Кака́я у вас краси́вая но́вая кварти́ра!
3. Кака́я больша́я ко́мната!

4. Кака́я све́тлая ку́хня!

СТУДЕ́НТ Б
1. Да, но там нет _____!
(контине́нт, лифт, меню́)

2. Да, но у нас нет _____!
(душ, молоко́, статья́)
3. Да, но там нет _____!
(окно́, бу́ква, пол)

4. Да, но _____ нет!
(сосе́д, вода́, стена́)

УПРАЖНЕ́НИЕ 6   У тебя́ есть мотоци́кл[†]?

Working with a classmate, compile a list of as many things as you can that both of you possess. Use complete <**нет** + Genitive> answers as needed. Here is a list of some items to start you off:

то́стер	сестра́	саксофо́н
пылесо́с	компью́тер	гита́ра
ко́шка	фен (*hair dryer*)	телефо́н
соба́ка	микроско́п[†]	муж
брат	мотоци́кл	???
рюкза́к	жена́	

ОБРАЗЕЦ: — У тебя́ есть мотоци́кл?
                      — Да. А у тебя́?
                                    or
                      — Нет, у меня́ нет мотоци́кла. (*Note Genitive case.*) А у тебя́?

◆ 4.4. POSSESSION PHRASES WITHOUT ЕСТЬ

Каки́е у вас пробле́мы?   *What kinds of problems do you have?*

У нас но́вый дом! И э́то прекра́сно!   *We have a new building! And that's wonderful!*

The manager of the new building (**Серге́й Петро́вич**) has already been informed by the angry residents that there *are* problems with the new apartments. In the first example above, he tries to establish what kinds of problems these are, hence he does not use **есть**. As the residents are leaving his office, he says it's wonderful that they have a new building. Again, **есть** is omitted because they all know the building is new. Omission of **есть** is generally the pattern when the existence (presence or absence) of an item or object is not in question, but rather one is stating or seeking a description, clarification, or specification. Here are some more examples:

EXISTENCE AT ISSUE: USE есть	EXISTENCE PRESUMED: DON'T USE есть
— У вас **есть** соба́ка? — Да. *or* Есть. *or* Да, есть.	— У вас **больша́я** соба́ка? — Да, больша́я.
— У него́ **есть** телеви́зор? — Нет, у него́ нет телеви́зора.	— У Джи́ма **япо́нский** (*Japanese*) телеви́зор? — Нет, америка́нский.
— У меня́ **есть** ва́нна, но нет воды́. — А у меня́ нет ва́нны!	— У них **но́вые** кварти́ры? — Да, и о́чень хоро́шие!

УПРАЖНЕНИЕ 7   To ЕСТЬ or not to ЕСТЬ?

Insert **есть** into the blanks where appropriate, i.e., where existence or possession rather than some quality of an item is at issue.

— У вас _____ [1] маши́на(*car*)?
— Да, _____ .[2]
— А кака́я у вас _____ [3] маши́на?
— У нас _____ [4] япо́нская (*Japanese*) маши́на.
— Твой брат говори́т (*says*), что у тебя́ ещё _____ [5] мотоци́кл. Э́то ве́рно (*is that true*)?
— Ве́рно, _____ .[6] У меня́ ста́рый америка́нский мотоци́кл.

УПРАЖНЕНИЕ 8   У когó (*Who has*) . . . ?

Refer to the table showing the «**у**» construction. Then fill in the blanks with the correct form of the pronoun used in the first sentence of each pair.

ОБРАЗЕЦ: Я журналист. *У меня* интерéсная профéссия.

1. Мы мнóго читáем. _____ хорóшая библиотéка.
2. Они пи́шут сочинéние. _____ интерéсная тéма.
3. Он живёт ря́дом. _____ краси́вая собáка.
4. Она живёт далекó. _____ большáя кóмната.
5. Ты мнóго рабóтаешь. _____ трýдная рабóта?
6. Вы живёте тут? _____ ужáсный сосéд.
7. Я пиани́ст. _____ нóвый роя́ль.

❖❖ 4.5. INTONATION IN POSSESSION QUESTIONS AND ANSWERS WITHOUT ЕСТЬ

When asking an «**у**» phrase question without **есть,** the *high* point of the sentence is the stressed syllable of the point of inquiry. The stressed syllable of the answer drops to the *low* intonation level.

LEVEL	THE QUESTION			THE ANSWER	
High		⌐ПÓН-			
Mid	У тебя́ я-	ский ⌐		Да, я-	
Low			телеви́зор?		⌐ПÓНский.

УПРАЖНЕНИЕ 9   У тебя́ есть . . . ?

Make up five questions using **есть** to find out whether your classmate has certain items. If he does have the item, follow up with a question (without **есть**) asking for a clarification or description of that item. Make sure you take turns asking questions.

ОБРАЗЕЦ: — У тебя́ есть рюкзáк?
— Нет, у меня́ нет рюкзакá. А у тебя́ есть компью́тер? . . .
or
— Да, у меня́ есть рюкзáк.
— А какóй у тебя́ рюкзáк?
— У меня́ большóй (нóвый, хорóший . . .) рюкзáк. А у тебя́ есть компью́тер? . . .

КУЛЬТУРА РЕЧИ

❖ ТАК ГОВОРЯТ: КОНЕ́ЧНО

Пробле́мы небольши́е: у вас нет ва́нны, у вас нет ду́ша, у вас о́чень плохо́й пол . . . Э́то, **коне́чно,** пло́хо. Но у нас но́вый дом! И э́то прекра́сно!

In the preceding example, Sergei Petrovich uses the word **коне́чно** (*of course*) parenthetically before he adds a contrasting comment.

Коне́чно may also be used in a response to questions about something very obvious:

— У тебя́ до́ма есть ва́нна?
— Коне́чно, есть! (*or* — Коне́чно!)

УПРАЖНЕНИЕ 10   Э́то, коне́чно, пло́хо

Working with a classmate, create a short dialogue in which one person reacts to another person's statement using a parenthetical **коне́чно,** then follows up this statement with additional contrastive information.

1. A friend says he has a small apartment. You tell him this, of course, is bad, but he has a very nice building.
2. A friend exclaims what a beautiful apartment you have. You point out that the apartment, of course, isn't bad, but the neighbor is a musician.

УПРАЖНЕНИЕ 11   Коне́чно!

Working with a classmate, create short dialogues similar to the one above in which a person uses **коне́чно** in his response to exclude any uncertainty or doubt.

1. Someone asks if you listen to the radio.
2. A friend asks if you read newspapers.

❖ САМОПРОВЕРКА: УПРАЖНЕНИЕ 12

Working on your own, try this self-test: Read a Russian sentence out loud, then give an idiomatic English equivalent without looking at the book. Then work from English to Russian. After you have completed the activity, try it with a classmate.

1. — У тебя́ есть пылесо́с?
   — Нет. А у тебя́?
   — Есть, но ста́рый.

1. *"Do you have a vacuum cleaner?"*
   "No. Do you?"
   "Yes, but it's an old one."

2. — Кака́я у вас соба́ка?
   — Пу́дель. А у вас то́же есть соба́ка?
   — Соба́ки нет, но есть ко́шка.

2. *"What kind of dog do you have?"*
   "A poodle. Do you have a dog, too?"
   "No dog, but I have a cat."

✤ ВОПРОСЫ И ОТВЕТЫ: УПРАЖНЕНИЕ 13

Working with a classmate, take turns asking and answering the following questions.

1. У тебя́ есть кварти́ра (ко́мната)?
2. Кака́я она́ — больша́я? Ма́ленькая?
3. Что у тебя́ — ва́нна и́ли душ?
4. У тебя́ есть стира́льная маши́на? Она́ но́вая? Хорошо́ рабо́тает?
5. А микроволно́вая печь у тебя́ есть?

✤ ДИАЛОГИ

ДИАЛОГ 1 У меня́ больша́я кварти́ра
(Describing an apartment)

    — У вас но́вая кварти́ра? Больша́я?
    — Да, больша́я и о́чень хоро́шая.
    — А дом то́же хоро́ший?
    — И дом хоро́ший, и сосе́ди хоро́шие.

ДИАЛОГ 2 У меня́ ужа́сная пробле́ма
(Discussing problems)

    — У меня́ ужа́сная пробле́ма.
    — У меня́ то́же. Кака́я у вас пробле́ма?
    — У меня́ нет ва́нны. А у вас?
    — У меня́ есть ва́нна, но нет ду́ша.
    — Э́то пло́хо, но не ужа́сно.

УПРАЖНЕНИЕ 14   Ваш диало́г

Make up a dialogue in which you have just moved into a new dorm room (or apartment) and are comparing what you and a fellow student have (furniture, room sizes, good neighbors, amenities, and so on).

✤ А ТЕПЕРЬ . . . : УПРАЖНЕНИЕ 15

Working with a classmate, use what you learned in Part 1 to . . .

1. ask if he has a refrigerator (vacuum cleaner, alarm clock, computer, and so on)
2. ask what kind of refrigerator (vacuum cleaner, alarm clock, computer, and so on) your classmate has
3. respond when asked a similar question that you do *not* have the item

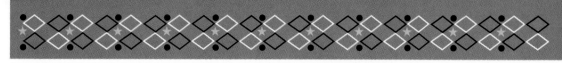

ЧАСТЬ ВТОРАЯ

С ЧЕГО НАЧАТЬ?

ЧТО ДЕЛАТЬ ВЕЧЕРОМ?

ОПЕРА   БАЛЕТ   РОК   ДЖАЗ   КЛАССИКА†

"Why didn't I study Russian in college?!"

ЧТО?
М. Му́соргский. «Бори́с Годуно́в»
П. Чайко́вский. «Щелку́нчик»
С. Проко́фьев. «Роме́о и Джулье́тта»
«Соли́сты Москвы́»
«Зву́ки джа́за»
Гру́ппа† «Парадо́кс»

ГДЕ?
Большо́й теа́тр
Большо́й **зал Моско́вской**† консервато́рии
Конце́ртный зал им.[2] Чайко́вского
Музе́й им. Гли́нки, конце́ртный зал
Моско́вский Дворе́ц молодёжи
Джаз† Арт **Клуб**†

ПА́ПА. Я люблю́ **о́перу.**†
МА́МА. А я — **бале́т.**†
ДЕ́ТИ. А мы лю́бим рок!

Что де́лать. . .?	*What should we do . . .*
я люблю́. . .	*I like . . .*
мы лю́бим. . .	*We like . . .*
«Щелку́нчик»	*"The Nutcracker"*
зал	*auditorium*
музе́й	*museum*
Дворе́ц молодёжи	*Youth Center*

---

[2]The form «**им.**» is an abbreviation for **и́мени,** the Genitive case of **и́мя.** When a cultural center, educational institution, etc., is named in honor of a prominent figure, the construction **им.** (or **и́мени**) plus that person's name in the Genitive case follows the name of the institution. In English, the name of the person precedes the name of the organization, as in The John F. Kennedy Center for the Performing Arts.

всё . . . *they can hear everything*

❖ ВНИЗУ́ ВСЁ СЛЫ́ШНО°

(*Sasha has just finished practicing the piano.*)

all / so БА́БУШКА. Э́то **всё**°? Ты так° ма́ло игра́ешь, Са́ша.

СА́ША. Я мно́го игра́ю, ба́бушка.

too / softly БА́БУШКА. И ты **сли́шком**° **ти́хо**° игра́ешь.

you can't / loudly СА́ША. Ба́бушка , у нас **нельзя́**° игра́ть **гро́мко**°. (*He knocks on the wall to show that it is not really soundproof.*) Внизу́ сосе́ди, всё слы́шно.

ДЕ́ДУШКА. (*Suddenly hearing everything and coming to life.*) Сосе́ди? А-а, симпати́чная блонди́нка†! Она́, коне́чно, лю́бит му́зыку.

everybody СА́ША. Но я игра́ю кла́ссику,† а её не **все**°[3] лю́бят.

only БА́БУШКА. Ты игра́ешь не **то́лько**° кла́ссику. Джаз и рок ты то́же игра́ешь.

(*Sasha begins to play a jazz tune loudly. Loud knocks from below are heard.*)

Вот. . . See! / say СА́ША. **Вот ви́дишь!**° Там (*pointing down*) всё слы́шно. А ты **говори́шь**°, что я ти́хо игра́ю.

unpleasant / woman БА́БУШКА. Э́то, коне́чно, не Ле́на, а её мать. О́чень **несимпати́чная**° **же́нщина.**° И не лю́бит му́зыку.

---

[3]The Russian word **все** (which is the plural of **весь,** *all*) requires a plural verb, unlike its English counterparts *everybody, everyone:* **все рабо́тают** *everybody works, everyone is working.* The neuter word **всё** *everything* requires a singular verb as it does in English: **всё рабо́тает** *everything works.*

| СА́ША. | Ба́бушка, ты не зна́ешь. **Мо́жет быть,°** у них **го́сти.°** Мо́жет быть, у Во́вы° за́втра **контро́льная.°** Мо́жет быть, Серге́й Петро́вич **спит.°** И почему́ ты говори́шь, что её мать несимпати́чная? | Мо́жет. . . *Maybe / guests* у. . . *Vova has / test / is sleeping* |

(*The doorbell rings.*)

БА́БУШКА.	Э́то, коне́чно, она́. (*Vasya, the plumber, enters.*)	
ВА́СЯ.	Здра́вствуйте. Отопле́ние° рабо́тает? (*He walks over to the radiator, turns something, and bangs the radiator loudly.*) Не рабо́тает. (*Seeing that Grandpa and Grandma did not hear him.*) Не ра-бо-та-ет. Понима́ете?	*heating*
БА́БУШКА.	Понима́ем . . .	
СА́ША.	(*relieved*) Понима́ем!	

УПРАЖНЕ́НИЕ 1   Под микроско́пом: Accusative case

Here are selected sentences from this reading. Each has at least one Accusative case form in it. Circle the Accusative forms.

1. Она́, коне́чно, лю́бит му́зыку.
2. Но я игра́ю кла́ссику . . .
3. . . . а её не все лю́бят.
4. Джаз и рок ты то́же игра́ешь.

◆ 4.6. -ИШЬ VERBS: BASIC (ГОВОРИ́ТЬ) TYPE

Почему́ ты **говори́шь,** что её мать несимпати́чная?	*Why do you say that her mother isn't nice?*
Она́, коне́чно, **лю́бит** му́зыку.	*She, of course, loves music.*
Не все **лю́бят** кла́ссику.	*Not everybody likes classical music.*

The second major group of Russian verbs is the -**ишь** conjugation.[4] It differs from the -**ешь** conjugation in three essential ways:

1. The **я**-form ending is -**ю,** whether the verb stem ends in a vowel or a consonant. (This ending is written -**у** only when required by the «**ви́жу**» spelling rule discussed below).
2. The vowel in the ending of the **ты, он/она́, мы,** and **вы** forms is -**и**- instead of -**е-/-ё-.**
3. The **они́**-form ending is -**ят** (-**ат** when required by the «**ви́жу**» spelling rule).

---

[4]Some textbooks call the -**ишь** verbs "second conjugation."

Compare the two types of endings in the following table:

	-ешь ENDINGS[5]	**-ишь ENDINGS**
	рабо́тать (*to work*)	**говори́ть** (*to say, speak, talk*)
я	рабо́та-**ю**	говор-**ю́**
ты	рабо́та-**ешь**	говор-**и́шь**
он, она́, оно́	рабо́та-**ет**	говор-**и́т**
мы	рабо́та-**ем**	говор-**и́м**
вы	рабо́та-**ете**	говор-**и́те**
они́	рабо́та-**ют**	говор-**я́т**

The three stress patterns (stem stress, ending stress, and shifting stress) mentioned in Lesson 3 in connection with the **-ешь** verbs also occur with **-ишь** verbs. The verb **смотре́ть** *to look* (*at*), *to watch* which you learned in Lesson 3 is a regular **-ишь** verb (**смотр-ю́, смо́тр-ишь, . . . смо́тр-ят**).

УПРАЖНЕ́НИЕ 2   Все говоря́т . . .

Provide forms of **говори́ть** and **люби́ть** to complete the following paragraph.

Моя́ сестра́ Мари́на хоро́шая пиани́стка. Все _____,[1] что она́ о́чень хорошо́ игра́ет. Мари́на _____,[2] что она́ _____[3] и кла́ссику, и джаз, и рок. Ба́бушка и де́душка _____,[4] что они́ _____[5] кла́ссику. А я _____[6]: — Ба́бушка, ты _____,[7] что ты _____[8] то́лько кла́ссику. А ра́зве рок — э́то плоха́я му́зыка? — Мо́жет быть, э́то хоро́шая му́зыка, но я её не люблю́.

УПРАЖНЕ́НИЕ 3   Во́ва пи́шет сочине́ние

Fill in the blanks with conjugated forms of the verbs **говори́ть, де́лать, знать, писа́ть, чита́ть.**

Сего́дня воскресе́нье, и мы все (*we all*) до́ма. Ма́ма на балко́не, она́ _____[1] письмо́ в газе́ту. Ле́на в столо́вой, она́ _____[2] по телефо́ну (*on the phone*). Она́ _____[3] ти́хо, и не всё слы́шно. Я _____[4] дома́шнее зада́ние, а па́па _____[5] газе́ту. Он, коне́чно, _____[6] о (*about*) спо́рте[†] и́ли о поли́тике[†]. Он _____,[7] что когда́ (*when*) он _____[8] об (*about*) эконо́мике[†], он пото́м пло́хо спит. Кро́ме того́, он _____,[9] что он уже́ всё _____[10] об эконо́мике.

❖❖ 4.7. STEM-CHANGING VERBS

Many Russian verbs of both the **-ешь** and **-ишь** types exhibit changes in the final consonant of the stem. At first, it is best simply to memorize the conjugation patterns of these verbs as you encounter them; then, as you progress, you will begin to see that they fall into several large groups. (Several of these groups are included for reference in Appendix H on page 353.) As you've seen, when these changes occur, they appear in all conjugated forms of **-ешь** verbs; for example **с → ш** in all forms of **писа́ть: пишу́,**

---

[5]Remember the two **-ешь** variations: (1) if the ending is stressed, you'll have **-ё-** endings (**живёшь, живёт, живём, живёте**), and (2) after a consonant you'll have **у**, not **ю** (**живу́, живу́т**).

пи́шешь, . . . пи́шут. In **-ишь** verbs, however, the stem change appears **only** in the **я** form, as shown in the following examples of **-ишь** verbs, one from each stress pattern:

	STEM STRESS ви́д - еть (to see)	ENDING STRESS сп - ать (to sleep)	SHIFTING STRESS люб - и́ть (to like, love)
	д → ж	п → пл	б → бл
я	ви́ж-у	спл-ю	любл-ю́
ты	ви́д-ишь	сп-ишь	лю́б-ишь
он, она́, оно́	ви́д-ит	сп-ит	лю́б-ит
мы	ви́д-им	сп-им	лю́б-им
вы	ви́д-ите	сп-и́те	лю́б-ите
они́	ви́д-ят	сп-ят	лю́б-ят

УПРАЖНЕНИЕ 4   Э́то на́ша кварти́ра

Fill in the blanks with conjugated forms of the verbs **говори́ть, спать, люби́ть.**
(*Natalya Ivanovna is showing her new apartment to a friend.*)

Э́то на́ша кварти́ра. Вот на́ша спа́льня. Тут _____[1] мы — муж и я. Ле́на _____[2] тут, э́то её ко́мната. У Во́вы то́же есть своя́ (*his own*) ко́мната. Бе́лка _____[3] в ко́мнате Во́вы и́ли в пере́дней (*hallway*). Мы _____,[4] когда́ (*when*) в кварти́ре ти́хо, но Во́ва и Ле́на _____[5] слу́шать му́зыку. Во́ва _____[6] рок, а Ле́на — кла́ссику. Кро́ме того́, у нас сосе́д-музыка́нт. Ле́на _____,[7] что он хорошо́ игра́ет. Я не зна́ю, хорошо́ он игра́ет и́ли пло́хо, но я зна́ю, что он игра́ет гро́мко. Что ты _____[8]? У тебя́ то́же сосе́д-музыка́нт? Како́й кошма́р!

❖ 4.8. SPELLING: THE «ВИ́ЖУ» RULE

The last major spelling rule of Russian, the «**ви́жу**» rule, is frequently encountered with **-ишь** verbs.

Never **-ю,** always **-у,** and ⎫
never **-я,** always **-а,** after ⎭ **ж, ч, ш, щ**

This rule explains why the **я** form of **ви́деть** (*to see*) is **ви́ж-у,** ending in **-у** (rather than **-ю**), and why the **они́** form of many other **-ишь** verbs that you will soon learn ends in **-ат** (rather than **-ят**).

УПРАЖНЕНИЕ 5   Мой брат и я

Complete the following sentences, using the verbs **говори́ть, люби́ть, спать, ви́деть.**

Мой брат _____,[1] что я мно́го _____[2]: «У́тром, когда́ (*when*) я иду́ на рабо́ту, ты спишь, ве́чером ты _____.[3] А что ты де́лаешь но́чью (*at night*), когда́ все _____[4]?» А я _____[5]: «Я _____[6] у́тром и ве́чером, потому́ что (*because*) но́чью я рабо́таю. Я _____[7] рабо́тать но́чью, когда́ в до́ме ти́хо. Но ты но́чью _____[8] и поэ́тому не _____,[9] что я _____[10]».

УПРАЖНЕ́НИЕ 6   Что вы лю́бите?

Work in groups of three or four. Student A asks student B a "leading question," student B answers and then addresses a question to student C, and so on. After the last student responds, she should then ask student A a question. Three "leading questions" are given after the example.

ОБРАЗЕ́Ц: A. (*to B*) Ты лю́бишь чита́ть детекти́вы[†]?

B. Нет, не о́чень. Я люблю́ чита́ть газе́ты. (*to C*) А что ты лю́бишь чита́ть?

C. Я то́же люблю́ чита́ть газе́ты. Кро́ме того́, я люблю́ чита́ть три́ллеры.[†] (*to D or back to A*) А ты? Что ты лю́бишь чита́ть?

D. or A. Я то́же люблю́ чита́ть три́ллеры. (Я люблю́ чита́ть газе́ты.// Я люблю́ чита́ть и газе́ты, и журна́лы, и детекти́вы.)

Additional "leading questions":

1. Ты лю́бишь игра́ть в баскетбо́л?
2. Каку́ю (*What kind of*) му́зыку ты лю́бишь?
3. Ты лю́бишь чита́ть журна́лы?

❖◇ О РОССИИ ❖◇❖◇❖◇❖◇❖◇❖◇❖◇❖

МУ́ЗЫКА В РОССИ́И

Са́ша игра́ет кла́ссику.

Russia's contribution to the world's treasury of classical music cannot be overestimated. The music of **Чайко́вский, Му́соргский, Ри́мский-Ко́рсаков, Проко́фьев, Страви́нский,** and **Шостако́вич** is performed throughout the world, enjoying special popularity in the United States. Composer **Серге́й Проко́фьев** lived in the United States from 1918 to 1922, and composer and pianist **Серге́й Рахма́нинов** lived in the United States from 1917 until his death in 1943.

Composer **Михаи́л Гли́нка**, who lived in the first half of the nineteenth century, is less known in the West. In Russia, however, he is considered the "founding father" of Russian classical music. During the Soviet period, when tsars were not especially popular, one of Glinka's operas, *A Life for the Tsar,* was "renamed" *Ivan Susanin* (after the main character, a patriotic peasant).

❖◇❖◇❖◇❖◇❖◇❖◇❖◇❖◇❖◇❖◇❖◇❖◇❖◇

❖◇ 4.9. GENITIVE CASE: <у + NOUN>

Мо́жет быть, **у Во́вы** за́втра контро́льная.   *Maybe Vova has a test tomorrow.*

У дире́ктора есть де́ти?   *Does the director have children?*

As you have seen, <**у** + Genitive *pronoun*> (**у меня́, у вас, у них,** and so on) expresses *to have.* You can also use <**у** + Genitive *noun*> forms (which you learned to use with

нет) to render "*have*" sentences:

сестра́ → у сестры́ . . .	(*my*) *sister has* . . .
Во́ва → у Во́вы . . .	*Vova has* . . .
Джим → у Джи́ма . . .	*Jim has* . . .
Са́ша → у Са́ши . . .	*Sasha has* . . .
Та́ня → у Та́ни . . .	*Tanya has* . . .

УПРАЖНЕНИЕ 7   У меня́ нет . . .

Fill in the blanks with Genitive case endings.

А. У меня́ нет брат_____,[1] но есть сестра́. У неё есть подру́га (*female friend*), а у подру́г_____[2] есть брат. Его́ зову́т Серге́й. Он замеча́тельно игра́ет в хоккей[†], а я о́чень люблю́ хоккей. Сего́дня бу́дет (*will be*) интере́сный хокке́йный матч[†], но у меня́ нет биле́т_____.[3] А у сестр_____[4] есть биле́т. Я говорю́: «О́ля! Ты не лю́бишь хоккей, а я люблю́». «Понима́ю, — говори́т О́ля. — У тебя́ нет биле́т_____[5]!»

Б. У па́п_____[6] сего́дня конфере́нция,[†] у ма́м_____[7] — семина́р[†], поэ́тому я бу́ду (*will be*) у тёт_____[8] Поли́н_____.[9] Но там ску́чно (*boring*). У неё нет компью́тер_____.[10] У неё нет магнитофо́н_____.[11] У неё да́же телеви́зор_____[12] нет.

УПРАЖНЕНИЕ 8   Asking who has what

Form groups of three and ask one another who has what. Because you know only singular forms of the Genitive, limit your answers to singular forms of each noun.

ОБРАЗЕЦ: — У кого́ есть при́нтер?
          — У меня́ есть компью́тер, но нет при́нтера.

          — У кого́ есть саксофо́н?
          — У Ребе́кки.

УПРАЖНЕНИЕ 9   У тебя . . . ?

Find three people in the room with at least one of the following:

симпати́чные сосе́ди
хоро́шая кварти́ра
но́вая микроволно́вая печь
больша́я ко́мната
тру́дная рабо́та
и́мпортная ме́бель
но́вый телеви́зор

❖❖ 4.10. GENITIVE: NOUN LINKAGE

Где **остано́вка автобуса**?	*Where's the bus stop?*
Ты не зна́ешь его́ **но́мер телефо́на**?	*Do you happen to know his phone number?*

In addition to showing possession, the Genitive case can be used to link two nouns, as phrases with 's and *of* often do in English:

POSSESSION:	пылесо́с сосе́да	*the neighbor's vacuum cleaner*
	кроссо́вки Во́вы	*Vova's sneakers*
OTHER:	а́дрес Ни́ны	*Nina's address*
	муж мое́й сестры́	*my sister's husband*
	день рожде́ния	*birthday*

УПРАЖНЕНИЕ 10   Но́вые фра́зы

The following phrases contain words you know (or can guess) to link two nouns, the second of which is the Genitive case. What do they mean in English? Note that some express possession or ownership, whereas others show some other kind of linkage.

но́мер телефо́на
а́дрес магази́на
кварти́ра ба́бушки
му́зыка Мо́царта
продю́сер фи́льма

рабо́та журнали́ста
дом-музе́й Пу́шкина
музе́й исто́рии авиа́ции
дире́ктор клу́ба
су́мка Ната́ши

КУЛЬТУРА РЕЧИ

❖ ТАК ГОВОРЯТ: У НАС, У ВАС

У нас нельзя́ игра́ть гро́мко.

You're not allowed to play loudly here (at our place).

In addition to expressing possession, phrases with «**у**» such as **у нас, у вас,** and so on, are commonly used to designate one's home, country, place of work, or other location with which one might be identified. Usually the location is clear from context, as in this reading when Sasha is talking about the new apartment. Here is another example (note how context determines the meaning of the «**у**» phrase):

В Аме́рике студе́нты рабо́тают,
   а **у нас** нет.

In America students work, but not here.
[The speaker is contrasting America with her country.]

УПРАЖНЕНИЕ 11   У нас, у вас . . .

How would you interpret the «**у**» phrases in the following sentences?

1. Мари́на рабо́тает у нас.
2. У вас хоро́ший кли́мат,[†] а у нас плохо́й.
3. У них в до́ме не рабо́тает лифт.

❖ САМОПРОВЕРКА: УПРАЖНЕНИЕ 12

Working on your own, try this self-test: Read a Russian sentence out loud, then give an idiomatic English equivalent without looking at the book. Then work from English to Russian. After you have completed the activity, try it with a classmate.

1. Почему́ ты так гро́мко говори́шь? Внизу́ все спят.
2. Э́то ва́ша сосе́дка? Óчень несимпати́чная же́нщина.
3. Я люблю́ игра́ть в ша́хматы. А ты? Ты то́же лю́бишь игра́ть в ша́хматы?
4. У дире́ктора есть де́ти?
5. Ты не зна́ешь, как зову́т жену́ дире́ктора?

1. *Why are you talking so loudly? Everybody's asleep downstairs.*
2. *Is that your neighbor? She's a very unpleasant woman.*
3. *I love to play chess. How about you? Do you like playing chess, too?*
4. *Does the director have children?*
5. *Do you happen to know what the director's wife's name is?*

❖ ВОПРОСЫ И ОТВЕТЫ: УПРАЖНЕНИЕ 13

1. Ты лю́бишь му́зыку?
2. У тебя́ есть компа́кт-ди́ски[†]?
3. Что ты лю́бишь — кла́ссику, джаз, рок, ка́нтри[†]?
4. Как по-тво́ему, все лю́бят кла́ссику? А рок?

❖❖ ДИАЛОГИ

ДИАЛОГ 1 А что де́лает . . . ?
(Making an inquiry over the phone)
A little boy answers the phone.

— Ми́ша, э́то тётя Ва́ря. Ты что, оди́н (*alone*) до́ма?
— Нет, я не оди́н. Ба́бушка, де́душка и ма́ма то́же до́ма.
— А что де́лает ба́бушка?
— Спит.
— А де́душка?
— Слу́шает му́зыку.
— А ма́ма?
— Ма́ма говори́т, что её нет (*she's not*) до́ма.

ДИАЛОГ 2 Я люблю́ бале́т!
(Choosing a performance to attend)
Looking at a theater schedule . . .

— Вот Большо́й теа́тр. За́втра там Му́соргский. «Бори́с Годуно́в».
— Я не люблю́ о́перу.
— А вот Музыка́льный теа́тр. Там «Роме́о и Джулье́тта». Бале́т
  Проко́фьева «Роме́о и Джулье́тта».
— Прекра́сно! Я о́чень люблю́ бале́т!

УПРАЖНЕНИЕ 14 Ваш диало́г

Make up a dialogue in which you and your roommate discuss what you hear through
the walls of your apartment, such as what music the neighbors listen to and whether it
disturbs you.

❖❖ А ТЕПЕРЬ . . . : УПРАЖНЕНИЕ 15

Working with a classmate, use what you learned in Part 2 to . . .

1. tell someone she's speaking too quietly
2. ask whether she likes opera (jazz, ballet, rock, . . .)
3. ask if she likes the group [*fill in a name*]
4. ask if she knows a classmate's telephone number

 С ЧЕГО НАЧАТЬ?

Кафедра языков и литературы

— Э́то на́ша **ка́федра.** На́ши профессора́ и **преподава́тели говоря́т по-ру́сски, по-францу́зски,**[†] **по-испа́нски,**[†] **по-италья́нски,**[†] **по-португа́льски,**[†] **по-неме́цки, по-кита́йски** и **по-япо́нски.**[†] И, коне́чно, мы все говори́м **по-англи́йски.**[†] Я **преподаю́** мой родно́й **язы́к** — ру́сский.

ка́федра	*department*
преподава́тель	*instructor*
говори́ть по-ру́сски	*to speak Russian*
…по-неме́цки	*… German*
…по-кита́йски	*… Chinese*
преподава́ть	*to teach*
родно́й	*native*
язы́к	*language*

✵ ЧТЕНИЕ ✵

Золоты́е. . . *Good with his hands*

❖ ЗОЛОТЫ́Е РУ́КИ°

(At the Silins'.)

	ЛЕ́НА.	Во́ва, ты куда́?
	ВО́ВА.	Гуля́ть.
homework	ЛЕ́НА.	А **уро́ки°?**
later (on) / let's go!	ВО́ВА.	Уро́ки — **пото́м.°** Бе́лка, **пошли́°!**

(Vova and Belka walk out to the elevator. When they reach the ground floor, the door won't open.)

	ВО́ВА.	Бе́лка? *(Belka squats.)* Бе́лка, стоп,† нельзя́!

Никого́. . . *There's no one there.*

help!

(He pushes the emergency button. No response.) **Никого́** нет° . . .
Нельзя́, Бе́лка! *(Yelling.)* Эй, эй, **помоги́те°!**

(Belka barks. The neighbors run up to the elevator.)

Бо́же. . . *Good heavens!*

	БА́БУШКА.	**Бо́же мой°,** лифт опя́ть не рабо́тает. *(She pushes the button several times.)* А там ма́льчик. Како́й кошма́р!
	ЛЕ́НА.	Э́то наш Во́ва и Бе́лка. *(Loudly.)* Во́ва, э́то вы?

Мы. . . *Sure it's us, who else!*

yesterday / work

know how to do

tools

saw / were

VOVA'S VOICE.	Мы, **кто же ещё°!**
ПРОФЕ́ССОР.	Что, лифт опя́ть не рабо́тает? Он и **вчера́°** не рабо́тал°.
БА́БУШКА.	В ли́фте ма́льчик и соба́ка. Что де́лать?
ПРОФЕ́ССОР.	Джим, вы всё **уме́ете.°** Помоги́те, пожа́луйста.
ДЖИМ.	Коне́чно, Илья́ Ильи́ч. У вас есть инструме́нты°?
ПРОФЕ́ССОР.	Да, я их вчера́ ви́дел.° Ка́жется, они́ **бы́ли°** в ку́хне. На по́лке и́ли на столе́. *(He goes to his apartment, returns with a set of tools, and gives them to Jim who immediately starts working on the elevator.)*
ВО́ВА.	Бе́лка, нельзя́! *(The door opens.)*, Ура́† !!!

БА́БУШКА.	Вы **молоде́ц,**° Джим! Молоде́ц!	
ВО́ВА.	Джим, вы америка́нец? Сэ́нк'ю!	*Good job!*
ДЖИМ.	Око́й, Во́ва! Ты говори́шь по-англи́йски? Do you speak English?	
ВО́ВА.	М-м-м . . . **Немно́го.**° В **шко́ле**† у меня́ **пятёрка,**[6] но . . .	
ПРОФЕ́ССОР.	(*Smiling.*) Ничего́, Во́ва, Джим немно́го говори́т по-ру́сски.	*A little*
ВО́ВА.	Джим, **расскажи́те**° **об**° Аме́рике.	
	(*Belka barks.*)	*tell (us) / about*
ЛЁНА.	(*To Jim.*) Извини́те. Во́ва! **Бы́стро**° на у́лицу!	
ВО́ВА.	Бе́лка, пошли́! Джим, спаси́бо, гудба́й!	*Quickly*
ПРОФЕ́ССОР.	(*To Lena and Grandma Kruglov.*) Джим — мой аспира́нт, **исто́рик,**† **у́чится**° у нас в университе́те.	
ЛЁНА.	О́чень прия́тно.	*is a student*
ПРОФЕ́ССОР.	Кро́ме того́, у Джи́ма золоты́е ру́ки.	
БА́БУШКА.	Ма́стер на все ру́ки.° Так°, Джим?	
ДЖИМ.	(*Slightly embarrassed, to Lena and Grandma.*) Здра́вствуйте, меня́ зову́т Джим Ри́чардсон.	*Ма́стер. . . jack-of-all-trades / Isn't that so?*

УПРАЖНЕ́НИЕ 1   Под микроско́пом: **Verb conjugation patterns**

Find an example of each of the following verbs in the reading and indicate for each whether its present tense conjugation follows the **-ешь** or the **-ишь** pattern: **ви́деть, де́лать, говори́ть, гуля́ть, рабо́тать.**

---

[6]**Пятёрка:** a "five", the top grade in Russian schools, equivalent to a grade of "A." See culture note on p. 151.

ГРАММАТИКА И ПРАКТИКА

❖❖ 4.11. PLAYING AN INSTRUMENT

Cа́ша хорошо́ **игра́ет на роя́ле.** *Sasha plays the piano well.*

Playing an instrument is rendered by <**игра́ть на** + Prepositional case> of the instrument.

УПРАЖНЕНИЕ 2   Ты игра́ешь на гита́ре?

Are there any musicians in your class? If you play an instrument, look up its Russian name and use the pattern **Я игра́ю на** . . . , with the name of the instrument in the Prepositional case.

ОБРАЗЕЦ: — Ты игра́ешь на гита́ре (на роя́ле, на фле́йте . . .)?
           — Да, я немно́го игра́ю на . . .
                 or
           — Нет, я игра́ю не на . . . , а на . . .

СЛОВА, СЛОВА, СЛОВА . . . ✪ *Вы лю́бите му́зыку?*

Since many words relating to music are shared among Western European languages, you may recognize most of the following words. Sort them into three groups: *instruments, types of music,* and *people or performers.* Are there any words that don't quite fit any of these categories?

анса́мбль	три́о	гита́ра
вальс	сона́та	кларне́т
кварте́т	увертю́ра	ритм
фле́йта	ту́ба	симфо́ния
саксофо́н	фортепиа́но	орга́н
виолонче́ль	дирижёр	орке́стр
контраба́с	аккордео́н	музыка́нт
тромбо́н	конце́рт	рок-му́зыка
о́пера	бале́т	

❖❖ О РОССИИ ❖❖❖❖❖❖❖❖❖❖❖❖❖❖❖

THE RUSSIAN ACADEMIC GRADING SYSTEM

В шко́ле у меня́ пятёрка…

Grades in Russian schools and colleges are assigned on a five-point scale, from 1 to 5, with 5 being the highest grade. The system (and how students refer to the grades) looks like this:

Отли́чно	5 (пятёрка)	Excellent
Хорошо́	4 (четвёрка)	Good
Удовлетвори́тельно	3 (тро́йка)	Satisfactory
Неудовлетвори́тельно	2 (дво́йка)	Poor
О́чень пло́хо	1 (едини́ца)	Very poor

Both 2 and 1 are failing grades and 1 is in fact very rarely given.

❖❖ 4.12. THE PREPOSITIONS В AND НА

В and **на** are among the most commonly used prepositions in Russian. Both govern the Prepositional case when used to indicate a location.

Uses of **в**
- *In, inside:*   Ле́на живёт в Москве́.
  Мой па́спорт в су́мке.

Uses of **на**
- *On:*   У них на балко́не цветы́. Кни́ги на столе́.
- *At* (a function or event):   Ди́ма на конце́рте. Лари́са на семина́ре.
- *To go by car* (*bus* and so on):   Они́ е́дут на маши́не (на авто́бусе, …).
- *To play an instrument*[7]:   Са́ша хорошо́ игра́ет на роя́ле.
- *Idiomatically:*

  —for some physical locations where you might expect **в**:

на стадио́не	*at/in the stadium*
на фотогра́фии	*in the photo*
на по́чте	*at the post office*

  —in the expression **на у́лице,** which can mean *on* the street, *in* the street, and, in a more general sense, *outside.* For example, **Во́ва на у́лице** most commonly means *Vova is outside.*

---

[7]Remember that *to play a sport or game* is rendered by <**игра́ть в** + Accusative>: **Макси́м и Ко́ля игра́ют в ша́хматы. Ива́н игра́ет в те́ннис.**

УПРАЖНЕНИЕ 3   Вы зна́ете геогра́фию?

Working with a classmate, see what you know about geography and world landmarks.

ОБРАЗЕ́Ц: — Где нахо́дится (*is*) Фра́нция?
— Фра́нция нахо́дится в Евро́пе.

1. _____ Где нахо́дится Нью-Йо́рк?
2. _____ Где нахо́дится музе́й Эрмита́ж?
3. _____ Где нахо́дится Ло́ндон?
4. _____ Где нахо́дится Сент-Лу́ис?
5. _____ Где нахо́дится река́ Амазо́нка?
6. _____ Где нахо́дится Оде́сса?
7. _____ Где нахо́дится Кремль?

а. на реке́ Те́мзе (*Thames River*)
б. в Аме́рике
в. на Чёрном мо́ре (*Black Sea*)
г. в Ю́жной Аме́рике
д. в Санкт-Петербу́рге
е. в Москве́
ж. на реке́ Миссиси́пи

УПРАЖНЕНИЕ 4   В or НА

Fill in the blanks with **в** or **на** as appropriate.

(*Two former classmates run into each other, and one of them is telling the other about her family.*)

Живём мы _____[1] Но́вгороде. Серге́й, мой муж, рабо́тает _____[2] шко́ле. Я рабо́таю _____[3] по́чте. Сын _____[4] Москве́, он у́чится _____[5] университе́те. А Ри́та, на́ша дочь, у́чится _____[6] музыка́льной (*music*) шко́ле. Она́ игра́ет _____[7] скри́пке.

УПРАЖНЕНИЕ 5   Где . . . ?

А. Answer the following questions based on what you learned in the Part 3 reading.

1. Где Во́ва и Бе́лка?
2. А где ба́бушка, Илья́ Ильи́ч и Джим?
3. Где у Ильи́ Ильича́ инструме́нты?
4. Где у́чится Во́ва?
5. А где у́чится Джим?

Б. Make up logical answers.

1. Где живу́т твои́ роди́тели?
2. Где нахо́дится твой университе́т?
3. Где живёт президе́нт США?
4. Где живёт президе́нт Росси́и?

◈ 4.13. *ABOUT:* О + PREPOSITIONAL (AND "BUFFER CONSONANTS")

Джим, расскажи́те **об Аме́рике.**   *Jim, tell us about America.*

The preposition **о** followed by the Prepositional case expresses *about.* When the preposition **о** precedes a word beginning with **а, э, и, о,** or **у,** the resulting two-vowel sequence is broken up by inserting the sound **б** in between them, making the phrase easier to pronounce. (This is similar to the use of *a* vs. *an* in English.) This **б** is called a "buffer consonant." For example:

Мы говори́м (чита́ем, пи́шем, ду́маем) . . .
    о де́душке, о конце́рте, о Москве́, о Япо́нии;

but

    об Аме́рике, об эколо́гии, об институ́те, об океа́не,
    об университе́те

Note that the phrases **О чём . . .?** (*About what?*) and **О ком . . .?** (*About whom?*) are used to make an inquiry: **О чём/О ком вы сейча́с ду́маете**? (*What/Whom are you thinking about now?*)

УПРАЖНЕ́НИЕ 6   Мы говори́м о . . .

A. What subjects do you find interesting? Complete the sentences below.

Я люблю́ говори́ть о (об) . . .
Я никогда́ не (*never*) говорю́ о (об) . . .
Когда́ (*when*) я пишу́ пи́сьма,
    я пишу́ о (об) . . .
Я люблю́ чита́ть о (об) . . .

аэро́бика
Аме́рика
бале́т
ко́смос
литерату́ра
му́зыка
о́пера
поли́тика
спорт
Росси́я
университе́т
???

Б. Now find someone else in the room with similar interests.

ОБРАЗЕ́Ц: — Ты лю́бишь чита́ть о ко́смосе?
            — Да, о́чень люблю́.
                or
            — Нет, не о́чень.

◈ 4.14. PAST TENSE

Что, лифт опя́ть не рабо́тает?   *What, the elevator's not working*
    Он и вчера́ не **рабо́тал.**   *again? It wasn't working yesterday*
                                        either.

Я их вчера́ **ви́дел.** Они́ **бы́ли**   *I saw them yesterday. They were*
    в ку́хне.   *in the kitchen.*

To form the past tense of the vast majority of verbs (both **-ешь** and **-ишь** types), simply delete the **-ть** infinitive ending and add one of four past tense endings.

	ENDING	EXAMPLES
Masculine singular (я, ты, он)	-л	рабóтал, гуля́л, ви́дел
Feminine singular (я, ты, онá)	-ла	рабóтала, гуля́ла, ви́дела
Neuter singular (онó)	-ло	рабóтало, гуля́ло, ви́дело
Formal or plural (мы, вы, они́)	-ли	рабóтали, гуля́ли, ви́дели

Unlike English, Russian has no compound past-tense forms such as *was reading, have read, had read,* and *had been reading.* A compound past form like *He was watching television* and a simple past form like *He watched television* are both expressed by **Он смотрéл телеви́зор.** The Russian past tense is always indicated by the ending of the verb, and no helping verbs (*have, had, has been, had been, was, were*) are needed.

УПРАЖНЕНИЕ 7   А что они́ дéлали вчерá?

Contrast today's activities with yesterday's, using the phrases provided; then make up five of your own.

1. Сегóдня Джим игрáет на роя́ле, а вчерá . . .
2. Сегóдня мы читáем газéты, а вчерá . . .
3. ???

а. слýшать рок-мýзыку (класси́ческую мýзыку, рáдио . . .)
б. игрáть в бейсбóл (тéннис, баскетбóл . . .)
в. писáть письмó, (сочинéние, статью)
г. читáть кни́ги (газéты, журнáлы . . .)
д. гуля́ть в пáрке
е. ???

УПРАЖНЕНИЕ 8 Что ты дéлал (дéлала) вчерá?

Tell three things you did yesterday (**читáл/а кни́гу, слýшал/а рáдио,** and so on) and ask what others did (**Вчерá ты . . .?**).

❖ 4.15. EXPRESSING *WAS, WERE*

Они́ **бы́ли** в кýхне.   *They were in the kitchen.*

Although the *present* tense equivalent of *to be* is not normally expressed in Russian (**я студéнтка**), the *past* tense forms are obligatory. These forms are derived from the infinitive **быть:**

он был
онá былá (note stressed feminine ending)
онó бы́ло
они́ бы́ли

These forms are used in sentences like **Онá былá дóма** (*She was at home*) and **Э́то бы́ло ужáсно** (*That was terrible*). (Do not confuse these sentences with instances of *was, were* as an auxiliary—such as *He was reading* or *They were speaking Japanese.* As you've seen, Russian does not have any past tense auxiliary verb.)

УПРАЖНЕНИЕ 9   Где ты был (была́) вчера́?

Ask a classmate where he was yesterday and what he was doing. Then ask both questions about his sister, brother, friend, parents, and so on. Be prepared to tell the class what you find out.

◇◆◇ О РОССИИ ◇◆◇◆◇◆◇◆◇◆◇◆◇◆◇

WHAT IS RUSSIAN RELATED TO?

Джим немно́го говори́т по-ру́сски.

Russian belongs to one of the world's largest language groups, the Indo-European family of languages. Scholars do not agree on much about the prehistoric people who spoke the ancestral Indo-European language, except that their earliest homeland was near the Black Sea, that some called themselves Aryans, and that they were the precursors not only of most Europeans, but also of Afghans, Iranians, Pakistanis, and northern Indians. As time passed, the common language of the Indo-Europeans gradually evolved into the major languages of those areas: the Indic languages (including Hindi, Urdu, and Bengali), the Iranian languages (including Persian and Kurdish), the Romance languages (including French, Italian, Portuguese, and Spanish), the Germanic languages (including English, Dutch, German, and the Scandinavian languages), the Slavic languages, and others.

   Russian belongs to the Slavic family, which has three major divisions—the East, West, and South Slavic groups. The chart below will help you relate the Slavic languages to one another.

SLAVIC LANGUAGE GROUPS		
Common Slavic	East	Russian* Ukrainian* Byelorussian*
	West	Polish Czech Slovak
	South	Serbian* Croatian Slovenian Bulgarian* Macedonian*

*This language is written in a Cyrillic alphabet.

◈◈ 4.16. TO SPEAK A LANGUAGE

Во́ва, ты **говори́шь по-англи́йски?**   *Vova, do you speak English?*

Джим немно́го **говори́т по-ру́сски.**   *Jim speaks a little Russian.*

To express speaking a certain language, the verb **говори́ть** is used with an adverb composed of **по-** plus a form derived from a nationality adjective like **ру́сский.** Note that the resulting form does not contain a final **-й.** Here are some examples:

говори́ть по-англи́йски	говори́ть по-неме́цки
говори́ть по-ара́бски	говори́ть по-ру́сски
говори́ть по-испа́нски	говори́ть по-францу́зски
говори́ть по-италья́нски	говори́ть по-япо́нски
говори́ть по-кита́йски	

Like days of the week and months of the year, nationalities and languages are not capitalized in Russian except as the first word of a sentence.

УПРАЖНЕНИЕ 10   Кто понима́ет, говори́т, пи́шет по-ру́сски? По-испа́нски?

Can you connect the names of the nationalities with their languages? Some of the nationalities are given in the singular, some in the plural. Choose the necessary verb forms (**говори́т** or **говоря́т,** and so on) to make ten sentences.

ОБРАЗЕ́Ц: *Францу́зы пи́шут по-францу́зски.*

америка́нцы		по-испа́нски
испа́нка		по-по́льски
мексика́нец		по-францу́зски
поля́к		по-болга́рски
ру́сские	говори́т, говоря́т	по-италья́нски
англича́нин	пи́шет, пи́шут	по-англи́йски
францу́з	понима́ет, понима́ют	по-ру́сски
италья́нцы	чита́ет, чита́ют	по-кита́йски
кана́дцы		по-япо́нски
чех		по-че́шски
кита́йцы		по-неме́цки
не́мец		
япо́нцы		
болга́рка		

УПРАЖНЕНИЕ 11   Ты говори́шь по-ру́сски?

Working with a classmate, find out about his or her knowledge of foreign languages by asking:

		по-ру́сски?
		по-испа́нски?
	говори́шь	по-по́льски?
Ты	чита́ешь	по-францу́зски?
	понима́ешь	по-италья́нски?
		по-япо́нски?
		по-неме́цки?
		???

КУЛЬТУРА РЕЧИ

❖❖ ТАК ГОВОРЯТ

This lesson's reading contains two particularly conversational phrases with equivalents or near-equivalents to English in meaning and usage:

Пошли! *Let's go!* Use this with a friend or a group of friends exactly as you would in English. It's actually an irregular past tense form that you'll learn later.

Что, . . . ? *What, . . . ?* (as in, **Что, лифт опять не работает?**) Use this to introduce a question that you're asking not so much to gain information, but rather to seek verification and/or to express surprise, perplexity, and so on.

УПРАЖНЕНИЕ 12   Что, . . . ?

Using **Что, . . . ?**, react to the following situations.

ОБРАЗЕЦ: Your roommate wants to wash his hands. He turns on the faucet, but nothing happens. He might say . . .
— **Что, (опять) нет воды?**

1. You brought some drinks to a friend's party. When you say they need to be chilled, your friend looks a bit upset that you didn't bring cold drinks. You might ask . . .
2. You're describing one of your neighbors, a musician who is always playing too loudly. Your friend looks at you as if he has experienced exactly the same thing. You might ask . . .
3. Your new roommate looks a little uncomfortable when you suggest playing basketball. You might ask . . .
4. A friend is complaining about having to walk up to his apartment on the fourth floor. You might say . . .
5. You offer to fix a friend's broken alarm clock, but when you tell him to get his tools, he just starts looking at the piles of junk around his messy apartment. You might ask . . .
6. You're visiting a friend and you spent the whole day walking around her city. When you tell her you're looking forward to a hot bath, she looks as if she's about to deliver some bad news. You might say . . .
7. You and a friend are in a museum carrying on a conversation at a relatively loud volume. A guard walks up to you and raises a finger to her lips. Your friend might say . . .

✧ САМОПРОВЕРКА: УПРАЖНЕНИЕ 13

Working on your own, try this self-test: Read a Russian sentence out loud, then give an idiomatic English equivalent without looking at the book. Then work from English to Russian. After you have completed the activity, try it with a classmate.

1. — Во́ва, ты говори́шь по-англи́йски?
   — Да, но не о́чень хорошо́.

2. — Ле́на, где ты была́?
   — У Та́ни.
   — Что вы де́лали?
   — Игра́ли в ша́хматы, говори́ли о поли́тике и слу́шали му́зыку.

3. — Ма́ма, ты не зна́ешь, где мои́ кни́ги?
   — Коне́чно, зна́ю! В ку́хне на столе́.

1. *"Vova, do you speak English?"*

   "Yes, but not very well."

2. *"Lena, where have you been?"*
   "At Tanya's."
   "What were you doing?"
   "Playing chess, talking about politics, and listening to music."

3. *"Mom, would you happen to know where my books are?"*
   "Of course I know! In the kitchen, on the table."

✧ ВОПРОСЫ И ОТВЕТЫ: УПРАЖНЕНИЕ 14

1. Ты говори́шь по-япо́нски и́ли по-кита́йски?
2. А по-англи́йски? А по-ру́сски?
3. Ты хорошо́ чита́ешь по-ру́сски? Ты бы́стро чита́ешь по-ру́сски?
4. Ты кана́дка и́ли америка́нка?
5. Как по-тво́ему, ты уже́ хорошо́ зна́ешь ру́сский язы́к?
6. Каки́е языки́ ты зна́ешь?
7. О чём ты лю́бишь чита́ть — о му́зыке, о поли́тике, о любви́ (*love*)?

✧ ДИАЛОГИ

ДИАЛОГ 1 Как по-ру́сски . . . ?
(Asking how to say something in Russian)

   — Как по-ру́сски *journalist*?
   — Журнали́ст, журнали́стка.
   — А как по-ру́сски *The journalist is writing an article*?
   — Журнали́ст (и́ли журнали́стка) пи́шет статьёй.
   — Спаси́бо.
   — Пожа́луйста.

ДИАЛОГ 2 Вы о́чень хорошо́ говори́те по-францу́зски
(Discussing knowledge of foreign languages)

   — Вы о́чень хорошо́ говори́те по-францу́зски. Вы жи́ли во Фра́нции?
   — Да, я жила́ там два го́да (*two years*). В Пари́же. Я говори́ла то́лько по-францу́зски.
   — А каки́е ещё языки́ (*what other languages*) вы зна́ете?
   — Я непло́хо говорю́ по-италья́нски и по-испа́нски. И (*smiling*) немно́го говорю́ по-ру́сски.

УПРАЖНЕНИЕ 15   Ваш диало́г

Make up a dialogue in which a curious friend asks all sorts of questions about things you did and places you were yesterday.

❖ А ТЕПЕРЬ...: УПРАЖНЕНИЕ 16

Working with a classmate, use what you learned in Part 3 to ...

1. tell what languages you speak and ask if your classmate also speaks those languages
2. ask how to say the name of some particular musical instrument in Russian
3. find out if your classmate plays that instrument
4. say what you like to read about and find out what your classmate likes to read about
5. say where you were and what you were doing yesterday, then ask your classmate where he was and what he was doing
6. say you saw something (a cat, a table, a dog ...) on the street yesterday and find out if your classmate also saw it

С ЧЕГО НАЧАТЬ?

АНОНИ́МНЫЕ† АЛКОГО́ЛИКИ†

Расскажи́те, пожа́луйста, кака́я у вас профе́ссия, где вы рабо́таете.

Я **почтальо́н**, рабо́таю на по́чте.

Я **официа́нтка**, рабо́таю в **рестора́не**.†

Я **юри́ст**. У меня́ ча́стная пра́ктика.†

Я **инжене́р**,† рабо́таю на **заво́де**.

Я **води́тель** такси́.†

Я био́лог,† рабо́таю в лаборато́рии.†

Я хи́мик.† Я рабо́таю в фи́рме.†

Я миллионе́р.† Я не рабо́таю.

води́тель	*driver*
заво́д	*factory*
официа́нт/официа́нтка	*waiter/waitress*
почтальо́н	*mail carrier*
ча́стный	*private*
юри́ст	*lawyer*

ЧТЕНИЕ

❖ ÓЧЕНЬ ПРИЯ́ТНО ПОЗНАКÓМИТЬСЯ°

Óчень… *Very nice to meet you.*

(Lena and Jim, still at the elevator, continue talking.)

ЛÉНА. Джим, вы хорошó говори́те по-ру́сски.

ДЖИМ. Нет, **ещё не**° óчень, но спаси́бо. Здесь, в Москвé, я говорю́ по-ру́сски, а дóма у меня́ нет **никакóй прáктики.**° Лéна, а вы живёте здесь, в э́том подъéзде, да?

ЛÉНА. Да, вторóй этáж. Э́то хорошó, что вторóй, **потому́ что**° наш лифт **никогдá**° не рабóтает.

ДЖИМ. А вы у́читесь и́ли рабóтаете?

ЛÉНА. Я студéнтка, учу́сь в университéте на **факультéте**° журнали́стики.[†] Джим, **мóжно**° задáть вам вопрóс°? Илья́ Ильи́ч говори́т, что вы всё умéете. Я знáю, что вы умéете **чини́ть**° ли́фты. А что ещё° вы умéете?

ДЖИМ. У меня́ **неплохóй**° **óпыт.**° У нас в Амéрике студéнты и аспирáнты **обы́чно**° рабóтают. Я тóже рабóтал, **когдá**° учи́лся в университéте. Я рабóтал в **магази́не электрóники**°, в автосéрвисе° и дáже на **би́рже.**°

ЛÉНА. Знáчит, вы не тóлько истóрик, но и **элéктрик,**[†] и **автомехáник,**[†] и дáже брóкер.[†]

ДЖИМ. Я, конéчно, не **настоя́щий**° брóкер, но я понимáю, как рабóтает **би́ржа.**

ЛÉНА. **Затó**° вы замечáтельный элéктрик. Э́то отли́чная профéссия!

ДЖИМ. И **всегдá**° есть рабóта!

ПРОФÉССОР. *(From a distance.)* Джим, где вы?

ДЖИМ. Иду́, Илья́ Ильи́ч. *(To Lena.)* Извини́те. Óчень прия́тно познакóмиться.

ЛÉНА. До свидáния, Джим.

ещё не… *not yet*
никакóй… *no practice at all*

потому́… *because*
never

department
may I / задáть… *ask you a question*
fix / что… *what else*
pretty good / *experience*
usually / *when*
магази́не… *electronics store* / *automotive shop*
stock exchange

real

But then
always

УПРАЖНЕНИЕ 1   Под микроскóпом: Prepositional case

There are nine examples of the Prepositional case in this reading. List them.

ГРАММАТИКА И ПРАКТИКА

◆◇О РОССИИ ◆◇◆◇◆◇◆◇◆◇◆◇◆◇

RESPONDING TO COMPLIMENTS

*ЛÉНА. **Вы хорошó говорúте по-рýсски.***
*ДЖИМ. **Нет, ещё не óчень, но спасúбо.***

Self-promotion is less acceptable in Russian culture than it is in American. Not only do you not "toot your own horn" in Russian culture, but indeed, even responses to praise—including well-deserved compliments—are rather subdued. When Russians are complimented, they invariably thank the person offering the compliment (**Спасúбо** or **Спасúбо за комплимéнт**), and often say something to show that the praise is not taken for granted.

УПРАЖНЕНИЕ 2   Комплимéнты

Working with a classmate, practice giving and replying to compliments. Select replies—which are appropriate for many situations—from the list on the right.

ОБРАЗÉЦ: — Ты хорошó говорúшь по-рýсски!
— Спасúбо, но я говорю́ ещё не óчень хорошó.

1. — Ты хорошó игрáешь в баскетбóл!
2. — У тебя óчень красúвый пóчерк (*handwriting*).
3. — У тебя харóшее произношéние (*pronunciation*)!
4. — У тебя золотые рýки!
5. — Ты прекрáсно танцýешь (*dance*)!
6. — Ты мáстер на все рýки!
7. — Ты так хорошó ирáешь на гитáре.
8. — Я читáю твою́ (*your*) статью́. Ты пúшешь óчень оригинáльно.
9. — Ты неплóхо знáешь граммáтику.[†]
10. — Ты так хорошó знáешь литератýру.[†]

⎰ — Спасúбо.
⎱ — Спасúбо за комплимéнт.
— Нет, ещё не óчень, но спасúбо.

❖❖ 4.17. DOUBLE NEGATIVES

Наш лифт **никогда́ не** рабо́тает.	*Our elevator never works.*
Никого́ нет.	*There's no one there.*

Two expressions of a negative in one sentence—**никогда́** and **не** in the example above—are perfectly proper in Russian. Many Russian question words can be prefixed with **ни-** and used in negative sentences. The most common negative form of **что** is **ничего́**. The pronoun **кто** becomes **никто́** in the Nominative and **никого́** in the Genitive and Accusative.

Мы **ничего́ не** де́лаем.	*We're not doing anything.*
Никто́ не зна́ет, где он.	*No one knows where he is.*

УПРАЖНЕНИЕ 3   Negatives

Look at the question words on the left and provide their negative forms in the blank:

ОБРАЗЕ́Ц: когда́   *никогда́*   never, not ever

1. кто   _____   no one, nobody, not . . . anyone
2. где   _____   (*location*) nowhere, not . . . anywhere
3. куда́   _____   (*direction*) nowhere, not . . . anywhere
4. как   _____   (in) no way, not . . . at all
5. како́й   _____   no, not . . . any

УПРАЖНЕНИЕ 4   Answering in the negative

Working with a classmate, respond negatively to the questions below. Remember to negate the verb with **не**.

ОБРАЗЕ́Ц: — Что ты пи́шешь? — *Я ничего́ не пишу́.*

1. — Где ты у́чишься?
2. — А где ты рабо́таешь?
3. — Что же ты де́лаешь?
4. — Что ты говори́шь?
5. — Ты не рабо́таешь, но зато́ твой оте́ц мно́го рабо́тает. Когда́ он спит?
6. — Я зна́ю, что ты тут не живёшь. А кто тут живёт?

❖❖ 4.18. PERMISSION AND PROHIBITION: *ONE MAY/MAY NOT*

Джим, **мо́жно** зада́ть вам вопро́с?	*Jim, may I ask you a question?*
У нас **нельзя́** игра́ть гро́мко.	*You can't play loudly at our place.*
Бе́лка, стоп, **нельзя́**!	*Belka, stop, don't!*

To express permission and prohibition, use the following words with an infinitive phrase.

PERMISSION = МÓЖНО	**PROHIBITION** = НЕЛЬЗЯ́
Здесь мо́жно кури́ть? *May one smoke here?*	У нас нельзя́ игра́ть гро́мко. *You can't (aren't allowed to) play loudly at our place.*

УПРАЖНЕНИЕ 5   Мо́жно и́ли нельзя́?

Complete the sentences below using **мо́жно** or **нельзя́**. More than one answer may be correct.

1. _____ гро́мко игра́ть на саксофо́не, когда́ сосе́ди спят.
2. Здесь _____ гуля́ть?
3. Ми́ша, _____ спать на балко́не!
4. _____ говори́ть по-ру́сски?
5. Почему́ ты говори́шь так ти́хо? Здесь _____ говори́ть гро́мко.
6. _____ зада́ть вам вопро́с?
7. _____ кури́ть (*smoke*) в ли́фте.

УПРАЖНЕНИЕ 6   У нас до́ма нельзя́ . . .

What rules are there at your house? What rules *should* there be? Working with one or two other classmates, make up some rules of your own, following the examples in the previous exercise.

❖❖ 4.19. REFLEXIVE VERB УЧИ́ТЬСЯ

Джим **у́чится** у нас в университе́те.	*Jim studies at our university.*
Я **учу́сь** на факульте́те журнали́стики.	*I am majoring in journalism.*

Some verbs, such as **учи́ться**, have a suffix attached. This suffix is spelled **-ся** after consonants and **-сь** after vowels. These verbs are called "reflexive" verbs; you will learn more about them later. For now, just learn the conjugation of the **-ишь** reflexive verb **учи́ться** (shown below). Note that the **я**-form ending has **-у-** (rather than **-ю-**) and the **они́**-form ending has **-а-** (rather than **-я-**) as required by the «**ви́жу**» spelling rule (Part 2).

ГОВОРИ́ТЬ *TO SAY, SPEAK, TALK* (for reference)	УЧИ́ТЬСЯ *TO STUDY, BE A STUDENT*
я говор **-ю́**	я уч-у́ **-сь**
ты говор **-и́шь**	ты у́ч-**ишь-ся**
он, она́ говор **-и́т**	он, она́ у́ч-**ит** **-ся**
мы говор **-и́м**	мы у́ч-**им** **-ся**
вы говор **-и́те**	вы у́ч-**ите** **-сь**
они́ говор **-я́т**	они́ у́ч-**ат** **-ся**

УПРАЖНЕНИЕ 7   Кто где у́чится?

Fill in the blanks using the verb **учи́ться**.

У нас больша́я семья́, и мы все где-нибу́дь *(somewhere)* _____.¹
Я _____² в университе́те, на факульте́те биоло́гии. Мои́ сёстры
Ве́ра и Ка́тя то́же _____³: Ве́ра _____⁴
в Политехни́ческом† институ́те, а Ка́тя — в шко́ле. Мой брат Артём уже́
рабо́тает. Он рабо́тает в лаборато́рии, а ве́чером _____⁵
на ку́рсах *(classes)* англи́йского языка́. Ма́ма то́же _____⁶
на ку́рсах англи́йского языка́. Па́па нигде́ не _____,⁷
но говори́т, что хо́чет *(wants)* _____.⁸ А ба́бушка говори́т: «Э́то
прекра́сно, что вы все _____⁹!»

О РОССИИ

GOING TO COLLEGE IN RUSSIA

Я учу́сь на факульте́те журнали́стики.

Russian institutions of higher learning include universities (**университе́ты**), institutes (**институ́ты**) and a smaller number of academies (**акаде́мии**). Until the late 1980s, **университе́ты** tended to concentrate on the pure sciences and the humanities, while **институ́ты** generally provided education in technology, engineering, architecture, medicine, law, and so on. Although this distinction still exists, the names (**университе́т** and **институ́т**) do not reflect it as clearly as before: since the late 1980s, many specialized **институ́ты** have changed their names to **университе́ты**.

Russian educational institutions differ in structure from their American counterparts. They are usually divided into administrative units called **факульте́ты**, which represent broad academic disciplines. In addition, some universities have divisions called **институ́ты**, which may then be divided into **факульте́ты**. For example, the **Росси́йский госуда́рственный гуманита́рный университе́т** (*Russian State University for the Humanities*) has individual **факульте́ты** such as **филосо́фский** (*philosophy*) **факульте́т** and **факульте́т информа́тики** (*computer science*). This university also has the **Институ́т эконо́мики, управле́ния и пра́ва** (*economics, management, and law*) with separate **факульте́ты** for each of those three areas. A **факульте́т** may have further subdivisions, called **отделе́ния**, for more narrow areas of specialization. Faculty with the same area of specialization are grouped into **ка́федры**. The American notion of "department" is commonly translated as **ка́федра**.

Each **факульте́т** provides specialized education from the very beginning of a course of study. As a result, Russians—unlike Americans—must select their future specialty before applying to an institution of higher learning. Moreover, Russian applicants must take a competitive entrance exam for the specific institution to which they apply because there are no national standardized college-entrance exams.

❖ **4.20.** *TO KNOW AND TO KNOW HOW*: ЗНАТЬ **AND** УМЕ́ТЬ

Я зна́ю, что вы **уме́ете** чини́ть лифты. А что ещё вы **уме́ете**?	*I know you know how to fix elevators. What else do you know how to do?*

Used by itself, the English verb *to know* refers to knowing someone or something. It is also used in the expression *to know how* (*to do something*). Russian distinguishes between these two meanings by using **знать** in the former case and **уме́ть** (also a regular vowel-stem **-ешь** verb) in the latter.

УПРАЖНЕ́НИЕ 8   Кто зна́ет (уме́ет) . . .?

Which of our characters knows (or knows how to do) each of the following?

1. _____ уме́ет игра́ть на роя́ле.
2. _____ зна́ет, что симпати́чная блонди́нка — их сосе́дка.
3. _____ уме́ет чини́ть лифты.
4. _____ зна́ют, что лифт пло́хо рабо́тает.
5. _____ зна́ет, как рабо́тает би́ржа (*stock exchange*).
6. _____ уме́ет игра́ть рок и джаз.

УПРАЖНЕ́НИЕ 9   Minisurvey: знать and уме́ть

How many of your classmates know how to play the violin? How many know the name of the author of *War and Peace* («**Война́ и мир**»)? Using one of the following models, ask at least six classmates and report your results.

1. Ты уме́ешь игра́ть на скри́пке? На гита́ре? На фле́йте?
2. Ты зна́ешь, кто а́втор[†] «Войны́ и ми́ра»? «Евге́ния Оне́гина»? «Мо́би Ди́ка»?

СЛОВА́, СЛОВА́, СЛОВА́ . . . ✪ *Professions and Occupations*

Many Russian words denoting professions, occupations, military ranks and the like are related to the English terms. You already know **музыка́нт, студе́нт, профе́ссор, журнали́ст,** and **пиани́ст.** Working with a classmate, read aloud the occupations in the following list and try to come up with the name of a famous person for each category. Compare your results with another pair of students and see how many overlap.

а́втор	лейтена́нт
актёр	ме́неджер
архите́ктор	секрета́рша
астроно́м	сержа́нт
ба́рмен	фи́зик
био́лог	фото́граф
гео́лог	хи́мик
инжене́р	шофёр
кло́ун	эле́ктрик
гео́граф	

КУЛЬТУРА РЕЧИ

❖ ТАК ГОВОРЯТ: ЗАТО́...

Зато́ is used to introduce a balancing or compensatory statement.

— Я, коне́чно, не настоя́щий бро́кер, но я понима́ю, как рабо́тает би́ржа.	*"Of course, I'm not a real broker, but I understand how the stock exchange works."*
— **Зато́** вы замеча́тельный эле́ктрик.	*"But then again, you're a wonderful electrician."*

УПРАЖНЕНИЕ 10   Зато́

Match each statement on the left with an appropriate follow-up compensatory statement on the right. Then, working with a classmate, see if you can make up a different follow-up statement for each of the items on the left.

1. _____ — И́горь Алекса́ндрович говори́т и по-францу́зски, и по-испа́нски, и по-италья́нски.

а. — Зато́ ты прекра́сно говори́шь по-испа́нски!

2. _____ — Я не о́чень хорошо́ говорю́ по-ру́сски.

б. — Зато́ у вас хоро́шая кварти́ра.

3. _____ — Мы живём далеко́.

в. — Зато́ *ты* говори́шь по-кита́йски!

❖ САМОПРОВЕРКА: УПРАЖНЕНИЕ 11

Working on your own, try this self-test: Read a Russian sentence out loud, then give an idiomatic English equivalent without looking at the book. Then work from English to Russian. After you have completed the activity, try it with a classmate.

1. — Зна́чит, вы живёте здесь?
— Да. Э́то мой подъе́зд. Второ́й эта́ж. Э́то хорошо́, что второ́й, потому́ что наш лифт никогда́ не рабо́тает.

2. — Ни́на, мо́жно зада́ть вам вопро́с? Вы у́читесь и́ли рабо́таете?
— Я студе́нтка, учу́сь в консервато́рии.

3. Я зна́ю, что вы уме́ете чини́ть ли́фты. А что ещё вы уме́ете?

1. *"So, you live here?"*
"Yes. This is my entrance. Second floor. It's good that it's the second, because our elevator never works."

2. *"Nina, can I ask you a question? Do you go to school or do you work?"*
"I'm a student. I study at the conservatory."

3. *I know you know how to fix elevators. What else do you know how to do?*

❖❖ ВОПРОСЫ И ОТВЕТЫ: УПРАЖНЕНИЕ 12

1. Ты у́чишься и́ли рабо́таешь?

*if the response is **учу́сь** …*	*if the response is **рабо́таю** …*
2. Где ты у́чишься?	**2.** Где ты рабо́таешь?
3. Ты студе́нтка и́ли аспира́нтка?	**3.** Ты мно́го рабо́таешь?

4. Ты хорошо́ говори́шь по-ру́сски?

5. У тебя́ есть пра́ктика в ру́сском языке́?

6. Ты мно́го чита́ешь по-ру́сски?

7. Ты до́ма говори́шь по-ру́сски?	**7.** Ты на рабо́те говори́шь по-ру́сски?

8. Твои́ роди́тели зна́ют ру́сский язы́к?

❖❖ ДИАЛОГИ

ДИАЛОГ 1 Я не уме́ю игра́ть на виолонче́ли
(Discussing musical abilities)

— Э́то твоя́ виолонче́ль? Я не зна́ла, что ты игра́ешь на виолонче́ли.

— Я не уме́ю игра́ть на виолонче́ли. Э́то виолонче́ль Ната́ши, мое́й
(*my*) сестры́.

— Она́ хорошо́ игра́ет?

— Коне́чно! Она́ преподаёт в консервато́рии.

— Мой брат у́чится в консервато́рии.

— Мо́жет быть, моя́ сестра́ его́ зна́ет.

ДИАЛОГ 2 О́чень прия́тно познако́миться
(Getting acquainted)

— Вы здесь живёте?

— Да, вот моя́ кварти́ра.

— Так мы сосе́ди! Меня́ зову́т Мари́я Анто́новна.

— А меня́ — Бори́с Васи́льевич. О́чень прия́тно познако́миться.

— О́чень прия́тно.

УПРАЖНЕНИЕ 13   Ваш диало́г

Create a dialogue in which you're getting acquainted with a new roommate or
classmate. Ask and answer questions about where you and she live, what you like to do,
what you know how to do, what languages you speak, what things you own, what you
like to read, talk, or write about, and so on.

❖❖ А ТЕПЕРЬ … : УПРАЖНЕНИЕ 14

Working with a classmate, use what you learned in Part 4 to …

1. find out if she works, and if so, where
2. tell your mother's (father's, …) occupation and where she (he) works
3. ask if your classmate's mother (father, …) works; if so, find out where
4. find out if your classmate knows how to play the piano (play chess, …)

УЧИСЬ УЧИТЬСЯ ⭐ *Good Study Practices*

1. *Always learn the* **я, ты,** *and* **они** *forms with each new infinitive.* This will tell you whether the verb is a **-ешь** or **-ишь** type, whether it has a stem change, and what its stress pattern is. This information will help you not only now but also in later lessons with other verb forms.

2. Every few days *go through the flash cards* you made for vocabulary and phrases of an earlier lesson, to refresh them in your memory.

3. *Build and use your own personal vocabulary* (your instructor can help you). You may want to say you collect stamps (**я собираю марки**), have a pet crocodile (**у меня дома есть крокодил**), or live in a cave (**я живу в пещере**—even if it's not true). Learn and use these expressions in class. Language learning means expressing ourselves, and we're all different. Through repeated use, your classmates will learn words and phrases from you, just as you will from them.

4. When homework or tests are corrected and returned, *go over any errors you made* to be sure you understand them; then make flash cards on those points and practice them so that you won't make the same errors again.

5. *Prepare for a test in the manner that you will be tested.* Before a written vocabulary test, practice writing out vocabulary words (especially English to Russian). Before an oral test, practice asking and answering questions with a friend. Before a test that will involve grammar, review the kinds of exercises in the textbook and the workbook that are likely to be on the test. If the test will involve English-to-Russian translation, practice translating sentences in the textbook or workbook from Russian to English and then translating them back into Russian without looking at the original (see, for example, the **Самопроверка** in each Part).

6. *Periodically read into a tape recorder* and listen critically to yourself. You will hear where your pronunciation and phrasing are awkward or hesitant, and then you can practice those words and phrases in context.

 # ИТАК…

❖❖ НОВЫЕ СЛОВА

NOUNS

Professions

автомеханик	auto mechanic (4)
водитель такси	taxi driver (4v)
инженер	engineer (4v)
историк	historian (3)
официант/официантка	waiter/waitress (4v)
почтальон	mail carrier (4v)
преподаватель/ преподавательница	instructor (in college); teacher (3v)
электрик	electrician (4)
юрист	lawyer (4v)

Places of work

биржа	stock exchange (4)
завод	plant; factory (4v)
лаборатория	laboratory (4v)
магазин электроники	electronics store (4)
ресторан	restaurant (4v)
фирма	firm; business; company (4v)

House, Apartment

ванна	bathtub (1)
вода (*Acc. sing.* воду)	water (1)
душ	shower (1)

Appliances, Gadgets

будильник	alarm clock (1v)
микроволновая печь	microwave oven (1v)
пылесос	vacuum cleaner (1v)

стира́льная маши́на	washing machine (1v)	нас	us (1)
то́стер [*pronounced* -тэ]	toaster (1v)	вас(*formal or pl.*)	you (1)
холоди́льник	refrigerator (1v)	их (них)	them (1)
электро́ника	electronics (4)		

Studies, University, School

ADJECTIVES

вопро́с	question (4)	моско́вский	Moscow (2v)
ка́федра	department (3v)	настоя́щий	real; true (4)
контро́льная	test; quiz (2)	неплохо́й	pretty good; not
noun, declines like adj.			(a) bad (4)
пра́ктика	practice (4)	несимпати́чный	unpleasant (2)
пятёрка	a "five" (top grade in	никако́й	no . . . (at all); not any (4)
	Russian schools) (3)	ужа́сный	horrible; terrible (1)
уро́к (*usu. pl.* уро́ки)	homework (3)		
факульте́т	department (4)	**VERBS**	
шко́ла	school (3)	быть[8]	to be (3)
язы́к	language (3v)	ви́деть (ви́ж-у,	to see (2)

Arts, Music, Entertainment

бале́т	ballet (2v)	ви́д-ишь, . . . ви́д-ят)	
гру́ппа	group (2v)	говори́ть (говор-ю́,	1. to speak; to talk;
джаз	jazz (2v)	говор-и́шь, . . . говор-я́т)	2. to say; to tell (2)
зал	hall; auditorium (2v)	есть	there is (are) (1)
клуб	club (2v)	люби́ть (любл-ю́,	1. to love; 2. to like (2v)
музе́й	museum (2v)	лю́б-ишь, . . . лю́б-ят)	
о́пера	opera (2v)	преподава́ть (препода-ю́,	to teach (3v)

Other Nouns

гость (*Gen. sing.*	guest (2)	препода-ёшь, . . .	
го́стя)/го́стья		препода-ю́т)	
день рожде́ния	birthday (2)	смотре́ть (смотр-ю́,	to look (at); to watch (2)
дире́ктор	director; manager (1)	смо́тр-ишь, . . . смо́тр-ят)	
же́нщина	woman (2)	спать (спл-ю́,	to sleep (2)
кошма́р	nightmare (1)	сп-ишь, . . . сп-ят)	
миллионе́р	millionaire (4v)	уме́ть (уме́-ю, уме́-ешь, . . .	to know how (to do some-
о́пыт	experience (4)	уме́-ют)	thing); to be able to (3)
пробле́ма	problem (1)	учи́ться (уч-у́сь,	to study; to be a
такси́ *neut. indecl.*	taxi; cab (4v)	у́ч-ишься, . . . у́ч-атся)	student (3)
у́жас	horror (1)	чини́ть (чин-ю́,	to fix; to repair (4)

PRONOUNS

чи́н-ишь, . . . чи́н-ят)	

все (*pl. of* весь)	everybody; everyone (2)	**ADVERBS**	
всё	everything; all (2)	бы́стро	quickly; fast (3)
никого́ *Gen. and Acc. of*	no one; nobody (4)	всегда́	always (4)
никто́		вчера́	yesterday (3)
никто́	no one; nobody (3)	гро́мко	loudly (2)

Genitive Pronouns

		ещё	else (3)
кого́	whom (1)	ещё не . . .	not yet (4)
чего́	what (1)	когда́	when (4)
меня́	me (1)	немно́го	a little (3)
тебя́ (*informal sg.*)	you (1)	никогда́	never (4)
его́ (него́)	him, it (1)	обы́чно	usually (4)
её (неё)	her, it (1)	по-англи́йски	(in) English (3v)
		по-испа́нски	(in) Spanish (3v)
		по-италья́нски	(in) Italian (3v)
		по-кита́йски	(in) Chinese (3v)

[8]For the time being use **быть** in the past tense only.

по-неме́цки — (in) German (3v)
по-португа́льски — (in) Portuguese (3v)
по-ру́сски — (in) Russian (3v)
пото́м — later (on) (3)
по-францу́зски — (in) French (3v)
по-япо́нски — (in) Japanese (3v)
сли́шком — too (2)
ти́хо — quietly; softly (2)
то́лько — only (2)

OTHER

же *particle (used for emphasis)* — surely; after all (3)

зато́ (*often* но зато́) — but (then); but on the other hand (4)

заче́м — what (does one need . . .) for; why (1)

мо́жно — one can; one may (4)

невозмо́жно — (it's/that's) impossible (1)

нельзя́ — one may not; it is forbidden (2)

нет *predicative (usu.* у + *Gen.* + нет + *Gen.*) — I (you, *etc.*) don't have . . . ; I (you, *etc.*) have no . . . (1)

о (об) (+ *Prep.*) — about; of (3)

IDIOMS AND EXPRESSIONS

Бо́же мой — Good heavens!; My goodness! (3)

Вот ви́дишь (ви́дите)! — You see!; See! (2)
Всё слы́шно. — I (we, and so on) can hear everything. (2)

говори́ть по-англи́йски (по-ру́сски, *etc.*) — to speak English (Russian, *etc.*) (3v)
золоты́е ру́ки (у + *Gen.*) — (one is) good with one's hands (3)

игра́ть на роя́ле (на гита́ре) — to play the piano (guitar) (3)
Кто (что) ещё? — Who (what) else? (3)
мо́жет быть *parenthetical* — maybe; perhaps (2)
Мо́жно зада́ть вам вопро́с? — May I ask you a question? (4)

Молоде́ц! — Good job!; Well done! (3)
О́чень прия́тно познако́миться. — (It's/It was) very nice to meet you. (4)
Помоги́те! — Help! (3)
потому́ что — because (4)
Пошли́! — Let's go! (3)
Прекра́сно! — It's (that's) wonderful! (1)
Расскажи́те о (об) . . . — Tell me (us) about . . . (3)
то есть (*often abbreviated* т. е.) — that is (1)

У меня́ (есть) . . . , у тебя́ (есть) . . . , *etc.* — I have . . . , you have . . . , *etc.* (1v)
Что де́лать? — What should (can) we (I) do? (2v)

❖❖ ЧТО Я ЗНАЮ, ЧТО Я УМЕЮ

Use this checklist to mark off what you've learned in this lesson:

☐ Using **есть** to ask whether someone possesses something (Part 1)
☐ Expressing possession: <**у** + Genitive nouns> (Part 2)
☐ Asking what kind of things someone has (Part 1)
☐ Saying someone or something is missing, lacking or absent <**нет** + Genitive> (Part 1)
☐ Linking nouns together with the Genitive case (Part 2)
☐ Conjugation of -**ишь** verbs (Part 2)
☐ Stem changes in -**ишь** verbs (Part 2)
☐ The «**ви́жу**» spelling rule (Part 2)
☐ Conjugating reflexive verbs like **учи́ться** (Part 4)
☐ Forming past tense of verbs (Part 3)
☐ Talking about playing a musical instrument (Part 3)
☐ Using the prepositions **в** and **на** (Part 3)
☐ Expressing English "about" in Russian (Part 3)
☐ Use of buffer consonants (Part 3)
☐ Saying what languages people speak (Part 3)
☐ Using double negatives (Part 4)
☐ Expressing permission and prohibition with **мо́жно** and **нельзя́** (Part 4)
☐ Distinguishing between "knowing" and "knowing how" (Part 4)

❖❖ ЭТО НАДО ЗНАТЬ

CASE USES

Here is a summary of the uses of the cases that you have learned to date:

CASE	USE (+ where discussed)	EXAMPLE
Nominative	Subject of a sentence (1/3)	Мо́жет быть, **Серге́й Петро́вич** спит. **Наш лифт** никогда́ не рабо́тает. У нас в Аме́рике **студе́нты** и **аспира́нты** обы́чно рабо́тают.
	Predicate nominative (1/3)	Моя́ сестра́ — **аспира́нтка.**
Accusative	Direct object of a verb (3/2)	Я зна́ю, что вы уме́ете чини́ть **ли́фты.** Ты игра́ешь не то́лько **кла́ссику. Джаз** и **рок** ты то́же игра́ешь.
	To show direction or destination: object of prepositions «**в**» and «**на**» (3/3)	Джим, а вы зна́ете, как е́хать **в аэропо́рт?**
	In the idiom «**игра́ть в**» (to play a sport or game) (3/4)	Ты лю́бишь игра́ть **в ша́хматы?**
Genitive	To show possession: object of preposition «**у**» (4/1, 4/2)	**У вас** но́вые кварти́ры! **У меня́** то́же. Мо́жет быть, **у Во́вы** за́втра контро́льная.
	With «**нет**» to state a lack or absence of something or someone (4/1)	У неё **нет ва́нны,** а у меня́ нет **ду́ша.** До́ма у меня́ **нет никако́й пра́ктики.**
	Noun linkage (4/2)	Я студе́нтка, учу́сь в университе́те на факульте́те **журнали́стики.** Ты зна́ешь его́ но́мер **телефо́на?** Вы не зна́ете, где остано́вка **авто́буса?**
Prepositional	To show location: object of prepositions «**в**» and «**на**» (3/1, 4/3)	Я рабо́тал **в магази́не** электро́ники, **в автосе́рвисе** и да́же **на би́рже.**
	In the idiom «**игра́ть на**» (to play a musical instrument) (4/3)	Са́ша хорошо́ игра́ет **на роя́ле.**
	To show means of transportation: object of preposition «**на**» (4/3)	Как вы сего́дня е́дете домо́й? **На маши́не** и́ли **на авто́бусе?**
	Object of the preposition «**о/об**» "about" (4/3)	Мы говори́ли **о де́душке.**

❖ ДОПОЛНИТЕЛЬНЫЕ ТЕКСТЫ

A. EVENTS CALENDAR

МУ́ЗЫКА	О́ПЕРА

Четве́рг, 23 октября́
Ка́мерный Бетхо́вен

Фортепиа́нный кварте́т "Клавио́ль" в соста́ве: И́горь Гусе́льников (фортепиа́но), Ди́на Аха́нова (скри́пка), Мари́на Судзило́вская (альт) и Серге́й Судзило́вский (виолонче́ль) — игра́ет ка́мерные произведе́ния Бетхо́вена.

Музе́й Скря́бина, 18.30. 241 19 01. Бол. Николопеско́вский пер., 11, Ⓜ "Смоле́нская"

Четве́рг, 23 октября́
Влади́мир Спивако́в

Худо́жественный руководи́тель ка́мерного орке́стра «Виртуо́зы Москвы́» игра́ет со́льную скрипи́чную програ́мму. У роя́ля — коре́йский пиани́ст Кун Ву Пек.

Конце́ртный зал им. Чайко́вского, 19.00. 299 36 81, 299 39 57. Триумфа́льная пл., 4/31, Ⓜ "Маяко́вская"

Пя́тница, 24 октября́
Дед и внук

Скрипачи́ Ви́ктор и И́горь Пика́йзен, альти́ст И́горь На́йдин из кварте́та им. Бороди́на́ и ка́мерный орке́стр "Cantus firmus" под управле́нием Алекса́ндра Хургина́. В програ́мме — произведе́ния Мо́царта.

Ма́лый зал Моско́вской консервато́рии, 19.00. 229 77 95. Бол. Ники́тская, 13, Ⓜ "Библиоте́ка им. Ле́нина", "Охо́тный ряд", "Арба́тская"

Среда́, 22 октября́
«Любо́вь к трём апельси́нам» С. Проко́фьева

Режиссёр Пи́тер Усти́нов. Спекта́кль сде́лан в европе́йской мане́ре. Домини́руют сти́льные моде́рновые декора́ции Оле́га Ше́йнциса.

Большо́й теа́тр, 19.00. 292 00 50, 292 99 86. Театра́льная пл., 1, Ⓜ "Театра́льная", "Охо́тный ряд"

Воскресе́нье, 26 октября́
«Ска́зка о царе́ Салта́не» Н. Ри́мского-Ко́рсакова

В спекта́кле Алекса́ндра Ти́теля мно́го режиссёрской фанта́зии и театра́льных трю́ков.

Музыка́льный теа́тр им. К. С. Станисла́вского и В. И. Немиро́вича-Да́нченко, 12.00. 229 06 49, 229 83 88. Б. Дми́тровка, 17, Ⓜ "Че́ховская"

Вто́рник, 28 октября́
Дивертисме́нт Росси́ни

Фрагме́нты коми́ческих о́пер Росси́ни «Севи́льский цирю́льник» и «Италья́нка в Алжи́ре». Кро́ме того́, впервы́е на моско́вской сце́не звуча́т фрагме́нты ме́нее изве́стных у нас о́пер компози́тора, в том числе́ уника́льный хор спа́сшихся евре́ев из о́перы «Моисе́й в Еги́пте».

Но́вая о́пера, 19.00. Репетицио́нная сце́на. 911 14 40. Тага́нская, 40/42, Ⓜ "Маркси́стская"

Му́зыка

1. Which composer's work will be performed at the **Музе́й Скря́бина**?
2. Which musicians will be performing in this quartet? Give the Russian words.
3. Where will **Влади́мир Спивако́в** be performing?
4. What is the name of his chamber orchestra?
5. What instrument will he be playing?
6. What is the name of the country his accompanist is from?
7. What is the relationship between **Ви́ктор** и **И́горь Пика́йзен**?
8. What instrument(s) do they play?
9. Which composer's music will they perform?

О́пера

1. Who is the composer of «**Любо́вь к трём апельси́нам**» [The Love for Three Oranges]?
2. What is the name of the venue where this opera is being performed?
3. Which venue is presenting music by an Italian composer?
4. What is the Italian composer's name?
5. Who is the composer of «**Ска́зка о царе́ Салта́не**» [The Tale of Tsar Sultan]?
6. Which opera would you go to if you want to see a matinee?
7. What are the phone numbers of the **Большо́й теа́тр**?

БАЛЕ́Т	ПОП РОК ШОУ

Пя́тница, 24 октября́
«**Спя́щая краса́вица**» П. Чайко́вского
Постано́вка Ю. Григоро́вича.
Большо́й теа́тр, 19.00. 292 00 50,
292 99 86. Театра́льная пл., 1,
Ⓜ «Театра́льная», «Охо́тный ряд»

Суббо́та, 25 октября́
«**Зо́лушка**» С. Проко́фьева
Спекта́кль хореографи́ческой шко́лы Михаи́ла
Лавро́вского.
Музыка́льный теа́тр им. К. С. Станисла́вского и
В. И. Немиро́вича-Да́нченко, 12.00. 229 06 49,
229 83 88. Б. Дми́тровка, 17,
Ⓜ «Че́ховская»

Суббо́та, 25 октября́
«**Роме́о и Джулье́тта**» С. Проко́фьева
Постано́вка В. Васи́льева.
Большо́й теа́тр, 19.00. 292 00 50,
292 99 86. Театра́льная пл., 1,
Ⓜ «Театра́льная», «Охо́тный ряд»

Четве́рг, 23 октября́
Гру́ппа «**Али́са**»
Моско́вский Дворе́ц молодёжи, 19.00.
245 84 21. Комсомо́льский пр., 28,
Ⓜ «Фру́нзенская»

Пя́тница, 24 октября́
А́втор–исполни́тель **Оле́г Митя́ев** и гитари́ст
Константи́н Тара́сов
Теа́тр эстра́ды. 19.00. 959 04 56.
Берсе́невская наб., 20/2, Ⓜ «Поля́нка»,
«Борови́цкая»

Суббо́та, 25 октября́
**Моско́вский Госуда́рственный ка́мерный
евре́йский хор**
Теа́тр эстра́ды, 19.00. 959 04 56.
Берсе́невская наб., 20/2,
Ⓜ «Поля́нка», «Борови́цкая»

Бале́т

1. You know the words «**спать**» and «**краси́вый**». What is the English title of the ballet «**Спя́щая краса́вица**»?
2. Who composed the music for this ballet?
3. Which ballet would you go to if you want to see a matinee?
4. Who is the composer of «**Зо́лушка**» [*Cinderella*] and «**Роме́о и Джулье́тта**»?
5. Which of these two ballets would you attend if you wanted to see the **Большо́й теа́тр**?
6. Which metro stops are closest to the **Большо́й теа́тр**?
7. What is the name of the square (**пло́щадь**) on which the **Большо́й теа́тр** is located?

Поп Рок Шоу

1. Which chamber choir might you be able to see?
2. Which rock group will be performing?
3. What instrument does **Константи́н Тара́сов** play?
4. Who is the writer-performer **Тара́сов** will be accompanying?
5. What is the name of the venue where they'll be performing?
6. What time do all these shows begin?
7. Which metro stops are near the **Теа́тр эстра́ды**?
8. At which metro stop would you get off for the **Моско́вский Дворе́ц молодёжи**?
9. What is the name of the **проспе́кт** where **Моско́вский Дворе́ц молодёжи** is located?

Б. ANECDOTE

«Мóжно и́ли нельзя́?»

A joke from the Soviet era

В Áнглии что мóжно, то мóжно, а что нельзя́, то нельзя́.
В Герма́нии всё нельзя́, крóме тогó, что мóжно.
В Амéрике всё мóжно, крóме тогó, что нельзя́.
Во Фра́нции всё мóжно, да́же то, что нельзя́.
В Совéтском Сою́зе всё нельзя́, да́же то, что мóжно.

что мóжно, то мóжно	*what is allowed, is allowed*
крóме тогó, что	*except for what . . .*
то, что	*that which*
Совéтский Сою́з	*Soviet Union*

RIDDLE

Я в óзере и мóре, а в водé меня́ нет. Кто я?

ДЖИМ В МОСКВЕ

Моско́вский теа́тр дра́мы и коме́дии на Тага́нке

In Part 1 of this lesson Jim and Vova learn a little more about each other. In Part 2 Jim writes a letter to his Russian professor in the United States. Part 3, which you'll see on video, introduces an enterprising young businessman named Viktor. And in Part 4, Jim and Professor Petrovsky are in a cafe where they meet Tanya, a student at the university.

Ви́ктор

In this lesson you will learn

- ✪ to use adjectives and possessives in three cases that you already know: Prepositional, Genitive, and Accusative

- ✪ to express *to want* and *to be able*

- ✪ about a very productive group of verbs (many of which are recognizable from English)

- ✪ to use reflexive verbs (such as учи́ться) in the past tense

- ✪ more about how to express going somewhere

- ✪ to point things out (*this one, that one*)

- ✪ to form more sophisticated sentences using *who, which, that*

- ✪ to emphasize or intensify what you are saying

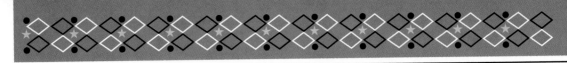

С ЧЕГО НАЧАТЬ?

— Это мои **однокла́ссники**. Это Ко́ля Са́харов. Он у́чится в Фина́нсовой[†] акаде́мии[†]. Ната́ша Кузьме́нко у́чится в РГГУ, на **юриди́ческом** факульте́те, Ди́ма Пале́й — в Моско́вском **экономи́ческом**[†] **институ́те**[†], а Мари́на Са́вина, на́ша бу́дущая **кинозвезда́** — в Институ́те кинематографии[†]!

бу́дущий	*future*
кинозвезда́	*movie star*
однокла́ссник/однокла́ссница	*classmate*
юриди́ческий	*law*

ЧТЕНИЕ

❖ МОЙ ОТÉЦ НЕ МИЛЛИОНÉР!

(*Jim and Vova are getting acquainted.*)

	ВÓВА.	Джим, где ты живёшь?
	ДЖИМ.	В Бóстоне.
	ВÓВА.	Нет, не в Амéрике, а здесь, в Москвé!
dormitory	ДЖИМ.	В **общежи́тии.**° В университéте хорóшее общежи́тие. И университéт бли́зко.
	ВÓВА.	У тебя́ большáя кóмната?
room / everywhere	ДЖИМ.	Кóмната большáя, но там **мéста**° нет, потому́ что **вездé**° кни́ги — на кни́жной пóлке, на кровáти и дáже на полу́.
	ВÓВА.	А у нас дóма вездé цветы́: в столóвой, на балкóне, в ку́хне. Лéнка лю́бит цветы́. Джим, а у тебя́ есть **маши́на**°?
car	ДЖИМ.	Здесь, в Москвé, нет, а дóма есть.
	ВÓВА.	А какáя маши́на? Не «феррáри»?
Ну... *what are you talking about*	ДЖИМ.	(*Laughing.*) **Ну что ты,**° Вóва! Мой отéц не миллионéр! У меня́ «фольксвáген».
parks / wants / to buy *advertisements /* Ничегó... *there's nothing*	ВÓВА.	(*Knowingly.*) Неплохáя маши́на. У нас тóже есть маши́на. «Лáда». Но **гаражá**† нет, и пáпа **парку́ет**° её на у́лице. Он **хóчет купи́ть**° гарáж, читáет **объявлéния,**° но **ничегó** нет° **бли́зко от**[1] дóма. А у тебя́ есть гарáж?
	ДЖИМ.	Нет. Я тóже парку́ю маши́ну на у́лице.
	ВÓВА.	У тебя́ в маши́не есть **рáдио**†?
often	ДЖИМ.	Конéчно. И магнитофóн есть. Я **чáсто**° слу́шаю ру́сские **кассéты.**†
so	ВÓВА.	Поэ́тому ты **так**° хорошó говори́шь по-ру́сски!

---

[1] **От** means *from*. The phrase **бли́зко от дóма** means *close to / near our house.*

УПРАЖНЕНИЕ 1   Под микроско́пом: Prepositional case

This reading has a large number of Prepositional case forms. Write down as many Prepositional case phrases (such as **в Бо́стоне**) as you can find. One of them includes an adjective *made from* a noun; another is an adjective *used as* a noun. Can you find them?

ГРАММАТИКА И ПРАКТИКА

◈ 5.1. PREPOSITIONAL CASE (SINGULAR): ADJECTIVES AND POSSESSIVES

В **мое́й** ко́мнате везде́ кни́ги — на **кни́жной** по́лке, на крова́ти . . . А у нас до́ма везде́ цветы́: в **столо́вой**, на балко́не, в ку́хне.	*There are books everywhere in my room—on the bookshelf, on the bed . . .* *And at our house there are flowers everywhere: in the dining room, on the balcony, in the kitchen.*

Not only nouns, but also adjectives, adjectives used as nouns, and possessives have Prepositional case endings. (So do pronouns, which you will learn in a later lesson.) Here is a summary of those endings. If you keep in mind what you have learned about hard/soft-series vowel letters, spelling rules (such as unstressed **o → e** after hushers), and the effects of stress, the apparent variations in the table turn out to be quite regular and predictable.

	NOMINATIVE CASE (dictionary form)	PREPOSITIONAL CASE ENDING	EXAMPLES
ADJECTIVES (including adjectives used as nouns)			
Masculine and neuter	но́в-ый (стол) больш-о́й (дом) хоро́ш-ий (рестора́н) интере́сн-ое (письмо́)	-ом/-ем	на но́в-**ом** столе́ в больш-**о́м** до́ме в хоро́ш-**ем** рестора́не в интере́сн-**ом** письме́
Feminine	кни́жн-ая (по́лка) столо́в-ая хоро́ш-ая (кварти́ра)	-ой/-ей	на кни́жн-**ой** по́лке в столо́в-**ой** в хоро́ш-**ей** кварти́ре
POSSESSIVES			
Masculine and neuter	мо-й / тво-й (дом) мо-ё / тво-ё (письмо́)	-ём	в мо-**ём** до́ме в тво-**ём** письме́
	наш / ваш (университе́т) на́ш-е / ва́ш-е (общежи́тие)	-ем	в на́ш-**ем** университе́те в ва́ш-**ем** общежи́тии
Feminine	мо-я́ / тво-я́ (кни́га) на́ш-а / ва́ш-а (у́лица)	-ей	в мо-**е́й** кни́ге на на́ш-**ей** у́лице

УПРАЖНЕ́НИЕ 2　Где…?

Match the questions on the left with the correct locations on the right.

1. _____ В како́м го́роде живёт и рабо́тает америка́нский президе́нт[†]?
2. _____ В како́й стране́ игра́ют в ре́гби[†]?
3. _____ Где живу́т жира́фы[†]? _____ А пингви́ны[†]?
4. _____ В како́м го́роде нахо́дится (is) Колизе́й (the Coliseum)?
5. _____ В како́й стране́ нахо́дится Пиза́нская ба́шня (Tower of Pisa)?
6. _____ В како́й стране́ нахо́дится Э́йфелева[†] ба́шня?
7. _____ В како́м го́роде нахо́дится музе́й Эрмита́ж?
8. _____ В како́й стране́ нахо́дятся дре́вние (ancient) пирами́ды[†]?
9. _____ В како́й кана́дской[†] прови́нции[†] нахо́дится Монреа́ль?
10. _____ В како́й стране́ в Ю́жной Аме́рике нахо́дится река́ Амазо́нка?
11. _____ В како́м го́роде нахо́дится Лувр[†]?
12. _____ Где нахо́дится Я́лта?
13. _____ В како́м америка́нском шта́те нахо́дится А́нкоридж?

а. в Австра́лии
б. в Вашингто́не
в. в Анта́рктике
г. в А́фрике
д. в Брази́лии
е. в Ита́лии
ж. в Квебе́ке
з. в Ри́ме
и. в Еги́пте
к. во Фра́нции
л. на Аля́ске[2]
м. в Пари́же
н. в Крыму́
о. в Санкт-Петербу́рге

УПРАЖНЕ́НИЕ 3　В но́вом до́ме

Working with a classmate, answer the questions using the cues provided, or make up answers of your own.

ОБРАЗЕ́Ц:　— Где ты парку́ешь маши́ну? (на́ша у́лица)
　　　　　　— На на́шей у́лице.

1. Где ты живёшь? (большо́й но́вый дом)
2. На како́м этаже́ ты живёшь? (второ́й)
3. А где твоя́ маши́на? (гара́ж)
4. Где рабо́тает твой оте́ц? (би́ржа)
5. А твоя́ мать? (шко́ла)
6. А где ты рабо́таешь? (но́вый магази́н электро́ники)

УПРАЖНЕ́НИЕ 4　Наш микрорайо́н

Fill in the blanks with the appropriate Nominative or Prepositional adjective endings, and in the numbered parentheses after each blank indicate the case used.

В наш_____ (_____)[1] микрорайо́не везде́ нов_____ (_____)[2] магази́ны. В наш_____ (_____)[3] до́ме есть магази́н «Проду́кты». Там

---

[2] **Аля́ска** and **Гава́йи** are the only two American states that require **на** (**на Аля́ске, на Гава́йях**) rather than **в** to show location. **На Гава́йях,** referring to the islands in the plural, uses a form you will learn in Lesson 9, Part 3.

есть хлеб, колбаса́, молоко́. Ря́дом больш_____ (_____)⁴ апте́ка и банк.
Кро́ме того́, на на́ш_____ (_____)⁵ у́лице есть магази́н «Телеви́зоры».
В э́том магази́не есть недоро́г_____ (*inexpensive*) (_____),⁶ но о́чень
хоро́ш_____ (_____)⁷ телеви́зоры, видеомагнитофо́ны, видеокассе́ты.

УПРАЖНЕНИЕ 5   Prepositional endings of nouns and adjectives

Answer the following questions, choosing the proper words or phrases from the list
below.

Бо́стон	университе́т
но́вый дом // кварти́ра № 6	у́лица
общежи́тие	шко́ла
университе́т // факульте́т журнали́стики	

1. В како́м го́роде живёт Джим в Аме́рике?
2. Где он у́чится в Москве́?
3. Где он живёт в Москве́?
4. А где живёт Во́ва?
5. Где у́чится Во́ва?
6. А где у́чится его́ сестра́ Ле́на?
7. Где Серге́й Петро́вич парку́ет маши́ну?

УПРАЖНЕНИЕ 6   Где живу́т твои́ роди́тели?

Find out where your classmates' family members live by asking questions such as the
following.

1. Где живу́т твои́ роди́тели? А ба́бушка и де́душка?
2. У тебя́ есть брат (бра́тья)? Где он живёт (они́ живу́т)?
3. У тебя́ есть сестра́ (сёстры)? Где она́ живёт (они́ живу́т)?
4. У тебя́ есть тётя (тёти)? Где она́ живёт (они́ живу́т)?
5. У тебя́ есть дя́дя (дя́ди)? Где он живёт (они́ живу́т)?
6. ???

◈◈ 5.2. NOUN IRREGULARITIES: SHIFTING-STRESS MASCULINES AND MASCULINE PREPOSITIONAL IN -ý

— Где газе́та? На **столе́**?   *"Where's the newspaper? On the table?"*
— Нет, она́ там, на **полу́**.   *"No, it's there, on the floor."*

A small number of masculine nouns are end-stressed whenever a case ending is added
(for example, **гара́ж** but **гаража́ нет** and **в гараже́; стол** but **на столе́**); others, as you
learned in Lesson 2, Part 3, are end-stressed in the plural only (**дома́, адреса́,
профессора́,** and so on). In addition, some masculine nouns (most with only
one-syllable) take a stressed -ý ending in the Prepositional case following **в** and **на**.
These forms are not predictable, so you may want to keep a running list of them as you
encounter them. To assist you, these forms are shown in the end-of-lesson and
end-of-book vocabulary lists (see, for example, the listing for **пол**).

УПРАЖНЕНИЕ 7   Где...?

Working with a classmate, answer the following questions using the correct preposition (**в** or **на**) and Prepositional case forms of a phrase from the right column. Various locations are possible for most items.

ОБРАЗЕЦ: — Где магазин «Хлеб»? (наш дом)
            — В нашем доме.

1. Где у вас телевизор?	большая комната
2. А где твой компьютер?	моя комната, стол
3. А твои книги?	книжная полка, стол и пол
4. Где ваша машина?	наш гараж
5. А где гараж?	наша улица

❖ О РОССИИ

PARKING PROBLEMS

Гаража нет, и папа паркует машину на улице. Он хочет купить гараж, но нет ничего близко от дома.

Very few Moscow apartment buildings provide garages for the residents. Hundreds of such buildings went up during the Soviet era, when most people could not buy cars at all; for residents of these buildings there was no need for garages. Now that car ownership is becoming more possible and popular in Russia, people in large cities face the problem of where to keep the vehicle when it's not in use. Parking on the street (**на улице**) — even if one can find a spot — or in the courtyard (**во дворе**) is not always permitted. Moreover, it's risky: parts are easily stolen from unattended cars (windshield wipers are said to be particularly vulnerable). Thus, many car owners try to buy (not rent) a carport/parking slot in privately owned "garage complexes." These complexes may be enclosed by a fence with gates for which the owner will have a key; they may even have a guard. They vary in terms of comfort, security, and price. Finding a garage complex near one's apartment is a particular challenge; some car owners have to travel to their garage by bus or metro, which has become the subject of many jokes (**анекдоты**). Thus, Vova's father is looking for a garage close to home, and he may eventually discover that, as in Paris, London or New York, owning a car can be more of a nuisance than using public transportation.

❖ 5.3. A PRODUCTIVE SUFFIX: -ОВАТЬ VERBS

Папа **паркует** машину на улице.   *Dad parks the car on the street.*

Infinitives ending in **-овать**, like **парковать**, form a huge subgroup of **-ешь** verbs. The **-ова-** portion is changed to **-у-**, then regular **-ешь** endings are added.

парк-**ова́**-ть	парк-**у́**-ю	парк-**у́**-ем
	парк-**у́**-ешь	парк-**у́**-ете
	парк-**у́**-ет	парк-**у́**-ют

Many of these verbs are easily recognizable from English.

УПРАЖНЕНИЕ 8   Guessing at -овать verbs

The following paragraph contains a number of -овать verbs whose meanings you can probably guess. Underline all the -овать verb forms, then write out the infinitive (dictionary form) for each. Finally, translate the paragraph into English, using context to guess the meaning of unfamiliar words.

ОБРАЗЕЦ: Па́па <u>парку́ет</u> маши́ну на у́лице.
паркова́ть: *Dad parks the car on the street.*

Во́ва де́лает уро́ки. Он пи́шет, что Аме́рика импорти́рует маши́ны и электро́нику, но он не зна́ет, что Аме́рика экспорти́рует. Пото́м он смо́трит телеви́зор: сена́торы аплоди́руют президе́нту, пото́м врачи́ рекоменду́ют но́вую дие́ту, пото́м конгрессме́ны критику́ют президе́нта, а популя́рный актёр его́ паро́ди́рует.

О РОССИИ

ФАКУЛЬТЕ́ТЫ

Ната́ша Кузьме́нко у́чится в РГГУ, на юриди́ческом факульте́те.

Knowing that there are structural differences between Russian and American university systems helps one understand why the first two lines in the following conversation can be interpreted in various ways.

— **На како́м факульте́те вы у́читесь?**
— **На биологи́ческом.**
— А ваш оте́ц то́же био́лог?
— Нет, он преподаёт на истфа́ке.

"What department are you in?"   *"What are you majoring in?"*
"I'm in the biology department."   *"Biology."*

"What's your major?"   *"What do you study?"*
"Biology."   *"I'm a biology major."*

The names of many **факульте́ты** are commonly referred to with abbreviated forms, such as **истфа́к** (**истори́ческий факульте́т**), **биофа́к** (**биологи́ческий факульте́т**), **мехма́т** (**меха́нико-математи́ческий факульте́т**), **филфа́к** (**филологи́ческий факульте́т**), and so on. **Филологи́ческий факульте́т** refers to the division of the university where students study literature and language.

Э́ти студе́нтки у́чатся в Санкт-Петербу́ргском университе́те.

УПРАЖНÉНИЕ 9   На каком факультéте вы ýчитесь?

You're a Russian student filling out an application that asks where you go to school. Practice giving various responses, including both the name of an institution and a department from this list.

> ОБРАЗÉЦ: — Где вы ýчитесь?
> — Я учýсь в Москóвском госудáрственном университéте на физи́ческом факультéте.

Москóвский госудáрственный университéт

биологи́ческий факультéт	социологи́ческий факультéт
географи́ческий факультéт	физи́ческий факультéт
геологи́ческий факультéт	филологи́ческий факультéт
факультéт журнали́стики	филосóфский факультéт
истори́ческий факультéт	хими́ческий факультéт
мехáнико-математи́ческий факультéт	экономи́ческий факультéт
факультéт фундаментáльной медици́ны	факультéт психолóгии

Москóвский университéт инженéрной экологии

> факультéт геофи́зики

Орéхово-Зýевский педагоги́ческий институ́т

> факультéт рýсского языкá, литерату́ры и культуролóгии

Санкт-Петербýргский госудáрственный техни́ческий университéт

> факультéт техни́ческой кибернéтики

СЛОВА, СЛОВА, СЛОВА … ✪ лóжные друзья́ (*False friends*)

На каком **факультéте** вы ýчитесь?   *What are you majoring in?*

The Russian cognates presented so far have generally had meanings similar to their counterparts in English, but there are also **лóжные друзья́** (*false friends*)— recognizable cognates whose meanings differ from their English counterparts. **Факультéт** is a good example, and there are many others. **Туалéт** means *bathroom* or *restroom*, not the *toilet* fixture (**унитáз**). **Фами́лия** means *last name*, not *family* (**семья́**). **Симпати́чный** means *likable*, not *sympathetic* (**сочýвственный**). Keep in mind that words borrowed from another language may assume meanings that differ from those in the source language.

◈ 5.4. TO WANT ХОТÉТЬ

Пáпа **хóчет** купи́ть гарáж.   *Dad wants to get a garage.*

The verb **хотéть** can, like its English counterpart, be used with noun phrases (*want something*) or infinitives (*want to do something*). It is one of the few truly irregular verbs in Russian. Note the following characteristics.

- the mutation of the final consonant in the stem (**ч-т**)
- the mixed endings (-**ешь** in the singular, -**ишь** in the plural)
- the unusual stress pattern

Since this verb is used so frequently, you should focus on learning its conjugation.

FORM OF ХОТÉТЬ	WITH NOUNS (*want something*)	WITH INFINITIVES (*want to do something*)
я хоч-у́ ты хо́ч-ешь он, она́ хо́ч-ет	Я хочу́ но́вый рюкза́к. Ты хо́чешь ко́фе? Он (она́) хо́чет маши́ну.	Я хочу́ слу́шать му́зыку. Что ты хо́чешь де́лать? Он (она́) хо́чет купи́ть маши́ну.
мы хот-и́м	Мы хоти́м магнитофо́н.	Мы хоти́м учи́ться в Моско́вском университе́те.
вы хот-и́те они́ хот-я́т	Вы хоти́те бутербро́д? Они́ хотя́т соба́ку.	Вы хоти́те гуля́ть? Они́ хотя́т жить в Санкт-Петербу́рге.

УПРАЖНЕНИЕ 10   Что мы хоти́м

Mike is writing a letter to a Russian friend and telling him about the family's discussion about whether to buy a new car. Fill in the blanks with the appropriate form of **хоте́ть.**

Мои́ роди́тели _____[1] купи́ть маши́ну, т. е., втору́ю маши́ну.
Па́па _____[2] «нисса́н». Ма́ма говори́т: «У нас уже́ есть оди́н
«нисса́н». Я не _____[3] ещё оди́н (*another*) «нисса́н»,
я _____[4] «мерседе́с»!» Но па́па говори́т, что «мерседе́с»—э́то
о́чень дорога́я маши́на.

 Сестра́ не _____[5] маши́ну: «Заче́м втора́я маши́на, когда́
есть авто́бусы? Кро́ме того́, у нас есть велосипе́ды (*bicycles*). Я не
понима́ю, почему́ вы все _____[6] ещё одну́ (*another*) маши́ну!
Тогда́ па́па спра́шивает (*asks*) меня́: «Майк, а что ты _____[7]?»
«Я? Я _____[8] на́шу ста́рую маши́ну!»

УПРАЖНЕНИЕ 11   Что ты хо́чешь?

You have just won $10,000 in a TV game show sponsored by a department store and have decided to buy your classmates one item each. Circulate around the class, making a list of who wants what. See if you come up with any duplicates on your list.

ОБРАЗЕ́Ц: — Что ты хо́чешь?
         — Я хочу́ но́вый компью́тер.

КУЛЬТУРА РЕЧИ

❖ ТАК ГОВОРЯТ: НУ ЧТО ТЫ (ВЫ)!

— А кака́я у тебя́ маши́на? Не
«ферра́ри»?
— **Ну что ты!** Я не миллионе́р!

*"What kind of car do you have?
A Ferrari?"*
*"What're you talking about! I'm
no millionaire!"*

The phrase **Ну что ты (вы)!** is used to express one's disagreement with or denial of some statement, or as a negative answer to a question. It can have a range of translations: *What do you mean! What are you talking about! What are you saying! Good heavens, no!* Here are some situations in which you might use this expression:

1. Someone tells you a prominent public figure died (but you saw him live on TV just last night).
2. One of your friends says she heard that you won $1 million in the lottery and that you're going to drop out of school and move to Tahiti (but you're still here working).
3. A friend asks if you'll be staying in a hotel when you visit Moscow (but of course you won't because you have relatives there).

УПРАЖНЕНИЕ 12   Ну что ты (вы)!

Make up a couple more situations where you think **Ну что ты (вы)!** might be appropriate.

❖ САМОПРОВЕРКА: УПРАЖНЕНИЕ 13

Working on your own, try this self-test: Read a Russian sentence out loud, then give an idiomatic English equivalent without looking at the book. Then work from English to Russian. After you have completed the activity, try it with a classmate.

1. У нас везде́ цветы́: на столе́, на балко́не, в ку́хне и да́же в туале́те.
2. — Где твоя́ соба́ка?
   — У меня́ в спа́льне. Спит на мое́й крова́ти.
   — А почему́ не на полу́?
   — Она́ не лю́бит спать на полу́.
3. Я не хочу́ паркова́ть маши́ну на у́лице.
4. — На како́м факульте́те ты у́чишься — на биологи́ческом?

   — Нет, я учу́сь на факульте́те психоло́гии.

1. *We have flowers everywhere: on the table, on the balcony, in the kitchen, and even in the bathroom.*
2. *"Where's your dog?"*
   "In my room. Sleeping on my bed."
   "Why not on the floor?"
   "She doesn't like sleeping on the floor."
3. *I don't want to park my car on the street.*
4. *"What department are you in? [What are you majoring in?] Biology?"*
   "No, I'm in the psychology department. [I'm majoring in psychology.]"

❖ ВОПРОСЫ И ОТВЕТЫ: УПРАЖНЕНИЕ 14

Working with a classmate, take turns asking and answering the following questions.

1. Где ты живёшь — до́ма, в общежи́тии, и́ли снима́ешь (*are you renting*) кварти́ру и́ли ко́мнату?
2. Твои́ роди́тели рабо́тают? Где они́ рабо́тают?
3. Ты лю́бишь смотре́ть телеви́зор? У тебя́ есть телеви́зор? А видеомагнитофо́н†?
4. А маши́на у тебя́ есть? Кака́я у тебя́ маши́на?
5. У тебя́ в маши́не есть магнитофо́н и́ли компа́кт-диск-пле́йер†? А до́ма? А ру́сские кассе́ты и компа́кт-ди́ски у тебя́ есть? Где ты их слу́шаешь?
6. Где ты парку́ешь маши́ну?

❖ ДИАЛОГИ

ДИАЛОГ 1 Где ты у́чишься?
(Asking where someone studies)

— Во́ва, на како́м факульте́те у́чится твоя́ сестра́?
— На факульте́те журнали́стики.
— А где ты у́чишься?
— В шко́ле.
— А где твоя́ шко́ла?
— На на́шей у́лице.

ДИАЛОГ 2 Ты зна́ешь, где . . . ?
(Clarifying directions)

— Ты зна́ешь, где Тверска́я у́лица?
— Да, коне́чно. В це́нтре.
— У тебя́ есть ка́рта Москвы́?
— Да, вот она́. Смотри́, вот Тверска́я.
— Но э́то у́лица Го́рького!
— Нет, э́то Тверска́я. Тверска́я — э́то о́чень ста́рое назва́ние (*name*). Пото́м э́то была́ у́лица Го́рького, а сейча́с — опя́ть Тверска́я!

УПРАЖНЕНИЕ 15   Ваш диало́г

Create a dialogue in which you ask someone the location of **Театра́льная пло́щадь**, the square by the **Большо́й теа́тр** that used to be called **пло́щадь Свердло́ва**.

❖ А ТЕПЕРЬ . . . : УПРАЖНЕНИЕ 16

Working with a classmate, use what you learned in Part 1 to . . .

1. find out the locations of pieces of furniture in his apartment or home
2. ask whether he has a car, and if so, what kind
3. find out what department he is studying in
4. ask if he wants to study in Russia

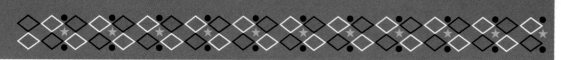

ЧАСТЬ ВТОРАЯ

 С ЧЕГО НАЧАТЬ?

Áнтон Пáвлович Чéхов
(1860, Таганрóг—1904, Баденвéйлер,
Гермáния†)

ПЬЕСЫ ЧЕХОВА

Три сестры
А.П. Чехов

Дядя Ваня
А.П. Чехов

Вишнёвый сад
А.П. Чехов

Иванов
А.П. Чехов

РАССКАЗЫ ЧЕХОВА

О любви

Волося большой
и Волося маленький

Моя жизнь

Скрипка
Ротшильда

Человек в
футляре

Дама с
собачкой

пьéса	*play*
расскáз	*short story*
«Вишнёвый сад»	*"The Cherry Orchard"*
«Человéк в футлáре»	*"The Man in a Case"*
«Дáма с собáчкой»	*"The Lady with a Lap Dog"*
жизнь	*life*
любóвь	*love*

188

ЧТЕНИЕ

❖ ХОДЯ́ЧАЯ ЭНЦИКЛОПЕ́ДИЯ°!

Ходя́чая. . . *A walking encyclopedia*

(*Jim is checking over part of a letter he is about to send to his American professor of Russian.*)

Моего́ нау́чного руководи́теля° Вы[3] зна́ете: э́то профе́ссор Петро́вский, Илья́ Ильи́ч Петро́вский. Он был у нас в университе́те **в про́шлом году́**.° Он говори́т, что хорошо́ Вас **по́мнит.**°

Илья́ Ильи́ч о́чень интере́сный **челове́к**° и у него́ замеча́тельная библиоте́ка. Кни́ги у него́ везде́: и в пере́дней,° и в **гости́ной**,° и в спа́льне. Да́же в туале́те есть кни́жная по́лка. У него́ есть не то́лько кни́ги, но и ста́рые ка́рты: Москва́, Санкт-Петербу́рг, **други́е**° города́, **ра́зные**° стра́ны.

Илья́ Ильи́ч о́чень хорошо́ зна́ет Москву́, все у́лицы и **пло́щади,**° их **назва́ния**° — ста́рые и но́вые, их **исто́рию.**° Я **ду́мал,**° что он москви́ч,° но он не москви́ч: он **роди́лся**° на Кавка́зе.°

Вчера́ мы **ходи́ли**° на вы́ставку° «Исто́рия Москвы́». Илья́ Ильи́ч — замеча́тельный **гид**°! Ходя́чая энциклопе́дия!

Моего́. . . *My (academic) adviser / В. . . last year remembers*
person
entryway / living room

other / different
squares
names / history / thought / Muscovite
was born / the Caucasus
went / exhibition
guide

УПРАЖНЕ́НИЕ 1   Под микроско́пом: Past tenses

In this reading there are four examples of past tense verbs. Circle them.

---

[3]Although pronoun forms are not normally capitalized except as the first word of a sentence, it is common when addressing one person formally to capitalize **Вы** (and its other case forms) in letters as a sign of respect for the recipient. Plural **вы** is never capitalized except as the first word of a sentence.

ГРАММАТИКА И ПРАКТИКА

❖❖ 5.5. ACCUSATIVE CASE: PRONOUNS

Он говори́т, что хорошо́ **вас** по́мнит.	*He says he remembers you well.*
Как **тебя́** зову́т?	*What's your name?*
Ты **меня́** не понима́ешь?	*Don't you understand me?*

You learned Accusative case forms of personal pronouns in the phrase **Как вас (тебя́,** and so on) **зову́т?** They are the same as the Genitive case forms (see Lesson 4, Part 1). As with the Genitive, the Accusative forms for *he, she, it, they* (**его́, её, их**) also take an initial letter **н-** when governed by a preposition; you'll see Accusative forms with **н- (него́, неё, них)** in later lessons. Here is a comparative table of pronoun forms in the Nominative, Accusative, and Genitive cases.

PRONOUNS: Nominative / Accusative / Genitive

INTERROGATIVES			PERSONAL PRONOUNS					
Nom.	**Acc.**	**Gen.**	**Nom.**	**Acc.**	**Gen.**	**Nom.**	**Acc.**	**Gen.**
кто	кого́	(у) кого́	я	меня́	(у) меня́	мы	нас	(у) нас
что	что	(у) чего́	ты	тебя́	(у) тебя́	вы	вас	(у) вас
			он, оно́	его́	(у) него́	они́	их	(у) них
			она́	её	(у) неё			

УПРАЖНЕНИЕ 2   Кого́, что?

Professor Petrovsky is making introductions. Supply the appropriate Accusative case pronouns in the following text.

Здра́вствуйте! _____¹ зову́т (*My name is*) Илья́ Ильи́ч Петро́вский. Это Джим Ри́чардсон, мой аспира́нт. Вы _____² (*him*) зна́ете? А _____³ (*me*)? Дава́йте познако́мимся! Я люблю́ ста́рые фи́льмы.† А вы _____⁴ (*them*) лю́бите? Я люблю́ му́зыку Мо́царта. А вы? Вы то́же _____⁵ (*it*) лю́бите? Я люблю́ пье́сы Че́хова. И вы _____⁶ (*them*) лю́бите? Вон иду́т мои́ сосе́ди. Вы _____⁷ (*them*) зна́ете? У Серге́я Петро́вича есть маши́на, и он парку́ет _____⁸ (*it*) на у́лице.

УПРАЖНЕНИЕ 3   People, places, and things

See which pair or small group of students in the class can be the first to provide at least three different completions for each of the following sentences.

1. Моя́ сестра́ (мать, ба́бушка) чита́ет _____.
2. Мой брат (па́па, де́душка) лю́бит _____.

3. Я хорошо́ по́мню _____.
4. Ты понима́ешь _____?
5. Мы ви́дим _____.
6. Я никогда́ не слу́шаю _____.

❖❖ 5.6. ACCUSATIVE CASE: ANIMATE MASCULINE NOUNS

Моего́ нау́чного **руководи́теля**
вы зна́ете . . .

You know my adviser . . .

When you learned the Accusative case forms of nouns in Lesson 3, Part 2, animate masculine nouns were excluded. These nouns actually have the same form in the Accusative as they have in the Genitive, which you learned in Lesson 4, Part 1. (This Genitive/Accusative overlap for masculine animate nouns also holds for the words that modify them, as you will see in Parts 3 and 4 of this lesson.)

Here are some more examples of masculine animate nouns in the Accusative.

Вы хорошо́ зна́ете **дире́ктора**? *Do you know the director well?*
Почему́ ты не слу́шаешь **преподава́теля**? *Why aren't you listening to the teacher?*
Валенти́на Серге́евна ждёт **му́жа**. *Valentina Sergeevna is waiting for her husband.*

Here is a summary of the regular noun endings in the Accusative that you have learned up to this point.

	NOMINATIVE CASE (dictionary form)	ACCUSATIVE CASE ENDING	EXAMPLES
«-а/-я» **Feminines and "masquerading masculines"**	сестр-а́ стать-я́ Во́в-а дя́д-я	Delete final -а/-я; add -у/-ю	сестр-у́ стать-ю́ Во́в-у дя́д-ю
Masculine animates	исто́рик америка́нец преподава́тель Серге́й	same as Genitive; (add -а/-я)	исто́рик-**а** америка́нц-**а** преподава́тел-**я** Серге́-**я**
All other types, singular and plural (except plural animates, which will be covered in Lesson 8, Part 4	Masculine журна́л роя́ль Feminine -ь мать ме́бель Neuter письм-о́ упражне́ни-е	No change	журна́л роя́ль мать ме́бель письм-**о́** упражне́ни-**е**

(Continued)

	NOMINATIVE CASE (dictionary form)	ACCUSATIVE CASE ENDING	EXAMPLES
<u>Plural</u> журна́л-ы роя́л-и дом-а́ газе́т-ы профе́сси-и пи́сьм-а упражне́ни-я		No change	журна́л-ы роя́л-и дом-а́ газе́т-ы профе́сси-и пи́сьм-а упражне́ни-я

УПРАЖНЕНИЕ 4   Кого́ вы зна́ете?

Complete the following sentences with the Accusative case forms of the nouns and pronouns in parentheses.

Вы зна́ете _____[1] (Ле́на)? Где она́? Я _____[2] (она́) не ви́жу. Кто э́та же́нщина? Э́то мать Ле́ны? Вы _____[3] (она́) зна́ете? А _____[4] (оте́ц) Ле́ны вы то́же зна́ете? Вы да́же зна́ете, как _____[5] (он) зову́т? Он, ка́жется, купи́л _____[6] (маши́на)? Где он _____[7] (она́) парку́ет? Как зову́т _____[8] (брат) Ле́ны? Вы _____[9] (он) хорошо́ зна́ете? Это её соба́ка? Вы да́же зна́ете, как зову́т _____[10] (её соба́ка)? Как вы хорошо́ _____[11] (они́) зна́ете!

УПРАЖНЕНИЕ 5   Кого́ вы ви́дите? Что вы ви́дите?

Work with a classmate to see who can come up with the longest list of people and objects in the room.

ОБРАЗЕ́Ц: Я ви́жу преподава́теля, Ната́шу, Ива́на, кни́гу, рюкза́к ...

✣○ РОССИИ ✣✣✣✣✣✣✣✣✣✣✣✣✣✣✣

РУ́ССКИЕ И КНИ́ГИ

Кни́ги у него́ везде́: и в пере́дней, и в гости́ной, и в спа́льне.

Russians love books. They read on buses, trains and subways, at bus and subway stops, at home. They read contemporary authors and classics of Russian literature such as **Пу́шкин, Го́голь, Толсто́й, Достое́вский, Че́хов, Ахма́това, Пастерна́к.** Translations from many languages of the world are published regularly: You'll find books by many British and American writers such as **Шекспи́р, Ди́ккенс, Уэ́ллс, Лонгфе́лло, По, Твен, Ло́ндон, Хемингуэ́й, Сте́йнбек, Во́ннегут, Сэ́линджер.** The former homes of especially esteemed writers and poets are often turned into museums, such as the **Дом-музе́й Че́хова.** Streets and squares in cities often bear authors' names, such as **пло́щадь Пу́шкина.**

УПРАЖНЕНИЕ 6   Кто это?

Which of the authors' names in the list below do you recognize?

Кристи Агата. МЕСТЬ НОФРЕТ. Пер. с англ. Переплет. 1992.

Кристи Агата, Тэй Джозефина, Маклой Элен. УБИЙСТВО ПОД
   РОЖДЕСТВО. Сборник. Пер. с англ. Переплет. 1990.

Лагин Лазарь. СТАРИК ХОТТАБЫЧ. Обложка. 1990.

Макбейн Эд. ЛЕГАВЫЕ. Пер. с англ. Переплет. 1993.

Макбейн Эд. 87-Й ПОЛИЦЕЙСКИЙ УЧАСТОК. Пер. с англ. Переплет. 1992.

Макдональд Росс. ДЕЛО ФЕРГЮСОНА. Пер. с англ. Переплет. 1992.

МЕТРОПОЛЬ. Альманах. Переплет. 1991.

Мирер Александр. ДОМ СКИТАЛЬЦЕВ. Переплет. 1992.

МУЗЕЙ ЧЕЛОВЕКА. Сборник. Обложка. 1990.

Набоков Владимир. ИСТРЕБЛЕНИЕ ТИРАНОВ. Обложка. 1991.

НЕИЗВЕСТНАЯ ЧЕРНАЯ КНИГА. Сборник (совместно с Яд–Вашем и
   Государственным архивом РФ). Обложка. 1993.

НЕЧЕЛОВЕК–НЕВИДИМКА. Сборник. Обложка. 1991.

НИКИФОРОВ ПАВЕЛ. Альбом. Обложка. 1993.

Оруэлл Джордж. СКОТСКИЙ ХУТОР. Пер. с англ. Обложка. 1989.

Пелевин Виктор. СИНИЙ ФОНАРЬ. Переплет. 1991.

По Эдгар Аллан. ПАДЕНИЕ ДОМА АШЕРОВ. Пер. с англ.
   Обложка. 1990.

УПРАЖНЕНИЕ 7   Английская и американская литература[†]

You are in Russia, and you're curious to see which English-language works are commonly available to Russians in translation. By making good guesses, match the Russian renditions to the original English titles.

1. _____ Великий Гэтсби
2. _____ Винни-Пух
3. _____ Гамлет
4. _____ Двенадцатая ночь
5. _____ Завтрак для чемпионов
6. _____ Как важно быть серьёзным
7. _____ Машина времени
8. _____ Алиса в стране чудес
9. _____ Приключения Гекльберри Финна
10. _____ Приключения Оливера Твиста
11. _____ Приключения Тома Сойера
12. _____ Рэгтайм
13. _____ Старик и море
14. _____ Трамвай «Желание»

а. A Streetcar Named Desire
б. Alice's Adventures in Wonderland
в. Breakfast of Champions
г. Hamlet
д. Oliver Twist
е. Ragtime
ж. The Adventures of Huckleberry Finn
з. The Adventures of Tom Sawyer
и. The Great Gatsby
к. The Importance of Being Earnest
л. The Old Man and The Sea
м. The Time Machine
н. Twelfth Night
о. Winnie the Pooh

◈ 5.7. REFLEXIVE VERBS: PAST TENSE FORMS

Он **родился** на Кавказе.   *He was born in the Caucasus.*

The principle behind reflexive endings that you learned for **учиться** in the present tense (see Lesson 4, Part 4) also holds true in the past tense: If the form ends in a consonant, add **-ся;** if it ends in a vowel, add **-сь.** Compare the following forms.

он роди́л-**ся**
она́ родила́-**сь**
они́ родили́-**сь**

УПРАЖНЕНИЕ 8   Дя́дя Сла́ва и тётя Све́та

Complete the following text with the past tense forms of the verbs **роди́ться**, **познако́миться**, and **учи́ться**.

Э́то мой дя́дя Сла́ва и его́ жена́, тётя Све́та. Дя́дя Сла́ва и тётя Све́та _____,[1] когда́ они́ _____[2] в университе́те. Дя́дя Сла́ва _____[3] в Новосиби́рске. Там жи́ли и рабо́тали его́ роди́тели. Он _____[4] в математи́ческой шко́ле. По́сле (after) шко́лы он рабо́тал — ка́жется, два и́ли три го́да. Пото́м он _____[5] в Новосиби́рском университе́те, на меха́нико-математи́ческом факульте́те. Тётя Све́та то́же _____[6] в университе́те, но на экономи́ческом факульте́те. Они́ _____[7] в университе́тском кафе́. Сейча́с они́ живу́т в Петербу́рге. Дя́дя Сла́ва рабо́тает в фи́рме «Нева́», а тётя Све́та преподаёт в университе́те.

✿ О РОССИИ ✿

НО́ВЫЕ НАЗВА́НИЯ В РОССИ́И

Илья́ Ильи́ч о́чень хорошо́ зна́ет Москву́, все у́лицы и пло́щади, их назва́ния — ста́рые и но́вые.

Throughout the history of Russia and the former Soviet Union, place names have undergone widespread changes to reflect the ideology of the times. After the Communist Revolution of 1917, thousands of places were renamed along communist lines, but since the overthrow of the Communist regime in 1991, many of these places have regained their former names. For example, Moscow's **у́лица Го́рького** (*Gorky Street*), named for the twentieth-century author **Макси́м Го́рький**, has regained its prerevolutionary name — **Тверска́я у́лица**. Similarly, **Ленингра́д** has been changed back to **Санкт-Петербу́рг**, **Го́рький** to **Ни́жний Но́вгород**, and **Кали́нин** to **Тверь**.

✧ 5.8. VERBS OF MOTION: ХОДИ́ЛИ КУДА́ = БЫ́ЛИ ГДЕ

Вчера́ мы **ходи́ли** на вы́ставку   *Yesterday we went to an exhibit,*
«Исто́рия Москвы́».   *"The History of Moscow."*

The verb **ходи́ть** is related in meaning to the verb **идти́** *to go* (*without implying the use of a vehicle*), but it carries a significant additional sense: It implies (among other things) *to make at least one round trip, to go somewhere and return*. It is therefore helpful to think of equating the following examples.

Вчера́ мы **ходи́ли на вы́ставку**.   Вчера́ мы **бы́ли на вы́ставке**.
  (куда́? — *Accusative*)   (где? — *Prepositional*)
We went to an exhibit.   *We were at an exhibit.*

For the time being you should use **ходи́ть** only in the past tense.

УПРАЖНЕНИЕ 9   В Москве

You and some friends are visiting Russia for the first time. You're at dinner with a Russian friend who is eager to hear what you've seen in Moscow. As she asks where you were today (yesterday, in the morning, and so on), the "tourists" should consult the list of places in Appendix K and respond, using the verb **ходи́ть** to say where you went. Then, working together, you should locate the sites on the map of Moscow.

ОБРАЗЕЦ: (*to first tourist*)   — Где ты была́ сего́дня?
            — Я ходи́ла в Большо́й теа́тр. (*The two of you locate it on the map.*)

    (*to another tourist*)   — А ты где был?

Москва́

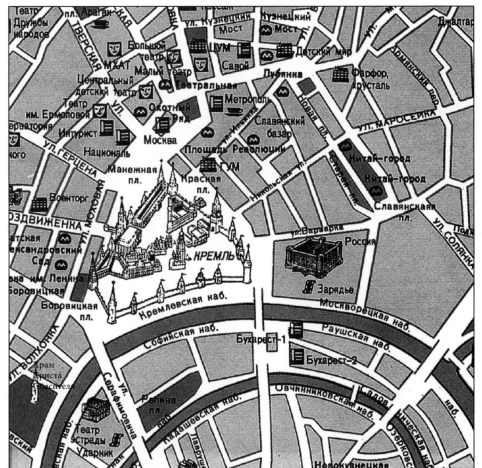

КУЛЬТУРА РЕЧИ

❖ **ТАК ГОВОРЯТ: НЕ ТОЛЬКО..., НО И...**

У него́ есть **не то́лько** кни́ги, **но и** ста́рые ка́рты.

He has not only books, but also old maps.

The phrase **не то́лько..., но и...** is used in Russian very much like *not only..., but also...* is used in English.

Третьяко́вская галере́я

УПРАЖНЕНИЕ 10   Не то́лько..., но и...

How would you use **не то́лько..., но и...** to complete the following phrases?

ОБРАЗЕ́Ц: Вчера́ тури́сты бы́ли не то́лько в Большо́м теа́тре, но и в Третьяко́вской галаре́е.

1. В э́том магази́не мо́жно купи́ть не то́лько колбасу́, но и...
2. Мы вчера́ ходи́ли не то́лько в музе́й, ...
3. Моя́ сестра́ игра́ет не то́лько на роя́ле, ...
4. Она́ игра́ет не то́лько кла́ссику, ...
5. На́ши сосе́ди бы́ли вчера́ не то́лько в кафе́, ...
6. Я говорю́ не то́лько по-англи́йски, ...
7. Я хочу́ купи́ть не то́лько пылесо́с, ...

УПРАЖНЕНИЕ 11   Linking phrases

Working with a classmate, make up sentences using pairs of phrases linked by **не то́лько..., но и...**.

ОБРАЗЕ́Ц: кана́дцы[†] — америка́нцы
В на́шем университе́те у́чатся не то́лько кана́дцы, но и америка́нцы.

1. детекти́вы — три́ллеры
2. компью́тер[†] — при́нтер[†]
3. профессора́ — аспира́нты
4. рестора́н — кафе́
5. расска́зы Че́хова — его́ пье́сы
6. университе́т — Технологи́ческий институ́т

❖ САМОПРОВЕРКА: УПРАЖНЕНИЕ 12

Working on your own, try this self-test: Read a Russian sentence out loud, then give an idiomatic English equivalent without looking at the book. Then work from English to Russian. After you have completed the activity, try it with a classmate.

1. Ты его не помнишь? А он говорит, что он тебя знает.

2. Я не понимаю Петра Петровича. Он очень много работает и мало отдыхает. Он не ходит в театр, не ходит в кино, не ходит на концёрты. Разве это жизнь?

3. — Где вы были вчера? — Ходили в кино. А вы?

4. Моя мать родилась в России, а отец — во Франции.

1. *Don't you remember him? He says he knows you.*

2. *I don't understand Pyotr Petrovich. He really works a lot and he doesn't rest much. He doesn't go to the theater, doesn't go the movies, doesn't go to concerts. Is that really a life?*

3. *"Where were you [pl.] yesterday?" "We went to the movies. How about you?"*

4. *My mother was born in Russia and my father in France.*

❖ ВОПРОСЫ И ОТВЕТЫ: УПРАЖНЕНИЕ 13

Working with a classmate, take turns asking and answering the following questions. For this exercise, one of you is a Russian exchange student who recently arrived and is asking about your university. The other will respond to her questions.

1. У вас в университете хорошая библиотека? А дома?

2. Вы часто работаете в библиотеке университета? Что вы там делаете?

3. Что ещё есть в библиотеке университета, кроме книг (*except books*)? Там есть карты? Видеокассеты[†]? CD-ROM'ы[†]? Телефонные[†] книги?

4. В вашей библиотеке есть русские книги и видеокассеты? Какие?

5. Вы хорошо знаете ваш университет, его историю? Это старый университет?

6. Я здесь в аспирантуре (*graduate school*)[4] на экономическом факультете. Вы не знаете моего (*my*) руководителя, профессора Андерсона?

7. Вы, кажется, были в России. Вы были в Москве? В Петербурге?

8. Вы хорошо знаете Москву — её улицы, станции метро (*metro stations*)? Вы знаете, какие названия старые, а какие новые?

9. А ваш город вы хорошо знаете? Вы хороший гид[†]?

---

[4]You already know the word **аспирант** *graduate student.* **Аспирантура** has the same root and means *graduate studies.* **В аспирантуре** is normally translated as *in graduate school.*

❖❖ О РОССИИ ❖❖❖❖❖❖❖❖❖❖

«МА́СТЕР И МАРГАРИ́ТА» МИХАЙ́ЛА БУЛГА́КОВА

Я о́чень люблю́ «Ма́стера и Маргари́ту».

The novel **Ма́стер и Маргари́та** by Mikhail Bulgakov (1891–1940) is one of the most fascinating and beloved works of twentieth-century Russian literature. In the former Soviet Union, the novel was first published with substantial cuts in the magazine «**Москва́**» in 1966–67—almost thirty years after Bulgakov's death in 1940. The novel has universal appeal: it has been translated into more than twenty languages. There are four English translations of the novel: by M. Ginsburg (1967, abridged version), M. Glenny (1967, complete version), D. Burgin and K. O'Connor (1995, complete text, annotated edition), and R. Pevear and L. Volokhonsky (1997, complete text, annotated edition).

In the novel, the first appearance of the devil and his motley crew in 1930s Moscow takes place in **Патриа́ршие пруды́,** Patriarch's Ponds, located near **Ма́лая Бро́нная** street in the heart of old Moscow. (**Патриа́рший** comes from the noun **патриа́рх**: the site is named in honor of the Patriarch of the Russian Orthodox Church.)

❖❖ ДИАЛОГИ

ДИАЛОГ 1 «Ма́стер и маргари́та»
(Discussing a writer)

— Джон, где ты был вчера́?
— Я ходи́л на вы́ставку (*exhibition*) «Ру́сская кни́га». Там бы́ли кни́ги Булга́кова.
— Ты лю́бишь Булга́кова?
— Да, я о́чень люблю́ «Ма́стера и Маргари́ту».
— Ты чита́л Булга́кова по-ру́сски?
— Ну что ты! По-англи́йски, коне́чно!

ДИАЛОГ 2 Вы не зна́ете, где . . . ?
(Finding a certain place)

— Вы не зна́ете, где Пионе́рские пруды́ (пруд = *pond*)?
— Э́то ста́рое назва́ние. Сейча́с э́то Патриа́ршие пруды́.
— А где они́?
— Они́ в друго́м райо́не, в це́нтре.
— Спаси́бо.

УПРАЖНЕНИЕ 14 Ваш диало́г

Create a dialogue in which you ask a classmate about a writer you like. Ask if she has read that writer, and if so, if she has read some particular work. If the author wrote in a foreign language, find out whether your classmate read it in that language. Then switch roles.

❖❖ А ТЕПЕРЬ . . . : УПРАЖНЕНИЕ 15

Working with a classmate, use what you learned in Part 2 to . . .

1. ask where she was living when she went to school (use **ходи́ть в шко́лу**)
2. ask if she was born in that city
3. find out whether she likes to read, and if so, what she likes to read (note: *novel* is **рома́н**)
4. ask if she has read **Че́хов, Шекспи́р, Пу́шкин, Твен, Го́голь**
5. find out if she went to the library (the gym, the movies, . . .) yesterday

С ЧЕГО НАЧАТЬ?

зубна́я па́ста

аспири́н†

зубна́я щётка

шокола́д†

туале́тная бума́га

мы́ло

шампу́нь†

пасти́лки от ка́шля

сигаре́ты†

откры́тка

— **Скажи́те, пожа́луйста,** где мо́жно купи́ть ка́рту Москвы́?
— В на́шем **кио́ске**†. Там есть всё. Вы там **мо́жете** купи́ть газе́ты и журна́лы, откры́тки, сигаре́ты, аспири́н, пасти́лки от ка́шля, зубну́ю щётку и зубну́ю па́сту, мы́ло, шампу́нь, туале́тную бума́гу, **проездны́е биле́ты,**[5] шокола́д . . .
— Не так бы́стро, пожа́луйста!

Вы мо́жете . . .	*You can . . .*
мы́ло	*soap*
пасти́лки от ка́шля	*cough drops*
проездно́й (биле́т)	*metro (bus, trolley, tram) pass*
Скажи́те, пожа́луйста, . . .	*Could you please tell me . . .*

---

[5]A **проездно́й биле́т** refers to a public transportation pass that gives the rider access to the subway, bus, trolley, and tram systems. The pass may cover only one form of transportation or a combination.

ЧТЕНИЕ

❖ БИ́ЗНЕС° ПО-МОСКО́ВСКИ°

business / Moscow style

(*A rainy morning. Residents of the building want to leave, but the rain and muddy ground are stopping them.*)

ЛЕ́НА.	Кака́я грязь°! У́жас!	*mud*
СА́ША.	Да, кошма́р!	
ПРОФЕ́ССОР.	(*Grumbling.*) Дом но́вый, а асфа́льта† нет.	
ЛЕ́НА.	**Нигде́**° не могу́ купи́ть **рези́новые**° **сапоги́.**° Нет моего́ **разме́ра.**°	*Nowhere / не. . . I can't / rubber / boots / size*
СА́ША.	Моего́ **то́же**° нет.	*Моего́. . . They don't have mine either.*

(*A young man appears in the doorway, wearing rain gear and carrying a box.*)

ВИ́КТОР.	У вас, ка́жется, пробле́мы?	
ПРОФЕ́ССОР.	Коне́чно, у нас пробле́мы. (*Gestures towards the conditions outside.*) Смотри́те!	
СА́ША.	Вы, коне́чно, нас не понима́ете, у вас есть сапоги́.	
ВИ́КТОР.	О́чень хорошо́ понима́ю и да́же могу́ **помо́чь.**°	*to help*
ВСЕ.	Как?	
ВИ́КТОР.	У меня́ есть рези́новые сапоги́. Все разме́ры.	
ПРОФЕ́ССОР.	И мы мо́жем их купи́ть?	
ВИ́КТОР.	Нет, я их не **продаю́.**°	*не. . . not selling*
СА́ША.	Но вы говори́те, что вы мо́жете помо́чь.	
ВИ́КТОР.	Да, я **действи́тельно**° могу́ помо́чь. Мой би́знес рабо́тает **так:**° **ка́ждое**° **у́тро**° я жду° вас здесь. Я **даю́**° **вам**° сапоги́. На **автобусной остано́вке**° вас ждёт мой **друг.**° Вы **отдаёте**° **ему́**° сапоги́ и **пла́тите**° **пятьсо́т**° **рубле́й.**°6	*really / like this* *every / morning / wait for / give / (to) you / bus stop friend / give back (to) him / pay / five hundred / rubles*
ПРОФЕ́ССОР.	Пятьсо́т рубле́й! Это **до́рого!**°	*expensive / friends*
ВИ́КТОР.	Вы ду́маете, это до́рого? Нет, дороги́е друзья́°, это **недо́рого.**° Пятьсо́т рубле́й — и у вас **чи́стые**° ту́фли и хоро́шее настрое́ние.°	*not expensive / clean / mood*
ЛЕ́НА.	А мой разме́р у вас есть?	

6500 rubles was an appropriate price at the time the video for this book was made. Currency fluctuations have been great since that time.

young women	ВИ́КТОР. Коне́чно. У меня́ есть все разме́ры. И краси́вые **де́вушки**°
get / for free	**получа́ют**° сапоги́ **беспла́тно.**°
discrimination	СА́ША. Э́то дискримина́ция°!
joke	ВИ́КТОР. Э́то **шу́тка.**° (*To Lena.*) Но вы действи́тельно о́чень краси́вая
	де́вушка.

УПРАЖНЕНИЕ 1   Под микроско́пом: Accusative case

There are ten Accusative case forms (nouns, noun phrases, pronouns) in this reading. Circle as many as you can find.

ГРАММАТИКА И ПРАКТИКА

❖ 5.9. INTENSIFIERS: ТАК, ТАКО́Й

Поэ́тому ты **так** хорошо́ говори́шь по-ру́сски!	*That's why you speak Russian so well!*

You already know one useful intensifier: **о́чень.**

О́ЧЕРЬ WITH VERBS	Я **о́чень люблю́** америка́нский рок.	*I like American rock a lot!*
О́ЧЕРЬ WITH ADVERBS	По-мо́ему, Са́ша **о́чень хорошо́** игра́ет кла́ссику.	*In my opinion, Sasha plays classical music really well.*
О́ЧЕРЬ WITH ADJECTIVES (+/− NOUN)	Э́то **о́чень больша́я ку́хня.**	*That's a very large kitchen.*

Two even stronger intensifiers are **так** and **тако́й** (-**а́я, -о́е, -и́е**). **Так** is used with adverbs and verbs, and is often translated as *so, so very, so much*. **Тако́й**, whose adjectival endings must agree with the item being intensified, is used with nouns and adjectives. It is often translated as *such, such a, so, a real*.

ТАК WITH VERBS	Я **так хочу́** его́ ви́деть!	*I want to see him so much!*
ТАК WITH ADVERBS	Джим **так хорошо́** говори́т по-ру́сски!	*Jim speaks Russian so well!*
ТАКО́Й WITH ADJECTIVES (+/− NOUN)	Э́то **така́я интере́сная кни́га!** Ле́на **така́я краси́вая!**	*It is such an interesting book! Lena is so beautiful!*
ТАКО́Й WITH NOUNS	Э́то **тако́й кошма́р!**	*It's a real nightmare!*

You can also express intense *negative* feelings or judgments this way.

Я **о́чень** (**так**) **не** люблю́ смотре́ть бейсбо́л!	*I really don't like watching baseball.*

Так and **о́чень** are essentially synonymous adverbs, with **так** being somewhat more emotional: **Я так люблю́ хокке́й!** is a little stronger than **Я о́чень люблю́ хокке́й.**

УПРАЖНЕНИЕ 2   Intensifiers

Insert **о́чень, так,** or a form of **тако́й** to intensify the statements below. More than one answer may be correct.

— Это ва́ша маши́на? У вас _____[1] краси́вая маши́на!

— Да, маши́на краси́вая. Но у меня́ _____[2] пробле́ма! У меня́ нет гаража́, а я _____[3] не люблю́ паркова́ть маши́ну на у́лице!

— Да, я вас _____[4] хорошо́ понима́ю. Я то́же _____[5] не люблю́ паркова́ть маши́ну на у́лице. А гара́ж в Москве́—э́то _____[6] до́рого!

— А вы не москви́ч? Вы америка́нец? Вы _____[7] хорошо́ говори́те по-ру́сски!

— У меня́ был _____[8] замеча́тельный преподава́тель!

УПРАЖНЕНИЕ 3   Кака́я у тебя́ мечта́?
(What do you dream about doing?)

How would answer the question **Кака́я у тебя́ мечта́?** Read through the following list and choose (or make up) an answer: **Я так хочу́...** Then go around the room and ask other students the same question; find out if anyone else shares your fondest hope or if other students share another hope.

жить в Санкт-Петербу́рге
учи́ться в Москве́
чита́ть кни́ги по-ру́сски
писа́ть интере́сные статьи́
игра́ть в Нью-Йо́ркском филармони́ческом орке́стре
рабо́тать в Библиоте́ке Конгре́сса
учи́ться на биологи́ческом факульте́те
???

◈ 5.10. *TO BE ABLE:* МОЧЬ

Нигде́ не **могу́** купи́ть рези́новые сапоги́.

I can't buy rubber boots anywhere.

Мочь is used with an infinitive. In the following conjugation note the stem-consonant mutation (**г-ж-г**), which also appears in other verbs you will learn.

я мог-у́	мы мо́ж-ем
ты мо́ж-ешь	вы мо́ж-ете
он, она́ мо́ж-ет	они́ мо́г-ут

УПРАЖНЕНИЕ 4   Мочь

Complete the following sentences with the correct forms of the verb **мочь**.

1. Идёт дождь (*it's raining*), везде́ грязь (*mud*). Ле́на говори́т: — Я нигде́ не _____ купи́ть рези́новые сапоги́!

2. «Мы то́же нигде́ не _____ их купи́ть», — ду́мают сосе́ди.

3. Ви́ктор говори́т, что он _____ помо́чь.

4. Профе́ссор Петро́вский спра́шивает (*asks*): — Как вы _____
помо́чь?

5. Ви́ктор говори́т: — Когда́ грязь, я _____ ждать вас здесь.
У меня́ есть сапоги́ — все разме́ры.

6. Профе́ссор Петро́вский говори́т: — И вы их продаёте — зна́чит,
мы _____ их купи́ть.

7. — Нет, — говори́т Ви́ктор. — Я их не продаю́, и вы не _____
их купи́ть.

УПРАЖНЕНИЕ 5   Де́душка и ба́бушка

Fill in the blanks, using present tense forms of the verbs **мочь** and **хоте́ть**.

Де́душка и ба́бушка _____[1] смотре́ть телеви́зор,
брат _____[2] рабо́тать на компью́тере[†], а ма́ма и па́па
_____[3] слу́шать му́зыку. Когда́ ба́бушка и де́душка
смо́трят телеви́зор, я не_____[4] его́ смотре́ть. Почему́
они́ _____[5] де́лать то, что (*what*) _____,[6]
а мы—я и сестра́—не _____[7]? «Де́ти, — говори́т ма́ма,
— вы _____[8] гуля́ть, чита́ть, игра́ть в ша́хматы. Почему́
вы всегда́ _____[9] смотре́ть телеви́зор?!»

❖ 5.11. GENITIVE SINGULAR: ADJECTIVES AND POSSESSIVES

Нет **моего́** разме́ра.   *They don't have my size.*

Adjectives and possessives that modify Genitive singular nouns have their own Genitive
singular endings. If you keep in mind what you have learned about hard/soft-series
vowel letters, spelling rules (unstressed **о** → **е** after hushers), and the effects of stress,
the apparent variations in the table turn out to be quite regular and predictable. Note
that the **-г-** in the ending **-ого/-его** is pronounced [**-в-**], as in the word **его́**.

	NOMINATIVE CASE (dictionary form)	GENITIVE SINGULAR ENDING	EXAMPLES
ADJECTIVES (including adjectives used as nouns)			
Masculine and neuter	проездно́й биле́т хоро́шее кре́сло	-ого/-его	У меня́ нет **проездно́го** биле́та. Тут нет **хоро́шего** кре́сла.
Feminine	зубна́я па́ста хоро́шая апте́ка	-ой/-ей	В кио́ске нет **зубно́й** па́сты. В на́шем райо́не нет **хоро́шей** апте́ки.
POSSESSIVES			
Masculine and neuter	ваш аспира́нт тво-ё письмо́	-его	У **ва́шего** аспира́нта интере́сная диссерта́ция. Тут нет **твоего́** письма́.
Feminine	мо-я́ сестра́	-ей	У **мое́й** сестры́ есть ка́рта Москвы́.

УПРАЖНЕНИЕ 6   «Наша школа»

Place the words in parentheses into the Genitive singular form. Be prepared to translate the resulting sentences into English and explain why the Genitive case is used.

Вот письмо от (*from*)_____[1] (моя сестра). Она просит (*is asking*) меня купить журнал «Наша школа». В этом журнале есть фотография†_____[2] (наш старый учитель *teacher*) и статья о нём (*about him*). В нашем киоске нет этого (*that*)_____[3] (журнал). Мой брат получает разные журналы, но_____[4] («Наша школа») у него нет. У_____[5] (мой друг) журнала тоже нет. Может быть, журнал есть у_____[6] (наш сосед Антон Иванович). Ведь он учитель.

УПРАЖНЕНИЕ 7   Новая квартира

You've just moved into an apartment and are telling a friend about it. Complete the descriptions below with the correct case endings. In the parentheses, indicate the case needed.

1. У нас большая новая квартира. Рядом автобусная остановка, но нет хорош_____ магазин_____ (_____).
2. В наш_____ дом_____ (_____) большие окна.
3. В наш_____ квартир_____ (_____) большая кухня, но нет балкон_____ (_____).
4. У мо_____ сестр_____ (_____) небольшая, но светлая комната.
5. Рядом живёт профессор математики. У этого стар_____ профессор_____ (_____) везде книги, даже в туалет_____ (_____)!
6. У кажд_____ сосед_____ (_____) есть место в больш_____ гараж_____ (_____).
7. У нас тоже есть место в гараж_____ (_____), но у нас нет машин_____ (_____)!

СЛОВА, СЛОВА, СЛОВА . . . ✪ ‹от + *Genitive*›

Папа хочет купить гараж, читает объявления, но нет ничего **близко от** дома.

Dad wants to get a garage. He reads the ads, but there's nothing near the house.

The preposition **от** is followed by the Genitive case. It generally means *from*, as in **Вот письмо от моей сестры**; it also combines with several adverbs that are already familiar to you.

близко от + Genitive	*close to, near*
далеко от + Genitive	*far from*
недалеко от + Genitive	*not far from*

УПРАЖНЕНИЕ 8   Далеко́ от. . . Недалеко́ от. . . Бли́зко от. . .

These phrases with **от** all require the Genitive case. Fill in the blanks with correct Genitive forms of the words and phrases provided in cues.

Мы живём в це́нтре Москвы́, недалеко́ от _____ [1] (Кра́сная пло́щадь). Мой муж преподаёт в Фина́нсовой акаде́мии. Э́то далеко́ от _____ [2] (мы), но е́хать туда́ удо́бно (*is convenient*). Мо́жно е́хать на метро́, и ста́нция метро́ недалеко́ от _____ [3] (наш дом). Я рабо́таю в большо́й апте́ке на Тверско́й. Э́то о́чень бли́зко от _____ [4] (мы). К сожале́нию (*Unfortunately*), на́ша дочь живёт далеко́ от _____ [5] (центр), и мы ви́дим её не о́чень ча́сто.

УПРАЖНЕНИЕ 9   Вы не зна́ете но́мер телефо́на. . .?

You work as an operator at Moscow State University (**Моско́вский госуда́рственный университе́т = МГУ**). Refer to the following page from the university phone book. Your classmate plays a caller who asks for the phone number of an academic department. He should work from the list in Appendix K and write down the number as you give it to him. Switch roles after requesting three numbers, then check them against the phone book to make sure you each wrote them down correctly.

ОБРАЗЕ́Ц: — Но́мер телефо́на филосо́фского факульте́та, пожа́луйста.
— [*Read numbers singly.*] 9-3-9-1-9-2-5.

им. М.В. ЛОМОНОСОВА МОСК. ГОС. (МГУ); 117234, Воробьевы Горы, МГУ   ☏ 939 1000
Биологический фак-т   ☏ 939 2776
Вычислительной математики и кибернетики фак-т   ☏ 939 2596
Географический фак-т   ☏ 939 2238
Геологический фак-т   ☏ 939 1301
Исторический фак-т   ☏ 939 3566
Подготовительные курсы   ☏ 939 2137
Почвоведения фак-т   ☏ 939 2947
Физический фак-т   ☏ 939 1682
Филологический фак-т   ☏ 939 5596
Философский фак-т   ☏ 939 1925
Химический фак-т   ☏ 939 1671
Экономический фак-т   ☏ 939 3495
Юридический фак-т   ☏ 939 2903
им. М.В. ЛОМОНОСОВА МОСК. ГОС. (МГУ); 121019, Моховая ул., 11   ☏ 203 6565
Журналистики фак-т; 121019, Моховая ул., 9   ☏ 203 6641
Психологии фак-т; 121019, Моховая ул., 8, к. 5   ☏ 203 6593
Стран Азии и Африки ин-т (ИСАА); 121019, Моховая ул., 11   ☏ 203 6476

УЧИСЬ УЧИТЬСЯ ✪ *Antonyms and Contrasts*

Many students find that consciously learning pairs of words with opposite or contrasting meanings helps them retain vocabulary. Try this not only with adjectives (**но́вый-ста́рый**) but also with adverbs (**бли́зко-далеко́**), nouns (**день-ночь**) and verbs (**говори́ть-слу́шать**).

УПРАЖНЕНИЕ 10   Анто́нимы

Write down three adjective-noun phrases that describe something you have (or wish you had). Use only the singular: **краси́вая ко́шка, больша́я кварти́ра, но́вый компью́тер, стра́нный** (*strange*) **сосе́д.** Then see how many other students can respond with a contrasting statement.

ОБРАЗЕ́Ц: — У меня́ но́вый компью́тер. А у тебя́?
              — А у меня́ ста́рый.
                        or
              — У меня́ то́же но́вый компью́тер.

The following contrasting adjective pairs may help:

но́вый — ста́рый
молодо́й (*young*) — ста́рый
лёгкий (*easy*) — тру́дный
большо́й — ма́ленький
симпати́чный — несимпати́чный
хоро́ший — плохо́й (и́ли ужа́сный)
чи́стый — гря́зный (*dirty*)

КУЛЬТУРА РЕЧИ

❖ ТАК ГОВОРЯ́Т: КА́ЖЕТСЯ

У вас, **ка́жется**, пробле́мы?

Я их вчера́ ви́дел, но не по́мню где. **Ка́жется**, в па́рке.

It seems you're having some problems.
I saw them yesterday, but I don't remember where. It seems like it was in the park.

The effect of inserting **ка́жется** into a question or statement is to add some uncertainty or doubt.

УПРАЖНЕНИЕ 11   Ка́жется

How would you use **ка́жется** to react in the following situations?

1. A friend points to an unfamiliar woman in front of your building and asks who she is. You think she might be your new neighbor.
2. Your roommate is getting ready to go out, and you think she's wearing something new.
3. You are studying in Moscow and learning the names of other students in the dorm. Someone mentions his roommate, Yoriko Nakajima. You think you've already met him and that he studies in the physics department.

❖ САМОПРОВЕРКА: УПРАЖНЕНИЕ 12

Working on your own, try this self-test: Read a Russian sentence out loud, then give an idiomatic English equivalent without looking at the book. Then work from English to Russian. After you have completed this activity, try it with a classmate.

1. Я нигде́ не могу́ купи́ть кроссо́вки. Нет моего́ разме́ра.
2. Твоя́ сестра́ о́чень тала́нтливая. Она́ так хорошо́ игра́ет Рахма́нинова!
3. От кого́ э́то письмо́? От твоего́ дру́га?
4. У тебя́ таки́е интере́сные кни́ги и ка́рты!

1. *I can't buy running shoes anywhere. They don't have my size.*
2. *Your sister's very talented. She plays Rachmaninov so well!*
3. *Who is that letter from? From your friend?*
4. *You have such interesting books and maps!*

❖ ВОПРОСЫ И ОТВЕТЫ: УПРАЖНЕНИЕ 13

1. Почему́ у тебя́ сего́дня плохо́е настрое́ние (*mood*)? У тебя́ всегда́ плохо́е настрое́ние? (*or*) У тебя́ сего́дня о́чень хоро́шее настрое́ние. У тебя́ всегда́ хоро́шее настрое́ние?
2. Ты живёшь бли́зко и́ли далеко́ от университе́та?
3. Ты живёшь в хоро́шем райо́не?
4. На како́м этаже́ ты живёшь?
5. На твое́й у́лице есть авто́бусная остано́вка?
6. В твоём райо́не есть магази́ны, где мо́жно купи́ть проду́кты? Они́ недалеко́ от до́ма?
7. А есть магази́н, где мо́жно купи́ть кроссо́вки, ту́фли, сапоги́? (*If the answer is no:*) Где мо́жно их купи́ть?
8. (*Depending on the response:*) Там есть кроссо́вки о́чень большо́го разме́ра? А о́чень ма́ленького?
9. В твоём райо́не есть магази́н «Спорт»? Э́то далеко́ от твоего́ до́ма? Там мо́жно купи́ть ковбо́йские[†] сапоги́?
10. Э́то дорого́й магази́н?

❖ ДИАЛОГИ

ДИАЛОГ 1 Кака́я грязь!
(Expressing dismay)

— Кака́я грязь (*mud*)!
— Да, кошма́р! Дом но́вый, а асфа́льта[†] нет.
— У нас то́же но́вый дом и то́же нет асфа́льта.
— Да, э́то ужа́сная пробле́ма.

ДИАЛОГ 2 Где мо́жно купи́ть . . . ?
(Asking where to buy things)

— Вы не зна́ете, где мо́жно купи́ть рези́новые сапоги́?
— Вот наш магази́н. Там есть рези́новые сапоги́.
— Все разме́ры?
— Не зна́ю. Мой разме́р у них есть. Мо́жет быть, ваш то́же есть.

УПРАЖНЕНИЕ 14   Ваш диало́г

Create a dialogue in which you and a friend are commiserating about being unable to find some things you need to buy.

❖ А ТЕПЕРЬ. . . : УПРАЖНЕНИЕ 15

Working with a classmate, use what you learned in Part 3 to . . .

1. complain about something you want to do, but cannot
2. compliment him on something he does well
3. remark that it seems he's been to Europe
4. ask if he knows the nice young musician who lives next door

С ЧЕГО НАЧАТЬ?

Я ем	I eat	овсянка	oatmeal
Я пью	I drink	яичница	fried eggs
Я опаздываю	I'm late	чёрный кофе	black coffee
ветчина	ham	сыр	cheese

❖ ЧТЕНИЕ ❖

❖ ОТЛИ́ЧНАЯ МЫСЛЬ°   *thought*

(Jim and Ilya Ilyich are sitting at a cafe not far from the university. Tanya enters, sees Ilya Ilyich and walks over.)

ТА́НЯ.	Здра́вствуйте, Илья́ Ильи́ч.
ПРОФ.	Та́ня! До́брый день, Та́ня. Познако́мьтесь, э́то Джим Ри́чардсон, наш аспира́нт. Джим, э́то Та́ня Жили́нская. Та́ня — дочь моего́ ста́рого дру́га, Андре́я Ви́кторовича Жили́нского, и, **кста́ти,°** *by the way*
	на́ша студе́нтка.
ДЖИМ, ТА́НЯ.	*(Simultaneously.)* О́чень прия́тно.
ПРОФ.	Где же наш официа́нт? Мо́жет быть, **э́тот°** **молодо́й челове́к°**? *that / молодо́й... young man*
ТА́НЯ.	Нет, Илья́ Ильи́ч, не э́тот, а вон **тот.°** Ви́дите высо́кого° **па́рня,°** *that one / tall / guy*
	кото́рый° открыва́ет° бутьı́лку°? Э́то ваш официа́нт. *who / is opening / bottle*
	(Explaining to Jim.) Мы ча́сто хо́дим в э́то кафе́, и я здесь всех° *everyone*
	зна́ю.

(She motions to the waiter, who comes over to the table.)   Что... *What can I get you?*

ОФИЦИА́НТ.	До́брый день! **Что бу́дете зака́зывать°**?
ПРОФ.	**Пре́жде всего́°** — **минера́льную во́ду.°** *(Looking at Tanya and*
	Jim.) Ко́фе? *(They nod.)* А что ещё?
ОФИЦИА́НТ.	Рекоменду́ю° минда́льные° **пиро́жные°** и шокола́дный° **торт°**.
ТА́НЯ.	Я хочу́ минда́льное пиро́жное.
ДЖИМ.	Шокола́дный торт, пожа́луйста.

Пре́жде... *First of all /*
  минера́льную... *mineral*
  water
I recommend / almond /
  pastries / chocolate / cake

Excellent / So ещё… *one more*	ПРОФ.	**Отли́чно!**° Ита́к,° минера́льная вода́, три ко́фе, минда́льное пиро́жное и шокола́дный торт. И … **ещё одно́**° минда́льное пиро́жное.

(Half an hour later.)

к… *unfortunately / have to /* *Check* *is planning to come*	ПРОФ.	Я, **к сожале́нию,**° **до́лжен**° идти́. (*To the waiter.*) **Счёт,**° пожа́луйста. Та́ня, когда́ Андре́й Ви́кторович **собира́ется**° в Москву́?
	ТА́НЯ.	Не зна́ю, Илья́ Ильи́ч.
rarely / go *bad* я… *it's my treat*	ПРОФ.	Я тепе́рь **ре́дко**° **е́зжу**° в Петербу́рг, а он — в Москву́. Это **нехорошо́.**° (*The waiter brings the bill. Jim and Tanya begin to reach for their money.*) Сего́дня **я угоща́ю.**°
	ДЖИМ, ТА́НЯ.	Спаси́бо, Илья́ Ильи́ч.
a major anniversary Кру́глая… *A good round* *figure* об… *don't say a word about* *it / will be / surprise / people*	ТА́НЯ.	Илья́ Ильи́ч, вы по́мните, что в январе́ у па́пы юбиле́й°? Кру́глая да́та.° Мо́жет быть, вы …
	ПРОФ.	Отли́чная мысль! Но об э́том (*puts his finger to his lips indicating a secret*) **ни сло́ва.**° Это бу́дет° **сюрпри́з.**° До свида́ния, молоды́е **лю́ди.**°
	ДЖИМ, ТА́НЯ.	До свида́ния, Илья́ Ильи́ч.
	ТА́НЯ.	(*Turning back to Jim.*) Где вы живёте, Джим?
	ДЖИМ.	В общежи́тии. А вы?
friend / are looking for *for now / у…* *at my aunt's* *is for rent*	ТА́НЯ.	Мы — моя́ **подру́га**° Све́та и я — **и́щем**° кварти́ру и́ли ко́мнату. А пока́° я живу́ у тёти.°
	ДЖИМ.	Я ви́дел объявле́ние, что сдаётся° ко́мната в до́ме, где живёт Илья́ Ильи́ч. У меня́ есть но́мер телефо́на.
Like	ТА́НЯ.	**Как**° говори́т Илья́ Ильи́ч, отли́чная мысль!

УПРАЖНЕ́НИЕ 1   Под микроско́пом: Recognizing cases

Below are some phrases taken from this reading. Identify the case of the italicized noun or noun phrase.

1. Та́ня — дочь *моего́ ста́рого дру́га.* (_____)

2. Где же *наш официа́нт*? (_____)

3. Ви́дите *высо́кого па́рня* … (_____)

4. …кото́рый открыва́ет *буты́лку*? (_____)

5. Рекоменду́ю *минда́льные пиро́жные и шокола́дный торт.* (_____)

6. Я хочу́ *минда́льное пиро́жное.* (_____)

7. Я тепе́рь ре́дко е́зжу в *Петербу́рг.* (_____)

8. В *общежи́тии.* (_____)

9. Мы …и́щем *кварти́ру и́ли ко́мнату.* (_____)

ГРАММАТИКА И ПРАКТИКА

❖ 5.12. PUNCTUATION: USES OF THE DASH

You have encountered the following uses of the dash (as distinct from the hyphen).

1. In affirmative equational (such as A = B) sentences

   Джим — америка́нец.
   Та́ня — дочь моего́ ста́рого дру́га.
   Вы — Са́ша и Алекса́ндр, а я — Джим и Джеймс.

2. To replace part of a sentence (especially the predicate) that can be easily understood from context

   | ОФИЦИА́НТ. | Что бу́дете зака́зывать? |
   | ПРОФЕ́ССОР. | Пре́жде всего́ — минера́льную во́ду. |

   Я ре́дко е́зжу в Петербу́рг, а он — в Москву́.

3. To set off a part of a sentence (such as an appositive) that specifies or explains the preceding word or phrase

   Мы — моя́ подру́га и я — и́щем кварти́ру и́ли ко́мнату.

As with many aspects of punctuation, these uses are not so much hard-and-fast rules as rather common tendencies. Note also that in typed or typeset material a space is usually left on each side of the dash (in contrast to English, where no space is left).

❖ 5.13. POINTING AND DISTINGUISHING THINGS: Э́ТО **VS.** Э́ТОТ

| Проф. | Где же наш официа́нт? Мо́жет быть, **э́тот** молодо́й челове́к? | *"Where's our waiter? Maybe it's that young man?"* |
| Та́ня. | Нет, Илья́ Ильи́ч, не **э́тот**, а вон тот. . . . **Э́то** ваш официа́нт. | *"No, Ilya Ilyich, not that one, but the one over there . . . . That's your waiter."* |

As you know, the demonstrative pronoun **э́то** (*this is, that is, these are, those are*) is used in sentences of introduction and naming, such as **э́то мой брат, а э́то моя́ сестра́.** (*this/that is my brother, and this/that is my sister.*) In these sentences, **э́то** never changes form. But suppose you want to distinguish one thing from other similar things, as in *This book* [as distinct from other nearby books] *is mine* or *That dog* [as distinct from other dogs in the same area] *is ours.* Then the words *this* and *that* are adjectives and their equivalents in Russian must reflect the gender, number and case of the noun with which they are used. Compare the following, noting how the English equivalents in the left column differ from those in the right.

Это мой ковёр.	Этот (*m.*) ковёр мой.
This is (that's) my rug.	*This (that) rug is mine.*
Это моё одея́ло.	Это (*neut.*) одея́ло моё.
This is (that's) my blanket.	*This (that) blanket is mine.*
Это моя́ поду́шка.	Эта (*f.*) поду́шка моя́.
This is (that's) my pillow.	*This (that) pillow is mine.*
Это мои́ карти́ны.	Эти (*pl.*) карти́ны мои́.
These (those) are my pictures.	*These (those) pictures are mine.*

УПРАЖНЕНИЕ 2   Это ваш дом?

Jim is showing some pictures of his home and family to Vova. Provide the correct form of **это** or **этот** (эта, это, эти), and circle those that are adjectival.

ДЖИМ.   _____[1] наш дом.

ВО́ВА.   Како́й большо́й! А _____[2] ва́ша маши́на?

ДЖИМ.   Да, _____[3] маши́на на́ша. И _____[4] мотоци́кл† то́же наш.

ВО́ВА.   А где твоя́ ко́мната?

ДЖИМ.   Вот _____[5] ко́мната — моя́. А _____[6] ко́мната—на́ша столо́вая.

ВО́ВА.   А кто _____[7]? Твои́ роди́тели?

ДЖИМ.   Нет, _____[8] не роди́тели. _____[9] на́ши сосе́ди. А вот моя́ ма́ма.

ВО́ВА.   А кто _____[10] лю́ди?

ДЖИМ.   _____[11] мой друг Ро́берт. А _____[12] профе́ссор Макке́нзи. Он преподаёт исто́рию Росси́и в на́шем университе́те.

❖ 5.14. CONTRASTING SIMILAR ITEMS: ЭТОТ, ТОТ

To contrast two of the same items, as in **this book** *is mine, and* **that book** *is hers,* the agreeing pronoun **тот** (*that*) is used to contrast with agreeing forms of **этот**. The form of **этот** or **тот** always agrees in gender, number, and case with the noun to which it refers. Compare the Nominative case forms of **этот** with those of **тот,** and note the unusual plural forms.

	THIS, THAT	THAT	EXAMPLES (NOMINATIVE)
Masculine	этот	тот	**этот** сыр (*this cheese*) **тот** шокола́д (*that chocolate*)
Feminine	эта	та	**эта** вы́ставка (*this exhibition*) **та** дие́та (*that diet*)
Neuter	это	то	**это** пиро́жное (*this pastry*) **то** мы́ло (*that soap*)
Plural (all genders)	эти	те	**эти** де́вочки (*these girls*) **те** ма́льчики (*those boys*)

УПРАЖНЕНИЕ 3   Этот и тот

Fill in the correct form of **э́тот** or **тот**.

1. _____ ка́рта о́чень краси́вая, а _____ о́чень некраси́вая.
2. Я не хочу́ чита́ть _____ журна́л.
3. _____ де́вушки и́щут (*are looking for*) ко́мнату.
4. _____ ма́льчик о́чень симпати́чный.
5. _____ студе́нт живёт в на́шем до́ме, а _____ в общежи́тии.
6. _____ дом наш.
7. _____ кни́ги интере́сные, а _____ не о́чень интере́сные.
8. _____ общежи́тие но́вое, а _____ ста́рое.

❖ 5.15. ACCUSATIVE CASE: ADJECTIVES AND POSSESSIVES

Моего́ нау́чного руководи́теля Вы зна́ете.	*You know my academic adviser.*
Ви́дите **высо́кого** па́рня, кото́рый открыва́ет буты́лку?	*Do you see the tall guy who's opening the bottle?*
Пре́жде всего́ — **минера́льную** во́ду.	*First of all [we'd like] mineral water.*

In Lesson 3, Part 2 you learned the Accusative case forms of most nouns; in Lesson 5, Part 2 you learned the Accusative case forms of animate masculine nouns and of personal pronouns. Now you are encountering adjectives and possessives in the Accusative case. You may have noticed that many are forms you're already familiar with. Only the feminine forms are new.

	NOMINATIVE CASE (dictionary form)	ACCUSATIVE CASE	EXAMPLES
ADJECTIVES (including adjectives used as nouns)			
Masculine inanimate **Neuter** **Plural inanimate**[7]	но́в-ый (стол) хоро́ш-ий (рестора́н) интере́сн-ое (письмо́) и́мпортн-ые (маши́ны)	Same as Nominative	но́в-**ый** (стол) хоро́ш-**ий** (рестора́н) интере́сн-**ое** (письмо́) и́мпортн-**ые** (маши́ны)
Masculine animate	люби́м-ый (компози́тор) хоро́ш-ий (врач)	Same as Genitive	люби́м-**ого** (компози́тора) хоро́ш-**его** (врача́)
Feminine	кни́жн-ая (по́лка) столо́в-ая	-ую	кни́жн-**ую** (по́лку) столо́в-**ую**
POSSESSIVES			
Masculine inanimate **Neuter** **Plural inanimate**	мо-й / наш (дом) мо-ё / наш-е (сочине́ние) тво-и́ / ваш-и (джи́нсы)	Same as Nominative	мо-**й**/наш (дом) мо-**ё**/наш-**е** (сочине́ние) тво-**и́**/ваш-**и** (джи́нсы)
Masculine animate	мо-й / ваш (друг)	Same as Genitive	мо-**его́** / ваш-**его** (дру́га)
Feminine	мо-я́ / тво-я́ (кни́га) наш-а / ваш-а (у́лица)	-ю -у	мо-**ю́** / тво-**ю́** (кни́гу) наш-**у**/ваш-**у** (у́лицу)

[7]When you learn plural animate forms in the Accusative—which are like plural Genitive forms—your knowledge of the Accusative case forms will be largely complete.

УПРАЖНЕНИЕ 4 A visit to the Silins'

Fill in the blanks in the following text by adding the correct Accusative case form of the adjectives, adjectival nouns, and possessives in parentheses.

(*Natalya Ivanovna's friend Veronika and her husband come to visit the Silins.*)

— Ната́ша, Серге́й, здра́вствуйте! Мы принесли́ (*brought*) _____¹ (шокола́дный) торт и _____² (хоро́ший) конья́к.† Ната́ша, я зна́ю, что ты на дие́те.† Тебе́ (*For you*) мы принесли́ _____ _____³ (минда́льные пиро́жные).

(*Later at the table*)

— Веро́ника, ты хо́чешь чай и́ли ко́фе?
— _____⁴ (Чёрный) ко́фе, пожа́луйста. И _____ _____⁵ (минда́льное пиро́жное). Ната́ша, мы вчера́ бы́ли в теа́тре. Ви́дели _____ _____⁶ (интере́сная но́вая) пье́су.
— А мы вчера́ ви́дели _____ _____⁷ (интере́сная ста́рая) пье́су — «_____⁸ (Вишнёвый) сад» Че́хова. Хо́чешь ещё одно́ _____⁹ (пиро́жное)?

(*The guests are leaving.*)

— Где моя́ су́мка? Никто́ не ви́дел _____ _____¹⁰ (моя́ су́мка)? Бе́лка, что ты де́лаешь?!
— Извини́, Веро́ника, на́ша Бе́лка о́чень лю́бит _____ _____¹¹ (дороги́е но́вые) су́мки.

УПРАЖНЕНИЕ 5 Моя́ сестра́ хорошо́ зна́ет америка́нскую му́зыку

Make up ten present tense sentences using the subjects, verbs, and objects listed in the following table. Remember to put the objects in the Accusative case.

ОБРАЗЕ́Ц: — *Мои́ однокла́ссники лю́бят ру́сскую литерату́ру.*

SUBJECTS	VERBS[8]	OBJECTS
Мой друг Ми́ша	знать	америка́нская му́зыка
Моя́ сестра́	игра́ть	дома́шнее зада́ние
Мои́ однокла́ссники	люби́ть	э́тот молодо́й журнали́ст
Твой нау́чный руководи́тель	писа́ть	ру́сская литерату́ра†
На́ша сосе́дка Мари́на	получа́ть	хоро́шая недорога́я кварти́ра
Э́ти молоды́е лю́ди	по́мнить	финáнсовые проблéмы
Наш преподава́тель (На́ша преподава́тельница) ру́сского языка́	понима́ть продава́ть хоте́ть чита́ть	дороги́е пода́рки (*gifts*) пье́са Че́хова «Три сестры́» интере́сные статьи́ и́мпортная ме́бель
???		???

---

[8]The verbs in the list are called *transitive* verbs because they can take a direct object. Contrast them with *intransitive* verbs, such as **роди́ться, гуля́ть,** and **мочь,** which do not take a direct object.

УПРАЖНЕНИЕ 6 Како́й рюкза́к ты хо́чешь?

You are preparing for a trip, and you still need to get a number of items. Answer the following questions, giving some details about exactly what you want. Use some of these adjectives in your answers.

большо́й	краси́вый	недорого́й
дорого́й	ма́ленький	но́вый
интере́сный	небольшо́й	хоро́ший

ОБРАЗЕ́Ц: — Како́й га́лстук ты хо́чешь?
— Я хочу́ недорого́й га́лстук.

1. Како́й рюкза́к ты хо́чешь?
2. Каку́ю су́мку ты хо́чешь?
3. Каки́е кроссо́вки ты хо́чешь?
4. Каку́ю запи́сную кни́жку (*address book*) ты хо́чешь?
5. Каки́е джи́нсы ты хо́чешь?
6. Како́й детекти́в ты хо́чешь?
7. Каку́ю блу́зку ты хо́чешь?
8. Каки́е брю́ки ты хо́чешь?

❖ 5.16. CLAUSE LINKS: КОТО́РЫЙ

Ви́дите высо́кого па́рня, **кото́рый** открыва́ет буты́лку?

Do you see the tall guy who's opening the bottle?

A relative clause is introduced by a form of the relative pronoun **кото́рый** (*who, which, that*). The number and the gender of **кото́рый** depend on what it refers to (its *antecedent*). **Кото́рый** takes regular *adjectival* endings.

Сосе́дка, **кото́рая** живёт на второ́м этаже́, о́чень симпати́чная.

The neighbor who lives on the second floor is very nice.

In this case, the antecedent **сосе́дка** is feminine singular, so **кото́рая** must be feminine singular to agree with it. The ending of **котóр-** is plural if the antecedent is plural.

Студе́нты, **кото́рые** живу́т здесь, говоря́т по-ру́сски.

The students who live here speak Russian.

Sometimes the words *which* and *that* are left out in English. Relative pronouns must always be included in Russian, however, and they are always preceded by a comma.[9]

УПРАЖНЕНИЕ 7 Кото́рый

Grandma Kruglov is introducing her new friends and neighbors. Fill in the blanks with the appropriate form of **кото́рый**.

Это Джим, аспира́нт университе́та, _____[1] хорошо́ говори́т по-ру́сски. А э́то Та́ня, студе́нтка университе́та, _____[2] зна́ет англи́йский язы́к. У Та́ни есть друзья́, _____[3] живу́т в на́шем до́ме, и есть друзья́, _____[4] живу́т в общежи́тии. Это мой

---

[9]These examples all have **кото́рый** in the Nominative. In future lessons you will learn how to use **кото́рый** in other cases.

внук Са́ша, студе́нт консервато́рии, _____ [5] прекра́сно игра́ет
и кла́ссику и джаз. Э́то молодо́й челове́к, _____ [6] говори́т, что
он бизнесме́н. А э́то Си́лины, на́ши сосе́ди, _____ [7] живу́т на
второ́м этаже́.

❖ 5.17. ROUND-TRIP AND HABITUAL TRAVEL: ХОДИ́ТЬ, Е́ЗДИТЬ

Вчера́ мы **ходи́ли** на вы́ставку «Исто́рия Москвы́».	*Yesterday we went to the exhibition, "The History of Moscow."*
Мы ча́сто **хо́дим** в э́то кафе́.	*We come to this cafe a lot.*
Я тепе́рь ре́дко **е́зжу** в Петербу́рг.	*I rarely go to St. Petersburg these days.*

All of the above sentences present the notion of making one or more trips to a particular destination and returning. Unlike the **идти́** and **е́хать** "go" sentences you encountered in Lesson Three, note that these trips are viewed by their respective speakers in complete terms, that is, *going to the exhibit (and coming home); repeatedly going to the cafe (over a period of time); going to St. Petersburg (such as on business trips and then returning to Moscow)*. "There and back" is the key element in the use of **ходи́ть** and its counterpart for vehicular/distance travel, **е́здить**. As the first example shows, these verbs can refer to a single round trip that has already been completed (hence past tense only); or, as the other two examples show, they can describe habitual trips. A destination is usually stated when these verbs are used.

Here are the conjugations of these verbs. In addition to their parallel usage, their conjugations are similar: You will notice that both are **-ишь** verbs with a **д > ж** stem-consonant mutation in the **я** form. But note the stress pattern difference: **ходи́ть** exhibits shifting stress, while **е́здить** exhibits stem stress.

ХОДИ́ТЬ *TO GO SOMEWHERE* (round trip)		Е́ЗДИТЬ *TO GO SOMEWHERE* (round trip, vehicle stated or assumed)	
я	хож-у́	я	е́зж-у
ты	хо́д -ишь	ты	е́зд -ишь
он, она́	хо́д -ит	он, она́	е́зд -ит
мы	хо́д -им	мы	е́зд -им
вы	хо́д -ите	вы	е́зд -ите
они́	хо́д -ят	они́	е́зд -ят

Reminder: use **е́здить** and **е́хать** when use of a vehicle is mentioned (such as when you're specifically stating that you're taking the bus or driving a car) or when vehicular travel can be inferred from the distance of the trip (such as when you're talking about going to another city). Otherwise, if you're just talking about going to school, a restaurant, a concert or a friend's house, use **ходи́ть** and **идти́**.

УПРАЖНЕНИЕ 8   На́ше расписа́ние (*schedule*)

Fill in the blanks in the following text with the appropriate present tense form of the verb **ходи́ть**.

Я _____¹ на рабо́ту ка́ждый день, а жена́—во вто́рник и в четве́рг. В понеде́льник и в четве́рг я _____² ве́чером в спортза́л. В понеде́льник, в сре́ду и в пя́тницу моя́ жена́ _____³ на ку́рсы англи́йского языка́ (*English language classes*). Мы ча́сто _____⁴ в кино́ (*to the movies*). Иногда́ (*sometimes*) мы _____⁵ в рестора́н. В воскресе́нье мы обы́чно _____⁶ в го́сти к мои́м роди́телям (*to my parents'*).

УПРАЖНЕНИЕ 9   Куда́ вы хо́дите . . . ?

When do you go where? Choose one element from each column to make up sentences.

ве́чером	я		на заня́тия (*to class*)
у́тром	мои́ друзья́		в рестора́н
в пя́тницу ве́чером	мой брат	ходи́ть	в бар†
в суббо́ту у́тром	моя́ сестра́		в спортза́л
	мои́ роди́тели		в кафе́
			на стадио́н
			???

УПРАЖНЕНИЕ 10   На́ши кани́кулы (*Our vacation*)

Fill in the blanks using appropriate past tense forms of the verbs **ходи́ть** and **е́здить**.

В про́шлом году́ я _____¹ во Флори́ду. Мы ка́ждый день _____² на пляж (*beach*). В спортза́л мы то́же _____³ ка́ждый день. Иногда́ (*sometimes*) мы _____⁴ на экску́рсии (*sightseeing tours*) и _____⁵ в музе́и. В кино́ (*movies*) мы _____⁶ ре́дко. Ве́чером мы обы́чно _____⁷ в кафе́ и́ли в рестора́н.

УПРАЖНЕНИЕ 11   Ходи́ть и́ли е́здить?

Complete the following sentences with the appropriate present or past tense form of **ходи́ть** or **е́здить**.

1. — Ты _____ и́ли _____ в университе́т?

   — _____ — я живу́ далеко́.

   or

   — _____ — я живу́ о́чень бли́зко.

2. — Где живу́т твои́ роди́тели? (*After a response*) Ты ча́сто _____ туда́?

3. — Как ты туда́ _____ — на авто́бусе? На маши́не? На по́езде (*by train*)?

4. — Ты был (была́) в Филаде́льфии? Когда́ ты туда́ _____?

КУЛЬТУРА РЕЧИ

❖❖ ТАК ГОВОРЯТ: СОБИРА́ТЬСЯ

Когда́ Андре́й Ви́кторович **собира́ется** в Москву́?

When is Andre Viktorovich planning to come (or: go) to Moscow?

The verb **собира́ться** is used when talking about what one is planning to do or, as in the above example, where one is planning to go. Note that the "go" verb is often omitted in this construction, hence the importance of context.

УПРАЖНЕ́НИЕ 12   Собира́ться

Who's planning to go where? Fill in the blanks with present tense forms of **собира́ться** and Accusative case forms of the cued destinations.

Наши пла́ны†

Куда́ мы _____ [1] на кани́кулы (*for vacation*)? Ма́ма и па́па _____ [2] в _____ [3] (Евро́па). Они́ лю́бят е́здить во _____ [4] (Фра́нция) и в _____ [5] (Ита́лия). Они́ е́дут в _____ [6] (Пари́ж), пото́м в _____ [7] (Рим), а оттуда — на Ка́при. Де́душка и ба́бушка _____ [8] в _____ [9] (Вермо́нт) — они́ е́здят туда́ ка́ждое ле́то (*summer*). Моя́ сестра́ Ли́за _____ [10] в _____ [11] (Калифо́рния) — она́ бу́дет (*will be*) там ме́сяц. Я _____ [12] быть до́ма. Я бу́ду (*will*) рабо́тать — я хочу́ зако́нчить (*finish*) диссерта́цию.

❖ САМОПРОВЕ́РКА: УПРАЖНЕ́НИЕ 13

Working on your own, try this self-test: Read a Russian sentence out loud, then give an idiomatic English equivalent without looking at the book. Then work from English to Russian. When you have completed this activity, try it with a classmate.

1. — Где мои́ кассе́ты? Э́то не они́ вон там, на столе́?
   — Нет, э́то мои́ кассе́ты. Твои́ на кни́жной по́лке. Вон там.

2. Когда́ мы жи́ли в Пари́же, мы ча́сто ходи́ли в музе́и и на конце́рты. И мы ча́сто е́здили в Ло́ндон!

3. Я вчера́ чита́ла о́чень интере́сную статью́ о ру́сской эконо́мике.

4. Ты зна́ешь моего́ бра́та? Нет? Вот он, на фотогра́фии†.

5. Я зна́ю официа́нта, кото́рый рабо́тает в э́том кафе́.

1. *"Where are my tapes? Isn't that them over there on the table?" "No, those are my tapes. Yours are on the bookshelf. Over there."*

2. *When we lived in Paris we often went to museums and concerts. And we frequently went to London!*

3. *Yesterday I was reading a very interesting article about the Russian economy.*

4. *Do you know my brother? No? Here's a picture of him.*

5. *I know the waiter who works in this cafe.*

❖ ВОПРОСЫ И ОТВЕТЫ: УПРАЖНЕНИЕ 14

1. Ты лю́бишь ходи́ть в рестора́н?
2. Ты ча́сто хо́дишь в рестора́н и в кафе́?
3. У тебя́ есть люби́мый рестора́н? Как он называ́ется (*What's it called*)?
4. Како́й э́то рестора́н — италья́нский, францу́зский, кита́йский, америка́нский? Э́то дорого́й рестора́н?
5. Что ты там зака́зываешь — сала́т,† суп,† бифште́кс†?
6. А ты лю́бишь пи́ццу† и га́мбургеры†?
7. Скажи́, пожа́луйста, в университе́те есть кафе́? Как оно́ называ́ется (*What's it called*)?
8. Ты ча́сто хо́дишь туда́? А твои́ друзья́ лю́бят ходи́ть туда́?
9. Что ты обы́чно пьёшь — чай, ко́фе, минера́льную во́ду? Или, мо́жет быть, во́дку†?
10. Ты лю́бишь фру́кты? А шокола́д? Шокола́дный торт? Пиро́жные?
11. Как ты ду́маешь, ты ешь мно́го и́ли ма́ло?

❖ ДИАЛОГИ

ДИАЛО́Г 1   Что бу́дете зака́зывать?
(Ordering food)

At a cafe. A man, a woman, and a waiter.

ОФИЦИА́НТ.   Что бу́дете зака́зывать?
ТО́ЛЯ.   Ва́ля, что бу́дем зака́зывать? Что ты хо́чешь?
ВА́ЛЯ.   Я хочу́ шокола́дный торт.
ТО́ЛЯ.   Но ты же на дие́те†!
ВА́ЛЯ.   Я была́ вчера́ на дие́те. Я не могу́ быть на дие́те ка́ждый день!

ДИАЛО́Г 2   Вы ча́сто е́здите туда́?
(Discussing travel)

Two acquaintances run into each other on the train to St. Petersburg.

— Вале́рий Петро́вич! Вы то́же е́дете в Петербу́рг на конфере́нцию†?
— В Петербу́рг, но не на конфере́нцию.
— Вы ча́сто е́здите туда́?
— Да, у меня́ там сын. А вы, ка́жется, живёте в Петербу́рге?
— Жил. Сейча́с я живу́ в Москве́. Но я то́же ча́сто е́зжу в Петербу́рг. У меня́ там ста́рые друзья́ — ведь я там учи́лся.

УПРАЖНЕНИЕ 15   Ваш диало́г

Create a dialogue in which you and a friend meet in a cafe for lunch or a snack. Decide what you want to eat and drink.

❖ А ТЕПЕРЬ . . . : УПРАЖНЕНИЕ 16

Working with a classmate, use what you learned in Part 4 to . . .

1. find out if she often travels to another city [*you choose the city*]
2. ask if she goes to the movies a lot
3. find out whether she likes mineral water (black coffee, tea . . .)
4. ask whether she knows the waiter who works in the cafe not far from the university
5. find out if she knows your instructor of history (Russian literature, . . .)

ИТАК…

NOUNS AND NOUN PHRASES

People, Their Behavior and Emotions

де́вушка	girl; young woman (3)
друг (*pl.* друзья́)	friend (3)
жизнь *f.*	life (2v)
люб(о́)вь (*Gen.* любви́) *f.*	love (2v)
лю́ди *pl.* (*sing.* челове́к)	people (4)
молодо́й челове́к	young man (4)
па́р(е)нь *m.*	guy; fellow (4)
подру́га	(female) friend (4)
сюрпри́з	surprise (4)
челове́к (*pl.* лю́ди)	person; man (2)
шу́тка	joke (3)

Studies, University

институ́т	institute (1v)
исто́рия	history (2)
кассе́та	cassette (1)
общежи́тие	dormitory (1)
однокла́ссник/ однокла́ссница	classmate (1v)
ра́дио	radio (1)

Literature, Theater, Art

кинозвезда́ (*pl.* кинозвёзды)	movie star (1v)
назва́ние	name (2)
пье́са	play (2v)
расска́з	(short) story (2v)

Food and Drinks

буты́лка	bottle (4)
ветчина́	ham (4v)
минера́льная вода́	mineral water (4)
овся́нка *coll.* (овся́ная ка́ша)	oatmeal (4v)
пиро́жное *noun, declines like adj.*	pastry (4)
счёт	check (4)
сыр	cheese (4v)
торт	cake (4)
фру́кты *usu. pl.*	fruit (4v)
чёрный ко́фе	black coffee (4v)
шокола́д	chocolate (3v)
яи́чница [*pronounced* -шн-]	fried eggs (4v)

Medicine, Personal Hygiene

аспири́н	aspirin (3v)
зубна́я па́ста	toothpaste (3v)
зубна́я щётка	toothbrush (3v)
мы́ло	soap (3v)
туале́тная бума́га	toilet paper (3v)
шампу́нь *m.*	shampoo (3v)

Transportation

авто́бусная остано́вка	bus stop (3)
гара́ж (*Gen. sing.* гаража́)	garage (1)
маши́на	car (1)
проездно́й *noun, declines like adj.* (проездно́й биле́т)	metro (bus, trolley, tram) pass (3v)

Other Nouns

би́знес	business (3)
гости́ная *noun, declines like adj.*	living room (2)
кио́ск	kiosk; stand (3v)
ме́сто	space; room (1)
объявле́ние	advertisement, ad (1)
откры́тка	postcard (3v)
пло́щадь *f.*	(city) square (2)
разме́р	size (3)
рубль (*Gen. sing.* рубля́) *m.*	ruble (3)
сапоги́ *pl.* (*sing.* сапо́г, *Gen. sing.* сапога́)	boots (3)
сигаре́та	cigarette (3v)
у́тро	morning (3)

PRONOUNS

кото́рый	who; that; which (4)
ничего́	nothing (1)
тот (та, то, те)	that; this one (4)
э́тот (э́та, э́то, э́ти)	this; that (4)

Accusative Pronouns

кого́	whom (2)
что	what (2)
меня́	me (2)
тебя́ (*informal sing.*)	you (2)
его́ (него́)	him, it (2)
её (неё)	her, it (2)
нас	us (2)
вас (*formal or pl.*)	you (2)
их (них)	them (2)

ADJECTIVES

до́лжен (должна́, должно́, должны́) (*used as predicate*)	must; have to (4)
дорого́й	expensive (3)
друго́й	other; another (2)
ка́ждый	every; each (3)
молодо́й	young (4)
недорого́й	inexpensive (3)
нехоро́ший	bad (4)
про́шлый	last (*preceding the present one*) (2)
ра́зный	1. different; 2. various (2)
рези́новый	rubber (*adj.*) (3)
тако́й	1. such (a); like that; this kind of; 2. (*with adj. + noun*) such (a); (*with adj.*) so (3)
чи́стый	clean (3)
экономи́ческий	economics (*adj.*) (institute) of economics (1v)
юриди́ческий	law (*adj.*); (department) of law (1v)

VERBS

дава́ть (да-ю́, да-ёшь, . . . да-ю́т)	to give (3)
ду́мать (ду́ма-ю, ду́ма-ешь, . . . ду́ма-ют)	to think (2)
е́здить (е́зж-у, е́зд-ишь, . . . е́зд-ят) *multidir.* of е́хать	to go (*by vehicle*) (4)
есть (ем, ешь, ест, еди́м, еди́те, едя́т)	to eat (4v)
ждать (жд-у, жд-ёшь, . . . жд-ут)	to wait (for) (3)
купи́ть[10]	to buy (1)
мочь (мог-у́, мо́ж-ешь, мо́ж-ет, мо́ж-ем, мо́ж-ете, мо́г-ут)	to be able (3v)
опа́здывать (опа́здыва-ю, опа́здыва-ешь, . . . опа́здыва-ют)	to be late (4v)
отдава́ть (отда-ю́, отда-ёшь, . . . отда-ю́т)	to return; to give (back) (3)
открыва́ть (открыва́-ю, открыва́-ешь, . . . открыва́-ют)	to open (4)
паркова́ть (парку́-ю, парку́-ешь, . . . парку́-ют)	to park (1)
пить (пь-ю, пь-ёшь, . . . пь-ют)	to drink (4v)
плати́ть (плач-у́, пла́т-ишь, . . . пла́т-ят)	to pay (3)
получа́ть (получа́-ю, получа́-ешь, . . . получа́-ют)	to receive; to get (3)
по́мнить (по́мн-ю, по́мн-ишь, . . . по́мн-ят)	to remember (2)
помо́чь[10]	to help (3)
продава́ть (прода-ю́, прода-ёшь, . . . прода-ю́т)	to sell (3)
роди́ться (*past* роди́лся, родила́сь, роди́лись)[10]	to be born (2)
собира́ться (собира́-юсь, собира́-ешься, . . . собира́-ются)	1. to be planning to go somewhere; 2. (+ *infin.*) to intend, to be about (to do something) (4)
ходи́ть (хож-у́, хо́д-ишь, . . . хо́-дят) *multidir.* of идти́	1. to go; 2. to walk (2)
хоте́ть (хоч-у́, хо́ч-ешь, хо́ч-ет, хот-и́м, хот-и́те, хот-я́т)	to want (1)

ADVERBS

беспла́тно	free (of charge); for free (3)
везде́	everywhere (1)
действи́тельно	really; indeed (3)
кста́ти	by the way; incidentally (4)
нигде́	nowhere (3)
по-моско́вски	Moscow style (3)
ре́дко	rarely (4)
так	1. (in) this way; like this; like that; thus (3); 2. (*with advs. and short-form adjs.*) so; (*with verbs*) so much (1)
то́же (*with a negated verb*)	either (3)
ча́сто	often (1)

---

[10]For the time being use **купи́ть** only in the infinitive or past tense. Use **помо́чь** only in the infinitive. Use only past tense forms of **роди́ться**.

OTHER

бли́зко от (+ *Gen.*)	close to, near (1)
далеко́ (недалеко́) от (+ *Gen.*)	far (not far) from (3)
ита́к	so; and so (4)
как	as, like (4)
от (+ *Gen.*)	from (1)
пятьсо́т	five hundred (3)

IDIOMS AND EXPRESSIONS

в про́шлом году́	last year (2)
ещё оди́н (одна́, одно́)	one more (4)
к сожале́нию *parenthetical*	unfortunately (4)
ни сло́ва	don't say (breathe) a word (about it) (4)
Ну что ты!	What are you talking about! What do you mean! (1)
Отли́чно (!)	Excellent! (4)
пре́жде всего́	first of all (4)
Скажи́те, пожа́луйста…	(Could you) please tell me … (3v)
Что бу́дете зака́зывать?	What can I get you?; Are you ready to order? (4)
Я угоща́ю *when offering to pay for another or others at a restaurant*	(It's) my treat; It's on me (4)

❖ ЧТО Я ЗНАЮ, ЧТО Я УМЕЮ

Use this checklist to mark off what you've learned in this lesson:

- ☐ Using adjectives and possessives in the Prepositional singular (Part 1)
- ☐ Using adjectives and possessives in the Genitive singular (Part 3)
- ☐ Using adjectives and possessives in the Accusative singular (Part 4)
- ☐ Using pronouns and animate masculine nouns in the Accusative singular (Part 2)
- ☐ About end-stressed masculine nouns and masculine nouns with -у́ ending in Prepositional singular (Part 1)
- ☐ Conjugating **-овать** verbs (Part 1)
- ☐ Forming the past tense of reflexive verbs (Part 2)
- ☐ Expressing *to want* with the verb **хоте́ть** (Part 1)
- ☐ Expressing *to be able* with the verb **мочь** (Part 3)
- ☐ Telling where you've been (**ходи́ли куда́ = бы́ли где**) (Part 2)
- ☐ Expressing round-trip and habitual travel with **ходи́ть, е́здить** (Part 4)
- ☐ Intensifying statements with **так** and **тако́й** (Part 3)
- ☐ Pointing out and distinguishing things with **э́то, э́тот** (Part 4)
- ☐ Contrasting similar items: **э́тот, тот** (Part 4)
- ☐ Linking clauses with **кото́рый** (Part 4)

❖❖ ЭТО НАДО ЗНАТЬ

NOUN CASE ENDINGS

Here is a summary of the noun case endings that you have learned so far.

NOUNS: Masculine

	BASIC ENDING	HARD CONSONANT	SOFT: -Ь	SOFT: -Й
SINGULAR				
Nom.	(*none*)	автóбус	календáрь	музéй
Acc.	*inanimate* = *Nom.*	автóбус	календáрь	музéй
	animate = *Gen.*			
Gen.	-а/-я	автóбуса	календаря́	музéя
Prep.	-е	автóбусе	календарé	музéе
PLURAL				
Nom.	-ы/-и	автóбусы	календари́	музéи
Acc.	*inanimate* = *Nom.*	автóбусы	календари́	музéи
	animate = *Gen.*[11]			

NOUNS: Neuter

	BASIC ENDING	HARD-SERIES VOWEL	SOFT: -ИЕ
SINGULAR			
Nom .	-о/-е	слóво	сочинéние
Acc.	-о/-е	слóво	сочинéние
Gen.	-а/-я	слóва	сочинéния
Prep.	-е, -и	слóве	сочинéнии
PLURAL			
Nom.	-а/-я	словá	сочинéния
Acc.	-а/-я	словá	сочинéния

NOUNS: Feminine

	BASIC ENDING	HARD-SERIES VOWEL	SOFT: -Я	SOFT: -ИЯ	SOFT: -Ь
SINGULAR					
Nom.	-а/-я, -ь	газéта	недéля	истóрия	кровáть
Acc.	-у/-ю, -ь	газéту	недéлю	истóрию	кровáть
Gen.	-ы/-и	газéты	недéли	истóрии	кровáти
Prep.	-е, -и	газéте	недéле	истóрии	кровáти
PLURAL					
Nom.	-ы/-и	газéты	недéли	истóрии	кровáти
Acc.	*inanimate* = *Nom.*	газéты	недéли	истóрии	кровáти
	animate = *Gen.*[11]				

[11]Not yet encountered actively.

❖ ДОПОЛНИТЕЛЬНЫЕ ТЕКСТЫ

А. МЕЛЬНИК[1], МАЛЬЧИК И ОСЁЛ[2]
С. МАРШАК

Мельник
На ослике[3]
Ехал
Верхом.[4]
Мальчик
За мельником
Плёлся
Пешком.[5]

—Глянь-ка,[6] —
Толкует[7]
Досужий[8] народ[9]: —
Дедушка
Едет,
А мальчик
Идёт!

Где это
Видано[10]?
Где это
Слыхано[11]?
Дедушка
Едет,
А мальчик
Идёт!

Дедушка
Быстро
Слезает
С седла,[12]
Внука
Сажает
Верхом
На осла.[13]

—Ишь ты[14]! —
Вдогонку
Кричит[15] пешеход[16]:—
Маленький
Едет,
А старый
Идёт!

Где это
Видано?
Где это
Слыхано?
Маленький
Едет,
А старый
Идёт!

Мельник
И мальчик
Садятся
Вдвоём[17] —
Оба[18]
На ослике
Едут
Верхом.

—Фу ты[19]! —
Смеётся[20]
Другой пешеход:
Деда[21]
И внука
Скотина[22]
Везёт[23]!

Где это
Видано?
Где это
Слыхано?
Деда
И внука
Скотина
Везёт!

Дедушка
С внуком[24]
Плетутся
Пешком.[25]
Ослик
На дедушке
Едет
Верхом.

—Тьфу ты[26]! —
Хохочет[27]
Народ у ворот[28]:—
Старый осёл
Молодого
Везёт!

Где это
Видано?
Где это
Слыхано?
Старый
Осёл
Молодого
Везёт!

---

1. *miller;* 2. *donkey, ass* (*also used figuratively of a person*); 3. *diminutive of* осёл; 4. на ослике ехал верхом *was riding a donkey;* 5. за мельником плёлся пешком *was trudging along behind the miller;* 6. *Take a look at that;* 7. *say;* 8. *idle;* 9. *people;* 10. Где это видано? *Who's ever seen such a thing?* 11. Где это слыхано? *Who's ever heard of such a thing?* 12. слезает с седла *dismounts* (*from the saddle*); 13. внука сажает верхом на осла *puts his grandson on the donkey;* 14. Ишь ты! *Look at that!* 15. вдогонку кричит *calls out;* 16. *pedestrian;* 17. садятся вдвоём *both get on;* 18. *both;* 19. фу ты *ugh!* 20. смеётся *laughs;* 21. дед *дедушка;* 22. *here: the donkey;* 23. *is carrying;* 24. дедушка с внуком = дедушка и внук; 25. плетутся пешком *are trudging along;* 26. тьфу ты! *bah!* 27. *laugh out loud;* 28. у ворот *at the gates.*[12]

---

[12]People are standing at the gates in the fences which surround their houses.

Б. КОНФЕРЕНЦИЯ

Институ́т этноло́гии и антрополо́гии Росси́йской акаде́мии нау́к, Моско́вский госуда́рственный университе́т и Росси́йский госуда́рственный гуманита́рный университе́т в сентябре́ 1996 го́да прово́дят нау́чную конфере́нцию молоды́х учёных и аспира́нтов «Этни́ческие и культу́рные стереоти́пы».

Акаде́мия нау́к	*Academy of Sciences*
проводи́ть	*to hold*
нау́чный	*academic, scientific*
учёный	*scholar*

ДОСКА ОБЪЯВЛЕНИЙ

Конференции. Симпозиумы. Встречи

Институт этнологии и антропологии Российской академии наук, Московский государственный университет и Российский государственный гуманитарный университет в сентябре 1996 года проводят научную конференцию молодых ученых и аспирантов «Этнические и культурные стереотипы».

На конференции предполагается обсудить следующие темы:
— сущность и значение этнических и культурных стереотипов;
— механизмы формирования и функционирования, условия существования и устойчивости стереотипов;
— социальные стереотипы и общественное сознание;
— стереотипы и социальная стратификация;
— мораль, этика, религия, искусство, литература, средства массовой информации и социальные стереотипы;
— стереотипы поведения, мысли и действия;
— стереотипы, экономика, политика;
— нормы социальной, культурной и этнической организации, нарушение их, участники и посредники, способы разрешения конфликтных ситуаций.

По всем интересующим вас вопросам обращаться:
117334, Москва, Ленинский проспект, 32-А, корпус В
Институт этнологии и антропологии РАН
Гузикова Тамара Семеновна (ИЭА РАН). Тел.: 938-53-07
Калабанов Александр Николаевич (ИЭА РАН).
Тел.: 938-57-19, 938-68-17;
факс: 938-06-00; e-mail antbrab @ iea. msk. su

Научные конференции и фестивали культуры 1996 года, организуемые Крымским центром гуманитарных исследований при содействии Министерства культуры Республики Крым и Госкомиздата Республики Крым:
15—21 сентября, Георгиевский монастырь «Литература и религия». VI Крымские Пушкинские чтения.
22—28 сентября, Гурзуф. Дни Адама Мицкевича в Крыму. Конференция и фестиваль польской культуры.
29 сентября — 5 октября, Алушта «Пути небесные русской литературы». V Шмелевские чтения.
20—26 октября, Ливадия «Геополитика славянства». III чтения Н. Я. Данилевского.
27 октября—2 ноября, Гурзуф. Дни французской культуры. Конференция и фестиваль.
Прием заявок и тезисов докладов прекращается за 3 месяца до начала конференции.
Дополнительная информация — в Крымском центре гуманитарных исследований:
333036, Республика Крым, г. Симферополь, ул. Ялтинская, 4, госуниверситет.
Тел.: (065-2) 23-39-32, 23-22-76. Факс: (065-2) 23-21-69.
E-mail: kazarin @ ccun. crinea. su; postmaster @ cdu. crinea. ua.

Восточно-Сибирская государственная академия культуры и искусств при содействии республиканских и областных комитетов культуры Восточно-Сибирского региона проводит с 20 по 26 июня 1996 года в г. Улан-Удэ международную научно-практическую конференцию «Восток — Запад — диалог культур».
Оргкомитет: 670005, Россия, Бурятия, г. Улан-Удэ, ул. Терешковой, 1. Восточно-Сибирская государственная академия культуры и искусств. Тел.: (830122) 38004; факс: (830122) 74477, 74696.

Почему выгодно размещать рекламу в журнале «Родина»

Журнал «Родина» издается седьмой год, выходит массовым тиражом.
Это издание, содержащее уникальную информацию, которая интересна всем, кто небезразличен к прошлому, настоящему и будущему России, пользуется постоянным спросом, что СДЕЛАЕТ ВАШУ РЕКЛАМУ «ДОЛГОИГРАЮЩЕЙ» И ДЕЙСТВЕННОЙ.

Журнал «Родина» постоянно презентуется на российских и международных конференциях, рассылается в Администрацию Президента РФ, Правительство РФ, министерства и ведомства РФ, в ведущие российские фирмы и банки, а это — ПРЕКРАСНЫЙ ИМИДЖ ДЛЯ ВАС И ВАШЕЙ КОМПАНИИ.

Журнал «Родина» реализуется по всей России, странам СНГ и 34-м зарубежным государствам. Аудитория читателей очень широка:
от преподавателей школ и вузов до руководителей производственных предприятий и банков, и все они — ВАШИ ПОТЕНЦИАЛЬНЫЕ ЗАКАЗЧИКИ.

Журнал «Родина» был признан Торгово-промышленной палатой РФ и Союзом журналистов РФ ЛУЧШИМ ЖУРНАЛОМ 1995 ГОДА.

Журнал «Родина» давно сотрудничает с крупнейшими российскими рекламодателями: РАО «Газпром», АО «Роснефть», «Промстройбанк», «Сбербанк России», «Внешторгбанк», АО «Ростелеком», Акцептный Дом «ЕЭС», АО «Росвооружение», НК «Лукойл» и др. НАРАВНЕ С НИМИ ВЫ ВОЙДЕТЕ В ИСТОРИЮ.

Журнал «Родина» издает ряд приложений — журнал «Источник», газета «Былое», журнал «Репетитор» (общим тиражом 130 тыс. экземпляров), — в которых МЫ ПУБЛИКУЕМ БЕСПЛАТНО РЕКЛАМУ НАШИХ ПОСТОЯННЫХ ЗАКАЗЧИКОВ.

Журнал «Родина» принимает заявки на рекламу и предоставляет большие скидки, а это — РЕАЛЬНАЯ ЭКОНОМИЯ ВАШИХ СРЕДСТВ.

О расценках на рекламу в нашем журнале вы узнаете по телефону: (095) 291-03-09; факс: (095) 202-34-39.

1. What kind of event is being announced?
2. What are the names of the three sponsoring institutions?
3. When did the event take place?
4. Who are the participants?
5. What is the title of the event?

6

НОВЫЕ СОСЕДИ, НОВЫЕ ДРУЗЬЯ

На по́чте

In Part 1 Lena and Sasha become better acquainted and decide to use the familiar form of address with each other. Lena also has to correct her younger brother's manners (a lesson he quickly applies!). In Part 2, which is on video, you'll meet two additional residents of the apartment building—students who've heard there's a room for rent. In Part 3, also on video, the local letter carrier deals with a mail mixup, and in Part 4 Tanya writes in her diary about the process of getting settled.

In this lesson you will learn

- ✪ to express doing something to or for someone
- ✪ to tell your age
- ✪ to use numerals from 1 to 100
- ✪ to express likes and dislikes
- ✪ to express future actions
- ✪ to give commands
- ✪ to ask about and give the date
- ✪ to say that someone needs something or has to do something
- ✪ to say whom you resemble
- ✪ about switching between formal and informal speech forms
- ✪ to write Russian addresses

Та́ня, Све́та и Татья́на Дми́триевна

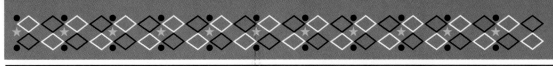

С ЧЕГО НАЧАТЬ?

Тут Са́шенька ма́ленький, **ему́ два го́да**.

А на э́той **фотогра́фии**[†] — Са́шенька и Валенти́на Васи́льевна, его́ пе́рвая **учи́тельница** му́зыки. О́чень **стро́гая!**

Э́то Кинг, наш пу́дель.[†]

А э́то его́ после́дний конце́рт в шко́ле.

ему́ два го́да	*he's two years old*
после́дний	*last*
стро́гая	*strict*
учи́тельница	*teacher*

❖ ЧТЕНИЕ ❖

❖ «ТЫ» И «ВЫ»

(Sasha runs into Lena and Vova in the stairwell when they are coming out of their apartment.)

СА́ША.	До́брый день.
ЛЕ́НА.	Приве́т, Са́ша. Скажи́те, что вы вчера́ игра́ли?
СА́ША.	Прелю́д† Ге́ршвина.
ЛЕ́НА.	Замеча́тельная му́зыка! *(She pauses.)* Са́ша, а **почему́ мы говори́м друг дру́гу «вы»**°?
СА́ША.	**Действи́тельно**°! **Дава́й**° говори́ть друг дру́гу «ты»!
ВО́ВА.	*(Knowingly.)* **Пра́вильно!**° Студе́нты всегда́ говоря́т друг дру́гу «ты». Са́ша, а **ты на како́м ку́рсе**°?
СА́ША.	На второ́м.
ЛЕ́НА.	Во́ва, а почему́ ты говори́шь Са́ше «ты»? Ты, **ме́жду про́чим,**° ещё не студе́нт. Ты же[1] зна́ешь, что **культу́рные**† лю́ди **говоря́т ста́ршим**° «вы».
ВО́ВА.	Са́ша не «ста́рший». Он **ещё**° то́лько на второ́м ку́рсе, а я уже́ **в шесто́м кла́ссе.**° И вообще́, Ле́нка, ты говори́шь, как на́ша учи́тельница. Это о́чень **ску́чно.**°
ЛЕ́НА.	Ах, ску́чно? *(To Sasha.)* Са́ша, **мне сты́дно**°, что у меня́ тако́й «культу́рный» брат! *(She looks at her watch.)* Я опа́здываю. Пока́! *(She runs down the stairs.)*
СА́ША.	Стро́гая у тебя́ сестра́.
ВО́ВА.	Она́ ду́мает, что она́ краси́вая, и поэ́тому **кома́ндует.**°
СА́ША.	Она́ действи́тельно о́чень краси́вая.

Marginal glosses (left column):

почему́... *why are we using* «*вы*» *with each other? /*

Right! / Let's
That's right!

ты... *what year are you in?*

by the way
говоря́т... *use* «*вы*» *with their elders*
still
в... *in the sixth grade*
boring
мне... *I'm ashamed*

bosses everyone around

---

[1]**Же** is used for emphasis. Although in some contexts it can be translated by *surely, after all,* and so on, in many contexts the best way to convey its meaning is through intonation and/or emphatic verbal constructions (for example, **Я же говори́л тебе́ об э́том!** *I **did** tell you about it!*).

(Just then a neighbor exits from the elevator with a small boy, Kolya. They approach Sasha and Vova.)

КО́ЛЯ.	Здра́вствуй, Во́ва.	
ВО́ВА.	**Тебе́ ско́лько лет°?**	*How old are you?*
КО́ЛЯ.	Пять.	
ВО́ВА.	А почему́ ты говори́шь мне «здра́вствуй»? (*Imitating Lena's tone.*) Ста́ршим на́до говори́ть «вы». Не «здра́вствуй», а «здра́вствуйте».	
СА́ША.	(*Laughing.*) Во́ва, у тебя́ непло́хо получа́ется!°	*Во́ва. . . Vova, that's pretty good!*
СОСЕ́ДКА.	Са́ша, Алекса́ндра Никола́евна до́ма?	
СА́ША.	Нет, она́ у сосе́дки.°	*у. . . at the neighbor's*
КО́ЛЯ.	Во́ва, а где твоя́ Бе́лка?	
ВО́ВА.	Не «твоя́», а «ва́ша». **Понима́ешь°?**	*Got it?*
КО́ЛЯ.	Да. Тепе́рь я бу́ду° говори́ть тебе́ «вы». И Бе́лке то́же. Во́ва, а ско́лько лет ва́шей Бе́лке?	*will*

УПРАЖНЕ́НИЕ 1   Под микроско́пом: Case recognition

Here are some sentences taken from this reading. Indicate the case of the boldfaced word or words.

1. _____ Скажи́те, **что** вы вчера́ игра́ли?
2. _____ Прелю́д **Ге́ршвина.**
3. _____ Са́ша, а ты **на како́м ку́рсе?**
4. _____ Ты говори́шь, как **на́ша учи́тельница.**
5. _____ Стро́гая **у тебя́** сестра́.
6. _____ Она́ действи́тельно о́чень **краси́вая.**

ГРАММА́ТИКА И ПРА́КТИКА

◇◇ О РОССИ́И ◇◇◇◇◇◇◇◇◇◇◇◇◇◇◇◇

«НА ТЫ» AND «НА ВЫ»

Во́ва, а почему́ ты говори́шь Са́ше «ты»?

For family members, the «**на ты**» form of address is the norm. Outside the family, whether a relationship is conducted «**на вы**» or «**на ты**» involves many factors such as age, status, gender, and intent. Children normally relate to one another «**на ты**», as do many people even into their early twenties. Their use of **ты** forms need not carry any special connotation other than that the speakers recognize themselves to be of approximately the same age and status. Children and young people almost always address adults (other than family members) «**на вы**,» while adults will likely address children of school age «**на ты**.» As young people enter adulthood they start being addressed «**на вы**» by adults. Among adults, **вы** forms are the norm; neighbors in an apartment complex and colleagues at work may know and talk to each other for years without ever switching to **ты** forms.

УПРАЖНЕНИЕ 2   «На ты» и́ли «на вы»?

Indicate whether you would address the following persons «**на ты**» or «**на вы**».

		«на ты»	«на вы»
1.	же́нщина, кото́рая рабо́тает в магази́не	☐	☐
2.	ма́ленький ма́льчик и́ли ма́ленькая де́вочка	☐	☐
3.	ва́ша соба́ка	☐	☐
4.	ваш преподава́тель	☐	☐
5.	ваш друг	☐	☐
6.	ва́ша ба́бушка	☐	☐
7.	ваш не о́чень молодо́й сосе́д	☐	☐
8.	администра́тор в ва́шем общежи́тии	☐	☐
9.	води́тель такси́	☐	☐

У Ч И С Ь   У Ч И Т Ь С Я ✪ *Learning Individual Words*

Except for scientific and technical vocabulary, remarkably few words in one language perfectly match their counterparts in another. Rather than exact translations, languages often have "approximate equivalents": A word in one language may mean more or less than its counterpart in another language. For example, there is no single Russian word for *student*. Russians must choose from at least three different words: **студе́нт** (*undergraduate student*), **аспира́нт** (*graduate student*), and **шко́льник** (*pupil in elementary through secondary school*). The reverse also occurs. There is no single English word for **рука́**, for example: In English you say either *hand* or *arm*. Sometimes there are no one-word equivalents at all: The particle **же**, which is used for intensification or emphasis, can be rendered only roughly by various phrases in English. This is why it is important to remember how a word is used as you learn it, rather than just memorizing lists.

❖ 6.1. DATIVE CASE

А почему́ ты говори́шь **мне** «здра́вствуй»?	*Why are you saying «**здра́вствуй**» to me?*

The Dative case has a number of functions in Russian, one of which is shown above: expressing *to whom* or *for whom* something is done. This function corresponds to the English *indirect object* of a verb. Here is another example.

Я чита́ю журна́л **бра́ту**.	*I'm reading a magazine to my brother.*

In this sentence, **я** is the subject, **чита́ю** is the verb, **журна́л** (in the Accusative case) is the direct object of the verb, and **бра́ту** (in the Dative case) is the indirect object.

Here is a summary of the basic Dative case forms presented in this lesson.

DATIVE CASE FORMS[2]

PRONOUNS

INTERROGATIVES		PERSONAL PRONOUNS			
Nom.	Dat.	Nom.	Dat.	Nom.	Dat.
кто	кому́	я	мне	мы	нам
что	чему́	ты	тебе́	вы	вам
		он, оно́	ему́	они́	им
		она́	ей		

OTHERS

	NOMINATIVE CASE (dictionary form)	DATIVE CASE ENDING	EXAMPLES
NOUNS			
Masculine and neuter	брат Серге́й роя́л-ь окн-о́ упражне́ни-е	-у/-ю	бра́т-у Серге́-ю роя́л-ю окн-у́ упражне́ни-ю
Feminine -а/-я and "masquerading masculines")[3]	сестр-а́ ку́хн-я Са́ш-а	-е	сестр-е́ ку́хн-е Са́ш-е
Feminine -ь	двер-ь мат-ь[4] доч-ь[4]	-и	две́р-и ма́т-ер-и до́ч-ер-и
ADJECTIVES (including adjectives used as nouns)			
Masculine and neuter	но́в-ый, -ое хоро́ш-ий, -ее дорог-о́й, -о́е	-ому/-ему	но́в-ому хоро́ш-ему дорог-о́му
Feminine	но́в-ая хоро́ш-ая	-ой/-ей	но́в-ой хоро́ш-ей
POSSESSIVES			
Masculine and neuter	мо-й, мо-ё ваш, ва́ш-е	-ему	мо-ему́ ва́ш-ему
Feminine	мо-я́ ва́ш-а	-ей	мо-е́й ва́ш-ей

---

[2]Note the internal patterns: (a) the similarities in the pronouns (**мне-тебе́, ему-кому́-чему, нам-вам-им**) and (b) the repetition of **-ому/-ему** and **-ой/-ей** in the adjective and possessive pronoun endings.

[3]Remember that masculine nouns ending in **-а/-я** (such as **па́па**) take the same endings as feminine nouns that end in **-а/-я**.

[4]The nouns **мать** and **дочь** insert the syllable **-ер-** before adding the **-и** ending.

УПРАЖНЕНИЕ 3   Кто . . . кому́?

Who said the following lines to whom? Match each statement in the left column with the proper combination in the right column.

Что говори́т		Кто — кому́?
1. _____ Прелю́д Ге́ршвина — э́то замеча́тельная му́зыка.		**а.** Ви́ктор — Ле́не
2. _____ Ты так хорошо́ говори́шь по-ру́сски.		**б.** Во́ва — Джи́му
3. _____ Пре́жде всего́ — минера́льную во́ду.		**в.** Во́ва — Ле́не
4. _____ Вы действи́тельно о́чень краси́вая де́вушка.		**г.** Джим — профе́ссору Петро́вскому
5. _____ У вас есть инструме́нты†?		**д.** Джим — Та́не
6. _____ Сдаётся ко́мната (*There's a room for rent*) в до́ме, где живёт Илья́ Ильи́ч.		**е.** Ле́на — Во́ве
7. _____ Ты говори́шь, как на́ша учи́тельница. Э́то о́чень ску́чно!		**ж.** Ле́на — Са́ше
8. _____ Все культу́рные лю́ди говоря́т ста́ршим «вы».		**з.** профе́ссор Петро́вский — официа́нту
9. _____ Как говори́т Илья́ Ильи́ч, отли́чная мысль (*thought*)!		**и.** Та́ня — Джи́му

УПРАЖНЕНИЕ 4   Кому́ Джим пи́шет пи́сьма?

Follow the example; describe to whom Jim writes letters.

ОБРАЗЕ́Ц: брат → *Джим пи́шет пи́сьма бра́ту.*

1. сестра́
2. мать
3. де́душка

4. оте́ц
5. ба́бушка
6. друг

УПРАЖНЕНИЕ 5   Что кому́

You and a friend are discussing birthday or holiday gifts you need to purchase. On the right are some suggested gifts. Pick at least five people and decide what you will give them, putting the gift and the recipient into the proper case forms. Feel free to add gifts and recipients of your own choosing.

ОБРАЗЕ́Ц: *Сестре́ я хочу́ купи́ть краси́вую ку́клу (doll).*

КОМУ́?		ЧТО?
де́душка		шампа́нское†
ма́ма		цветы́
мой преподава́тель му́зыки	. . . я хочу́ купи́ть . . .	компа́кт-диск† рок-му́зыки
ста́рший (*older*) брат		кассе́та
мла́дший (*younger*) брат		то́стер

КОМУ́?		ЧТО?
ста́ршая (мла́дшая)		шокола́дный торт
сестра́		но́вый при́нтер
оте́ц		часы́
друг	. . . я хочу́ купи́ть . . .	футбо́лка
ба́бушка		???
мой дя́дя		
моя́ тётя		
???		

◈ 6.2. TELLING YOUR AGE: СКО́ЛЬКО ТЕБЕ́ ЛЕТ? (AND CARDINAL NUMERALS THROUGH 49)

— Ско́лько тебе́ лет?   *"How old are you?"*
— Мне двена́дцать лет.   *"I'm twelve years old."*

When expressing someone's age, that person's name (or the pronoun referring to that person) is in the Dative case. Here is the age-telling formula.

<name (or pronoun) in Dative + numeral + "year" word>

The "year" word is determined by the numeral used with it, as follows:

год with numerals ending in the word **оди́н**
го́да with numerals ending in the words **два, три, четы́ре**
лет with all other numerals

With other quantity words such as **мно́го, ма́ло,** and **ско́лько** the "year" word **лет** is always used. Here are some typical age-related questions and answers:

— Ско́лько тебе́ (ей, Джи́му, Во́ве, Ле́не, твоему́ бра́ту . . .) лет?
— Мне (ей, Джи́му, Во́ве, Ле́не, моему́ бра́ту . . .) . . . (see the following table)

Note: An older person may ask a young person his or her age, and young people may ask the ages of their peers. However, it is generally inappropriate to ask the age of an adult with whom one would normally use the «на вы» form of address.

СЛОВА, СЛОВА, СЛОВА . . . ✪ *Numerals 13–40*

13 тринáдцать		**18** восемнáдцать	
14 четы́рнадцать		**19** девятнáдцать	
15 пятнáдцать		**20** двáдцать	
16 шестнáдцать		**30** три́дцать	
17 семнáдцать		**40** сóрок	

NUMERALS AND AGES

ГОД	ГÓДА	ЛЕТ
оди́н **год**	два (три, четы́ре) **гóда**	оди́ннадцать **лет**
двáдцать оди́н **год**	двáдцать два (двáдцать три, двáдцать четы́ре) **гóда**	двенáдцать **лет**
три́дцать оди́н **год**	три́дцать два (три́дцать три, три́дцать четы́ре) **гóда**	тринáдцать **лет**
сóрок оди́н **год**	сóрок два (сóрок три, сóрок четы́ре) **гóда**	четы́рнадцать **лет**
		пятнáдцать **лет**
		двáдцать **лет**
		двáдцать пять **лет**
		три́дцать шесть **лет**
		сóрок семь **лет**

УПРАЖНЕНИЕ 6   Скóлько тебé лет?

Ask your classmates **Скóлько тебé лет?** and give your own age when you are asked. Write down (in figures) the age you hear, show it to the person whom you've asked to be sure you understood correctly, and repeat aloud the answer you heard (**Тебé девятнáдцать лет, двáдцать три гóда,** and so on).

УПРАЖНЕНИЕ 7   Скóлько лет твоéй сестрé?

Using the Dative case forms of **мать, отéц, брат, сестрá,** ask others how old their family members are [for example, **Скóлько лет твоемý (вáшему) дéдушке?**[5]], and give answers about your own family.

❖❖ 6.3. APPROXIMATE AGE AND CARDINAL NUMERALS 50–100

If you are not sure of someone's age, simply put the "year" word in front of the numeral to render the idea of *about, approximately.*

Áнне **сóрок пять лет.**	*Anna is forty-five years old.*
Áнне **лет сóрок пять.**	*Anna is about forty-five years old.*

---

[5]As a reminder, masculine nouns that end in **-а/-я** take feminine endings when declined, but adjectives and past tense verb forms used with them follow biology and take masculine endings.

СЛОВА, СЛОВА, СЛОВА . . . *Numerals 50–100*

50 пятьдеся́т	**80** во́семьдесят
60 шестьдеся́т	**90** девяно́сто
70 се́мьдесят	**100** сто

Note the following particulars of spelling and pronunciation.

1. Whereas the numerals 11–30 are spelled with a **мя́гкий знак** at the end of the word, the numerals 50–80 have a **мя́гкий знак** in the middle of the word.

2. The stress is on the last syllable for 50 and 60, but on the first syllable for 70 and 80.

УПРАЖНЕНИЕ 8   Ско́лько ему́ (ей) лет?

Locate a picture of a famous personality (e.g., a politician, sports figure or entertainer), and find out when she or he was born. Bring the picture into class and ask other students **Как ты ду́маешь, ско́лько ему́ (ей) лет?** Consider an answer correct if someone gives an exact age or uses the "approximate age" construction to come within +/− five years of the right age.

> ОБРАЗЕЦ: — Как ты ду́маешь, ско́лько лет на́шему президе́нту?
> — По-мо́ему, ему́ (ей) лет 55 (пятьдеся́т пять).

КУЛЬТУРА РЕЧИ

❖ ТАК ГОВОРЯТ: ДРУГ ДРУ́ГУ

Са́ша, а почему́ мы говори́м **друг дру́гу** «вы»?	*Sasha, why are we saying «вы» to each other?*

In this phrase the first **друг** never changes; the second one shows the appropriate case ending, and is always masculine singular. If a preposition is involved, it goes between the two words: **Они́ всегда́ ду́мают друг о дру́ге.** *(They're always thinking about each other.)*

УПРАЖНЕНИЕ 9   Друг дру́гу

Here are some more examples using the *each other* construction. Indicate the case of the expression and translate each sentence into English.

Алексе́й и Валенти́на лю́бят друг дру́га. Они́ всё зна́ют друг о дру́ге, потому́ что у них нет секре́тов (*secrets*) друг от дру́га. Они́ хорошо́ понима́ют друг дру́га и всегда́ помога́ют (*help*) друг дру́гу.

УПРАЖНЕНИЕ 10   Each other . . .

Which of the following verbs and phrases could you use in sentences about yourself, your friends, or your family?

ОБРАЗЕЦ: Мой брат и моя́ сестра́ *не понима́ют друг дру́га.*

. . . друг дру́га . . . (ждать; ви́деть; люби́ть; слу́шать; понима́ть; всегда́ по́мнить)
. . . друг о дру́ге . . . (ду́мать; говори́ть; всё знать)
. . . друг дру́гу . . . (де́лать пода́рки (*gifts*); писа́ть пи́сьма)

❖ САМОПРОВЕРКА: УПРАЖНЕНИЕ 11

Working on your own, try this self-test: Read a Russian sentence out loud, then give an idiomatic English equivalent without looking at the book. Then work from English to Russian. After you have completed the activity, try it with a classmate.

1. Студе́нты обы́чно говоря́т
   друг дру́гу «ты».
2. — Са́ша, ты на како́м ку́рсе?
   — На второ́м.

3. — Ле́на, что ты де́лаешь?
   — Пишу́ письмо́.
   — А кому́ ты пи́шешь?
   — Подру́ге, кото́рая живёт в
   Петербу́рге.

4. — Вот фотогра́фия моего́
   отца́. Как по-тво́ему,
   ско́лько ему́ тут лет?
   — По-мо́ему, ему́ лет 45.

1. *Students usually address each
   other using «**ты**».*
2. *"Sasha, what year of school are
   you in?"*
   "Second year."

3. *"Lena, what are you doing?"*
   "Writing a letter."
   "Whom are you writing to?"
   "A friend who lives in Petersburg."

4. *"Here's a picture of my father.
   What do you think—how old is
   he here?"*
   "I think he's about forty-five."

❖ ВОПРОСЫ И ОТВЕТЫ: УПРАЖНЕНИЕ 12

Use the following questions to role play an interview with a Russian whom you don't know very well, played by a classmate.

1. Вы лю́бите му́зыку? Каку́ю му́зыку вы лю́бите — класси́ческую, джаз,
   рок?
2. Вы лю́бите му́зыку Ге́ршвина? А му́зыку Мо́царта?
3. А му́зыку Чайко́вского вы лю́бите? Вы зна́ете его́ бале́ты и о́перы?
4. Вы игра́ете на роя́ле? На скри́пке? На гита́ре? На саксофо́не?
5. Вы игра́ете кла́ссику? А джаз? А ка́нтри? А рок?
6. Расскажи́те мне о ва́шей семье́. У вас есть бра́тья и сёстры? Как его́
   (её, их) зову́т? Ско́лько ему́ (ей, им) лет?
7. Ваш брат (ва́ша сестра́) у́чится и́ли рабо́тает? Где он (она́) у́чится
   (рабо́тает)?
8. Скажи́те, ру́сские студе́нты говоря́т друг дру́гу «ты» и́ли «вы»? Кому́ вы
   говори́те «ты» и кому́ «вы»?
9. А ва́шему преподава́телю вы говори́те «ты» и́ли «вы»?

❖❖ ДИАЛОГИ

ДИАЛОГ 1 Ско́лько лет твоему́ дру́гу?
(Discussing age)

— Ско́лько лет твоему́ дру́гу?
— Два́дцать три.
— Где он у́чится?
— В университе́те.
— На како́м факульте́те?
— На хими́ческом.
— А на како́м ку́рсе?
— На второ́м.

ДИАЛОГ 2 Ей то́лько оди́ннадцать лет
(Discussing age)

— Твоя́ сестра́ о́чень краси́вая.
— Она́ то́же так ду́мает.
— Ско́лько ей лет?
— Она́ ещё ма́ленькая, ей то́лько оди́ннадцать лет.
— А тебе́ ско́лько?
— Мне уже́ четы́рнадцать!

УПРАЖНЕНИЕ 13   Ваш диало́г

Create a dialogue in which you are showing a Russian acquaintance a picture of your family or friends. Your classmate takes an immediate interest in them, asking their ages and other things about them: likes and dislikes, whether they are students, what they are majoring in, and so on.

❖❖ А ТЕПЕРЬ . . . : УПРАЖНЕНИЕ 14

Working with a classmate, use what you learned in Part 1 to . . .

1. ask whom he writes letters to
2. tell what you've bought for someone
3. ask about the age of someone you both know
4. guess at the age of your favorite movie stars (sports stars, musicians, TV news anchors, actors, . . .)

 # С ЧЕГО НАЧАТЬ?

ПРОДАЁМ:
- Хоро́шие котте́джи,† уча́стки, Пя́тницкое ш. т. 284-35-14.
- Банк, т. 368-30-48.
- Дом кирпи́чный в Звени́городе, т. 334-96-19.

СДАЁМ:
- **О́фисы.**† Тел.: 274-57-34.
- **Двухко́мнатную кварти́ру** в це́нтре. Тел.: 921-12-67.

двухко́мнатная кварти́ра	*two-room apartment*
сдава́ть	*to rent (out)*
уча́сток	*plot of land*
шоссе́	*highway*
кирпи́чный	*brick*

УПРАЖНЕ́НИЕ 1   Объявле́ния

1. What kind of texts are these?
2. What do the abbreviations «**т.**» and «**тел.**» stand for?
3. Find the abbreviation for *highway*.
4. Which phone number would you call to get information on buying a cottage or a plot of land? On buying a house?
5. What is the name of the town where this house is located?
6. What else is for sale in these ads?
7. What kind of apartment is available for rent? Where is it located?
8. What else is available for rent?

ЧТЕНИЕ

❖ ВЫ СДАЁТЕ КÓМНАТУ?

(The doorbell rings in Tatyana Dmitrievna's apartment: Sveta and Tanya have come to see about renting a room.)

СВÉТА.	Здра́вствуйте. Вы Татья́на Дми́триевна и вы сдаёте ко́мнату?	
ТАТЬЯ́НА ДМ.	Да, я Татья́на Дми́триевна. А **отку́да вы зна́ете,**° что я сдаю ко́мнату?	Отку́да. . . ? *How do you happen to know . . . ?*
ТА́НЯ.	Я вчера́ ви́дела Джи́ма, америка́нского аспира́нта. Он **сказа́л**° мне, что вы сдаёте ко́мнату.	*told*
ТАТЬЯ́НА ДМ.	Да-да. Заходи́те, пожа́луйста.	
СВÉТА, ТА́НЯ.	Спаси́бо.	
ТАТЬЯ́НА ДМ.	Это моя́ ко́мната, а э́ту° ко́мнату я сдаю.	*this*
СВÉТА, ТА́НЯ.	Кака́я хоро́шая ко́мната!	
СВÉТА.	Та́ня, смотри́, и ме́бель есть: крова́ти, сту́лья, кни́жные по́лки, **шкаф.**°	*cabinet*
ТА́НЯ.	А стол?	
ТАТЬЯ́НА ДМ.	К сожале́нию, у меня́ то́лько оди́н стол. Но у меня́ есть **идéя.**[†] Напиши́те° объявле́ние и пове́сьте° в подъе́зде. У нас симпати́чные сосе́ди. Мо́жет быть, у них есть ли́шний° стол.	*Write / put (it) up* *spare*
СВÉТА.	Да, э́то хоро́шая идéя.	
ТАТЬЯ́НА ДМ.	Я ра́да,° что вам ко́мната **нра́вится.**°	*glad /* вам. . . *you like the room*
СВÉТА.	Нам нра́вится ко́мната и нра́вится **хозя́йка.**° У вас о́чень хорошо́, везде́ кни́ги.	*landlady*
ТАТЬЯ́НА ДМ.	Да, мы — мой сын и я — о́чень лю́бим кни́ги.	
СВÉТА.	Ваш сын? Он то́же здесь живёт?	

в... *in the (military) service*	ТАТЬЯ́НА ДМ.	Да, но сейча́с он **в а́рмии,**° поэ́тому я сдаю́ его́ ко́мнату.
	СВЕ́ТА.	(*Noticing a photograph on the wall.*) Э́то он на фотогра́фии?
	ТАТЬЯ́НА ДМ.	Да, э́то он.
похо́ж... *[he] looks like you* *Too bad*	СВЕ́ТА.	Како́й симпати́чный! И о́чень **похо́ж на вас.**° **Жаль,**° что он далеко́. Ой, извини́те, Татья́на Дми́триевна, вы ещё не зна́ете, как нас зову́т. Я Све́та Ле́бедева.
	ТА́НЯ.	А я Та́ня Жили́нская. Я учу́сь в университе́те на **истори́ческом**[†] факульте́те.
	ТАТЬЯ́НА ДМ.	О́чень прия́тно. Так вы студе́нтка моего́ сосе́да Ильи́ Ильича́?
	ТА́НЯ.	Да. Он замеча́тельный преподава́тель. Студе́нты о́чень лю́бят его́.
	ТАТЬЯ́НА ДМ.	А вы, Све́та, где у́читесь?
скоро́й... *ambulance service*	СВЕ́ТА.	В **медици́нском**[†] институ́те. У меня́ и роди́тели, и брат — врачи́. Я учу́сь на второ́м ку́рсе и немно́го рабо́таю. На **скоро́й по́мощи.**°
всё... *everything's fine /* наш... *our very own /* *cost*	ТАТЬЯ́НА ДМ.	Ну, де́вушки, я о́чень ра́да, что моя́ кварти́ра вам нра́вится. Зна́чит, **всё в поря́дке.**° И у нас есть наш **со́бственный**° врач!
	СВЕ́ТА.	Всё хорошо́! Татья́на Дми́триевна, а ско́лько э́то **сто́ит**°?

(*Tatyana Dmitrievna smiles and takes the girls into the living room.*)

your

Две студе́нтки хотя́т
купи́ть стол. Е́сли у
вас есть ли́шний стол,
пожа́луйста, напиши́те
на э́том объявле́нии свой°
но́мер телефо́на.[†]

УПРАЖНЕ́НИЕ 2   Под микроско́пом: Who's who?

See if you can match the characters on the left with their descriptions on the right without looking at the text.

1. _____ Све́та Ле́бедева.

2. _____ Профе́ссор Петро́вский.
3. _____ Сын Татья́ны Дми́триевны.
4. _____ Та́ня Жили́нская.

5. _____ Татья́на Дми́триевна и её сын.

6. _____ Татья́на Дми́триевна.

а. Он замеча́тельный преподава́тель.
б. Она́ сдаёт ко́мнату.
в. Он сейча́с в а́рмии.
г. У неё и роди́тели, и брат — врачи́.
д. Она́ у́чится в университе́те на истори́ческом факульте́те.
е. Они́ о́чень лю́бят кни́ги.

ГРАММАТИКА И ПРАКТИКА

❖ 6.4. LIKING SOMETHING: (МНЕ) НРА́ВИТСЯ...

Нам **нра́вится** ко́мната и **нра́вится** хозя́йка.	*We like the room and (we) like the landlady.*

A particularly common use of the Dative case is in **нра́вится (нра́вятся)** constructions. Sentences like these can be regarded as "turned around" from the English equivalent: The Russian sentence structure uses *room* and *landlady* as the subjects and places *we* in the Dative: literally, *the room is pleasing to us and the landlady is pleasing (to us)*. Use **нра́вится** for singular subjects and **нра́вятся** for plural subjects. Note that the singular **нра́вится** can be used with infinitives as well: **Нам нра́вится слу́шать кла́ссику.** (*We like listening to classical music.*)

Вам **нра́вится** ва́ша но́вая кварти́ра?	*Do you like your new apartment?*
Вам **нра́вятся** ва́ши но́вые сосе́ди?	*Do you like your new neighbors?*

УПРАЖНЕНИЕ 3   Что ему́ (ей) нра́вится?

By now you know the characters well enough to be able to talk about some of their likes and dislikes. For example, **Во́ве нра́вится Джим; Во́ва говори́т, что Ле́не нра́вится кома́ндовать**. Make up some similar sentences; include information about your own likes and dislikes if you wish (**Мне нра́вится ва́ша маши́на**). Here are some things you might talk about.

1. твоя́ фотогра́фия
2. э́ти краси́вые котте́джи
3. мой но́вый о́фис
4. игра́ть Ге́ршвина
5. ва́ша двухко́мнатная кварти́ра
6. рабо́тать на ско́рой по́мощи
7. э́ти кни́жные шкафы́
8. ???

УПРАЖНЕНИЕ 4   Что тебе́ (вам) нра́вится?

Find out who likes what in your class by asking your classmates **Тебе́ (вам) нра́вится (нра́вятся) . . . ?** (Use **вам** when addressing your instructor.) Here are some phrases you might want to use in answering these questions (a simple **да** or **нет** sometimes seems a little brusque): **Да, мне нра́вится . . .** or **Да, мне о́чень нра́вится . . . ; Нет, мне не о́чень нра́вится . . .** , or the very strongly negative **Нет, мне совсе́м не нра́вится . . .** (*I don't like . . . at all*).

1. рок-му́зыка
2. класси́ческая му́зыка
3. фильм «Да́ма с соба́чкой» («А́нна Каре́нина» . . .)
4. смотре́ть, как игра́ют хоро́шие тенниси́сты
5. фи́льмы у́жасов (*horror films*)

6. жить в общежи́тии
7. америка́нский футбо́л
8. фотографи́ровать†
9. га́мбургеры в Макдо́налдсе
10. му́зыка Чайко́вского
11. ???

❖❖ 6.5. НРА́ВИТЬСЯ **AND** ЛЮБИ́ТЬ

As is the case with the English verbs *to like* and *to love,* the Russian verbs **нра́виться** and **люби́ть** overlap somewhat in meaning. **Люби́ть** denotes a greater depth of feeling toward, and/or a longer-term attachment to, the person or thing in question.

Андре́й и Ната́ша **лю́бят** друг дру́га.	*Andrei and Natasha love each other.*
Я о́чень **люблю́** му́зыку Мо́царта.	*I really love Mozart's music.*
Мари́на **лю́бит** шокола́д.	*Marina loves chocolate.*
Мы **лю́бим** игра́ть в волейбо́л.	*We love to play volleyball.*

Нра́виться is the only choice for describing first impressions. To express a very positive first impression, or a very positive attitude toward something familiar but not truly "loved," **о́чень нра́виться** is used.

Мне **нра́вится** ваш го́род.	*I like your town.*
Мне **о́чень нра́вится** твоё но́вое пла́тье!	*I really like your new dress!*
Вам **нра́вятся** расска́зы Че́хова?	*Do you like Chekhov's short stories?*

In some instances, **люби́ть** and **о́чень нра́виться** are virtually interchangeable.

Мне **о́чень нра́вится** класси́ческая му́зыка.
Я **люблю́** класси́ческую му́зыку.

While the meanings of these two verbs overlap somewhat, it is important to keep their distinct grammatical constructions separate.

люби́ть: <Nom. subject + **люби́ть** + Acc. object or verb infinitive>
нра́виться: <Dat. indirect object + **нра́вится/нра́вятся** + Nom. subject or verb infinitive>

As with other "set" constructions in Russian, word order may vary depending on the speaker's intended emphasis.

УПРАЖНЕНИЕ 5   Тебе́ нра́вится рок-му́зыка?

What is most and least popular among the students in your class? For each item listed, place one checkmark showing the degree to which you like or enjoy it. Then combine the ratings of the class as a whole.

	+2 Я о́чень люблю́…	+1 Я люблю́…	−1 Я не люблю́…	−2 Я о́чень (совсе́м) не люблю́…
1. игра́ть в бейсбо́л	——	——	——	——
2. о́пера	——	——	——	——
3. гуля́ть в па́рке	——	——	——	——
4. фи́льмы Кли́нта И́ствуда	——	——	——	——
5. де́лать дома́шнее зада́ние	——	——	——	——
6. игра́ть в ша́хматы	——	——	——	——
7. му́зыка Ге́ршвина	——	——	——	——
8. игра́ть в бридж†	——	——	——	——
9. класси́ческая му́зыка	——	——	——	——

	+2 Мне о́чень нра́вится (нра́вятся)…	+1 Мне нра́вится (нра́вятся)…	−1 Мне не нра́вится (нра́вятся)…	−2 Мне о́чень (совсе́м) не нра́вится (нра́вятся)…
1. игра́ть в гольф	——	——	——	——
2. бале́т	——	——	——	——
3. гото́вить (to cook)	——	——	——	——
4. фи́льмы Ву́ди А́ллена	——	——	——	——
5. игра́ть в ка́рты	——	——	——	——
6. пье́сы Че́хова	——	——	——	——
7. встава́ть в 5 часо́в утра́ (to get up at 5 a.m.)	——	——	——	——
8. слу́шать джаз	——	——	——	——
9. фи́льмы у́жасов (horror films)	——	——	——	——

❖ 6.6. VERBS: THE FUTURE *WILL, WILL BE*

Тепе́рь я **бу́ду говори́ть** тебе́ «вы».

Now (from now on) I'll use «вы» with you.

Но об э́том ни сло́ва. Э́то **бу́дет** сюрпри́з.

Don't say a word about it. It'll be a surprise.

Что **бу́дете зака́зывать?**

What'll you have?

As you know, Russian doesn't normally express *to be* in the present tense. Russian does, however, express *will / will be* in the future via the verb **быть,** which is conjugated as follows.

я бу́д-у	мы бу́д-ем
ты бу́д-ешь	вы бу́д-ете
он, она́ бу́д-ет	они́ бу́д-ут

Forms of **быть** can be used alone to mean *will be* (**э́то *бу́дет* сюрпри́з**) as well as with some infinitives to express future meanings (**я *бу́ду говори́ть* тебе́ «вы»**). Note that any Russian sentence referring to the future (such as **я *бу́ду* в Москве́**) retains the future tense even when used with **когда́** or **е́сли: Когда́ (Е́сли) я *бу́ду* в Москве́, . . .** (*When (If) I will be in Moscow, . . .*). This is a good example of where Russian is more consistent than English, which changes the future *will be* to present tense after *when* or *if*: *When I am in Moscow, I will speak only Russian*. You'll learn more about the future in Lesson 7; for now, use only those future constructions you have encountered in the text.

УПРАЖНЕ́НИЕ 6   Где ты бу́дешь . . . ?

You and a classmate are on the phone trying to find a time you can study together for an upcoming exam. Your schedule is below; your classmate's is in Appendix K. By alternating questions, find a time and location convenient for both of you.

ОБРАЗЕ́Ц: CLASSMATE: Где ты бу́дешь за́втра у́тром?
YOU: За́втра у́тром? За́втра у́тром я бу́ду до́ма. А где ты бу́дешь за́втра у́тром?

YOUR SCHEDULE	сего́дня	за́втра	послеза́втра (*the day after tomorrow*)
у́тром	(present time)	до́ма	в университе́те
днём (*in the afternoon*)	на рабо́те	в университе́те	на рабо́те
ве́чером	до́ма	на рабо́те	до́ма

УПРАЖНЕ́НИЕ 7   В Москве́

You and your friend John are about to go on a summer study program in Moscow. You have gone to see your Russian instructor, who is very interested in hearing about your plans. Fill in the blanks with missing forms of the verb **быть.**

— Где вы _____[1] жить в Москве́? В общежи́тии?
— Нет, я _____[2] жить у друзе́й.
— Ва́ши друзья́ _____[3] ле́том (*in the summer*) в Москве́?
— Нет, они́ _____[4] на да́че (*summer cottage*). Я _____[5] жить у них на да́че и _____[6] е́здить отту́да в университе́т.
— Что вы _____[7] де́лать в Москве́?
— Я _____[8] ходи́ть на ле́кции[†] и на семина́ры[†]. Мои́ друзья́ говоря́т, что мы _____[9] ходи́ть в музе́и и теа́тры.
— А вы не зна́ете, где Джон _____[10] жить?

— Зна́ю. В ру́сской семье́. Он говори́т, что е́сли он _____[11] жить в ру́сской семье́, он _____[12] говори́ть то́лько по-ру́сски.

— А вы то́же _____[13] говори́ть то́лько по-ру́сски?

— Коне́чно! Кро́ме того́, я _____[14] чита́ть по-ру́сски и смотре́ть ру́сское телеви́дение (*television*). Но пи́сьма домо́й я _____[15] писа́ть по-англи́йски.

УПРАЖНЕНИЕ 8   Что ты бу́дешь де́лать?

Based on the preceding conversation, imagine that you and a classmate are discussing your (or her) upcoming summer of study in Russia. See how many questions you can ask and answer using the following cues:

1. Где ты бу́дешь там жить?
2. Ты бу́дешь там учи́ться и́ли рабо́тать?
3. Где ты бу́дешь учи́ться? / Где ты бу́дешь рабо́тать?
4. Ты бу́дешь ходи́ть в музе́и?
5. Ты бу́дешь смотре́ть ру́сское телеви́дение (*television*)?
6. Ты бу́дешь говори́ть и чита́ть то́лько по-ру́сски?
7. Ты бу́дешь писа́ть мне пи́сьма?

СЛОВА, СЛОВА, СЛОВА . . . ✪ *Nouns Ending in -ция/-сия*

Hundreds of Russian nouns ending in **-ция/-сия** correspond directly to English nouns ending in *-tion/-sion*. You have already encountered at least two.

дискримина́ция
профе́ссия

УПРАЖНЕНИЕ 9   Guessing cognates

How many of the following cognates can you guess the meaning of? Read them aloud to a classmate; notice that the stress is always on the last vowel preceding the **-ия** ending.

авиа́ция	ликвида́ция	электрифика́ция
коми́ссия	рекоменда́ция	пе́нсия
депре́ссия	реа́кция	конденса́ция
делега́ция	экспеди́ция	тради́ция
навига́ция	инстру́кция	колле́кция
града́ция	диску́ссия	экску́рсия
диссерта́ция	репроду́кция	

❖ 6.7. COMMAND FORMS (IMPERATIVES)

Преподава́тель говори́т: — **Чита́йте** гро́мко!	*The teacher says, "Read loudly!"*

By now you have encountered a number of command forms (imperatives) and may have noticed some patterns developing. Specifically, note that the imperative endings **-й, -йте** (the «на ты» and «на вы» forms, respectively) are used with verb stems that end in a vowel (such as **чита-**), while the endings **-и, -ите** are used with verb stems that end in a consonant (such as **пиш-**). To find the verb stem, simply drop the **-ют/-ут** or **-ят/-ат** ending from the conjugated **они́** form of the verb (**чита́-ют, пи́ш-ут**).

-Й(ТЕ) ENDING (FOLLOWS VOWEL STEMS)	-Й(ТЕ) ENDING (FOLLOWS CONSONANT STEMS)
Слу́шай(те)!	Пиши́(те)!
Чита́й(те)!	Помоги́(те)!
Игра́й(те)!	Смотри́(те)!
Рабо́тай(те)!	Жди(те)!

УПРАЖНЕНИЕ 10 Imperatives (императи́вы)

Match the situation on the left with a logical command form on the right.

1. You're stuck in an elevator.
2. In a dark movie theater, you step on someone's toe.
3. You're baby-sitting. You have put the kids to bed, but they keep talking.
4. You are in charge of a work crew.
5. You're a newspaper editor and you need your reporter's story in 20 minutes.

Извини́те!
Помоги́те!
Слу́шайте!
Рабо́тайте!
Спи́те!
Пиши́те!
Чита́йте!
Гуля́йте!
Говори́те!
Игра́йте!
Смотри́те!

КУЛЬТУРА РЕЧИ

❖ ТАК ГОВОРЯТ: **EXPRESSING REGRET:** К СОЖАЛЕ́НИЮ **AND** ЖАЛЬ, ЧТО . . .

Like **Извини́те,** which you know, these two new phrases are used much like the parallel phrases are used in English.

Я, **к сожале́нию**, до́лжен идти́.	*Unfortunately, I have to leave.*
К сожале́нию, у меня́ то́лько оди́н стол.	*Unfortunately, I have only one table.*
Жаль, что он далеко́.	*Too bad he's far away.*

УПРАЖНЕНИЕ 11   Apologizing and expressing regret

Match the situations with a possible statement of apology or regret that might be made in response.

1. _____ Your brother hasn't shown up for a job interview. The employer calls your house.

2. _____ You are caught in a traffic jam and are late for an appointment. You call on your cell phone to let someone know.

3. _____ You are going to the movies, and you call a friend to invite her to go with you. Her roommate answers the phone.

4. _____ You and your friends are discussing your instructors. One of your friends says that a popular professor is on leave.

5. _____ A neighbor asks if you have the phone number of the plumber who did such a good job in your apartment building last year.

6. _____ You're known to be great at repairing things. A friend calls and asks you for help: his refrigerator broke down.

7. _____ You made friends with a Russian family in St. Petersburg and would like to send them a souvenir. A friend of yours is going to Russia, but only to Moscow.

а. К сожале́нию, у меня́ нет его́ но́мера телефо́на.
or К сожале́нию, я не по́мню его́ но́мер телефо́на.

б. Жаль, что ты е́дешь в Москву́, а не в Петербу́рг.
or Жаль, что ты не е́дешь в Петербу́рг.

в. К сожале́нию, её нет до́ма.

г. Извини́те, что я опа́здываю.

д. К сожале́нию, я не зна́ю, где он.

е. Извини́, но я не уме́ю чини́ть холоди́льники.
or К сожале́нию, я не уме́ю чини́ть холоди́льники.
or Извини́, но я не могу́ тебе́ помо́чь. К сожале́нию, я не уме́ю чини́ть холоди́льники.

ж. Жаль, что он (она́) в э́том году́ не преподаёт.

❖ САМОПРОВЕРКА: УПРАЖНЕНИЕ 12

Working on your own, try this self-test: Read a Russian sentence out loud, then give an idiomatic English equivalent without looking at the book. Then work from English to Russian. After you have completed the activity, try it with a classmate.

1. Говори́ ти́хо. Ба́бушка спит.

2. Жаль, что ты не лю́бишь рок. У меня́ есть хоро́ший компа́кт-диск.

3. Нам нра́вится ко́мната и нра́вится хозя́йка.

4. Об э́том ни сло́ва. Э́то бу́дет сюрпри́з.

5. Когда́ вы бу́дете в Москве́, где вы бу́дете жить? Что вы бу́дете де́лать?

6. Скажи́те, что вы вчера́ игра́ли?

1. *Talk quietly. Grandma's sleeping.*

2. *Too bad you don't like rock. I have a good CD.*

3. *We like the room and (we) like the landlady.*

4. *Don't say a word about it. It'll be a surprise.*

5. *When you're in Moscow, where will you be living? What will you be doing?*

6. *Tell me, what were you playing yesterday.*

❖❖ ВОПРОСЫ И ОТВЕТЫ: УПРАЖНЕНИЕ 13

Working with a classmate, take turns asking and answering the following questions.

1. Ты живёшь в своём (*your own*) до́ме и́ли снима́ешь (*rent*) кварти́ру?
2. Где живёт твой друг (твоя́ подру́га)?
3. Снима́ть (*Renting*) кварти́ру в твоём го́роде — до́рого и́ли недо́рого?
4. Тебе́ нра́вится твоя́ кварти́ра?
5. Кака́я ме́бель у тебя́ в ко́мнате?
6. Где ты у́чишься? На како́м факульте́те?
7. Ты рабо́таешь? Где?
8. Ты живёшь далеко́ от университе́та и́ли недалеко́?
9. У тебя́ есть маши́на? А гара́ж? (*If no*) Где ты парку́ешь маши́ну? Кака́я у тебя́ маши́на?

❖ ДИАЛО́ГИ

ДИАЛО́Г 1 Каку́ю му́зыку ты лю́бишь?
(Expressing likes and dislikes)

— Тебе́ нра́вится э́та му́зыка?
— Совсе́м не нра́вится.
— А каку́ю му́зыку ты лю́бишь?
— Я люблю́ кла́ссику.

ДИАЛО́Г 2 Э́то беспла́тно!
(Discussing living arrangements)

— Ты живёшь далеко́ от университе́та?
— Далеко́, но зато́ у меня́ хоро́шая кварти́ра. Двух ко́мнатная.
— Э́то, наве́рно (*most likely*), о́чень до́рого?
— Нет, э́то беспла́тно: э́то кварти́ра моего́ дя́ди. Он сейча́с в А́нглии, а мы живём в его́ кварти́ре.
— Кто «мы»?
— Я и его́ соба́ка.
— Тепе́рь я понима́ю, почему́ э́то беспла́тно!

УПРАЖНЕ́НИЕ 14   Ваш диало́г

Create a dialogue with a prospective landlord or landlady in which you discuss a room (or apartment) available for rent. You might discuss what you like or don't like about the room (apartment) and ask about the other tenants.

❖ А ТЕПЕ́РЬ . . . : УПРАЖНЕ́НИЕ 15

Working with a classmate, use what you learned in Part 2 to . . .

1. discuss some likes and dislikes that you both have
2. find out what she will be doing tomorrow afternoon and evening
3. express regret or offer an apology over something that you did not do or that did not go as planned

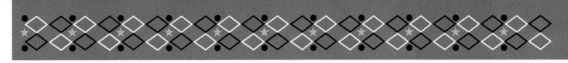
С ЧЕГО НАЧАТЬ?

— Али́са, **конве́рты** и **ма́рки** продаю́т в тре́тьем окне́. Джек, **телегра́ммы принима́ют** в пя́том окне́. **Обме́на валю́ты** тут нет, но ря́дом есть банк.

валю́та	*foreign currency*
обме́н	*exchange*
принима́ть	*to accept; to take*

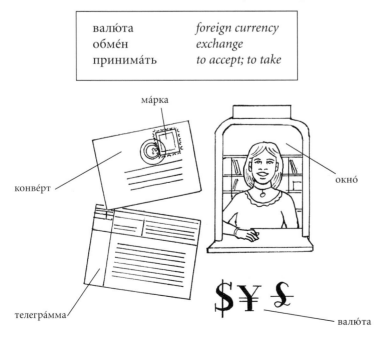

ма́рка

конве́рт

окно́

телегра́мма

валю́та

ЧТЕНИЕ

mail

◈◈ НА́ША ПО́ЧТА°

(Grandma Silin is standing in the lobby.
The professor checks his mailbox and sees that
the mail hasn't been delivered yet.)

	ПРОФЕ́ССОР.	Алекса́ндра Никола́евна, вы не зна́ете, когда́ бу́дет по́чта?
вон... *there comes*	БА́БУШКА.	Зна́ю, Илья́ Ильи́ч: *(motioning toward the window)* вон идёт° почтальо́н.

(Sergei Petrovich walks in.)

как... *How are you?*	СЕРГЕ́Й ПЕТР.	До́брый день, Алекса́ндра Никола́евна, **как здоро́вье?**[6o] Скажи́те, по́чта уже́ была́?
Нет... *Not yet.*	БА́БУШКА.	**Нет ещё.°** Я жду почтальо́на.
	ПОЧТАЛЬО́Н.	*(Walks in.)* Здра́вствуйте.
	ПРОФЕ́ССОР И СОСЕ́ДИ.	Здра́вствуйте.
Пя́тая... *Apartment five* [printed matter] package / (It's) heavy / Most likely	ПОЧТАЛЬО́Н.	*(Coming up to the professor.)* **Пя́тая** кварти́ра.° Вам два письма́ и **бандеро́ль.° Тяжёлая.° Наве́рно,°** кни́ги. *(Gives it to the professor.)*
	ВО́ВА.	Илья́ Ильи́ч, каки́е краси́вые ма́рки!
	ПРОФЕ́ССОР.	*(He takes out the letter and offers the envelope to Vova.)* Пожа́луйста, Во́ва, э́то тебе́.
	ВО́ВА.	Спаси́бо, Илья́ Ильи́ч... а тут на конве́рте а́дрес.[7]
записно́й... *address book*	ПРОФЕ́ССОР.	У меня́ есть э́тот а́дрес в **записно́й кни́жке.°**
Деся́тая... *Apartment ten /* pension payment	ПОЧТАЛЬО́Н.	**Деся́тая** кварти́ра.° Вам письмо́ и пе́нсия.° Нет, две[8] пе́нсии.
	БА́БУШКА.	О, пе́нсия — э́то хорошо́!

(The mail carrier hands out letters and newspapers.)

	СА́ША.	Извини́те, мы получа́ем «Изве́стия»,[9] а э́то «Моско́вские но́вости».
	ЛЁНА.	А мы получа́ем «Моско́вские но́вости», а э́то «Изве́стия».

---

[6] **Как ва́ше здоро́вье?** is appropriate only when addressing people middle-aged and older. It is generally not used with younger people, among whom the equivalent is **Как дела́?**

[7] Return addresses are not included in Russian personal letters, so before Vova takes the envelope, he checks to make sure Ilya Ilyich has this address.

[8] **две** is the form of **два** used with feminine nouns.

[9] «**Изве́стия**» - *News*; «**Моско́вские но́вости**» - *Moscow News*; «**Литерату́рная газе́та**» - *Literary News*; «**Коммерса́нтъ**» - *Businessman*

ПРОФЕ́ССОР.	А где моя́ «Литерату́рная† газе́та»?	
СЕРГЕ́Й ПЕТР.	Вот она́, у меня́. Где мой «Коммерса́нтъ»?	
ПРОФЕ́ССОР.	У меня́.	
ПОЧТАЛЬО́Н.	**Не волну́йтесь.°** Не волну́йтесь, ваш дом но́вый, а я на по́чте рабо́таю **неда́вно.°** Я ещё не всё зна́ю. Пи́сьма ва́ши? Не чужи́е°?	*Don't worry.* *Я... I haven't been working at the post office very long. /*
ВСЕ.	Нет, нет!	*somebody else's*
ПОЧТАЛЬО́Н.	**Замеча́тельно!°** **Гла́вное°** — э́то пи́сьма. А газе́ты — э́то не пробле́ма. Вы, **мужчи́ны,°** отдаёте друг дру́гу газе́ты. (*To Silin.*) Вам — «Коммерса́нтъ», (*to the professor*) а вам — «Литерату́рная газе́та». Тепе́рь всё в поря́дке. (*Taking another letter out of her bag.*) Скажи́те, а кто э́то — Си́лин В. С.?	*Wonderful! / The main thing* *gentlemen*
СЕРГЕ́Й ПЕТР.	Я Си́лин, но мои́ инициа́лы† — С. П.	
ПОЧТАЛЬО́Н.	Нет, тут на конве́рте Си́лину В. С.	
БА́БУШКА.	Серге́й Петро́вич, э́то же ваш Во́ва!	
СЕРГЕ́Й ПЕТР.	Действи́тельно, Во́ва! И уже́ инициа́лы! Как бы́стро **расту́т°** на́ши де́ти!	*grow up*

УПРАЖНЕ́НИЕ 1   Под микроско́пом: Dative forms

There are five sentences containing Dative pronouns and pronoun phrases as indirect objects in this reading. Locate them and write them out, underlining the Dative forms.

ГРАММА́ТИКА И ПРА́КТИКА

О РОССИИ

ADDRESSING ENVELOPES

Илья́ Ильи́ч, а тут на конве́рте а́дрес.

Russians traditionally addressed envelopes in the following manner: (**Куда́**) the country (for international mail), then the city, postal code (**и́ндекс**), street, building, apartment, and finally (**Кому́**) the addressee, whose name is in the Dative case. The sender's address (**А́дрес отправи́теля**) was usually placed directly below that of the addressee. Some newer envelopes follow a different pattern, much like our own: the addressee's name (**Кому́**) appears on the first line in the Dative case, followed by the destination (**Куда́**) and finally, the postal code; the return address (marked **От кого́** and **Отку́да**) is in the upper left corner. Both formats have a series of boxes in the lower left corner where the postal code is written in large block numerals. Note the following abbreviations commonly used in writing addresses: **г. = го́род, ул. = у́лица, д. = дом, корп. = ко́рпус** (*a separate building within a building complex*),

кв. = кварти́ра. When you send a letter to Russia from the United States, it is appropriate to put the complete address in Russian in the manner described above, then add *To:* [*city*], *Russia* in English at the bottom.

УПРАЖНЕНИЕ 2   Addressing envelopes

Address envelopes to the following recipients. Use appropriate abbreviations.

1. И. И. Серге́ев, у́лица Тверска́я, дом 24, кварти́ра 362, Москва́ 123100
2. Н. В. Жили́нская, Кондра́тьевский проспе́кт, дом 15, ко́рпус 2, кварти́ра 134, Санкт-Петербу́рг 195197

❖❖ 6.8. NUMERALS: CASE USAGE WITH 1–4

К сожале́нию, у меня́ то́лько **оди́н стол.**	*Unfortunately, I have only one table.*
Вам **два письма́** и бандеро́ль.	*There are two letters and a [printed matter] package for you.*
Вам письмо́ и пе́нсия. Нет, **две пе́нсии.**	*For you there's a letter and a pension payment. No, two payments.*

All the preceding sentences contain a numeral that expresses a quantity. With the exception of **оди́н,** *cardinal* numerals (those that express a quantity) in Russian are followed by the Genitive case of the items being counted, as shown in the following table.[10]

NUMERAL	WHAT HAPPENS	EXAMPLES
1 (оди́н, одна́, одно́)	The form of this number changes to match the gender of the noun.	У меня́ **оди́н стол, одна́ ла́мпа** и **одно́ кре́сло.**
2 (два, две)	**а.** **Два** precedes masculine and neuter nouns; **две** precedes feminine nouns. **6.** The items being counted are in Genitive singular.	У меня́ **два бра́та** и **две сестры́.** На столе́ **два письма́.** В ко́мнате **две крова́ти.**
3 (три), **4** (четы́ре)	The items being counted are in Genitive singular.	В коридо́ре **три студе́нта.** В э́том до́ме **четы́ре кварти́ры.**

УПРАЖНЕ́НИЕ 3   Scavenger hunt

Using the numerals **оди́н, два/две, три, четы́ре,** find out who in your class has how many of the following. To do so, first state how many you have and then ask **А у тебя́?**

ОБРАЗЕ́Ц: — У меня́ до́ма два телефо́на. А у тебя́?
                   — У меня́ оди́н телефо́н. *or* У меня́ нет телефо́на.

1. телеви́зор
2. компью́тер
3. сестра́
4. брат
5. ко́шка
6. соба́ка
7. телефо́н
8. маши́на
9. ла́мпа
10. кре́сло
11. спа́льня
12. туале́т
13. при́нтер
14. ???

---

[10]It is this "numeral governance" that requires **оди́н год** but **два, три, четы́ре го́да** (Genitive singular). The word **лет** used with other numbers is a special Genitive plural about which you will learn more later.

СЛОВА, СЛОВА, СЛОВА . . . ✪ *Ordinal Numerals 5–30*

Пя́тая кварти́ра. Вам два письма́ и. . . .   *Fifth apartment. You get two letters and . . .*

Деся́тая кварти́ра. вам письмо́ и. . . .   *Tenth apartment. There's a letter for you and . . .*

You already know the ordinal numerals *first, second, third, fourth*; here are the ordinals through the thirties (which you need to give calendar dates, among other things).

	Ordinals	**Cardinals (*for reference*)**
1st	пе́рвый	(оди́н)
2nd	второ́й	(два)
3rd	тре́тий	(три)
4th	четвёртый	(четы́ре)
5th	пя́тый	(пять)
6th	шесто́й	(шесть)
7th	седьмо́й	(семь)
8th	восьмо́й	(во́семь)
9th	девя́тый	(де́вять)
10th	деся́тый	(де́сять)
11th	оди́ннадцатый	(оди́ннадцать)
12th	двена́дцатый	(двена́дцать)
13th	трина́дцатый	(трина́дцать)
14th	четы́рнадцатый	(четы́рнадцать)
15th	пятна́дцатый	(пятна́дцать)
16th	шестна́дцатый	(шестна́дцать)
17th	семна́дцатый	(семна́дцать)
18th	восемна́дцатый	(восемна́дцать)
19th	девятна́дцатый	(девятна́дцать)
20th	двадца́тый	(два́дцать)
21st	два́дцать пе́рвый	(два́дцать оди́н)
22nd	два́дцать второ́й	(два́дцать два)
30th	тридца́тый	(три́дцать)
31st	три́дцать пе́рвый	(три́дцать оди́н)

Except for the forms of **тре́тий** (*third*), the ordinal numerals have regular adjective endings. Here are the forms of **тре́тий.**

	MASCULINE	**NEUTER**	**FEMININE**
Nom.	тре́тий (эта́ж)	тре́тье (сло́во)	тре́тья (кварти́ра)
Acc.	*Nom./Gen.*	тре́тье	тре́тью
Gen.	тре́тьего		тре́тьей
Prep.	тре́тьем		тре́тьей
Dat.	тре́тьему		тре́тьей

УПРАЖНЕНИЕ 4   Пе́рвый челове́к в ко́смосе

Who was the first man in space? The first woman? The first person on the moon?
Match the items in the left-hand column with those on the right.

1. _____ Пе́рвый челове́к в
ко́смосе (*space*)
2. _____ Тре́тий день неде́ли
3. _____ Шесто́й ме́сяц го́да
4. _____ Второ́й ме́сяц го́да
5. _____ Пе́рвая же́нщина в ко́смосе
6. _____ Деся́тая бу́ква
англи́йского алфави́та†
7. _____ Пя́тая бу́ква ру́сского алфави́та
8. _____ Четвёртый ме́сяц
уче́бного го́да (*school year*)
9. _____ Шестна́дцатый америка́нский
президе́нт
10. _____ Пе́рвый америка́нский
университе́т

а. J
б. Валенти́на Терешко́ва
в. ноя́брь и́ли дека́брь
г. среда́
д. Д
е. Ю́рий Гага́рин
ж. Авраа́м Ли́нкольн
з. февра́ль
и. Га́рвардский университе́т
к. ию́нь

УПРАЖНЕНИЕ 5   Где он живёт?

Study the floor plan of the apartment building[11] on page 44; then close your book and
see if you and another student can reconstruct who lives where.

ОБРАЗЕ́Ц: — Ты по́мнишь, где живёт профе́ссор Петро́вский?
— Да, он живёт на второ́м этаже́, в пя́той кварти́ре.

УПРАЖНЕНИЕ 6   На како́м этаже́ ты живёшь?

Ask classmates what floor they live on and find out who lives on the highest floor.

ОБРАЗЕ́Ц: — На како́м этаже́ ты живёшь?
— На второ́м.

СЛОВА́, СЛОВА́, СЛОВА́ . . . ✪ *Months (Ме́сяцы)*
in Nominative and Genitive

NOMINATIVE	GENITIVE	NOMINATIVE	GENITIVE
янва́рь	января́	ию́ль	ию́ля
февра́ль	февраля́	а́вгуст	а́вгуста
март	ма́рта	сентя́брь	сентября́
апре́ль	апре́ля	октя́брь	октября́
май	ма́я	ноя́брь	ноября́
ию́нь	ию́ня	дека́брь	декабря́

---

[11]Russian and American systems for numbering floors are usually the same: **пе́рвый эта́ж** = *first*
or *ground floor.*

◈◈ 6.9. CALENDAR DATES (DAY + DATE + MONTH)

— Извини́те, **како́е сего́дня число́?**	*"Excuse me, what's today's date?"*
— Сего́дня? Сего́дня **17** (**семна́дцатое**) **февраля́.**	*"Today? Today is the 17th of February."*

To answer the question **Како́е сего́дня число́?** (*What's the date today?*), Russian uses the following pattern.

<ordinal numeral (Nom.; always neuter) + month (Gen.)>

Remember, all the names of months (see previous page) are masculine, as is the word **календа́рь**. Note their Genitive case forms, paying particular attention to where the stress falls: It stays on the stem for the six months beginning with March but shifts to the ending for the six months beginning with September.

If you wish also to give the day of the week, you can begin with that day in the Nominative: **Сего́дня среда́, два́дцать второ́е (два́дцать тре́тье, . . .) ма́рта.**

УПРАЖНЕ́НИЕ 7   Како́е сего́дня число́?

Working with a classmate, take turns pointing to a date on the calendar and asking what the date is.

ОБРАЗЕ́Ц: (*Pointing to March 22.*)— Како́е сего́дня число́?
— Сего́дня два́дцать второ́е ма́рта.

КАЛЕНДА́РЬ

	ЯНВАРЬ	ФЕВРАЛЬ	МАРТ
Пн	6 13 20 27	3 10 17 24	3 10 17 24 31
Вт	⑦ 14 21 28	4 11 18 25	4 11 18 25
Ср	① 8 15 22 29	5 12 19 26	5 12 19 26
Чт	2 9 16 23 30	6 13 20 27	6 13 20 27
Пт	3 10 17 24 31	7 14 21 28	7 14 21 28
Сб	4 11 18 25	1 8 15 22	1 ⑧ 15 22 29
Вс	5 12 19 26	2 9 16 23	2 9 16 23 30

	АПРЕЛЬ	МАЙ	ИЮНЬ
Пн	7 14 21 28	5 12 19 26	2 9 16 23 30
Вт	1 8 15 22 29	6 13 20 27	3 10 17 24
Ср	2 9 16 23 30	7 14 21 28	4 11 18 25
Чт	3 10 17 24	1 8 15 22 29	5 12 19 26
Пт	4 11 18 25	2 ⑨ 16 23 30	6 13 20 27
Сб	5 12 19 26	3 10 17 24 31	7 14 21 28
Вс	6 13 20 27	4 11 18 25	1 8 15 22 29

	ИЮЛЬ	АВГУСТ	СЕНТЯБРЬ
Пн	7 14 21 28	4 11 18 25	1 8 15 22 29
Вт	1 8 15 22 29	5 12 19 26	2 9 16 23 30
Ср	2 9 16 23 30	6 13 20 27	3 10 17 24
Чт	3 10 17 24	7 14 21 28	4 11 18 25
Пт	4 11 18 25	1 8 15 22 29	5 12 19 26
Сб	5 12 19 26	2 9 16 23 30	6 13 20 27
Вс	6 13 20 27	3 10 17 24 31	7 14 21 28

	ОКТЯБРЬ	НОЯБРЬ	ДЕКАБРЬ
Пн	6 13 20 27	3 10 17 24	1 8 15 22 29
Вт	7 14 21 28	4 11 18 25	2 9 16 23 30
Ср	1 8 15 22 29	5 12 19 26	3 10 17 24 31
Чт	2 9 16 23 30	6 13 20 27	4 11 18 25
Пт	3 10 17 24 31	⑦ 14 21 28	5 12 19 26
Сб	4 11 18 25	1 8 15 22 29	6 13 20 27
Вс	5 12 19 26	2 9 16 23 30	7 14 21 28

УПРАЖНЕНИЕ 8   Days and dates

Without pointing, give a date and see if your classmate, looking at his own copy of the calendar, can respond with the day of the week. Take turns giving the date and responding with the day.

ОБРАЗЕЦ: — Три́дцать пе́рвое января́.
              — Э́то пя́тница.

❖ 6.10. ADDITIONAL MEANINGS OF «У» PHRASES

— Са́ша, Алекса́ндра Никола́евна до́ма?	*"Sasha, is Aleksandra Nikolaevna at home?"*
— Нет, она́ **у сосе́дки.**	*"No, she's at a neighbor's."*
Джим — мой аспира́нт, исто́рик, у́чится **у нас в университе́те.**	*Jim is my graduate student, a historian, (who's) studying at our university.*
У нас в Аме́рике студе́нты и аспира́нты обы́чно рабо́тают.	*At home in America students and grad students usually work.*
У меня́ и роди́тели, и брат — врачи́.	*My parents and my brother are all doctors.*

You have learned to use «**у**» phrases to express possession: **У меня́ япо́нская маши́на** (*I have a Japanese car.*). «**У**» phrases are also used with a person (or a pronoun referring to a person) to express location at that person's home, place of business, or even in his city or country. In the last of the preceding examples an «**у**» phrase is used like a possessive to establish the relationship between the speaker and his family members. Here are some more examples showing location.

— Извини́те, Ната́лья Ива́новна, Во́ва до́ма?	*"Excuse me, Natalya Ivanovna, is Vova home?"*
— Нет, Ко́ля, он **у ба́бушки.**	*"No, Kolya, he's at (his) grandmother's."*
А пока́ я живу́ **у тёти.**	*For the time being I'm living at my aunt's place.*

УПРАЖНЕНИЕ 9   У нас, у вас

You're getting acquainted with a Russian student. Here are some questions he is asking you about America and your life. How will you answer these questions?

1. У вас студе́нты рабо́тают? Где они́ обы́чно рабо́тают?
2. У вас тут есть недороги́е рестора́ны?
3. У вас в университе́те есть спортза́л?
4. Како́й у вас са́мый популя́рный (*the most popular*) вид спо́рта (*kind of sport*)?
5. Где у вас мо́жно купи́ть конве́рты и ма́рки?
6. У вас есть кни́жный магази́н?
7. У вас в библиоте́ке есть ру́сские кни́ги?

◆О РОССИИ◆

НОМЕР ТЕЛЕФОНА

У меня́ есть его́ но́мер телефо́на.

Tanya and Sveta will have a new telephone number when they move into their room at Tatyana Dmitrievna's apartment. Russian telephone numbers are not standardized. In the largest cities (**Москва́, Санкт-Петербу́рг**), they consist of seven digits, which are written and spoken XXX-XX-XX. In less populous cities (such as **Хаба́ровск,** population about 615,000, located in eastern Russia on the border with China), they may be made up of only six numbers, which are written and spoken XX-XX-XX. Finally, in many small towns and villages (such as **Баба́ево,** population under 50,000, located about 300 miles north of Moscow and about 200 miles east of St. Petersburg), phone numbers consist of only five numbers. Such numbers are usually read X-XX-XX.

УПРАЖНЕНИЕ 10 Но́мер телефо́на

You are doing an internship at the **КАМАЗ** truck factory (**Ка́мский автомоби́льный заво́д**) in **На́бережные Челны́** (population about 300,000, located about 150 miles east of **Каза́нь** on the **Ка́ма** river). A colleague from the factory is giving you the phone numbers of some of your co-workers. Write down the names and numbers as a classmate reads them aloud to you in Russian, then change the names and numbers around (or make up new ones) and dictate them for your classmate to write down.

Андре́й	22-47-83
Валенти́на	91-17-74
Лари́са	65-36-59
Константи́н	70-39-12
Ю́рий	19-51-48
Зо́я	90-62-86

Таксофо́н *Pay phone*

УПРАЖНЕНИЕ 11   Какóй твой нóмер телефóна?

Compile a list of the actual phone numbers of five of your classmates. (Although Russians usually give seven-digit phone numbers as XXX-XX-XX, imagine that you are in a noisy café, so your classmates must give you their numbers this way: X-X-X-XX-XX.)

УПРАЖНЕНИЕ 12   Там есть нóмер телефóна . . . ?

Below is a page from a city information book that gives phone numbers for various restaurants, movie theaters, and clubs. A classmate will ask you for the phone numbers of certain establishments listed in Appendix K and write them down as you read them aloud. After you do three items, switch roles. Then check to see that you each wrote down all the phone numbers correctly.

РЕСТОРАНЫ		КЛУБЫ	
«ФОНТАН»		**«ГАЙДАРОВЕЦ»**	
Муравьева-Амурского, 50.	33-49-10	К. Маркса, 82.	39-16-54
«ЧУДЕСНИЦА»		**з-да Гражданской авиации**	
Московская, 2.	33-67-71	пер. Гражданский, 1.	33-37-72
«ШАШЛЫЧНАЯ»		**«ИСКОРКА»**	
Краснореченская, 98.		Рокоссовского, 29.	52-66-34
Директор	36-05-03	**комбината Хлебопродуктов**	
Склад	36-10-19	Краснореченская, 90.	51-48-97
«ЭКСПРЕСС»		**«ЛАСТОЧКА»**	
Серышева, 74.	35-72-06	Дзержинского, 68.	34-20-95
		«МАТРОССКИЙ»	
КИНОТЕАТРЫ		Краснофлотская, 1	7-73-22
«АМУР»		**«СЕМЬЯ»**	
Известковая, 19.	34-36-96	Советская, 52.	35-79-45
«ВОСХОД»		**«СИГНАЛ»**	
Краснореченская, 38.		Пушкина, 6.	33-58-31
Директор	55-21-71		
Кассы	55-21-62	**«АЛЬТЕРНАТИВА»**	
Автоответчик	55-21-70	Фрунзе, 3.	33-03-67
«ГИГАНТ»		**поселка ВОРОНЕЖ-2**	7-79-35
Муравьева-Амурского, 19.		**«РАДУГА»**	
Директор	33-53-93	Краснореченская, 85.	55-25-24
Бухгалтерия	33-33-28		
Техnorук	33-18-13	**«ОРЛЕНОК»**	
Администратор	33-09-02	Костромская, 46б.	37-25-44
Автоответчик	33-99-69		

455

КУЛЬТУРА РЕЧИ

❖◈ **ТАК ГОВОРЯТ: ДЕЙСТВИ́ТЕЛЬНО**

Да, я **действи́тельно** могу́ помо́чь.	*Yes, I can indeed help.*
Но вы **действи́тельно** о́чень краси́вая де́вушка.	*But you really are a very pretty girl.*
Действи́тельно! Дава́й говори́ть друг дру́гу «ты»!	*Right! Let's use «ты» with each other!*
— Серге́й Петро́вич, э́то же ваш Во́ва!	*"Sergei Petrovich, that's your Vova!"*
— **Действи́тельно**, Во́ва! И уже́ инициа́лы! Как бы́стро расту́т на́ши де́ти!	*"It's Vova, indeed! And [he's] already [using] initials! How quickly our children grow up!"*

The adverb **действи́тельно** is used to confirm something that may not be obvious (but is obvious to the speaker). It may be used parenthetically and is rendered in a number of ways in English, depending on its context.

УПРАЖНЕ́НИЕ 13   Действи́тельно

Match the statements on the left with likely responses on the right. Then decide which of our characters made or might have made each statement.

1. _____ — Ната́ша говори́т, что
   кварти́ра плоха́я.
   (_____)

2. _____ — Моя́ пе́рвая
   учи́тельница му́зыки
   была́ стро́гая.
   (_____)

3. _____ — Во́ва, почему́ ты
   говори́шь Са́ше «ты»?
   (_____)

4. _____ — Вы действи́тельно
   сдаёте ко́мнату?
   (_____)

5. _____ — Кто э́то на фотогра́фии?
   Наве́рно, ваш сын?
   (_____)

6. _____ — Ле́на ду́мает, что она́
   краси́вая, и поэ́тому
   кома́ндует.[†]
   (_____)

а. — Действи́тельно, Во́ва,
   почему́ ты говори́шь мне
   «ты»? (_____)

б. — Кварти́ра действи́тельно
   плоха́я.
   (_____)

в. — Да, э́то действи́тельно мой
   сын. (_____)

г. — Да, она́ действи́тельно
   была́ о́чень стро́гая.
   (_____)

д. — Она́ действи́тельно о́чень
   краси́вая.
   (_____)

е. — Да, я действи́тельно сдаю́
   ко́мнату.
   (_____)

❖ САМОПРОВЕРКА: УПРАЖНЕНИЕ 14

Working on your own, try this self-test: Read a Russian sentence out loud, then give an idiomatic English equivalent without looking at the book. Then work from English to Russian. After you have completed the activity, try it with a classmate.

1. Вам письмо́, две газе́ты и три журна́ла.

   1. For you there's a letter, two newspapers and three magazines.

2. — Извини́те, како́е сего́дня число́?

   — Сего́дня? Сего́дня 17 (семна́дцатое) февраля́.

   2. "Excuse me, what's the date today?"
   "Today? Today's February 17th."

3. — Извини́те, Мари́на Влади́мировна, Сла́ва до́ма?

   — Нет, Ми́ша, он у де́душки.

   3. "Excuse me, Marina Vladimirovna, is Slava home?"
   "No, Misha, he's at (his) grandfather's."

4. У нас в университе́те о́чень лю́бят спорт.

   4. They really like sports at our university.

❖ ВОПРОСЫ И ОТВЕТЫ: УПРАЖНЕНИЕ 15

1. Ты лю́бишь получа́ть по́чту? Ты получа́ешь мно́го по́чты?
2. Ты лю́бишь получа́ть пи́сьма? А писа́ть пи́сьма ты лю́бишь?
3. Кому́ ты пи́шешь пи́сьма?
4. (*Depending on the response to #3.*) А твоя́ подру́га (твоя́ ба́бушка, твои́ ру́сские друзья́) пи́шет (пи́шут) тебе́?
5. Ты ча́сто получа́ешь бандеро́ли? Что ты получа́ешь — кни́ги, компа́кт-ди́ски?
6. Ты получа́ешь «Моско́вские но́вости»?
7. Твой почтальо́н — мужчи́на и́ли же́нщина?
8. Он молодо́й и́ли ста́рый (Она́ молода́я и́ли ста́рая)?
9. Ты получа́ешь иногда́ (*sometimes*) чужу́ю (*other people's*) по́чту? Что ты де́лаешь, когда́ ты получа́ешь чужу́ю по́чту?

Почтальо́н

❖ **ДИАЛОГИ**

ДИАЛОГ 1 Ваш па́спорт?
(Asking for your mail in a post office)

— Пожа́луйста, да́йте (*give*) мою́ по́чту.
— Фами́лия?
— Ольхо́вская.
— Ваш па́спорт?
— Вот он, пожа́луйста.
— Вот ва́ша по́чта. Два письма́ и две газе́ты.

ДИАЛОГ 2 По́чта уже́ была́?
(Asking about mail)

— По́чта уже́ была́?
— Да, вот она́. Письмо́ па́пе, письмо́ мне и два письма́ тебе́.
— А кому́ бандеро́ль?
— Бандеро́ль то́же тебе́. Она́ тяжёлая. Наве́рно, кни́ги.
— Да, э́то а́нгло-ру́сский слова́рь (*dictionary*).

УПРАЖНЕНИЕ 16   Ваш диало́г

Create a three- or four-way dialogue in which you help a new mail carrier distribute mail in your apartment building.

❖ **А ТЕПЕРЬ . . . : УПРАЖНЕНИЕ 17**

Working with a classmate, use what you learned in Part 3 to . . .
1. practice giving quantities of things (up to four) that you can see in your classroom, for example: **Я ви́жу три рюкзака́** (avoid animate nouns like **студе́нтка, преподава́тель**)
2. ask and tell the day and date (use a calendar to quiz each other)
3. ask and give each other's telephone number (in the form X-X-X-XX-XX)

ЧАСТЬ ЧЕТВЁРТАЯ

 С ЧЕГО НАЧАТЬ?

ВАСИ́ЛИЙ ПЕТРО́ВИЧ И НАДЕ́ЖДА ИВА́НОВНА В РЕСТОРА́НЕ

— Рестора́н дорого́й, а **гото́вят** пло́хо.

— **Пи́во тёплое.**

— Официа́нты **гру́бые.**

— Всё **невку́сно.**

— Ну что ты! Рестора́н недорого́й. И гото́вят замеча́тельно.

— **Да нет,** пи́во **холо́дное!**

— Ну что ты! фициа́нты о́чень **ве́жливые!**

— По-мо́ему, всё о́чень **вку́сно!**

ве́жливый	*polite*
вку́сно	*delicious*
гото́вить	*to cook*
гру́бый	*rude*
Да нет, . . .	*Not at all*
невку́сно	*tasteless*
пи́во	*beer*
тёплый	*warm*
холо́дный	*cold*

✖ ЧТЕНИЕ ✖

❖ **НАМ НРА́ВИТСЯ Э́ТА ИДЕ́Я!**

An excerpt from Tanya's diary

Or rather

to buy / almost / всё… *everything we need / True /* нам…
we were incredibly lucky
Сиди́м… *We're sitting /*
having a conversation /
Suddenly / we hear / a noise
landing / there's / elderly
is angry / не смей… *don't*
you dare / throw out /
for / Мне… *I don't need*
a table / sure / At that moment
are renting / Антиква́рная…
A real antique!
present / Isn't that so /
Че́рез… *A minute later*
brings over / asks
как… *how about /*
a housewarming / definitely

Ита́к, у нас есть кварти́ра. Верне́е,° не кварти́ра, а ко́мната, зато́ о́чень хоро́шая. В кварти́ре то́лько мы и Татья́на Дми́триевна, на́ша хозя́йка.

Нам да́же не на́до покупа́ть° ме́бель: в ко́мнате есть **почти́° всё, что ну́жно.° Пра́вда,°** не́ было стола́: у Татья́ны Дми́триевны то́лько оди́н стол. Но **нам необыкнове́нно повезло́.°**

Сиди́м мы° на ку́хне и **разгова́риваем. Вдруг° слы́шим** шум° на ле́стнице. Открыва́ем дверь и ви́дим: на площа́дке° **стои́т°** стол, а ря́дом — пожила́я° же́нщина и симпати́чный па́рень. Она́ се́рдится°: «Са́ша, не смей° выбра́сывать° стол! На чём ты бу́дешь писа́ть?» А он говори́т: «Ба́бушка, но у меня́ в ко́мнате уже́ стои́т роя́ль и нет ме́ста **для°** стола́! Мне стол не **ну́жен.°** Писа́ть я могу́ и на роя́ле, а игра́ть на столе́ я не могу́. Кро́ме того́, я его́ не выбра́сываю — я **уве́рен,°** что у нас есть сосе́ди, кото́рые …» **Тут°** он ви́дит нас: «Де́вушки, вы тут живёте?» «Да, мы **снима́ем°** тут ко́мнату». «Вам не ну́жен стол? Антиква́рная вещь»!° — «О́чень ну́жен!» — «Вам нра́вится наш стол? О́чень нра́вится? Отли́чно! Э́то наш **пода́рок°** вам. **Пра́вда,°** ба́бушка?» **Че́рез мину́ту°** стол уже́ стои́т у нас! Татья́на Дми́триевна **прино́сит°** варе́нье,[12] и мы все пьём чай. Са́ша **спра́шивает,°** как **насчёт° новосе́лья.°** Нам всем нра́вится э́та иде́я! У нас **обяза́тельно°** бу́дет новосе́лье!

---

[12]Serving tea with jam (**чай с варе́ньем**) is a favorite custom among some Russians.

УПРАЖНЕНИЕ 1   Под микроско́пом: Personal pronouns

The reading contains many examples of the personal pronouns in various case forms. In addition to six different Nominative (N) forms, there are two Accusatives (A), two Genitives (G) and three Datives (D), some of which are used more than once. Find them in the reading, underline the phrases in which they occur, and place the appropriate letter (N, A, G, D) above each pronoun.

ГРАММАТИКА И ПРАКТИКА

6.11. MISSING, LACKING IN THE PAST AND FUTURE: <НÉ БЫЛО, НЕ БУ́ДЕТ + GENITIVE>

Пра́вда, **не́ было стола́**.   *True, there was no table.*

In Lesson 4 you learned the unvarying present tense construction <**нет** + Genitive> to say that someone (something) is missing or lacking (**Ле́ны нет до́ма, Воды́ нет!**) or that you don't have something (**У неё нет ва́нны, а у меня́ нет ду́ша**). Similarly, the Genitive is linked with the set phrases **не́ было** and **не бу́дет** for expressing these meanings in the past and future, respectively.

Present: <**нет** + Genitive>
Past: <**не́ было** + Genitive> (Note: this is pronounced as one word, with the stress clearly on the **не́:** [né́byla].)
Future: <**не бу́дет** + Genitive>

PRESENT	PAST	FUTURE
Ле́на до́ма?	Ле́на **была́** до́ма?	Ле́на **бу́дет** до́ма?
Ле́ны нет до́ма.	**Ле́ны не́ было** до́ма.	**Ле́ны не бу́дет** до́ма.
У нас больша́я кварти́ра.	У нас **была́** больша́я кварти́ра.	У нас **бу́дет** больша́я кварти́ра.
У него́ **нет дипло́ма.**†	У него́ **не́ было дипло́ма.**	У него́ **не бу́дет дипло́ма.**

УПРАЖНЕНИЕ 2   У Ка́ти

Fill in the blanks with the correct Genitive forms for the words in parentheses.

В про́шлом году́ я жила́ два ме́сяца в кварти́ре мое́й подру́ги Ка́ти. _____[1] (Ка́тя) не́ было: она́ была́ в Росси́и. У неё больша́я двухко́мнатная кварти́ра. Сейча́с там есть всё, что ну́жно, но в про́шлом году́ там почти́ не́ было _____[2] (ме́бель).

Не́ было _____ ³ (стол). Не́ было _____ ⁴ (кре́сло).
Не́ было да́же _____ ⁵ (крова́ть), и я спала́ на ста́ром дива́не.
Кро́ме того́, там не́ было _____ ⁶ (отопле́ние) (*heating*).
Обы́чно у нас в Аризо́не тепло́ и отопле́ние не нужно́, но в про́шлом году́
была́ холо́дная о́сень (*autumn*). У меня́ не́ было _____ ⁷
(тёплое одея́ло), и мне бы́ло хо́лодно (*I was cold*). Я купи́ла одея́ло. Пото́м
я купи́ла тёплый сви́тер, потому́ что _____ ⁸ (свитер) у меня́
то́же не́ было. Коне́чно, хорошо́ жить в большо́й кварти́ре, но мне
бо́льше (*more*) нра́вится моя́ ма́ленькая и о́чень тёплая кварти́ра.

УПРАЖНЕ́НИЕ 3   У нас не́ было . . .

You and some friends are discussing the terrible living accommodations you had last
year. Form a chain where you take turns listing things that your apartment did and did
not have.

> ОБРАЗЕ́Ц: А. — В про́шлом году́ у нас не́ было телеви́зора.
> Б. — У нас был телеви́зор, но не́ было холоди́льника.
> В. — Холоди́льник у нас был, но не́ было . . .

❖❖ 6.12. TELLING WHAT YOU NEED

В ко́мнате есть почти́ всё, что **ну́жно.**	*In the room there's almost everything that's needed.*
Мне стол не **ну́жен.**	*I don't need a table.*

To express something you need, place the person who needs the item in the Dative,
followed by the form of **ну́жен** (**нужна́, ну́жно, нужны́**) that agrees in gender and
number with the item. That item is the grammatical subject, so it's in the Nominative.
Compare this structure with the examples that follow.

<Dat. of person + **ну́жен** (**нужна́, ну́жно, нужны́**) + Nom. of item needed>

Мне **нужна́** хоро́шая кварти́ра.	*I need a good apartment.*
Мое́й сестре́ **ну́жен** но́вый компью́тер.	*My sister needs a new computer.*
Тебе́ **нужны́** но́вые сапоги́.	*You need new boots.*

УПРАЖНЕ́НИЕ 4   Что нам ну́жно?

You're moving into an unfurnished apartment and you're interested in shopping for
furniture and appliances. A friend of yours also needs to buy some things. Make up ten
exchanges (some with adjectives, some without) about things you do (or don't) need
and things you do (or don't) have. Some suggested items are given below. Avoid plural
nouns for now.

> ОБРАЗЕ́Ц: — Мне ну́жен стол. У меня́ есть сту́лья, но нет стола́. А у
> тебя́?
> — У меня́ стол есть. Стол мне не ну́жен, но мне нужна́
> хоро́шая ла́мпа. А тебе́ ла́мпа не нужна́?

но́вая крова́ть	дива́н	кни́жная по́лка
кни́жный шкаф	поду́шка	хоро́шее кре́сло
тёплое одея́ло	краси́вый ковёр	буди́льник
карти́на	большо́й холоди́льник	???
но́вый пылесо́с		

◈ 6.13. WHAT ONE MUST (NOT) DO: <DATIVE + (НЕ) НА́ДО + INFINITIVE>

Нам да́же **не на́до** покупа́ть ме́бель.   *We don't even have to buy furniture.*

The formula below shows the most common way to express something that someone must (or shouldn't) do or something that someone has to (or doesn't have to) do.

<Dative of person + (**не**) **на́до** + infinitive>

If no person is expressed, the meaning becomes generic: *one must (not), you (don't) have to.*

Кро́ме того́, **на́до** писа́ть интере́сно,   *Besides, one must (you have to)*
оригина́льно.   *write interestingly, creatively.*
Не на́до здесь фотографи́ровать.   *You're not supposed to (you shouldn't)*
                                             take pictures here.

УПРАЖНЕНИЕ 5   How to do something

Match the situation on the left with a possible solution or necessary action on the right. Various combinations are possible.

1. _____ To get good grades . . .
2. _____ To be a historian . . .
3. _____ To become a famous pianist . . .
4. _____ To earn money . . .
5. _____ If one is a journalist . . .
6. _____ To make a living as a pianist . . .

а. на́до мно́го чита́ть.
б. на́до писа́ть хорошо́ и интере́сно.
в. на́до мно́го рабо́тать.
г. на́до мно́го игра́ть.
д. на́до хорошо́ учи́ться.
е. на́до име́ть (*have*) тала́нт.[†]

УПРАЖНЕНИЕ 6   Что на́до де́лать?

Match the situation on the left with a likely response or rejoinder on the right.

1. _____ За́втра день рожде́ния де́душки.
2. _____ Све́те и Та́не не нра́вится их кварти́ра.
3. _____ Са́ша игра́ет на роя́ле ве́чером.
4. _____ У Во́вы большо́е дома́шнее зада́ние.
5. _____ Джим хо́чет хорошо́ говори́ть по-ру́сски.
6. _____ У Си́линых сего́дня го́сти.
7. _____ Ле́на пи́шет статью́ для газе́ты.

а. Ему́ на́до игра́ть ти́хо.
б. Им на́до иска́ть другу́ю кварти́ру.
в. Ей на́до писа́ть интере́сно, оригина́льно.
г. Ему́ не на́до сего́дня ве́чером смотре́ть телеви́зор.
д. Ната́лье Ива́новне на́до купи́ть торт.
е. Ему́ на́до слу́шать ру́сские кассе́ты.
ж. На́до купи́ть ему́ пода́рок.

◈ 6.14. SHORT-FORM ADJECTIVES

Я, к сожале́нию, **до́лжен** идти́.	*I, unfortunately, must be going.*
Како́й симпати́чный! И о́чень **похо́ж** на вас.	*How nice-looking! And (he looks) a lot like you.*
Я **ра́да**, что вам ко́мната нра́вится.	*I'm glad that you like the room.*
Кро́ме того́, я его́ не выбра́сываю — я **уве́рен**, что у нас есть сосе́ди, кото́рые . . .	*Besides, I'm not throwing it out; I'm sure that we have neighbors who . . .*

Short-form adjectives are used only predicatively (in effect, following a noun, pronoun, or **быть**), hence they have no case forms: they reflect only the gender and number of the noun or pronoun to which they refer (their *antecedent*). You have seen many short-form adjectives used to express emotions, often with the neuter subject **э́то: Э́то о́чень ску́чно, Э́то хорошо́, Э́то здо́рово!, Э́то ужа́сно!, Э́то прекра́сно!, Э́то до́рого!** Here are four other short-form adjectives that you have already encountered.

	ОН . . .	ОНА́ . . .	ОНО́ . . .	ОНИ́ . . .
should, supposed to	до́лжен	должна́	должно́	должны́
similar, alike	похо́ж	похо́жа	похо́же	похо́жи
glad, pleased	рад	ра́да	(*not common*)	ра́ды
sure, positive	уве́рен	уве́рена	уве́рено	уве́рены

Usage notes:

1. **До́лжен** (from the noun **долг** *debt*) expresses an obligation (*should, ought to, supposed to*). It is normally accompanied by an infinitive to express something one *should do:* **Я, к сожале́нию, до́лжен идти́.** In this meaning, **до́лжен** in some ways overlaps the meaning of **на́до,** but the latter expresses actions viewed as necessities rather than as obligations or duties.

2. *Should not* is usually expressed as **не на́до: Са́ша, не на́до игра́ть так гро́мко!** (*Sasha, you shouldn't play so loud!*)

3. **Похо́ж** is usually accompanied by <**на** + Accusative> to show to whom or what the subject is similar: **Твоя́ сестра́ похо́жа на тебя́?**

УПРАЖНЕНИЕ 7   *Short-form adjectives*

Sasha and Sveta are going to a concert at the conservatory. Sasha has come to get Sveta and she is showing him some family photos. Fill in the blanks of the following conversation with the correct form of one of the short-form adjectives **до́лжен, похо́ж, рад, уве́рен.**

СА́ША.	Све́та, кто э́то на фотогра́фии?
СВЕ́ТА.	Э́то мои́ роди́тели. Ма́ме тут 23 го́да, а па́пе 25.
СА́ША.	Ты о́чень _____¹ на ма́му!
СВЕ́ТА.	А когда́ я была́ ма́ленькая, я была́ _____² на па́пу.
СА́ША.	Я о́чень _____,³ что ты лю́бишь класси́ческую му́зыку. Я _____,⁴ что конце́рт бу́дет хоро́ший. Бу́дет игра́ть мой друг И́горь Нико́льский. Э́то о́чень тала́нтливый† виолончели́ст. Уже́ 7 часо́в? Мы _____⁵ идти́. Конце́рт начина́ется (*starts*) че́рез час.

УПРАЖНЕНИЕ 8   Я о́чень рад (ра́да), что...

What has recently caused you to be happy? Complete the sentence **Я рад (ра́да), что ...** in three or four ways and then share your statements with a classmate. Some possibilities might include the following.

...что сего́дня хоро́шая пого́да (*weather*).
...что у меня́ больша́я кварти́ра.
...что я учу́сь в э́том университе́те (ко́лледже), а не в [*name of another institution*].
...что мой сосе́д по ко́мнате (*roommate*) лю́бит гото́вить.
...что мои́ сосе́ди (не) музыка́нты.
...что у меня́ больша́я кварти́ра и есть ко́мната для госте́й (*guests*).
...что у меня́ есть биле́ты на конце́рт [*name of a musician or group*].
...что мои́ бра́тья хорошо́ у́чатся.
...что у нас в университе́те хоро́ший спортза́л.
...???

 # КУЛЬТУРА РЕЧИ

ТАК ГОВОРЯТ: **CONNECTORS AND SEQUENCERS:** КСТА́ТИ, ПРЕ́ЖДЕ ВСЕГО́, КРО́МЕ ТОГО́

Та́ня — дочь моего́ ста́рого дру́га, Андре́я Ви́кторовича Жили́нского и, **кста́ти,** на́ша студе́нтка.	*Tanya is the daughter of my old friend, Andrei Viktorovich Zhilinskii and, by the way, one of our students.*
— До́брый день! Что бу́дете зака́зывать?	*"Hello! What can I get you?"*
— **Пре́жде всего́** — минера́льную во́ду.	*"First of all, mineral water."*
Мне стол не ну́жен. Пи́сать я могу́ и на роя́ле, а игра́ть на столе́ я не могу́. **Кро́ме того́,** я его́ не выбра́сываю.	*I don't need the table. I can write on the piano, but I can't play on the table. Besides, I'm not throwing it out.*

In conversation (and especially in extended discourse) it's important to use connecting phrases. These act like language signposts to mark links, examples, extensions, or contrasts in someone's ideas. All languages have such signposts, and their use makes it easier to understand both speech and writing.

УПРАЖНЕНИЕ 9 Кста́ти, пре́жде всего́, кро́ме того́

Complete the following sentences with the connector or sequencer phrase that best fits the context: **кста́ти, пре́жде всего́,** or **кро́ме того́.**

1. Вчера́ я был (была́) в кни́жном магази́не. _____, я там ви́дел (ви́дела) но́вый слова́рь сино́нимов (*dictionary of synonyms*). По́мнишь, ты мне говори́л о нём?

2. — Ри́чард, вы бы́ли два ме́сяца в Санкт-Петербу́рге. Расскажи́те нам, что вы там де́лали.

   — _____ я хочу́ рассказа́ть (*tell*) об э́том замеча́тельном го́роде и о его́ исто́рии.

3. Е́сли ты хо́чешь хорошо́ знать ру́сский язы́к, тебе́ на́до слу́шать ру́сские ка́ссеты и смотре́ть ру́сское телеви́дение (*television*). _____, тебе́ на́до чита́ть и говори́ть по-ру́сски.

4. — Вита́лий, ты по́мнишь, что мы идём ве́чером на новосе́лье?

   — _____, ты купи́л шокола́дный торт?

5. — До́ктор, мне ну́жен ваш совет (*advice*). Я о́чень пло́хо сплю.

   — _____, вам на́до мно́го отдыха́ть и мно́го гуля́ть.

   — _____, по́мните, что вам нельзя́ есть ве́чером.

❖ САМОПРОВЕРКА: УПРАЖНЕНИЕ 10

Working on your own, try this self-test: Read a Russian sentence out loud, then give an idiomatic English equivalent without looking at the book. Then work from English to Russian. After you have completed the activity, try it with a classmate.

1. На́м да́же не на́до покупа́ть ме́бель: в ко́мнате есть почти́ всё, что ну́жно.

2. Спаси́бо, мне не ну́жен стол. Я бу́ду жить в общежи́тии. Ко́мнаты там о́чень ма́ленькие, и, к сожале́нию, для стола́ не бу́дет ме́ста.

3. У тебя́ но́вая кварти́ра? Замеча́тельно! А как насчёт новосе́лья?

4. Э́то ва́ша дочь на фотогра́фии? Кака́я симпати́чная де́вочка! Она́ о́чень похо́жа на вас.

1. *We don't even have to buy furniture: there's almost everything we need in the room.*

2. *Thanks, I don't need a table. I'll be living in the dorm. The rooms there are really small and, unfortunately, there won't be room for a table.*

3. *You have a new apartment? Wonderful! So how about a housewarming?*

4. *Is that your daughter in the picture? What a cute little girl! She looks a lot like you.*

❖ ВОПРОСЫ И ОТВЕТЫ: УПРАЖНЕНИЕ 11

Working with a classmate, take turns asking and answering the following questions, posed by a sociologist who is doing a survey on student life.

1. Вы живёте в общежи́тии и́ли снима́ете кварти́ру (ко́мнату)?

2. Ва́ше общежи́тие (Ва́ша кварти́ра/ко́мната) далеко́ от университе́та?

3. В общежи́тии есть ме́бель? А в ва́шей кварти́ре (ко́мнате) есть ме́бель? Вам не на́до покупа́ть ме́бель?

4. У вас есть всё, что вам ну́жно? У вас есть компью́тер? А при́нтер? Что ещё?

5. Вам нра́вится всё но́вое и́ли всё ста́рое? Вы предпочита́ете (*prefer*) антиква́рные ве́щи (*antiques*) и́ли моде́рн†?

6. У вас есть сосе́ди? Они́ симпати́чные? Они́ молоды́е и́ли пожилы́е (*elderly*)? Они́ да́рят (*give*) вам пода́рки? А вы им?

❖ ДИАЛОГИ

ДИАЛОГ 1 Я могу́ дать (*give*) вам . . .
(Giving things to others)

— Вам нра́вится ва́ша но́вая кварти́ра?
— О́чень нра́вится.
— Там есть ме́бель?
— Там всё есть, нет то́лько стола́.
— У меня́ есть ли́шний стол. Он большо́й, о́чень хоро́ший. Я могу́ дать его́ вам.
— Спаси́бо.

ДИАЛОГ 2 Мне о́чень ну́жно кре́сло
(Doing a favor for someone)

— В мое́й но́вой кварти́ре есть стол, сту́лья, ла́мпы, кофе́йный сто́лик (*coffee table*). Там о́чень краси́вый ковёр. Есть почти́ всё, что ну́жно, но, к сожале́нию, нет кре́сла, а мне о́чень ну́жно кре́сло.
— Я зна́ю, что мои́ сосе́ди продаю́т ме́бель. У них есть отли́чное кре́сло, но я не зна́ю, продаю́т они́ его́ и́ли нет. Е́сли хо́чешь, я могу́ спроси́ть (*ask*).
— Спаси́бо!

УПРАЖНЕНИЕ 12   Ваш диало́г

You and another student have decided to rent a small apartment. Discuss what furniture you each have and what you need to buy.

❖ А ТЕПЕ́РЬ . . . : УПРАЖНЕНИЕ 13

Working with a classmate, use what you learned in Part 4 to . . .

1. tell her something that you need in your apartment and find out if she also needs that item
2. find out what else she needs
3. tell her something that you do *not* need there
4. tell her where you need to be tomorrow
5. ask whether she works and, if so, whether she has to work all day (**весь день**) tomorrow

ИТАК...

❖ НОВЫЕ СЛОВА

NOUNS AND NOUN PHRASES

Studies, University

истори́ческий факульте́т	history department (2)
класс	grade (in school) (1)
курс	year (of college) (1)
учи́тель (*pl.* учителя́)/ учи́тельница	teacher (1v)

Mail and Post Office

бандеро́ль *f.*	package (containing printed matter) (3)
валю́та	foreign currency (3v)
конве́рт	envelope (3v)
ма́рка	stamp (3v)
обме́н	exchange (3v)
по́чта	mail (3)
телегра́мма	telegram (3v)

House and Home

двухко́мнатная кварти́ра	two-room apartment (2v)
новосе́лье	housewarming (4)
пода́р(о)к	present; gift (4)
фотогра́фия	photograph (1v)
хозя́ин/хозя́йка	landlord/landlady (2)
шкаф (*Prep. sing.* в шкафу́, *pl.* шкафы́)	wardrobe; cabinet (2)
шоссе́ [*pronounced* -сэ́]	highway (2v)

Other Nouns

а́рмия	army (2)
гла́вное *noun, declines like adj.*	the main thing (3)
записна́я кни́жка	notebook; address book (3)
иде́я	idea (2)
лет (*Gen. pl. of* год)	years (1)
мину́та	minute (4)
мужчи́на	man; gentleman (3)
о́фис	office (2v)
пи́во	beer (4v)
ско́рая по́мощь	ambulance service (2)
ста́ршие *noun, declines like adj.* (*pl. only*)	one's elders (1)

ADJECTIVES

ве́жливый	polite (4v)
вку́сный	tasty; delicious (4v)
гру́бый	rude (4v)
истори́ческий	historical; history (*adj.*) (2)
культу́рный	cultured (1)
медици́нский	medical (2)
невку́сный	unpalatable; tasteless (4v)
ну́жен (нужна́, ну́жно, нужны́)	1. needed; 2. (+ *Dat.*) one needs (4)
рад (ра́да, ра́ды)	glad; pleased (4)
ску́чный	boring (1)
стро́гий	strict (1v)
тёплый	warm (4v)
тяжёлый	heavy (3)
уве́рен (уве́рена, уве́рено, уве́рены)	sure; certain (4)
холо́дный	cold (4v)

PRONOUNS

Dative Pronouns

кому́	(to / for) whom (1)
мне	(to / for) me (1)
тебе́ (*informal sing.*)	(to / for) you (1)
ему́ (нему́)	(to / for) him, it (1)
ей (ней)	(to / for) her, it (1)
нам	(to / for) us (1)
вам (*formal or pl.*)	(to / for) you (1)
им (ним)	(to / for) them (1)

NUMERALS

Cardinals

трина́дцать	thirteen (1)
четы́рнадцать	fourteen (1)
пятна́дцать	fifteen (1)
шестна́дцать	sixteen (1)
семна́дцать	seventeen (1)
восемна́дцать	eighteen (1)
девятна́дцать	nineteen (1)
два́дцать	twenty (1)
три́дцать	thirty (1)
со́рок	forty (1)
пятьдеся́т	fifty (1)
шестьдеся́т	sixty (1)

сéмьдесят — seventy (1)
вóсемьдесят — eighty (1)
девянóсто — ninety (1)
сто — hundred (1)

Ordinals

пя́тый — fifth (3)
шестóй — sixth (1)
седьмóй — seventh (3)
восьмóй — eighth (3)
девя́тый — ninth (3)
деся́тый — tenth (3)
одиннадцатый — eleventh (3)
двенáдцатый — twelfth (3)
тринáдцатый — thirteenth (3)
четы́рнадцатый — fourteenth (3)
пятнáдцатый — fifteenth (3)
шестнáдцатый — sixteenth (3)
семнáдцатый — seventeenth (3)
восемнáдцатый — eighteenth (3)
девятнáдцатый — nineteenth (3)
двадцáтый — twentieth (3)
тридцáтый — thirtieth (3)

VERBS

быть (бýду, бýдешь, ... бýдут) — will; will be (2)
готóвить(готóвл-ю, готóв-ишь, ... готóв-ят) — to cook (4v)
нрáвиться (*usu. 3rd pers.* нрáв-ится, нрáв-ятся) (+ *Dat.*) — to be pleasing (to someone) (2)
принимáть (принимá-ю, принимá-ешь, ... принимá-ют) — to accept; to take (3v)
приносúть (принош-ý, принóс-ишь, ... принóс-ят) — to bring (over) (4)
разговáривать (разговáрива-ю, разговáрива-ешь, ... разговáрива-ют) — to talk; to speak (4)
растú (растý, растёшь, ... растýт; *past* рос, рослá, рослó, рослú) — to grow up (3)
сдавáть (сда-ю, сда-ёшь, ... сда-ют) — to rent out (an apartment) (2v)
сказáть[13] — to say; to tell (2)

слы́шать (слы́ш-у, слы́ш-ишь, ... слы́ш-ат) — to hear (4)
снимáть (снимá-ю, снимá-ешь, ... снимá-ют) — to rent (4)
спрáшивать (спрáшива-ю, спрáшива-ешь, ... спрáшива-ют) (*usu.* + *Acc. or,* <о + *Prep.*>) — to ask (about); to inquire (4)
стóить (*usu. 3rd. pers.* стóит, стóят) — to cost (2)
стоя́ть (сто-ю́, сто-и́шь, ... сто-я́т) — to stand; to be; there is (are) (4)

ADVERBS

вдруг — suddenly (4)
ещё — still (1)
недáвно — recently; (*with past verbs*) not long ago; (*with present verbs*) not ... very long (3)
обяза́тельно — absolutely; definitely; by all means (4)
почтú — almost (4)
скóлько — how many; how much (1)
скýчно — boringly; (it's/that's) boring (1)
тут — at this point; at that moment (4)

OTHER

Да нет, ... — Not at all ... (4v)
для (+ *Gen.*) — for: **Тут нет мéста для столá.** *There is no room for a table here.* (4)
жаль — (that's) too bad; it's/that's a pity! (2)
навéрно (навéрное) *parenthetical* — most likely; probably (3)
прáвда *parenthetical* — true; granted (4)
у (+ *Gen.*) *indicates someone's home, place of work, etc.* — at: **у бáбушки** *at Grandma's* (1)

---

[13]For the time being use **сказáть** in the infinitive or past tense only.

IDIOMS AND EXPRESSIONS

в а́рмии	in the (military) service (2)	Как (ва́ше) здоро́вье?	How are you? (3)
в шесто́м кла́ссе	in the sixth grade (1)	как насчёт (+ *Gen.*)?	how about . . . ? (4)
Всё в поря́дке.	Everything is in order; Everything's fine. (2)	Како́е сего́дня число́?	What's the date today? (3)
		ме́жду про́чим	by the way; incidentally (1)
всё, что ну́жно	everything we need; everything one needs (4)	*parenthetical*	
		Мне сты́дно.	I'm ashamed. (1)
говори́ть (+ *Dat.*) «вы»	to address (someone) formally; to use «вы» with someone (1)	на второ́м ку́рсе	in second year (of college) (1)
		На како́м ты (вы) ку́рсе?	What year (of college) are you in? (1)
говори́ть (+ *Dat.*) «ты»	to address (someone) in a familiar fashion; to use «ты» with someone (1)	Нам (необыкнове́нно) повезло́.	We were (incredibly) lucky. (4)
		Не волну́йся (Не волну́йтесь)!	Don't worry! (3)
Да нет	Not at all; On the contrary (4)	Нет ещё (Ещё нет)	Not yet. (3)
Дава́й говори́ть друг дру́гу «ты»!	Let's use «ты» with each other. (1)	Отку́да вы зна́ете (ты зна́ешь)?	How do you (happen to) know? (2)
Действи́тельно!	Right! (1)	Понима́ешь?	Got it? (1)
друг дру́га (друг дру́гу, друг о дру́ге, *etc.*)	(to, about, *etc.*) each other; (to, about, *etc.*) one another (1)	похо́ж на (+ *Acc.*)	resemble; look like: **Он похо́ж на вас.** *He looks like you.* (2)
Ему́ (ей) два го́да.	He (she) is two years old. (1v)	Пра́вда?	Isn't that so? (4)
		Ско́лько ему́ (ей) лет?	How old is he (she)? (1)
Замеча́тельно!	Great!; Wonderful! (3)	Ско́лько это сто́ит?	How much does this cost? (2)
		Ты в како́м кла́ссе?	What grade are you in? (1)
		че́рез мину́ту	a minute later (4)

❖ ЧТО Я ЗНАЮ, ЧТО Я УМЕЮ

Use this checklist to mark off what you've learned in this lesson:

- ☐ Using nouns, pronouns, possessives and adjectives in the Dative case (Part 1)
- ☐ Expressing indirect objects (*to whom* or *for whom* something is done) (Part 1)
- ☐ Telling exact and approximate age (Part 1)
- ☐ Expressing *to like* and *to love* with **нра́виться** and **люби́ть** (Part 2)
- ☐ Saying what things you need (Part 4)
- ☐ Telling what you have to do (Part 4)
- ☐ Expressing actions in the future (Part 2)
- ☐ Expressing absence in the past and future (Part 4)
- ☐ Giving commands (Part 2)
- ☐ Using Genitive singular case forms with 1–4 (Part 3)
- ☐ Additional meanings of «у» phrases (Part 3)
- ☐ Asking and giving the date (Part 3)
- ☐ Using short-form adjectives (Part 4)

❖ ЭТО НАДО ЗНАТЬ

Here is a summary of pronouns, possessives, and adjectives in the cases you have learned so far.

PERSONAL PRONOUNS								INTERROGATIVES	
Nom.	я	ты	он, оно́	она́	мы	вы	они́	кто	что
Acc.	меня́	тебя́	(н)его́[1]	(н)её	нас	вас	(н)их	кого́	что
Gen.	меня́	тебя́	(н)его́	(н)её	нас	вас	(н)их	кого́	чего́
Prep.	*forms will be given in Lesson 7*								
Dat.	мне	тебе́	(н)ему́	(н)ей	нам	вам	(н)им	кому́	чему́

[1]Case forms of the third-person personal pronouns (**он, оно́, она́, они́**) add an initial **н-** when they are governed by a preposition, e.g., **У него́ есть маши́на.**

POSSESSIVES				
	MASCULINE	**NEUTER**	**FEMININE**	**PLURAL**
Nom.	мой / наш[1]	моё / на́ше	моя́ / на́ша	мои́ / на́ши
Acc.	*inanimate = Nom.* *animate = Gen.*	моё / на́ше	мою́ / на́шу	*inanimate = Nom.* *animate = Gen.*
Gen.	моего́ / на́шего		мое́й / на́шей	*forms given in L. 8*
Prep.	моём / на́шем		мое́й / на́шей	*forms given in L. 9*
Dat.	моему́ / на́шему		мое́й / на́шей	*forms given in L. 9*

[1]**Твой** is like **мой**; **ваш** is like **наш**.
Note: The third-person possessives (**его́, её, их**) never change and they never add an initial **н-**, e.g., **У его́ бра́та есть маши́на.**

ADJECTIVES				
	MASCULINE	**NEUTER**	**FEMININE**	**PLURAL**
Nom.	-ый: но́вый (хоро́ший)[1] -о́й: молодо́й	-ое: но́вое (хоро́шее)	-ая: но́вая	-ые: но́вые (хоро́шие)
Acc.	*inanimate = Nom.* *animate = Gen.*	-ое: но́вое (хоро́шее)	-ую: но́вую	*inanimate = Nom.* *animate = Gen.*
Gen.	-ого: но́вого (хоро́шего)		-ой: но́вой (хоро́шей)	*forms given in Lesson 8*
Prep.	-ом: но́вом (хоро́шем)		-ой: но́вой (хоро́шей)	*forms given in Lesson 9*
Dat.	-ому: но́вому (хоро́шему)		-ой: но́вой (хоро́шей)	*forms given in Lesson 9*

[1]As the examples with **хоро́ший** show, many adjective endings reflect the spelling rules. According to the «**кни́ги**» rule, **ы** is replaced with **и** after hushers (**ж, ч, ш, щ**) and velars (**г, к, х**). According to the «**хоро́шее**» rule, unstressed **о** is replaced with **е** after hushers (**ж, ч, ш, щ**) and **ц**.

❖ ДОПОЛНИТЕЛЬНЫЕ ТЕКСТЫ

A. **CARTOON FROM** АРГУМЕ́НТЫ И ФА́КТЫ

Рисунок Виктора Федорова

Б. **FROM** АНЕКДО́ТЫ ОТ НИКУ́ЛИНА

— А ско́лько лет твоему́ де́душке?
— Не зна́ю. Но он у нас уже́ о́чень да́вно (*for a long time*).

B. **AD FROM** *BUSINESS WEEK INTERNATIONAL*

1. What type of information would you expect to find in a subscription ad?

Look briefly at the advertisement without reading anything in detail.
2. What is the name of the publication being advertised?

Read through the next three questions, then skim the first paragraph to find answers.
3. Is this publication a newspaper or a magazine?
4. Relying on cognates, can you figure out who is the intended audience of this publication?
5. What language is it published in?

Look at the figures near the bottom of the ad.
6. What do you think these figures represent?
7. Circle all the numeral phrases that require Genitive singular.
8. What do you think the word **нóмер** means in this context?
9. How long does the subscription for $90 last?
10. How much money do you save if you buy a two-year subscription? A three-year?

Look at the text below the figures.
11. What two international currencies can be used to pay for the subscription?
12. What do you think **креди́тные ка́рточки** are?
13. Are they accepted for payment?
14. Do you know anyone who subscribes to this magazine?

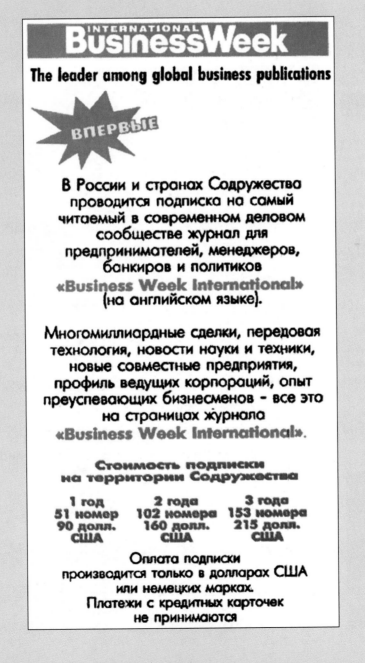

УРОК

7

Молоды́е лю́ди в Росси́и

ЖИЗНЬ ИДЁТ

In Part 1, which is on the video, Sasha calls on the two young women who have just moved into Tatyana Dmitrievna's apartment; the three of them get acquainted and start planning a housewarming party. In Part 2 Natalya Ivanovna's initial happiness at having their phone hooked up quickly turns to dismay. In Part 3, the beginning of which is on the video, Jim gets invited to the party—and promises to make a unique contribution. And in Part 4 Sveta writes a letter to her mother, telling her about their new surroundings and acquaintances.

In this lesson you will learn

- ☆ to talk about studying
- ☆ how to say when something happens (days and times)
- ☆ how to tell time
- ☆ how Russian verbs show a process versus a result
- ☆ about expressing thanks
- ☆ to relate what someone else has said
- ☆ how to say whether or not something happened

Та́ня

С ЧЕГО НАЧАТЬ?

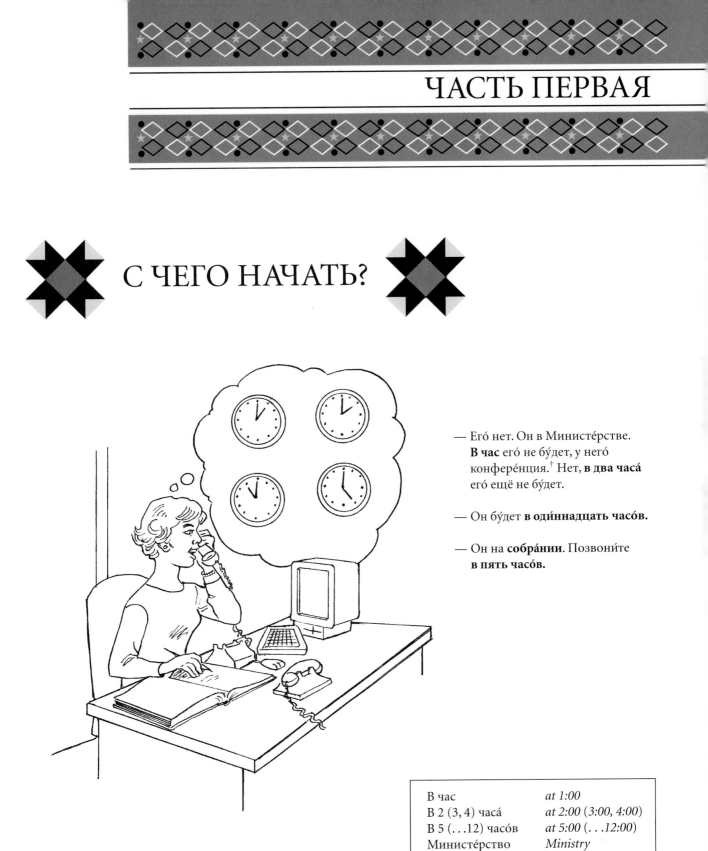

— Егó нет. Он в Министéрстве. **В час** егó не бýдет, у негó конферéнция.[†] Нет, **в два часá** егó ещё не бýдет.

— Он бýдет **в одиннадцать часóв.**

— Он на **собрáнии.** Позвонúте **в пять часóв.**

В час	*at 1:00*
В 2 (3, 4) часá	*at 2:00 (3:00, 4:00)*
В 5 (. . .12) часóв	*at 5:00 (. . .12:00)*
Министéрство	*Ministry*
собрáние	*meeting*
позвонúте	*call*

ЧТЕНИЕ

❖❖ КОГДА́ БУ́ДЕТ НОВОСЕ́ЛЬЕ?

(Sasha Kruglov rings the doorbell of apartment 7. Tatyana Dmitrievna opens the door.)

До́брый. . . *Good evening*	СА́ША.	**До́брый ве́чер,**° Татья́на Дми́триевна. Ва́ши де́вушки до́ма?
	ТАТЬЯ́НА ДМ.	До́брый ве́чер, Са́ша. Де́вушки до́ма. Заходи́те.

(Sasha knocks at Sveta and Tanya's door.)

Come in.	СВЕ́ТА.	**Войди́те.**°
	СА́ША.	Приве́т!
	СВЕ́ТА И ТА́НЯ.	Приве́т, Са́ша.
Как. . . *How are you doing?*	СА́ША.	**Как пожива́ете?**°
что. . . *what sort of. . . are those? / cards*	СВЕ́ТА.	Хорошо́ пожива́ем, спаси́бо. А как у тебя́ дела́?
	СА́ША.	Всё хорошо́. Све́та, а **что э́то за**° **ка́рточки?**°
English / am studying have learned	СВЕ́ТА.	Э́то **англи́йские**° слова́, кото́рые я **учу́**.° Спра́ва — слова́, кото́рые я зна́ю, я их у́же **вы́учила.**° Сле́ва — слова́, кото́рые ещё на́до вы́учить.
I see	СА́ША.	**Поня́тно.**° Интере́сная систе́ма.† А когда́ ва́ше новосе́лье?
	ТА́НЯ.	Наве́рное, в суббо́ту и́ли в воскресе́нье. Пя́тница — то́же
convenient		**удо́бный**° день, но Све́та в пя́тницу рабо́тает.
	СВЕ́ТА.	Да, в понеде́льник, в сре́ду и в пя́тницу я рабо́таю ве́чером.
Really?	СА́ША.	**Пра́вда?**° А где ты рабо́таешь?
	СВЕ́ТА.	На ско́рой по́мощи.
	СА́ША.	А что ты там де́лаешь?
медици́нская. . . *nurse*	СВЕ́ТА.	Я медици́нская сестра́.°
Но. . . *But you're only in second year, aren't you?*	СА́ША.	Но ты **ведь** у́чишься то́лько на второ́м ку́рсе?°

СВЕ́ТА. **Ве́рно,°** но **до°** институ́та я **зако́нчила°** медици́нское учи́лище.° | *That's true / before / graduated from / медици́нское. . . nursing school*
У меня́ **дипло́м**[†] медсестры́.[1]

СА́ША. Молоде́ц! Ты рабо́таешь то́лько ве́чером?

СВЕ́ТА. Ве́чером и **но́чью.°** А у́тром и **днём°** у меня́ **заня́тия.°** | *at night / in the afternoon / classes / is it hard*

СА́ША. А **тру́дно°** рабо́тать на ско́рой по́мощи?

СВЕ́ТА. Коне́чно, тру́дно. Но э́то хоро́шая пра́ктика и неплохо́й **за́работок.°** | *pay*

СА́ША. Та́ня, а ты то́же рабо́таешь?

ТА́НЯ. Сейча́с я не рабо́таю. **Ле́том°** я рабо́тала два ме́сяца. А сейча́с нет **вре́мени,°** на́до мно́го **занима́ться.°** | *In the summer time / to study*

СА́ША. Понима́ю — я то́же мно́го занима́юсь. **Ла́дно,°** де́вочки, не хочу́ вам **меша́ть.°** Так когда́ бу́дет новосе́лье? Я **предлага́ю°** в суббо́ту. Хорошо́? | *All right to bother / suggest*

СВЕ́ТА. Хорошо́. В семь часо́в? Как ты ду́маешь, Та́ня?

ТА́НЯ. В семь часо́в — **э́то удо́бно.°** | *э́то. . . that's okay*

СА́ША. Мо́жно **пригласи́ть°** на́шу сосе́дку Ле́ну Си́лину. **Вы не возража́ете?°** Она́ то́же студе́нтка и живёт здесь ря́дом, в 6-ой кварти́ре. | *invite*   *Вы. . . Do you mind?*

ТА́НЯ. Коне́чно, не возража́ем. А где она́ у́чится?

СА́ША. В университе́те, на факульте́те журнали́стики.

СВЕ́ТА. Три де́вушки и оди́н Са́ша . . .

СА́ША. Я ду́маю, кого́ ещё мо́жно пригласи́ть.

ТА́НЯ. Мо́жно пригласи́ть Джи́ма. Э́то америка́нец, аспира́нт профе́ссора Петро́вского.

СА́ША. **Прекра́сная°** иде́я! Ита́к, Све́та, Та́ня, Ле́на, Джим и я. **Отли́чная компа́ния!°** | *Wonderful / Отли́чная. . . Sounds like a great group!*

Приглашаем на новоселье

---

[1]медсестры́ = медици́нской сестры́

УПРАЖНЕНИЕ 1 Под микроско́пом: A job ad

<table>
<tr><td>

ПРИГЛАША́ЕМ НА РАБО́ТУ

(можно по совместительству) по конкурсу

электро́нщиков и программи́стов.

Для владеющих английским языком возможна работа в Западной Европе.

Присылать конверт с обратным адресом, телефон, желательно резюме и фото.

125047 , Москва , а/я 19."ПАНОРА́МА".

</td><td>

Here is an ad from a newspaper. If you make some good guesses, you'll find answers to the following questions.

1. What kinds of specialists are being sought?
2. What language must they know?
3. Where will they work? (Hint: **за́пад** = *west*)
4. What information should be sent to the employer (four items, all cognates)?

</td></tr>
</table>

ГРА́ММА́ТИКА И ПРА́КТИКА

❖❖ 7.1. TO STUDY: УЧИ́ТЬ **AND** ЗАНИМА́ТЬСЯ

Это англи́йские слова́, кото́рые я **учу́.**	*These are English words that I'm studying.*
Сейча́с нет вре́мени, на́до мно́го **занима́ться.**	*There's no time now, I have to study a lot.*

Use <**учи́ть** + Accusative> to mean *to memorize* or, colloquially, *to study* (*something specific such as vocabulary words, lines in a play, a foreign language*). Use **занима́ться** (without an object) to mean *to study* (*in general*), *to do homework.*

УПРАЖНЕНИЕ 2 Учи́ть и́ли занима́ться?

Fill in each blank with an appropriate form of **учи́ть** or **занима́ться.** Use the context to determine whether present or past tense forms are required.[2]

Моя́ сестра́ о́чень хорошо́ говори́т по-францу́зски. Она́ _____*у́чит*_____ [1] францу́зский язы́к 10 лет. Она́ мно́го _____.[2] Она́ чита́ет францу́зские кни́ги и _____ [3] но́вые слова́. Она́ зна́ет не то́лько францу́зский язы́к, но и италья́нский. Она́ _____ [4] италья́нский то́лько два го́да, но уже́ хорошо́ говори́т по-италья́нски. Ле́том она́ была́ в Ита́лии, во Флоре́нции. Там она́ ча́сто ходи́ла в музе́и и _____ [5] не о́чень мно́го, но сейча́с она́ опя́ть мно́го _____,[6] смо́трит италья́нские фи́льмы, _____ [7] грамма́тику. Ме́жду про́чим, она́ тепе́рь ча́сто получа́ет пи́сьма из Флоре́нции. Мо́жет быть, она́ и́менно (*precisely*) поэ́тому так мно́го _____ [8]?

---

[2]Remember that Russian uses the present tense to describe actions that began in the past and are still going on: Она́ у́чит францу́зский язы́к 10 лет. (*She has been studying French for ten years.*)

УПРАЖНЕ́НИЕ 3   Talking about studying

Are your study habits at all like those of your classmates? Interview a classmate and be prepared to tell about what you learned. Use questions like the following:

1. Где ты обы́чно занима́ешься? В библиоте́ке? До́ма? У дру́га?
2. Где твои́ друзья́ обы́чно занима́ются?
3. Ты лю́бишь занима́ться?
4. Како́й язы́к (каки́е языки́) ты учи́л (учи́ла) в шко́ле?
5. Что ещё ты учи́л (учи́ла) в шко́ле?
6. Что ты де́лал (де́лала) вчера́ ве́чером — занима́лся (занима́лась), смотре́л (смотре́ла) телеви́зор, слу́шал (слу́шала) му́зыку?
7. Где ты занима́лся (занима́лась) вчера́ ве́чером?
8. Ты смо́тришь телеви́зор, когда́ ты занима́ешься?
9. Когда́ ты обы́чно занима́ешься — у́тром, днём, ве́чером и́ли но́чью?
10. Когда́ ты вчера́ учи́л (учи́ла) ру́сский язы́к — у́тром, днём, ве́чером и́ли но́чью?

❖ 7.2. "ON" A CERTAIN DAY OF THE WEEK: В СУББО́ТУ

У нас бу́дет новосе́лье и́ли в **суббо́ту** и́ли в **воскресе́нье**.

We'll have our housewarming either on Saturday or on Sunday.

	ДЕКА́БРЬ			
пн		4	11	18	25
вт		5	12	19	26
ср		6	13	20	27
чт		7	14	21	28
пт	1	8	15	22	29
сб	2	9	16	23	30
вс	3	10	17	24	

To express *on* a certain day of the week, use the preposition **в** followed by the day of the week in the Accusative. Note in the table below that each of these <**в** + day> combinations is pronounced as one word; pay particular attention to the voicing assimilation.

NOMINATIVE FORMS	TO SAY <*ON* + A PARTICULAR DAY OF THE WEEK> USE <В + ACCUSATIVE>
понеде́льник (*cf.* неде́ля)	в понеде́льник [фпан-]
вто́рник (*cf.* второ́й)	во вто́рник [вафто́р-]
среда́ (середи́на = *middle*)	в сре́ду [фсре́-]
четве́рг (*cf.* четы́ре)	в четве́рг [фчит-]
пя́тница (*cf.* пять)	в пя́тницу [фпя́т-]
суббо́та (*cf. sabbath*)	в суббо́ту [фсуб-]
воскресе́нье	в воскресе́нье [ввас-]

УПРАЖНЕНИЕ 4 Что бу́дет в университе́те в суббо́ту?

What interesting events will occur on your campus next week? Fill in the following table with as many events as you can, then compare your list with those of your classmates. Some suggestions (including a number of cognates) are provided below to help you get started.

ОБРАЗЕ́Ц: — Что бу́дет в университе́те в суббо́ту?
— В суббо́ту бу́дет баскетбо́льный матч.

понеде́льник	
вто́рник	
среда́	
четве́рг	
пя́тница	
суббо́та	
воскресе́нье	

баскетбо́льный матч
рок-конце́рт
семина́р профе́ссора Петро́вского (or some other professor)
францу́зский фильм
футбо́льный матч
ле́кция о Да́рвине
деба́ты†

❖❖ 7.3. INTRODUCTION TO ASPECT

Све́та всё у́тро **учи́ла** англи́йские слова́. Вот слова́, кото́рые она́ **вы́учила.**

Sveta studied English (vocab) words all morning. Here are the words that she learned.

Russian verbs reflect a feature called *aspect.* There are two aspects: *imperfective* (such as **учи́ла,** from the imperfective infinitive **учи́ть**) and *perfective* (such as **вы́учила,** from the perfective infinitive **вы́учить**[3]). English has a similar option, though it is not formally called 'aspect.' For example, the sentence below left shows action in progress and corresponds to the Russian imperfective aspect; the sentence on the right shows one-time completed action and corresponds to the Russian perfective aspect.

*I saw her as she **was crossing** the street.*   *She **crossed** the street and entered the building.*

The first thing to learn is the meaning of aspect. Most of the verbs you have learned so far have been of the imperfective aspect, which typically denotes an ongoing, repeated,

---

[3]When the perfective is shown by the prefix **вы́-,** that prefix is always stressed.

or habitual action. (Thus, all present-tense actions are by definition expressed via the imperfective aspect.) Verbs of the imperfective aspect *describe;* they are often used in general contexts.

Here are examples of the imperfective aspect in all three tenses. Pay particular attention to the ongoing or repetitive meaning that each contains.

Present tense (always imperfective aspect)

Студе́нты **говоря́т** друг дру́гу «ты».	*Students say **ты** to each other.*
На авто́бусной остано́вке вас **ждёт** мой друг. Вы **отдаёте** ему́ сапоги́ и **пла́тите** пятьсо́т рубле́й.	*My friend waits for you at the bus stop. You give him the boots and pay 500 rubles.*
Я учу́сь на второ́м ку́рсе и немно́го **рабо́таю.**	*I'm a second-year student, and I [also] work a little.*

Imperfective aspect, past tense

Скажи́те, что вы вчера́ **игра́ли?**	*Tell me, what were you playing yesterday?*
В про́шлом году́ Ва́ня **жил** в обшежи́тии и ча́сто **занима́лся** в библиоте́ке.	*Last year Vanya lived in the dorm and frequently studied at the library.*
Ле́том я **рабо́тала** два ме́сяца.	*In the summer I worked for two months.*

Imperfective aspect, future tense

На чём ты **бу́дешь писа́ть?**	*What are you going to write on?*
Тепе́рь я **бу́ду говори́ть** тебе́ «вы».	*From now on I'll address you formally.*

In contrast to the imperfective aspect, verbs of the perfective aspect have a restricted, very focused meaning: When using a perfective verb the speaker seeks to convey the notion of completion or result. So far you have seen just a few instances of perfective verbs. Here are some that will be familiar; pay attention to their completive or resultative nature.

Perfective aspect, past tense

Спра́ва — слова́, кото́рые я зна́ю, я их уже́ **вы́учила.**	*On the right are words that I know; I've already learned them.*
Профе́ссор Петро́вский **роди́лся** на Кавка́зе.	*Professor Petrovsky was born in the Caucasus.*
До институ́та я **зако́нчила** медици́нское учи́лище.	*Before [entering] the institute I finished nursing school.*

You will soon encounter examples of perfective verbs in the future; meanwhile, here are some examples of perfective infinitives that you have seen.

Па́па хо́чет **купи́ть** гара́ж.	*Dad wants to buy a garage.*
Джим, мо́жно **зада́ть** вам вопро́с?	*Jim, may I ask you a question?*
О́чень хорошо́ понима́ю и да́же могу́ **помо́чь.**	*I understand quite well and I can even help out.*
Мо́жно **пригласи́ть** на́шу сосе́дку Ле́ну Си́лину.	*We could invite our neighbor, Lena Silina.*

You may have noted that the past-tense endings are the same for imperfective and perfective verbs; and you will soon see that the future perfective endings are also familiar. Thus, remember that *aspect is a matter of stems, not endings.*

УПРАЖНЕНИЕ 5   Imperfective infinitives

Look back at the reading in Lesson 3, Part 1. Underline each conjugated verb form. Then make an alphabetical list, by infinitive, of all of the verbs you underlined. (There will be eight, all imperfective.)

❖❖ 7.4. THE PERFECTIVE ASPECT: ONE-TIME COMPLETION

Imperfective

— Что ты **де́лал** вчера́ ве́чером?
— Я **писа́л** курсову́ю.

"What did you do last night?"
"I was writing a paper."

Perfective

— Ты **написа́л** её?
— Коне́чно, **написа́л**.

"Did you finish writing it?"
"Of course I finished it."

To grasp the perfective aspect, concentrate on its fundamental meaning: a single completed action. Use the perfective to convey the sense of one-time completion; use the imperfective in nearly all other situations. In the example above, the verbs under the left-hand drawing (**де́лал, писа́л**) are imperfective; they describe an action that took place over a period of time. Under the right-hand drawing, **написа́л** (from the perfective infinitive **написа́ть**), focuses attention on the completion/result of the evening's writing.

УПРАЖНЕНИЕ 6   Identifying "one-time completion"

Nine of the following sentences describe one-time completed action in the past or future that would most likely be rendered in Russian with the perfective aspect. Which are they? (Do not try to translate the sentences.)

1. I usually get up at 6.00.
2. But this morning I overslept.
3. I got up at 7:30.
4. My cat was waiting for his breakfast.
5. My roommate was reading the paper.
6. I fed the cat and drank a cup of coffee.
7. As I drove to campus I listened to the news on the radio.
8. I arrived at 8:15.
9. Then I realized that I'd forgotten the history paper . . .
10. that I had written last night.
11. When I got to class my instructor asked, . . .
12. "Will you bring it tomorrow?"
13. "For sure," I said.
14. I usually don't forget things.

УПРАЖНЕНИЕ 7   Perfective verbs: Расскáз профéссора Петрóвского

Fill in the blanks in Professor Petrovsky's story, choosing from the perfective verbs given in the following list. Insert the correct past tense or infinitive form to complete the story. Then translate the story into English.

купи́ть	опозда́ть (*pfv. of* опа́здывать)
роди́ться	вы́пить (*pfv. of* пить)
позвони́ть	поздра́вить (*to congratulate*)
пригласи́ть	

Сего́дня я _____¹ на ле́кцию. Я о́чень ре́дко опа́здываю, но вчера́ я _____² То есть, не вчера́, а сего́дня. Вчера́ _____³ мой ста́рый друг — мы вме́сте (*together*) учи́лись в аспиранту́ре (*graduate school*). «Мо́жешь меня́ _____⁴! У нас сего́дня _____⁵ внук! Я тепе́рь де́душка!» Я _____⁶ его́, а он _____⁷ меня́ в го́сти. Я _____⁸ шокола́дный торт для ба́бушки и буты́лку конья́ка† для де́душки. Конья́к мы _____⁹, и в результа́те (*as a result*) я сего́дня у́тром не слы́шал, как звони́л буди́льник.

◈ 7.5. THE IMPERFECTIVE ASPECT: ONGOING, REPEATED, OR HABITUAL/CHARACTERISTIC ACTIONS OR STATES

Сейча́с я не **рабо́таю.** Ле́том я **рабо́тала** два ме́сяца.	*I'm not working now. In the summer I worked for two months.*

The imperfective aspect is associated with ongoing, repeated, or habitual/characteristic actions or states in the present, past, or future tense. Words and expressions such as **всегда́, иногда́, ка́ждый день, никогда́, обы́чно,** and **ча́сто** convey repetition or frequency and are commonly associated with the imperfective aspect. Words that express time frames are also frequently associated with the imperfective aspect, regardless of the tense. These words include adverbs that relate to "season" or "part of day" (see **Слова, Слова, Слова . . .** on the next page) during which an activity—such as watching TV, spending time at the beach, or doing one's homework—might take place. And of course, all present tense verbs are imperfective by definition.

УПРАЖНЕНИЕ 8   Жизнь Джи́ма

Read the following paragraphs in which Jim is telling Lena about his life in America and in Russia. Underline the imperfective verbs and try to link them to other words or phrases associated with ongoing, repeated, or habitual/characteristic actions or states.

Когда́ я учи́лся в шко́ле, я ма́ло занима́лся. У меня́ всегда́ бы́ло свобо́дное (*free*) вре́мя. Я игра́л в баскетбо́л, смотре́л телеви́зор и мно́го чита́л. Когда́ я учи́лся в ко́лледже, я мно́го занима́лся. Я ка́ждый день рабо́тал в библиоте́ке, а ве́чером занима́лся до́ма. Иногда́ я приглаша́л дру́га, и мы вме́сте смотре́ли телеви́зор. Ещё я игра́л в те́ннис и мно́го чита́л. Я всегда́ люби́л чита́ть о поли́тике. Мы получа́ли газе́ту «Бо́стон Гло́уб», и я чита́л её ка́ждый день.

Сейча́с я то́же мно́го чита́ю, но не газе́ты, а кни́ги по исто́рии (*history books*). Иногда́ (*sometimes*) я смотрю́ телеви́зор. У меня́ никогда́ нет вре́мени, поэ́тому в те́ннис я игра́ю не о́чень ча́сто, а в баскетбо́л совсе́м не (*not at all*) игра́ю. Но я люблю́ слу́шать му́зыку. У меня́ есть кассе́ты и компа́кт-ди́ски, и я слу́шаю хоро́шую му́зыку ка́ждый день.

УПРАЖНЕНИЕ 9   More imperfective infinitives

Go back to **Упражнение 8** and make an alphabetized list of the infinitives of imperfective verbs encountered there.

СЛОВА, СЛОВА, СЛОВА . . . ✪ *Когда́? Parts of the Day and Seasons of the Year*

— Ты рабо́таешь то́лько **ве́чером?**   *"Do you work only in the evening?"*
— **Ве́чером** и **но́чью.** А **у́тром**   *"In the evening and at night. In the*
и **днём** у меня́ заня́тия.   *morning and afternoon I have*
                          classes."

Сейча́с я не рабо́таю. **Ле́том**   *I'm not working now. In the summer*
я рабо́тала два ме́сяца.   *I worked for two months.*

To answer **когда́**-type questions, you'll need the following two sets of adverbs. Note that **но́чью** generally refers to the hours between midnight and dawn.

у́тром (*in the morning*)   **ле́том** (*in the summer*)
днём (*in the afternoon*)   **о́сенью** (*in the fall*)
ве́чером (*in the evening*)   **зимо́й** (*in the winter*)
но́чью (*at night*)   **весно́й** (*in the spring*)

У́тром Све́та у́чится в институ́те.

Днём и **ве́чером** Све́та занима́ется до́ма.

Ве́чером Све́та рабо́тает на ско́рой по́мощи.

Но́чью Све́та спит.

The terms referring to parts of the day can combine with **вчера́, сего́дня, за́втра.** Note that the English expression *last night,* as in *What did you do last night?* is normally expressed as **вчера́ ве́чером.** Therefore **сего́дня ве́чером** means *tonight,* and **за́втра ве́чером** means *tomorrow night.*

УПРАЖНЕНИЕ 10 Когда́ э́то бу́дет (бы́ло)?

Complete the table below to provide the Russian for each of the following English phrases:

this afternoon	yesterday morning	tomorrow morning
this evening	yesterday afternoon	tomorrow afternoon
	last night	tomorrow evening

	сего́дня	вчера́	за́втра
у́тром	сего́дня у́тром *this morning*		
днём			
ве́чером			

УПРАЖНЕНИЕ 11 Что ты де́лал (де́лала) ...?

Take a survey of your classmates. Find out what each person was doing last night and whether some of them were doing the same thing. Your classmates may answer using some of the following phrases:

де́лать дома́шнее зада́ние
занима́ться в библиоте́ке
игра́ть в волейбо́л (ка́рты ...)
писа́ть курсову́ю
рабо́тать в (на) ...

слу́шать ра́дио
  (компа́кт-ди́ски, ...)
смотре́ть телеви́зор
учи́ть но́вые слова́
чита́ть журна́лы

УПРАЖНЕНИЕ 12 "Repetition/duration" adverbs and the imperfective aspect

Here is a list of adverbs that suggest repetition or duration. Using these words and any imperfective verbs you know, work with a classmate to make up seven sentences that might apply to you. Try to use the past and future tenses as well as the present tense.

ОБРАЗЕЦ: обы́чно → *Я обы́чно занима́юсь до́ма, но вчера́ я занима́лся в библиоте́ке.*

всегда́
обы́чно
ка́ждый день
иногда́ (*sometimes*)

ча́сто
ре́дко
никогда́ не

❖ 7.6. ASPECT: IMPERFECTIVE AND PERFECTIVE COUNTERPARTS

Nearly all Russian verbs have an imperfective form, and most of these have a perfective counterpart that conveys the meaning of specific, one-time completion of that action in the past or future. When aspectual pairs occur together in this book, they will typically be presented thus: imperfective / perfective. Remember: *Perfective verbs have no present tense.* Below are three common pairs of imperfective and perfective counterparts.

IMPERFECTIVE INFINITIVE	PERFECTIVE INFINITIVE
писа́ть—*to write, to be writing*	**написа́ть**—*to finish writing (a particular thing)*
чита́ть—*to read, to be reading*	**прочита́ть**—*to read (something) all the way through, to finish reading (something)*
учи́ть—*to study, to be studying (something specific)*	**вы́учить**—*to learn, to memorize (something specific)*

УПРАЖНЕНИЕ 13   Imperfective and perfective infinitives

Read the text below and underline all the verbs you encounter. Then make a list of their infinitives, placing them in two columns: (a) imperfective infinitives; (b) perfective infinitives. In some cases, you may see perfective forms based on imperfective verbs you already know. Based on how the verbs are used in context, you should be able to determine whether they are imperfective or perfective.

На про́шлой неде́ле я купи́л но́вую ста́рую маши́ну. Э́то не шу́тка — я говорю́ серьёзно (*I'm serious!*)! Мои́ пе́рвые две маши́ны бы́ли о́чень ста́рые. Э́то моя́ тре́тья маши́на, и она́ то́же ста́рая, но для меня́ она́ но́вая. Хоти́те послу́шать, как я её купи́л? Вчера́ ве́чером позвони́л мой друг Дени́с и сказа́л, что его́ сосе́д Па́вел Петре́нко продаёт маши́ну. Я зна́ю Па́вла, он о́чень хоро́ший па́рень. Кро́ме того́, он автомеха́ник и рабо́тает в автосе́рвисе.† У тако́го челове́ка мо́жно купи́ть маши́ну. Я спроси́л (*asked*) Дени́са, кака́я у Па́вла маши́на, но он не знал, и я сказа́л, что хочу́ посмотре́ть её. Че́рез час Па́вел позвони́л мне и пригласи́л посмотре́ть маши́ну. Мне нра́вятся кра́сные маши́ны, и маши́на Па́вла — кра́сная «Ла́да» — мне о́чень понра́вилась. Ме́жду про́чим, я заплати́л за (*paid for*) неё о́чень ма́ло!

УПРАЖНЕНИЕ 14   Selecting the correct aspect

Choosing from the list of three verb pairs (six infinitives) below, select the aspect that fits the context and fill in the correct verb form. Use only the present tense or the past tense. Where you use the perfective aspect, be prepared to explain how the context suggests one-time completion.

писа́ть / написа́ть (*to write*)
учи́ть / вы́учить *to study / learn [something]*
чита́ть / прочита́ть (*to read*)

Кварти́ра Татья́ны Дми́триевны. 8 часо́в ве́чера (*p.m.*). Что де́лают Татья́на Дми́триевна, Та́ня и Све́та? Татья́на Дми́триевна _____¹ журна́л, Та́ня _____² письмо́, а Све́та _____³ англи́йские слова́.

Свете нравится английский язык, она _____ [4] по-английски

и _____ [5] английские слова каждый день. Вчера

она _____ [6] английскую статью и _____ [7] 30 слов.

Таня уже _____ [8] два письма и сейчас _____ [9]

письмо своей (*her*) подруге Кристине, которая живёт в Нью-Йорке. Вчера

вечером Таня тоже _____ [10] письма. У неё есть друзья,

которые живут в Петербурге, и она часто _____ [11] им. Татьяна

Дмитриевна любит читать. Она много _____ .[12]

Она _____ [13] газеты и журналы каждый день. Вчера

она _____ [14] в газете «Московские новости» интересную

статью.

❖ КУЛЬТУРА РЕЧИ ❖

❖ ТАК ГОВОРЯТ: ЧТО ЭТО ЗА . . . ?

— Света, а **что это за** карточки?

"Sveta, what kind of cards are those?"

— Это английские слова, которые я учу.

"They're English vocab words that I'm studying."

The question phrase <**что это за** + Nominative . . . ?> can be used to ask someone to provide further details about the item named.

УПРАЖНЕНИЕ 15   Что это за . . . ?

Use the phrase **что это за . . . ?** to ask about the items mentioned in the following scenarios. Note that the phrase may begin with «**a**» when used in response to a statement: **А что это за . . . ?**

ОБРАЗЕЦ: Your friend is a mechanic and he owns a lot of tools. You see him holding an unfamiliar tool in his hands.
— *Что это за инструмент?*

1. Your father says that he has subscribed to a magazine, the name of which you have never heard.
2. Your older sister is a graduate student doing dissertation research. She returns home after three months of field work and brings stacks of cards with her.
3. One of your friends suggests going out to see a new film.

❖ САМОПРОВЕРКА: УПРАЖНЕНИЕ 16

Working on your own, try this self-test: Read a Russian sentence out loud, then give an idiomatic English equivalent without looking at the book. Then work from English to Russian. After you have completed the activity, try it with a classmate.

1. — Что ты де́лала вчера́
     ве́чером?
   — Занима́лась.
   — А что бу́дешь де́лать
     сего́дня ве́чером?
   — Опя́ть бу́ду занима́ться.
   — Ты так мно́го занима́ешься!

2. — (*Noticing a friend's stack of
     vocabulary cards.*) Что э́то,
     опя́ть англи́йские слова́?
   — Да. Э́то слова́, кото́рые я
     уже́ вы́учила. (*Pointing to
     another stack of cards.*) А э́то
     слова́, кото́рые я должна́
     вы́учить сего́дня.

3. — Ты рабо́таешь то́лько
     ве́чером?
   — Ве́чером и но́чью. А у́тром
     и днём у меня́ заня́тия.

4. О́сенью я бу́ду учи́ться в
   Санкт-Петербу́рге.

1. "*What were you doing last
      night?*"
   "*Studying.*"
   "*And what are you going to do
      tonight?*"
   "*I'm going to be studying again.*"
   "*You sure study a lot!*"

2. (Noticing a friend's stack of
   vocabulary cards.) "*What are
   those, English words again?*"
   "*Yup. These are the words that
   I've already learned.* (Pointing
   to another stack of cards.)
   *And those are words that I'm
   supposed to learn today.*"

3. "*Do you work only in the
      evening?*"
   "*In the evening and at night.
   In the morning and afternoon
   I have classes.*"

4. *In the fall I'm going to be going
   to school in St. Petersburg.*

❖ ВОПРОСЫ И ОТВЕТЫ: УПРАЖНЕНИЕ 17

Work with a classmate to complete the following activity: One of you plays the role of an American student and the other plays a visitor from Russia who is asking about working and studying in America.

1. Вы рабо́таете и́ли то́лько у́читесь?
2. Где вы у́читесь? На како́м ку́рсе?
3. Где вы рабо́таете?
4. Где ча́сто рабо́тают америка́нские студе́нты?
5. Вы снима́ете ко́мнату? Кварти́ру? Живёте в общежи́тии? Живёте до́ма?
6. Ва́ши роди́тели рабо́тают? Где рабо́тает ваш оте́ц/ва́ша мать?
7. Где у́чится ваш брат (ва́ша сестра́, ваш друг, ва́ша подру́га)?

❖ ДИАЛОГИ

ДИАЛОГ 1 Когда́ бу́дет . . . ?
(Scheduling a social event)

— Ни́на, когда́ у вас бу́дет новосе́лье?
— Я ещё не зна́ю. Наве́рно, в пя́тницу и́ли в суббо́ту.
— Пя́тница — э́то удо́бный день. И суббо́та то́же. Я хочу́ пригласи́ть моего́
   дру́га Са́шу. Мо́жно?
— Коне́чно.

ДИАЛОГ 2 Приходи́ к нам (*come over to our place*) **в воскресе́нье**
(Extending and accepting invitations[4])

— Приходи́ к нам в воскресе́нье.
— Спаси́бо. А кого́ ещё вы приглаша́ете?
— Мы хоти́м пригласи́ть Лю́ду, Ка́тю, Ма́шу, Серёжу и Оле́га.
— Отли́чная компа́ния! Мо́жно пригласи́ть ещё Джо́на, на́шего аспира́нта.
  Он в Москве́ неда́вно.
— Прекра́сная иде́я! Пригласи́ его́, пожа́луйста!

УПРАЖНЕ́НИЕ 18   Ваш диало́г

Create a dialogue in which you are planning a housewarming party at your new apartment. With a friend, decide which evening it will be (juggling work, school, and study schedules) and whom you should invite.

◆❖ А ТЕПЕ́РЬ . . . : УПРАЖНЕ́НИЕ 19

Working with a classmate, use what you learned in Part 1 to . . .

1. ask when he usually studies (morning, afternoon, evening, night)
2. ask when and where he will be studying tonight
3. ask what he is going to be studying
4. ask if he worked in the summer, and if so, where

---

[4]Contemporary Russian has no simple equivalent of the English word *party* to refer to a wide range of private social gatherings.

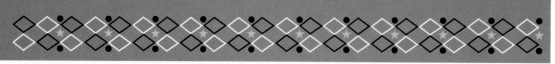

ЧАСТЬ ВТОРАЯ

С ЧЕГО НАЧАТЬ?

Извини́те, что беспоко́ю вас.	*Sorry to bother you.*	Что но́вого?	*What's new?*
совсе́м не	*not at all*	Э́то звони́т...	*This is . . . calling.*
Спаси́бо за приглаше́ние.	*Thanks for the invitation.*	Я перезвоню́.	*I'll call back.*
футбо́л	*soccer*		

 ЧТЕНИЕ

❖ Я ТЕБЕ́ ПОЗВОНЮ́°

СА́ША.	(*On the phone.*) Ле́на, приве́т! Мо́жешь меня́ поздра́вить: пять мину́т **наза́д°** у нас **на́чал°** рабо́тать телефо́н! 155-20-10 (сто пятьдеся́т пять, два́дцать, де́сять). **Послу́шай,°** Ле́на, я тебя́ приглаша́ю в суббо́ту на новосе́лье. Я тебе́ пото́м всё **объясню́.°**
НАТА́ЛЬЯ ИВ.	(*From the other room.*) Ле́на, мне ну́жен телефо́н. А тебе́, кста́ти, **пора́°** в университе́т. Ты **опозда́ешь°** на ле́кции.
ЛЕ́НА.	(*To her mother.*) Сейча́с! (*To Sasha.*) Са́ша, извини́, ма́ме ну́жен телефо́н. Перезвони́° че́рез **полчаса́,°** хорошо́? Или я тебе́ позвоню́.

(*Lena hangs up, but before Natalya Ivanovna can dial, the phone rings.*)

FIRST CALLER.	(*Shouts.*) Э́то **спра́вочная?°**
НАТ. ИВ.	**Вы не туда́ попа́ли.°** Э́то кварти́ра.
FIRST CALLER.	Извини́те, пожа́луйста.

(*Hangs up. Telephone immediately rings again.*)

SECOND CALLER.	**Попроси́те,°** пожа́луйста, Серге́я Петро́вича.
НАТ. ИВ.	Его́ нет, он на рабо́те.
SECOND CALLER.	**Прости́те,°** а кто э́то? Его́ жена́? Здра́вствуйте. **Э́то говори́т°** Алексе́й Грачёв, его́ ста́рый **знако́мый.°** Я в Москве́ **в командиро́вке.°** Вы не мо́жете **дать°** мне его́ телефо́н?
НАТ. ИВ.	Пожа́луйста, 193-14-41.

(*Hangs up. Telephone immediately rings a third time.*)

THIRD CALLER.	Э́то спра́вочная?
НАТ. ИВ.	(*Getting angry.*) Како́й но́мер вы **набира́ете?°**
THIRD CALLER.	155-94-89.
НАТ. ИВ.	Вы не туда́ попа́ли. (*Hangs up.*) Нет, э́то ужа́сно! Наш но́мер 155-94-79, а спра́вочная — 155-94-89. Тепе́рь нам бу́дут звони́ть днём и но́чью.° (*Telephone rings again.*)

Я. . . *I'll call you.*

Мо́жешь. . . *Congratulate me! / ago / started*
Listen

will explain

it's time (to go)
will be late

Call back
half an hour

Information
Вы. . . *You got the wrong number.*

May I speak with . . .

Excuse me / Э́то. . . *This is . . . speaking*
его́. . . *an old acquaintance of his*
в. . . *on a business trip / give*

are you dialing

днём. . . *day and night*

	НАТ. ИВ.	(*Picks up the phone and shouts.*) Это не спра́вочная! (*Hangs up. It rings again. Lena answers.*)
	ЛЁНА.	Слу́шаю.
(*Would you*) *get* что... *what happened?*	СЕРГЕ́Й ПЕТР.	Ле́на, э́то ты? У вас там всё в поря́дке? **Позови́**° ма́му. (*When Natalya Ivanovna comes to the phone.*) Ната́ша, э́то я. (*No response.*) Ната́ша! Ната́ша, **что случи́лось?**°
	НАТ. ИВ.	(*Icily.*) Ты зна́ешь, како́й у нас но́мер телефо́на?
city	СЕРГЕ́Й ПЕТР.	Ната́ша...
	НАТ. ИВ.	Ты зна́ешь, что наш но́мер 155-94-79, а но́мер городско́й° спра́вочной — 155-94-89...
Не мо́жет... *That can't be!*	СЕРГЕ́Й ПЕТР.	**Не мо́жет быть!**°
end up [*calling*] / *here*	НАТ. ИВ.	... и что лю́ди, кото́рые звоня́т туда́, **попада́ют**° **сюда́?**° (*Raising her voice*) Телефо́н то́лько сего́дня на́чал рабо́тать, а нам уже́ **всё вре́мя**° звоня́т. Не нам, а в спра́вочную (*With tragic overtones in her voice.*) Но́мер телефо́на похо́ж на но́мер спра́вочной.... Лю́ди бу́дут звони́ть днём и но́чью! Ра́зве мо́жно так жить?! (*Changing to a business-like mode.*) Серге́й, пожа́луйста, поменя́й° наш но́мер телефо́на. Неме́дленно.°
all the time		
change *right now*		
Я... *I don't want to hear a thing about it!* / *Hello!* До́брое... *Good morning.* Одну́... *Just a minute!* Возьми́... *Pick up the phone.*	СЕРГЕ́Й ПЕТР.	Но Ната́ша...
	НАТ. ИВ.	**Я ничего́ не хочу́ слы́шать!**° (*Hangs up; the phone immediately rings again.*) **Алло́!**[5]°
	СА́ША.	(*Cautiously*) **До́брое у́тро.**° Это Ле́на?
	НАТ. ИВ.	Нет, э́то Ната́лья Ива́новна. Здра́вствуйте, Са́ша. **Одну́ мину́ту!**° Ле́на, **возьми́ тру́бку.**°
That's strange.	ЛЁНА.	(*Comes to phone.*) Са́ша, приве́т!
	СА́ША.	Ле́на, како́й у вас но́мер телефо́на? 155-94-79? **Стра́нно.**° Я звони́л мину́т пять наза́д, но, ка́жется, не туда́ попа́л. **Кака́я-то**° же́нщина серди́то° кри́кнула,° что э́то не спра́вочная, и пове́сила тру́бку.° Наве́рно, номера́ похо́жи. Не повезло́ ей.° (*Lena smiles to herself.*) Ну, как насчёт новосе́лья?
Some / *angrily* / *shouted* *hung up* / Не повезло́... *A tough break for her!* С... *I'd be glad to!* *It's settled, then!*	ЛЁНА.	**С удово́льствием!**°
	СА́ША.	**Договори́лись!**°

УПРАЖНЕ́НИЕ 1 Под микроско́пом: Linking infinitives to conjugated forms

Below left is a list of imperfective/perfective verb pairs, of which one member or the other is used in this reading (some but not all are used in the infinitive). Find at least one example of each pair in the reading and underline it. Then circle the corresponding infinitive in the list. Finally, match the infinitive pairs on the left with the English meanings on the right.

1. _____ веша́ть / пове́сить
2. _____ звони́ть / позвони́ть
3. _____ перезва́нивать / перезвони́ть
4. _____ крича́ть / кри́кнуть
5. _____ меня́ть / поменя́ть
6. _____ набира́ть / набра́ть
7. _____ начина́ть / нача́ть

а. to begin
б. to call (on the telephone)
в. to call back (on the telephone)
г. to change
д. to congratulate
е. to dial (telephone)
ж. to hang (something) up (e.g., on a wall or bulletin board)

---

[5]**Алло́** is typically pronounced with a soft **л**: [алё].

8. _____ поздравля́ть / поздра́вить   з. to happen, occur
9. _____ попада́ть / попа́сть   и. to hear
10. _____ случа́ться / случи́ться   к. to listen
11. _____ слу́шать / послу́шать   л. to reach, get to
12. _____ слы́шать / услы́шать   м. to shout

ГРАММАТИКА И ПРАКТИКА

◆ 7.7. ASPECT: *TO BEGIN* (OR *FINISH*) DOING SOMETHING

Пять мину́т наза́д у нас **на́чал рабо́тать** телефо́н!

Обы́чно я **начина́ю де́лать** дома́шнее зада́ние в семь часо́в, а вчера́ я **начала́** (де́лать дома́шнее зада́ние) в во́семь.

Обы́чно я **конча́ю занима́ться** в де́сять часо́в, а вчера́ ве́чером я **ко́нчила** (занима́ться) в оди́ннадцать.

Our phone began working five minutes ago!

Usually I begin doing my homework at 7:00, but today I started at 8:00.

Usually I finish studying at 10:00, but last night I finished at 11:00.

When the verbs **начина́ть / нача́ть** *to begin* and **конча́ть / ко́нчить** *to finish* are followed by another verb, the second verb is always an imperfective infinitive.

УПРАЖНЕНИЕ 2   To begin or finish doing something

Ask a classmate the following questions.

1. Когда́ ты обы́чно начина́ешь де́лать дома́шнее зада́ние? А когда́ ты вчера́ на́чал (начала́) де́лать его́?

2. Как до́лго (*how long*) ты обы́чно де́лаешь дома́шнее зада́ние? (Час? Два часа́? Три часа́? Четы́ре часа́?)

3. Ты рабо́таешь? Ты рабо́таешь ка́ждый день? Когда́ ты обы́чно начина́ешь рабо́тать? А когда́ ты конча́ешь рабо́тать?

4. Ты, ка́жется, до́лжен (должна́) написа́ть курсову́ю рабо́ту. Ты уже́ на́чал (начала́) её писа́ть? Когда́ ты на́чал (начала́) её писа́ть? А когда́ ты ду́маешь её зако́нчить?

5. Ты вчера́ мно́го занима́лся (занима́лась)? Когда́ ты ко́нчил (ко́нчила) занима́ться? А когда́ на́чал (начала́)?

6. Ты смо́тришь телеви́зор ве́чером? Ты смотре́л (смотре́ла) телеви́зор вчера́ ве́чером? Как до́лго ты смотре́л (смотре́ла) телеви́зор? Что ты смотре́л (смотре́ла)? Когда́ ты на́чал (начала́) / ко́нчил (ко́нчила) смотре́ть?

❖ 7.8. TIME "WHEN": КОГДА . . . ? В СЕМЬ ЧАСОВ

— Так **когда** будет новоселье? Я предлагаю **в семь часов**. Хорошо?	*"So, when will the housewarming be. I suggest at 7:00. Okay?"*
— В субботу **в семь часов** — это удобно.	*"On Saturday at 7:00—that's okay."*

To express "at" a certain time, use the following construction.

<**в** + number + "hour" word>

The "hour" word changes according to the number.

at 1:00 . . . (час, no number)	*at 2:00, 3:00, 4:00 . . .* (часа́)	*at any other time . . .* (часо́в)	
в час	в два часа́	в пять часов	в де́вять часов
	в три часа́	в шесть часов	в де́сять часов
	в четы́ре часа́	в семь часов	в оди́ннадцать часов
		в во́семь часов	в двена́дцать часов

СЛОВА, СЛОВА, СЛОВА . . . ✪ *Час*

Do not mistakenly say **оди́н час** for *one o'clock*. **Оди́н час** means *one hour*. In addition to **Когда́?**, you might also hear **В кото́ром часу́?** *At what time?* in this context.

УПРАЖНЕНИЕ 3   Making an appointment

You've arrived at the institution in St. Petersburg where you'll be studying for a semester and you need to meet with **Ири́на Серге́евна,** with whom you'll have private Russian lessons. You call her office and try to make an appointment for later in the week. You'll first have to find out which day she is free, then at what time. (Your fellow student, who will take the part of a department secretary, has the week's appointment book for **Ири́на Серге́евна** in Appendix K.)

> ОБРАЗЕЦ: — Ири́на Серге́евна свобо́дна (*free*) во вто́рник?
> — К сожале́нию, во вто́рник её не бу́дет.
> — А в сре́ду?
> — В сре́ду у́тром у неё заня́тия.
> — А в два часа́…?

◈ 7.9. EXPRESSING THANKS

Спаси́бо, Илья́ Ильи́ч.	*Thanks, Ilya Ilyich.*
Большо́е **спаси́бо.**	*Thanks a lot.*
Спаси́бо за приглаше́ние.	*Thanks for the invitation.*

To simply thank someone, use **Спаси́бо.** This can be intensified by saying **Большо́е спаси́бо.** To express what you are thanking someone for, use the construction <**Спаси́бо за** + Accusative>.

УПРАЖНЕНИЕ 4   Спаси́бо за…

How would you thank someone for the following things? Use <**Спаси́бо за** + Accusative>.

бандеро́ль	варе́нье (*jam*)	информа́ция[†]
зубна́я па́ста	ка́рточки	прия́тный (*pleasant*)
микроволно́вая печь	вино́ (*wine*)	ве́чер
откры́тка	пасти́лки от ка́шля	одея́ло
пода́рок	приглаше́ние	пи́во
фотогра́фия	чемода́н	проездно́й биле́т
		торт

◈ 7.10. ASPECT IN THE FUTURE: IMPERFECTIVE

В суббо́ту они́ **бу́дут пра́здновать** новосе́лье.	*On Saturday they'll celebrate their housewarming.*

The future tense that you learned in Lesson 6, Part 2, was actually the imperfective future. To review, this is the aspect/tense combination that describes ongoing, repeated, or habitual/characteristic actions or states in the future. It consists of a conjugated form of **быть** followed by an imperfective infinitive. Here are some examples of the imperfective future:

Я **бу́ду рабо́тать** весь ве́чер.	*I'll be working all evening.*
В суббо́ту она́ **бу́дет отдыха́ть.**	*On Saturday she's going to relax.*
Ле́том мы **бу́дем учи́ться** в Москве́.	*In the summer we'll be studying in Moscow.*

УПРАЖНЕНИЕ 5   Что ты бу́дешь де́лать . . . ?

Take a survey of your classmates. Find out what each person will be doing tonight and whether some of them will be doing the same thing. Your classmates may answer using some of the following phrases:

занима́ться в библиоте́ке
игра́ть в волейбо́л (ка́рты, баскетбо́л . . .)
писа́ть курсову́ю
рабо́тать в (на) . . .
слу́шать ра́дио (компа́кт-ди́ски, ру́сские кассе́ты)
смотре́ть телеви́зор
учи́ть но́вые слова́
чита́ть журна́лы
???

УПРАЖНЕНИЕ 6   Где ты бу́дешь ле́том? Что ты бу́дешь де́лать?

A friend is telling you about her summer plans. Tell your friend what you will be doing during the summer.

1. — Я бу́ду во Флори́де.
   — Ты бу́дешь во Флори́де, а мы бу́дем в . . .
2. — Я бу́ду загора́ть (*sunbathe*) на пля́же (*beach*).
   — Ты бу́дешь загора́ть на пля́же, а я бу́ду . . .
3. — Я бу́ду смотре́ть ковбо́йские† фи́льмы.
   — Ты бу́дешь смотре́ть ковбо́йские фи́льмы, а я бу́ду . . .
4. — Я бу́ду ка́ждый день учи́ть англи́йские слова́.
   — Ты бу́дешь учи́ть англи́йские слова́, а мы бу́дем . . .
5. — Я бу́ду чита́ть интере́сные кни́ги.
   — Ты бу́дешь чита́ть интере́сные кни́ги, а я бу́ду . . .
6. — Я бу́ду ка́ждый день смотре́ть телеви́зор.
   — Ты бу́дешь ка́ждый день смотре́ть телеви́зор, а мы бу́дем . . .

УПРАЖНЕНИЕ 7   Coordinating schedules

The following is a page from a day planner. Fill it in with things that you are doing during the coming week. Then, without showing it to anyone, try to find someone in the class with whom you can arrange a mutually convenient time to study Russian.

ОБРАЗЕ́Ц: — Дава́й учи́ть ру́сский язы́к вме́сте (*together*). Что ты де́лаешь в сре́ду ве́чером?
   — В сре́ду ве́чером я рабо́таю. Мо́жет быть, днём? У тебя́ есть вре́мя днём?
   — К сожале́нию, у меня́ в час заня́тия. Но у меня́ есть вре́мя у́тром. Мо́жет быть, в 10 часо́в?

	ПН	ВТ	СР		ЧТ	ПТ	СБ	ВС
8.00								
9.00								
10.00								
11.00								
12.00								
1.00								
2.00								
3.00								
4.00								
5.00								
6.00								

❖ 7.11. ASPECT IN THE FUTURE: PERFECTIVE

Я тебе́ **позвоню́** че́рез полчаса́, хорошо́?	*I'll call you back in half an hour, OK?*
А тебе́, кста́ти, пора́ в университе́т. Ты **опозда́ешь** на ле́кции.	*And by the way, it's time for you to go to the university. You'll be late for classes.*
Я тебе́ пото́м всё **объясню́.**	*I'll explain everything to you later.*

The effect of the perfective future, like that of the perfective past, is to convey a one-time completed action, often with focus on a result. In this case the speaker is referring to a future action viewed in its entirety, such as "I'll buy a new computer after work tonight." That meaning is conveyed via the use of the perfective infinitive or one of its conjugated forms.

The future tense of the perfective looks a lot like the present tense of the imperfective: The endings are the same **-ешь** and **-ишь** endings you have already learned, and there is no **быть** auxiliary. For that reason, the present tense conjugations of imperfective verbs and the future tense conjugations of perfective verbs will henceforth be referred to as "nonpast" forms because they exhibit the same endings. But the meaning of the perfective future is clearly different from that of the present, and for that reason it is important to distinguish between the two types of infinitives.

Present *(always imperfective)*	**Perfective future**
читáть	**прочитáть**
Лéтом я **читáю** детекти́вы и три́ллеры.	Лéтом я **прочитáю** все пьéсы Шекспи́ра.
In the summer I read mysteries and thrillers.	*(This) summer I'll read all of Shakespeare's plays.*
запи́сывать; говори́ть	**записáть; сказáть**
Я всегдá **запи́сываю** всё, что вы **говори́те.**	Я **запишу́** всё, что вы **скáжете.**
I always write down everything you say.	*I'll write down everything you say.*
начинáть	**начáть**
Обы́чно мы **начинáем** рабóтать в 4 часá.	Сегóдня мы **начнём** рабóтать в 5 часóв.
Usually we start working at 4:00.	*Today we'll start working at 5:00.*

УПРАЖНЕНИЕ 8   Determining aspect in the future

A friend of yours is telling you about her plans for the weekend. Five of her statements below refer to activities that, were she speaking Russian, she'd probably render in the perfective future. Which are they? (Do not try to translate the sentences.)

1. I'll be working late on Friday night.
2. We'll close the shop at midnight.
3. When I get home I'll feed the cat.
4. On Saturday I'll sleep until noon.
5. I'll spend all Saturday afternoon shopping.
6. In addition to groceries, I'll buy a gift for my friend.
7. We'll be celebrating her birthday on Saturday night.
8. I'll get her a new CD.
9. What will we do at the party?
10. We'll be dancing, singing, playing cards, and eating.
11. Then on Sunday afternoon I'll definitely finish writing my history term paper no matter what.
12. And on Sunday evening I'll study my Russian in the library.

УПРАЖНЕНИЕ 9   Matching with perfective future

Complete the sentences on the left by selecting logical endings from the fragments on the right. Then underline each perfective verb and translate the resulting sentences. Here is a list of the verbs used in this exercise: You've already learned the imperfectives; the perfectives are to the right of the slash.

дéлать / сдéлать	*to do*	приноси́ть / принести́	*to bring*
идти́ / пойти́	*to go*	серди́ться / рассерди́ться	*to get angry*
набирáть / набрáть	*to dial*	спрáшивать / спроси́ть	*to ask*
отдыхáть / отдохну́ть	*to rest*	учи́ть / вы́учить	*to study, learn*

ОБРАЗЕЦ: Я <u>спрошу́</u> у сестры́ . . . когда́ у неё бу́дет вре́мя нам помо́чь.
I'll ask my sister when she'll have time to help us.

1. _____ Я не пойду́ сего́дня в теа́тр, . . .
2. _____ Е́сли я бу́ду игра́ть гро́мко, . . .
3. _____ Когда́ ты сде́лаешь дома́шнее зада́ние, . . .
4. _____ Е́сли ты принесёшь пи́ццу, . . .
5. _____ Я не хочу́ с ним говори́ть: я наберу́ но́мер, . . .
6. _____ Е́сли я сейча́с отдохну́, . . .
7. _____ Когда́ я вы́учу италья́нский язы́к, . . .

а. а ты говори́.
б. мо́жешь посмотре́ть телеви́зор.
в. потому́ что у меня́ мно́го рабо́ты.
г. сосе́ди рассе́рдятся.
д. я бу́ду учи́ть испа́нский.
е. я не бу́ду ничего́ гото́вить.
ж. я смогу́ занима́ться всю ночь.

УПРАЖНЕНИЕ 10   Perfective futures

Here is a list of imperfective infinitives and their perfective counterparts. Use the perfective future of the appropriate verb to complete the following text.

дари́ть / подари́ть (подарю́, пода́ришь, . . . пода́рят)	*to give (as a present)*
звони́ть / позвони́ть (позвоню́, позвони́шь, . . . позвоня́т)	*to call; to phone*
идти́ / пойти́ (пойду́, пойдёшь, . . . пойду́т)	*to go*
покупа́ть / купи́ть (куплю́, ку́пишь, . . . ку́пят)	*to buy*
приглаша́ть / пригласи́ть (приглашу́, пригласи́шь, . . . приглася́т)	*to invite*
приноси́ть / принести́ (принесу́, принесёшь, . . . принесу́т)	*to bring*
спра́шивать / спроси́ть (спрошу́, спро́сишь, . . . спро́сят)	*to ask*

В пя́тницу у мое́й подру́ги Ребе́кки день рожде́ния (*birthday*). Ребе́кка
сказа́ла, что она́ _____¹ Дже́ка, Серге́я и Ю́лю.
А я _____² И́горя. Мы все _____³ в кафе́.
Я ещё не купи́ла Ребе́кке пода́рок, но я обяза́тельно _____⁴
его́ сего́дня и́ли за́втра. Сейча́с я _____⁵
Ю́ле и _____,⁶ что она́ _____⁷ Ребе́кке.
Я, наве́рно, _____⁸ ей компа́кт-ди́ски, а
И́горь _____⁹ цветы́ и конфе́ты (*candy*).

УПРАЖНЕНИЕ 11   Сего́дня ве́чером я . . .

What do you plan to get done this evening? See if your classmates intend to accomplish the same things as you.

ОБРАЗЕЦ: *Сего́дня ве́чером я вы́учу слова́. А ты?*

куплю́ пода́рок ма́ме (бра́ту, сестре́, отцу́ . . .)
напишу́ курсову́ю (письмо́ роди́телям (*to my parents*), письмо́ дру́гу . . .)
позвоню́ де́душке (ба́бушке, дру́гу, подру́ге . . .)
посмотрю́ но́вости (*the news*) по телеви́зору
приглашу́ дру́га на новосе́лье
прочита́ю статью́ о Росси́и (об Ива́не Гро́зном *Ivan the Terrible*)
сде́лаю дома́шнее зада́ние

❖ 7.12. ASPECT AND TENSE: SUMMARY

The imperfective has present, past, and future tenses; the perfective has only past and future tenses. The table below shows how aspect and tense interact.

TENSE	IMPERFECTIVE ASPECT Expresses ongoing, repeated, or habitual action or state.	PERFECTIVE ASPECT Expresses one-time completion.
Present	я пишу́	*Does not exist.*
Past	я писа́л (писа́ла)	я написа́л (написа́ла)
Future	я бу́ду писа́ть	я напишу́

КУЛЬТУРА РЕЧИ

❖ ТАК ГОВОРЯТ: ПОРА́

А **тебе́**, кста́ти, **пора́ в университе́т.** Ты опозда́ешь на ле́кции.	*And it's time for you, by the way, to go to the university. You'll be late to class.*
Ма́мочка, **мне пора́ в институ́т.**	*Mom, it's time for me to go to the institute.*

The construction <Dative + **пора́** + **в/на** + destination in the Accusative> renders *it's time [for someone] to go [somewhere]*. The "go" verb is usually omitted, and if the referential context is clear (for example, everyone is standing around with bags packed) the simple **Пора́!** is sufficient to say *It's time (to go)!*

УПРАЖНЕНИЕ 12   Пора́

How might you use **пора́** constructions in the following situations?

1. Say it's time for you to go to class.
2. It's your little brother's bedtime. Say it's time for him to sleep.
3. Your mother is running late. Tell her it's time to go to work.
4. You and some friends have been at a party. Say it's time for you (pl.) to go home.

❖ САМОПРОВЕРКА: УПРАЖНЕНИЕ 13

Working on your own, try this self-test: Read a Russian sentence out loud, then give an idiomatic English equivalent without looking at the book. Then work from English to Russian. After you have completed the activity, try it with a classmate.

1. Обы́чно я начина́ю занима́ться в семь часо́в, а вчера́ я начала́ (занима́ться) в шесть.

2. — Так когда́ бу́дет новосе́лье? Я предлага́ю в во́семь часо́в. Хорошо́?
   — В пя́тницу в во́семь часо́в — э́то удо́бно.

3. — Ири́на Серге́евна свобо́дна во вто́рник?
   — К сожале́нию, во вто́рник её не бу́дет.
   — А в сре́ду?
   — В сре́ду у́тром у неё заня́тия.

4. Перезвони́ че́рез полчаса́, хорошо́? И́ли я тебе́ позвоню́.

5. Ле́том я прочита́ю все пье́сы Шекспи́ра.

1. *Usually I start studying at 7:00, but yesterday I started at 6:00.*

2. *"So, when will the housewarming be. I suggest at 8:00. Okay?"*

   "On Friday at 8:00—that's okay."

3. *"Is Irina Sergeyevna free on Tuesday?"*
   "Unfortunately on Tuesday she won't be here."
   "And on Wednesday?"
   "On Wednesday morning she has class."

4. *Call back in a half hour, okay? Or I'll call you.*

5. *(This) summer I'll read all of Shakespeare's plays.*

❖ ВОПРОСЫ И ОТВЕТЫ: УПРАЖНЕНИЕ 14

Working with a classmate, take turns asking and answering the following questions.

1. У тебя́ до́ма есть телефо́н? А на рабо́те?
2. Како́й у тебя́ но́мер телефо́на?
3. Э́то твой дома́шний телефо́н?
4. Кому́ ты ча́сто звони́шь?
5. А кто тебе́ ча́сто звони́т?
6. Ты ча́сто звони́шь в спра́вочную?
7. Ва́ша спра́вочная хорошо́ рабо́тает?
8. У тебя́ есть со́товый телефо́н (*cell phone*)?

❖ ДИАЛОГИ

ДИАЛОГ 1   Ни́на до́ма?
(Asking for someone on the phone)

— Алло́, я слу́шаю.
— До́брый день. Скажи́те, пожа́луйста, Ни́на до́ма?
— Её нет. Она́ в университе́те.
— Вы не зна́ете, когда́ она́ бу́дет до́ма?
— Позвони́те, пожа́луйста, ве́чером.
— Хорошо́, спаси́бо. До свида́ния.

ДИАЛОГ 2 **Мне о́чень жаль . . .**
(Turning down an invitation)

— Ни́на, в воскресе́нье в университе́те конце́рт рок-му́зыки. Я тебя́
приглаша́ю.
— Спаси́бо, но в воскресе́нье я не могу́.
— О́чень жаль. Конце́рт бу́дет о́чень хоро́ший.
— Мне то́же о́чень жа́ль, но в воскресе́нье у нас бу́дут го́сти, и мне на́до быть
до́ма.

УПРАЖНЕНИЕ 15   **Ваш диало́г**

Create a dialogue in which you call a friend to discuss your respective plans for the
evening. (Depending on whether you plan to finish something, you may be using the
perfective future, the imperfective future, or both.)

❖❖ А ТЕПЕРЬ . . . : УПРАЖНЕНИЕ 16

Working with a classmate, sit back to back and pretend you are speaking on the phone.
Use what you learned in Part 2 to . . .

1. find out if you've reached the person you were calling and identify yourself as
   the caller
2. say you can't hear at all and you'll call back
3. find out what she's going to be doing tonight
4. ask whether she works, and if so, what time she starts working
5. tell her to call you on Wednesday (Thursday, . . .) (she may or may not be
   interested)

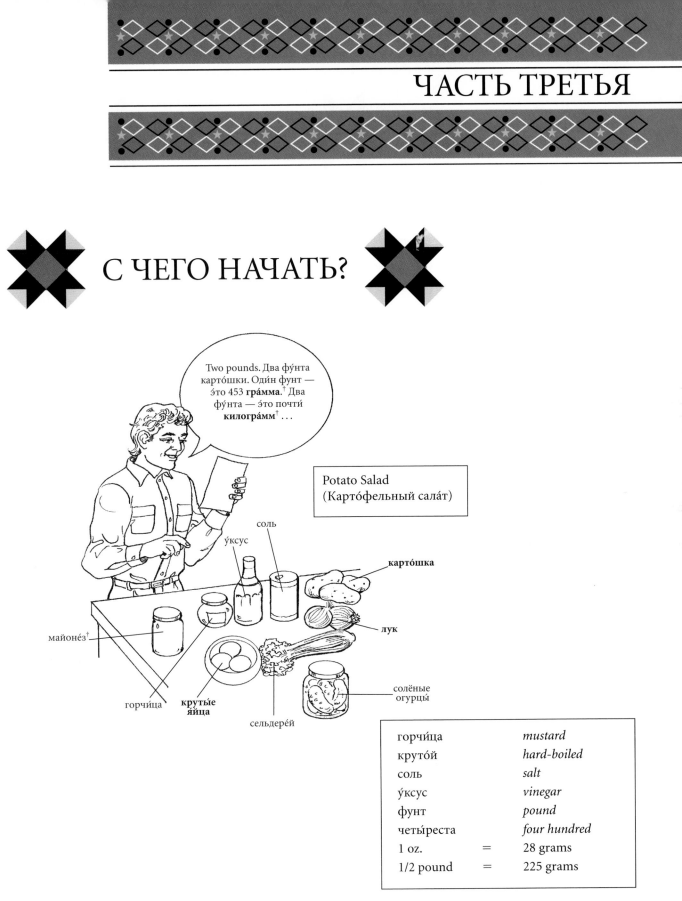

С ЧЕГО НАЧАТЬ?

Two pounds. Два фу́нта карто́шки. Оди́н фунт — э́то 453 **гра́мма.**[†] Два фу́нта — э́то почти́ **килогра́мм**[†] . . .

Potato Salad
(Карто́фельный сала́т)

соль

у́ксус

карто́шка

майоне́з[†]

лук

горчи́ца

круты́е яйца

сельдере́й

соле́ные огурцы́

горчи́ца		mustard
крутой		hard-boiled
соль		salt
у́ксус		vinegar
фунт		pound
четы́реста		four hundred
1 oz.	=	28 grams
1/2 pound	=	225 grams

309

ЧТЕНИЕ

Что... *What should I bring?*	◆ **ЧТО ПРИНЕСТИ?**°

(The telephone rings in Tatyana Dmitrievna's apartment. Tanya lifts the receiver.)

	ТА́НЯ.	Алло́, я слу́шаю.
May I speak to ...	ДЖИМ.	До́брое у́тро. Это Джим. **Мо́жно попроси́ть**° Та́ню?
	ТА́НЯ.	Здра́вствуй, Джим. Это я. Как хорошо́, что ты звони́шь. Мы неда́вно о тебе́ говори́ли.
	ДЖИМ.	Да? А почему́?
celebrate	ТА́НЯ.	Потому́ что Све́та и я бу́дем **пра́здновать**° новосе́лье и приглаша́ем тебя́.
	ДЖИМ.	Спаси́бо. А когда́ бу́дет новосе́лье?
в... *at seven in the evening*	ТА́НЯ.	В суббо́ту, в семь часо́в **ве́чера.**° Пожа́луйста, не опа́здывай.
	ДЖИМ.	Я никогда́ не опа́здываю. Что принести́?
wine	ТА́НЯ.	Спаси́бо, ничего́ не ну́жно. Сыр, колбасу́ и **вино́**° мы уже́ купи́ли. А гото́вить ты, наве́рное, не уме́ешь.
offend	ДЖИМ.	Я? Не уме́ю гото́вить? Та́ня, ты меня́ **обижа́ешь.**° Я уме́ю гото́вить
vegetables / meat / fish		и **о́вощи,**° и **мя́со,**° и **ры́бу.**° *(Jokingly.)* Ме́жду про́чим, мои́ друзья́
make		говоря́т, что я гото́влю совсе́м непло́хо. Я могу́ **пригото́вить**°
картофельный... *potato*		карто́фельный сала́т° и́ли мясно́й руле́т.° И́ли пи́ццу.†
salad / мясной... *meat loaf*	ТА́НЯ.	Пи́цца — это замеча́тельно! Мы все о́чень лю́бим пи́ццу, но не уме́ем её гото́вить.
will make	ДЖИМ.	Хорошо́, я **сде́лаю**° пи́ццу.
	ТА́НЯ.	А у нас мужчи́ны не о́чень лю́б т гото́вить.
many	ДЖИМ.	В Аме́рике **мно́гие**° мужчи́ны хорошо́ гото́вят. Муж и жена́ ча́сто
готовят... *fix dinner /* по...		гото́вят **обе́д**° **по о́череди.**° Кста́ти, и у вас, и у нас почти́ все шеф-
take turns		повара́° — мужчи́ны. Зна́чит, у вас то́же есть мужчи́ны, кото́рые
head chefs		лю́бят гото́вить.
learn (how to)	ТА́НЯ.	А как ты научи́лся° гото́вить?
a	ДЖИМ.	Когда́ я был на второ́м ку́рсе, мой друг Джеф, я и одна́° де́вушка,
together		Нико́ль, **вме́сте**° снима́ли кварти́ру. Мы гото́вили по о́череди. Джеф о́чень хорошо́ гото́вит. Нико́ль то́же. Мне бы́ло сты́дно, что я не уме́ю гото́вить, и я научи́лся.

ТА́НЯ.	У вас па́рни и де́вушки мо́гут снима́ть кварти́ру вме́сте?
ДЖИМ.	Да, мно́гие э́то де́лают.
ТА́НЯ.	Как интере́сно! А у нас э́то не при́нято.° Ты обяза́тельно до́лжен **рассказа́ть**° мне об э́том. Но не сейча́с. Сейча́с гла́вное — э́то новосе́лье. Джим, ты, ка́жется, у́чишься игра́ть на гита́ре?
ДЖИМ.	(*Smiling.*) Я всё **по́нял.**° Мы — пи́цца, гита́ра и я — бу́дем у вас в суббо́ту, **ро́вно**° в семь часо́в ве́чера.
ТА́НЯ.	Ждём!°

y. . . *we don't do that here*
tell

understood
on the dot
We'll be expecting you!

УПРАЖНЕ́НИЕ 1   Под микроско́пом: Linking aspectual meaning to form

For each of the English sentences below, find the corresponding Russian sentence in the reading. Copy the sentence onto a separate sheet of paper, underline the Russian equivalent of the boldfaced English verb, and give its aspect, tense, and the infinitive from which it is derived.

ОБРАЗЕ́Ц: We **were** just (recently) **talking** about you.

Мы неда́вно о тебе́ <u>говори́ли.</u> (*impfv. past;* говори́ть)

1. Sveta and I **will be celebrating** a housewarming. . . .
2. I can **fix** a potato salad or a meatloaf. (*Infinitive used; no tense*)
3. OK, I'll **make** a pizza.
4. We've already **bought** cheese, sausage and wine.
5. My friend Jeff, I, and a girl, Nicole, **were renting** an apartment together.
6. By the way, my friends say I don't **cook** too badly.

В го́сти

О РОССИИ

VISITING RUSSIANS AT HOME

Я никогда́ не опа́здываю. Что принести́?

When Jim goes to the **новосе́лье,** he will probably take not only his guitar and homemade pizza, but also a small gift for the hosts. Flowers are customary, but only in odd numbers (three and higher), and never yellow: even numbers are considered bad luck, and yellow is a symbol of parting or betrayal. Most likely the hosts will invite their guests to the table soon after their arrival. The meal generally begins with a selection of appetizers, immediately followed by several varied and plentiful courses. Toasts may be made throughout the meal.

ГРАММАТИКА И ПРАКТИКА

СЛОВА, СЛОВА, СЛОВА . . . ✪ *Мно́гие*

В Аме́рике **мно́гие** мужчи́ны хорошо́ гото́вят.   *In America many men cook well.*
Да, **мно́гие** э́то де́лают.   *Yes, many (people) do that.*

The word **мно́гие** *many* (*but not all*) can be both an adjective (as in the first example) or a noun (as in the second). It is always plural.

◈◈ **О РОССИИ** ◈◈◈◈◈◈◈◈◈◈◈◈◈◈◈◈◈

GENDER RELATIONS IN RUSSIA

А у нас мужчи́ны не о́чень лю́бят гото́вить.

Despite the large number of Russian women who work outside the home, gender relations in Russia are generally more traditional than they are in the United States. Not many Russian men readily spend time cooking and housekeeping, and single students rarely rent an apartment with those of the opposite sex.

In the area of etiquette, many Russian men exhibit a certain degree of chivalry. They often hold doors, coats, and bags for women; compliment them on their appearance; and may even kiss the hand of a woman upon meeting. Russian men virtually always pay the expenses on a date. Such behavior should not be construed as sexist, but rather understood as a different cultural norm.

◈◈◈◈◈◈◈◈◈◈◈◈◈◈◈◈◈◈◈◈◈◈◈◈

СЛОВА, СЛОВА, СЛОВА . . . ✪ *The Neuter Pronoun э́то*

— У вас па́рни и де́вушки мо́гут снима́ть   *"In your country men and women can rent*
   кварти́ру вме́сте?   *an apartment together?"*
— Да, мно́гие **э́то** де́лают.   *"Yes, lots of people do it."*
— Как интере́сно! А у нас **э́то** не при́нято.   *"How interesting! That's not done here.*
   Ты обяза́тельно до́лжен рассказа́ть   *You'll definitely have to tell me about it."*
   мне об **э́том.**

The neuter pronoun **э́то,** like English *it* or *that,* can serve as a connector in speech when one refers back to a previous statement or topic of discussion. For example, **э́то** is used in the preceding conversation to refer to the concept of men and women renting an apartment together.

❖ 7.13. PREPOSITIONAL CASE OF PRONOUNS AND ЭТО

Мы неда́вно **о тебе́** говори́ли.	*We were just (recently) talking about you.*
Ты обяза́тельно до́лжен рассказа́ть мне **об э́том.**	*You absolutely must tell me about that.*
Но **об э́том** ни сло́ва. Э́то бу́дет сюрпри́з.	*Don't say a word about this. It'll be a surprise.*

You have already learned Prepositional case singular endings for nouns, adjectives and possessives. Here are the forms of the Prepositional case pronouns and the demonstrative pronoun **э́то**. Note that **о** becomes **об** before **э́том** and **обо** before **мне**; **обо** has no stress of its own, but rather is pronounced with the word that follows it.

PRONOUNS: Nominative / Prepositional

INTERROGATIVES		PERSONAL PRONOUNS			
Nom.	**Prep.**	**Nom.**	**Prep.**	**Nom.**	**Prep.**
кто	(о) ком	я	(обо) мне	мы	(о) нас
что	(о) чём	ты	(о) тебе́	вы	(о) вас
		он, оно́	(о) нём	они́	(о) них
DEMONSTRATIVE		она́	(о) ней		
э́то	(об) э́том				

УПРАЖНЕНИЕ 2   Мы неда́вно о тебе́ говори́ли

Fill in the blanks with appropriate Prepositional case pronouns.

ОБРАЗЕ́Ц: — Са́ша, мы говори́ли о тебе́ вчера́ ве́чером.
　　　　　 — Обо _____*мне*_____? А почему́?

1. — О чём э́та кни́га?
   — О поэ́зии (*poetry*). Я ма́ло зна́ю о _____.
2. — Твои́ но́вые друзья́ пи́шут тебе́?
   — Нет, я ничего́ о _____ не зна́ю.
3. — О́чень интере́сная статья́!
   — О _____ она́?
4. — Расскажи́ мне о своём ста́ршем бра́те.
   — Что ты хо́чешь знать о _____?
5. — Я хочу́ пое́хать (*to go*) в о́тпуск (*vacation*) в А́фрику. Что ты об _____ ду́маешь?
6. — Тебе́ нра́вится э́тот расска́з?
   — Да, о́чень. В _____ мно́го ю́мора.[†]
7. — О чём вы говори́ли?
   — Не о *чём*, а о _____. О тебе́.
8. — Э́то твой рюкза́к?
   — Да, спаси́бо. В _____ все мои́ кни́ги!

УПРАЖНЕНИЕ 3   О чём вы ча́сто ду́маете?

As a psychologist, you must explore the inner life of your patients (classmates) by asking the following questions.

1. О чём вы ча́сто ду́маете?
2. О ком вы ча́сто ду́маете?
3. О ком вы ча́сто говори́те?

✧ 7.14. *WHAT TIME IS IT?* AND *A.M., P.M.*

— Скажи́те, пожа́луйста, **кото́рый час?**	*"Can you please tell me what time it is?"*
— Сейча́с **два часа́.**	*"It's (now) two o'clock."*

Use **Кото́рый час?** to ask someone the time. If someone asks you the time, use the following formula to respond with a round hour.

<(**сейча́с** +) number + "hour" word>

If you wish to give the minutes as well, the easiest way is simply to delete the "hour" word and add the number of minutes, a construction directly parallel to English.

Сейча́с два два́дцать пять.   *It's two twenty-five.*

Like most other European nations, Russia uses a 24-hour clock for official purposes (for example, on train, plane, and bus schedules). But in everyday conversation, the following time-of-day designators are used.

8 часо́в **утра́**	*8 A.M.*
час **дня**	*1 P.M.*
7 часо́в **ве́чера**	*7 P.M.*
2 часа́ **но́чи**	*2 A.M.*

Do not confuse these forms—which are the Genitive case—with the adverbial forms **у́тром, днём, ве́чером, но́чью**. The Genitive forms **утра́** (for *morning*), **дня** (for the *afternoon*), **ве́чера** (for the *evening*), and **но́чи** (through the *night*) are used as English uses A.M. and P.M. when giving a particular time of day: **10 часо́в утра́** (*10 A.M.*) and **10 часо́в ве́чера** (*10 P.M.*).

— А когда́ бу́дет новосе́лье?	*"So when will the housewarming be?"*
— В суббо́ту, в семь часо́в ве́чера.	*"On Saturday at 7:00 P.M."*

УПРАЖНЕНИЕ 4   Когда́ начина́ется переда́ча . . . ? (*When does the program X start?*)

Look at the following TV schedule. Find three programs you might like to watch. Write down the names and channels, and then close your book. Your classmate will keep his book open. Ask your classmate when each of the programs starts. (You may need to tell him what channel schedule to look at.) After he looks up the times for the programs you chose, switch roles and do the programs he chose.

ОБРАЗЕ́Ц: — Когда́ начина́ется переда́ча «Футбо́л-кла́сс»? Кана́л
           (*channel*) РТР [эр-тэ-эр] Росси́йские университе́ты.
           — Она́ начина́ется в 9.00 (де́вять часо́в) утра́.

10 ИЮНЯ   СУББОТА

ПЕРВЫЙ КАНАЛ

РТР

2x2 ТЕЛЕКАНАЛ

РТР РОССИЙСКИЕ УНИВЕРСИТЕТЫ

5 САНКТ-ПЕТЕРБУРГ

TV6 МОСКВА

ПЕРВЫЙ КАНАЛ

7.30 «Телеутро»
8.45 Слово пастыря
9.00, 15.00, 1.40 Новости
9.20 «Лего-го!»
9.50 «СЕКРЕТЫ МОЕГО ЛЕТА». Телесериал для детей
10.25 Утренняя почта
11.00 «Смак»
11.15 Здоровье. «Помоги себе сам»
11.50 Провинция. «Русская линия»
12.20 «Радуга»
12.40 Век кино. «ШПИОН В ЧЕРНОМ». (Великобритания)
14.05 Мультфильм
14.25 «Зеркало»
15.20 «Большие гонки»
15.50 К 50-летию Победы. «Будь проклята война». Док. фильм. Фильм 2-й «Сожженная земля»
16.40 В мире животных
17.20 «Смехопанорама»
18.00, 21.00 Время
18.25 Брэйн-ринг
19.15 «ЖАНДАРМ И ИНОПЛАНЕТЯНЕ». Худ.фильм (Франция)
20.45 Спокойной ночи, малыши!
21.45 «ПРИКЛЮЧЕНИЯ ЧАСТНОГО ДЕТЕКТИВА НЕСТОРА БУРМЫ». Телесериал
22.30 «Что? Где? Когда?»
23.35 «До и после»
0.30 «Визит к «Кинотавру»...». Дневник кинофестиваля
0.40 Теннис. Открытый чемпионат Франции. Финал

***

2.05 «ЛЕТНОЕ ПРОИСШЕСТВИЕ». Телефильм. 1-я серия
3.10 «Белорусская эстрада»

РТР

8.00, 14.00, 20.00, 23.00 Вести
8.20 Звезды говорят
8.25 Программа передач
8.30 «Продленка»
8.45 «От винта»
9.00 Пилигрим
9.45 Парламентская неделя
10.30 Футбол без границ
11.15 До Москвы — далеко
12.00 Любимые комедии. «ПЕС БАРБОС И НЕОБЫЧАЙНЫЙ КРОСС», «САМОГОНЩИКИ»
12.45 «В эфире — невидимки»
13.10 Мировая деревня
13.40 Крестьянский вопрос
14.20 Де-факто
14.35 Домашний экран. «МЕГРЭ И ПОРЯДОЧНЫЕ ЛЮДИ». Худ. фильм из сериала «Расследования комиссара Мегрэ». Часть 1-я (Франция)
15.30 Баскетбол. Финал НБА. Передача из США
16.30 Кинофиша
16.45 Праздник каждый день
16.55 Футбол. Чемпионат России. «Спартак» (Москва) — «Локомотив» (Москва)
18.55 «Музыка на десерт»
19.10 Кто мы? «Не в силе Бог, а в правде»
20.25 Киномарафон. «ПУГАЛО». Худ. фильм (США)
22.40 Танц-экспресс
23.30 Река времени
23.35 Автомиг
23.40 «Золотые страницы «Грэмми». Музыкальная программа

2x2 ТЕЛЕКАНАЛ

6.30 Религиозная программа
8.00 Телегазета 2x2
8.15 О строительстве, ремонте и житейских мелочах
8.45 Секреты С. Зверева
9.00 Информационная программа «С 9 до 11»
9.15 «Конан». Мультсериал (США)
11.00, 12.00, 13.00, 14.00, 15.00, 16.00, 17.00, 17.54, 23.01 Новости 2x2
11.05 «Экспедиция». Док. сериал (Венесуэла)
12.10 «Комильфо»
12.30 «Мой чемпион»
13.05 «ДЖОН РОСС». Худ. фильм. 1-я и 2-я серии (США)
14.12 «КАЖДЫЙ ОХОТНИК ЖЕЛАЕТ ЗНАТЬ». Худ. фильм
15.35 «ТОПАЗ». Телесериал (Венесуэла)
16.42 «КАССАНДРА». Телесериал (Венесуэла)
23.11 Экспресс-камера
23.22 «КОМИССАР ШИМАНСКИЙ». Телесериал (Германия)
1.17 «Спид-инфо-видео»
1.37 «Музыкальные новости BIZ TV»

МТК МОСКОВСКАЯ ПРОГРАММА

18.00 Прогноз погоды
18.04 «КОБРА». Телесериал
19.00 Подмосковье
19.30 Причал № 6
20.00 Автосфера
20.30 Без долгов
20.45 Окно
21.30 Все это кино
21.55 Прогноз погоды
22.00 Новости недели

РТР РОССИЙСКИЕ УНИВЕРСИТЕТЫ

8.00 Возвращение к Богу. М. Моргулис
8.30 «Данило и Ненила». Мультфильм. Фильм 1-й и 2-й СЕМЕЙНЫЙ КАНАЛ Ведущий — журналист А. Бедеров
8.55 Анонс Семейного канала
9.00 Футбол-класс
9.15 Десять уроков рисования
9.35 «И это кино». 10-я серия (Франция)
10.00, 14.35, 17.20 Гостиная Семейного канала
10.20 Домовладелец
10.35 СИВ. «Новости кино»
10.55 Нужные вещи
11.15 Медицина для Вас
11.30, 14.30, 17.45 СИВ. Новости
11.35 Научные субботы
12.10 «Открытое письмо». Док. фильм
12.55 Пенсион
13.00 «ШКОЛЬНЫЙ УЧИТЕЛЬ». Сериал (Франция)
13.50 В семейном блокноте
14.15 «Коктейль» для любопытных
15.00 Волейбол. Мировая лига. Россия — Япония
16.10 «Пригласительный билет»
16.55 Удачный день
17.00 СИВ. «Мода: от Кардена до комода»

НТВ

18.00 Детям. «Том и Джерри в детстве», «Семейка Флинстоун». Мультсериалы (США)
19.00 Сегодня
19.35 Телеигра. «Ключи от форта Байяр». (Франция)
20.50 Детям и взрослым. «Авиаторы». Мультфильм
21.00 Сериал по выходным. «ВОЗВРАЩЕНИЕ АРСЕНА ЛЮПЕНА». (Франция)
22.05 «Куклы»
22.25 Кино 80-х. «ЧЕРНАЯ РОЗА — ЭМБЛЕМА ПЕЧАЛИ, КРАСНАЯ РОЗА — ЭМБЛЕМА ЛЮБВИ». Худ. фильм (02:11:27)
0.45 «Третий глаз»
1.30 «Его жена — курица», «Когда-то давно», «Укрощение велосипеда», «Козел-музыкант». Мультфильмы для взрослых

5 САНКТ-ПЕТЕРБУРГ

7.30 Христос во всем мире
8.00 — 11.00 «ДОБРОЕ УТРО»
9.30 «Живьем...»
11.00 Стиль жизни
11.15 Информ-ТВ. Европейский калейдоскоп
11.45 «Жар-птица». Телефильм-балет
12.30 Объектив. «Красок звучные ступени», «Экспертиза века». Док. фильмы
13.10 «Моя музыка». А. Лиепа и его княгинюшка
13.40 Теледоктор
13.55 Программа теледня
14.00 Тест
14.15 Киноканал «Осень». «БЕЛАЯ ПТИЦА С ЧЕРНОЙ ОТМЕТИНОЙ». Худ. фильм
16.00 Футбол. Чемпионат России. «Зенит» (СПБ) — «Луч» (Владивосток)
17.45 «Пусть приплывут дельфины». Телефильм
18.05 «Полосатый хит»
18.45 Программа телевечера
18.50 Экономика и мы
19.05 Телеблиц
19.10 Большой фестиваль
19.30, 22.40 Информ-ТВ
19.50 «Песни нашей памяти»
20.10 Детектив на телеэкране. «Побег». Телеспектакль
22.20 «Наобум»
22.55 Программа телезавтра
23.00 «Оранж-ТВ представляет канал: «Не хочешь — не смотри»
0.00 «Хрустальный ключ». Фестиваль видеоклипов
0.20 «ЗАМОК ПОМПОН РУЖ». Телесериал (Германия)

TV6 МОСКВА

8.00 Дорожный патруль
8.10 Кинотеатр ТВ-6. «ДОНСКАЯ ПОВЕСТЬ»
9.45 Сказки братьев Гримм: «Бременские музыканты»
10.10 «Ералаш»
10.25 Детский сеанс. «АНДРЕЙ И ЗЛОЙ ЧАРОДЕЙ». Мультсериал
11.40 Доброе утро с Л. Лейкиным
12.00 Вояджер». 11-я серия
13.00 Воен-ТВ
13.30 Кинотеатр ТВ-6. «ФАНТАЗИИ ФАРЯТЬЕВА»
16.00 Ток-шоу «Я САМА». «Вот я своего и добилась...»
17.00 Звезды эстрады. Ангел. В.Казаченко
18.40 «Пульс моды» (MTV)
19.00 «Хорошо забытое...»: «Песня-74»
20.00 Катастрофы недели
20.30 Кинотеатр ТВ-6. Сатирический киножурнал «Фитиль»

«ДАЙТЕ ЖАЛОБНУЮ КНИГУ». Худ. фильм
22.20 Кинотеатр ТВ-6. «КУЛАЧНЫЙ БОЕЦ»
0.00 Дорожный патруль
0.10 «На грани» (MTV)
0.55 Ночной сеанс. «АНАТОМИЯ ЛЮБВИ» (Польша) (до 2.20)

СУББОТА

УПРАЖНЕНИЕ 5   Когда́ ты обы́чно . . . ?

Tell when you ordinarily do the following things. Give a specific hour if it makes sense (for example, **в семь часо́в утра́**); otherwise use a general part of the day (for example, **у́тром**).

1. Когда́ ты обы́чно смо́тришь телеви́зор?
2. Когда́ ты обы́чно игра́ешь в баскетбо́л?
3. Когда́ ты обы́чно занима́ешься?
4. Когда́ ты обы́чно начина́ешь занима́ться?
5. Когда́ ты обы́чно зака́нчиваешь занима́ться?
6. Когда́ ты обы́чно гото́вишь обе́д?
7. Когда́ ты обы́чно говори́шь по телефо́ну?
8. Когда́ ты обы́чно получа́ешь по́чту?

◈ 7.15. VERBS OF "STUDYING"

В про́шлом году́ моя́ сестра́ **учи́лась** в Росси́и.	*Last year my sister was studying in Russia.*
Обы́чно я **занима́юсь** до́ма, но сего́дня ве́чером я **бу́ду занима́ться** в библиоте́ке.	*Usually I study at home, but tonight I'll be studying in the library.*
В шко́ле я **учи́л** францу́зский язы́к, а в университе́те **учу́** ру́сский и испа́нский.	*In school I studied French, but in college I'm studying Russian and Spanish.*

As you have already seen, the English verb *to study* covers a range of activities which are rendered by distinct Russian verbs. You might find it useful, when you see the word *study,* to think of a substitute phrase that helps orient you toward the correct Russian verb. In the summary that follows, note how the English meanings and Russian renderings of *study* are presented from the general to the specific. Try keeping that principle in mind as you learn to use these verbs. Note that many of these verbs have no true perfective forms; that is, they express process or state over a period of time rather than result.

1. to study = *to be a student, to attend school* = **учи́ться** (no perfective in this meaning)
   This verb is used to talk about whether you go to school, where you go to school, what department you're in, what year you're in, what kind of student you are, and so on.

— А вы **у́читесь** и́ли рабо́таете?	*"So do you go to school or do you work?"*
— Я студе́нтка, **учу́сь** в университе́те на факульте́те журнали́стики.	*"I'm a student. I study in the journalism department at the university."*
— А где вы **у́читесь**?	*"Where do you go to school?"*
— В медици́нском институ́те. **Я учу́сь** на второ́м ку́рсе.	*"At a medical school. I'm a second-year student."*
Моя́ сестра́ хорошо́ **у́чится.**	*My sister is a good student.*

2. to study = *to prepare for classes, to do homework* = **занима́ться** (no perfective in this meaning)
This verb is used to talk about how much time you spend preparing for classes, where you do it, when you do it, and so on.

Я мно́го **занима́юсь.**	*I study a lot.*
Моя́ подру́га лю́бит **занима́ться** в библиоте́ке.	*My friend likes studying in the library.*
Мой брат ча́сто **занима́ется** но́чью.	*My brother frequently does his homework late at night.*

3. to study = *to learn (or memorize) something specific* = <**учи́ть / вы́учить**
   (+ Accusative direct object)>
This verb is used to talk about something specific that you're learning, such as vocabulary words, lines in a play, a foreign language and so on.

Э́то англи́йские слова́, кото́рые я **учу́.** Спра́ва — слова́, кото́рые я зна́ю, я их уже́ **вы́учила.** Сле́ва — слова́, кото́рые ещё на́до **вы́учить.**	*These are English vocab words that I'm learning. On the right are the words I know. I've already memorized them. On the left are the words I still have to learn.*
— Что де́лает Бори́с?	*"What's Boris doing?"*
— **У́чит** францу́зский.	*"He's studying French."*

Све́та всё у́тро учи́ла англи́йские слова́.

Вот слова́, кото́рые она́ вы́учила.

4. to study = *to study a particular subject over time* = <**изуча́ть** (+ Accusative direct object)> (perfective not introduced at this time)
This verb is used to describe a subject studied in depth over a substantial period of time, such as when one majors or minors in that subject in college.

Джим **изуча́ет** ру́сскую исто́рию.   *Jim studies Russian history.*

5. to study = *to study for an exam, to prepare for an exam (in a certain subject)* = **гото́виться / подгото́виться к экза́мену** (<**по** + Dative>)
This phrase is used when you want to talk specifically about preparing for an exam. Remember that **гото́вить** can mean *to cook, to prepare (food)*; the reflexive verb **гото́виться** means *to prepare oneself* for something, in this case, for an exam **к экза́мену**. **Экза́мен** is usually qualified by the phrase <**по** + Dative> to indicate the subject being tested: **экза́мен по исто́рии** (*an exam in history, a history exam*), **экза́мен по фи́зике,** and so on.

Я не могу́ пойти́ сего́дня ве́чером   *I can't go to the movies tonight.*
в кино́. Мне на́до **гото́виться**   *I have to get ready for a history*
к экза́мену по исто́рии.   *exam.*

6. to study = *to take an academic subject*
The following exchange is a colloquial way of talking about what academic subjects someone is taking.

— Каки́е у тебя́ предме́ты в э́том   *"What subjects are you taking (What*
  семе́стре?   *courses do you have) this semester?"*
— У меня́ хи́мия, исто́рия и ру́сский   *"I have chemistry, history, and*
  язы́к.   *Russian."*

УПРАЖНЕНИЕ 6   Verbs of studying

Fill in the blanks with forms of **учи́ться**, **изуча́ть**, **занима́ться**, and **гото́виться / подгото́виться.**

A. Мой друг Гри́ша у́чится в университе́те, как и я, но я_____[1]
на факульте́те иностра́нных языко́в (*foreign languages*),
а Гри́ша_____[2] на биологи́ческом факульте́те.
Я_____[3] францу́зский язы́к и литерату́ру[†],
а он_____[4] биоло́гию[†]. Мы о́ба (*both*)_____[5]
хорошо́. Ме́жду про́чим, Гри́ша то́же_____[6] францу́зский, и
иногда́ я помога́ю (*help*) ему́_____[7] к экза́мену.

Б. Это было 10 лет назад, когда мой брат Коля ещё _____¹
в школе. Он _____² очень плохо. Каждый день учительница
звонила нашим родителям (*our parents*) и говорила: «Ваш сын очень
плохо _____³». Родители говорили Коле, что он должен
больше (*more*) _____,⁴ а он отвечал (*answered*), что он всё
знает. Когда Коля был в 9-ом классе, он полюбил (*came to like*) историю.
Он начал больше _____⁵. Он очень
хорошо _____⁶ к экзамену по истории и получил «отлично».
Сейчас он _____⁷ в университете на историческом
факультете. Он _____⁸ историю России.

УПРАЖНЕНИЕ 7   Verbs of studying: past tense

Complete **Упражнение 6A** again, this time using the past tense. Begin as follows and
make all necessary changes.

Это было 10 лет назад. Мой друг Гриша учился в университете . . .

УПРАЖНЕНИЕ 8   Как учится Вова? А Лёна?

Complete the following paragraphs with forms of **учиться, учить / выучить,** or
изучать as required by context.

A. Вова _____¹ в школе. Он _____² два языка:
английский и немецкий. Он _____³ неплохо. Его любимый
предмет (*subject*) — английский язык. Ему очень нравятся ковбойские
фильмы. Он говорит, что фильмы помогают ему _____⁴
новые слова. Он _____⁵ английские слова каждый день
и уже _____⁶ все трудные глаголы (*verbs*). Он говорит, что
когда он закончит школу, он будет _____⁷ в университете.
Там он будет _____⁸ не только английский и немецкий, но и
французский.

Б. Когда Лёна училась в школе, она _____¹ русскую литературу[†]
и французский язык. Сейчас она _____² в университете.
Здесь она _____³ английскую литературу и английский язык.
Вчера вечером она _____⁴ английские глаголы.
Она _____⁵ 50 глаголов и знает их хорошо.

УЧИСЬ УЧИТЬСЯ ⭐ *Verbs and the Cases They Govern*

Some verbs that take a direct object in English (*transitive* verbs) take the Dative
case in Russian. **Звонить / позвонить** (*to call someone on the phone*) is one:
Я тебе позвоню (*I'll call you*). **Помогать / помочь** (*to help someone*) also
requires Dative: **Вова помогает Джиму** (*Vova helps Jim*). **Мешать** is another:
Я не хочу вам мешать! (*I don't want to disturb you*). It would be a good idea to
start a list of "non-Accusative" verbs and write down new ones as you encounter
them.

КУЛЬТУРА РЕЧИ

❖ ТАК ГОВОРЯТ: МÉЖДУ ПРÓЧИМ; ПО ÓЧЕРЕДИ

Ты, **мéжду прóчим**, ещё не студéнт.	*You, by the way, are not yet a student (not yet in college.)*
Мéжду прóчим, мои друзья́ говоря́т, что я готóвлю совсéм неплóхо.	*By the way, my friends say that I'm a pretty good cook.*
Муж и жена́ ча́сто готóвят обéд **по óчереди**.	*A husband and wife often take turns doing the cooking.*
Мы готóвили **по óчереди**.	*We took turns doing the cooking.*

УПРАЖНÉНИЕ 9   По óчереди

Match the expression using **по óчереди** with the appropriate situation.

1. _____ You and your roommate each have to make a few phone calls, but you have only one line.

2. _____ Your roommate doesn't like cooking, and you initially volunteered to do most of it. Now you're tired of it, and you want your roommate to do her share.

3. _____ Several kids are simultaneously trying to ask questions in class, interrupting one another. The teacher tells them to take turns asking questions.

а. Пожа́луйста, задава́йте вопрóсы по óчереди.

б. Дава́й (*Let's*) звони́ть по óчереди.

в. Дава́й (*Let's*) готóвить по óчереди.

❖ САМОПРОВÉРКА: УПРАЖНÉНИЕ 10

Working on your own, try this self-test: Read a Russian sentence out loud, then give an idiomatic English equivalent without looking at the book. Then work from English to Russian. After you have completed the activity, try it with a classmate.

1. Ты обяза́тельно дóлжен (должна́) рассказа́ть мне об э́том.

2. Почему́ вы всё врéмя говори́те обо мне?

3. В Амéрике мнóгие мужчи́ны хорошó готóвят.

4. — Скажи́те, пожа́луйста, котóрый час?

   — Сейча́с два часа́.

5. Они́ должны́ быть здесь в пя́тницу, в 9 часóв вéчера.

1. *You absolutely must tell me about that.*

2. *Why are you always talking about me?*

3. *In America many men cook well.*

4. *"Can you please tell me what time it is?"*

   "It's (now) two o'clock."

5. *They're supposed to be here on Friday at 9:00 p.m.*

❖ ВОПРОСЫ И ОТВЕТЫ: УПРАЖНЕНИЕ 11

1. Ты умéешь готóвить? Ты хорошó готóвишь?
2. Что ты умéешь готóвить?
3. Ты лю́бишь готóвить? А есть?
4. Что ты обы́чно готóвишь на зáвтрак (*breakfast*)?
5. Что ты предпочитáешь (*prefer*) — яи́чницу и́ли круты́е я́йца?
6. Что ты обы́чно готóвишь на обéд?
7. Ты лю́бишь борщ (*borsch*)? Ты умéешь готóвить борщ? А суп?
8. А блины́ ты лю́бишь? Ты умéешь их готóвить?
9. Ты лю́бишь óвощи? (*If yes*) Каки́е? А фру́кты ты лю́бишь?
10. Каку́ю ку́хню (*cuisine*) ты предпочитáешь (*prefer*) — францу́зскую, италья́нскую, кита́йскую, япóнскую, ру́сскую?

❖ ДИАЛОГИ

ДИАЛОГ 1   Мóжно попроси́ть . . . ?
(On the phone: Asking to speak to someone who is absent)

— Дóбрый день (Дóброе у́тро/Дóбрый вéчер). Мóжно попроси́ть Вáсю?
— Дóбрый день (Дóброе у́тро/Дóбрый вéчер). Вáси нет, он в университéте.
— А когдá он бу́дет дóма?
— Позвони́те вéчером (чéрез час, зáвтра у́тром).

ДИАЛОГ 2   Приглашéние
(Extending an invitation)

— В воскресéнье мои́ друзья́ бу́дут прáздновать новосéлье. Они́ пригласи́ли меня́, а я приглашáю тебя́.
— А э́то удóбно? Ведь я их не знáю.
— Конéчно, удóбно.
— Что принести́?
— Мóжно принести́ сыр и колбасу́. И́ли лимонáд (*soda pop*).

УПРАЖНЕНИЕ 12   Ваш диалóг

Create a dialogue in which you've just gotten back to town after an extended holiday. Call a friend and exchange information about where you were, what you saw, what you did, and so on.

❖ А ТЕПЕРЬ . . . : УПРАЖНЕНИЕ 13

Working with a classmate, use what you learned in Part 3 to . . .

1. find out what time it is
2. ask who usually cooks at his home
3. find out if he cooks, and if so, if he likes doing it
4. ask if he's a good cook, and what he likes to cook

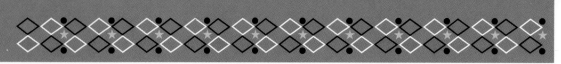

ЧАСТЬ ЧЕТВЁРТАЯ

С ЧЕГО НАЧАТЬ?

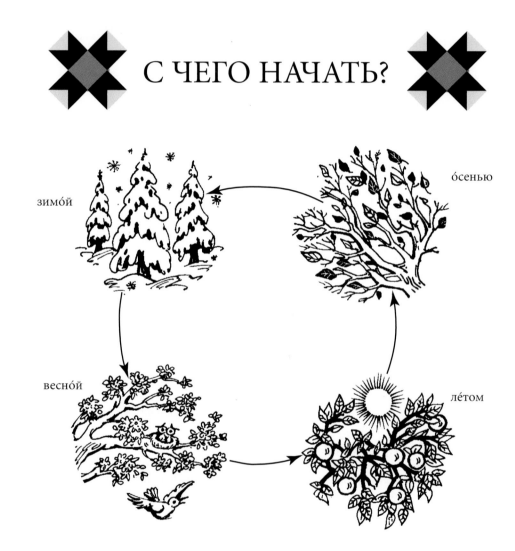

зимóй

óсенью

веснóй

лéтом

�֍ ЧТЕНИЕ ✖

❖ БЫ́ЛО О́ЧЕНЬ ВЕ́СЕЛО!°

Бы́ло...! *It was a lot of fun!*

14-XI

Дорога́я ма́мочка!

У меня́ замеча́тельная **но́вость**°: мы **наконе́ц**° **нашли́**° ко́мнату, кото́рая нам о́чень **понра́вилась,**° и уже́ перее́хали.° Нам нра́вится райо́н и нра́вится, что дом но́вый. Пра́вда, э́то далеко́ от це́нтра, но зато́ авто́бусная остано́вка ря́дом и метро́ бли́зко.

news / finally / found / кото́рая... which we really liked / moved

На́ша хозя́йка, Татья́на Дми́триевна, — о́чень **прия́тная**° же́нщина. Она́ библио́граф,† рабо́тает в библиоте́ке. Когда́ мы **сня́ли**° ко́мнату, там бы́ло всё, что ну́жно. Пра́вда, не́ было стола́, но нам повезло́: у на́шего сосе́да Са́ши Кругло́ва был стол, кото́рый ему́ был не ну́жен, и он **подари́л**° э́тот стол нам.

nice
rented

gave

Вообще́,° сосе́ди у нас хоро́шие. Са́ша Кругло́в — студе́нт консервато́рии, пиани́ст. В на́шем подъе́зде живёт Илья́ Ильи́ч Петро́вский — он преподаёт у Та́ни на факульте́те. Она́ говори́т, что он о́чень хорошо́ чита́ет ле́кции.° Вчера́ мы вме́сте жда́ли авто́буса, и он **спроси́л**° меня́, люблю́ **ли я**° **литерату́ру**.† Я **сказа́ла,**° что да, о́чень люблю́. **Тогда́**° он улыбну́лся° и спроси́л, по́мню ли я, каку́ю литерату́рную† герои́ню° зову́т Татья́на Дми́триевна — как на́шу хозя́йку. Я не могла́ вспо́мнить.° Тут мы **уви́дели**° авто́бус, и Илья́ Ильи́ч «**помо́г**»° мне: он спроси́л, хорошо́ ли я зна́ю «Евге́ния Оне́гина».⁶ Действи́тельно, Татья́на в «Евге́нии Оне́гине» — то́же Татья́на Дми́триевна!

All in all

о́чень... is a really good lecturer / asked / люблю́... whether I like / said / Then / smiled / heroine recall / saw / helped

В про́шлую суббо́ту мы пра́здновали новосе́лье. Бы́ли на́ши сосе́ди — Са́ша Кругло́в и Ле́на Си́лина (она́ у́чится в университе́те, на факульте́те журнали́стики). Ещё мы пригласи́ли Джи́ма Ри́чардсона. Джим — аспира́нт профе́ссора Петро́вского, он прие́хал в Москву́ на год.° Был ещё оди́н гость — бизнесме́н† Ви́ктор. Он **пришёл**° к Татья́не Дми́триевне° по де́лу,° и она́ нас познако́мила с ним.° Он нам понра́вился, и мы пригласи́ли его́ оста́ться.° Джим принёс° гита́ру, и мы пе́ли° ру́сские и америка́нские **пе́сни.**° Бы́ло о́чень ве́село!

came / на... for a year
came / к... to Tatyana Dmitrievna's / по... on business
нас... introduced us to him / to stay
brought / sang / songs

Ма́мочка, мне пора́ в институ́т. Кре́пко целу́ю.°

Кре́пко... *Lots of love*

Све́та

---

⁶«**Евге́ний Оне́гин**» is the title of a famous novel in verse by A. S. Pushkin.

УПРАЖНЕНИЕ 1 Под микроскопом

In her letter home Sveta has used many perfective verbs to tell her mother about particular events that have taken place since her last letter. Circle at least one in each paragraph (most paragraphs contain more than one). After finding the perfective verbs, copy them onto a list and beside each, provide its infinitive form.

ГРАММАТИКА И ПРАКТИКА

◈◈◈ О РОССИИ ◈◈◈◈◈◈◈◈◈◈◈

ПУ́ШКИН И «ЕВГЕ́НИЙ ОНЕ́ГИН»

Илья́ Ильи́ч спроси́л, хорошо́ ли я зна́ю «Евге́ния Оне́гина».

Алекса́ндр Серге́евич Пу́шкин (1799–1837) is revered by Russians as their greatest poet. One of his most renowned works is his novel in verse, **«Евге́ний Оне́гин»** (*Eugene Onegin*), named for its alienated antihero who first rejects, then longs for **Татья́на,** a romantic girl possessing the strong and deep character **Оне́гин** lacks. The poem presents a lush panorama of Russian life, and is the basis for Tchaikovsky's opera of the same name. Other operas inspired by the works of Pushkin include the following: Glinka's **«Русла́н и Людми́ла»** (*Ruslan and Ludmila*), Mussorgsky's **«Бори́с Годуно́в»** (*Boris Godunov*), Tchaikovsky's **«Пи́ковая да́ма»** (*The Queen of Spades*), and two works by Rimsky-Korsakov: **«Ска́зка о царе́ Салта́не»** (*The Tale of Tsar Saltan*) and **«Золото́й петушо́к»** (*The Golden Cockerel*).

◈ 7.16. PAST TENSE OF VERBS LIKE МОЧЬ / СМОЧЬ

Я не **могла́** вспо́мнить. Тут мы уви́дели авто́бус, и Илья́ Ильи́ч «**помо́г**» мне . . . .

I couldn't recall. Just then we saw the bus, and Ilya Ilyich "helped" me . . . .

The past tense of many verbs ending in **-чь** follows the pattern of the past tense of **мочь / смочь**.

	МОЧЬ	**СМОЧЬ**	**ПОМОЧЬ**
он	мог	смог	помог
оно́	мог-ло́	смог-ло́	помог-ло́
она́	мог-ла́	смог-ла́	помог-ла́
они́	мог-ли́	смог-ли́	помог-ли́

УПРАЖНЕНИЕ 2   The verbs мочь / смочь and помо́чь

Complete the following text with an appropriate form of **мочь / смочь** or **помо́чь**.

Я не_____¹ жить без (*without*) телеви́зора. Вчера́ мой
телеви́зор не рабо́тал. Не́ было зву́ка. Я не_____² почини́ть
его́ и попроси́л (*asked*) моего́ дру́га Вади́ма мне_____.³ Вади́м
сказа́л, что он не_____⁴ мне_____,⁵ потому́ что
не уме́ет чини́ть телеви́зоры, но что у него́ есть друг (его́ зову́т Же́ня),
кото́рый уме́ет чини́ть всё. Вади́м позвони́л Же́не на рабо́ту, а пото́м
позвони́л мне и сказа́л, что Же́ня_____⁶ мне. Но у Же́ни
мно́го рабо́ты, и он_____⁷ прийти́ то́лько в 9 часо́в ве́чера. Он
действи́тельно пришёл в 9. Он почини́л (*fixed*) телеви́зор о́чень бы́стро, и
мы все_____⁸ посмотре́ть фигу́рное ката́ние (*figure skating*).

◈ 7.17. PAST TENSE OF -ТИ́ VERBS

Джим **принёс** гита́ру.	*Jim brought his guitar.*
Он **пришёл** к Татья́не Дми́триевне по де́лу.	*He had come to see Tatiana Dmitrievna on business.*
Мы наконе́ц **нашли́** ко́мнату, кото́рая нам о́чень понра́вилась.	*We finally found a room that we really liked.*
Уро́ки — пото́м. Бе́лка, **пошли́**!	*Homework—later. Belka, let's go!*

Although the Russian past tense is remarkably regular, a few verbs present different patterns, particularly those that end in **-ти́.** Infinitives in **-ти́** lose this stressed ending in all forms (just as other verbs lose **-ть**). When an infinitive has this stressed **-ти́** ending, all other forms of the verb (past, non-past, imperatives) are also end-stressed. Here, for example, is a table with the past tense of the perfective verb **принести́** *to bring*. Note that the masculine form has no **-л** and it has **-ё-** rather than **-е-.**

	принес-ти́
он	принёс
оно́	принес-ла́
она́	принес-ло́
они́	принес-ли́

Many other **-ти́** verbs are actually based on the verb **идти́** (*to go*), where **-йти́** is a "combining" form of **идти́** used with prefixes.

All prefixed **-йти́** forms are perfective, almost all are end-stressed, and all are conjugated similarly. Here is a table comparing the past tense of three more **-йти́** verbs you have seen: **прийти́** (*to come; to arrive*), **найти́** (*to find*), **пойти́** (*to go*). In the following table the prefixes have been separated by a hyphen to help you see the pattern.

	при-йти́	**на-йти́**	**по-йти́**
он	при-шёл	на-шёл	по-шёл
оно́	при-шло́	на-шло́	по-шло́
она́	при-шла́	на-шла́	по-шла́
они́	при-шли́	на-шли́	по-шли́

Remember that if you are asking a question with **кто** always use the masculine singular form: **Кто принёс гита́ру? Кто нашёл твой рюкза́к?**

УПРАЖНЕНИЕ 3   Verbs in -ти́

Fill in the blanks in the following text with an appropriate form of **принести́, прийти́, найти́,** or **пойти́.**

Моя́ подру́га Ю́ля — студе́нтка Моско́вского университе́та. Сейча́с она́ у́чится в на́шем университе́те. Вчера́ она́ _____[1] ко мне (*to my place*) и сказа́ла, что не мо́жет _____[2] свой (*her*) па́спорт. Я _____[3] к ней в общежи́тие (*to her dormitory*), но мы ничего́ не _____.[4] Тогда́ мы вме́сте _____[5] в Междунаро́дный отде́л (*Office of International Programs*) университе́та. Ю́ля _____[6] ви́зу и други́е докуме́нты.† Когда́ она́ рассказа́ла дире́ктору Междунаро́дного отде́ла, что случи́лось (*happened*), он улыбну́лся (*smiled*) и сказа́л: «Ваш па́спорт у нас. Его́ _____[7] оди́н наш аспира́нт. Он _____[8] к нам (*to our place*) полчаса́ наза́д и сказа́л, что _____[9] па́спорт ру́сской студе́нтки. Он _____[10] его́ в университе́тском кафе́». Ю́ля была́ о́чень ра́да, что па́спорт нашёлся (*was found*), и мы _____[11] в университе́тское кафе́ пить ко́фе.

УПРАЖНЕНИЕ 4   Когда́ они́ пришли́? Что они́ принесли́?

Your neighbors had a party this weekend, but you and your classmate were not invited. Now you're on the phone piecing together what each of you knows about the event. Take turns asking when different people arrived and what they brought with them, and fill in the table below. (Your classmate's table is in Appendix K.)

ОБРАЗЕ́Ц: — Когда́ пришла́ Ната́ша?
— Она́ пришла́ в шесть часо́в.
— Кто принёс пласти́нки?
— Пласти́нки принесла́ Лю́да.
— Кто пришёл в 6:00 (шесть часо́в)?
— В 6:00 (шесть часо́в) пришли́ Мари́на и Ко́ля.

КТО?	КОГДА?	ЧТО?
Стёпа	6:00	
Áлла		гитáру
Тóля		пи́ццу
	7:00	цветы́
Вáля и Ви́тя		пирожки́

◇ О РОССИИ ◇◇◇◇◇◇◇◇◇◇◇◇◇◇◇◇◇◇◇

WRITING A PERSONAL LETTER

> *18.12.2001 г.*
>   *Дорогóй Гéна!*
> *Спаси́бо за интерéсное письмó. Извини́, что я давнó не писáла.*
> . . . .
> *Привéт пáпе и мáме. Пиши́.*
>   *Вéра*

14 – XI

Дорогая мамочка! Получила ли ты моё последнее письмо? Всё ли в порядке дома? Неделю назад мы – Таня и я – сняли очень хорошую комнату. Нашу хозяйку зовут Татьяна Дмитриевна, она работает в библиотеке. Нам очень нравится и хозяйка, и наша комната. Когда мы сняли комнату, там было всё, что нужно, но не было стола. Мы повесили объявление в подъезде, и наш сосед Саша Круглов (он музыкант, учится в консерватории) подарил нам стол. Сейчас у нас всё есть. . . . Мамочка, мне пора в институт. Крепко целую. Света.

A personal letter in Russia typically includes the following four features.

1. The date is usually written numerically in the order day, month, and year, with dashes, slashes or dots separating the three, followed by **г.** (for **гóда** *of the year*). Some Russians use a Roman numeral for the month.

2. The return address is usually given on the envelope rather than in the letter itself.

3. The greeting **Дорогóй (Дорогáя),** followed by the addressee's name (or name and patronymic), is usually indented and followed by an exclamation mark.

4. Appropriate closings depend on how close the relationship is between the writer and the addressee. Generally the writer extends greetings to other known members of the family and may urge the addressee to write back soon.

◇◆◇◆◇◆◇◆◇◆◇◆◇◆◇◆◇◆◇◆◇◆◇◆◇◆◇◆◇◆◇◆◇◆◇

◆ 7.18. REPORTED SPEECH

Онá сéрдится: «Сáша, не смей выбрáсывать стол! На чём ты бýдешь писáть?»	*She gets angry: "Sasha, don't you dare throw out the table! What will you write on?"*
Онá говори́т, что он óчень хорошó читáет лéкции.	*She says that he gives good lectures.*

When you want to report what someone else has said, you can quote that person directly or you can convey the thought without necessarily using the same words. Consider the following examples.

а. — Я принесу́ гита́ру.	*"I'll bring (my) guitar."*
б. Джим сказа́л: — Я принесу́ гита́ру.	*Jim said, "I'll bring (my) guitar."*
в. Джим сказа́л, что он **принесёт** гита́ру.	*Jim said that he would bring (his) guitar.*

In the first example Jim is talking. In the second, someone is stating Jim's exact words in the form of a direct quote. In the third, which shows reported speech, someone gives the substance of what Jim said without directly quoting him. Whereas reported speech in English often involves changes in verb tense (as in the third example), reported speech in Russian retains the original tense and aspect used by the speaker (in this case, future tense and perfective aspect). The only change is that of person (in this case, from **я** to **он**). As in English, other appropriate changes are made as well; for example, **мой** or **наш** might logically have to change to **его́** or **их,** respectively.

УПРАЖНЕНИЕ 5   Что говори́т Ве́ра?

Your friend Vera has told you over the phone about the kind of day she expects to have. Tell a classmate what she said to you.

ОБРАЗЕ́Ц: — Сего́дня у меня́ мно́го рабо́ты.
             — *Ве́ра говори́т, что сего́дня у неё мно́го рабо́ты.*

1. — У́тром я пойду́ в спортза́л.
2. — Пото́м мне на́до пригото́вить карто́фельный сала́т (*potato salad*).
3. — Когда́ я пригото́влю карто́фельный сала́т, я позвоню́ Та́не.
4. — Я приглашу́ её в кино́.
5. — В 3 часа́ мне на́до быть в университе́те.
6. — Там бу́дет интере́сная ле́кция.
7. — По́сле ле́кции бу́дет диску́ссия.[†]
8. — Пото́м я пойду́ в магази́н и куплю́ пода́рок ма́ме.
9. — Я хочу́ купи́ть ей компа́кт-ди́ски.
10. — Ве́чером я бу́ду до́ма. Я бу́ду смотре́ть телеви́зор.

◈ 7.19. *WHETHER (OR NOT)*: INQUIRIES USING ЛИ

Кака́я ра́зница, симпати́чный он **и́ли нет!**	*What difference does it make whether he's cute!*
Вчера́ мы вме́сте жда́ли авто́буса, и он спроси́л меня́, **люблю́ ли я** литерату́ру.	*Yesterday we were waiting for a bus together and he asked me if I like literature.*
Он улыбну́лся и спроси́л, **по́мню ли я,** каку́ю литерату́рную геро́иню зову́т Татья́на Дми́триевна.	*He smiled and asked whether I know what literary heroine is named Tatyana Dmitrievna.*
Он спроси́л, **хорошо́ ли я зна́ю** «Евге́ния Оне́гина».	*He asked whether I know* Eugene Onegin *well.*

There are two ways to embed "whether (or not)" questions in a sentence. In conversational Russian, place the focus of the inquiry (which is often the verb) at the beginning of the dependent clause and **и́ли нет** at the end.

Я не зна́ю, **купи́л** он маши́ну **и́ли нет.**

In a more formal style, the focus of inquiry is still placed at the beginning of the dependent clause, where it is followed by the particle **ли.**

Я не зна́ю, **купи́л ли** он маши́ну.

УПРАЖНЕНИЕ 6 *Whether (if) questions*

Translate the following sentences using **и́ли нет** or **ли.**

ОБРАЗЕ́Ц: Ask him whether (if) he wants to play basketball. →
Спроси́ его́, хо́чет ли он игра́ть в баскетбо́л (хо́чет он игра́ть в баскетбо́л и́ли нет).

1. (ли *or* и́ли нет) Ask Tanya whether (if) she wants to go to the movies.
Спроси́ Та́ню, . . .
2. (ли) Professor Petrovsky wants to know whether (if) I love Pushkin.
Профе́ссор Петро́вский хо́чет знать, . . .
3. (ли) Ask Lena whether (if) she knows Eugene Onegin well.
Спроси́ Ле́ну, . . .
4. (ли *or* и́ли нет) Tanya is asking Jim whether (if) he found his backpack.
Та́ня спра́шивает Джи́ма, . . .
5. (ли *or* и́ли нет) Sveta asked Jim whether (if) he brought a guitar.
Све́та спроси́ла Джи́ма, . . .
6. (ли *or* и́ли нет) We will ask Jim whether (if) he likes pirozhki.
Мы спро́сим Джи́ма, . . .

СЛОВА, СЛОВА, СЛОВА . . . ✪ *To Wait For: <жда́ть + Genitive> vs. <жда́ть + Accusative>*

| Вчера́ мы вме́сте жда́ли **авто́буса.** . . . | *Yesterday we were waiting for a bus together.* . . . |

Жда́ть (*to wait for*) takes either the Accusative or the Genitive case, depending on the definiteness of the object. Abstract nouns and nouns expressing general notions are used in the Genitive, while nouns denoting persons and concrete/specific objects are used in the Accusative. This difference is usually rendered in English by one's choice of the indefinite or definite article.

| Мы ждём **авто́буса.** (Genitive) | *We're waiting for a bus.* (The speaker is telling the listener, in general terms, why he's there.) |
| Мы ждём **авто́бус.** (Accusative) | *We're waiting for the bus.* (The speaker has a particular bus in mind and assumes the reference is also shared by the listener.) |

КУЛЬТУРА РЕЧИ

❖❖ ТАК ГОВОРЯТ: — ПРА́ВДА? — НЕ МО́ЖЕТ БЫТЬ!

If you look up **пра́вда** in a dictionary, the first meaning you'll see is *truth,* which was also the name of a famous Soviet newspaper. But **пра́вда** has a wide range of conversational use: It can express concession, surprise, astonishment, disbelief, irony, and so on. The phrase **Не мо́жет быть!** is used to react to something with doubt or amazement. Consider the following examples.

Пра́вда, э́то далеко́ от це́нтра, но зато́ . . .	*Granted it's far from downtown, but . . .*
Пра́вда, не́ было стола́.	*True, there was no table.*
Э́то наш пода́рок вам. **Пра́вда,** ба́бушка?»	*It's our gift to you. Right, Grandma?*
— В понеде́льник, в сре́ду и в пя́тницу я рабо́таю ве́чером.	*"On Mondays, Wednesdays, and Fridays I work in the evening."*
— **Пра́вда?** А где ты рабо́таешь?	*"Oh, really? Where do you work?"*
— Ты зна́ешь, что наш но́мер 155-94-79, а но́мер городско́й спра́вочной — 155-94-89 . . .	*"You know our number is 155-94-79, and the city information number is 155-94-89 . . ."*
— **Не мо́жет быть!**	*"That can't be!"*

УПРАЖНЕНИЕ 7   — Пра́вда? — Не мо́жет быть!

How good a liar are you? Working with a classmate, make statements about yourself or someone you know. If your classmate thinks you're telling the truth, she will respond: **Пра́вда?** You can then respond: **Че́стное сло́во!** (*Honest!*). If your classmate thinks you've made the statement up, she will respond: **Не мо́жет быть!** You can then respond: **Э́то шу́тка!** Some sample opening statements are provided to help you get started.

1. В воскресе́нье но́чью у нас бы́ло небольшо́е землетрясе́ние (*earthquake*).
2. Я хорошо́ говорю́ по-испа́нски и по-неме́цки.
3. Мой брат игра́ет в рок-гру́ппе.
4. Вчера́ я ви́дела в универса́ме Джея Ле́но.
5. ???

❖❖ САМОПРОВЕ́РКА: УПРАЖНЕНИЕ 8

Working on your own, try this self-test: Read a Russian sentence out loud, then give an idiomatic English equivalent without looking at the book. Then work from English to Russian. After you have completed the activity, try it with a classmate.

1. Я не могла́ вспо́мнить. Тут мы уви́дели авто́бус, и Илья́ Ильи́ч «помо́г» мне . . . .

1. *I couldn't recall. Just then we saw the bus, and Ilya Ilyich "helped" me . . . .*

2. Мы наконе́ц нашли́ ко́мнату, кото́рая нам о́чень понра́вилась.

3. Он пришёл к Татья́не Дми́триевне по де́лу.

4. Джим сказа́л, что он принесёт гита́ру и пригото́вит пи́ццу.

5. Вчера́ мы вме́сте жда́ли авто́буса, и он спроси́л меня́, люблю́ ли я литерату́ру.

2. *We finally found a room that we really liked.*

3. *He had come to see Tatiana Dmitrievna on business.*

4. *Jim said he'd bring his guitar and make pizza.*

5. *Yesterday we were waiting for a bus together and he asked me if I like literature.*

❖ ВОПРОСЫ И ОТВЕТЫ: УПРАЖНЕНИЕ 9

1. Тебе́ нра́вится твоя́ кварти́ра (твой дом)?

2. Ты живёшь в но́вом до́ме и́ли в ста́ром?

3. Ты снима́ешь кварти́ру? (*If yes*) Когда́ ты её снял (сняла́)?

4. Когда́ ты туда́ перее́хал (перее́хала) (*moved*)?

5. Ты живёшь в це́нтре? Далеко́ (Недалеко́) от це́нтра?

6. Что тебе́ нра́вится и что не нра́вится в твоём райо́не?

7. Метро́ и авто́бус далеко́ от твоего́ до́ма?

8. Где рабо́тает твой хозя́ин (твоя́ хозя́йка)?

9. У тебя́ бы́ло новосе́лье, когда́ ты перее́хал (перее́хала) на э́ту кварти́ру? (*If yes*) Кого́ ты пригласи́л (пригласи́ла) на новосе́лье?

10. Ты мно́го чита́ешь? Каки́е кни́ги ты лю́бишь?

11. Каки́е америка́нские писа́тели (*writers*) тебе́ нра́вятся? А ру́сские?

12. Кто твои́ люби́мые литерату́рные геро́и (*heroes*)?

❖ ДИАЛОГИ

ДИАЛОГ 1 Вы давно́ тут живёте?
(Discussing living arrangements)

— Та́ня, познако́мьтесь, э́то Ми́ша и его́ друг Ко́ля. Они́ снима́ют ко́мнату у на́шей сосе́дки.

— Ми́ша, вы давно́ тут живёте?

— Нет, не о́чень. Мы сня́ли ко́мнату ме́сяц наза́д.

— Вам тут нра́вится?

— Да, нам нра́вятся и ко́мната и хозя́йка. И авто́бусная остано́вка бли́зко.

ДИАЛОГ 2 Ты уже́ снял кварти́ру?
(Discussing living arrangements)

— Ты уже́ снял кварти́ру?

— Да. В о́чень хоро́шем райо́не.

— Ты там живёшь оди́н?

— Нет, коне́чно! Мы снима́ем большу́ю кварти́ру. Мне така́я больша́я кварти́ра не нужна́. Кро́ме того́, э́то до́рого.

— Кто э́то «мы»?

— Мы — э́то я и мои́ шко́льные друзья́ Ва́дик Росто́вцев и Пе́тя Гузе́нко. Мы всё де́лаем по о́череди: покупа́ем проду́кты, гото́вим, убира́ем (*clean*) кварти́ру. В воскресе́нье моя́ о́чередь (*turn*) гото́вить обе́д. Ребя́та (*The guys*) говоря́т, что я гото́влю непло́хо. Приходи́ к нам (*to our place*) в воскресе́нье обе́дать (*to have dinner*)!

УПРАЖНЕНИЕ 10   Ваш диалóг

You're interested in learning more about someone your roommate was talking to today in the library. Create a dialogue in which you ask what she knows about this person: where she lives, what she likes to do, what kind of music she likes, when she generally studies in the library, if she works and where, and so on.

❖❖ А ТЕПÉРЬ ...: УПРАЖНЕНИЕ 11

Working with a classmate, use what you learned in Part 4 to ...

1. find out if she knows whether a mutual friend likes Gershwin (or some other composer or musician whom you like)
2. say that you need to study your Russian tonight, and invite her to study at your place
3. tell her that you couldn't study last night because you had to work
4. ask if she was in class yesterday; if so, does she know whether the teacher talked about the term paper
5. ask if she is going to the library this afternoon; tell her you're going home because you're waiting for a letter

ИТАК ...

❖❖ НОВЫЕ СЛОВА

NOUNS AND NOUN PHRASES

Food and Drinks

винó	wine (3)
картóшка *coll.*	potatoes (3v)
крутóе яйцó	hard-boiled egg (3v)
лук	onions (3v)
мя́со	meat (3)
обéд	dinner; afternoon meal (3)
óвощи	vegetables (3)
ры́ба	fish (3)
яйцó (*pl.* я́йца)	egg (3v)

Time

вéчер	evening (1)
врéмя (*Gen., Dat., and Prep. sing.* врéмени) *neut.*	time (1)

полчаса́	half an hour (2)
час (*Gen. sing.* ча́са *but* 2, 3, 4 часа́; *Prep. sing.* в... часу́; *pl.* часы́)	1. hour; 2. (*when telling time*) o'clock (1v)

Studies and Work

диплóм	diploma (1)
заня́тия *pl. only*	classes (1)
зáработ(о)к (*Gen. sing.* зáработка)	pay (1)
литератýра	literature (4)
собрáние	meeting (1v)
экзáмен	exam (3)

Leisure

знакóмый/знакóмая *noun, declines like adj.*	acquaintance (2)
пéсня	song (4)
приглашéние	invitation (2v)
футбóл	soccer (2v)

Other Nouns

грамм	gram (3v)
ка́рточка	card (1)
килогра́мм	kilogram (3v)
мно́гие *noun, declines like adj.*	many people; many (3)
но́вость (*pl.* но́вости)	news (4)
спра́вочная *noun, declines like adj.*	information; directory assistance (2)

PRONOUNS

Prepositional Pronouns

(о) ком	(about) whom (3)
(о) чём	(about) what (3)
(об) э́том	(about) this, that, it (3)
(обо) мне	(about) me (3)
(о) тебе́ (*informal sing.*)	(about) you (3)
(о) нём	(about) him, it (3)
(о) ней	(about) her, it (3)
(о) нас	(about) us (3)
(о) вас (*formal or pl.*)	(about) you (3)
(о) них	(about) them (3)

ADJECTIVES

англи́йский	English (1)
како́й-то	some (2)
мно́гие *pl. only*	many (3)
прекра́сный	wonderful (1)
прия́тный	nice; pleasant (4)
удо́бный	convenient (1)

VERBS

VERBS WITH WHICH YOU ARE FAMILIAR WHOSE ASPECTUAL PAIR IS INTRODUCED IN LESSON 7

ви́деть (ви́ж-у, ви́д-ишь, … ви́д-ят) *pfv.* уви́деть	to see (4)
говори́ть (говор-ю́, говор-и́шь, … говор-я́т) *pfv.* сказа́ть (скаж-у́, ска́ж-ешь, … ска́ж-ут)	1. (*impfv. only*) to speak; to talk; 2. to say; to tell (4)
гото́вить (гото́вл-ю, гото́в-ишь, … гото́в-ят) *pfv.* приготовить	to cook (3)
дава́ть (да-ю́, да-ёшь, … да-ю́т) *pfv.* дать (да-м, да-шь, да-ст, дад-и́м, дад-и́те, дад-у́т; *past* дал, дала́, да́ло, да́ли)	to give (2)
де́лать (де́ла-ю, де́ла-ешь, … де́ла-ют) *pfv.* сде́лать	1. to do; 2. to make (3)
нра́виться (*usu. 3rd person* нра́в-ится, нра́в-ятся) (+ *Dat.*) *pfv.* понра́виться	to be pleasing (to someone) (4)
опа́здывать (опа́здыва-ю, опа́здыва-ешь, … опа́здыва-ют) *pfv.* опозда́ть (опозда́-ю, опозда́-ешь, … опозда́-ют)	to be late (2)
мочь (мог-у́, мо́ж-ешь, … мог-ут *pfv.* смочь *past* мог, могла́, могло́, могли́)	to be able (4)
писа́ть (пиш-у́, пи́ш-ешь, … пи́ш-ут) *pfv.* написа́ть	to write (1)
покупа́ть (покупа́-ю, покупа́-ешь, … покупа́-ют) *pfv.* купи́ть (купл-ю́, ку́п-ишь, … ку́п-ят)	to buy (2)
помога́ть (помога́-ю, помога́-ешь, … помога́-ют) (+ *Dat.*) *pfv.* помо́чь (помог-у́, помо́ж-ешь, … помо́г-ут; *past* помо́г, помогла́, помогло́, помогли́)	to help (4)

понима́ть (понима́-ю, понима́-ешь, . . . понима́-ют) *pfv.* поня́ть (пойм-у́, пойм-ёшь, . . . пойм-у́т; *past* по́нял, поняла́, по́няло, по́няли)	to understand (3)
приноси́ть (принош-у́, принос-ишь, . . . принос-ят) *pfv.* принести́ (принес-у́, принес-ёшь, . . . принес-у́т; *past* принёс, принесла́, принесло́, принесли́)	to bring (3)
слу́шать (слу́ша-ю, слу́ша-ешь, . . . слу́ша-ют) *pfv.* послу́шать	to listen (to) (2)
снима́ть (снима́-ю, снима́-ешь, . . . снима́-ют) *pfv.* снять (сним-у́, сни́м-ешь, . . . сни́м-ут; *past* снял, сняла́, сня́ло, сня́ли)	to rent (4)
спра́шивать (спра́шива-ю, спра́шива-ешь, . . . спра́шива-ют) *pfv.* спроси́ть (спрош-у́, спро́с-ишь, . . . спро́с-ят)	1. (+ *Acc.* or <у + *Gen.*>) to ask (someone); 2. (+ *Acc.* or <o + *Prep.*>) to ask (about); to inquire (4)
чита́ть (чита́-ю, чита́-ешь, . . . чита́-ют) *pfv.* прочита́ть	to read (1)

NEW VERBS ENCOUNTERED AND ACTIVE IN LESSON 7

дари́ть (дар-ю́, да́р-ишь, . . . да́р-ят)(+ *Dat.* + *Acc.*) *pfv.* подари́ть	to give (*as a present*) (4)
зака́нчивать (зака́нчива-ю, зака́нчива-ешь, . . . зака́нчива-ют) *pfv.* зако́нчить (зако́нч-у, зако́нч-ишь, . . . зако́нч-ат)	to finish (1)
занима́ться (занима́-юсь, занима́-ешься, . . . занима́-ются) *no pfv. in this meaning*	to study (1)
звони́ть (звон-ю́, звон-и́шь, . . . звон-я́т) (+ *Dat.*) *pfv.* позвони́ть	to call; to phone (1v)
изуча́ть (изуча́-ю, изуча́-ешь, . . . изуча́-ют) *pfv. not introduced at this time*	to study (in depth) (3)
конча́ть (конча́-ю, конча́-ешь, . . . конча́-ют) *pfv.* ко́нчить (ко́нч-у, ко́нч-ишь, . . . ко́нч-ат)	to finish (2)
меша́ть (меша́-ю, меша́-ешь, . . . меш-а́ют) *pfv.* помеша́ть (+ *Dat.*)	to bother; to disturb (1)
находи́ть (нахож-у́, нахо́д-ишь, . . . нахо́д-ят) *pfv.* найти́ (найд-у́, найд-ёшь, . . . найд-у́т; *past* нашёл, нашла́, нашло́, нашли́)	to find (4)
начина́ть (начина́-ю, начина́-ешь, . . . начина́-ют) *pfv.* нача́ть (начн-у́, начн-ёшь, . . . начн-у́т; *past* на́чал, начала́, на́чало, на́чали)	to begin (2)
объясня́ть (объясня́-ю, объясня́-ешь, . . . объясня́-ют) *pfv.* объясни́ть (объясн-ю́, объясн-и́шь, . . . объясн-я́т)	to explain (2)

попада́ть (попада́-ю, попада́-ешь, . . . попада́-ют) *куда́* *pfv.* попа́сть (попад-у́, попад-ёшь, . . . попад-у́т; *past* попа́л, попа́ла, попа́ло, попа́ли)	to end up calling (some place) (2)
пра́здновать (пра́здну-ю, пра́здну-ешь, . . . пра́здну-ют) *pfv.* отпра́здновать	to celebrate (3)
предлага́ть (предлага́-ю, предлага́-ешь, . . . предлага́-ют) *pfv.* предложи́ть (предлож-у́, предло́ж-ишь, . . . предло́ж-ат)	1. to offer; 2. to suggest (1)
приглаша́ть (приглаша́-ю, приглаша́-ешь, . . . приглаша́-ют) *pfv.* пригласи́ть (приглаш-у́, приглас-и́шь, . . . приглас-я́т)	to invite (1)
приходи́ть (прихож-у́, прихо́д-ишь, . . . прихо́д-ят) *pfv.* прийти́ (прид-у́, прид-ёшь, . . . прид-у́т; *past* пришёл, пришла́, пришло́, пришли́)	to come; to arrive; to come back (4)
расска́зывать (расска́зыва-ю, расска́зыва-ешь, . . . расска́зыва-ют) *pfv.* рассказа́ть (расскаж-у́, расска́ж-ешь, . . . расска́ж-ут)	to tell; to relate (3)
учи́ть (уч-у́, у́ч-ишь, . . . у́ч-ат) *pfv.* вы́учить (вы́уч-у, вы́уч-ишь, . . . вы́уч-ат)	to study (something); (to try) to memorize (1) *pfv.* learn; to memorize (1)

ADVERBS

весно́й	in the spring (1)
вме́сте	together (3)
вообще́	all in all (4)
днём	in the afternoon (1)
зимо́й	in the winter (1)
ле́том	in the summer (1)
наза́д (*or* тому́ наза́д)	ago (2)
наконе́ц	finally (4)
но́чью	at night (1)
о́сенью	in the fall (1)
сюда́ (*indicates direction*)	here; this way (2)
тогда́	then (4)
тру́дно	(it's/that's) difficult; (it's/that's) hard (1)

OTHER

алло́ *said when answering the phone*	hello (2)
ведь *particle used for emphasis; often omitted in translation*	you know; why; after all (1)
до (+ *Gen.*)	before (1)
ли *conj.*	if; whether (4)

IDIOMS AND EXPRESSIONS

Бы́ло о́чень ве́село.	It was a lot of fun.; We had a lot of fun. (4)
в два (три, четы́ре) часа́	at two (three, four) o'clock (1v)
в два часа́ но́чи	at two a. m. (3)
в командиро́вке	on a business trip (2)
в кото́ром часу́?	at what time?; when? (2)
в пять (шесть, семь, . . .) часо́в	at five (six, seven, . . .) o'clock (1v)
в пять часо́в утра́	at five a. m. (3)
в семь часо́в ве́чера	at seven p. m. (3)
в три часа́ дня	at three p. m. (3)
в час	at one o'clock (1v)
Ве́рно!	That's true!; That's right! (1)
возьми́ тру́бку	pick up the phone (2)
Войди́те.	Come in. (1)
всё вре́мя	all the time; constantly; keep (doing something) (2)
Вы не возража́ете (Ты не возража́ешь)?	Do you mind ? (1)
Вы не туда́ попа́ли. *over the telephone*	You dialed (got) the wrong number. (2)
гото́вить обе́д	to fix dinner (3)
гото́виться (гото́вл-юсь, гото́в-ишься, . . . гото́в-ятся) / подгото́виться к экза́мену	to prepare for an exam; to study for an exam (3)

До́брое у́тро!	Good morning! (2)	Прости́те!	Excuse me! (2)
До́брый ве́чер!	Good evening! (1)	ро́вно в семь часо́в	at seven o'clock sharp; at seven on the dot (3)
Договори́лись!	It's settled, then!; Agreed! (2)	с удово́льствием	I'd be glad to; gladly; with pleasure (2)
Извини́те, что беспоко́ю вас (Извини́те, что я вас беспоко́ю).	Sorry to bother you. (2v)	совсе́м не	not at all (2v)
		Спаси́бо за приглаше́ние.	Thanks for the invitation. (2v)
Как пожива́ете?	How are you doing? (1)		
Кото́рый час?	What time is it? (3)	Стра́нно.	That's strange. (2)
Ла́дно.	All right. Okay. (1)	Что но́вого?	What's new? (2v)
Мо́жно попроси́ть …?	May I speak to …? (3)	Что принести́?	What should I bring? (3)
on the phone		Что случи́лось?	What happened? (2)
Не мо́жет быть!	That can't be!; Unbelievable! (2)	Что э́то за …?	What sort of … is that (are those)? (1)
Одну́ мину́ту!	Just a minute! (2)	экза́мен по исто́рии	history exam (3)
Отли́чная компа́ния!	What a great group! (1)	Э́то говори́т …	This is … speaking. (2)
по о́череди	to take turns (doing something) (3)	Э́то звони́т …	This is … calling. (2v)
		Э́то удо́бно.	It's/That's okay. (1)
Позови́ (ма́му).	(Would you) get mom? (2)	Я ничего́ не хочу́ слы́шать!	I don't want to hear a thing about it! (2)
Поня́тно.	I understand; I see. (1)	Я перезвоню́.	I'll call back. (2v)
Попроси́те (к телефо́ну) …	May I speak with …? (2)		
пора́ (+*Dat.*) (*куда́*) *impersonal*	it's time (for someone to go someplace) (2)		

❖ ЧТО Я ЗНАЮ, ЧТО Я УМЕЮ

Use this checklist to mark off what you've learned in this lesson:

- ☐ Distinguishing between studying in general and studying something specific (Part 1)
- ☐ Talking about studying (Part 4)
- ☐ Imperfective versus perfective aspect (Part 1)
- ☐ To begin or finish doing something (Part 2)
- ☐ Using -чь verbs and -ти verbs in the past tense (Part 4)
- ☐ Using the verb ждать (*to wait*) (Part 4)
- ☐ Reporting what other people have said (Part 4)
- ☐ Asking/saying whether or not something happened (Part 4)
- ☐ Saying what day of the week something happened (Part 1)
- ☐ Expressing parts of the day and seasons of the year (Part 1)
- ☐ Saying what time something happened (Part 2)
- ☐ Asking and telling time (Part 3)
- ☐ Expressing thanks (Part 2)
- ☐ Using the neuter pronoun э́то (Part 3)
- ☐ Using pronouns in the Prepositional case (Part 3)

❖ ЭТО НАДО ЗНАТЬ

A. BASIC NONPAST VERB CONJUGATION PATTERNS IN RUSSIAN

SUMMARY OF -ешь / ёшь ENDINGS

	VOWEL STEMS	CONSONANT STEMS
я	-ю	-у
ты	-ешь / -ёшь	
он, она́, оно́	-ет / -ёт	
мы	-ем / -ём	
вы	-ете / -ёте	
они́	-ют	-ут

For the **-ешь/-ёшь** conjugation, endings with **-ё-** rather than **-е-** occur only with verbs that are end-stressed.

SUMMARY OF -ишь ENDINGS

ALL STEMS
-ю (-у *after hushers*)
-ишь
-ит
-им
-ите
-ят (-ат *after hushers*)

For the **-ишь** conjugation, remember the «**ви́жу**» rule: The endings **-ю** and **-ят** are spelled **-у** and **-ат** after hushers.

EXAMPLES OF -ешь / ёшь VERBS

STEM OR SHIFTING STRESS (-ешь endings)		ENDING STRESS (-ёшь endings)	
Vowel stem	Consonant stem	Vowel stem	Consonant stem
де́лать	**писа́ть**	**дава́ть**	**идти́**
(де́ла-)	(пиш-)	(да-)	(ид-)
де́ла-ю	пиш-у́	да-ю́	ид-у́
де́ла-ешь	пи́ш-ешь	да-ёшь	ид-ёшь
де́ла-ет	пи́ш-ет	да-ёт	ид-ёт
де́ла-ем	пи́ш-ем	да-ём	ид-ём
де́ла-ете	пи́ш-ете	да-ёте	ид-ёте
де́ла-ют	пи́ш-ут	да-ю́т	ид-у́т

EXAMPLES OF -ишь VERBS

ALL STRESS PATTERNS	
Most stems	Stems with hushers
говори́ть	**слы́шать**
(говор-)	(слы́ш-)
говор-ю́	слы́ш-у
говор-и́шь	слы́ш-ишь
говор-и́т	слы́ш-ит
говор-и́м	слы́ш-им
говор-и́те	слы́ш-ите
говор-я́т	слы́ш-ат

Б. SYSTEMATIC STEM CHANGES

-овать VERBS: -ова- → -у- парко́ва́ть		-ава́ть VERBS: -ва- DELETED дава́ть	
парк-у́-ю	парк-у́-ем	да-ю́	да-ём
парк-у́-ешь	парк-у́-ете	да-ёшь	да-ёте
парк-у́-ет	парк-у́-ют	да-ёт	да-ю́т

Similarly: **рекомендова́ть, кома́ндовать, пра́здновать,** and so on.

Similarly: **преподава́ть, отдава́ть, продава́ть, сдава́ть,** and so on.

B. CONSONANT SHIFTS IN VERB CONJUGATIONS

The final consonant in some verb stems changes when nonpast endings are added. With **-ешь/-ёшь** verbs, this change carries through all forms; with **-ишь** verbs, the change occurs only in the **я** form.

-ешь/-ёшь VERBS LIKE писа́ть (с → ш IN ALL FORMS)		-ишь VERBS LIKE пригласи́ть (с → ш IN я FORM ONLY)	
пиш-у́	пи́ш-ем	приглаш-у́	приглас-и́м
пи́ш-ешь	пиш-ете	приглас-и́шь	приглас-и́те
пи́ш-ет	пи́ш-ут	приглас-и́т	приглас-я́т

Shifts in stem-final consonants are very systematic; for example, whenever **-с-** shifts, it will always change to **-ш-**. Here are some other shifts that you have seen. See if you can think of other examples for each of these patterns.

б → бл	люби́ть	люблю́, лю́бишь
в → вл	гото́вить	гото́влю, гото́вишь
м → мл	познако́мить	познако́млю, познако́мишь
п → пл	спать	сплю, спишь
д → ж	ви́деть	ви́жу, ви́дишь
з → ж	сказа́ть	скажу́, ска́жешь
с → ш	писа́ть	пишу́, пи́шешь
ск→щ	иска́ть	ищу́, и́щешь
т→ч	плати́ть	плачу́, пла́тишь

❖ ДОПОЛНИ́ТЕЛЬНЫЕ ТЕКСТЫ

A. FROM АНЕКДО́ТЫ ОТ НИКУЛИ́НА

— Зна́ешь, ма́ма, наш сосе́д о́чень до́брый челове́к.

— Почему́ ты так ду́маешь?

were sitting / kids' room
drum / Came in
small knife
find out
is / inside of

— Мы сиде́ли° в де́тской,° и Том как всегда́ игра́л на бараба́не.° Вошёл° сосе́д, подари́л То́му краси́вый но́жик° и спроси́л его́, не хо́чет ли он узна́ть,° что нахо́дится° внутри́° бараба́на.

Б. FROM TABLE OF CONTENTS. *HARPER'S BAZAAR*, JAN-FEB 1998

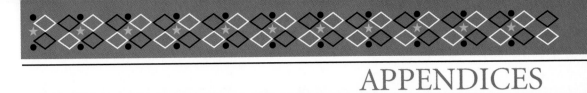

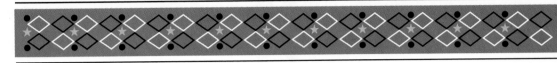

APPENDICES

APPENDIX A

❖ COMMON USES OF RUSSIAN CASES[1]

CASE	USES	EXAMPLES
Nominative Имени́тельный (кто, что)	*(Dictionary form)* 1. Subject of sentence or clause 2. Predicate nominative	студе́нтка Он зна́ет, где живёт **э́та студе́нтка.** Она́ **хоро́шая студе́нтка.**
Accusative Вини́тельный (кого́, что)	1. Direct object 2. Object of prepositions **в, на, за, под,** when indicating motion toward a goal 3. A game or sport that is the object of preposition **в** 4. A day, hour, or minute that is the object of preposition **в,** indicating time when (**когда́?**) 5. Time or distance covered 6. Object of preposition **че́рез**	Я купи́ла **ру́чку.** Ма́ма пошла́ на **по́чту.** Они́ игра́ют в **те́ннис.** Вади́м придёт в **пя́тницу.** Я был там **неде́лю.** Ма́ша прие́дет че́рез **неде́лю.**
Genitive Роди́тельный (кого́, чего́)	1. Ownership 2. Linking 3. Object of prepositions **у, от, до, из, для, без, о́коло, кро́ме, ми́мо, во́зле, и́з-за, про́тив,** and **с** when **с** means *from* 4. To indicate the absence or lack of someone or something (used with **нет, не́ было, не бу́дет**) 5. Nonspecific direct object of a negated verb 6. After numbers (singular after 2–4; plural after 5–20) 7. With certain verbs including **боя́ться.** Some verbs like **иска́ть, ждать, хоте́ть, жела́ть, проси́ть** take Genitive if the object is indefinite. 8. The date on which an event occurred or will occur 9. Partitive *some*	Э́то каранда́ш **Бори́са.** Остано́вка **авто́буса** там. Я получи́ла письмо́ от **Ива́на.** Они́ е́дут с **конце́рта.** Там нет **шко́лы.** Мы не слы́шим **никако́й му́зыки.** Три **биле́та,** два́дцать **биле́тов.** **Чего́** ты бои́шься? Жела́ем вам уда́чи. Мой брат прие́дет **второ́го ма́я.** Нале́й мне **со́ка.**

[1]Some of these uses, and the Instrumental case, will be first encountered in Book 2.

CASE	USES	EXAMPLES
Prepositional Предло́жный (о ком, о чём)	1. Object of preposition **о (об)**	Мы лю́бим говори́ть об **исто́рии.**
	2. Object of prepositions **в** or **на** when indicating location	Кни́га на **столе́.**
	3. **Неде́ле** is the object of preposition **на,** indicating time when (**когда́?**)	Э́то бы́ло на **про́шлой неде́ле.**
	4. A month, year, or larger unit is the object of preposition **в,** indicating time when (**когда́?**)	Э́то бы́ло в **ма́рте.**
	5. Object of preposition **на** when indicating means of transportation	Све́та е́дет на **маши́не.**
Dative Да́тельный (кому́, чему́)	1. Indirect object (*to* or *for* someone)	Она́ дала́ **мне** кни́гу.
	2. With certain verbs, including **помога́ть, сове́товать, отвеча́ть, меша́ть, звони́ть, обеща́ть**	Мари́на помога́ет **бра́ту.**
	3. With the verb **нра́виться** and with constructions containing **мо́жно, ну́жно, тепло́,** and so on	**Мне** нра́вится кла́ссика. **Нам** ну́жно позвони́ть ма́ме.
	4. The person or thing whose age is indicated	**Мое́й сестре́** шесть лет.
	5. Object of prepositions **к, по**	Мы за́втра пое́дем к **Бори́су.**
Instrumental Твори́тельный (кем, чем)	1. The means by which something is done, especially mode of travel	Студе́нтка пи́шет **ру́чкой.** Све́та е́дет **авто́бусом.**
	2. Object of prepositions **за, под, над, пе́ред,** or **ме́жду,** when indicating location. (**За** and **под** take other cases in other situations.)	Челове́к стои́т пе́ред **до́мом.**
	3. Complement of many reflexive verbs: **занима́ться, по́льзоваться, интересова́ться, каза́ться, станови́ться**	Мы занима́емся **ру́сским языко́м.**
	4. Complement of the verbs **стать** and **быть**	Я хочу́ стать **настоя́щим бизнесме́ном.**
	5. Adverbs indicating time of day and seasons are identical to instrumental of corresponding nouns.	Я встал ра́но **у́тром.** Он рабо́тает **ле́том.**
	6. Object of preposition **с** when **с** means *together with*	Я люблю́ разгова́ривать с **Ири́ной.**

APPENDIX B

❖ SPELLING RULES

RULE	AFTER Г, К, Х	AFTER Ж, Ч, Ш, Щ	AFTER Ц
«Кни́ги» rule: **и** (not **ы**)	и	и	
«Хоро́шее» rule: **e** (not unstressed **o**)		e	e
«Ви́жу» rule: **у** (not **ю**), and **a** (not **я**)		у, а	

	NOMINATIVE PLURAL FOR NOUNS ENDING IN		
	-Ь	-Я	-Й
«Роя́ли» rule: **и** (not **ы**)	и	и	и

APPENDIX C

❖ DECLENSIONS: NOUNS

MASCULINE SINGULAR

CASE	ENDINGS	HARD	SOFT: -ь	SOFT: -й	SOFT: -ий
Nominative КТО, ЧТО	(none)	автóбус	календáрь	музéй	гéний
Accusative КОГО, ЧТО	inanimate = 　Nominative; animate = 　Genitive	автóбус	календáрь	музéй	гéния
Genitive КОГÓ, ЧЕГÓ	-а/-я	автóбуса	календаря́	музéя	гéния
Prepositional О КОМ, О ЧЁМ	-е, -и	автóбусе	календарé	музéе	гéнии
Dative КОМУ́, ЧЕМУ́	-у/-ю	автóбусу	календарю́	музéю	гéнию
Instrumental КЕМ, ЧЕМ	-ом/-ем (-ём)	автóбусом	календарём	музéем	гéнием

MASCULINE PLURAL

CASE	ENDINGS	HARD	SOFT: -ь	SOFT: -й	SOFT: -ий
Nominative	-ы/-и	автóбусы	календари́	музéи	гéнии
Accusative	inanimate = 　Nominative; animate = 　Genitive	автóбусы	календари́	музéи	гéниев
Genitive	-ов/-ев, -ей	автóбусов	календарéй	музéев	гéниев
Prepositional	-ах/-ях	автóбусах	календаря́х	музéях	гéниях
Dative	-ам/-ям	автóбусам	календаря́м	музéям	гéниям
Instrumental	-ами/-ями	автóбусами	календаря́ми	музéями	гéниями

NEUTER SINGULAR

CASE	ENDINGS	HARD	SOFT: -ИЕ	SOFT: -ЬЕ	-МЯ
Nominative ЧТО	-о/-е	сло́во	сочине́ние	воскресе́нье	и́мя
Accusative ЧТО	-о/-е	сло́во	сочине́ние	воскресе́нье	и́мя
Genitive ЧЕГО́	-а/-я	сло́ва	сочине́ния	воскресе́нья	и́мени
Prepositional О ЧЁМ	-е, -и	сло́ве	сочине́нии	воскресе́нье	и́мени
Dative ЧЕМУ́	-у/-ю	сло́ву	сочине́нию	воскресе́нью	и́мени
Instrumental ЧЕМ	-ом/-ем	сло́вом	сочине́нием	воскресе́ньем	и́менем

NEUTER PLURAL

CASE	ENDINGS	HARD	SOFT: -ИЕ	SOFT: -ЬЕ	-МЯ
Nominative	-а/-я	слова́	сочине́ния	воскресе́нья	имена́
Accusative	-а/-я	слова́	сочине́ния	воскресе́нья	имена́
Genitive	("zero" ending)	слов	сочине́ний	воскресе́ний[1]	имён
Prepositional	-ах/-ях	слова́х	сочине́ниях	воскресе́ньях	имена́х
Dative	-ам/-ям	слова́м	сочине́ниям	воскресе́ньям	имена́м
Instrumental	-ами/-ями	слова́ми	сочине́ниями	воскресе́ньями	имена́ми

[1]The neuter noun **пла́тье** (*dress*) has the ending **-ев** in the Genitive plural (**пла́тьев**).

FEMININE SINGULAR

CASE	ENDINGS	HARD	SOFT: -Я	SOFT: -Ь	SOFT: -ИЯ	SOFT: -ЬЯ
Nominative КТО, ЧТО	**-а/-я, -ь**	газе́т**а**	неде́л**я**	крова́т**ь**	акаде́ми**я**	статья́
Accusative КОГО́, ЧТО	**-у/-ю, -ь**	газе́т**у**	неде́л**ю**	крова́т**ь**	акаде́ми**ю**	статью́
Genitive КОГО́, ЧЕГО́	**-ы/-и**	газе́т**ы**	неде́л**и**	крова́т**и**	акаде́ми**и**	статьи́
Prepositional О КОМ, О ЧЁМ	**-е, -и**	газе́т**е**	неде́л**е**	крова́т**и**	акаде́ми**и**	статье́
Dative КОМУ́, ЧЕМУ́	**-е, -и**	газе́т**е**	неде́л**е**	крова́т**и**	акаде́ми**и**	статье́
Instrumental КЕМ, ЧЕМ	**-ой/-ей, -ью**	газе́т**ой**	неде́л**ей**	крова́т**ью**	акаде́ми**ей**	статьёй

FEMININE PLURAL

CASE	ENDINGS	HARD	SOFT: -Я	SOFT: -Ь	SOFT: -ИЯ	SOFT: -ЬЯ
Nominative	**-ы/-и**	газе́т**ы**	неде́л**и**	крова́т**и**	акаде́ми**и**	статьи́
Accusative	inanimate = Nominative; animate = Genitive	газе́т**ы**	неде́л**и**	крова́т**и**	акаде́ми**и**	статьи́
Genitive	("zero" ending)	газе́т	неде́л**ь**	крова́т**ей**	акаде́ми**й**	стате́й
Prepositional	**-ах/-ях**	газе́т**ах**	неде́л**ях**	крова́т**ях**	акаде́ми**ях**	статья́х
Dative	**-ам/-ям**	газе́т**ам**	неде́л**ям**	крова́т**ям**	акаде́ми**ям**	статья́м
Instrumental	**-ами/-ями**	газе́т**ами**	неде́л**ями**	крова́т**ями**	акаде́ми**ями**	статья́ми

APPENDIX D

❖ DECLENSIONS: PRONOUNS

INTERROGATIVE/RELATIVE, PERSONAL, REFLEXIVE

CASE	INTERROG./RELATIVE		PERSONAL								REFLEX.
Nominative	кто	что	я	ты	он	онó	онá	мы	вы	они́	(none)
Accusative	когó	что	меня́	тебя́	егó[1]	егó[1]	её[1]	нас	вас	их[1]	себя́
Genitive	когó	чегó	меня́	тебя́	егó[1]	егó[1]	её[1]	нас	вас	их[1]	себя́
Prepositional	ком	чём	мне	тебé	нём	нём	ней	нас	вас	них	себé
Dative	комý	чемý	мне	тебé	емý[1]	емý[1]	ей[1]	нам	вам	им[1]	себé
Instrumental	кем	чем	мной	тобóй	им[1]	им[1]	ей[1]	на́ми	ва́ми	и́ми[1]	собóй

DEMONSTRATIVE

CASE	ЭТОТ MASC.	ЭТОТ NEUT.	ЭТОТ FEM.	ЭТОТ PLUR.	ТОТ MASC.	ТОТ NEUT.	ТОТ FEM.	ТОТ PLUR.
Nominative	э́тот	э́то	э́та	э́ти	тот	то	та	те
Accusative (For masculine and plural: inanimate = Nominative; animate = Genitive)	э́тот/ э́того	э́то	э́ту	э́ти/ э́тих	тот/ тогó	то	ту	те/ тех
Genitive	э́того		э́той	э́тих	тогó		той	тех
Prepositional	э́том		э́той	э́тих	том		той	тех
Dative	э́тому		э́той	э́тим	томý		той	тем
Instrumental	э́тим		э́той	э́тими	тем		той	тéми

---

[1]These forms take a prefixed «н-» when governed by a preposition, e.g., **у негó.**

DETERMINATIVE

CASE	MASCULINE	NEUTER	FEMININE	PLURAL
Nominative	весь	всё	вся	все
Accusative (For masculine and plural: inanimate = Nominative; animate = Genitive)	весь/ всего	всё	всю	все/ всех
Genitive	всего		всей	всех
Prepositional	всём		всей	всех
Dative	всему́		всей	всем
Instrumental	всем		всей	всéми

POSSESSIVE: МОЙ (ТВОЙ, СВОЙ)

CASE	MASCULINE	NEUTER	FEMININE	PLURAL
Nominative	мой	моё	моя́	мои́
Accusative (For masculine and plural: inanimate = Nominative; animate = Genitive)	мой/ моего́	моё	мою́	мои́/ мои́х
Genitive	моего́		моéй	мои́х
Prepositional	моём		моéй	мои́х
Dative	моему́		моéй	мои́м
Instrumental	мои́м		моéй	мои́ми

POSSESSIVE: НАШ (ВАШ)

CASE	MASCULINE	NEUTER	FEMININE	PLURAL
Nominative	наш	на́ше	на́ша	на́ши
Accusative (For masculine and plural: inanimate = Nominative; animate = Genitive)	наш/ на́шего	на́ше	на́шу	на́ши/ на́ших
Genitive	на́шего		на́шей	на́ших
Prepositional	на́шем		на́шей	на́ших
Dative	на́шему		на́шей	на́шим
Instrumental	на́шим		на́шей	на́шими

POSSESSIVE INTERROGATIVE

CASE	MASCULINE	NEUTER	FEMININE	PLURAL
Nominative	чей	чьё	чья	чьи
Accusative (For masculine and plural: inanimate = Nominative; animate = Genitive)	чей/ чьего́	чьё	чью	чьи/ чьих
Genitive	чьего́		чьей	чьих
Prepositional	чьём		чьей	чьих
Dative	чьему́		чьей	чьим
Instrumental	чьим		чьей	чьи́ми

❖ DECLENSIONS: ADJECTIVES

MASCULINE

CASE	ENDINGS	UNSTRESSED ENDING	STRESSED ENDING	SOFT
Nominative	-ый (-ой)/-ий	но́вый (хоро́ший)	молодо́й	ли́шний
Accusative (For masculine and plural: inanimate = Nominative; animate = Genitive)	-ый (-ой)/-ий; -ого/-его	но́вый (хоро́ший)/ но́вого (хоро́шего)	молодо́й/ молодо́го	ли́шний/ ли́шнего
Genitive	-ого/-его	но́вого (хоро́шего)	молодо́го	ли́шнего
Prepositional	-ом/-ем	но́вом (хоро́шем)	молодо́м	ли́шнем
Dative	-ому/-ему	но́вому (хоро́шему)	молодо́му	ли́шнему
Instrumental	-ым/-им	но́вым (хоро́шим)	молоды́м	ли́шним

NEUTER

CASE	ENDINGS	HARD	SOFT
Nominative	-ое/-ее	но́вое (хоро́шее)	ли́шнее
Accusative	-ое/-ее	но́вое (хоро́шее)	ли́шнее
Genitive	-ого/-его	но́вого (хоро́шего)	ли́шнего
Prepositional	-ом/-ем	но́вом (хоро́шем)	ли́шнем
Dative	-ому/-ему	но́вому (хоро́шему)	ли́шнему
Instrumental	-ым/-им	но́вым (хоро́шим)	ли́шним

FEMININE

CASE	ENDINGS	HARD	SOFT
Nominative	-ая/-яя	но́вая (хоро́шая)	ли́шняя
Accusative	-ую/-юю	но́вую (хоро́шую)	ли́шнюю
Genitive	-ой/-ей	но́вой (хоро́шей)	ли́шней
Prepositional	-ой/-ей	но́вой (хоро́шей)	ли́шней
Dative	-ой/-ей	но́вой (хоро́шей)	ли́шней
Instrumental	-ой/-ей	но́вой (хоро́шей)	ли́шней

PLURAL, ALL GENDERS

CASE	ENDINGS	HARD	SOFT
Nominative	-ые/-ие	но́вые (хоро́шие)	ли́шние
Accusative (For masculine and plural: inanimate = Nominative; animate = Genitive)	-ые/-ие; -ых/-их	но́вые (хоро́шие)/ но́вых (хоро́ших)	ли́шние/ ли́шних
Genitive	-ых/-их	но́вых (хоро́ших)	ли́шних
Prepositional	-ых/-их	но́вых (хоро́ших)	ли́шних
Dative	-ым/-им	но́вым (хоро́шим)	ли́шним
Instrumental	-ыми/-ими	но́выми (хоро́шими)	ли́шними

APPENDIX F

❖ NUMERALS

	CARDINAL	ORDINAL		CARDINAL	ORDINAL
0	ноль (*or* нуль)[1]	нулево́й, -а́я, -о́е, -ы́е	50	пятьдеся́т	пятидеся́тый
			60	шестьдеся́т	шестидеся́тый
1	оди́н	пе́рвый, -ая, -ое, -ые	70	се́мьдесят	семидеся́тый
2	два	второ́й, -а́я, -о́е, -ы́е	80	во́семьдесят	восьмидеся́тый
3	три	тре́тий, тре́тья, тре́тье, тре́тьи	90	девяно́сто	девяно́стый
4	четы́ре	четвёртый			
5	пять	пя́тый	100	сто	со́тый
6	шесть	шесто́й	200	две́сти	двухсо́тый
7	семь	седьмо́й	300	три́ста	трёхсо́тый
8	во́семь	восьмо́й	400	четы́реста	четырёхсо́тый
9	де́вять	девя́тый	500	пятьсо́т	пятисо́тый
10	де́сять	деся́тый	600	шестьсо́т	шестисо́тый
			700	семьсо́т	семисо́тый
11	оди́ннадцать	оди́ннадцатый	800	восемьсо́т	восьмисо́тый
12	двена́дцать	двена́дцатый	900	девятьсо́т	девятисо́тый
13	трина́дцать	трина́дцатый			
14	четы́рнадцать	четы́рнадцатый	1000	ты́сяча	ты́сячный
15	пятна́дцать	пятна́дцатый	2000	две ты́сячи	двухты́сячный
16	шестна́дцать	шестна́дцатый	3000	три ты́сячи	трёхты́сячный
17	семна́дцать	семна́дцатый	4000	четы́ре ты́сячи	четырёхты́сячный
18	восемна́дцать	восемна́дцатый	5000	пять ты́сяч	пятиты́сячный
19	девятна́дцать	девятна́дцатый	6000	шесть ты́сяч	шеститы́сячный
			7000	семь ты́сяч	семиты́сячный
20	два́дцать	двадца́тый	8000	во́семь ты́сяч	восьмиты́сячный
30	три́дцать	тридца́тый	9000	де́вять ты́сяч	девятиты́сячный
40	со́рок	сороково́й			

[1]Both **ноль** and **нуль** are masculine nouns.

APPENDIX G

❖ DECLENSIONS: CARDINAL NUMERALS

1–2

| CASE | ОДИ́Н | | | | ДВА | |
	MASC.	NEUT.	FEM.	PLUR.	MASC. AND NEUT.	FEM.
Nominative	оди́н	одно́	одна́	одни́	два	две
Accusative (For masculine and plural: inanimate = Nominative; animate = Genitive)	оди́н/ одного́	одно́	одну́	одни́/ одни́х	два/ двух	две/ двух
Genitive	одного́	одного́	одно́й	одни́х	двух	двух
Prepositional	одно́м	одно́м	одно́й	одни́х	двух	двух
Dative	одному́	одному́	одно́й	одни́м	двум	двум
Instrumental	одни́м	одни́м	одно́й	одни́ми	двумя́	двумя́

3–4

CASE	ТРИ	ЧЕТЫ́РЕ
Nominative	три	четы́ре
Accusative (For masculine and plural: inanimate = Nominative; animate = Genitive)	три/ трёх	четы́ре/ четырёх
Genitive	трёх	четырёх
Prepositional	трёх	четырёх
Dative	трём	четырём
Instrumental	тремя́	четырьмя́

5 AND HIGHER

CASE	
Nominative	пять
Accusative	пять
Genitive	пяти́
Prepositional	пяти́
Dative	пяти́
Instrumental	пятью́

APPENDIX H

❖ CONJUGATIONS

-ешь / -ёшь ENDINGS

	VOWEL STEMS	CONSONANT STEMS
я	-ю	-у
ты	-ешь / -ёшь	
он, она́, оно́	-ет / -ёт	
мы	-ем / -ём	
вы	-ете / -ёте	
они́	-ют	-ут

For the **-ешь/-ёшь** conjugation, endings with -ё- rather than -е- occur only with verbs that are end-stressed.

-ишь ENDINGS

ALL STEMS
-ю (-у *after hushers*)
-ишь
-ит
-им
-ите
-ят (-ат *after hushers*)

For the **-ишь** conjugation, remember the «**ви́жу**» rule: The endings **-ю** and **-ят** are spelled **-у** and **-ат** after hushers.

EXAMPLES OF -ешь / -ёшь VERBS

STEM OR SHIFTING STRESS (-ешь endings)		ENDING STRESS (-ёшь endings)	
Vowel stem	Consonant stem	Vowel stem	Consonant stem
де́лать	**писа́ть**	**дава́ть**	**идти́**
(де́ла-)	(пиш-)	(да-)	(ид-)
де́ла-ю	пиш-у́	да-ю́	ид-у́
де́ла-ешь	пи́ш-ешь	да-ёшь	ид-ёшь
де́ла-ет	пи́ш-ет	да-ёт	ид-ёт
де́ла-ем	пи́ш-ем	да-ём	ид-ём
де́ла-ете	пи́ш-ете	да-ёте	ид-ёте
де́ла-ют	пи́ш-ут	да-ю́т	ид-у́т

EXAMPLES OF -ишь VERBS

ALL STRESS PATTERNS	
Most stems	Stems with hushers
говори́ть	**слы́шать**
(говор-)	(слы́ш-)
говор-ю́	слы́ш-у
говор-и́шь	слы́ш-ишь
говор-и́т	слы́ш-ит
говор-и́м	слы́ш-им
говор-и́те	слы́ш-ите
говор-я́т	слы́ш-ат

CONSONANT SHIFTS

The final consonant in some verb stems changes when nonpast endings are added. With **-ешь/-ёшь** verbs, this change carries through all forms; with **-ишь** verbs, the change occurs only in the **я** form.

-ешь/-ёшь VERBS LIKE писа́ть (с → ш IN ALL FORMS)		-ишь VERBS LIKE пригласи́ть (с → ш IN я FORM ONLY)	
пиш-у́	пи́ш-ем	приглаш-у́	приглас-и́м
пи́ш-ешь	пи́ш-ете	приглас-и́шь	приглас-и́те
пи́ш-ет	пи́ш-ут	приглас-и́т	приглас-я́т

Shifts in stem-final consonants are very systematic; for example, whenever **-с-** shifts, it will always change to **-ш-**.

б → бл[1]	люби́ть	люблю́, лю́бишь, . . . лю́бят
в → вл[1]	гото́вить	гото́влю, гото́вишь, . . . гото́вят
м → мл[1]	познако́мить	познако́млю, познако́мишь, . . . познако́мят
п → пл[1]	спать	сплю, спишь, . . . спят
д → ж	ви́деть	ви́жу, ви́дишь, . . . ви́дят
з → ж	сказа́ть	скажу́, ска́жешь, . . . ска́жут
с → ш	писа́ть	пишу́, пи́шешь, . . . пи́шут
ск → щ	иска́ть	ищу́, и́щешь, . . . и́щут
т → ч	плати́ть	плачу́, пла́тишь, . . . пла́тят

OTHER SYSTEMATIC STEM CHANGES

-овать VERBS: -ова- → -у- парков́ать		-авать VERBS: -ва- DELETED дава́ть	
парк-у́-ю	парк-у́-ем	да-ю́	да-ём
парк-у́-ешь	парк-у́-ете	да-ёшь	да-ёте
парк-у́-ет	парк-у́-ют	да-ёт	да-ю́т

(Similarly, **рекомендова́ть, кома́ндовать, пра́здновать,** and so on.)

(Similarly, **преподава́ть, отдава́ть, продава́ть, сдава́ть,** and so on.)

---

[1]Note that -л- insertion occurs only with labial consonants (**б, в, м, п**) and only in the **я** form.

 APPENDIX I

❖ AMERICAN STATES, CANADIAN PROVINCES, AMERICAN AND CANADIAN CITIES

АМЕРИКА́НСКИЕ ШТА́ТЫ

А́йдахо	Калифо́рния	Нью-Йо́рк
А́йова	Ка́нзас	Нью-Ме́ксико
Алаба́ма	Кенту́кки	Нью-Хе́мпшир
Аля́ска	Колора́до	Ога́йо
Аризо́на	Конне́ктикут	Оклахо́ма
Арканза́с	Луизиа́на	О́регон
Вайо́минг	Массачу́сетс	Пенсильва́ния
Вашингто́н	Миннесо́та	Род-А́йленд
Вермо́нт	Миссиси́пи	Се́верная Дако́та
Вирги́ния	Миссу́ри	Се́верная Кароли́на
Виско́нсин	Мичига́н	Теннесси́
Гава́йи	Монта́на	Теха́с
Де́лавэр	Мэн	Флори́да
Джо́рджия	Мэ́риленд	Ю́жная Дако́та
За́падная Вирги́ния	Небра́ска	Ю́жная Кароли́на
Иллино́йс	Нева́да	Ю́та
Индиа́на	Нью-Дже́рси	

КАНА́ДСКИЕ ПРОВИ́НЦИИ

Альбе́рта	Но́вая Шотла́ндия	О́стров При́нца
Брита́нская Колу́мбия	Нью-Бра́нсуик	Эдуа́рда
Квебе́к	Ньюфаундле́нд	Саска́чеван
Манито́ба	Онта́рио	

АМЕРИКА́НСКИЕ И КАНА́ДСКИЕ ГОРОДА́

Атла́нта	Майа́ми	Про́виденс
Би́рмингем	Ме́мфис	Реджа́йна
Бо́стон	Милуо́ки	Ри́чмонд
Бу́ффало	Миннеа́полис	Ро́ли
Ванку́вер	Монреа́ль (m.)	Ро́честер
Вашингто́н	Моби́л	Сан-Дие́го
Викто́рия	На́швилл	Сан-Франци́ско
Гонолу́лу	Неа́поль (m.)	Сент-Лу́ис
Да́ллас	Но́вый Орлеа́н	Сент-По́л
Де-Мо́йн	Нью-Йо́рк	Сиэ́тл
Детро́йт	Нью́арк	Солт-Лейк-Си́ти
Де́нвер	Оде́сса	Та́лса
Дувр	О́кленд	Торо́нто
Индиана́полис	О́ксфорд	Уи́лмингтон
Ка́нзас-Си́ти	О́лбани	Филаде́льфия
Квебе́к	О́маха	Фи́никс
Кли́вленд	Отта́ва	Хью́стон
Лас-Ве́гас	Пи́ттсбург	Цинцинна́ти
Литл-Ро́к	Пли́мут	Чика́го
Лос-А́нджелес	По́ртленд	Эдмонтон
Лу́исвилл	По́ртсмут	

APPENDIX J

❖ SELECTED EVENTS IN RUSSIAN AND WESTERN HISTORY

YEAR	NOTABLE EVENTS IN RUSSIAN HISTORY	IMPORTANT EVENTS ELSEWHERE
800	Cyril and Methodius devise Slavic alphabet (863) **Рю́рик** rules **Но́вгород** (862–879)	Reign of Charlemagne (768–814)
900	Rise of **Ки́ев. Влади́мир** accepts Christianity as state religion (988–990)	
1000		Battle of Hastings (1066) First Crusade (1099)
1100	**Москва́** first mentioned in chronicles (1147)	Rise of independent towns in Europe
1200	**Тата́ры** invade Russia (1237–1240), beginning **тата́рское и́го** (*Tatar yoke*)	
1300	**Дми́трий Донско́й** defeats Tatars (1380)	Outbreak of the plague in Europe (1348) Renaissance begins (midcentury)
1400	**Тата́ры** decline; **Москва́** rises **Царь Ива́н III** reigns 1462–1505	Columbus discovers America (1492)
1500	**Царь Ива́н IV** ("the Terrible") reigns 1533–1584; "Time of Troubles" begins with his death	Protestant Reformation begins (1517); Queen Elizabeth I reigns (1558–1603)
1600	Founding of **Рома́нов** dynasty (1613) Old Believers break from Russian Orthodox Church (1654–1656) **Царь Пётр I** ("the Great") reforms Russia, ruling 1682–1725	Pilgrims land at Plymouth Rock (1620) Thirty Years' War in Europe (1618–1648)
1700	**Санкт-Петербу́рг** founded (1703) **Цари́ца Екатери́на II** ("the Great") reigns (1762–1796)	American Declaration of Independence (1776) Constitution of **США** (USA) ratified (1787) **Францу́зская револю́ция** (1789)

YEAR	NOTABLE EVENTS IN RUSSIAN HISTORY	IMPORTANT EVENTS ELSEWHERE
1800	**Ру́сские** under **Алекса́ндр I** defeat Napoleon's Grand Army (1812) Crimean War (1853–1856) **Алекса́ндр II** frees serfs (1861)	**Наполео́н** rules France (1804–1815) Gold rush in California (1848) Civil War in **США** (1861–1865); **Авраа́м Ли́нкольн** ends slavery (1863)
1900	**Росси́я** enters WWI (1914), as do **А́нглия и Фра́нция** **Царь Никола́й II** abdicates in March, 1917; **Влади́мир Ле́нин** and the **большевики́** seize power in October/November 1917; devastating civil war 1917–1921 **СССР** (USSR) created; death of **Ле́нин** (1924); **Ста́лин** takes control **Ста́лин** industrializes and collectivizes **СССР;** millions killed in purges (1930s) **Фаши́сты** (Nazis) invade **СССР** (June 1941) WWII allied victory: **А́нглия, СССР, США, Фра́нция** (1945)	**США** enters WWI (1917) Roaring Twenties; Jazz Age Stock market crash in **США** (1929) Attack on Pearl Harbor brings **США** into WWII (December 1941)
1950	**Ста́лин** dies (1953); **Хрущёв** takes power, denounces **Ста́лин** **Спу́тник** (first artificial satellite) launched (1957) **Бре́жнев** ousts **Хрущёв** (1964) **Горбачёв** takes power (1985) Communist regimes in Central Europe collapse (1989–1990) **Е́льцин** elected **президе́нт;** end of **СССР** and Communist rule (August 21, 1991) **Пу́тин** elected **президе́нт** (March 2000)	Korean War (1950–1953) Cuban missile crisis (1962) Vietnam War (1960–1975) Persian Gulf War (1991)

APPENDIX K

❖ INFO-GAP ACTIVITIES

УРОК 2: ЧАСТЬ ПЕРВАЯ

УПРАЖНЕНИЕ 8   Ва́ша фами́лия? (p. 45)

One of you is visiting an important Russian official. The other student plays the guard on duty, who will not let visitors in until they provide relevant information about themselves. As the "guard" asks the following questions, the "visitor" responds with his or her own name and the address and phone number given here. After the guard writes down the responses, the visitor should check to see that the address and phone number are written correctly. Then switch roles and continue.

Guard's questions:

1. Ва́ша фами́лия?
2. Ва́ше и́мя?
3. Ваш а́дрес?
4. Ваш но́мер телефо́на?

Your answers are numbers 1, 3, and 5 below. Your classmate will answer your "guard" questions on numbers 2, 4, and 6 below.

	го́род	у́лица	дом	кварти́ра	но́мер телефо́на
1.	Москва́	Азо́вская	3	7	416–38–27
2.	_____	_____	__	__	_____
3.	Смоле́нск	Че́хова	8	2	50–63–74
4.	_____	_____	__	__	_____
5.	Волгогра́д	Маяко́вского	11	10	40–61–53
6.	_____	_____	__	__	_____

УРОК 2: ЧАСТЬ ЧЕТВЁРТАЯ

УПРАЖНЕНИЕ 7   Intonation (p. 72)

Work with a classmate, using the following sentences and the corresponding sentences on page 72. Take turns reading them aloud. When a sentence is read to you, indicate whether you have heard a statement, a question, or an exclamation.

What you read:

1. Э́то твоя́ ба́бушка?
2. Кака́я краси́вая ку́хня!
3. Са́ша до́ма.
4. Како́й у́жас!

What your classmate reads:

	STATEMENT	QUESTION	EXCLAMATION
	☐	☐	☐
	☐	☐	☐
	☐	☐	☐
	☐	☐	☐

УРОК 5: ЧАСТЬ ВТОРАЯ

УПРАЖНЕНИЕ 9　В Москве́ (p. 195)

Each "tourist" should pick one of these destinations and be prepared to respond when asked, **Я ходи́л (ходи́ла) в/на** + destination in accusative. All of the destinations use **в** except for **на Кра́сную пло́щадь.**

Кремль (the central, oldest part of the city; originally a fortress)

Кра́сная пло́щадь (a central square adjoining the Kremlin)

Большо́й теа́тр (the most famous Russian theater; home of the Bolshoi Ballet and Opera companies)

гости́ница «Росси́я» (one of the largest hotels in the world)

Храм Васи́лия Блаже́нного (the famous cathedral on Red Square; not on map; between the **Кремль** and the **«Росси́я»**; see cover of textbook)

ГУМ *pronounced* [гум] (**Госуда́рственный универса́льный магази́н;** a large shopping center **на Кра́сной пло́щади**)

МХАТ *pronounced* [ммм-ХАТ] (**Моско́вский Худо́жественный академи́ческий теа́тр;** a famous theater where Chekhov's plays were first staged)

Де́тский мир (a large store selling toys and other goods for children)

УРОК 5: ЧАСТЬ ТРЕТЬЯ

УПРАЖНЕНИЕ 9　Вы не зна́ете но́мер телефо́на . . . ? (p. 206)

You are calling the operator at Moscow State University (**Моско́вский госуда́рственный университе́т = МГУ**). Ask for the phone number of an academic department listed below and write it in the space provided. Switch roles after requesting three numbers, then check them against the phone book to make sure you each wrote them down correctly.

ОБРАЗЕ́Ц:　—Но́мер телефо́на филосо́фского факульте́та, пожа́луйста.
　　　　　　—[*Read numbers singly.*] 9-3-9-1-9-2-5.

ФАКУЛЬТЕ́Т	НО́МЕР ТЕЛЕФО́НА
Биологи́ческий фак-т	_____
Географи́ческий фак-т	_____
Экономи́ческий фак-т	_____
(Switch roles)	
Истори́ческий фак-т	_____
Филологи́ческий фак-т	_____
Хими́ческий фак-т	_____

УРОК 6: ЧАСТЬ ВТОРАЯ

УПРАЖНЕНИЕ 5   Где ты бу́дешь . . . ? (p. 246)

You and a classmate are on the phone trying to find a time you can study together for an upcoming exam. Your schedule is below; your classmate's is on page 246. By alternating questions, find a time and location convenient for both of you.

ОБРАЗЕЦ: YOU: Где ты бу́дешь за́втра у́тром?

CLASSMATE: За́втра у́тром? За́втра у́тром я бу́ду до́ма. А где <u>ты</u> бу́дешь за́втра у́тром?

YOUR SCHEDULE	сего́дня	за́втра	послеза́втра (*the day after tomorrow*)
у́тром	(present time)	в университе́те	в университе́те
днём (*in the afternoon*)	до́ма	на рабо́те	до́ма
ве́чером	в университе́те	до́ма	на рабо́те

УРОК 6: ЧАСТЬ ТРЕТЬЯ

УПРАЖНЕНИЕ 12   Там есть но́мер телефо́на . . . ? (p. 261)

Your classmate is looking at a page from a city information book that gives phone numbers for various restaurants, movie theaters and clubs. You will ask him for the phone numbers of the establishments listed below and write them down as he reads them aloud. After you do three items, switch roles. Then check to see that you each wrote down all the phone numbers correctly.

1. Там есть но́мер телефо́на кинотеа́тра «Аму́р»?
2. Дай (*Give*) мне, пожа́луйста, телефо́н клу́ба «Сигна́л».
3. Како́й но́мер телефо́на рестора́на «Экспре́сс»?

   (*Switch roles.*)

4. Скажи́, пожа́луйста, како́й но́мер телефо́на рестора́на «Фонта́н»?
5. Како́й но́мер телефо́на клу́ба «Ла́сточка»?
6. Там есть но́мер кинотеа́тра «Восхо́д»?

УРОК 7: ЧАСТЬ ВТОРАЯ

УПРАЖНЕНИЕ 3   Making an appointment (p. 301)

You are keeping an appointment book for **Ири́на Серге́евна,** a Russian language teacher in St. Petersburg. Your classmate is playing the role of a student who is trying to find out when she is free later in the week.

> ОБРАЗЕ́Ц: — Ири́на Серге́евна свобо́дна (*free*) во вто́рник?
> — К сожале́нию, во вто́рник её не бу́дет.
> — А в сре́ду?
> — В сре́ду у́тром у неё заня́тия.
> — А в два часа́? . . .

The only time **Ири́на Серге́евна** is free is Thursday afternoon at 3:00. Whatever other day and time your classmate proposes, select from the following answers.

её не бу́дет   она́ бу́дет на ле́кции
у неё заня́тия   у неё уже́ есть студе́нт/студе́нтка
у неё семина́р   она́ бу́дет в командиро́вке, etc.

УРОК 7: ЧАСТЬ ЧЕТВЁРТАЯ

УПРАЖНЕНИЕ 4   Когда́ они́ пришли́? Что они́ принесли́? (p. 326)

Your neighbors had a party this weekend, but you and your classmate were not invited. Now you're on the phone piecing together what each of you knows about the event. Take turns asking when different people arrived and what they brought with them, and fill in the table below (Your classmate's table is on page 327).

> ОБРАЗЕ́Ц: — Когда́ пришла́ Ната́ша?
> — Она́ пришла́ в шесть часо́в.
> — Кто принёс пласти́нки?
> — Пласти́нки принесла́ Лю́да.
> — Кто пришёл в 6:00 (шесть часо́в)?
> — В 6:00 (шесть часо́в) пришли́ Мари́на и Ко́ля.

КТО?	КОГДА́?	ЧТО?
Стёпа		буты́лку вина́
	7:00	гита́ру
То́ля	6:00	
Ка́тя	7:00	
	8:00	пирожки́

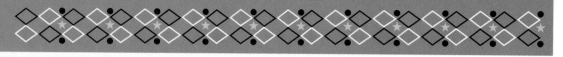

RUSSIAN-ENGLISH GLOSSARY

Key

Acc.	Accusative	*infin.*	infinitive	*pl.*	plural
adj.	adjective	*Instr.*	Instrumental	*Prep.*	Prepositional
Dat.	Dative	*m.*	masculine	*pres.*	present
f.	feminine	*multidir.*	multidirectional	*sing.*	singular
Gen.	Genitive	*neut.*	neuter	*unidir.*	unidirectional
impfv.	imperfective	*pers.*	person	*usu.*	usually
indecl.	indeclinable	*pfv.*	perfective	*v.*	visuals

The numbers in parentheses after each Russian equivalent indicate the lesson and part in which the Russian word or phrase was first used as active; Russian words followed by numbers in brackets are passive vocabulary. The letter "v" after the lesson/part number indicates that the given word first appears in a visual vocabulary display. Bold numbers introduce separate meanings for a given word. The Russian letters **E** and **Ё** are treated as a single letter. Russian words in parentheses do not count in the alphabetical ordering. Verbs not marked as perfective are imperfective. Verbs for which key forms are not given are conjugated like **читáть**.

А

а 1. and; **2.** but (1/1)
áвгуст August (1/4)
Австрáлия Australia (1/2)
автóбус bus (3/4)
  остановка автóбуса bus stop (3/4)
автóбусный bus (*adj.*)
  автóбусная остановка bus stop (5/3)
автомехáник auto mechanic (4/4)
автосéрвис automotive shop [4/4]
áдрес (*pl.* адресá) address (2/1)
Áзия Asia (1/2)
академия academy [5/1v]
алкогóлик alcoholic [4/4v]
аллó (*said when answering the phone*)
  hello (7/2)

альт viola [3/3v]
альтист/альтистка violist [3/3v]
Амéрика America (1/2)
америкáн(е)ц/американка (*Gen. pl.* американок)
  an American (2/1)
американский American (*adj.*) (3/3)
английский English (*adj.*) (7/1)
  по-английски in English (4/3v)
анонимный anonymous [4/4v]
антиквáрный antique (*adj.*)
  антиквáрная вещь a real antique [6/4]
апрéль *m.* April (1/4)
аптéка drugstore; pharmacy (3/3)
áрмия army (6/2)
  в áрмии in the [military] service (6/2)
аспирин aspirin (5/3v)

аспира́нт/аспира́нтка (*Gen. pl.* аспира́нток) graduate student (1/3)

асфа́льт asphalt [5/3]

А́фрика Africa (1/2)

ах ah!; oh! [6/1]

аэропо́рт (*Prep. sing.* в аэропорту́) airport (3/4)

Б

ба́бушка (*Gen. pl.* ба́бушек) grandmother (2/1v)

бале́т ballet (4/2v)

балко́н balcony (2/2v)

бандеро́ль *f.* package (containing printed matter) (6/3)

банк bank (3/4v)

беспла́тно free (of charge); for free (5/3)

библио́граф bibliographer [7/4]

библиоте́ка library; home library (3/4v)

би́знес [*pronounced* -нэ-] business (5/3)

бизнесме́н [*pronounced* -нэ-] businessman [7/4]

биле́т ticket (1/4)

    проездно́й биле́т metro (bus, trolley, tram) pass (5/3v)

био́лог biologist [4/4v]

би́ржа stock exchange (4/4)

бли́зко *used as predicate* (it's/that's) near; (it's/that's) close (2/4v)

    бли́зко от (+ *Gen.*) close to; near (5/3)

блонди́н/блонди́нка (*Gen. pl.* блонди́нок) blond (4/2)

блу́зка (*Gen. pl.* блу́зок) blouse (1/3)

Бо́же мой! Good heavens!; My goodness! (4/3)

большо́й big; large (2/2)

    Большо́й теа́тр Bolshoi Theater [4/2v]

брат (*pl.* бра́тья, *Gen. pl.* бра́тьев) brother (2/1v)

бро́кер (stock) broker [4/4]

брю́ки (*Gen.* брюк) *pl.* pants; trousers (1/3)

буди́льник alarm clock (4/1v)

бу́дущий future (*adj.*) [5/1v]

бу́ква letter (*of the alphabet*) (1/2)

бутербро́д sandwich (1/2)

буты́лка (*Gen. pl.* буты́лок) bottle (5/4)

буфе́т snack bar (1/2)

Бы́ло о́чень ве́село. It was a lot of fun; We had a lot of fun. (7/4)

бы́стро quickly; fast (4/3)

быть (*future* бу́ду, бу́дешь, … бу́дут; *past* был, была́, бы́ло, бы́ли) to be (*past* 4/3, *future* 6/2)

    мо́жет быть *parenthetical* maybe; perhaps (4/2)

    Не мо́жет быть! That can't be!; Unbelievable! (7/2)

В

в 1. (+ *Prep.—to denote location*) in; at: **в Москве́** in Moscow, **в теа́тре** at the theater (3/1); **2.** (+ *Acc. to denote a destination*) to; into: **я иду́ в апте́ку.** I'm going to the pharmacy. (3/3); **3.** (+ *Prep.—with time units of a month or more*) in: **в январе́** in January; **4.** (+ *Acc.—to indicate a time of day*) **в четы́ре часа́** at four o'clock (7/1v); **5.** (+ *Acc. with days of the week*) **в суббо́ту** on Saturday (7/1)

    в а́рмии in the [military] service (6/2)

    в два часа́ но́чи at two a.m. (7/3)

    в два (три, четы́ре) часа́ at two (three) o'clock (7/1v)

    в командиро́вке on a business trip (7/2)

    в кото́ром часу́? at what time?; when? (7/2)

    в про́шлом году́ last year (5/2)

    в пять часо́в утра́ at five a.m. (7/3)

    в пять (шесть, семь, *etc.***) часо́в** at five (six, seven, *etc.*) o'clock (7/1v)

    в семь часо́в ве́чера at 7 p.m. (7/3)

    в три часа́ дня at 3 p.m. (7/3)

    в час at one o'clock (7/1v)

    в шесто́м кла́ссе in the sixth grade (6/1)

    игра́ть в ша́хматы to play chess (3/1)

ва́за vase [3/2v]

валю́та foreign currency (6/3v)

вам *Dat. of* вы (6/1)

ва́ми *Instr. of* вы (9/1)

ва́нна bathtub (4/1)

ва́нная *noun, declines like adj.* bathroom (2/2v)

варе́нье jam [6/4]

вас *Gen., Acc., and Prep. of* вы (4/1, 5/2, 7/3)

ваш (**ва́ша, ва́ше, ва́ши**) *formal or pl.* your; yours (1/4)

Вашингто́н Washington (1/2)

вдруг suddenly (6/4)

ведь *particle* (*used for emphasis; often omitted in translation*) you know; why; after all (7/1)

ве́жливый polite (6/4v)

везде́ everywhere (5/1)

везти́ (везёт; *past* везло́)/**повезти́** (+ *Dat.*) *impersonal* to have good luck; to be lucky

    Нам необыкнове́нно повезло́. We were incredibly lucky; We really lucked out. (6/4)

    Не повезло́ ей! That's tough luck for her! [7/2]

верне́е *parenthetical* (or) rather [6/4]

Ве́рно! That's true!; That's right! (7/1)

ве́село merrily

    Бы́ло о́чень ве́село. It was a lot of fun; We had a lot of fun. (7/4)

весна́ spring
   весно́й in the spring (7/1)
весь (вся, всё, все) 1. *adj.* all; the whole; all of (2/4);
   2. все (*pl. only*) *pronoun* everybody; everyone (4/2);
   3. всё (*neut. sing. only*) everything; all (4/2)
ветерина́рный veterinary [2/4]
ветчина́ ham (5/4v)
ве́чер evening (7/1)
   в семь часо́в ве́чера at 7 p.m. (7/3)
   До́брый ве́чер! Good evening! (7/1)
ве́чером in the evening (3/3v)
ве́шать/пове́сить (пове́шу, пове́сишь, . . . пове́сят) to
   hang; to hang up [7/2]
   Пове́сьте объявле́ние. Put up a sign. [6/2]
   пове́сить тру́бку to hang up the phone [7/2]
вещь *f.* thing
   антиква́рная вещь a real antique [6/4]
ви́деть (ви́жу, ви́дишь, . . . ви́дят)**/уви́деть** to see (4/2)
   (*pfv.* 7/4)
   Вот ви́дишь (ви́дите)! You see!; See! (4/2)
   как ви́дишь (как ви́дите) as you (can) see (3/2)
ви́за visa (1/4)
вино́ wine (7/3)
виолончели́ст/виолончели́стка (*Gen. pl.*
   виолончели́сток) cellist (3/3v)
виолонче́ль *f.* cello (3/3v)
«Вишнёвый сад» *The Cherry Orchard* (5/2v)
вку́сный tasty; delicious (6/4v)
вме́сте together (7/3)
внизу́ downstairs; below (2/4)
внук/вну́чка (*Gen. pl.* вну́чек) grandson/
   granddaughter (2/1)
вода́ (*Acc. sing.* во́ду) water (4/1)
   минера́льная вода́ mineral water (5/4)
води́тель такси́ taxi driver (4/4v)
возража́ть/возрази́ть (возражу́, возрази́шь, . . .
   возразя́т) to object; to have an objection [7/1]
   Вы не возража́ете (Ты не возража́ешь)? Do you
   mind? (7/1)
Возьми́ тру́бку. Pick up the phone. [7/2]
Войди́те. Come in. (7/1)
волнова́ться (волну́юсь, волну́ешься, . . . волну́ются)
   to worry; to be nervous
   Не волну́йся (Не волну́йтесь)! Don't worry! (6/3)
вон (over) there (2/2)
вообще́ all in all (7/4)
   И вообще́. . . (*used to introduce a statement which is
   more general than what precedes it*)
   and . . . anyway (3/1)
вопро́с question (4/4)
   Мо́жно зада́ть вам вопро́с? May I ask you a
   question? (4/4)

восемна́дцатый eighteenth (6/3)
восемна́дцать eighteen (6/1)
во́семь eight (2/1)
во́семьдесят eighty (6/1)
воскресе́нье Sunday (1/4)
восьмо́й eighth (6/3)
вот here (is/are) (1/4)
   Вот ви́дишь (ви́дите)! You see!; See! (4/2)
врач (*Gen. sing.* врача́) physician; doctor (1/3)
вре́мя (*Gen., Dat., and Prep. sing.* вре́мени; *Instr. sing.*
   вре́менем; *pl.* времена́; *Gen. pl.* времён) *neut.*
   time (7/1)
   всё вре́мя all the time; constantly; keep (doing
   something) (7/2)
все (*pl. of* весь) *pronoun* everybody; everyone (4/2)
всё everything; all (4/2)
   Всё в поря́дке. Everything is in order.; Everything's
   fine. (6/2)
   всё вре́мя all the time; constantly; keep (doing
   something) (7/2)
   Всё слы́шно. I (we, *etc.*) can hear everything. (4/2)
   всё, что ну́жно everything that's needed; everything
   we need (6/4)
   пре́жде всего́ first of all (5/4)
   Э́то всё? Is that all? (4/2)
всегда́ always (4/4)
вспомина́ть/вспо́мнить (вспо́мню, вспо́мнишь, . . .
   вспо́мнят) to recall [7/4]
вто́рник Tuesday (1/4)
второ́й second (2/4)
вчера́ yesterday (4/3)
вы *formal or pl.* you (1/3)
выбра́сывать/вы́бросить (вы́брошу, вы́бросишь, . . .
   вы́бросят) to throw out; to throw away [6/4]
выи́грывать/вы́играть to win (3/1)
высо́кий 1. high; **2.** tall (5/4)
вы́ставка exhibition [5/2]
вы́учить (вы́учу, вы́учишь, . . . вы́учат) *pfv.* to learn; to
   memorize (*impfv.* **учи́ть**) (7/1)

Г

газе́та newspaper (1/2)
га́лстук tie (1/3)
гара́ж (*Gen. sing.* гаража́) garage (5/1)
где where (1/3)
геогра́фия geography (1/2)
Герма́ния Germany [5/2v]
герои́ня heroine [7/4]
гид guide [5/2]
гита́ра guitar (3/3v)
гитари́ст/гитари́стка guitarist (3/3v)

гла́вное *noun, declines like adj.* the main thing (6/3)

говори́ть (говорю́, говори́шь, . . . говоря́т)/**сказа́ть** (скажу́, ска́жешь, . . . ска́жут) **1.** (*impfv. only*) to speak; to talk; **2.** to say; to tell (4/2) (*pfv.* 7/4)

    говори́ть (+ *Dat.*) **«вы»** to address (someone) formally; to use «вы» with someone (6/1)

    говори́ть по-англи́йски (по-ру́сски, *etc.*) to speak English (Russian, *etc.*) (4/3v)

    говори́ть (+ *Dat.*) **«ты»** to address (someone) in a familiar fashion; to use «ты» with someone (6/1)

    Дава́й говори́ть друг дру́гу «ты»! Let's use «ты» with each other. (6/1)

год (*Prep. sing.* в году́, *pl.* го́ды, *Gen. pl.* лет) year (1/4)

    в про́шлом году́ last year (5/2)

    Ему́ (ей) два го́да. He (she) is two years old. (6/1v)

    на́ год for a year [7/4]

го́род (*pl.* города́) city; town (1/2)

городско́й city, municipal (*adj.*) [7/2]

горчи́ца mustard [7/3v]

гости́ная *noun, declines like adj.* living room (5/2)

гость (*Gen. sing.* го́стя, *Gen. pl.* госте́й)/**го́стья** guest (4/2)

гото́вить (гото́влю, гото́вишь, . . . гото́вят)/**приготóвить 1.** to prepare; **2.** to cook (6/4v) (*pfv.* 7/3)

    гото́вить/приготóвить обéд to fix dinner (7/3)

гото́виться (гото́влюсь, гото́вишься, . . . гото́вятся)/**подгото́виться (к экза́мену)** to prepare (for an exam) [7/3]

грамм gram (7/3v)

гро́мко loudly (4/2)

    Как гро́мко он игра́ет! He plays so loud! (2/3)

гру́бый rude (6/4v)

гру́ппа (performing) group; section; class (at a university, *etc.*) (4/2v)

грязь (*Prep. sing.* в грязи́) *f.* mud [5/3]

гуля́ть/погуля́ть to walk; to go for a walk; to take a walk (3/1v)

Д

да yes (1/3)

Да нет, . . . Not at all . . . ; On the contrary . . . (6/4v)

дава́й(те) *particle* let's . . . [6/1]

    Дава́й говори́ть друг дру́гу «ты»! Let's use «ты» with each other. (6/1)

    Дава́йте познако́мимся. Let's introduce ourselves; Let's get acquainted (2/3)

дава́ть (даю́, даёшь, . . . даю́т)/**дать** (дам, дашь, даст, дади́м, дади́те, даду́т; *past* дал, дала́, дало́, да́ли) (+ *Dat.* + *Acc.*) to give (5/3) (*pfv.* 7/2)

да́же *particle* even (3/2)

далеко́ far; far away (2/2)

    далеко́ (недалеко́) от (+ *Gen.*) far (not far) from (5/3)

«Да́ма с соба́чкой» *The Lady with a Lap Dog* [5/2v]

дари́ть (дарю́, да́ришь, . . . да́рят)/**подари́ть** (+ *Dat.* + *acc.*) to give (as a present) (7/4)

да́та date

    кру́глая да́та (good) round figure [5/4]

дать (дам, дашь, даст, дади́м, дади́те, даду́т; *past* дал, дала́, дало́, да́ли) *pfv.* to give (7/2) (*impfv.* дава́ть 5/3)

два (*f.* две) two (2/1)

    в два часа́ at two o'clock (7/1v)

двадца́тый twentieth (6/3)

два́дцать twenty (6/1)

двена́дцатый twelfth (6/3)

двена́дцать twelve (2/1)

дверь (*Prep. sing.* о две́ри, на двери́; *Gen. pl.* двере́й) *f.* door (2/2v)

Дворе́ц молодёжи Youth Center [4/2v]

двою́родная сестра́ cousin (female) (2/1v)

двою́родный брат cousin (male) (2/1v)

двухко́мнатная кварти́ра two-room apartment (6/2v)

де́вочка (*Gen. pl.* де́вочек) (little) girl (2/2)

де́вушка (*Gen. pl.* де́вушек) girl; young woman (5/3)

девяно́сто ninety (6/1)

девятна́дцатый nineteenth (6/3)

девятна́дцать nineteen (6/1)

девя́тый ninth (6/3)

де́вять nine (2/1)

де́душка (*Gen. pl.* де́душек) grandfather (2/1v)

действи́тельно really; indeed; actually (5/3)

    Действи́тельно! Right! (6/1)

дека́брь (*Gen. sing.* декабря́) *m.* December (1/4)

де́лать/сде́лать 1. to do; **2.** to make (3/1) (*pfv.* 7/3)

    Что делать? What should (can) I (we) do? (4/2v)

де́ло (*pl.* дела́, *Gen. pl.* дел) matter; business [7/4]

    Как (у тебя́, у вас) дела́? How are things (with you)?; How are you doing? (1/2)

    по де́лу on business [7/4]

д(е)нь (*Gen. pl.* дней) *m.* day (1/4)

    в три часа́ дня at 3 p.m. (7/1)

    день рожде́ния birthday (4/2)

    днём и но́чью day and night [7/2]

    До́брый день! Good day!; Good afternoon! (3/2)

    Како́й сего́дня день? What day is today? (1/4)

деся́тый tenth (6/3)

де́сять ten (2/1)

детекти́в mystery (novel) [3/2]

де́ти (*Gen.* дете́й, *Dat.* де́тям, *Instr.* детьми́) *pl.* (*sing.* ребён(о)к) children (2/1v)

джаз jazz (4/2v)

джи́нсы (*Gen.* джи́нсов) *pl.* jeans (1/3)

дива́н couch (2/3v)

дие́та diet (5/4v)

дипло́м diploma (7/1)

дире́ктор director, manager (of a building) (4/1)

дискримина́ция discrimination [5/3]

для (+ *Gen.*) for: **Тут нет ме́ста для стола́.** There is no room for a table here. (6/4)

днём in the afternoon (7/1)

 днём и но́чью day and night, constantly [7/2]

до (+ *Gen.*) before: **До институ́та я зако́нчила медици́нское учи́лище.** I finished a nursing school before the institute. [7/1]

 До свида́ния. Goodbye (1/2)

до́брый 1. kind; **2.** good

 До́брое у́тро! Good morning! (7/2)

 До́брый ве́чер! Good evening! (7/1)

 До́брый день! Good day!; Good afternoon! (3/2)

 Договори́лись! It's settled, then!; Agreed! (7/2)

до́лжен (**должна́, должно́, должны́**) (*used as predicate*) **1.** must; have to; **2.** should (5/4)

дом (*pl.* дома́) **1.** house; **2.** building; **3.** apartment building (2/1)

до́ма at home (1/3)

дома́шний home (*adj.*)

 дома́шнее зада́ние homework (assignment) (3/3)

домо́й (*indicates direction*) home (3/4v)

дорого́й 1. dear (2/3); **2.** expensive (5/3)

доска́ chalkboard

 Иди́те к доске́! Go to the board. [1/4]

до́ченька *affectionate* daughter [3/1]

дочь (*Gen., Dat., and Prep. sing.* до́чери, *Instr. sing.* до́черью, *pl.* до́чери, *Gen. pl.* дочере́й) *f.* daughter (2/1)

друг (*pl.* друзья́, *Gen. pl.* друзе́й) friend (5/3)

друг дру́га (**друг дру́гу, друг о дру́ге,** *etc.*) (to, about, *etc.*) each other; (to, about, *etc.*) one another (6/1)

 Дава́й говори́ть друг дру́гу «ты»! Let's use «ты» with each other. (6/1)

друго́й other; another (5/2)

ду́мать/поду́мать to think (5/2)

душ shower (4/1)

дя́дя (*Gen. pl.* дя́дей) *m.* uncle (2/1v)

Е

«Евге́ний Оне́гин» *Eugene Onegin* (a novel in verse by A. S. Pushkin) [7/4]

Евро́па Europe (1/2)

его́ 1. *Gen. and Acc. of* **он** *and* **оно́** (4/1, 5/2); **2.** *possessive* his; its (1/4)

её 1. *Gen. and Acc. of* **она́** (4/1, 5/2); **2.** *possessive* her; hers; its (1/4)

е́здить (**е́зжу, е́здишь, . . . , е́здят**) *multidir.* to go (*by vehicle*); to ride; to drive (5/4) (*unidir.* **е́хать** 3/3)

ей *Dat. and Instr. of* **она́** (6/1, 9/1)

ему́ *Dat. of* **он** *and* **оно́** (6/1)

е́сли if (3/2)

есть[1] (**ем, ешь, ест, еди́м, еди́те, едя́т;** *past* **ел, е́ла, е́ло, е́ли**)/**съесть** to eat (5/4v)

есть[2] *3rd person sing. present of* **быть 1.** there is (are) (4/1v); **2.** *with* **у меня́** (**у тебя́,** *etc.*) I (you, *etc.*) have: **У вас есть телеви́зор?** Do you have a television? (4/1v)

 Тут есть . . . ? Is (Are) there . . . here? [3/4]

е́хать (**е́ду, е́дешь, . . . е́дут**) *unidir.*/**пое́хать** to go (*by vehicle*); to ride; to drive (3/3)

ещё 1. still (6/1); **2.** yet; **3.** else (4/3)

 ещё не . . . not yet; not . . . yet (4/4)

 ещё оди́н (**одна́, одно́**) one more (5/4)

 Кто (**что**) **ещё?** Who (what) else? (4/3)

 Нет ещё (**Ещё нет**). Not yet. (6/3)

Ж

жаке́т (woman's) suit jacket (1/3)

жаль (that's) too bad; it's/that's a pity! (6/2)

ждать (**жду, ждёшь, . . . ждут;** *past* **ждал, ждала́, жда́ло, жда́ли**) **1.** to wait (for) (5/3); **2.** to expect

 Ждём! We'll be expecting you! [7/3]

же *particle* (*used for emphasis*) surely; after all (4/3)

 Мы, кто же ещё! Sure it's us, who else? [4/3]

жена́ (*pl.* жёны, *Gen. pl.* жён) wife (2/1v)

 муж и жена́ Кругло́вы Mr. and Mrs. Kruglov; the Kruglovs, husband and wife (2/2)

же́нщина woman (4/2)

жизнь *f.* life (5/2v)

жить (**живу́, живёшь, . . . живу́т;** *past* **жил, жила́, жи́ло, жи́ли**) to live (3/1) (*3rd pers. only* 2/1)

журна́л magazine; journal (1/2)

журнали́ст/журнали́стка (*Gen. pl.* журнали́сток) journalist (2/4)

журнали́стика journalism [4/4]

 факульте́т журнали́стики journalism department [4/4]

З

заво́д plant; factory (4/4v)

за́втра tomorrow (1/4)

задава́ть (**задаю́, задаёшь, . . . задаю́т**)/**зада́ть** (**зада́м, зада́шь, зада́ст, задади́м, задади́те, зададу́т;** *past* за́дал, задала́, за́дало, за́дали) **вопро́с** (+ *Dat.*) to ask (someone) a question [4/4]

Мо́жно зада́ть вам вопро́с? May I ask you a question? (4/4)

зада́ние assignment

    дома́шнее зада́ние homework (assignment) (3/3)

зака́зывать/заказа́ть (закажу́, зака́жешь, . . . зака́жут) to order; to reserve [5/4]

    Что бу́дете зака́зывать? What can I get you?; Are you ready to order?; What'll you have? (5/4)

зака́нчивать/зако́нчить (зако́нчу, зако́нчишь, . . . зако́нчат) to finish (7/1)

закрыва́ть/закры́ть (закро́ю, закро́ешь, . . . закро́ют) to close; to shut [*pfv.* 4/1]

зал (performance) hall; auditorium (4/2v)

замеча́тельно wonderfully; marvelously; *used as predicate* (it's/that's) wonderful; (it's/that's) marvelous

    Замеча́тельно! Great!; Wonderful! (6/3)

замеча́тельный wonderful; marvelous (3/3)

занима́ться to study (prepare for classes) (7/1)

заня́тия *pl. only* classes (7/1)

записна́я кни́жка notebook; address book (6/3)

за́работ(о)к (*Gen. sing.* за́работка) pay (7/1)

зато́ (*often* но зато́) but (then); but on the other hand (4/4)

Заходи́(те)! Come in! (3/2)

зачём what (does one need . . .) for; why (4/1)

звони́ть (звоню́, звони́шь, . . . звоня́т)/**позвони́ть** (+ *Dat.*) to call; to phone (7/1v)

звук sound (1/2)

здесь here (1/3)

здо́рово *used as predicate* (it's/that's) wonderful

    Это здо́рово! It's/That's great! (2/2)

здоро́вье health

    Как ва́ше здоро́вье? How are you? (6/3)

Здра́вствуй(те)! Hello! (1/2)

зима́ winter

    зимо́й in the winter (7/1)

знако́мить (знако́млю, знако́мишь, . . . знако́мят)/**познако́мить** (+ *Acc.* + **с** + *Instr.*) to introduce (someone to someone) [7/4]

знако́миться (знако́млюсь, знако́мишься, . . . знако́мятся)/**познако́миться** to get acquainted

    Дава́йте познако́мимся. Let's get acquainted; Let's introduce ourselves. (2/3)

    О́чень прия́тно познако́миться. (It's/It was) very nice to meet you. (4/4)

    Познако́мьтесь, э́то . . . . (*when introducing someone*) I'd like you to meet . . . ; Meet . . . ; Let me introduce . . . (2/3)

знако́мый/знако́мая *noun, declines like adj.* acquaintance (7/2)

знать to know (3/1) (*1st pers. only* 1/1)

    Вы не зна́ете . . . ? Do you happen to know . . . ? (3/4)

зна́чит *parenthetical* so; then (3/4)

зову́т (*3rd pers. pl. of* **звать**)

    Как тебя́ (вас) зову́т? What is your name? (1/1)

    Меня́ зову́т . . . My name is . . . (1/1)

золото́й gold; golden

    золоты́е ру́ки (**у** + *Gen.*) (one is) good with one's hands (4/3)

зубна́я па́ста toothpaste (5/3v)

зубна́я щётка toothbrush (5/3v)

И

и and (1/3)

И вообще́. . . *used to introduce a statement which is more general than what precedes it* and . . . anyway (3/1)

игра́ть to play (*3rd pers. only* 2/3) (3/1)

    игра́ть в ша́хматы to play chess (3/1)

    игра́ть на роя́ле (гита́ре, *etc.*) to play the piano (the guitar, *etc.*) (4/3)

    Как гро́мко он игра́ет! He plays so loud! (2/3)

иде́я idea (6/2)

идти́ (иду́, идёшь, . . . иду́т; *past* шёл, шла, шло, шли) *unidir.*/**пойти́** (пойду́, пойдёшь, . . . пойду́т; *past* пошёл, пошла́, пошло́, пошли́) **1.** to go; **2.** *impfv. only* to walk; **3.** *pfv. only* to set out (3/3)

    Иди́те к доске́! Go to the board. [1/4]

    Иди́те сюда́! Come here. [1/4]

Извини́(те) Excuse me! (1/2)

    Извини́те, что беспоко́ю вас (Извини́те, что я вас беспоко́ю). Sorry to bother you. (7/2v)

изуча́ть to study (in depth) (7/3)

и́ли or (2/3)

им *Dat. of* они́ (6/1), *Instr. of* он *and* оно́ (9/1)

и́менно precisely; exactly [3/1]

и́ми *Instr. of* они́ (9/1)

и́мпортный imported (3/2)

и́мя (*Gen., Dat., and Prep. sing.* и́мени, *Instr. sing.* и́менем, *pl.* имена́, *Gen. pl.* имён) *neut.* (first) name (1/2)

    Как ва́ше и́мя и о́тчество? What're your name and patronymic? (1/2)

инжене́р engineer (4/4v)

инициа́лы (*usually pl.*) initials (6/3)

институ́т institute (5/1v)

    Моско́вский экономи́ческий институ́т Moscow Institute of Economics [5/1v]

    юриди́ческий институ́т law school (5/1v)

инструме́нт tool [4/3]

интере́сно interestingly; engagingly; *used as predicate* (it's/that's) interesting (3/1)

интере́сный interesting (3/1)

иска́ть (ищу́, и́щешь, . . . и́щут) to look for [5/4]

испа́нский Spanish (*adj.*)

   по-испа́нски in Spanish (4/3v)

исто́рик historian (4/3)

истори́ческий historical; history (*adj.*) (6/2)

   истори́ческий факульте́т history department (6/2)

исто́рия history (5/2)

ита́к so; and so (5/4)

италья́нский Italian (*adj.*)

   по-италья́нски in Italian (4/3v)

их 1. *Gen. and Acc. of* **они́** (4/1, 5/2); **2.** *possessive* their; theirs (1/4)

ию́ль *m.* July (1/4)

ию́нь *m.* June (1/4)

К

к (+ *Dat.*) to [7/4]

   к сожале́нию *parenthetical* unfortunately (5/4)

Кавка́з the Caucasus [5/2]

ка́ждый every; each (5/3)

ка́жется *parenthetical* it seems (2/4)

как 1. how (1/1); **2.** as, like (5/4)

   Как (ва́ше) здоро́вье? How are you? (6/3)

   Как ва́ше и́мя и о́тчество? What's your name and patronymic? (1/2)

   как ви́дишь (как ви́дите) as you (can) see (3/2)

   Как вы пожива́ете? How are you doing? (7/1)

   Как гро́мко он игра́ет! He plays so loud! (2/3)

   Как дела́? How are things?; How are you doing? (1/2)

   Как насчёт (+ *Gen.*) . . . ? How about . . . ? (6/4)

   Как по-ру́сски . . . ? What's the Russian for . . . ? (1/4)

   Как тебя́ (вас) зову́т? What is your name? (1/1)

   Как у тебя́ (у вас) дела́? How're things with you?; How are you doing? (1/2)

како́й 1. which; what (3/1); **2.** what sort of; what is (are) . . . like?; **3.** what a . . . (2/2)

   кака́я ра́зница what's the difference?; what difference does it make? (3/2)

   Како́е сего́дня число́? What's the date today? (6/3)

   Како́й сего́дня день? What day is today? (1/4)

   Како́й у́жас! That's horrible!; How awful! (2/2)

како́й-то some (7/2)

календа́рь (*Gen. sing.* календаря́) *m.* calendar (1/4)

Кана́да Canada (1/2)

каранда́ш (*Gen. sing.* карандаша́) pencil (1/3)

ка́рта map (3/4)

карти́на picture; painting (3/2v)

карто́фельный сала́т potato salad [7/3]

ка́рточка (*Gen. pl.* ка́рточек) card (7/1)

карто́шка *colloquial* potatoes (7/3v)

кассе́та casette (5/1)

кафе́ *neut. indecl.* café (3/4v)

ка́федра department (4/3v)

кварте́т quartet [3/3v]

кварти́ра apartment (2/1)

   двухко́мнатная кварти́ра two-room apartment (6/2v)

кем *Instr. of* **кто** (9/1)

килогра́мм kilogram (7/3v)

кинематогра́фия cinematography [5/1v]

кинозвезда́ (*pl.* кинозвёзды) movie star [5/1v]

кио́ск kiosk; stand (5/3v)

кирпи́чный brick (*adj.*) [6/2v]

кита́йский Chinese (*adj.*)

   по-кита́йски in Chinese (4/3v)

кларне́т clarinet [3/3v]

класс 1. (*a group of students*) class (in school): **Мы учи́лись в одно́м кла́ссе.** We were in the same class in school. (6/1); **2.** grade (in school) **Ты в како́м кла́ссе?** What grade are you in? **Я в шесто́м кла́ссе.** I'm in the sixth grade (6/1)

кла́ссика 1. the classics; **2.** classical music [4/2]

класси́ческий classical (3/3)

клуб club (4/2v)

кни́га book (1/3)

кни́жка *diminutive of* кни́га

   записна́я кни́жка notebook; address book (6/3)

кни́жная по́лка bookshelf (2/3v)

ков(ё)р (*Gen. sing.* ковра́) carpet; rug (3/2v)

когда́ when (4/4)

кого́ *Gen. and Acc. of* **кто** (4/1, 5/2)

колбаса́ sausage (3/4)

ком *Prep. of* **кто** (7/3)

командиро́вка business trip [7/2]

   в командиро́вке on a business trip (7/2)

кома́ндовать (кома́ндую, кома́ндуешь, . . . кома́ндуют) to boss (someone, everyone) around [6/1]

ко́мната room (2/2)

компа́ния group (of people) [7/1]

   Отли́чная компа́ния! What a great group! (7/1)

компози́тор composer (3/3)

кому́ *Dat. of* **кто** (6/1)

конве́рт envelope (6/3v)

коне́чно *parenthetical* of course (3/2)

консервато́рия conservatory (3/3v)

контине́нт continent (1/2)

контраба́с double bass; bass; bass viol (3/3v)

контро́льная *noun, declines like adj.* test; quiz (4/2) конфере́нция conference [7/1v]

концéрт concert (3/3)

концéртный concert (*adj.*) [4/2v]

конча́ть/ко́нчить (ко́нчу, ко́нчишь, . . . ко́нчат) to finish (7/2)

костю́м suit (1/3)

кот (*Gen. sing.* кота́) tomcat (2/4)

кото́рый who; that; which (5/4)

  в кото́ром часу́? at what time?; when? (7/2)

  Кото́рый час? What time is it? (7/3)

котте́дж [*pronounced* -тэ-] cottage [6/2v]

ко́фе *m. indecl.* coffee (1/2)

кофе́йный сто́лик coffee table (2/3v)

ко́шка (*Gen. pl.* ко́шек) cat (2/4)

кошма́р nightmare (4/1)

краси́вый beautiful; good-looking; handsome (2/4)

кре́пко целу́ю (*usu. at the end of a letter to a close relative, sweetheart, or friend*) lots of love [7/4]

кре́сло armchair; easy chair (3/2)

крича́ть (кричу́, кричи́шь, . . . крича́т)/**кри́кнуть** (кри́кну, кри́кнешь, . . . кри́кнут) to shout [7/2]

крова́ть *f.* bed (3/2v)

кро́ме того́ *parenthetical* besides (that); moreover (3/1)

кроссо́вки (*Gen. pl.* кроссо́вок) *pl.* (*sing.* кроссо́вка) sneakers (1/3)

кру́глая да́та (good) round figure [5/4]

круто́е яйцо́ hard-boiled egg (7/3v)

кста́ти by the way; incidentally (5/4)

кто who (1/1)

  Кто ещё? Who else? (4/3)

  Кто э́то? Who's that (this)? (1/1)

куда́ (*indicates direction*) where (to) (3/3)

культу́рный cultured (6/1)

купи́ть (куплю́, ку́пишь, . . . ку́пят) *pfv.* to buy (*infin. only 5/1*) (*impfv.* покупа́ть 7/3)

курс year (of college) (6/1)

  На како́м ты (вы) ку́рсе? What year are you in? (6/1)

  на второ́м ку́рсе in second-year (of college) (6/1)

курсова́я *noun, declines like adj.;* (**курсова́я рабо́та**) term paper (3/1)

ку́ртка (casual) jacket (1/3)

ку́хня kitchen (2/2v)

Л

лаборато́рия laboratory (4/4v)

Ла́дно. All right; Okay. (7/1)

ла́мпа lamp (3/2v)

ле́кция lecture

  хорошо́ чита́ть ле́кции to be a good lecturer [7/4]

ле́стница [*pronounced* -сн-] stairs; staircase [2/2v]

лет (*Gen. pl. of* год) years (6/1)

  Ско́лько ему́ лет? How old is he? (6/1)

ле́то summer

  ле́том in the summer (7/1)

ли 1. *conjunction* if; whether; **Он спроси́л меня́, люблю́ ли я литерату́ру.** He asked me whether I liked literature. (7/4); 2. *interrogative particle* **Зна́ете ли вы об э́том?** Do you know about this?

литерату́ра literature (7/4)

литерату́рный literary (7/4)

лифт elevator (2/2v)

ли́шний spare; extra (6/2)

Лос-А́нджелес Los Angeles (1/2)

лук onions (7/3v)

люби́мый favorite (3/3)

люби́ть (люблю́, лю́бишь, . . . лю́бят) **1.** to love; **2.** to like (4/2v)

люб(о́)вь (*Gen.* любви́, *Instr.* любо́вью) *f.* love (5/2v)

лю́ди (*Gen.* люде́й *but* пять, шесть, *etc.*, челове́к; *Dat.* лю́дям, *Instr.* людьми́) *pl.* (*sing.* челове́к) people (5/4)

М

магази́н store; shop (2/4v)

магази́н электро́ники electronics store (4/4)

магнитофо́н tape recorder; tape player (2/3v)

май May (1/4)

майоне́з mayonnaise [7/3v]

ма́ленький small; little (2/2)

ма́ло (+ *Gen.*) **1.** little (3/3); **2.** few

ма́льчик boy (2/2)

ма́ма mom; mother (2/2)

ма́мочка *affectionate* mom; mother dear [7/4]

ма́рка (*Gen. pl.* ма́рок) stamp (6/3v)

март March (1/4)

ма́стер master

  ма́стер на все ру́ки jack-of-all-trades [4/3]

мат *chess* mate; checkmate [3/1]

мать (*Gen., Dat., and Prep. sing.* ма́тери, *pl.* ма́тери, **Instr. sing.** ма́терью, *Gen. pl.* матере́й) *f.* mother (2/1v)

маши́на car (5/1)

ме́бель *f.* furniture (3/2)

медици́нский medical (6/2)

  медици́нская сестра́ (медсестра́) nurse [7/1]

  медици́нское учи́лище nursing school [7/1]

медсестра́ nurse [7/1]

ме́жду про́чим *parenthetical* by the way; incidentally (6/1)

меню́ *neut. indecl.* menu (1/2)

меня́ *Gen. and Acc. of* **я** (4/1, 5/2)

Меня́ (его́, её) зову́т . . . My (His, Her) name is . . . (1/1)

меня́ть (меня́ю, меня́ешь, . . . меня́ют)/**поменя́ть** to change [7/2]

ме́сто (*pl.* места́) **1.** place; **2.** space; room (5/1)

ме́сяц month (1/4)

метро́ *neut. indecl.* subway; metro (2/4v)

меша́ть/помеша́ть (+ *Dat.*) to bother; to disturb (7/1)

Не хочу́ вам меша́ть. I don't want to bother you. [7/1]

микроволно́вая печь *f.* microwave oven (4/1v)

микрорайо́н neighborhood (3/4)

ми́ксер mixer; blender [4/1v]

миллионе́р millionaire (4/4v)

минда́льное пиро́жное almond pastry [5/4]

минера́льный mineral (*adj.*)

минера́льная вода́ mineral water (5/4)

министе́рство ministry [7/1v]

ми́нус minus

плю́сы и ми́нусы pluses and minuses [2/4v]

мину́та minute (6/4)

Одну́ мину́ту! Just a minute! [7/2]

мне *Dat. and Prep. of* **я** (6/1, 7/3)

мно́гие *pl. only* many; (*when used as a noun*) many people (7/3)

мно́го (+ *Gen.*) much; many (3/1v)

мной *Instr. of* **я** (9/1)

мо́жет быть *parenthetical* maybe; perhaps (4/2)

Не мо́жет быть! That can't be!; Unbelievable! [7/2]

Мо́жешь меня́ поздра́вить! Congratulate me! [7/2]

мо́жно one can; one may (4/4)

Мо́жно зада́ть вам вопро́с? May I ask you a question? (4/4)

(*on the phone*) **Мо́жно попроси́ть. . .?** May I speak to . . .? (7/3)

мой (**моя́, моё, мой**) my; mine (1/4)

Молоде́ц! Good job!; Well done! (4/3)

молодо́й young (5/4)

молодо́й челове́к young man (5/4)

молоко́ milk (3/4)

моро́женое *noun, declines like adj.* ice cream (1/2)

Москва́ Moscow (1/2)

москви́ч (*Gen. sing.* москвича́)/**москви́чка** (*Gen. pl.* москви́чек) Muscovite; resident of Moscow [5/2]

моско́вский Moscow (*adj.*) (4/2v)

Моско́вский экономи́ческий институ́т Moscow Institute of Economics [5/1v]

по-моско́вски Moscow style [5/3]

мочь (могу́, мо́жешь, . . ., мо́гут; *past* мог, могла́, могло́, могли́)/**смочь** to be able (5/3v) (*pfv.* 7/4)

муж (*pl.* мужья́, *Gen. pl.* мужей) husband (2/1v)

муж и жена́ Кругло́вы Mr. and Mrs. Kruglov; the Kruglovs, husband and wife (2/1)

мужчи́на man; gentleman (6/3)

музе́й museum (4/2v)

му́зыка music (3/3)

музыка́нт musician (1/3)

мы we (1/3)

мы́ло soap (5/3v)

мысль *f.* thought [5/4]

мясно́й руле́т meat loaf [7/3]

мя́со meat (7/3)

Н

на 1. (+ *Prep.—to denote location*) on: **на по́лке** on the shelf (3/2v); **2.** (+ *Acc.—to denote a destination*) to: **Она́ идёт на по́чту.** She is going to the post office. (3/3); **3.** (+ *Prep.—at an event, an open place, etc.*) at: **на конце́рте** at a concert; **на стадио́не** at the stadium (3/1v); **4.** (+ *Acc. to denote how long the result of an action is in effect*) for: **Мне э́та кни́га нужна́ на два дня.** I need this book for two days.

игра́ть на роя́ле (гита́ре, *etc.*) to play the piano (the guitar, *etc.*) (4/3)

на́ год for a year [7/4]

на второ́м ку́рсе (to be) a second-year student (6/1)

На како́м ты (вы) ку́рсе? What year (of college) are you in? (6/1)

На како́м факульте́те вы у́читесь? What department are you in? What are you majoring in? [4/4]

набира́ть/набра́ть (наберу́, наберёшь, . . . наберу́т) **но́мер** to dial (the phone) [7/2]

наве́рно (наве́рное) *parenthetical* most likely; probably (6/3)

на́до (+ *Dat.*+ *infin.*) (one) has to; (one) must (3/1)

наза́д back

(**тому́**) **наза́д** ago [7/2]

три го́да (тому́) наза́д three years ago

назва́ние name (5/2)

найти́ (найду́, найдёшь, . . . найду́т; *past* нашёл, нашла́, нашло́, нашли́) *pfv.* to find (*impfv.* **находи́ть**) (7/4)

наконе́ц finally; at last (7/4)

нале́во to the left; on the left (3/4)

нам *Dat. of* **мы** (6/1)

Нам необыкнове́нно повезло́. We were incredibly lucky; We really lucked out. (6/4)

на́ми *Instr. of* **мы** (9/1)

написа́ть (напишу́, напи́шешь, . . . напи́шут) *pfv.* to write (7/1) (*impfv.* **писа́ть** 3/1v)

Напиши́те! Write (it) down. [6/2]

напра́во to the right; on the right (3/4)

нас *Gen., Acc., and Prep. of* **мы** (4/1, 5/2, 7/3)

настоя́щий 1. present; **2.** real; true (4/4)

настрое́ние mood [5/3]

научи́ться (научу́сь, нау́чишься, . . . нау́чатся)
(+ *Dat. or* + *infin.*) *pfv.* to learn (how to); to learn
(to do something) [7/3] (*impfv.* **учи́ться** 4/3)

нау́чный руководи́тель *m.* (academic) adviser [5/2]

находи́ть (нахожу́, нахо́дишь, . . . нахо́дят)/**найти́**
(найду́, найдёшь, . . . найду́т; *past* нашёл, нашла́,
нашло́, нашли́) to find (7/4)

нача́ло beginning; start

начина́ть/нача́ть (начну́, начнёшь, . . . начну́т)
to begin; to start (7/2)

наш (на́ша, на́ше, на́ши) our; ours (1/4)

не not (1/1)
(*over the telephone*) **Вы не туда́ попа́ли.** You dialed
(got) the wrong number (7/2)

Не волну́йся (Не волну́йтесь)! Don't worry! (6/3)

Не мо́жет быть! That can't be!; Unbelievable! (7/2)

Не повезло́ ей! That's tough luck for her! [7/2]

не при́нято it is not (considered)
appropriate (7/3)

У нас э́то не при́нято. We don't do that
(here). [7/3]

небольшо́й not large (3/4)

невку́сный unpalatable; tasteless (6/4v)

невозмо́жно *used as predicate* (it's/that's)
impossible (4/1)

него́ *variant of* **его́** (*Gen. and Acc. of* **он** *and* **оно́**) *used
after prepositions* (4/1, 5/2)

неда́вно recently; (*with past verbs*) not long ago; (*with
present verbs*) not . . . very long (6/3)

Я на по́чте рабо́таю неда́вно. I haven't been
working at the post office very long. (6/3)

недалеко́ от (+ *Gen.*) not far from (5/3)

неде́ля week (1/4)

недорого́й inexpensive (5/3)

неё *variant of* **её** (*Gen. and Acc. of* **она́**) *used after
prepositions* (4/1, 5/2)

ней *variant of* **ей** (*Dat., Prep., and Instr. of* **она́**) *used after
prepositions* (6/1) (7/3)

нелегко́ *used as predicate* (it's/that's) not easy; (it's/that's)
difficult (3/1)

нельзя́ one may not; it is forbidden (4/2)

нём *Prep. of* **он** *and* **оно́** (7/3)

неме́дленно right now; at once; immediately [7/2]

неме́цкий German (*adj.*)
по-неме́цки in German (4/3v)

немно́го (+ *Gen.*) a little (4/3)

нему́ *variant of* **ему́** (*Dat. of* **он** *and* **оно́**) *used after
prepositions* (6/1)

необыкнове́нно incredibly [6/4]

Нам необыкнове́нно повезло́. We were incredibly
lucky; We really lucked out. (6/4)

непло́хо quite well; pretty well; *used as predicate*
(it's/that's) not bad (1/2)

неплохо́й pretty good; not (a) bad (4/4)

несимпати́чный unpleasant (4/2)

нет 1. (*used at the beginning of a negative response*) no
(1/3); **2.** not: **Вы идёте и́ли нет?** Are you going or
not?; **3.** *predicative* (+ *Gen.*) there isn't (there
aren't); there's (there are) no . . . : **Там нет ли́фта.**
There's no elevator there. (4/1); **4.** *predicative* (*usu.*
у + *Gen.* + **нет** + *Gen.*) I (you, *etc.*) don't have . . . ;
I (you, *etc.*) have no . . . : **У меня́ нет соба́ки.**
I don't have a dog. (4/1)

Ещё нет (Нет ещё) Not yet. (6/3)

нехоро́ший bad (5/4)

нехорошо́ *used as predicate* (it's/that's) bad (5/4)

ни сло́ва don't say (breathe) a word (about it) (5/4)

нигде́ nowhere (5/3)

никако́й no . . . (at all); not any (4/4)

никогда́ never (4/4)

никого́ *Gen. and Acc. of* **никто́** (4/3)

Никого́ нет. There's nobody there (here). [4/3]

никто́ no one; nobody (4/3)

ним *variant of* **им** (*Dat. of* **они́;** *Instr. of* **он** *and* **оно́**) *used
after prepositions* (6/1)

ни́ми *variant of* **и́ми** (*Instr. of* **они́**) *used after
prepositions*

них *variant of* **их** (*Gen., Acc., and Prep. of* **они́**) *used after
prepositions* (4/1, 5/2, 7/3)

ничего́ nothing (5/1)
(*in response to an apology*) **Ничего́!** That's okay!;
That's all right! (2/3)
(*in response to* **Как дела́?**) **Ничего́.** Okay; all right; not
(too) bad (1/2)

но but (3/4)

новосе́лье housewarming (6/4)

но́вость (*pl.* но́вости, *Gen. pl.* новосте́й) *f.* news (7/4)

но́вый new (2/1)
Что но́вого? What's new? (7/2v)

ноль (*or* **нуль**) (*Gen. sing.* ноля́ *or* нуля́) *m.* zero (2/1)

но́мер (*pl.* номера́) number (2/1)
но́мер телефо́на (tele)phone number (2/1)

ночь *f.* night
в два часа́ но́чи at two a.m. (7/3)
но́чью at night (7/1)

ноя́брь (*Gen. sing.* ноября́) *m.* November (1/4)

нра́виться (*usu. 3rd pers.* нра́вится, нра́вятся)/
понра́виться (+ *Dat.*) to like; to be pleasing
(to someone) (6/2, *pfv.* 7/4)

Нам нра́вится ко́мната. We like the room. (6/2)

ну well (2/2)

   Ну чтó ты! What are you talking about!; What do you mean! (5/1)

нýжен (нужнá, нýжно, нужны́) 1. needed; **2.** (+ *Dat.*) one needs (6/4)

   всё, что нýжно everything that's needed; everything we need (6/4)

нуль (*or* **ноль**) (*Gen. sing.* нуля́ *or* ноля́) *m.* zero (2/1)

Нью-Йóрк New York (1/2)

О

о (об, обо) (+ *prep*) about; of (4/3)

обéд dinner; afternoon meal; lunch (7/3)

   готóвить (готóвлю, готóвишь, . . . готóвят)/**приготóвить обéд** to fix dinner (7/3)

обижáть/обúдеть (обúжу, обúдишь, . . . обúдят) to offend [7/3]

обмéн exchange (6/3v)

   обмéн валю́ты currency exchange

общежи́тие dormitory (5/1)

объявлéние advertisement; ad, sign (5/1)

   Повéсьте объявлéние. Put up a sign. [6/2]

объяснять/объясни́ть (объясню́, объясни́шь, . . . объясня́т) to explain (7/2)

обы́чно usually (4/4)

обязáтельно absolutely; definitely; by all means (6/4)

óвощи vegetables (7/3)

овсянка (овсяная кáша) *colloquial* oatmeal (5/4v)

огур(é)ц (*Gen. sing.* огурцá) cucumber

   солёный огурéц pickle [7/3v]

одеяло blanket (3/2v)

оди́н (однá, однó, одни́) 1. *numeral* one (2/1); **2.** a; a certain [7/3]

   ещё оди́н (однá, однó) one more (5/4)

   Однý мину́ту! Just a minute! (7/2)

оди́ннадцать eleven (2/1)

оди́ннадцатый eleventh (6/3)

однокла́ссник/однокла́ссница classmate (5/1v)

Однý мину́ту! Just a minute! (7/2)

океáн ocean (1/2)

окнó (*pl.* óкна, *Gen. pl.* óкон) window (2/2v)

октябрь (*Gen. sing.* октября́) *m.* October (1/4)

он he; it (1/3)

онá she; it (1/3)

они́ they (1/3)

онó it (1/3)

опáздывать/опоздáть (опоздáю, опоздáешь, . . . опоздáют) to be late (5/4v) (*pfv.* 7/2)

óпера opera (4/2v)

опоздáть (опоздáю, опоздáешь, . . . опоздáют) *pfv.* to be late (7/2) (*impfv.* **опáздывать** 5/4v)

óпыт experience (4/4)

опять again (3/1)

оригинáльно creatively; *used as predicate* (it's/that's) creative (3/1)

óсень *f.* fall, autumn

   óсенью in the fall (7/1)

оставáться (остаю́сь, остаёшься, . . . остаю́тся)/**остáться** (остáнусь, остáнешься, . . . остáнутся) to remain; to stay [7/4]

остановка (of a bus, train, *etc.*) stop

   автóбусная остановка bus stop (5/3)

   остановка автóбуса bus stop (3/4)

остáться (остáнусь, остáнешься, . . . остáнутся) *pfv.* to remain; to stay (*impfv.* **оставáться**) [7/4]

от (+ *Gen.*) from (5/1)

   блúзко от near; close to (5/3)

   далекó (недалекó) от far (not far) from (5/3)

отдавáть (отдаю́, отдаёшь, . . . отдаю́т)/**отдáть** (отдáм, отдáшь, отдáст, отдади́м, отдади́те, отдаду́т; *past* óтдал, отдалá, óтдало, óтдали) to return; to give (back) (5/3)

отдыхáть/отдохну́ть (отдохну́, отдохнёшь, . . . отдохну́т) to rest (3/1v)

от(é)ц (*Gen. sing.* отцá) father (2/1v)

открывáть/откры́ть (открóю, открóешь, . . . открóют) to open (5/4) [*pfv. infin. only* 4/1]

   Открóйте кни́гу на страни́це . . . . Open your book to page . . . . [1/4]

   Открóйте окнó! Open the window! [1/4]

откры́тка (*Gen. pl.* откры́ток) postcard (5/3v)

откýда 1. from where: **Откýда вы?** Where are you from?; **2.** how: **Откýда вы знáете (ты знáешь)?** How do you (happen to) know? (6/2)

отли́чно excellently

   Отли́чно Excellent! (5/4)

отли́чный excellent (3/2)

   Отли́чная компáния! What a great group! (7/1)

отоплéние heating [4/2]

отпрáздновать (отпрáздную, отпрáзднуешь, . . . отпрáзднуют) *pfv.* to celebrate (*impfv.* **прáздновать**) (7/3)

оттýда from there (3/4v)

óтчество patronymic (1/2)

   Как вáше и́мя и óтчество? What're your name and patronymic? (1/2)

óфис office (6/2v)

официáнт/официáнтка (*Gen. pl.* официáнток) waiter/waitress (4/4v)

óчень very (1/2)

   óчень приятно! (*when meeting someone*) Pleased to meet you; Nice to meet you! (1/2)

Óчень прия́тно познако́миться. (It's/It was) very nice to meet you. (4/4)

Óчень рад. Pleased to meet you. (2/3)

óчередь *f.* turn

по óчереди to take turns (doing something); taking turns (7/3)

П

па́па dad (2/2)

па́р(е)нь (*gen sing.* па́рня, *Gen. pl.* парне́й) *m.* guy; fellow (5/4)

паркова́ть (парку́ю, парку́ешь, . . . парку́ют) to park (5/1)

па́спорт (*pl.* паспорта́) passport (1/4)

пасти́лки от ка́шля cough drops [5/3v]

пе́нсия pension; pension payment [6/3]

пе́рвый first (2/4)

пере́дняя *noun, declines like adj.* entryway [5/2]

переезжа́ть/перее́хать (перее́ду, перее́дешь, . . . перее́дут) to move (to a new residence) [7/4]

перезва́нивать/перезвони́ть to call again; to call back [7/2v]

Я перезвоню́. I'll call back. (7/2v)

пе́сня (*gen pl.* пе́сен) song (7/4)

петь (пою́, поёшь, . . . пою́т)/**спеть** to sing [7/4]

пиани́ст/пиани́стка (*Gen. pl.* пиани́сток) pianist (2/1)

пи́во beer (6/4v)

пиджа́к (*Gen. sing.* пиджака́) (man's) suit jacket (1/3)

пиро́жное *noun, declines like adj.* pastry (5/4)

пирож(о́)к (*Gen. sing.* пирожка́) pirozhok (*small filled pastry*) (1/2)

писа́ть (пишу́, пи́шешь, . . . пи́шут)/**написа́ть** to write (3/1v) (*pfv.* 7/1)

письмо́ (*pl.* пи́сьма, *Gen. pl.* пи́сем) letter (1/3)

пить (пью, пьёшь, . . . пьют)/**вы́пить** (вы́пью, вы́пьешь, . . . вы́пьют) to drink; *usu. pfv.* to drink up (5/4v)

пи́цца pizza [7/3]

Пиши́те! Write. [1/4]

плати́ть (плачу́, пла́тишь, . . . пла́тят)/**заплати́ть** (**за** + *Acc.*) to pay (for) (5/3)

пло́хо badly; *used as predicate* (it's/that's) bad (1/2)

плохо́й bad (2/4)

площа́дка landing (of a staircase) [6/4]

пло́щадь (*Gen. pl.* площаде́й) *f.* (city) square (5/2)

плюс plus

плю́сы и ми́нусы pluses and minuses [2/4v]

по (+ *Dat.*) by; on

по де́лу on business [7/4]

по óчереди to take turns (doing something) (7/3)

по-англи́йски (**по-ру́сски**, *etc.*) (in) English (Russian, *etc.*) (4/3v)

говори́ть по-англи́йски (**по-ру́сски**, *etc.*) to speak English (Russian, *etc.*) (4/3v)

писа́ть по-англи́йски (**по-ру́сски**, *etc.*) to write in English (Russian, *etc.*) (4/3v)

повезти́ (повезёт; *past* повезло́) (+ *Dat.*) *pfv. impersonal* to have good luck; to be lucky (*impfv.* **везти́**)

Нам необыкнове́нно повезло́. We were incredibly lucky; We really lucked out. (6/4)

Не повезло́ ей! That's tough luck for her! [7/2]

пове́сить (пове́шу, пове́сишь, . . . пове́сят) *pfv.* to hang; to hang up (*impfv.* **ве́шать**) [7/2]

ве́шать/пове́сить (пове́шу, пове́сишь, . . . пове́сят) **тру́бку** to hang up the phone [7/2]

Пове́сьте объявле́ние. Put up a sign [6/2]

Повтори́те! Repeat. [1/4]

подари́ть (подарю́, пода́ришь, . . . пода́рят) (+ *Dat.* + *Acc.*) *pfv.* to give (*as a present*) (*impfv.* **дари́ть**) (7/4)

пода́р(о)к (*Gen. sing.* пода́рка) gift; present (6/4)

подру́га (female) friend (5/4)

поду́шка (*Gen. pl.* поду́шек) pillow; cushion (2/3v)

подъе́зд entrance (to a building) (2/4)

пожа́луйста 1. please; **2.** You're welcome!; **3.** Here you are! (1/2)

пожило́й elderly; middle-aged [6/4]

позвони́ть (позвоню́, позвони́шь, . . . позвоня́т) (+ *Dat.*) *pfv.* to call; to phone (*impfv.* **звони́ть**) (7/1v)

поздравля́ть/поздра́вить (поздра́влю, поздра́вишь, . . . поздра́вят) (+ *Acc.* + **с** + *Instr.*) to congratulate

Мо́жешь меня́ поздра́вить! Congratulate me! [7/2]

познако́мить (познако́млю, познако́мишь, . . . познако́мят) (+ *Acc.* + **с** + *Instr.*) *pfv.* to introduce (someone to someone) [7/4] (*impfv.* **знако́мить**)

познако́миться (познако́млюсь, познако́мишься, . . . познако́мятся) *pfv.* to get acquainted (*impfv.* **знако́миться**)

Дава́йте познако́мимся. Let's introduce ourselves.; Let's get acquainted. (2/3)

Óчень прия́тно познако́миться. (It's/It was) very nice to meet you. (4/4)

Познако́мьтесь, э́то . . . . (*when introducing someone*) I'd like you to meet . . . ; Meet . . . ; Let me introduce. . . (2/3)

Позови́ ма́му. (Would you) get Mom? (7/2)

по-испа́нски (in) Spanish (4/3v)

по-италья́нски (in) Italian (4/3v)

пока́ 1. for the time being; for now [5/4]; **2. Пока́!** *informal* Bye!; See you later (1/2)

по-кита́йски (in) Chinese (4/3v)

покупа́ть/купи́ть (куплю́, ку́пишь, . . . ку́пят) to buy (*pfv. infin. only* 5/1) (7/2)

пол (*Prep. sing.* на полу́, *pl.* полы́) floor (2/2v)

поликли́ника outpatient clinic (3/4v).

по́лка (*Gen. pl.* по́лок) shelf (3/2v)

    кни́жная по́лка bookshelf (2/3v)

получа́ть/получи́ть (получу́, полу́чишь, . . . полу́чат) to receive; to get (5/3)

получа́ться/получи́ться (полу́чится, полу́чатся) (**у** + *gen*; *3rd pers. only*) to turn out

    У тебя́ непло́хо получа́ется! That's pretty good! [6/1]

полчаса́ half an hour (7/2)

поменя́ть *pfv.* to change (*impfv.* **меня́ть**) [7/2]

помеша́ть (+ *Dat.*) *pfv.* to bother; to disturb (*impfv.* **меша́ть**) (7/1)

по́мнить (по́мню, по́мнишь, . . . по́мнят) to remember (5/2)

помога́ть/помо́чь (помогу́, помо́жешь, . . . помо́гут; *past* помо́г, помогла́, помогло́, помогли́) (+ *Dat.*) to help (*pfv. infin. only* 5/3) (7/4)

Помоги́те! Help! (4/3)

по-мо́ему *parenthetical* in my opinion (3/1)

по-моско́вски Moscow style (5/3)

помо́чь (помогу́, помо́жешь, . . . помо́гут; *past* помо́г, помогла́, помогло́, помогли́) (+ *Dat.*) *pfv.* to help (*pfv. infin. only* 5/3) (*impfv.* **помога́ть** 7/4)

по́мощь *f.* help; assistance

    ско́рая по́мощь ambulance service (6/2)

понеде́льник Monday (1/4)

по-неме́цки (in) German (4/3v)

понима́ть/поня́ть (пойму́, поймёшь, . . . пойму́т; *past* по́нял, поняла́, по́няло, по́няли) to understand (3/1) (*pfv.* 7/3)

Понима́ешь? Got it? (6/1)

понра́виться (*usu. 3rd pers.* понра́вится, понра́вятся) (+ *Dat.*) *pfv.* to like, to be pleasing (to someone) (7/4) (*impfv.* **нра́виться** 6/2)

Поня́тно. *used as predicate* I understand; I see. (7/1)

попада́ть/попа́сть (попаду́, попадёшь, . . . попаду́т; *past* попа́л, попа́ла, попа́ло, попа́ли) *куда* to end up calling (some place) (7/2)

    (*over the telephone*) **Вы не туда́ попа́ли.** You dialed (got) the wrong number (7/2)

по-португа́льски (in) Portuguese (4/3v)

попроси́ть (попрошу́, попро́сишь, . . . попро́сят) *pfv.* to ask for; to request (*impfv.* **проси́ть**)

    (*on the phone*) **Мо́жно попроси́ть . . . ?** May I speak to . . . ? (7/3)

    Попроси́те (к телефо́ну) . . . May I speak with . . . ? (7/2)

пора́ (+ *Dat.*) (*куда*) *impersonal* it's time (*for someone to go some place*): **Тебе́ пора́ в университе́т.** It's time for you to go to the university. (7/2)

португа́льский Portuguese (*adj.*)

    по-португа́льски in Portuguese (4/3v)

по-ру́сски (in) Russian (4/3v)

    говори́ть (писа́ть, чита́ть) по-ру́сски to speak (write, read) (in) Russian (4/3v)

поря́док order

    Всё в поря́дке. Everything's OK. (6/2)

после́дний last (in a series) [6/1v]

послу́шать *pfv.* to listen (to) (7/2) (*impfv.* **слу́шать** 3/3)

потол(о́)к (*pl.* потолки́) ceiling (2/2v)

пото́м 1. then; after that (3/4v); 2. later (on) (4/3)

потому́ что because (4/4)

по-францу́зски (in) French (4/3v)

похо́ж (похо́жа, похо́же, похо́жи) на (+ *Acc.*) resemble; look like: **Он похо́ж на вас.** He looks like you. (6/2)

почему́ why (2/3)

по́чта 1. mail (6/3); 2. post office (3/4v)

почтальо́н mail carrier (4/4v)

почти́ almost (6/4)

Пошли́! Let's go! (4/3)

поэ́тому that's why; therefore; so (3/1)

по-япо́нски (in) Japanese (4/3v)

пра́вда 1. truth 2. *parenthetical* true; granted; to be sure (6/4); 3. **Пра́вда?** Really?; Isn't that so? (6/4)

пра́вильно correctly

    Пра́вильно! That's right!; That's correct! (6/1)

пра́здновать (пра́здную, пра́зднуешь, . . . пра́зднуют)/**отпра́здновать** to celebrate (7/3)

пра́ктика practice (4/4)

    ча́стная пра́ктика private practice [4/4v]

предлага́ть/предложи́ть (предложу́, предло́жишь, . . . предло́жат) 1. to offer; 2. to suggest (7/1)

предпочита́ть/предпоче́сть (предпочту́, предпочтёшь, . . . предпочту́т; *past* предпочёл, предпочла́, предпочло́, предпочли́) to prefer [3/4]

пре́жде всего́ first of all (5/4)

прекра́сно wonderfully

    Прекра́сно! It's (that's) wonderful! (4/1)

    Э́то прекра́сно! It's (that's) wonderful! (4/1)

прекра́сный wonderful (7/1)

прелю́д prelude [6/1]

преподава́тель/преподава́тельница instructor (in college); teacher (4/3v) преподава́ть (преподаю́, преподаёшь, . . . преподаю́т) to teach (4/3v)

Приве́т! *informal* Hi!; Hello there! (1/1)

приглаша́ть/пригласи́ть (приглашу́, пригласи́шь, . . . приглася́т) to invite (7/1)

приглаше́ние invitation (7/2v)

приготóвить (приготóвлю, приготóвишь, . . . приготóвят) *pfv.* **1.** to prepare; **2.** to cook (7/3) (*impfv.* **готóвить** 6/4v)

приезжа́ть/прие́хать (прие́ду, прие́дешь, . . . прие́дут) to come (*by vehicle*); to arrive [7/4]

прийти́ (приду́, придёшь, . . . приду́т; *past* пришёл, пришла́, пришло́, пришли́) *pfv.* to come; to arrive; to come back (*impfv.* **приходи́ть**) (7/4)

прилета́ть/прилете́ть (прилечу́, прилети́шь, . . . прилетя́т) to arrive (by plane) [3/4]

принести́ (принесу́, принесёшь, . . . принесу́т; *past* принёс, принесла́ принесло́, принесли́) *pfv.* to bring (over) (7/3) (*impfv.* **приноси́ть** 6/4)

принима́ть/приня́ть (приму́, при́мешь, . . . при́мут; *past* при́нял, приняла́, при́няло, при́няли) to accept; to take (6/3v)

приноси́ть (приношу́, прино́сишь, . . . прино́сят)/**принести́** (принесу́, принесёшь, . . . принесу́т; *past* принёс, принесла́ принесло́, принесли́) to bring (over) (6/4) (*pfv.* 7/3)

при́нято it is customary (to . . .); it is accepted; it is (considered) appropriate [7/3]

У нас э́то не при́нято. We don't do that (here). [7/3]

приходи́ть (прихожу́, прихо́дишь, . . . прихо́дят)/**прийти́** (приду́, придёшь, . . . приду́т; *past* пришёл, пришла́, пришло́, пришли́) to come; to arrive; to come back (7/4)

прия́тно *used as predicate* (it's/that's) pleasant; (it's/that's) nice

О́чень прия́тно! (*when meeting someone*) Pleased to meet you; Nice to meet you! (1/2)

О́чень прия́тно познако́миться. (It's/It was) very nice to meet you. (4/4)

прия́тный nice; pleasant (7/4)

пробле́ма problem (4/1)

продава́ть (продаю́, продаёшь, . . . продаю́т)/**прода́ть** (прода́м, прода́шь, прода́ст, продади́м, продади́те, продаду́т; *past* про́дал, продала́, про́дало, про́дали) (+ *Dat.* + *Acc.*) to sell (5/3)

Продолжа́йте! Continue. [1/4]

проду́кты *pl.* (*Gen.* проду́ктов) groceries (3/4)

проездно́й *noun, declines like adj.*, **проездно́й биле́т** metro (bus, trolley, tram) pass (5/3v)

проси́ть (прошу́, про́сишь, . . . про́сят)/**попроси́ть** to ask for; to request

(*on the phone*) **Мо́жно попроси́ть . . . ?** May I speak to . . . ? (7/3)

Попроси́те (к телефо́ну) . . . May I speak with . . . ? (7/2)

Прости́те! Excuse me! (7/2)

прочита́ть *pfv.* to read (7/1) (*impfv.* **чита́ть** 3/1)

профе́ссия profession (3/1)

профе́ссор (*pl.* профессора́) professor (2/1)

про́шлый last (*preceding the present one*) (5/2)

в про́шлом году́ last year (5/2)

пу́дель *m.* poodle (6/1v)

пуло́вер V-neck sweater (1/3)

пылесо́с vacuum cleaner (4/1v)

пье́са play (5/2v)

пятёрка a "five" (top grade in Russian schools, equivalent to a grade of "A") (4/3)

пятна́дцатый fifteenth (6/3)

пятна́дцать fifteen (6/1)

пя́тница Friday (1/4)

пя́тый fifth (6/3)

пять five (2/1)

пятьдеся́т fifty (6/1)

пятьсо́т five hundred (5/3)

Р

рабо́та **1.** work (3/1v); **2.** job

рабо́тать to work (3/1v)

рад (ра́да, ра́до, ра́ды) glad; pleased (6/4)

О́чень рад. Pleased to meet you. (2/3)

ра́дио radio (5/1)

ра́зве really?: **Ра́зве э́то тру́дная те́ма?** Is it really a difficult topic? (3/1)

разгова́ривать to talk; to speak (6/4)

разме́р size (5/3)

ра́зница difference

Кака́я ра́зница? What's the difference?; What difference does it make? (3/2)

ра́зный **1.** different; **2.** various (5/2)

райо́н district; section (of town) (3/4)

расска́з (short) story (5/2v)

расска́зывать/рассказа́ть (расскажу́, расска́жешь, . . . расска́жут) to tell; to relate (7/3)

Расскажи́те (о) . . . Tell us (me) (about) . . . (4/3)

расти́ (расту́, растёшь, . . . расту́т; *past* рос, росла́, росло́, росли́)/**вы́расти** (вы́расту, вы́растешь, . . . вы́растут; *past* вы́рос, вы́росла, вы́росло, вы́росли) **1.** to grow; **2.** to grow up (6/3)

ребён(о)к (*pl.* ребя́та, *Gen. pl.* ребя́т; *or pl.* де́ти, *Gen. pl.* дете́й) child (2/1v, де́ти)

ре́дко rarely (5/4)

рези́новый rubber (*adj.*) (5/3)

река́ (*Acc.* реку́ or ре́ку; *pl.* ре́ки, *Gen. pl.* рек) river (1/2)

рекомендова́ть (рекоменду́ю, рекоменду́ешь, . . . рекоменду́ют) to recommend [5/4]

рестора́н restaurant (4/4v)

ро́вно exactly (7/3)

   ро́вно в семь часо́в at seven o'clock sharp; at seven on the dot (7/3)

роди́тели (*Gen.* роди́телей) *pl.* parents (2/1v)

роди́ться (*past* роди́лся, родила́сь, роди́лись) to be born (5/2)

родно́й native [4/3v]

рожде́ние birth

   день рожде́ния birthday (4/2)

рок rock (music) (3/3)

Росси́я Russia (1/2)

роя́ль *m.* piano; grand piano (2/3v)

руба́шка (*Gen. pl.* руба́шек) shirt (1/3)

рубль (*Gen. sing.* рубля́) *m.* ruble (5/3)

рука́ (*Acc. sing.* ру́ку, *pl.* ру́ки) 1. hand; 2. arm

   золоты́е ру́ки (у + *Gen.*) (one is) good with one's hands (4/3)

   ма́стер на все ру́ки jack-of-all-trades [4/3]

руководи́тель *m.* leader; supervisor

   нау́чный руководи́тель *m.* (academic) adviser [5/2]

ру́сский 1. *adj.* Russian; 2. **ру́сский/ру́сская** (**ру́сские**) *noun, declines like adj.* a Russian (2/2)

   по-ру́сски in Russian (4/3v)

ру́чка (*Gen. pl.* ру́чек) pen (1/3)

ры́ба fish (7/3)

рюкза́к (*Gen.* рюкзака́) backpack; knapsack (1/4)

ря́дом (right) nearby; next door (3/4)

С

с (со) (+ *Instr.*) with

с удово́льствием I'd be glad to; gladly; with pleasure (7/2)

саксофо́н saxophone (3/3v)

саксофони́ст saxophonist (3/3v)

Санкт-Петербу́рг Saint (St.) Petersburg (1/2)

сапоги́ (*Gen.* сапо́г) *pl.* (*sing.* сапо́г, *Gen. sing.* сапога́) boots (5/3)

све́тлый bright; light (3/2)

сви́тер [*pronounced* -тэ-] (*pl.* сви́теры *and* свитера́) (high-neck) sweater (1/3)

свой *when owner is the subject* one's own [6/3]

сдава́ть (сдаю́, сдаёшь, . . . сдаю́т)/**сдать** (сдам, сдашь, сдаст, сдади́м, сдади́те, сдаду́т; *past* сдал, сдала́, сда́ло, сда́ли) to rent out (an apartment) (6/2v)

сдава́ться *impfv. only* to be for rent [5/4]

сде́лать *pfv.* 1. to do; 2. to make (7/3) (*impfv.* **де́лать** 3/1)

Се́верная Аме́рика North America (1/2)

сего́дня today (1/4)

   Како́е сего́дня число́? What's the date today? (6/3)

   Како́й сего́дня день? What day is today? (1/4)

седьмо́й seventh (6/3)

сейча́с 1. now; right now (3/4); 2. right away; at once (3/1)

   Сейча́с! (*when being called by someone*) I'll be right there! (2/4)

   (Сейча́с . . .) (+ *clock time*). It's (now) . . . o'clock. (7/3)

сельдере́й celery [7/3v]

семна́дцатый seventeenth (6/3)

семна́дцать seventeen (6/1)

семь seven (2/1)

се́мьдесят seventy (6/1)

семья́ (*pl.* се́мьи, *Gen. pl.* семе́й, *Dat. pl.* се́мьям) family (2/1v)

сентя́брь (*Gen. sing.* сентября́) *m.* September (1/4)

серди́то angrily [7/2]

серди́ться (сержу́сь, се́рдишься, . . . се́рдятся)/ **рассерди́ться** to be (get) angry (at) [6/4]

сестра́ (*pl.* сёстры, *Gen. pl.* сестёр, *Dat. pl.* сёстрам) sister (2/1v)

   медици́нская сестра́ (медсестра́) nurse [7/1]

сигаре́та cigarette (5/3v)

сиде́ть (сижу́, сиди́шь, . . . сидя́т) to sit; to be sitting [6/4]

симпати́чный nice; likable (3/2)

систе́ма system [7/1]

Сиэ́тл Seattle (1/2)

сказа́ть (скажу́, ска́жешь, . . . ска́жут) *pfv.* to say; to tell (*pfv. past only* 6/2) (*pfv.* 7/4) (*impfv.* **говори́ть** 4/2)

   Скажи́те, пожа́луйста. . . Please tell me . . . ; Could you please tell me . . . ? (5/3v)

ско́лько (+ *Gen.*) how many; how much (6/1)

   Ско́лько ему́ (ей) лет? How old is he (she)? (6/1)

   Ско́лько э́то сто́ит? How much does this cost? (6/2)

ско́рая по́мощь ambulance service (6/2)

скрипа́ч/скрипа́чка violinist (3/3v)

скри́пка violin (3/3v)

ску́чно boringly; *used as predicate* (it's/that's) boring (6/1)

ску́чный boring; tiresome (6/1)

сле́ва on the left (2/2)

сли́шком too; excessively (4/2)

сло́во (*pl.* слова́, *Gen. pl.* слов, *dat pl.* слова́м) word (1/2)
   ни сло́ва don't say (breathe) a word (about it) (5/4)
случа́ться/случи́ться (случи́тся, случа́тся) (*3rd pers. only*) to happen; to occur [7/2]
слу́шать/послу́шать to listen (to) (3/3) (*pfv.* 7/2)
   Слу́шайте. Listen! [1/4]
слы́шать (слы́шу, слы́шишь, . . . слы́шат)/**услы́шать** to hear (6/4)
   Я ничего́ не хочу́ слы́шать! I don't want to hear a thing about it! (7/2)
сметь to dare **Не смей** . . . Don't you dare . . . [6/4]
смотре́ть (смотрю́, смо́тришь, . . . смо́трят)/**посмотре́ть 1.** to look (at); **2.** to watch (*impfv. infin. only* 3/4) (4/2)
   Смотри́те! Look! (3/4)
смочь (смогу́, смо́жешь, . . . смо́гут; *past* смог, смогла́, смогло́, смогли́) *pfv.* to be able (7/4) (*impfv.* **мочь** 5/3)
снима́ть/снять (сниму́, сни́мешь, . . . сни́мут; *past* снял, сняла́, сня́ло, сня́ли) to rent (6/4) (*pfv.* 7/4)
соба́ка dog (2/1)
собира́ться/собра́ться (соберу́сь, собере́шься, . . . соберу́тся) **1.** to be planning to go somewhere; **2.** (+ *infin.*) to intend, to be about (to do something) (5/4)
собра́ние meeting (7/1v)
со́бственный one's own [6/2]
совсе́м не not at all (7/2v)
сок juice (1/2)
соле́ный огуре́ц pickle [7/3v]
соли́ст/соли́стка soloist [4/2v]
соль *f.* salt [7/3v]
со́рок forty (6/3)
сосе́д (*pl.* сосе́ди, *Gen. pl.* сосе́дей)/**сосе́дка** (*Gen. pl.* сосе́док) neighbor (2/2)
сочине́ние (*a writing assignment*) composition (3/1v)
спа́льня bedroom (2/2v)
спаси́бо thank you; thanks (1/2)
   Спаси́бо за приглаше́ние. Thanks for the invitation. (7/2v)
   (*in response to* **Как дела́?**) **Хорошо́, спаси́бо.** Fine, thanks (1/2)
спать (сплю, спишь, . . . спят) to sleep (4/2)
спортза́л gym; gymnasium (3/4v)
спра́ва on the right (2/2)
спра́вочная *noun, declines like adj.* information; directory assistance (7/2)
спра́шивать/спроси́ть (спрошу́, спро́сишь, . . . спро́сят) **1.** (+ *Acc.* or **y** + *Gen.*) to ask (someone); **2.** (+ *Acc.* or **o** + *Prep.*) to ask (about); to inquire (6/4) (*pfv.* 7/4)

среда́ (*Acc. sing.* сре́ду) Wednesday (1/4)
стадио́н stadium (1/3)
ста́ршие *noun, declines like adj.* (*pl. only*) one's elders (6/1)
ста́рый old (2/4v)
статья́ (*Gen. pl.* стате́й) article (3/1)
стена́ (*pl.* сте́ны) wall (2/2v)
стира́льная маши́на washing machine (4/1v)
сто (one) hundred (6/1)
сто́ить (сто́ит, сто́ят) (*usu. 3rd. pers.*) to cost (6/2)
   Ско́лько э́то сто́ит? How much does this cost? (6/2)
стол (*Gen. sing.* стола́) table (3/2v)
столо́вая *noun, declines like adj.* dining room (2/2v)
стоя́ть (стою́, стои́шь, . . . стоя́т) **1.** to stand; to be; there is (are); **2.** to be (located) (6/4): **Кни́ги стоя́т в кни́жном шкафу́.** The books are in the bookcase.
страна́ (*pl.* стра́ны) country (1/2)
Стра́нно. That's strange. (7/2)
стро́гий strict (6/1v)
студе́нт/студе́нтка (*Gen. pl.* студе́нток) student (1/3)
стул (*pl.* сту́лья, *Gen. pl.* сту́льев) chair (3/2)
сты́дно it's a shame
   Мне сты́дно. I'm ashamed. (6/1)
суббо́та Saturday (1/4)
су́мка (*Gen. pl.* су́мок) bag (1/4)
счёт (*pl.* счета́) (*in a café, restaurant, etc.*) check (5/4)
США (**Соединённые Шта́ты Аме́рики**) USA (United States of America) (1/2)
сын (*pl.* сыновья́, *Gen. pl.* сынове́й) son (2/1)
сыр cheese (5/4)
сюда́ (*indicates direction*) here; this way (7/2)
сюрпри́з surprise (5/4)

Т

так 1. (in) this way; like this; like that; thus (5/3); **2.** так . . . (*with adverbs and short-form adjectives*) so; (*with verbs*) so much (5/1); **3.** *particle* so; then (2/3)
   Так э́то . . . So this is (these are). . . (3/2)
тако́й 1. such (a); like that; this kind of; **2.** (*with adj.* + *noun*) such (a); (*with adj.*) so; (*with noun*) a real . . . (5/3)
такси́ *neut., indecl.* taxi; cab (4/4)
   води́тель такси́ taxi driver (4/4v)
там there (1/4)
тамо́жня customs [1/4]
твой (**твоя́, твоё, твои́**) *informal* your; yours (1/4)

теа́тр theater (1/3)

тебе́ *Dat. and Prep. of* **ты** (6/1, 7/3)

тебя́ *Gen. and Acc. of* **ты** (4/1, 5/2)

   Как тебя́ зову́т? What's your name? (1/1)

телеви́зор television (set); TV (set) (3/2v)

телегра́мма telegram (6/3v)

телефо́н telephone (3/1)

   но́мер телефо́на (tele)phone number (2/1)

те́ма topic; subject; theme (3/1)

те́ннис [*pronounced* тэ-] tennis (3/4)

тенниси́ст/тенниси́стка [*pronounced* тэ-]
   tennis player [3/4]

тепе́рь now (3/3)

тёплый warm (6/4v)

тётя (*Gen. pl.* тётей) aunt (2/1v)

ти́хо quietly; softly (4/2)

то *neut. of* **тот**

то есть (*often abbreviated* **т.е.**) that is (4/1)

тобо́й *Instr. of* **ты**

тогда́ then (7/4)

то́же 1. also; too (2/1); **2.** (*with a negated verb*)
   either (5/3)

то́лько *only* (4/2)

торт cake (5/4)

то́стер [-тэ-] toaster (4/1v)

тот (**та, то, те**) that; that one (5/4)

тре́тий (**тре́тья, тре́тье, тре́тьи**) third (2/4)

три three (2/1)

   в три часа́ at three o'clock (7/1v)

тридца́тый thirtieth (6/3)

три́дцать thirty (6/1)

три́ллер thriller [3/1v]

трина́дцатый thirteenth (6/3)

трина́дцать thirteen (6/1)

тромбо́н trombone [3/3v]

труба́ trumpet (3/3v)

тру́бка (*Gen. pl.* тру́бок) (telephone) receiver

   ве́шать/пове́сить (пове́шу, пове́сишь, . . . пове́сят)
     тру́бку to hang up the phone [7/2]

   возьми́ тру́бку pick up the phone (7/2)

тру́дно *used as predicate* (it's/that's) difficult; (it's/that's)
   hard (7/1)

тру́дный difficult; hard (3/1)

туале́т bathroom; restroom (2/2)

   туале́тная бума́га toilet paper (5/3v)

туда́ (*indicates direction*) there (3/4)

   (*over the telephone*) **Вы не туда́ попа́ли.** You dialed
   (got) the wrong number (7/2)

ту́мбочка (*Gen. pl.* ту́мбочек) night table [3/2v]

тут 1. here (2/4); **2.** at this point; at that moment (6/4)

   Тут есть . . . ? Is (Are) there . . . here? [3/4]

ту́фли (*Gen.* ту́фель) *pl.* (*sing.* ту́фля) shoes (1/3)

ты *informal* you (1/3)

   Ну что́ ты! What are you talking about!; What do
   you mean! (5/1)

   Ты не возража́ешь? Do you mind? (7/1)

тяжёлый heavy (6/3)

У

у (+ *Gen.*) **1.** (*indicates someone's home, place of work, etc.*)
   at: **Пока́ я живу́ у тёти.** For the time being, I live at
   my aunt's. (6/3); **2.** (*indicates possession*) **У неё есть**
   брат. She has a brother. (4/1)

   У нас э́то не при́нято. We don't do that (here). (7/3)

   У тебя́ неплохо́ получа́ется. That's pretty good! (6/1)

уве́рен (**уве́рена, уве́рено, уве́рены**) sure; certain (6/4)

уви́деть (уви́жу, уви́дишь, . . . уви́дят) *pfv.* to see (7/4)
   (*impfv.* **ви́деть** 4/2)

угоща́ть/угости́ть (угощу́, угости́шь, . . . угостя́т) to
   treat (someone) to

   Я угоща́ю. (It's) my treat; (It's) on me. [5/4]

уда́рник drummer [3/3v]

уда́рные drums [3/3v]

удо́бно: Это удо́бно. It's/That's okay. (7/1)

удо́бный convenient (7/1)

у́жас horror (4/1)

   Како́й у́жас! That's horrible!; How awful! (2/2)

ужа́сно horribly; *used as predicate* (it's/that's) horrible;
   (it's/that's) terrible

   Это ужа́сно! It's/That's horrible!; How awful! (2/3)

ужа́сный horrible; terrible (4/1)

уже́ already (3/1)

у́ксус vinegar [7/3v]

улыба́ться/улыбну́ться (улыбну́сь, улыбнёшься, . . .
   улыбну́тся) to smile [7/4]

у́лица street (2/1)

уме́ть (уме́ю, уме́ешь, . . . уме́ют) to know how (to do
   something); to be able (to) (4/3)

универса́м supermarket (3/4v)

университе́т university (3/4v)

упражне́ние exercise (1/3)

Ура́! Hurrah! (4/3)

уро́к 1. lesson; **2.** (*usually pl.* уро́ки) homework (4/3)

у́тро (*Gen. sing.* у́тра *but* до утра́) morning (5/3)

   в пять часо́в утра́ at five a.m. (7/3)

   До́брое у́тро! Good morning! (7/2)

   у́тром in the morning (3/3v)

уча́ст(о)к (*Gen. sing.* уча́стка) plot (of land) [6/2v]

учи́лище (specialized) school

   медици́нское учи́лище nursing school [7/1]

учи́тель (*pl.* учителя́)/**учи́тельница** teacher (6/1v)

учи́ть (учу́, у́чишь, . . . у́чат)/**вы́учить** (вы́учу, вы́учишь, . . . вы́учат) to study (something); *usu. pfv.* to learn; (to try) to memorize (7/1)

учи́ться (учу́сь, у́чишься, . . . у́чатся)/**научи́ться**
    1. *impfv. only* to study; to be a student (4/3);
    2. (+ *Dat.* or + *infin.*) to learn (how to); to learn (to do something) [7/3]
    Где вы у́читесь? Where do you study? (4/3)

Ф

факульте́т department (4/4)
    истори́ческий факульте́т history department (6/2)
    На како́м факульте́те вы у́читесь? What department are you in? What are you majoring in? [4/4]
    факульте́т журнали́стики journalism department [4/4]
фами́лия last name (1/2)
февра́ль (*Gen. sing.* февраля́) *m.* February (1/4)
фина́нсовый financial [5/1v]
фи́рма firm; business; company (4/4v)
фле́йта flute [3/3v]
флейти́ст/флейти́стка flutist [3/3v]
фотогра́фия photograph (6/1v)
францу́зский French (*adj.*)
    по-францу́зски in French (4/3v)
фру́кты *usu. pl.* fruit (5/4v)
фунт pound [7/3v]
футбо́л soccer (7/2v)
футбо́лка (*Gen. pl.* футбо́лок) t-shirt (1/3)

Х

хи́мик chemist [4/4v]
хлеб bread (3/4)
ходи́ть (хожу́, хо́дишь, . . . хо́дят) *multidir.* of идти́
    1. to go; **2.** to walk (5/2)
    ходя́чая энциклопе́дия walking encyclopedia [5/2]
хозя́ин (*pl.* хозя́ева)/**хозя́йка** (*Gen. pl.* хозя́ек) landlord/landlady (6/2)
холоди́льник refrigerator (4/1v)
холо́дный cold (6/4v)
хоро́ший good; nice (2/2)
хорошо́ well; *used as predicate* (it's/that's) good (1/2)
    (*in response to* Как дела́?) **Хорошо́, спаси́бо.** Fine, thanks (1/2)
    хорошо́ чита́ть ле́кции to be a good lecturer [7/4]
хоте́ть (хочу́, хо́чешь, хо́чет, хоти́м, хоти́те, хотя́т) to want (5/1)
    Не хочу́ вам меша́ть. I don't want to bother you. [7/1]

Ц

цвет(о́)к (*Gen. sing.* цветка́, *pl.* цветы́, *Gen. pl.* цвето́в) flower (3/2v)
целова́ть (целу́ю, целу́ешь, . . . целу́ют)/**поцелова́ть** to kiss
    кре́пко целу́ю (*usu. at the end of a letter to a close relative, sweetheart, or friend*) lots of love [7/4]
центр **1.** center; **2.** (= центр го́рода) downtown (2/2)
цирк circus [3/1]

Ч

чай tea (1/2)
час (*gen sing.* ча́са *but* два, три, четы́ре часа́; *Prep. sing.* в . . . часу́; *pl.* часы́) **1.** hour; **2.** (*when telling time*) o'clock (7/1v)
    в два (три, четы́ре) часа́ at two (three, four) o'clock (7/1v)
    в кото́ром часу́? at what time?; when? (7/2)
    в пять (шесть, семь, *etc.*) **часо́в** at five (six, seven, *etc.*) o'clock (7/1v)
    в час at one o'clock (7/1v)
    Кото́рый час? What time is it? (7/3)
ча́стный private
    ча́стная пра́ктика private practice [4/4v]
ча́сто often (5/1)
часы́ (*Gen.* часо́в) *pl.* clock; watch (2/3v)
чего́ *Gen. of* что (4/1)
чей (чья, чьё, чьи) **1.** *interrogative* whose?; **2.** *relative* whose (2/2)
челове́к (*pl.* лю́ди, *Gen. pl.* люде́й, but пять, шесть, *etc.*, челове́к) person; man (5/2)
    молодо́й челове́к young man (5/4)
    «Челове́к в футля́ре» *The Man in a Case* [5/2v]
чем *Instr. of* что (9/1)
чём *Prep. of* что (7/3)
чемода́н suitcase (1/4)
чему́ *Dat. of* что (6/1)
че́рез (+ *Acc.*) (*indicates time from the present or from the indicated moment*) in: **че́рез две неде́ли** in two weeks (6/4)
    че́рез мину́ту a minute later (6/4)
чёрный ко́фе black coffee (5/4v)
четве́рг (*Gen. sing.* четверга́) Thursday (1/4)
четвёртый fourth (2/4)
четы́ре four (2/1)
    в четы́ре часа́ at four o'clock (7/1v)
четы́реста four hundred [7/3]
четы́рнадцатый fourteenth (6/1)
четы́рнадцать fourteen (6/3)

Чика́го Chicago (1/2)

чини́ть (чиню́, чи́нишь, . . . чи́нят)/**почини́ть**
  to fix; to repair (4/4)

число́ 1. number; **2.** day (*of the month*); date
  Како́е сего́дня число́? What's the date today? (6/3)

чи́стый clean (5/3)

чита́ть/прочита́ть to read (3/1) (*pfv.* 7/1)
  хорошо́ чита́ть ле́кции to be a good lecturer [7/4]
  Чита́йте! Read. [1/4]
  чита́ть ле́кции to give lectures [7/4]

что 1. *interrogative* what? (1/3); **2.** *relative* that; what (3/4)
  всё, что ну́жно everything that's needed (6/4)
  Ну что ты! What are you talking about!;
    What do you mean! (5/1)
  Что бу́дете зака́зывать? What can I get you?; Are
    you ready to order?; What'll you have? (5/4)
  Что де́лать? What should (can) I (we) do? (4/2v)
  Что ещё? What else? (4/3)
  что ж well (3/1)
  Что но́вого? What's new? (7/2v)
  Что принести́? What should I (we) bring? (7/3)
  Что случи́лось? What happened? (7/2)
  что тако́е . . . what . . . is [3/1]
  Что-что? Beg your pardon? (3/1)
  Что э́то? What's that (this)? (1/3)
  Что э́то за . . . ? What sort of . . . is that
    (are those)? (7/1)

чужо́й someone else's [6/3]

Ш

шампу́нь *m.* shampoo (5/3v)

шах *chess* check [3/1]

ша́хматы chess (3/1)
  игра́ть в ша́хматы to play chess (3/1)

шестна́дцатый sixteenth (6/3)

шестна́дцать sixteen (6/1)

шесто́й sixth (6/3)
  в шесто́м кла́ссе in the sixth grade (6/1)

шесть six (2/1)

шестьдеся́т sixty (6/1)

шеф-по́вар chef [7/3]

шкаф (*Prep. sing.* в шкафу́, *pl.* шкафы́) wardrobe,
    armoire; cabinet; closet (6/2)

шко́ла school (4/3)

шко́льник/шко́льница schoolboy/schoolgirl (2/1)

шокола́д chocolate (5/3v)

шокола́дный chocolate (*adj.*) [5/4]

шоссе́ [*pronounced* -сэ] highway (6/2v)

шум noise [6/4]

шу́тка (*Gen. pl.* шу́ток) joke (5/3)

Э

экза́мен exam, test (7/3)
  экза́мен по исто́рии history exam (7/3)

экономи́ческий economics (*adj.*); (institute) of
    economics (5/1v)
  Моско́вский экономи́ческий институ́т Moscow
    Institute of Economics [5/1v]

эле́ктрик electrician (4/4)

электро́ника electronics (4/4)
  магази́н электро́ники electronics store (4/4)

энциклопе́дия encyclopedia
  ходя́чая энциклопе́дия walking encyclopedia [5/2]

эта́ж (*Gen. sing.* этажа́, *Gen. pl.* этаже́й) floor;
    story (2/2)

Э́то . . . This (That) is; These (Those) are . . . (1/1)
  Э́то всё? Is that all? (4/2)
  Э́то говори́т. . . . This is . . . speaking. (7/2)
  Э́то звони́т. . . . This is . . . calling. (7/2v)
  Э́то здо́рово! It's/That's great! (2/2)
  Э́то прекра́сно! It's/That's wonderful! (4/1)
  Э́то удо́бно. It's/That's okay (convenient). (7/1)
  Э́то ужа́сно! It's/That's horrible!; How
    awful! (2/3)

э́тот (**э́та, э́то, э́ти**) this; that (5/4)

Ю

юбиле́й anniversary [5/4]

ю́бка (*Gen. pl.* ю́бок) skirt (1/3)

Ю́жная Аме́рика South America (1/2)

юриди́ческий law (*adj.*); (department) of law (5/1v)
  юриди́ческий институ́т law school

юри́ст lawyer (4/4v)

Я

я I (1/3)
  Я в шесто́м кла́ссе. I'm in the sixth grade (6/1)
  Я на второ́м ку́рсе. I'm in second year
    (of college) (6/1)
  Я ничего́ не хочу́ слы́шать! I don't want to hear a
    thing about it! (7/2)
  Я перезвоню́. I'll call back. (7/2v)
  Я угоща́ю. (It's) my treat; (It's) on me. (5/4)

язы́к (*Gen. sing.* языка́) language (4/3v)

яйцо́ (*pl.* я́йца, *Gen. pl.* яи́ц) egg (7/3v)
  круто́е яйцо́ hard-boiled egg (7/3v)
  яи́чница [*pronounced* -шн-] fried eggs (5/4v)

янва́рь (*Gen. sing.* января́) *m.* January (1/4)

япо́нский Japanese (*adj.*)
  по-япо́нски in Japanese

ENGLISH-RUSSIAN GLOSSARY

Key

Acc.	Accusative	*infin.*	infinitive	*pl.*	plural
adj.	adjective	*Instr.*	Instrumental	*Prep.*	Prepositional
Dat.	Dative	*m.*	masculine	*pres.*	present
f.	feminine	*multidir.*	multidirectional	*sing.*	singular
Gen.	Genitive	*neut.*	neuter	*unidir.*	unidirectional
impfv.	imperfective	*pers.*	person	*usu.*	usually
indecl.	indeclinable	*pfv.*	perfective	*v.*	visuals

The numbers in parentheses after each Russian equivalent indicate the lesson and part in which the Russian word or phrase was first used as active; Russian words followed by numbers in brackets are passive vocabulary. The letter "v" after the lesson/part number indicates that the given word first appears in a visual vocabulary display. Bold numbers introduce separate meanings for a given word. The Russian letters **E** and **Ё** are treated as a single letter. Verbs not marked as perfective are imperfective. Verbs for which key forms are not given are conjugated like **читáть.**

A

a, a certain оди́н (однá, однó, одни́) [7/3]

a.m. (*midnight to dawn*) нóчи; (*dawn to noon*) утрá
   at 2:00 a.m. в два часá нóчи (7/3)
   at 5:00 a.m. в пять часóв утрá (7/3)

able: be able 1. мочь (могý, мóжешь, . . . мóгут; *past* мог, моглá, моглó, моглú)/смочь (*impfv.* 5/3v) (7/4); **2.** (*be able, know how* [*to do something*]) умéть (умéю, умéешь, . . . умéют) (4/3)

about о (об, обо) (+ *Prep.*) (4/3)
   be about (to do something) собирáться/собрáться (соберýсь, соберёшься, . . . соберýтся) (+ *infin.*) (*impfv.* 5/4)
   how about как насчёт (+ *Gen.*)

absolutely обязáтельно (6/4)

academic advisor нау́чный руководи́тель [5/2]

academy академия [5/1v]

accept принимáть/приня́ть (примý, при́мешь, . . . при́мут; *past* при́нял, принялá, при́няло, при́няли) (*impfv.* 6/3v)
   accepted: That's not accepted here. Это у нас не при́нято. [7/3]

acquaint: to get acquainted (with) знакóмиться (знакóмлюсь, знакóмишься, . . . знакóмятся)/познакóмиться (+ с + *Instr.*)
   Let's get acquainted. Давáйте познакóмимся. (2/3)

acquaintance знакóмый/знакóмая *noun, declines like adj.* (7/2)

actually действи́тельно (5/3)

address áдрес (*pl.* адресá) (2/1)
   address book записнáя кни́жка (6/3)

address (someone) formally говори́ть (+ *Dat.*)
«вы» (6/1)

address (someone) in a familiar fashion, address
someone informally говори́ть (+ *Dat.*) «ты» (6/1)

advertisement объявле́ние (5/1)

adviser (academic) нау́чный руководи́тель (5/2)

Africa А́фрика (1/2)

after all (*used for emphasis*) *particle* ведь (7/1);
(*used for emphasis*) *particle* же (4/3)

after that пото́м (4/3)

afternoon: afternoon meal обе́д (7/3)

  Good afternoon! До́брый день! (3/2)

  in the afternoon днём (7/1)

again опя́ть (3/1)

ago наза́д; (тому́) наза́д (7/2)

  not long ago неда́вно (*with past verbs*) (6/3)

  three years ago три го́да (тому́) наза́д

Agreed! Договори́лись! (7/2)

ah! ах! [6/1]

airport аэропо́рт (*Prep. sing.* в аэропорту́) (3/4)

alarm clock буди́льник (4/1v)

alcoholic алкого́лик [4/4v]

all (of) (*the whole*) **1.** весь (вся, всё, все) *adj.* [2/4];
    2. (*everything*) *pronoun* всё (4/2)

  all in all вообще́ (7/4)

  All right. (*in response to* Как дела́?) Ничего́. (1/2)

  All right. (*used to express agreement*) Ла́дно. (7/1)

  all the time всё вре́мя (7/2)

  Is that all? Э́то всё? (4/2)

  It's (that's) all right. Э́то удо́бно. (7/1)

  not at all совсе́м не (7/2v)

  That's all right! (*in response to an apology*)
    Ничего́! (2/2)

almond pastry минда́льное пиро́жное [5/4]

almost почти́ (6/4)

already уже́ (3/1)

also то́же (2/1)

always всегда́ (4/4)

ambulance service ско́рая по́мощь (6/2)

America Аме́рика (1/2)

American *adj.* америка́нский (3/3)

American: an American америка́н(е)ц/америка́нка
    (*Gen. pl.* америка́нок) (2/1)

and и (1/3); (*indicating a contrast*) а (1/1)

  and . . . anyway И вообще́. . . . *used to introduce*
    a statement which is more general than what
    precedes it) (3/1)

  and so ита́к (5/4)

angrily серди́то [7/2]

angry: get (be) angry (at) серди́ться (сержу́сь,
    се́рдишься, . . . се́рдятся)/рассерди́ться
    (на + *Acc.*) [*impfv.* 6/4]

anniversary: a major anniversary юбиле́й [5/4]

anonymous анони́мный [4/4v]

another друго́й (5/2)

antique антиква́рный

  a real antique антиква́рная вещь [6/4]

any: not any никако́й (4/4)

anyway: and . . . anyway И вообще́. . . . *used to introduce*
    a statement which is more general than what
    precedes it (3/1)

apartment кварти́ра (2/1)

  two-room apartment двухко́мнатная
    кварти́ра (6/2v)

apartment building дом (*pl.* дома́) (2/1)

appropriate при́нято [7/3]

  We don't do that here; It's not considered
    appropriate. У нас э́то не при́нято. (7/3)

April апре́ль *m.* (1/4)

arm рука́ (*Acc. sing.* ру́ку, *pl.* ру́ки)

armchair (easy chair) кре́сло (*Gen. pl.* кре́сел) (3/2)

armoire шкаф (*Prep. sing.* в шкафу́, *pl.* шкафы́) (6/2)

army а́рмия (6/2)

arrive 1. приходи́ть (прихожу́, прихо́дишь, . . .
    прихо́дят)/прийти́ (приду́, придёшь, . . . приду́т;
    past пришёл, пришла́, пришло́, пришли́) (*impfv.*
    7/4); **2.** (*by vehicle*) приезжа́ть/прие́хать (прие́ду,
    прие́дешь, . . . прие́дут) [7/4]; **3.** (*by plane*)
    прилета́ть/прилете́ть (прилечу́, прилети́шь, . . .
    прилетя́т) [3/4]

article (in a newspaper) статья́ (*Gen. pl.* стате́й) (3/1)

as как (5/4)

  as you (can) see как ви́дишь (как ви́дите) (3/2)

ashamed: I'm ashamed. Мне сты́дно. (6/1)

Asia А́зия (1/2)

ask 1. (*ask someone*) спра́шивать/спроси́ть
    (спрошу́, спро́сишь, . . . спро́сят) (+ *Acc. or*
    у + *Gen.*) (*impfv.* 6/4; *pfv.* 7/4); **2.** (*ask about,*
    inquire) спра́шивать/спроси́ть (спрошу́,
    спро́сишь, . . . спро́сят) (+ *Acc. or* о + *Prep.*)
    (*impfv.* 6/4; 7/4)

  Ask . . . to come to the phone. Попроси́те к
    телефо́ну. . . . (7/2)

  May I ask you a question? Мо́жно зада́ть вам
    вопро́с? (4/4)

asphalt асфа́льт [5/3]

aspirin аспири́н (5/3v)

assignment зада́ние (3/3)

  homework assignment дома́шнее зада́ние (3/3)

at 1. (*an event, an open place,* etc.) на (+ *Prep.*):
    at the concert на конце́рте (3/1v); (*other*
    locations) в (+ *Prep.*): **at the theater** в теа́тре
    (3/1); **2.** (*indicates clock time*) в (+ *Acc.*): **at two**
    (three, four) o'clock в два (три, четы́ре)

часа́ (7/1v); **3.** (*indicates someone's home, place of work,* etc.) у (+ *Gen.*): **For the time being, I live at my aunt's.** Пока́ я живу́ у тёти. (6/3)
   at home до́ма (1/3)
   at last наконе́ц (7/4)
   at night но́чью (7/1)
   at once неме́дленно [7/2], сейча́с (3/1)
   at this point, at that moment тут (6/4)
   at what time? в кото́ром часу́? (7/2)
auditorium зал (4/2v)
August а́вгуст (1/4)
aunt тётя (*Gen. pl.* тётей) (2/1v)
Australia Австра́лия (1/2)
auto mechanic автомеха́ник (4/4)
automotive shop автосе́рвис [4/4]
autumn о́сень *f.*
   in the autumn о́сенью (7/1)
awful: How awful! Како́й у́жас! (2/2), Э́то ужа́сно! (2/3)

B

backpack рюкза́к (*Gen. sing.* рукзака́) (1/4)
bad плохо́й (2/4); нехоро́ший (5/4)
   (it's/that's) bad пло́хо *used as predicate* (1/2); нехорошо́ *used as predicate* (5/4)
   (it's/that's) not bad непло́хо *used as predicate* (1/2)
   (it's/that's) too bad жаль (6/2)
   not (a) bad неплохо́й (4/4)
badly пло́хо (1/2)
bag су́мка (*Gen. pl.* су́мок) (1/4)
balcony балко́н (2/2v)
ballet бале́т (4/2v)
bank банк (3/4v)
bass (bass viol) контраба́с (3/3v)
bathroom 1. (*for bathing*) ва́нная *noun, declines like adj.* (2/2v); **2.** (*lavatory*) туале́т (2/2v)
bathtub ва́нна (4/1)
be быть (*future* бу́ду, бу́дешь, . . . бу́дут; *past* был, была́, бы́ло, бы́ли) (*past* 4/3, *future* 5/4)
   That can't be! Не мо́жет быть! (7/2)
   To be sure, . . . Пра́вда, . . . *parenthetical* (6/4)
beautiful краси́вый (2/4)
because потому́ что (4/4)
bed крова́ть *f.* (3/2v)
bedroom спа́льня (*Gen. pl.* спа́лен) (2/2v)
beer пи́во (6/4v)
before до (+ *Gen.*): **I finished a nursing school before the institute.** До институ́та я зако́нчила медици́нское учи́лище. (7/1)
Beg your pardon? Что-что? (3/1)

begin начина́ть/нача́ть (начну́, начнёшь, . . . начну́т; *past* на́чал, начала́, на́чало, на́чали) (7/2)
beginning нача́ло
below внизу́ (2/4)
besides (that) кро́ме того́ *parenthetical* (3/1)
bibliographer библио́граф [7/4]
big большо́й (2/2)
biologist био́лог [4/4v]
birthday день рожде́ния (4/2)
black coffee чёрный ко́фе (5/4v)
blanket одея́ло (3/2v)
blender ми́ксер [4/1v]
blond: a blond блонди́н/блонди́нка (*Gen. pl.* блонди́нок) [4/2]
blouse блу́зка (*Gen. pl.* блу́зок) (1/3)
board доска́
   Go to the board. Иди́те к доске́. [1/4]
Bolshoi Theater Большо́й теа́тр [4/2v]
book кни́га (1/3)
   address book записна́я кни́жка (6/3)
bookshelf кни́жная по́лка (2/3v)
boots сапоги́ (*Gen.* сапо́г) *pl.* (*sing.* сапо́г, *Gen. sing.* сапога́) (5/3)
boring ску́чный (6/1)
   (it's/that's) boring, tiresome ску́чно *used as predicate:* Э́то ску́чно. (6/1)
born: be born роди́ться (*past* роди́лся, родила́сь, роди́ли́сь) (5/2)
boss (someone, everyone) around кома́ндовать (кома́ндую, кома́ндуешь, . . . кома́ндуют) [6/1]
bother меша́ть/помеша́ть (+ *Dat.*) (7/1)
   I don't want to bother you. Не хочу́ вам меша́ть. [7/1]
   Sorry to bother you. Извини́те, что я вас беспоко́ю. (7/2v)
bottle буты́лка (*Gen. pl.* буты́лок) (5/4)
boy ма́льчик (2/2)
bread хлеб (3/4)
breathe: Don't breathe a word (about it) ни сло́ва (5/4)
brick *adj.* кирпи́чный [6/2v]
bright све́тлый (3/2)
bring (over) приноси́ть (приношу́, прино́сишь, . . . прино́сят)/принести́ (принесу́, принесёшь, . . . принесу́т; *past* принёс, принесла́, принесло́, принесли́) (*impfv.* 6/4; *pfv.* 7/3)
   What should I bring? Что принести́? (7/3)
broker бро́кер [4/4]
brother брат (*pl.* бра́тья, *Gen. pl.* бра́тьев) (2/1v)
building дом (*pl.* дома́) (2/1)
   apartment building дом (*pl.* дома́) (2/1)

bus автобус (3/4)
    bus stop автобусная остановка (5/3); остановка
        (*Gen. pl.* остановок) автобуса (3/4)
business 1. бизнес (5/3); фирма (4/4v); **2.** дело
    (*pl.* дела) [7/4]
    business trip командировка [7/2]
    on a business trip в командировке (7/2)
    on business по делу [7/4]
businessman бизнесмен [7/4]
but 1. но (3/4); **2.** а (1/1)
    but on the other hand (но) зато (4/4)
buy покупать/купить (куплю, купишь, . . . купят)
    (*pfv. infin. only* 5/1) (7/2)
by all means обязательно (6/4)
by the way кстати (5/4); между прочим
    parenthetical (6/1)
Bye! (*informal*) Пока! (1/2)

C

cab (*taxicab*) такси (4/4)
cabinet шкаф (*Prep. sing.* в шкафу, *pl.* шкафы) (6/2)
café кафе *neut. indecl.* (3/4v)
cake торт (5/4)
calendar календарь *m.* (*Gen. sing.* календаря) (1/4)
call (*on the phone*) звонить (звоню, звонишь, . . .
    звонят)/позвонить (+ *Dat.*) (7/1v)
    call again, call back перезванивать/перезвонить
        (перезвоню, перезвонишь, . . .
        перезвонят) [7/2v]
    end up calling (some place) попадать/попасть
        (попаду, попадёшь, . . . попадут; *past* попал,
        попала, попало, попали) куда (7/2)
    I'll call back. Я перезвоню. (7/2v)
    This is . . . calling. Это звонит. . . . (7/2v)
can (*be able*) **1.** мочь (могу, можешь, . . . могут; *past* мог,
    могла, могло, могли)/смочь (*impfv.* 5/3v) (7/4);
    2. (be able, know how [to do something]) уметь
    (умею, умеешь, . . . умеют) (4/3)
    I (we, etc.) can hear everything. Всё слышно. (4/2)
    one can, one may можно (4/4)
    one cannot (may not) нельзя (4/2)
Canada Канада (1/2)
car машина (5/1)
card карточка (*Gen. pl.* карточек) (7/1)
carpet ков(ё)р (*Gen. sing.* ковра) (3/2v)
cassette кассета (5/1)
cat кошка (*Gen. pl.* кошек) (2/4)
Caucasus, the Кавказ [5/2]
ceiling потол(о)к (*Gen. sing.* потолка) (2/2v)
celebrate праздновать (праздную, празднуешь, . . .
    празднуют)/отпраздновать (7/3)

celery сельдерей [7/3v]
cellist виолончелист/виолончелистка (*Gen. pl.*
    виолончелисток) (3/3v)
cello виолончель *f.* (3/3v)
center: Youth Center Дворец молодёжи (4/2v)
certain уверен (уверена, уверены) (6/4)
chair стул (*pl.* стулья, *Gen. pl.* стульев) (3/2)
    armchair (easy chair) кресло (*Gen. pl.* кресел) (3/2)
change менять (меняю, меняешь, . . . меняют)/
    поменять [7/2]
check 1. (*in a cafe, restaurant,* etc.) счёт (*pl.* счета) (5/4);
    2. (*in chess*) шах [3/1]
checkmate мат (*in chess*) [3/1]
cheese сыр (5/4v)
chef шеф-повар (*pl.* шеф-повара) [7/3]
chemist химик [4/4v]
Cherry Orchard, The «Вишнёвый сад» [5/2v]
chess шахматы (3/1)
    play chess играть в шахматы (3/1)
Chicago Чикаго (1/2)
child ребён(о)к
children дети (*Gen.* детей, *Dat.* детям, *Instr.*
    детьми) *pl.* (2/1v)
Chinese *adj.* китайский
    (in) Chinese по-китайски (4/3v)
chocolate шоколад (5/3v); *adj.* шоколадный [5/4]
cigarette сигарета (5/3v)
cinematography кинематография [5/1v]
circus цирк [3/1]
city город (*pl.* города) (1/2v); *adj.* городской [7/2]
clarinet кларнет [3/3v]
class (*group of students in elementary or high school*)
    класс (6/1)
    We were in the same class in school. Мы учились
        в одном классе. (6/1)
classes занятия *pl. only* (7/1)
classical классический (3/3)
    classical music классика [4/2]
classics, the классика [4/2]
classmate одноклассник/одноклассница (5/1v)
clean *adj.* чистый (5/3)
clinic (*outpatient*) поликлиника (3/4v)
clock часы (*Gen.* часов) *pl.* (2/3v)
    alarm clock будильник (4/1v)
close[1] близко (2/4v)
    close (to) близко от (+ *Gen.*) (5/3)
    (it's/that's) close близко *used as predicate* (2/4v)
close[2] закрывать/закрыть (закрою, закроешь, . . .
    закроют) [*pfv.* 4/1]
closet шкаф (*Prep. sing.* в шкафу, *pl.* шкафы) (6/2)
club клуб (4/2v)
coffee кофе *m. indecl.* (1/2)

black coffee чёрный ко́фе (5/4v)

    coffee table кофе́йный сто́лик [2/3v]

cold *adj.* холо́дный (6/4v)

come; come back 1. приходи́ть (прихожу́, прихо́дишь, . . . прихо́дят)/прийти́ (приду́, придёшь, . . . приду́т; *past* пришёл, пришла́, пришло́, пришли́) (*impfv.* 7/4); **2.** (*by vehicle*) приезжа́ть/прие́хать (прие́ду, прие́дешь, . . . прие́дут) [7/4]

    Come here. Иди́(те) сюда́. [1/4]

    Come in! Заходи́(те)! (3/2); Войди́(те). (7/1)

company фи́рма (4/4v)

composer компози́тор (3/3)

composition (*a writing assignment*) сочи́нение (3/1v)

concert конце́рт (3/3); *adj.* конце́ртный (4/2v)

conference конфере́нция [7/1v]

Congratulate me! Мо́жешь меня́ поздра́вить! [7/2]

conservatory консервато́рия (3/3v)

constantly всё вре́мя (7/2); днём и но́чью [7/2]

continent контине́нт (1/2)

Continue. Продолжа́й(те)! [1/4]

convenient удо́бный (7/1)

cook гото́вить (гото́влю, гото́вишь, . . . гото́вят)/ пригото́вить (*impfv.* 6/4v; *pfv.* 7/3)

    cook (fix) dinner гото́вить (гото́влю, гото́вишь, . . . гото́вят)/пригото́вить обе́д

correct: That's correct. Пра́вильно! [6/1]

cost сто́ить (*usu. 3rd person* сто́ит, сто́ят) (6/2)

    How much does that cost? Ско́лько э́то сто́ит? (6/2)

cottage котте́дж [*pronounced* -тэ-] [6/2v]

couch дива́н (2/3v)

cough drops пасти́лки от ка́шля [5/3v]

could: Could you please tell me . . . ? Скажи́те, пожа́луйста . . . (5/3v)

country страна́ (*pl.* стра́ны) (1/2)

cousin двою́родный брат/двою́родная сестра́ (2/1v)

creative: (it's/that's) creative оригина́льно *used as predicate* (3/1)

creatively оригина́льно (3/1)

cucumber огур(е́)ц (*Gen. sing.* огурца́)

cultured культу́рный (6/1)

currency: foreign currency валю́та (6/3v)

cushion поду́шка (*Gen. pl.* поду́шек) (2/3v)

customary: it is customary (to . . .) при́нято [7/3]

customs тамо́жня [1/4]

D

dad па́па (2/2)

dare сметь (сме́ю, сме́ешь, . . . сме́ют)

    Don't you dare. . . . Не смей. . . . (+ *infin.*) [6/4]

date 1. (*day of the month*) число́ (*pl.* чи́сла, *Gen. pl.* чи́сел); **2.** (*a time on the calendar*) да́та [5/4]

    (good) round figure кру́глая да́та [5/4]

    What's today's date? What's the date today? Како́е сего́дня число́? (6/3)

daughter дочь *f.* (*Gen., Dat., and Prep. sing.* до́чери, *Instr. sing.* до́черью, *pl.* до́чери, *Gen. pl.* дочере́й) (2/1); (*affectionate*) до́ченька [3/1]

day 1. д(е)нь *m.* (*Gen. sing.* дня) (1/4); **2.** (*day of the month, date*) число́ (*pl.* чи́сла, *Gen. pl.* чи́сел)

    day and night днём и но́чью [7/2]

    Good day! До́брый день! (3/2)

    What is today? What day is it today? Како́й сего́дня день? (1/4)

dear дорого́й (2/3)

December дека́брь *m.* (*Gen. sing.* декабря́) (1/4)

definitely обяза́тельно (6/4)

delicious вку́сный (6/4v)

department (*academic*) факульте́т (4/4); ка́федра (4/3v)

    history department истори́ческий факульте́т (6/2)

    journalism department факульте́т журнали́стики [4/4]

    What department are you in? На како́м факульте́те вы у́читесь? [4/4]

dial (*the phone*) набира́ть/набра́ть (наберу́, наберёшь, . . . наберу́т; *past* набра́л, набрала́, набра́ло, набра́ли) но́мер [7/2]

    You dialed the wrong number. Вы не туда́ попа́ли. (7/2)

diet дие́та [5/4v]

difference ра́зница [3/2]

    What's the difference? What difference does it make? Кака́я ра́зница? (3/2)

different ра́зный (5/2)

difficult тру́дный (3/1)

    (it's/that's) difficult тру́дно *used as predicate* (7/1), нелегко́ *used as predicate* (3/1)

dining room столо́вая *noun, declines like adj.* (2/2v)

dinner обе́д (7/3)

    cook (fix) dinner гото́вить (гото́влю, гото́вишь, . . . гото́вят)/пригото́вить обе́д

diploma дипло́м (7/1)

director дире́ктор (*pl.* директора́) (4/1)

directory assistance спра́вочная *noun, declines like adj.* (7/2)

discrimination дискримина́ция [5/3]

district райо́н (3/4)

disturb меша́ть/помеша́ть (+ *Dat.*) (7/1)

do де́лать/сде́лать (*impfv.* 3/1; *pfv.* 7/3)

    How are you doing? Как (у тебя́, у вас) дела́? (1/2)

    What should (can) we (I) do? Что де́лать? (4/2v)

doctor врач (*Gen. sing.* врача́) (1/3)

dog собáка (2/1)

don't:

    don't say a word about it ни слóва (5/4)

    Don't worry! Не волнýйся! (Не волнýйтесь!) (6/3)

    Don't you dare. . . . Не смей. . . . (+ *infin.*) [6/4]

door дверь *f.* (*Prep. sing.* о двéри, на двери; *Gen. pl.* дверéй) (2/2v)

dormitory общежитие (5/1)

double bass контрабáс (3/3v)

downstairs внизý (2/4)

downtown центр (= центр гóрода) (2/2)

drink пить (пью, пьёшь, . . . пьют)/выпить (выпью, выпьешь, . . . выпьют) (*impfv.* 5/4v)

drive (*go by vehicle*) *multidir.* éздить (éзжу, éздишь, . . . éздят); *unidir.* éхать (éду, éдешь, . . . éдут)/поéхать (*unidir.* 3/3; *multidir.* 5/4)

driver водитель (4/4v)

    taxi driver водитель такси (4/4v)

drugstore аптéка (3/3)

drummer удáрник [3/3v]

drums удáрные [3/3v]

E

each кáждый (5/3)

each other: (to, about, *etc.***) each other** друг дрýга (друг дрýгу, друг о дрýге, *etc.*) (6/1)

    Let's use «ты» with each other. Давáй говорить друг дрýгу «ты». (6/1)

easy chair крéсло (*Gen. pl.* крéсел) (3/2)

easy: (it's/that's) not easy нелегкó *used as predicate* (3/1)

eat есть (ем, ешь, ест, едим, едите, едя́т; *past* ел, éла, éло, éли)/съесть (*impfv.* 5/4v)

economics *adj.* экономический (5/1v)

    Moscow Institute of Economics Москóвский эконономический институ́т (5/1v)

egg яйцó (*pl.* я́йца, *Gen. pl.* яиц) (7/3v)

    fried eggs яичница [*pronounced* -шн-] (5/4v)

    hard-boiled egg крутóе яйцó (7/3v)

eight вóсемь (2/1)

eighteen восемнáдцать (6/1)

eighteenth восемнáдцатый (6/3)

eighth восьмóй (6/3)

eighty вóсемьдесят (6/1)

either *with a negated verb* тóже (5/3): **Я тóже не знáю.** I don't know either.

elderly пожилóй [6/4]

elders стáршие *noun, declines like adj.* (*pl. only*) (6/1)

electrician эле́ктрик (4/4)

electronics электрóника (4/4)

    electronics store магазин электрóники (4/4)

elevator лифт (2/2v)

eleven одиннадцать (2/1)

eleventh одиннадцатый (6/3)

else ещё (4/3)

    Sure it's us, who else! Мы, кто же ещё! [4/3]

    Who (what) else? Кто (что) ещё? (4/4)

encyclopedia: walking encyclopedia ходя́чая энциклопéдия [5/2]

end up calling (some place) попадáть/попáсть (попадý, попадёшь, . . . попадýт; *past* попáл, попáла, попáло, попáли) кудá (7/2)

engagingly интерéсно (3/1)

engineer инженéр (4/4v)

English *adj.* англи́йский (7/1)

    (in) English по-англи́йски (4/3v)

    speak English говори́ть по-англи́йски (4/3v)

entrance (*to a building*) подъéзд (2/4)

entryway (*in a home*) передняя *noun, declines like adj.* [5/2]

envelope конвéрт (6/3v)

Eugene Onegin «Евгéний Онéгин» [7/4]

Europe Еврóпа (1/2)

even *particle* дáже (3/2)

evening вéчер (*pl.* вечерá) (7/1)

    Good evening! Дóбрый вéчер! (7/1)

    in the evening вéчером (3/3v)

every кáждый (5/3)

everybody, everyone *pronoun, pl. only* все (4/2)

everything (*all*) *pronoun* всё (4/2)

    Everything is in order; Everything's fine. Всё в поря́дке. (6/2)

    Everything we need; everything one needs всё, что нýжно (6/4)

    I (we, *etc.***) can hear everything.** Всё слы́шно. (4/2)

everywhere вездé (5/1)

exactly и́менно [3/1]; (*with clock time*) рóвно [7/3]

    at seven o'clock sharp; at seven on the dot рóвно в семь часóв (7/3)

examination экзáмен (7/3)

    history exam экзáмен по истóрии (7/3)

excellent отли́чный (3/2)

Excellent! Отли́чно! (5/4)

excessively сли́шком (4/2)

exchange обмéн (6/3v)

Excuse me! Извини(те). (1/2); Прости(те)! (7/2)

exercise упражнéние (1/3)

exhibition вы́ставка (*Gen. pl.* вы́ставок) (5/2)

expect: We'll be expecting you! Ждём! [7/3]

expensive дорогóй (5/3)

experience óпыт (4/4)

explain объясня́ть (объясня́ю, объясня́ешь, . . . объясня́ют)/объясни́ть (объясню́, объясни́шь, . . . объясня́т) (7/2)

extra ли́шний [6/2]

F

factory заво́д (4/4v)

fall о́сень *f.*
  in the fall о́сенью (7/1)

family семья́ (*pl.* се́мьи, *Gen. pl.* семе́й, *Dat. pl.* се́мьям) (2/1v)

far (away) далеко́ (2/2)
  far (not far) from далеко́ (недалеко́) от (+ *Gen.*) (5/3)

fast бы́стро (4/3)

father от(е́)ц (*Gen. sing.* отца́) (2/1v)

favorite люби́мый (3/3)

February февра́ль *m.* (*Gen. sing.* февраля́) (1/4)

fellow па́р(е)нь *m.* (*Gen. sing.* па́рня, *Gen. pl.* парне́й) (5/4)

few ма́ло (+ *Gen. pl.*) (8/3)

fifteen пятна́дцать (6/1)

fifteenth пятна́дцатый (6/3)

fifth пя́тый (6/3)

fifty пятьдеся́т (6/1)

figure: good round figure (*date*) кру́глая да́та [5/4]

film star кинозвезда́ (*pl.* кинозвёзды) (5/1v)

finally наконе́ц (7/4)

financial фина́нсовый [5/1v]

find находи́ть (нахожу́, нахо́дишь, . . . нахо́дят)/найти́ (найду́, найдёшь, . . . найду́т; *past* нашёл, нашла́, нашло́, нашли́) (7/4)

fine:
  Everything's fine. Всё в поря́дке. (6/2)
  Fine, thanks. (*in response to* Как дела́?) Хорошо́, спаси́бо. (1/2)

finish зака́нчивать/зако́нчить (зако́нчу, зако́нчишь, . . . зако́нчат) (7/1); конча́ть/ ко́нчить (ко́нчу, ко́нчишь, . . . ко́нчат) (7/2)

firm фи́рма (4/4v)

first пе́рвый (2/4)
  first of all пре́жде всего́ (5/4)

fish ры́ба (7/3)

five пять (2/1); (*grade in Russian schools, equivalent to a grade of "A"*) пятёрка (4/3)

five hundred пятьсо́т (5/3)

fix (*repair*) чини́ть (чиню́, чи́нишь, . . . чи́нят)/ почини́ть (*impfv.* 4/4)
  fix dinner гото́вить (гото́влю, гото́вишь, . . . гото́вят)/приготовить обе́д (7/3)

floor 1. пол (*Prep. sing.* на полу́, *pl.* полы́) (2/2v); **2.** (*level in a building*) эта́ж (*Gen. sing.* этажа́, *Gen. pl.* этаже́й) (2/2)

flower цвет(о́)к (*Gen. sing.* цветка́, *pl.* цветы́, *Gen. pl.* цвето́в) (3/2v)

flute флейта (3/3v)

flutist флейти́ст/флейти́стка (*Gen. pl.* флейти́сток) [3/3v]

for 1. для (+ *Gen.*): **There's no room for a table here.** Тут нет ме́ста для стола́. (6/4); **2.** (*to denote how long the result of an action is in effect*) на (+ *Acc.*) **I need this book for two days.** Мне нужна́ э́та кни́га на два дня.
  for a year на́ год [7/4]
  for free беспла́тно (5/3)
  for now, for the time being пока́ [5/4]

forbidden: it is forbidden нельзя́ (4/2)

foreign currency валю́та (6/3v)

formally: to address (someone) formally говори́ть (+ *Dat.*) «вы» (6/1)

forty со́рок (6/1)

four четы́ре (2/1)

four hundred четы́реста [7/3v]

fourteen четы́рнадцать (6/1)

fourteenth четы́рнадцатый (6/3)

fourth четвёртый (2/4)

free (of charge); for free беспла́тно (5/3)

French *adj.* францу́зский
  (in) French по-францу́зски (4/3v)

Friday пя́тница (1/4)

fried eggs яи́чница [*pronounced* -шн-] (5/4v)

friend друг (*pl.* друзья́, *Gen. pl.* друзе́й) (5/3)/подру́га (5/4)

from от (+ *Gen.*) (5/1)
  far (not far) from далеко́ (недалеко́) от (+ *Gen.*) (5/3)
  from there отту́да (3/4v)
  from where отку́да [6/2]

fruit фру́кты (*Gen. pl.* фру́ктов) *usu. pl.* (5/4v)

fun: It was a lot of fun. We had a lot of fun. Бы́ло о́чень ве́село. (7/4)

furniture ме́бель *f.* (3/2)

future *adj.* бу́дущий [5/1v]

G

garage гара́ж (*Gen.* гаража́) (5/1)
  get (buy) a garage купи́ть гара́ж [5/1]

gentleman мужчи́на (6/3)

geography геогра́фия (1/2)

German *adj.* неме́цкий
 (in) German по-неме́цки (4/3v)
Germany Герма́ния [5/2v]
get (*receive*) получа́ть/получи́ть (получу́, полу́чишь, . . . полу́чат) (5/3)
 get (buy) a garage купи́ть гара́ж [5/1]
 Got it? Понима́ешь? (6/1)
 Let's get acquainted. Дава́йте познако́мимся. (2/3)
 What can I get you? (*in a restaurant,* etc.) Что бу́дете зака́зывать? (5/4)
 Would you get (Mom). Позови́ (ма́му). (7/2)
 You got the wrong number. (*over the phone*) Вы не туда́ попа́ли. (7/2)
gift пода́р(о)к (*Gen. sing.* пода́рка) (6/4)
girl 1. (*young woman*) де́вушка (*Gen. pl.* де́вушек) (5/3); **2.** (*little girl*) де́вочка (*Gen. pl.* де́вочек) (2/2)
give 1. дава́ть (даю́, даёшь, . . . даю́т)/дать (дам, дашь, даст, дади́м, дади́те, даду́т; *past* дал, дала́, да́ло, да́ли) (+ *Dat.* + *Acc.*) (*impfv.* 5/3; *pfv.* 7/2); **2.** (*as a present*) дари́ть (дарю́, да́ришь, . . . да́рят)/подари́ть (+ *Dat.* + *Acc.*) (7/4); **3.** (*give back*) отдава́ть (отдаю́, отдаёшь, . . . отдаю́т)/отда́ть (отда́м, отда́шь, отда́ст, отдади́м, отдади́те, отдаду́т; *past* о́тдал, отдала́, о́тдало, о́тдали) (*impfv.* 5/3)
 give lectures чита́ть ле́кции [7/4]
glad рад (ра́да, ра́до, ра́ды) (6/4)
gladly с удово́льствием (7/2)
go 1. *multidir.* ходи́ть (хожу́, хо́дишь, . . . хо́дят); *unidir.* идти́ (иду́, идёшь, . . . иду́т; *past* шёл, шла, шло, шли)/пойти́ (пойду́, пойдёшь, . . . пойду́т; *past* пошёл, пошла́, пошло́, пошли́) (*unidir.* 3/3; *multidir.* 5/2); **2.** (*by vehicle*) *multidir.* е́здить (е́зжу, е́здишь, . . . е́здят); *unidir.* е́хать (е́ду, е́дешь, . . . е́дут)/пое́хать (*unidir.* 3/3; *multidir.* 5/4)
 be planning to go somewhere собира́ться/собра́ться (соберу́сь, соберёшься, . . . соберу́тся) (*impfv.* 5/4)
 go for a walk гуля́ть (гуля́ю, гуля́ешь, . . . гуля́ют)/погуля́ть (*impfv.* 3/1v)
 Go to the board. Иди́(те) к доске́. [1/4]
 Let's go! Пошли́! (4/3)
good 1. хоро́ший (2/2); **2.** до́брый
 Good afternoon! Good day! До́брый день! (3/2)
 Good evening! До́брый ве́чер! (7/1)
 Good heavens! Бо́же мой! (4/3)
 Good job! Молоде́ц! (4/3)
 Good morning! До́брое у́тро! (7/2)

 (it's/that's) good хорошо́ *used as predicate* (1/2)
 (one is) good with one's hands золоты́е ру́ки (у + *Gen.*) (4/3)
 pretty good неплохо́й (4/4)
 That's pretty good! У тебя́ непло́хо получа́ется! [6/1]
Good-bye! До свида́ния! (1/2)
good-looking краси́вый (2/4)
Got it? Понима́ешь? (6/1)
grade (in school) класс (6/1)
 in the sixth grade в шесто́м кла́ссе (6/1)
 What grade are you in? Ты в како́м кла́ссе? (6/1)
graduate student аспира́нт/аспира́нтка (*Gen. pl.* аспира́нток) (1/3)
gram грамм (*Gen. pl.* грамм *or* гра́ммов) (7/3v)
granddaughter вну́чка (*Gen. pl.* вну́чек) (2/1)
grandfather де́душка *m.* (*Gen. pl.* де́душек) (2/1v)
grandmother ба́бушка (*Gen. pl.* ба́бушек) (2/1v)
grandson внук (2/1)
Granted, . . . Пра́вда, . . . (6/4)
Great! Замеча́тельно! (6/3); **That's great!** Э́то здо́рово! (2/2)
groceries проду́кты *pl.* (*Gen.* проду́ктов) (3/4)
group (of people) компа́ния [7/1]; **What a great group!** Отли́чная компа́ния! (7/1)
group (performing) гру́ппа (4/2v)
grow; grow up расти́ (расту́, растёшь, . . . расту́т; *past* рос, росла́, росло́, росли́)/вы́расти (вы́расту, вы́растешь, . . . вы́растут; *past* вы́рос, вы́росла, вы́росло, вы́росли) (*impfv.* 6/3)
guest гость *m.* (*Gen. sing.* го́стя, *Gen. pl.* госте́й)/го́стья (4/2)
guide гид [5/2]
guitar гита́ра (3/3v)
guitarist гитари́ст/гитари́стка (*Gen. pl.* гитари́сток) (3/3v)
guy па́р(е)нь *m.* (*Gen. sing.* па́рня, *Gen. pl.* парне́й) (5/4)
gym, gymnasium спортза́л (3/4v)

Н

half an hour полчаса́ (7/2)
hall: performance hall зал (4/2v)
hallway (*entryway*) пере́дняя *noun, declines like adj.* [5/2]
ham ветчина́ (5/4v)
hand рука́ (*Acc. sing.* ру́ку, *pl.* ру́ки)
 but on the other hand (но) зато́ (4/4)
 (one is) good with one's hands золоты́е ру́ки (у + *Gen.*) (4/3)
handsome краси́вый (2/4)
hang (up) ве́шать/пове́сить (пове́шу, пове́сишь, . . . пове́сят)

hang (up) (an advertisement) повесь(те) (объявление) [6/2]

hang up (the phone) вешать/повесить трубку [7/2]

happen случа́ться/случи́ться (случи́тся, случа́тся) *3rd pers. only* [7/2]

  Do you happen to know . . . ? Вы не зна́ете . . . ? (3/4)

  What happened? Что случи́лось? (7/2)

hard тру́дный (3/1)

  (it's/that's) difficult тру́дно *used as predicate* (7/1), нелегко́ *used as predicate* (3/1)

hard-boiled egg круто́е яйцо́ (7/3v)

have:

  have good luck везти́ (везёт; *past* везло́)/повезти́ (+ *Dat.*) *impersonal*

  have to на́до (+ *Dat.* + *infin.*) (3/1); до́лжен (должна́, должно́, должны́) (5/4)

  I (you, *etc.*) have. . . . У меня́ (у тебя́) (есть). . . . (4/1v)

  I (you, *etc.*) have no. . . .; I (you, *etc.*) don't have. . . . У меня́, (у тебя́, *etc.*) нет. . . . (+ *Gen.*): **I don't have a dog.** У меня́ нет соба́ки. (4/1)

  We had a lot of fun. Бы́ло о́чень ве́село. (7/4)

he он (1/3)

health здоро́вье

hear слы́шать (слы́шу, слы́шишь, . . . слы́шат)/услы́шать (*impfv.* 6/4)

  I (we, *etc.*) can hear everything. Всё слы́шно. (4/2)

  I don't want to hear a thing about it! Я ничего́ не хочу́ слы́шать! (7/2)

heating отопле́ние [4/2]

heavy тяжёлый (6/3)

Hello there!; Hi! Приве́т! (*informal*) (1/1)

hello (*said when answering the phone*) алло́ (7/2)

Hello! Здра́вствуйте! (1/2)

help помога́ть/помо́чь (помогу́, помо́жешь, . . . помо́гут; *past* помо́г, помогла́, помогло́, помогли́) (+ *Dat.*) (*pfv.* 5/3; 7/4)

Help! Помоги́(те)! (4/3)

her 1. *personal pronoun* её (*Gen. and Acc. of* она́ 4/1, 5/2), ей (*Dat. and Instr. of* она́ 6/1, 9/1); *after prepositions* неё, ней; ней (*Prep. of* она́ 7/3); **2.** *possessive* её (1/4); **3.** (*when possessor is subject*) свой (своя́, своё, свой)

hers 1. *possessive* её (1/4); **2.** (*when possessor is subject*) свой (своя́, своё, свой)

here 1. здесь (1/3), тут (2/4); **2.** (*indicates direction*) this way сюда́ (7/2)

  Come here. Иди́те сюда́. [1/4]

  here (is/are) вот (1/4)

  Here you are. Пожа́луйста. (1/2)

heroine герои́ня [7/4]

hers *possessive* её (1/4)

Hi! Приве́т! (*informal*) (1/1)

high высо́кий [5/4]

high-neck sweater сви́тер (*pl.* сви́теры *or* свитера́) (1/3)

highway шоссе́ (6/2v)

him его́ (*Gen. and Acc. of* он 4/1, 5/2), ему́ (*Dat. of* он 6/1), им (*Instr. of* он 9/1); *after prepositions* него́, нему́, ним; нём (*Prep. of* он 7/3)

his 1. *possessive* его́ (1/4); **2.** (*when possessor is subject*) свой (своя́, своё, свой)

historian исто́рик (4/3)

historical истори́ческий (6/2)

history исто́рия (5/2); *adj.* истори́ческий (6/2)

  history department истори́ческий факульте́т (6/2)

home 1. (*at home*) до́ма (1/3); **2.** (*indicates direction*) домо́й (3/4v); **3.** *adj.* дома́шний [3/3]

home library библиоте́ка (3/4v)

homework (assignment) дома́шнее зада́ние (3/3); уро́к (*usu. pl.* уро́ки) (4/3)

horrible ужа́сный (4/1)

  (it's/that's) horrible ужа́сно *used as predicate* (4/1), Это ужа́сно! (2/3), Како́й у́жас! (2/2)

horror у́жас (4/1)

hour час (*Gen.* ча́са *but* два, три, четы́ре часа́; *Prep. sing.* в . . . часу́; *pl.* часы́) (7/1)

  half an hour полчаса́ (7/2)

house дом (*pl.* дома́) (2/1)

housewarming новосе́лье (6/4)

how как (1/1)

  How about . . . ? Как насчёт . . . ? (+ *Gen.*) (6/4)

  How are things (with you)? Как (у тебя́, у вас) дела́? (1/2)

  How are you? Как (ва́ше) здоро́вье? (6/3)

  How are you (doing)? Как у тебя́ (у вас) дела́? (1/2); Как (вы) пожива́ете? (7/1)

  How awful! Како́й у́жас! (2/2)

  How do you (happen to) know? Отку́да вы зна́ете (ты зна́ешь)? (6/2)

  How much does that cost? Ско́лько э́то сто́ит? (6/2)

  how many, how much ско́лько (+ *Gen.*) (6/1)

  How old is he (she)? Ско́лько ему́ (ей) лет? (6/1)

  How're things? Как дела́? (1/2)

  know how (to do something) уме́ть (уме́ю, уме́ешь, . . . уме́ют) (4/3)

hundred (one) сто (6/1)

Hurrah! Ура́! (4/3)

husband муж (*pl.* мужья́, *Gen. pl.* муже́й) (2/1v)

I

I я (1/3)

ice cream моро́женое *noun, declines like adj.* (1/2)

idea иде́я (6/2)

if 1. éсли (3/2); **2.** (*whether*) ли *conjunction*: **He asked me if I liked literature.** Он спроси́л меня́, люблю́ ли я литерату́ру. (7/4)

immediately неме́дленно [7/2]

imported и́мпортный (3/2)

impossible: (it's/that's) impossible невозмо́жно *used as predicate* (4/1)

in 1. (*indicates location*) в (+ *Prep.*): **in Moscow** в Москве́ (3/1); **2.** (*with time units of a month or more*) **in January** в январе́ [5/4]; **3.** (*indicates time from the present* or *from the indicated moment*) че́рез (+ *Acc.*): **in a minute** че́рез мину́ту (6/4)

  Come in! Заходи́(те)! (3/2); Войди́(те). (7/1)

  (in) English (Russian) по-англи́йски (по-ру́сски) (4/3v)

  in my opinion по-мо́ему *parenthetical* (3/1)

  in the afternoon днём (7/1)

  in the evening ве́чером (3/3v)

  in the fall о́сенью (7/1)

  in the morning у́тром (3/3v)

  in second year (of college) на второ́м ку́рсе (6/1)

  in the sixth grade в шесто́м кла́ссе (6/1)

  in the spring весно́й (7/1)

  in the summer ле́том (7/1)

  in the winter зимо́й (7/1)

  in the [military] service в а́рмии (6/2)

incidentally кста́ти (5/4); ме́жду про́чим *parenthetical* (6/1)

incredibly необыкнове́нно [6/4]

indeed действи́тельно (5/3)

inexpensive недорого́й (5/3)

informally: to address (someone) informally: говори́ть (+ *Dat.*) «ты» (6/1)

information (*directory assistance*) спра́вочная *noun, declines like adj.* (7/2)

initials и́нициалы [6/3]

inquire спра́шивать/спроси́ть (спрошу́, спро́сишь, . . . спро́сят) (+ *Acc. or* о + *Prep.*) (*impfv.* 6/4; *pfv.* 7/4)

institute институ́т (5/1v)

  Moscow Institute of Economics Моско́вский экономи́ческий институ́т (5/1v)

instructor (*in college*) преподава́тель/ преподава́тельница (4/3v)

intend to (do something) собира́ться/собра́ться (соберу́сь, соберёшься, . . . соберу́тся) (+ *infin.*) (*impfv.* 5/4)

interesting интере́сный (3/1)

  (it's/that's) interesting интере́сно *used as predicate*

interestingly интере́сно (3/1)

into в (+ *Acc.*) (3/3)

introduce (someone to) знако́мить (знако́млю, знако́мишь, . . . знако́мят)/познако́мить (+ *Acc.* + с + *Instr.*) [7/4]

  Let me introduce . . . Познако́мьтесь, э́то. . . (2/3)

  Let's introduce ourselves. Дава́йте познако́мимся. (2/3)

invitation приглаше́ние (7/2v)

invite приглаша́ть/пригласи́ть (приглашу́, пригласи́шь, . . . приглася́т) (7/1)

Is (Isn't) that so? Пра́вда? (6/4); так? [4/3]

it он, она́, оно́ (1/3)

  Gen. and Acc. его́, её, его́ (4/1, 5/2)

  Dat. ему́, ей, ему́ (6/1)

  Prep. нём, ней, нём (7/3)

  Instr. им, ей, им (9/1)

Italian *adj.* италья́нский

  (in) Italian по-италья́нски (4/3v)

its 1. *possessive* его́, её; **2.** (*when possessor is subject*) свой (своя́, своё, свой)

J

jack-of-all-trades ма́стер на все ру́ки [4/3]

jacket:

  casual jacket ку́ртка (*Gen. pl.* ку́рток) (1/3)

  (man's) suit jacket пиджа́к (*Gen. sing.* пиджака́) (1/3)

  (woman's) suit jacket жаке́т (1/3)

jam варе́нье [6/4]

January янва́рь *m.* (*Gen. sing.* января́) (1/4)

Japanese *adj.* япо́нский

  (in) Japanese по-япо́нски (4/3v)

jazz джаз (4/2v)

jeans джи́нсы (*Gen.* джи́нсов) *pl.* (1/3)

job рабо́та (3/1v)

  Good job! Молоде́ц! (4/3)

joke шу́тка (*Gen. pl.* шу́ток) (5/3)

journal журна́л (1/2)

journalism журнали́стика [4/4]

  journalism department факульте́т журнали́стики [4/4]

journalist журнали́ст/журнали́стка (*Gen. pl.* журнали́сток) (2/4)

juice сок (1/2)

July ию́ль *m.* (1/4)

June ию́нь *m.* (1/4)

K

keep (doing something) всё вре́мя: **They keep calling us.** Нам все вре́мя звоня́т. (7/2)

kilogram килогра́мм (*Gen. pl.* килогра́мм *or* килогра́ммов) (7/3v)

kind: what kind of какой
kiosk киоск (5/3v)
kitchen кухня (*Gen. pl.* кухонь) (2/2v)
knapsack рюкзак (*Gen. sing.* рюкзака) (1/4)
know знать (*1st pers. sing. only* 1/1; 3/1)
   Do you (happen to) know . . . ? Вы не
     знаете . . . ? (3/4)
   everyone knows все знают [3/1]
   How do you know? Откуда ты знаешь
     (вы знаете)? (6/2)
   you know ведь (7/1)
   know how (to do something) уметь (умею,
     умеешь, . . . умеют) (4/3)

L

laboratory лаборатория (4/4v)
Lady with a Lap Dog, The «Дама с собачкой» [5/2v]
lamp лампа (3/2v)
landing (of a staircase) площадка (*Gen. pl.*
   площадок) (6/4)
landlady хозяйка (*Gen. pl.* хозяек) (6/2)
landlord хозяин (*pl.* хозяева, *Gen. pl.* хозяев) (6/2)
language язык (*Gen. sing.* языка) (4/3v)
large большой (2/2)
last 1. (*in a series*) последний [6/1v]; **2.** (*preceding the*
   present one) прошлый (5/2)
   at last наконец (7/4)
   last name фамилия (1/2)
   last year в прошлом году (5/2)
late: be late опаздывать/опоздать (опоздаю,
   опоздаешь, . . . опоздают) (*impfv.* 5/4v;
   pfv. 7/2)
later (on) потом (4/3)
   a minute later через минуту (6/4)
law *adj.* юридический (5/1v)
   law school юридический институт (5/1v)
lawyer юрист (4/4v)
learn 1. ([*try*] *to memorize*) учить (учу, учишь, . . .
   учат)/выучить (выучу, выучишь, . . . выучат)
   ([*memorize*] *usu. pfv.*) (7/1); **2.** (*learn* [*how to*]; *learn*
   [*to do something*]) учиться (учусь, учишься, . . .
   учатся)/научиться (+ *infin.*) [7/3]
lecture лекция
   give lectures читать лекции [7/4]
   lecture well, be a good lecturer хорошо читать
     лекции [7/4]
left:
   on the left слева (2/2); налево (3/4)
   to the left налево (3/4)
lesson урок

Let's. . . . *particle* Давай(те). . . . [6/1]
   Let's introduce ourselves; Let's get acquainted!
     Давайте познакомимся! (2/3)
   Let's use «ты» with each other. Давай говорить друг
     другу «ты»! (6/1)
   Let's go! Пошли! (4/3)
letter 1. (*of the alphabet*) буква (1/2); **2.** (*correspondence*)
   письмо (*pl.* письма, *Gen. pl.* писем) (1/3)
library библиотека (3/4v)
life жизнь *f.* (5/2v)
light, bright светлый (3/2)
likable симпатичный (3/2)
like[1] **1.** любить (люблю, любишь, . . . любят) (4/2v);
   2. нравиться (*usu. 3rd. pers.* нравится,
   нравятся)/понравиться (+ *Dat.*): **We like the**
   room. Нам нравится комната. (7/4)
   I'd like you to meet. . . . Познакомьтесь,
     это. . . . (2/3)
like[2] как (5/4)
   like this, like that так (5/3)
likely: most likely наверно (наверное)
   parenthetical (6/3)
listen (to) слушать/послушать (*impfv.* 3/3; *pfv.* 7/2)
   Listen. Слушай(те)! (1/4)
literary литературный [7/4]
literature литература (7/4)
little 1. (*small*) маленький (2/2); **2.** (*quantity*) мало
   (+ *Gen.*) (3/3)
   a little немного (+ *Gen.*) (4/3)
   little girl девочка (*Gen. pl.* девочек) (2/2)
live жить (живу, живёшь, . . . живут; *past* жил, жила,
   жило, жили) (*3rd pers. only* 2/1; 3/1)
living room гостиная *noun, declines like adj.* (5/2)
located: be located стоять (стою, стоишь, . . .
   стоят) (6/4)
long: not . . . very long недавно *with present tense*
   verbs (6/3)
   I haven't been working at the post office long. Я на
     почте работаю недавно. [6/3]
   not long ago недавно *with past tense verbs* (6/3)
look (at) смотреть (смотрю, смотришь, . . .
   смотрят)/посмотреть (*impfv. infin. only* 3/4;
   impfv. 4/2); **Look!** Смотри(те)! [1/4]
look for искать (ищу, ищешь, . . . ищут) [5/4]
look like похож (похожа, похожи) на (+ *Acc.*): **He looks**
   like you. Он похож на вас. (6/2)
Los Angeles Лос-Анджелес (1/2)
lots: lots of love (*usu. at the end of a letter to a close*
   relative, sweetheart, or friend) Крепко целую [7/4]
loudly громко (4/2)
   He plays so loud! Как громко он играет! (2/3)

love 1. *noun* люб(о́)вь *f.* (*Gen.* любви́, *Instr.* любо́вью) (5/2v); **2.** *verb* люби́ть (люблю́, лю́бишь, . . . лю́бят) (4/2v)

    lots of love (*usu. at the end of a letter to a close relative, sweetheart, or friend*) Кре́пко целу́ю [7/4]

luck: have good luck, be lucky везти́ (везёт; *past* везло́)/повезти́ (+ *Dat.*) impersonal

    That's tough luck for her! Не повезло́ ей! [7/2]

    We really lucked out; We were incredibly lucky. Нам необыкнове́нно повезло́. (6/4)

lunch обе́д (7/3)

M

magazine журна́л (1/2)

mail по́чта (6/3)

mail carrier почтальо́н (4/4v)

main: the main thing гла́вное *noun, declines like adj.*

major: What are you majoring in? На како́м факульте́те вы у́читесь? [4/4]

make де́лать/сде́лать (*impfv.* 3/1; *pfv.* 7/3)

Man in a Case, The «Челове́к в футля́ре» [5/2v]

man 1. мужчи́на (6/3); **2.** челове́к (*pl.* лю́ди, *Gen. pl.* люде́й *but* пять, шесть, *etc.* челове́к) (5/2)

    young man молодо́й челове́к (5/4)

manager (*of a building*) дире́ктор (*pl.* директора́) (4/1)

manner: in this manner так (5/3)

many 1. мно́го (+ *Gen. pl.*) (8/3); **2.** (*many people*) мно́гие *indef. pron., declines like adj.; pl. only* (7/3)

    how many ско́лько (+ *Gen.*) (6/1)

map ка́рта (3/4)

March март (1/4)

marvelous замеча́тельный (3/3)

    (it's/that's) marvelous замеча́тельно (6/3)

mate (*in chess*) мат (*in chess*) [3/1]

May май (1/4)

may: one can, one may мо́жно (4/4)

    May I ask you a question? Мо́жно зада́ть вам вопро́с? (4/4)

    May I speak to . . . ? (*on the phone*) Мо́жно попроси́ть . . . ? (7/3); Попроси́те (к телефо́ну). . . . (7/2)

    (one) may not нельзя́ (4/2)

maybe мо́жет быть *parenthetical* (4/2)

mayonnaise майоне́з [7/3v]

me меня́ (*Gen. and Acc. of* я 4/1, 5/2), мне (*Dat. and Prep. of* я 6/1, 7/3), мной (*Instr. of* я 9/1)

mean: What do you mean! Ну что ты (вы)! (5/1)

meat мя́со (7/3)

meat loaf мясно́й руле́т [7/3]

medical медици́нский (6/2)

meet:

    I'd like you to meet. . . . ; Meet. . . . Познако́мьтесь, э́то. . . . (2/3)

    (It's/It was) very nice to meet you. О́чень прия́тно познако́миться. (4/4); О́чень прия́тно. (1/2); О́чень рад. (2/3)

meeting собра́ние (7/1v)

memorize вы́учить (вы́учу, вы́учишь, . . . вы́учат) (*pfv.* 7/1)

menu меню́ *neut. indecl.* (1/2)

merrily ве́село

metro метро́ *neut. indecl.* (2/4v)

metro (bus, trolley, tram) pass проездно́й *noun, declines like adj.; or* проездно́й биле́т (5/3v)

microwave oven микроволно́вая печь (4/1v)

middle-aged пожило́й [6/4]

milk молоко́ (3/4)

millionaire миллионе́р (4/4v)

mind: Do you mind? Вы не возража́ете? (Ты не возража́ешь?) (7/1)

mine *possessive* мой (моя́, моё, мои́) (1/4)

mineral water минера́льная вода́ (5/4)

ministry министе́рство [7/1v]

minuses: pluses and minuses плю́сы и ми́нусы [2/4v]

minute мину́та (6/4)

    a minute later че́рез мину́ту (6/4)

    Just a minute! Одну́ мину́ту! (7/2)

mixer ми́ксер [4/1v]

mom ма́ма (2/2); (*affectionate*) ма́мочка [7/4]

moment: at that moment тут (6/4)

Monday понеде́льник (1/4)

month ме́сяц [1/4]

mood настрое́ние [5/3]

more: one more ещё оди́н (одна́, одно́) (5/4)

moreover кро́ме того́ *parenthetical* (3/1)

morning у́тро (5/3)

    Good morning! До́брое у́тро! (7/2)

    in the morning у́тром (3/3v)

Moscow Москва́ (1/2); *adj.* моско́вский [4/2v]

    Moscow Institute of Economics Моско́вский экономи́ческий институ́т [5/1v]

    resident of Moscow (Muscovite) москви́ч (*Gen.* москвича́)/москви́чка (*Gen. pl.* москви́чек) [5/2]

    Moscow style по-моско́вски [5/3]

most likely наве́рно (наве́рное) *parenthetical* (6/3)

mother мать *f.* (*Gen., Dat., and Prep. sing.* ма́тери, *Instr. sing.* ма́терью, *pl.* ма́тери, *Gen. pl.* матере́й) (2/1v); ма́ма (2/2)

move (to a new residence) переезжа́ть/перее́хать (перее́ду, перее́дешь, . . . перее́дут) [7/4]

movie star кинозвезда́ (*pl.* кинозвёзды) (5/1v)

Mr. and Mrs. Kruglov муж и жена́ Кругло́вы (2/1)

much мно́го (+ *Gen.*) (3/1v)
    how much ско́лько (+ *Gen.*) (6/1)
mud грязь *f.* (*Prep sing.* в грязи́) [5/3]
municipal городско́й [7/2]
Muscovite; resident of Moscow москви́ч (*Gen. sing.*
    москвича́)/москви́чка (*Gen. pl.* москви́чек) [5/2]
museum музе́й (4/2v)
music му́зыка (3/3)
musician музыка́нт (1/3)
must на́до (+ *Dat.* + *infin.*) (3/1); до́лжен (должна́,
    должно́, должны́) (5/4)
mustard горчи́ца [7/3v]
my 1. мой (моя́, моё, мой) (1/4); **2.** (*when possessor is
    subject*) свой (своя́, своё, свой)
    My goodness! Бо́же мой! (4/3)
    My name is. . . . Меня́ зову́т. . . . (1/1)
mystery (novel) детекти́в [3/2]

N

name 1. (*first name*) и́мя (*Gen., Dat., and Prep. sing.*
    и́мени, *Instr. sing.* и́менем, *pl.* имена́, *Gen. pl.*
    имён) *neut.* (1/2); **2.** (*last name*) фами́лия (1/2);
    3. назва́ние (5/2)
    My (his, her) name is. . . . Меня́ (его́, её) зову́т. . . . (1/1)
    What are your name and patronymic? Как ва́ше и́мя
    и о́тчество? (1/2)
    What is your name? Как тебя́ (вас) зову́т? (1/1)
native родно́й [4/3v]
near:
    (it's/that's) near бли́зко (2/4v)
    near (to) бли́зко от (+ *Gen.*) (5/3)
nearby (right nearby) ря́дом (3/4)
need:
    What (does one need . . . for? Заче́м . . . ? (4/1)
    everything we need; everything one needs;
    everything that's needed всё, что ну́жно (6/4)
needed ну́жен (нужна́, ну́жно, нужны́) (+ *Dat.*) (6/4)
neighbor сосе́д (*pl.* сосе́ди, *Gen. pl.* сосе́дей)/сосе́дка
    (*Gen. pl.* сосе́док) (2/2)
neighborhood микрорайо́н (3/4)
never никогда́ (4/4)
New York Нью-Йо́рк (1/2)
new но́вый (2/1)
    What's new? Что но́вого? (7/2v)
news но́вость *f.* (*pl.* но́вости, *Gen. pl.* новосте́й) (7/4)
newspaper газе́та (1/2)
next door ря́дом (3/4)
nice прия́тный (7/4), симпати́чный (3/2),
    хоро́ший (2/2)
    (It's/It was) very nice to meet you. Очень прия́тно
    познако́миться. (4/4)

(it's/that's) nice прия́тно *used as predicate*
    Nice to meet you. Очень прия́тно! (1/2)
night table ту́мбочка (*Gen. pl.* ту́мбочек) [3/2v]
night:
    at night но́чью (7/1)
    day and night днём и но́чью [7/2]
nightmare кошма́р (4/1)
nine де́вять (2/1)
nineteen девятна́дцать (6/1)
nineteenth девятна́дцатый (6/3)
ninety девяно́сто (6/1)
ninth девя́тый (6/3)
no 1. (*used at the beginning of a negative response*) нет
    (1/3); **2.** нет. . . . (+ *Gen.* + y + *Gen.*): **I (you,** *etc.*)
    have no. . . . У меня́, (у тебя́, *etc.*) нет. . . . (+ *Gen.*)
    not any, no . . . at all никако́й (4/4)
no one, nobody никто́ (*Gen. and Acc.* никого́) (4/3)
    There's nobody (no one) there. Никого́ нет. (4/3)
noise шум [6/4]
North America Се́верная Аме́рика (1/2)
Not at all, ... (*to introduce a contradiction to what has
    just been stated*) Да нет, ... (6/4v)
not 1. не (1/1); **2.** нет. . . . (+ *Gen.* + y + *Gen.*): **I (you,** *etc.*)
    don't have. . . . У меня́, (у тебя́, *etc.*) нет. . . .
    (+ *Gen.*)
    (it's/that's) not bad непло́хо *used as predicate* (1/2)
    (it's/that's) not easy нелегко́ *used as predicate* (3/1)
    not (a) bad непло́хой (4/4)
    not any никако́й (4/4)
    not at all совсе́м не (7/2v); да нет (6/4v)
    not far from недалеко́ от (+ *Gen.*) (5/3)
    not large небольшо́й (3/4)
    not long ago неда́вно *with past tense verbs* (6/3)
    not (too) bad ничего́ (1/2)
    not . . . very long неда́вно *with present tense*
    verbs (6/3)
    not yet ещё не. . . . (4/4)
    Not yet. Нет ещё. (Ещё нет.) (6/3)
    . . . or not . . . или нет?
notebook записна́я кни́жка (6/3)
nothing ничего́ (5/1)
November ноя́брь *m.* (*Gen. sing.* ноября́) (1/4)
now тепе́рь (3/3); сейча́с (3/4)
    right now сейча́с (3/4)
    right now, at once неме́дленно [7/2]
nowhere нигде́ (5/3)
number но́мер (*pl.* номера́) (2/1)
    phone number но́мер телефо́на (2/1)
    You dialed (got) the wrong number. (*on the phone*)
    Вы не туда́ попа́ли. (7/2)
nurse медици́нская сестра́ (медсестра́) [7/1]
nursing school медици́нское учи́лище [7/1]

O

o'clock:

    at one o'clock в час (7/1v)

    at two (three, four) o'clock в два (три, четы́ре) часа́ (7/1v)

    at five (six, seven, *etc.***) o'clock** в пять (шесть, семь, *etc.*) часо́в (7/1v)

    It's . . . o'clock. (Сейча́с . . .) (+ *time*) (7/3)

oatmeal овся́нка *colloquial* (5/4v)

object (have an objection) возража́ть/возрази́ть (возражу́, возрази́шь, . . . возразя́т) [7/1]

occur случа́ться/случи́ться (случи́тся, случа́тся) *3rd pers. only* [7/2]

ocean океа́н (1/2)

October октя́брь *m.* (*Gen. sing.* октября́) (1/4)

of course коне́чно *parenthetical* (3/2)

offend обижа́ть/оби́деть (оби́жу, оби́дишь, . . . оби́дят) [7/3]

offer предлага́ть/предложи́ть (предложу́, предложи́шь, . . . предложа́т) (7/1)

office о́фис (6/2v)

often ча́сто (5/1)

oh! ах! [6/1]

Okay. Ла́дно. (7/1)

    It's/That's okay. Это удо́бно. (7/1)

    It's/That's okay. (*in response to an apology*) Ничего́. (2/3)

    Okay (all right; not too bad). (*in response to* Как дела́?) Ничего́. (1/2)

old ста́рый (2/4v)

    He's (she's) two (five) years old. Ему́ (ей) два го́да (пять лет). (6/1v)

    How old is he (she)? Ско́лько ему́ (ей) лет? (6/1)

on 1. (*to denote location*) на (+ *Prep.*): **on the shelf** на по́лке (3/2v); **2.** (*on a day of the week*) в (+ *Acc.*): **on Saturday** в суббо́ту (7/1)

    but on the other hand (но) зато́ (4/4)

    It's on me. Я угоща́ю.

    on a business trip в командиро́вке (7/2)

    on business по де́лу [7/4]

    On the contrary . . . Да нет . . . (6/4v)

    on the left сле́ва (2/2); нале́во (3/4)

    on the right спра́ва (2/2); напра́во (3/4)

one (*numeral*) оди́н (одна́, одно́, одни́) (2/1)

    one more ещё оди́н (одна́, одно́) (5/4)

one another: (to, about, *etc.***) one another** друг дру́га (друг дру́гу, друг о дру́ге, *etc.*) (6/1)

one hundred сто (6/1)

one's own со́бственный [6/2]; *when owner is also subject* свой (своя́, своё, свои́) [6/3v]

onion(s) лук (7/3v)

only то́лько (4/2)

open открыва́ть/откры́ть (откро́ю, откро́ешь, . . . откро́ют) [*pfv. infin. only* 4/1] (*impfv.* 5/4)

    Open the window. Откро́й(те) окно́! [1/4]

    Open your book to page. . . . Откро́й(те) кни́гу на страни́це. . . . [1/4]

opera о́пера (4/2v)

opinion: in my opinion по-мо́ему (3/1)

or и́ли (2/3)

    or rather верне́е [6/4]

order 1. (*proper order*) поря́д(о)к (*Gen. sing.* поря́дка); **2.** зака́зывать/заказа́ть (закажу́, зака́жешь, . . . зака́жут) [5/4]

    Are you ready to order? Что бу́дете зака́зывать? (5/4)

    Everything is in order, everything's fine. Всё в поря́дке. (6/2)

other друго́й (5/2)

    but on the other hand (но) зато́ (4/4)

our 1. *possessive* наш (на́ша, на́ше, на́ши) (1/4); **2.** (*when possessor is subject*) свой (своя́, своё, свой)

ours *possessive* наш (на́ша, на́ше, на́ши) (1/4)

outpatient clinic поликли́ника (3/4v)

over there вон (2/2)

own: one's (my, your, *etc.***)** *possessive* свой [6/3v]; **one's own** *adj.* со́бственный [6/2]

P

p.m. (*noon to evening*) дня; (*evening to midnight*) ве́чера

    at 3:00 p.m. в три часа́ дня (7/3)

    at 7:00 p.m. в семь часо́в ве́чера (7/3)

package (*containing printed matter*) бандеро́ль *f.* (6/3)

painting карти́на (3/2v)

pants брю́ки (1/3)

paper (*term paper*) курсова́я *noun, declines like adj.*; курсова́я рабо́та (3/1)

parcel (*containing printed matter*) бандеро́ль *f.* (6/3)

Pardon? (Beg your pardon?) Что-что? (3/1)

parents роди́тели (*Gen. pl.* роди́телей) *pl.* (2/1v)

park паркова́ть (парку́ю, парку́ешь, . . . парку́ют) (5/1)

pass: metro (bus, trolley, tram) pass проездно́й *noun, declines like adj.*; проездно́й биле́т (5/3v)

passport па́спорт (*pl.* паспорта́) (1/4)

pastry пиро́жное *noun, declines like adj.* (5/4)

patronymic о́тчество (1/2)

    What are your name and patronymic? Как ва́ше и́мя и о́тчество? (1/2)

pay 1. *noun* за́работ(о)к (*Gen. sing.* за́работка) (7/1); **2.** *verb* pay (for) плати́ть (плачу́, пла́тишь, . . . пла́тят)/заплати́ть (за + *Acc.*) (*impfv.* 5/3)

pen ру́чка (*Gen. pl.* ру́чек) (1/3)

pencil каранда́ш (*Gen. sing.* карандаша́) (1/3)

pension, pension payment пéнсия [6/3]

people лю́ди (*Gen.* люде́й *but* пять, шесть, *etc.* челове́к; *Dat.* лю́дям, *Instr.* людьми́) *pl.* (*sing.* челове́к) (5/4)

performance hall зал (4/2v)

perhaps мо́жет быть *parenthetical* (4/2)

person челове́к (*pl.* лю́ди, *Gen. pl.* люде́й *but* пять, шесть, *etc.* челове́к) (5/2)

pharmacy апте́ка (3/3)

phone (telephone) 1. *noun* телефо́н; **2.** *verb* звони́ть (звоню́, звони́шь, . . . звоня́т)/позвони́ть (+ *Dat.*) (7/1v)

   hang up the phone ве́шать/пове́сить тру́бку [7/2]

   pick up the phone возьми́(те) тру́бку (7/2)

   phone number но́мер телефо́на (2/1)

photograph фотогра́фия (6/1v)

physician врач (*Gen. sing.* врача́) (1/3)

pianist пиани́ст/пиани́стка (*Gen. pl.* пиани́сток) (2/1)

piano; grand piano роя́ль *m.* (2/3v)

   play (the) piano игра́ть на роя́ле (4/3)

pick up: pick up the phone возьми́(те) тру́бку (7/2)

pickle солёный огур(é)ц [*pl.* солёные огурцы́] [7/3v]

picture карти́на (3/2v)

pillow поду́шка (*Gen. pl.* поду́шек) (2/3v)

pirozhok (*small filled pastry*) пирож(о́)к (*Gen. sing.* пирожка́) (1/2)

pity: it's/that's a pity жаль (6/2)

pizza пи́цца [7/3]

place (*location*) ме́сто (5/1)

plan, intend to (do something) собира́ться/собра́ться (соберу́сь, соберёшься, . . . соберу́тся) (+ *infin.*) (*impfv.* 5/4)

plant (*factory*) заво́д (4/4v)

play 1. *verb* игра́ть (*3rd pers. sing. only* 2/3; 3/1); **2.** *noun* (*drama*) пье́са (5/2v)

   He plays so loud! Как гро́мко он игра́ет! (2/3)

   play chess (tennis, *etc.*) игра́ть в ша́хматы (те́ннис, *etc.*) (3/2)

   play the piano (guitar, *etc.*) игра́ть на роя́ле (гита́ре, *etc.*) (4/3)

pleasant прия́тный (7/4)

please 1. *verb* **be pleasing (to)** нра́виться (*usu. 3rd. pers.* нра́вится, нра́вятся)/понра́виться (+ *Dat.*): **We like the room.** Нам нра́вится ко́мната. (7/4) (*impfv.* 6/2; *pfv.* 7/4); **2.** *adv.* пожа́луйста (1/2)

   Please tell me. . . . Скажи́те, пожа́луйста. . . . (5/3v)

pleased рад (ра́да, ра́до, ра́ды) (6/4)

   Pleased to meet you. О́чень прия́тно. (1/2), О́чень рад. (2/3)

pleasure: with pleasure с удово́льствием (7/2)

plot (*of land*) уча́ст(о)к (*Gen. sing.* уча́стка) [6/2v]

pluses and minuses плю́сы и ми́нусы [2/4v]

point: at this point тут (6/4)

polite ве́жливый (6/4v)

poodle пу́дель *m.* [6/1v]

Portuguese *adj.* португа́льский

   (in) Portuguese по-португа́льски (4/3v)

post office по́чта (3/4v)

postcard откры́тка (*Gen. pl.* откры́ток) (5/3v)

potatoes карто́шка *colloquial* (7/3v)

   potato salad карто́фельный сала́т [7/3]

pound фунт [7/3v]

practice пра́ктика (4/4)

precisely и́менно [3/1]

prefer предпочита́ть/предпоче́сть (предпочту́, предпочтёшь, . . . предпочту́т; *past* предпочёл, предпочла́, предпочло́, предпочли́) [3/4]

prelude прелю́д [6/1]

prepare гото́вить (гото́влю, гото́вишь, . . . гото́вят)/пригото́вить (*impfv.* 6/4v; *pfv.* 7/3)

   prepare for an exam гото́виться (гото́влюсь, гото́вишься, . . . гото́вятся)/подгото́виться к экза́мену (7/3)

present (*gift*) пода́р(о)к (*Gen. sing.* пода́рка) (6/4)

pretty good неплохо́й (4/4)

   That's pretty good! У тебя́ непло́хо получа́ется. [6/1]

pretty well непло́хо (1/2)

printed-matter parcel бандеро́ль *f.* (6/3)

private *adj.* ча́стный [4/4v]

   private practice ча́стная пра́ктика [4/4v]

probably наве́рно (наве́рное) *parenthetical* (6/3)

problem пробле́ма (4/1)

profession профе́ссия (3/1)

professor профе́ссор (*pl.* профессора́) (2/1)

put: put up (a sign, an advertisement) пове́сь(те) (объявле́ние) [6/2]

Q

quartet кварте́т [3/3v]

question вопро́с (4/4)

   May I ask you a question? Мо́жно зада́ть вам вопро́с? (4/4)

quickly бы́стро (4/3)

quietly ти́хо (4/2)

quite совсе́м

   quite well (совсе́м) непло́хо (1/2)

quiz контро́льная *noun, declines like adj.* (4/2)

R

radio ра́дио (5/1)

rarely ре́дко (5/4)

rather; or rather верне́е [6/4]

read чита́ть/прочита́ть (*impfv.* 3/1v, *pfv.* 7/1)
   Read. Чита́й(те)! [1/4]
real настоя́щий (4/4)
   a real. . . . (*with noun*) тако́й (5/3)
really 1. действи́тельно (5/3); **2. Really? Is that so?**
   Пра́вда? [7/1]; **3.** ра́зве (3/1)
   Is that really a difficult topic? Ра́зве э́то тру́дная
   те́ма? (3/1)
recall вспомина́ть/вспо́мнить (вспо́мню,
   вспо́мнишь, . . . вспо́мнят) [7/4]
receive получа́ть/получи́ть (получу́, полу́чишь, . . .
   полу́чат) (5/3)
receiver (*telephone*) тру́бка [7/2]
recently неда́вно (6/3)
recommend рекомендова́ть (рекоменду́ю,
   рекоменду́ешь, . . . рекоменду́ют) [5/4]
refrigerator холоди́льник (4/1v)
relate (*tell, narrate*) расска́зывать/рассказа́ть
   (расскажу́, расска́жешь, . . . расска́жут) (7/3)
remain остава́ться (остаю́сь, остаёшься, . . . остаю́тся)/
   оста́ться (оста́нусь, оста́нешься, . . .
   оста́нутся) [7/4]
remember по́мнить (по́мню, по́мнишь, . . .
   по́мнят) (5/2)
rent (*from someone*) снима́ть/снять (сниму́,
   сни́мешь, . . . сни́мут; *past* снял, сняла́, сня́ло,
   сня́ли) (*impfv.* 6/4; *pfv.* 7/4)
   be for rent сдава́ться (сдаётся, сдаю́тся) *3rd pers.*
   impfv. only [5/4]
   rent out (*an apartment*) (*to someone*) сдава́ть (сдаю́,
   сдаёшь, . . . сдаю́т)/сдать (сдам, сдашь, сдаст,
   сдади́м, сдади́те, сдаду́т; *past* сдал, сдала́, сда́ло,
   сда́ли) (6/2v)
repair чини́ть (чиню́, чи́нишь, . . . чи́нят)/почини́ть
   (*impfv.* 4/4)
Repeat. Повтори́(те)! [1/4]
resemble похо́ж (похо́жа, похо́жи) на (+ *Acc.*): **He**
   looks like you. Он похо́ж на вас. (6/2)
rest отдыха́ть/отдохну́ть (отдохну́, отдохнёшь, . . .
   отдохну́т) (*impfv.* 3/1v)
restaurant рестора́н (4/4v)
restroom туале́т (2/2)
return (*give back*) отдава́ть (отдаю́, отдаёшь, . . .
   отдаю́т)/отда́ть (отда́м, отда́шь, отда́ст, отдади́м,
   отдади́те, отдаду́т; *past* о́тдал, отдала́, о́тдало,
   о́тдали) (*impfv.* 5/3)
ride *multidir.* е́здить (е́зжу, е́здишь, . . . е́здят); *unidir.*
   е́хать (е́ду, е́дешь, . . . е́дут)/пое́хать (*unidir.* 3/3;
   multidir. 5/4)
right:
   All right. Ла́дно. (7/1)

I'll be right there! (*when being called by someone*)
   Сейча́с! (2/4)
   on the right спра́ва (2/2); напра́во (3/4)
   Right! Действи́тельно! (6/1)
   right away; at once сейча́с (3/1)
   right nearby (совсе́м) ря́дом (3/4)
   right now сейча́с (3/4); неме́дленно [7/2]
   That's right! Ве́рно! (7/1); Пра́вильно! [6/1]
   to the right напра́во (3/4)
river река́ (*Acc.* ре́ку *or* реку́; *pl.* ре́ки) (1/2)
rock (*music*) рок (3/3)
room 1. (*a room*) ко́мната (2/2); **2.** (*space*) ме́сто (5/1)
round figure (*date*) кру́глая да́та [5/4]
rubber *adj.* рези́новый (5/3)
ruble рубль *m.* (*Gen. sing.* рубля́) (5/3)
rude гру́бый (6/4v)
rug ков(ё)р (*Gen. sing.* ковра́) (3/2v)
Russia Росси́я (1/2)
Russian 1. ру́сский *adj.* (2/2) ; **2.** (*a Russian*)
   ру́сский/ру́сская (ру́сские) *noun,*
   declines like adj. (2/2) ; **3.** (*in Russian*)
   по-ру́сски (4/3v)
   speak Russian говори́ть по-ру́сски (4/3v)
   What's the Russian for . . . ? Как по-ру́сски . . . ? (1/4)

S

Saint Petersburg Санкт-Петербу́рг (1/2)
salad: potato salad карто́фельный сала́т [7/3]
salary за́работок (*Gen. sing.* за́работка) [7/1]
salt соль *f.* [7/3v]
sandwich бутербро́д (1/2)
Saturday суббо́та (1/4)
sausage колбаса́ (3/4)
saxophone саксофо́н (3/3v)
saxophonist саксофони́ст (3/3v)
say говори́ть (говорю́, говори́шь, . . . говоря́т)/сказа́ть
   (скажу́, ска́жешь, . . . ска́жут) (*impfv.* 4/2; *pfv. past*
   only 6/2; *pfv.* 7/4)
   Don't say a word (**about it**) ни сло́ва (5/4)
school шко́ла (4/3)
   nursing school медици́нское учи́лище [7/1]
schoolboy шко́льник (2/1)
schoolgirl шко́льница (2/1)
Seattle Сиэ́тл (1/2)
second второ́й (2/4)
section (*of town*) райо́н (3/4); (*class*) гру́ппа
see ви́деть (ви́жу, ви́дишь, . . . ви́дят)/уви́деть
   (*impfv.* 4/2; *pfv.* 7/4)
   as you (can) see как ви́дишь (ви́дите) (3/2)
   I see (understand). Поня́тно. (7/1)

See you later! Пока! (1/2)

See! You see! Вот видишь (видите)! (4/2)

seem: it seems ка́жется *parenthetical* (2/4)

sell продава́ть (продаю́, продаёшь, . . . продаю́т)/ прода́ть (прода́м, прода́шь, . . . прода́ст, продади́м, продади́те, продаду́т; *past* про́дал, продала́, про́дало, про́дали) (+ *Dat.* + *Acc.*) (*impfv.* 5/3)

September сентя́брь *m.* (*Gen. sing.* сентября́) (1/4)

service:

ambulance service ско́рая по́мощь (6/2)

in the [military] service в а́рмии (6/2)

settled: It's settled, then! Договори́лись! (7/2)

seven семь (2/1)

seventeen семна́дцать (6/1)

seventeenth семна́дцатый (6/3)

seventh седьмо́й (6/3)

seventy се́мьдесят (6/1)

shampoo шампу́нь *m.* (5/3v)

sharp: at 7:00 sharp ро́вно в семь часо́в (7/3)

she она́ (1/3)

shelf по́лка (*Gen. pl.* по́лок) (3/2v)

bookshelf кни́жная по́лка (2/3v)

shirt руба́шка (*Gen. pl.* руба́шек) (1/3)

shoes ту́фли (*Gen.* ту́фель) *pl.* (*sing.* ту́фля) (1/3)

shop магази́н (2/4v)

short story расска́з (5/2v)

should до́лжен (должна́, должно́, должны́) (5/4)

shout крича́ть/кри́кнуть (кри́кну, кри́кнешь, . . . кри́кнут) [7/2]

shower душ (4/1)

shut закрыва́ть/закры́ть (закро́ю, закро́ешь, . . . закро́ют) [4/1]

sign: (advertising) sign объявле́ние (5/1)

sing петь (пою́, поёшь, . . . пою́т)/спеть [7/4]

sister сестра́ (*pl.* сёстры, *Gen. pl.* сестёр, *Dat. pl.* сёстрам) (2/1v)

sit, be sitting сиде́ть (сижу́, сиди́шь, . . . сидя́т) [6/4]

six шесть (2/1)

sixteen шестна́дцать (6/1)

sixteenth шестна́дцатый (6/3)

sixth шесто́й (6/3)

sixty шестьдеся́т (6/1)

size разме́р (5/3)

skirt ю́бка (*Gen. pl.* ю́бок) (1/3)

sleep спать (сплю, спишь, . . . спят) (4/2)

small ма́ленький (2/2)

smile улыба́ться (улыба́юсь, улыба́ешься, . . . улыба́ются)/улыбну́ться (улыбну́сь, улыбнёшься, . . . улыбну́тся) [7/4]

snack bar буфе́т (1/2)

sneakers кроссо́вки (*Gen. pl.* кроссо́вок) *pl.* (*sing.* кроссо́вка) (1/3)

so 1. (*intensifier with adverbs and short-form adjectives*) так (5/1); (*intensifier with adj.*) тако́й (5/3); **2.** *particle* так (2/3); **3.** Зна́чит, . . . (3/4); **4.** ита́к (5/4); **5.** (*therefore*) поэ́тому (3/1)

So this is (these are) . . . ? Так э́то . . . ? (3/2)

so much *intensifier with verbs* так (5/1)

Is (Isn't) that so? так? [4/3], Пра́вда? [7/1]

soap мы́ло (5/3v)

soccer футбо́л (7/2v)

softly ти́хо (4/2)

soloist соли́ст/соли́стка (*Gen. pl.* соли́сток) [4/2v]

some како́й-то (7/2)

someone else's чужо́й [6/3]

son сын (*pl.* сыновья́, *Gen. pl.* сынове́й) (2/1)

song пе́сня (*Gen. pl.* пе́сен) (7/4)

sorry: Sorry to bother you. Извини́те, что я вас беспоко́ю. (7/2v)

sound звук (1/2)

South America Ю́жная Аме́рика (1/2)

space (room) ме́сто (5/1)

Spanish *adj.* испа́нский

(in) Spanish по-испа́нски (4/3v)

spare ли́шний [6/2]

speak 1. говори́ть (говорю́, говори́шь, . . . говоря́т) *impfv. only* (4/2); **2.** разгова́ривать (6/4)

speak English (Russian) говори́ть по-англи́йски (по-ру́сски) (4/3v)

May I speak with . . . ? (*on the phone*) Мо́жно попроси́ть . . . ? (7/3); Попроси́те (к телефо́ну). . . . (7/2)

This is . . . speaking. Это говори́т. . . . (7/2)

spring весна́

in the spring весно́й (7/1)

square: (city) square пло́щадь *f.* (*Gen. pl.* площаде́й) (5/2)

St. Petersburg Санкт-Петербу́рг (1/2)

stadium стадио́н (1/3)

stairs; staircase ле́стница [*pronounced* -сн-] (2/2v)

stamp ма́рка (*Gen. pl.* ма́рок) (6/3v)

stand кио́ск (5/3v)

stand (*be standing*) стоя́ть (стою́, стои́шь, . . . стоя́т) (6/4)

star: movie star кинозвезда́ (*pl.* кинозвёзды) (5/1v)

start 1. *noun* нача́ло; **2.** *verb* начина́ть/нача́ть (начну́, начнёшь, . . . начну́т; *past* на́чал, начала́, на́чало, на́чали) (7/2)

stay остава́ться (остаю́сь, остаёшься, . . . остаю́тся)/оста́ться (оста́нусь, оста́нешься, . . . оста́нутся) [7/4]

still ещё (6/1)

stock exchange би́ржа (4/4)

stockbroker бро́кер [4/4]

stop (*of a bus, train,* etc.) остано́вка (*Gen. pl.* остано́вок) (3/4)

   bus stop авто́бусная остано́вка (5/3); остано́вка авто́буса (3/4)

store магази́н (2/4v)

   electronics store магази́н электро́ники (4/4)

story (*level in a building*) эта́ж (*Gen.* этажа́, *Gen. pl.* этаже́й) (2/2)

story: (short) story расска́з (5/2v)

strange: That's strange. Стра́нно. (7/2)

street у́лица (2/1)

strict стро́гий (6/1v)

student студе́нт/студе́нтка (*Gen. pl.* студе́нток) (1/3)

   graduate student аспира́нт/аспира́нтка (*Gen. pl.* аспира́нток) (1/3)

   I'm a second-year student. Я на второ́м ку́рсе. (6/1)

study 1. (*something specific*) учи́ть (учу́, у́чишь, . . . у́чат)/вы́учить (вы́учу, вы́учишь, . . . вы́учат) (7/1); **2.** (*in depth*) изуча́ть (7/3); **3.** (*be a student*) учи́ться (учу́сь, у́чишься, . . . у́чатся) *impfv. only* (4/3); **4.** (*do homework*) занима́ться (занима́юсь, занима́ешься, . . . занима́ются) (7/1)

   study for an exam гото́виться (гото́влюсь, гото́вишься, . . . гото́вятся)/подгото́виться к экза́мену (7/3)

   Where do you study? (Where do you go to school?) Где вы у́читесь? (4/3)

subject те́ма (3/1)

subway метро́ *neut. indecl.* (2/4v)

such (a) тако́й *with* <(*adj.* +) *noun*> (5/3)

suddenly вдруг (6/4)

suggest предлага́ть/предложи́ть (предложу́, предло́жишь, . . . предло́жат) (7/1)

suit костю́м [1/3]

suit jacket 1. (*man's*) пиджа́к (*Gen.* пиджака́) (1/3); **2.** (*woman's*) жаке́т (1/3)

suitcase чемода́н (1/4)

summer ле́то

   in the summer ле́том (7/1)

Sunday воскресе́нье (1/4)

supermarket универса́м (3/4v)

sure уве́рен (уве́рена, уве́рены) (6/4)

   To be sure, ... Пра́вда, ... *parenthetical* (6/4)

   Sure it's us, who else! Мы, кто же ещё! [4/3]

surely *particle* же (*used for emphasis*) [6/1]

surprise сюрпри́з (5/4)

sweater: (high-neck) sweater сви́тер (*pl.* сви́теры *or* свитера́) (1/3); **(V-neck) sweater** пуло́вер (1/3)

system систе́ма [7/1]

T

table стол (*Gen. sing.* стола́) (3/2v)

   night table ту́мбочка (*Gen. pl.* ту́мбочек) [3/2v]

take принима́ть/приня́ть (приму́, при́мешь, . . . при́мут; при́нял, приняла́, при́няло, при́няли) (*impfv.* 6/3v)

   take a walk гуля́ть (гуля́ю, гуля́ешь, . . . гуля́ют)/погуля́ть (*impfv.* 3/1v)

   take turns (doing something) по о́череди (7/3)

talk 1. говори́ть (говорю́, говори́шь, . . . говоря́т) *impfv. only* (4/2); **2.** разгова́ривать (6/4)

   What are you talking about! Ну что ты! (5/1)

tall высо́кий [5/4]

tape recorder/player магнитофо́н (2/3v)

tasteless (*unpalatable*) невку́сный (6/4v)

tasty вку́сный (6/4v)

taxi driver води́тель такси́ (4/4v)

taxi; taxicab такси́

tea чай (1/2)

teach преподава́ть (преподаю́, преподаёшь, . . . преподаю́т) (4/3v)

teacher (*in college*) преподава́тель *m.*/преподава́тельница (4/3v); (*in school*) учи́тель *m.* (*pl.* учителя́)/учи́тельница (6/1v)

telegram телегра́мма (6/3v)

telephone телефо́н (3/1)

   telephone number но́мер телефо́на (2/1)

   telephone receiver тру́бка [7/2]

television (set); TV (set) телеви́зор (3/2v)

tell говори́ть (говорю́, говори́шь, . . . говоря́т)/сказа́ть (скажу́, ска́жешь, . . . ска́жут) (*impfv.* 4/2; *pfv. past only* 6/2; *pfv.* 7/4); (*relate, narrate*) расска́зывать/рассказа́ть (расскажу́, расска́жешь, . . . расска́жут) (7/3)

   (Could you) please tell me. . . . Скажи́те, пожа́луйста. . . . (5/3v)

   Tell (us) about. . . . Расскажи́те о (об). . . . (4/3)

ten де́сять (2/1)

tennis те́ннис (3/4)

tennis player тенниси́ст/тенниси́стка (*Gen. pl.* тенниси́сток) [3/4]

tenth деся́тый (6/3)

term paper курсова́я *noun, declines like adj.*, курсова́я рабо́та (3/1)

terrible ужа́сный (4/1)

   (It's/That's) terrible! Это ужа́сно! (2/3)

test контро́льная *noun, declines like adj.* (4/2); экза́мен (7/3)

   study (prepare) for an exam гото́виться (гото́влюсь, гото́вишься, . . . гото́вятся)/подгото́виться к экза́мену

Thank you; Thanks. Спаси́бо. (1/2)

    Thanks for the invitation. Спаси́бо за приглаше́ние. (7/2v)

that 1. (*that one, in contrast to* э́тот) *demonstrative* тот (та, то, те) (5/4); э́тот (э́та, э́то, э́ти) (5/4); **2.** (*that is. . . .*) э́то. . . .: **That is my brother.** Э́то мой брат (1/1); **3.** *relative conjunction* что (3/4); **4.** кото́рый (5/4)

    about that об э́том (7/3)

    like that так (5/3)

    That's all right (okay) (*in response to an apology*). Ничего́. (2/3)

    That can't be! Не мо́жет быть! (7/2)

    that is; i.e. то есть *often abbreviated* т.е. (4/1)

    That's right (correct)! Пра́вильно! [6/1]; Ве́рно! (7/1)

    That's strange. Стра́нно. (7/2)

    That's wonderful! Э́то прекра́сно! (4/1)

    that's why поэ́тому (3/1)

theater теа́тр (1/3)

their 1. *possessive* их (1/4); **2.** (*when possessor is subject*) свой (своя́, своё, свои́)

theirs *possessive* их (1/4)

them их (*Gen. and Acc. of* они́ 5/2), им (*Dat. of* они́ 6/1), и́ми (*Instr. of* они́); *after prepositions* них, ним, ни́ми; них (*Prep. of* они́ 7/3)

theme те́ма (3/1)

then 1. тогда́ (7/4); **2.** пото́м (4/3); **3.** (*so then*) Зна́чит, ... (3/4); **4.** *particle* так (2/3)

    but then (но) зато́ (4/4)

there 1. там (1/4); **2.** (*indicates direction*) туда́ (3/4); **3.** (*over there*) вон (2/2)

there is (are) есть (4/1v)

    from there отту́да (3/4v)

    Is (are) there . . . here? Тут есть . . . ? [3/4]

    there is (are) no. . . .; there isn't (aren't) нет (+ *Gen.*): **There's no elevator there.** Там нет ли́фта. (4/1)

therefore поэ́тому (3/1)

these are. . . . э́то. . . . (1/1)

they они́ (1/3)

thing вещь *f.*

    How are things with you? Как (у тебя́, у вас) дела́? (1/2)

    the main thing гла́вное *noun, declines like adj.* (6/3)

think ду́мать/поду́мать (*impfv.* 5/2)

third тре́тий (тре́тья, тре́тье, тре́тьи) (2/4)

thirteen трина́дцать (6/1)

thirteenth трина́дцатый (6/3)

thirtieth тридца́тый (6/3)

thirty три́дцать (6/1)

this 1. э́тот (э́та, э́то, э́ти) (5/4); **2.** (*this is. . . .*) э́то. . . . (1/1)

    about this об э́том (7/3)

    like this так (5/3)

This is . . . calling. Э́то звони́т. . . . (7/2v)

This is . . . speaking. Э́то говори́т. . . . (7/2)

those are. . . . э́то. . . . (1/1)

thought мысль *f.* [5/4]

three три (2/1)

thriller три́ллер [3/1v]

throw out (*throw away*) выбра́сывать/вы́бросить (вы́брошу, вы́бросишь, . . . вы́бросят) [6/4]

Thursday четве́рг (*Gen.* четверга́) (1/4)

thus так (5/3)

ticket биле́т (1/4)

tie га́лстук (1/3)

time вре́мя (*Gen., Dat., and Prep. sing.* вре́мени, *Instr. sing.* вре́менем) *neut.* (7/1)

    all the time всё вре́мя (7/2)

    At what time? В кото́ром часу́? (7/2)

    for the time being пока́ [5/4]

    it's time (*for someone to go some place*) пора́ (+ *Dat.*) (куда́) (7/2)

    What time is it? Кото́рый час? (7/3)

tiresome ску́чный (6/1)

to 1. (*to an event, an open place,* etc.) на (+ *Acc.*): **She's going to a concert.** Она́ идёт на конце́рт. (3/3); (*to other destinations*) в (+ *Acc.*): **I'm going to the pharmacy.** Я иду́ в апте́ку. (3/3); **2.** (*to a person's home, office,* etc.) к (+ *Dat.*): **I'm going to the doctor.** Я иду́ к врачу́. [7/4]

    to the left нале́во (3/4)

toaster то́стер [*pronounced* -тэ-] (4/1v)

today сего́дня (1/4)

together вме́сте (7/3)

toilet paper туале́тная бума́га (5/3v)

tomcat кот (*Gen. sing.* кота́) (2/4)

tomorrow за́втра (1/4)

too 1. (*excessively*) сли́шком (4/2); **2.** (*also*) то́же (2/1)

    (that's) too bad жаль (6/2)

tool инструме́нт [4/3]

toothbrush зубна́я щётка (5/3v)

toothpaste зубна́я па́ста (5/3v)

topic те́ма (3/1)

tough: That's tough luck for her! Не повезло́ ей! [7/2]

town го́род (*pl.* города́) (1/2)

treat (someone) to угоща́ть/угости́ть (угощу́, угости́шь, . . . угостя́т) [5/4]

    (It's) my treat; It's on me. Я угоща́ю. (5/4)

trip: business trip командиро́вка [7/2]

    on a business trip в командиро́вке (7/2)

trombone тромбо́н [3/3v]

trousers брю́ки (1/3)

true настоя́щий (4/4)

    true (To be sure, ...) Пра́вда, ... *parenthetical* (6/4)

    That's true! Ве́рно! (7/1)

trumpet труба́ (3/3v)
truth пра́вда
T-shirt футбо́лка (*Gen. pl.* футбо́лок) (1/3)
Tuesday вто́рник (1/4)
turn о́чередь *f.*
    take turns (doing something) по о́череди (7/3)
twelfth двена́дцатый (6/3)
twelve двена́дцать (2/1)
twentieth двадца́тый (6/3)
twenty два́дцать (6/1)
two два (2/1)
two-room apartment двухко́мнатная кварти́ра (6/2v)

U

Unbelievable! Не мо́жет быть! (7/2)
uncle дя́дя *m.* (*Gen. pl.* дя́дей) (2/1v)
understand понима́ть/поня́ть (пойму́, поймёшь, . . .
    пойму́т; *past* по́нял, поняла́, по́няло, по́няли)
    (*impfv.* 3/1; *pfv.* 7/3)
    I understand, I see. Поня́тно. (7/1)
unfortunately *parenthetical* к сожале́нию (5/4)
university университе́т (3/4v)
unpalatable невку́сный (6/4v)
unpleasant несимпати́чный (4/2)
us нас (*Gen., Acc., and Prep. of* мы 4/1, 5/2, 7/3), нам
    (*Dat. of* мы 6/1), на́ми (*Instr. of* мы)
USA (United States of America) США (Соединённые
    Шта́ты Аме́рики) (1/2)
use: use «ты» («вы») with someone говори́ть (+ *Dat.*)
    «ты» («вы»)
    Let's use «ты» with each other. Дава́й говори́ть друг
    дру́гу «ты». (6/1)
usually обы́чно (4/4)

V

vacuum cleaner пылесо́с (4/1v)
various ра́зный (5/2)
vase ва́за [3/2v]
vegetables о́вощи (*Gen.* овоще́й) *pl.* (7/3)
very о́чень (1/2)
veterinary ветерина́рный [2/4]
vinegar у́ксус [7/3v]
viola альт [3/3v]
violin скри́пка (*Gen. pl.* скри́пок) (3/3v)
violinist скрипа́ч/скрипа́чка (*Gen. pl.*
    скрипа́чек) (3/3v)
violist альти́ст/альти́стка (*Gen. pl.* альти́сток) [3/3v]
visa ви́за (1/4)
V-neck sweater пуло́вер (1/3)

W

wait (for) ждать (жду, ждёшь, . . . ждут; *past* ждал,
    ждала́, жда́ло, жда́ли) (5/3)
waiter официа́нт (4/4v)
waitress официа́нтка (*Gen. pl.* официа́нток) (4/4v)
walk 1. (*impfv. only*) *multidir.* ходи́ть (хожу́, хо́дишь, . . .
    хо́дят); *unidir.* идти́ (иду́, идёшь, . . . иду́т; *past*
    шёл, шла, шло, шли) (3/3; 5/2); **2.** гуля́ть (гуля́ю,
    гуля́ешь, . . . гуля́ют)/погуля́ть (*impfv.* 3/1v)
    to go for a walk, to take a walk гуля́ть (гуля́ю,
    гуля́ешь, . . . гуля́ют)/погуля́ть (*impfv.* 3/1v)
walking encyclopedia ходя́чая энциклопе́дия [5/2]
wall стена́ (*Acc. sing.* сте́ну, *pl.* сте́ны) (2/2v)
want хоте́ть (хочу́, хо́чешь, хо́чет, хоти́м, хоти́те,
    хотя́т) (5/1)
wardrobe шкаф (*Prep. sing.* в шкафу́, *pl.* шкафы́) (6/2)
warm тёплый (6/4v)
washing machine стира́льная маши́на (4/1v)
Washington Вашингто́н (1/2)
watch 1. *noun* часы́ (*Gen.* часо́в) *pl.* (2/3v); **2.** *verb*
    смотре́ть (смотрю́, смо́тришь, . . . смо́трят)/
    посмотре́ть (*impf. infin. only* 3/4; 4/2)
    watch the news on TV смотре́ть но́вости по
    телеви́зору
water вода́ (*Acc. sing.* во́ду) (4/1)
    mineral water минера́льная вода́ (5/4)
way:
    by the way кста́ти (5/4)
    this way так (5/3)
we мы (1/3)
We'll be expecting you! Ждём! [7/3]
Wednesday среда́ (*Acc. sing.* сре́ду) (1/4)
week неде́ля (1/4)
welcome: You're welcome! Пожа́луйста! (1/2)
well 1. хорошо́ (1/2); **2.** ну (2/2); что ж (3/1)
    pretty well, quite well непло́хо (1/2)
    Well done! Молоде́ц! (4/3)
what 1. *interrogative, relative* что (*Nom. and* Acc. 1/3,
    5/2), чего́ (*Gen. of* что 4/1), чему́ (*Dat. of* что 6/1),
    чем (*Instr. of* что), чём (*Prep. of* что 7/3); **2.** (*what
    kind* [*sort*] *of*) како́й (3/1)
    At what time? В кото́ром часу́? (7/2)
    what a. . . . како́й. . . . (2/2)
    What are you talking about! Ну что ты! (5/1)
    What can I get you? Что бу́дете зака́зывать? (5/4)
    What (day) is (it) today? Како́й сего́дня день? (1/4)
    What do you mean? Ну что ты! (5/1)
    what (does one need . . .) for? заче́м . . . ? (4/1)
    What else? Что ещё? (4/4)
    What grade are you in? Ты в како́м кла́ссе? (6/1)
    What happened? Что случи́лось? (7/2)

what . . . is что тако́е. . . . (3/1)

What is your name? Как тебя́ (вас) зову́т? (1/1)

What kind of . . . ? Како́й . . . ? (3/1)

What'll you have? Что бу́дете зака́зывать? (5/4)

What're your name and patronymic? Как ва́ше и́мя и о́тчество? (1/2)

What should (can) we (I) do? Что де́лать? (4/2v)

What sort of . . . is that/are those? Что э́то за . . . ? (7/1)

What's new? Что но́вого? (7/2v)

What's the Russian for . . . ? Как по-ру́сски . . . ? (1/4)

What's the difference? What difference does it make? Кака́я ра́зница? (3/2)

What's this/that? Что э́то? (1/3)

What time is it? Кото́рый час? (7/3)

What's today's date? What's the date today? Како́е сего́дня число́? (6/3)

when 1. когда́ (4/4); 2. (at what time) в кото́ром часу́ (7/2)

where 1. где (1/3); 2. (indicates direction) куда́ (3/3)

from where отку́да (6/2)

Where are you from? Отку́да вы (ты)?

whether conjunction ли (7/4)

which 1. како́й (3/1); 2. кото́рый (5/4)

who 1. кто (1/1); 2. кото́рый (5/4)

Who else? Кто ещё? (4/3)

Who's this/that? Кто э́то? (1/1)

whole: the whole (all of) adj. весь (вся, всё, все) [2/4]

whom кого́ (Gen. and Acc. of кто 4/1, 5/2), кому́ (Dat. of кто 6/1), кем (Instr. of кто), ком (Prep. of кто 7/3)

whose чей (чья, чьё, чьи) (2/2)

why 1. почему́ (2/3); заче́м (4/1); 2. (used for emphasis) particle ведь (3/1)

wife жена́ (pl. жёны, Gen. pl. жён) (2/1v)

win выи́грывать/вы́играть [3/1]

window окно́ (pl. о́кна, Gen. pl. о́кон) (2/2v)

wine вино́ (pl. ви́на) (7/3)

winter зима́ (Acc. sing. зи́му) (7/4v)

in the winter зимо́й (7/1)

with: with pleasure (gladly) с удово́льствием (7/2)

woman же́нщина (4/2)

young woman де́вушка (Gen. pl. де́вушек) (5/3)

wonderful замеча́тельный (3/3); прекра́сный (7/1)

It's (that's) wonderful! Прекра́сно! (4/1), Замеча́тельно! (6/3), Здо́рово! (2/2)

Wonderful! Замеча́тельно! (6/3); Здо́рово! (2/2)

wonderfully замеча́тельно (6/3)

word сло́во (pl. слова́, Gen. pl. слов, Dat. pl. слова́м) (1/2)

Don't breathe (say) a word (about it). Ни сло́ва. (5/4)

work 1. noun рабо́та (3/1v); 2. verb рабо́тать (3/1v)

I haven't been working at the post office long. Я на по́чте рабо́таю неда́вно. [6/3]

worry: **Don't worry!** Не волну́йся! (Не волну́йтесь!) (6/3)

write писа́ть (пишу́, пи́шешь, . . . пи́шут)/написа́ть (impfv. 3/1; pfv. 7/1)

Write! Пиши́(те)! [1/4]

Write (it) down! Напиши́(те)! [6/2]

write in English (Russian, etc.) писа́ть (пишу́, пи́шешь, . . . пи́шут) по-англи́йски (по-ру́сски, etc.) (4/3)

wrong: **You dialed the wrong number.** (on the phone) Вы не туда́ попа́ли. (7/2)

Y

year год (Prep. sing. в году́, pl. го́ды, Gen. pl. лет) (1/4); 2. (in college) курс: **in second year (of college)** на второ́м ку́рсе (6/1)

for a year на́ год [7/4]

He's (she's) two (five) years old. Ему́ (ей) два го́да (пять лет). (6/1v)

last year в про́шлом году́ (5/2)

What year (in college) are you in? Ты (вы) на како́м ку́рсе? (6/1)

yes да (1/3)

yesterday вчера́ (4/3)

yet ещё

not yet; not . . . yet ещё не. . . . (4/4)

Not yet. Нет ещё. (Ещё нет.) (6/3)

you informal sing. ты (1/2), тебя́ (Gen. and Acc. of ты 4/1, 5/2), тебе́ (Dat. and Prep. of ты 6/1, 7/3), тобо́й (Instr. of ты 9/1); formal or pl. вы (1/3), вас (Gen., Acc., and Prep. of вы 4/1, 5/2, 7/3), вам (Dat. of вы 6/1), ва́ми (Instr. of вы 9/1)

You're welcome! Пожа́луйста. (1/2)

young молодо́й (5/4)

young man молодо́й челове́к (5/4)

young woman де́вушка (Gen. pl. де́вушек) (5/3)

your 1. possessive твой (твоя́, твоё, твои́) (1/4) informal sing.; ваш (ва́ша, ва́ше, ва́ши) formal or pl. (1/4); 2. (when possessor is subject) свой (своя́, своё, свои́)

What's your name? Как тебя́ (вас) зову́т?

yours possessive твой (твоя́, твоё, твои́) (1/4) informal sing.; ваш (ва́ша, ва́ше, ва́ши) formal or pl. (1/4)

Youth Center Дворе́ц молодёжи [4/2v]

Z

zero ноль (or нуль) m. (Gen. ноля́ or нуля́) (2/1)

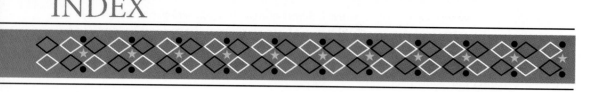

INDEX

The *n* notation indicates a footnote; the page number precedes the *n* and the note number follows.

Sophia Lubensky is Professor of Russian at the Department of Languages, Literatures, and Cultures at the University at Albany/State University of New York, where she teaches language, translation, and stylistics. She received her Ph.D. in linguistics from the University of Leningrad (now St. Petersburg), and holds M.A.s in Classics and English as well. She has published articles on linguistics, lexicography, and language teaching, and has reviewed numerous linguistic and literary publications, including a wide scope of monolingual and bilingual dictionaries. In addition to teaching and researching, Lubensky has worked as a translator, interpreter, and editor in the United States and Russia. In 1995 Lubensky culminated fourteen years of research in bilingual lexicography with the publication of her *Russian-English Dictionary of Idioms* (Random House). In 1997 the Russian edition of the dictionary was published in Moscow (Jazyki Russkoj Kul'tury).

Gerard L. Ervin is Associate Professor (emeritus) of Slavic Languages at the Ohio State University, where he founded the Foreign Language Center. He has taught French and Spanish at the secondary school level and Russian, foreign-language methods, and English as a second language at the college level. A past president of the American Council on the Teaching of Foreign Languages (ACTFL), Ervin has also taught at the U.S. Air Force Academy and the University of Arizona. In addition to authoring or coauthoring a variety of instructional materials for several languages, Ervin has written and lectured widely on language teaching, is Executive Director of the American Association of Teachers of Slavic and East European Languages (AATSEEL), and is cofounder of the Foreign Language Education Forum on CompuServe.

Larry McLellan teaches Russian and coordinates the Russian language program at the University of California, Santa Barbara, where he received the University Council/American Federation of Teachers Award for Excellence in Teaching in 1998. He has also taught at the University of California, Berkeley, where he received an M.A. and is a Ph.D. candidate in Slavic Linguistics. He has previously worked as a developmental editor of Russian textbook materials, as a leader for student and tourist groups in Russia, and as a program assistant at the Kennan Institute for Advanced Russian Studies in Washington, D.C.

Donald K. Jarvis is Professor of Russian and director of the Faculty Center at Brigham Young University. He has also served there as dean of General Education and chair of the Department of Asian and Slavic Languages. He is the author of *Junior Faculty Development: A Handbook* (Modern Language Association 1991) and other publications dealing with language teaching and faculty development, including *Teaching, Learning, Acquiring Russian,* edited with Sophia Lubensky (Slavica 1984). A past president of the American Council of Teachers of Russian and the American Association of Teachers of Slavic and East European Languages, Jarvis consults for a range of universities, professional organizations, and government agencies.

Grateful acknowledgment is made for use of the following:

Page xxix–xxx Aleksandr Zudin; *1* Vikentii Bragin, Dmitrii Antonov; *14* Steve Small; *15* A. Ovchinnikov/ITAR-TASS/Sovfoto; *28* E. Manewal/Superstock, Inc.; *38 Komsomol'skaia pravda* 26 June–3 July 1998, #117 (21850), p. 22; *39* Tass/Sovfoto; *42 Sem' dnei; 56* Peter Menzel/Stock Boston; *67* pet ad *Sem' dnei* 1998, p. 66; *70* Wolfgang Kaehler; *80* ITAR/TASS; ad for Titanic from *Pravda, Pravda* 28 May 1998 #69 (497); *81* James Balog/Tony Stone Images; *85* Dave Bartruff; *89* Tass/Sovfoto; *91* picture from *Novaia gazeta* No. 6 (478), 16–22 February 1998; *99* furniture ad from *Sem' dnei* 1998; *106* V. Khristoforov/ITAR-TASS/Sovfoto; *117* Chevy ad from *Itogi; 126* Tass/Sovfoto; *129* Vikentii Bragin, Dmitrii Antonov; *176* Vikentii Bragin, Dmitrii Antonov; *183* Jeff Greenberg/International Stock Photo; *188* Tass/Sovfoto; *194* Vikentii Bragin, Dmitri Antonov; *195* "Moskva putevoditel'," © Izdatel'stvo Aist, Moskva, 1993; *206 Adres Moskva 94/95* (Moskva/Munchen: Julius Meinl, 1994), p. 322; *227* conference announcement from *Rodina,* 1996, p. 83; *228* Richard Sylvester; *260* Vikentii Bragin, Dmitrii Antonov; *263* G. Khamelyanin/ITAR-TASS/Sovfoto; *278* cartoon from *Novoe vremia* No. 8, 1997; *279* ad from *International Business Week,* No. 7, 1993, p. 8; *280* ITAR-TASS/Sovfoto; *283* Izdate'stvo Sovetskiy khudozhnik; *311* A. Rukhadze/ITAR-TASS/Sovfoto; *315 TV Park* (Moskva), © "TV Park," 1995; *338* table of contents from *Harper's Bazaar,* January–February 1998, p. 10.

NOTES

Ирландия

Шотландия

Англия

Норвегия

Швеция

Финляндия

Ледовитый океан

Новая Земля

Мурманск

Баренцево море

Карск море

Германия

Чешская республика

Эстония
Латвия

Литва

Польша

Белоруссия

Словакия

Венгрия

Румыния

Украина

Молдавия

Болгария

Ладожское озеро

Петрозаводск

Белое море

Архангельск

Псков

Санкт-Петербург
Новгород

Тверь

Смоленск

Вологда

Онежское озеро

Двина

Москва

Москва ★

Тула

Курск

Ярославль
Кострома

Нижний Новгород

Воронеж
Пенза

Казань

Ижевск

Пермь

Обь

Р О С С И Я

Екатеринбург

Челябинск

Уфа

Саратов

Волга

Урал

Иртыш

Омск

Новосиб

Ростов-на-Дону

Крым

Дон

Астрахань

чёрное море

Грузия

Кавказ

Каспийское море

Аральское море

Казахстан

озеро Балхаш

Турция

Кипр

Армения

Узбекистан

Киргизия

Средиземное море

Израиль

Ливан

Сирия

Азербайджан

Ирак

Туркменистан

Таджикистан

Иордания

Иран

Афганистан

Индия

Саудовская Аравия

Кувейт

Пакистан